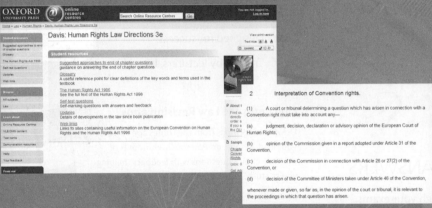

human rights law

DIRECTIONS

3rd edition

DR HOWARD DAVIS
Reader in Public Law,
Bournemouth University

OXFORD
UNIVERSITY PRESS

OXFORD
UNIVERSITY PRESS

Great Clarendon Street, Oxford, OX2 6DP,
United Kingdom

Oxford University Press is a department of the University of Oxford.
It furthers the University's objective of excellence in research, scholarship,
and education by publishing worldwide. Oxford is a registered trade mark of
Oxford University Press in the UK and in certain other countries

© Oxford University Press 2013

The moral rights of the author have been asserted

First editon 2007
Second editon 2009

Impression: 1

Public sector information reproduced under Open Government Licence v1.0
(http://www.nationalarchives.gov.uk/doc/open-government-licence/open-government-licence.htm)

Crown Copyright material reproduced with the permission of the
Controller, HMSO (under the terms of the Click Use licence)

British Library Cataloguing in Publication Data

Data available

ISBN 978-0-19-966937-0

Printed in Great Britain by
Ashford Colour Press Ltd, Gosport, Hampshire

Dedication

To Stella, Lydia and Edmund

Guide to the book

Human Rights Law Directions is enriched with a range of features designed to help support and reinforce your learning. This guided tour shows you how to fully utilise your textbook and get the most out of your study.

Chapter overview

> ### Chapter overview
>
> - The importance of fair trials and the rule of law.
> - The scope of Article 6: trials determining civil rights and obligations or a criminal charge.
> - The general right to a fair trial: express and implied rights found in Article 6(1) which apply to both civil and criminal trials (eg equality of

Each chapter begins with a bulleted outline of the main concepts and ideas you will encounter. These serve as a helpful guide to what you can expect to learn.

Definition boxes

> **reservations and derogations**
>
> Making a reservation can be contrasted with the power to 'derogate' under Article 15. A derogation is a suspension of agreed Convention obligations. States can only derogate in times of war or national emergency and cannot derogate in respect of the most fundamental rights, such as the right not to be tortured. Derogation is discussed in Chapter 7, section 7.2.

Key terms are highlighted in colour when they first appear and are clearly explained in definition boxes.

Key points

> **KEY POINT** The advocacy of violence by officials raises different issues. International law bans 'propaganda for war' (Article 20 ICCPR) and such a ban should extend to public officials. However, the lawful use of force can be legitimate for a state, and so propaganda for war is unlikely to exclude reasoned arguments for lawful war. Arguing for unlawful war could, of course, raise an Article 20 point.

Important rules, facts and examples are emphasised to draw your attention to essential concepts and developments, as well as clarify potential areas of confusion.

Discussion topic boxes

> **discussion topic**
>
> **The right to silence is not necessary to a fair trial?**
>
> The right to silence is controversial and, as indicated above, has been restricted. The right to silence is defended on grounds that include:
>
> - The best way to maintain the fundamental dimensions of a fair trial is by a s[...] unambiguously, the burden of proof onto the prosecution.
> - It discourages improper compulsion of defendants and so helps to avoid justice.
> - There may be many legitimate reasons why a person would be best advised

Broader themes and questions on areas of controversy are explored and discussed, encouraging you to develop a critical perspective and consider the wider issues in a methodical way.

Case close-up boxes

> **case close-up**
>
> *R (Countryside Alliance) v Attorney General* [2007] UKHL 52
> The Hunting Act 2004 banned hunting with dogs. The Countryside Alliance sought a declaration of incompatibility under section 4 HRA 1998 that, among the Act was incompatible with rights of their members in Article 1 of the First Pro[...] of Lords accepted that Article 1 was engaged. Specifically: the ban interfered w[...]

Summaries of cases are highlighted for ease of reference.

Further study boxes

further study

Critical articles include: Barendt, E. 'Free Speech and Abortion' [2003] *Pub[lic Law...]* ter). Supportive articles include: Geddes, A. 'What Future for Political Advertis[ing in the] Kingdom's Television Screens?' [2002] *Public Law* 615 (Winter)—commentin[g on the] Appeal's decision.

Valuable sources for critical evaluation and deeper research on particular topics of interest are identified. The author explains the significance of the source and what you should look out for in your further study, to give you the option of delving deeper into the subject in a focused way.

Cross-references

cross reference
See Lindsay, in section 23.7.2, for an example of a disproportionate exercise of this power.

23.6.4 The seizure of goods to guarantee [the] payment of taxes

Since this is expressly mentioned in the third sentence of Article 1, seizur[e of goods to guarantee payment of] taxes is accepted as a legitimate activity by the state over which it is giv[en a wide margin of] appreciation (see, for example, *Gasus Dosier- und Fördertechnik GmbH [v The Netherlands* (1995)] 20 EHRR 403).

The book is made easy to navigate through the use of clearly marked cross-references that pinpoint particular sections or pages of the book where related themes or cases are covered.

Chapter summaries

Summary

- The protection of belief itself is absolute in the sense that, unless there are grou[nds for dero]gation under Article 15, the state cannot interfere with religious and other be[liefs. States] have a duty to secure religious freedom.

- Manifestations of belief can be restricted by the state subject to the provisions [of Article 9(2).] The important point here is to distinguish between actions which manifest be[lief and those] which simply are motivated by belief. The latter do not raise issues under Article [9.]

The central points and concepts covered in each chapter are distilled into summaries at the end of chapters. These provide a mechanism for you to reinforce your understanding and can be used as a revision tool.

End of chapter questions

Questions

1 After finishing his final exams, Charles is expelled from university for a discipl[inary offence] and he also fails his degree. Under the university regulations neither the disci[plinary board] (which has the power of expulsion) nor the examinations board (which deter[mines his] degree), gives him a right to be heard. Comment on his allegation that his rig[ht to a fair] trial has been violated.

For suggested approaches, please visit the Online Resource Centre.

2 The Prison Service is creating an entirely new set of procedures dealing with [discip]line and you have been charged with ensuring compliance with Article 6 for [rules to] be used in the prisons housing the most dangerous prisoners. You are asked [to advise:] (a) whether Article 6 is involved and, if so, in which situations; (b) what speci[fic rights Art]icle 6 provides; and (c) whether those rights can be restricted to prevent, for [example,] intimidation of one prisoner by another.

Problem questions and essay type questions at the end of each chapter will help you to develop analysis and problem solving skills. The Online Resource Centre that accompanies this book provides suggested approaches to answering these questions and will help you to develop your own successful approach to assessments and examinations.

Further reading

Further reading

- Lester, A. and Pannick, D. (see Preface) Chapter 4, Article 9
- Ahdar, R. and Leigh, F. *Religious Freedom in the Liberal State* (2005) Oxford: O[UP]
- Taylor, P. *Freedom of Religion* (2005) Cambridge: CUP
- Evans, C. *Freedom of Religion under the ECHR* (2001) Oxford: OUP
- Addison, N. *Religious Discrimination and Hatred Law* (2007) London: Routledge

Selected further reading is included at the end of each chapter to provide a springboard for further study. This will help you to take your learning further and guide you to some of the key academic literature in the field.

Guide to the Online Resource Centre

The Online Resource Centre that accompanies this book provides students and lecturers with ready-to-use teaching and learning resources. They are free of charge and are designed to maximize the learning experience.

www.oxfordtextbooks.co.uk/orc/davis_directions3e/

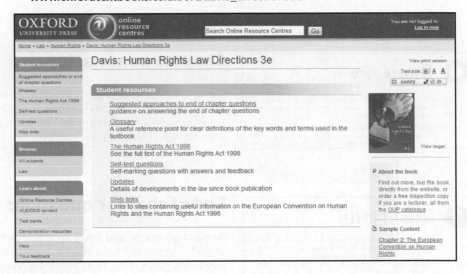

For Students

Accessible to all, with no registration or password required, enabling you to get the most from your textbook.

Web links

A selection of annotated web links chosen by the author allow you to easily research those topics that are of particular interest to you. These links are checked regularly to ensure they remain up to date.

Regular updates

An indispensable resource allowing you to access changes and developments in the law that have occurred since publication of the book. These are added to the website twice a year, with specific chapter references, to enable you to easily identify which material has been superseded or supplemented. Updates allow you to keep up to date with developments without buying a new book.

Davis: Human Rights Law Directions 2e

Chapter 2

Significant reform of the Convention system is proposed by individual cases.

Suggested approaches to end of chapter questions

Guidance is given on answering the end of chapter questions. These will help you to develop your skills in constructing a well-balanced argument.

Chapter 9

Question 1

- Consider whether there is state responsibility under for suffering in a private care home. (See, in particul

- Does it matter that the suffering is not inflicted by a s information, etc? (See 9.8)

Flashcard glossary

A series of interactive flashcards containing key terms and concepts to test your understanding of human rights law.

Actio popularis
Cases brought by pressure groups or individuals on behalf of the p of the public. Most legal systems restrict them to some extent, sinc to be used for what might be thought of as political disputes; Parlia forum for those. The public interest is represented in the courts by England and Wales, the Attorney General.

'Articles' and 'sections'
The ECHR, which is an act of the Council of Europe (see Chapter 'Articles'. The HRA 1998, which is an act of the UK Parliament, is c

---

Human Rights Act 1998

The full text of the Human Rights Act 1998 to use as a reference throughout your human rights studies.

---

2   Interpretation of Convention rights.

(1)   A court or tribunal determining a question which has arisen Convention right must take into account any—

(a)   judgment, decision, declaration or advisory opinion of the E Human Rights,

(b)   opinion of the Commission given in a report adopted under Convention,

---

Multiple choice questions

A selection of multiple choice questions, arranged by chapter, allows you to quickly assess your knowledge of the various topics in human rights.

Which one of the following statements best expresses the way in which the International Covenant on Civil and Political Rights (ICCPR) helps to secure human rig exception of the UN?

◯ The ICCPR is a list of civil and political rights agreed to by most UN states, but it is essentially an expression of aspirations (hopes and intentions) and does no obligations on states that are binding in international law.
◯ The ICCPR is a list of obligations accepted by signatory states, but there is no effective enforcement procedure available because it relies entirely on states r Human Rights Committee on their own behaviour
◯ The ICCPR is a list of obligations accepted by signatory states, it is enforced through the reporting process of the UN Human Rights Committee and there is a al Protocol by which states can grant their citizens a right of complaint.
◯ The ICCPR is a list of obligations accepted by signatory states, but there is no effective enforcement procedure available, in particular, there is no process for complaints against the behaviour of their own states.

New to this edition

This edition has been fully revised as of September 2012, and key updates include:

- Discussion of new procedures and reform proposals for the European Court of Human Rights.
- Developments concerning the application of the Convention outside Europe.
- Clarification of the UK Supreme Court's consolidated view of the relationship between itself and the European Court.
- A fuller section on external legal sources for the interpretation of the Convention.
- Material on medical law, deportations and public order has been integrated with the chapters on the relevant applicable articles.
- A chapter devoted to prisoners' rights.
- Full treatment of prisoners' rights to vote (in the chapter on Article 3 of the First Protocol).
- Chapter 26 on human rights and terrorism has been brought up to date in terms of changes to UK law since 2010.
- Extended treatment of issues of controversy in the UK such as right to privacy and its balance with freedom of expression and the right to manifest religious belief in employment.
- Proposals for change to human rights law in the UK.

Preface the basics

Two texts

This book is an introduction to human rights law in the United Kingdom. Primarily, it involves consideration of two texts: the European Convention on Human Rights (ECHR) and the Human Rights Act 1998 (HRA).

1. ECHR

- This contains a list of human rights and freedoms which are applied by the European Court of Human Rights (ECtHR).

- The Convention, being international law and neither an Act of Parliament nor rule of common law, is not part of UK law. Therefore the Convention cannot be directly enforced in UK courts.

2. HRA

- This is an Act of the UK Parliament and therefore part of the law of the UK, which creates legal rights and duties enforced in UK courts.

- The HRA gives effect to the rights and freedoms in the ECHR in UK law. It does this in specific ways.

Sources

ECHR

The text of the Convention is available on the Council of Europe website by following links to 'Human Rights' and then 'Basic Texts'. The Convention needs to be read with Protocol 1 and Protocol 13. The website is updated and contains changes to the Convention that result from the coming into effect of Protocol 14.

Strasbourg case law can be read, amongst other sources, in the European Human Rights Reports (EHRR); these are on Westlaw. Alternatively HUDOC is the Court of Human Rights' searchable database, to which there is free access.

Human Rights Act 1998

Googling 'the Human Rights Act 1998' leads to the original text, including the Schedules. The text has been subject to minor amendments, the most important of which are

- references in section 1(1)(c) to Protocol 6 are now to Protocol 13;
- derogations in Schedule 3 Part 1 have been withdrawn.

UK cases are reported through the standard law reports series. In this book the neutral citation is given to allow ease of internet use. The cases are available on BAILII, which gives free access.

Terminology

- 'Articles': the ECHR is divided into 'Articles'.
- 'Sections': the HRA is divided into 'sections'.
- 'Convention rights': the name given to the Articles from the ECHR which are given effect through the HRA.
- 'Schedule': a sort of appendix to an Act of Parliament. Schedule 1 HRA contains the 'Convention rights'.

Properly, the Articles in the ECHR given further effect in UK law by means of the HRA should be referred to as 'Article ? of Schedule 1 HRA'. For brevity reference in this book will just be to 'Article ?' whether under the ECHR or through the HRA.

United Kingdom

The HRA applies throughout the United Kingdom. The term 'UK law' is used in relation to general themes. Much of the book is on the application of Convention law to the law of England and Wales. This is made clear, as appropriate, in the text. There are three chapters looking in more detail at the application of human rights law to prisoners, to police powers and to the media.

Further reading

There are a number of in-depth studies of the Act and the Convention. Two works are referred to, where appropriate, in the 'Further reading' section at the end of each chapter.

- Lester, A, Pannick, D. and Herberg, J. *Human Rights Law and Practice* 3rd edn (2009) London: Lexis Nexis (this gives a full, detailed examination of Convention and UK law. It is available online via LexisNexisButterworths (Athens)).
- Amos, M. *Human Rights Law* (2006) Oxford: Hart Publishing (a detailed analysis focused on UK case law under the HRA).

Outline contents

xiii

Detailed contents

Table of cases

Table of cases

xlii

Table of legislation

Statutory Instruments

Treaties and Conventions

Part 1

Human rights: the European Convention, the Human Rights Act and pervasive principles

1

Human rights: the idea and the law

Chapter overview

- The idea of human rights.
- Issues relating to political, legal and constitutional theory.
- What human rights do we have?
- The international context of law-based human rights protection.

Introduction

Terrorist suspects are subjected to treatment that causes them severe pain and psychological disturbance; there is no effective investigation when an Asian man is put in a cell with a white racist who murders him; two men are convicted of a vicious murder and given long sentences on the basis of evidence they did not know about and could not challenge; the law prevents a newspaper from publishing articles investigating the responsibility of a drug company for marketing a tranquilliser which, when used by pregnant women, caused serious birth defects.

These are all examples of human rights abuses. They all involve the United Kingdom and were chosen because this book is about the protection of human rights in the United Kingdom. In fact, as some of the cases considered in this book demonstrate, these examples are somewhat at the mild end of the full spectrum of human rights abuses found in other parts of Europe or, emphatically, in the rest of the world.

In this chapter the idea of human rights is introduced, as are a range of political and constitutional issues to which they give rise. There is also an introduction to the general history of the international protection of human rights from which the United Kingdom system is derived.

4

 ## 1.1 General idea of human rights

1.1.1 Human dignity

The general idea of human rights is to give practical effect to an intuition or a feeling which, it is believed, all reasonable human beings share and which marks out our common humanity. This intuition or feeling is that in whatever we do, we need to accord proper respect to the dignity of all individual human beings. States and governments, in particular, must ensure that individual dignity is respected in their laws and practices. No matter how noble or popular a cause, no matter how much a policy may contribute to the overall wealth, security or common good of society, it is necessary to limit our actions in such a way as to respect the human dignity of all the individuals affected. The need to respect human dignity applies when states and governments act for the general good; the need applies all the stronger when government policies are oppressive, dictatorial or simply negligent.

Dignity is hard to define but at its core are two ideas.

Autonomy

Autonomy describes the freedom to live according to one's own sense of values and not to be compelled to live under the domination of others; not to be merely an object serving the interests of others but a 'person' with interests and desires of his or her own and the ability to pursue them. Obligations requiring obedience to the will of others (such as under an employment contract, for example) can be entered into but they must be voluntary, at least in the sense of not being compelled by the law. Put simply, autonomy is at the heart of what it means to be, and to be recognised as, an individual person.

Democracy

Dignity implies some idea of democracy and self-rule: the right to participate in the processes of government and the formation of the law and the choice of policies through which our common social interest is pursued. Such participation is mainly indirect (through voting for representatives), but there needs to be a place for more direct participation too (through other forms of political activity such as meetings, marches and demonstrations).

1.1.2 Philosophical underpinnings

The philosophical justification for this idea of human rights is difficult to make. That there are basic entitlements on which personhood and individuality depend and which act to restrain the actions of others, including state officials, has proved hard to establish in a universally convincing way. Under a religious justification, for instance, the Ten Commandments, reinforced by Christ's injunction to 'love thy neighbour as thyself', can be restated as rights (the right to life, for instance, being a necessary consequence of the injunction 'thou shalt not kill', and so on). Similar deductions can be derived from the texts and precepts of the other great religions. But for many, divine authority is too mysterious, or non-existent, to satisfy as an explanation for rights.

For natural lawyers (and American revolutionaries of the eighteenth century) rights are based on 'self-evident truths'. These are self-evident in the sense of being derived, using the 'reason' with which we are all endowed by nature, from simple reflection on the basic social conditions necessary for individual freedom (Finnis). Immanuel Kant (1724–1804) provides us with a philosophically sophisticated understanding of autonomy rooted in the possibilities of reason and expressing the values of the 'enlightenment'.

The horrors of the first half of the twentieth century, however, led many to reject the possibility of 'reason' as the ultimate guide. Today, perhaps, it is 'science' that has authority. If so, a better explanation for human rights may lie in evolution—an evolving tendency to compassion in human beings explains our current pursuit of human rights (Gearty). 'Postmodernists', on the other hand, deny the possibility of an *a priori* single principle that explains human rights.

It is clearly difficult to get agreement on the point of human rights if the aim is to describe some essential fact of human life from which human rights are derived. An alternative, 'political', approach is to ask whether there are social and political purposes for which human rights have a particular justificatory role. Thus it has been argued that human rights are defined and limited by being those values which are capable of justifying a just war; specifically, these days, military intervention in the affairs of a sovereign state (Rawls; Raz). Others have suggested a wider definition of human rights by which they are the discourse in terms of which progressive politics is now conducted (Gearty).

Lawyers (in their capacity as such) do not have to resolve these problems. They are concerned to identify and interpret the 'human rights' that have been agreed in the sense that they are found in international treaties or national legal systems etc. Philosophers (and lawyers too) then identify the values that best explain and justify the fact that we have those rights. The idea of individual 'autonomy', for example, emerges, *ex post*, as a presumed, underlying value which explains and justifies our having rights such as the right to life, not to be tortured, to freedom of expression, etc. (Griffin 2008).

1.1.3 **Legal protection**

Human rights involve the idea that it is possible and desirable to identify the fundamental attributes of human dignity and to express these attributes as legal rules. The idea is that human rights are not just desirable but obligatory. They are part of the law, they should be enforced by courts and should be legally binding on states and their governments, and there should be procedures and remedies by which a person's rights can be upheld. Legal protection means that it is sovereign states, such as the United Kingdom, which, through their institutions (government, Parliament and courts) have the primary responsibility for securing human rights for their populations.

1.1.4 **Respecting difference**

Recognising human dignity implies the recognition of basic standards to be applied to all individuals, standards which reflect our common humanity. It also involves the recognition of difference. The point is that individuals hold different beliefs on religion and on politics, have different senses of right and wrong, different desires and interests, etc. The idea of human rights is that these differences are basic to what we are, both as private individuals and as citizens acting with others in society—in commerce, politics, religion, etc. Respecting common humanity implies allowing such differences to flourish.

1.1.5 **The nice and the nasty**

Most individuals, as persons, are 'alright', some are very nice, but some are peculiarly nasty. One of the things that is hardest to accept about human rights is that they are shared by the good and the bad alike. The most violent murderers or vicious racists are entitled to the protection of their human rights. Of course, these are not rights to enable them to murder or pursue racist activities. But even the worst of persons is entitled to proper treatment in prison, and to a fair trial and other basic rights.

1.1.6 **Rights and freedom—absolute and qualified rights**

At the heart of the theory of human rights is the recognition that individual lives are led in a social context and that it is entirely legitimate for states to place reasonable restraints on individuals in order to pursue the common good by advancing common interests and protecting general security. Thus identifying the rights individuals have will usually involve, first, recognising that individual freedom may be qualified by duties owed to others; second, that individual freedom must be qualified by recognising the rights of others; and, third, that identifying rights may require a 'balancing' or 'weighing' of individual interests or desires with the pursuit of legitimate social purposes. There are some exceptions: no one should be tortured, for example, or denied a fair trial just because there is a strong public interest that would be benefited. These are sometimes referred to as 'absolute' rights. But very often the language of human rights law is the language of the fair balance and a recognition that the particular content of an individual right can depend upon the socio-political context in which it is claimed. Often, but not exclusively, this relates to a claimed right to some freedom—to be private or to speak, for example. The importance of 'balance' and 'context' will become clear in the examination of the specific rights derived from the European Convention on Human Rights that forms much of the text of this book. It is found both in the text of the Convention and in the interpretation and application of the Convention by the European Court of Human Rights (ECtHR).

1.1.7 **Universalism**

One of the difficult questions about human rights is whether they are 'universal' and apply equally to all men and women throughout the world, or whether they are culturally specific. The latter can mean that, in some cultures, the concept of human rights simply makes no sense. Thus, it might be argued, in cultures which emphasise obedience and duty to God or to traditional structures of authority, the idea of basic individual entitlements which must be respected by such authority may make little sense.

The argument that human rights are culturally specific can also mean that the content of human rights—what particular rights we have—differs between cultures. Thus what counts as 'fair' in the context of a fair trial, or what particular limits to freedom of speech are 'necessary', may differ culture to culture. One argument, for instance, is that human rights embody so-called 'Western values'. They promote a particular form of individual freedom which is necessary for the consumer capitalism of the West but which is inappropriate for non-capitalist societies that have not fully embraced the capitalist way and are seeking other ways forward or simply to maintain pre-capitalist traditions. Other cultures may emphasise concepts of obedience and service over individualism. The African conception, for example, embodied in the African Charter, refers to the 'historical tradition and values of African civilization', stresses anti-colonialism and gives significant emphasis to the rights of 'peoples' and to the importance of familial relationships. The point is that such concepts are, as much as individual freedom, attached to ideas of personhood and of human dignity and so are not simply contradictions of human rights. From such perspectives, the claims of human rights can seem a form of cultural imperialism.

The claim to cultural relativism in human rights often misses some of the main points of the universalist approach.

- Some rights, like the prohibition of torture, are hard to make culturally relative.
- A universalist has no difficulty in accepting that the content of other rights, like freedom of expression, is culturally specific. All a universalist insists on is to protect the core, the central, meaning of such a right. The suppression of political speech is likely to be inconsistent with a universalist conception of freedom of speech in a way that restricting pornography, for example, is not.
- Cultural relativism about human rights, particularly about the core of the freedom human rights should offer, can be simply a mask for dictatorship and tyranny. Likewise the opponents of such oppressive regimes may find themselves bereft of effective argument and intellectual resources for their campaigns.
- There can also be arguments about what rights we have that may appear to be relativist but which, in fact, are about what rights, universally, we ought to have. Thus feminists may take the view that mainstream human rights embody the values of a patriarchal society. If this is true it is an argument for expanding our understanding of rights to ensure they are genuinely universal; it does not reinforce the argument for cultural relativism.

Political, legal and constitutional theory

1.2

To approach a theoretical understanding of human rights, it can be helpful to consider the matter at three different levels: political theory, legal theory and constitutional theory. These can be very complex and abstract. The aim in what follows is no more than to introduce some

1.2.1 **Political theory**

A political theory is a set of general ideas about how government and state power can best be understood and justified, and under what conditions it can be said that citizens have real obligations to obey the laws of the country they live in. Political theory is important because the fundamental point of human rights is that basic entitlements of the autonomous person are to be protected by the law and the state.

Liberalism, broadly defined

Human rights presuppose the truth of what might be called 'liberal' theories of politics, using the term 'liberal' in a very broad and inclusive way and certainly not with a 'large L' (ie not confined to Liberal political parties). Put in very general terms, human rights assume that, whatever else a political theory proposes, it must accept that the only thing with ultimate, non-instrumental, moral value is the human individual. The state, associations, groups, cultures, etc may be necessary for human flourishing and may make demands on the freedom of individuals, but they should not be ends in themselves and should not have ultimate moral significance into which the individual can be merged, subordinated or sacrificed. Liberal theories require that the 'private', an individual's sovereignty over his or her own affairs, must be accepted to some extent (even though the precise place where private and public matters divide is endlessly controversial). Liberal theories also require that government should be ultimately based on the consent of the governed (even though the nature and form that consent takes may be equally controversial).

John Locke (whose *Second Treatise on Government* was published in 1690), writing in part to justify the Glorious Revolution 1688 (the assumption of the monarchy by William III and Mary II on the basis of some general conditions imposed by Parliament), has given the classic justification of a liberal form of government. Locke destroyed the idea that the authority of government was traditional and ultimately divine. Rather, he asserted that individual rights to 'life, liberty and estates (property)' were natural to mankind. Through reason mankind understands that these rights need protection. The authority of legitimate government stems, therefore, from the people consenting to law and government in so far as it protects these basic rights. Government failure in this regard might justify revolution.

In the second half of the twentieth century liberal ideas have been reformulated, especially by John Rawls, initially in *A Theory of Justice*. The idea of natural rights is replaced by an attempt to work out what basic principles, to be reflected in constitutions and laws, would be chosen by people who have to choose without knowing whether they themselves would be winners or losers from the outcome. The argument is that reasonable people would choose, and give normal priority to, a system of equal basic rights and liberties. Such a system requires everyone's rights, including those of the least well off, to be recognised. (Rawls's work is complex and has been developed over the years.)

Non-liberal theories

Political theories which, for instance, depend upon enforcing the superiority of one race over another (Nazism) or which invest the state with a monopoly of moral or social truth to which the masses must subscribe (Stalinism) or which subordinate the law to the word of God as this is interpreted by an untouchable class of clerics, are theories which are unlikely to leave much room for recognising and supporting human rights.

Even non-authoritarian political theories, such as anarchism (not the bomb-throwing kind), may be hard to reconcile, theoretically, with human rights. Anarchism is a political theory that explores the possibility that individuals in their communities can conduct their affairs in the absence of states, laws and rules. Freed from these restraints, communities will develop their own inclusive and informal ways of self-government. But human rights imply entitlements embodied in authoritative, binding rules, which we call law. It implies the separation of powers by which the rules are impartially enforced by officials who are institutionally separated from the procedures by which social goals are chosen. This commitment to 'law', central to human rights, is hard to reconcile with anarchist approaches to politics.

This is no more than a suggestion that some general political theories may be incompatible with human rights. Of course the real problem, from a human rights point of view, is less the ideas and more the practices of violence and oppression by which non-liberal states conduct their affairs (this should not be taken to imply that liberal states never use oppression and violence).

1.2.2 **Rights and utility**

Utilitarian approaches to government do not sit easily with human rights. Utilitarians take the view that the proper standard for evaluating government actions relates to its outcomes. A policy is to be evaluated by one standard only, which is whether it maximises the common good or the well-being of individuals. Human rights theory, on the other hand, argues that policies must respect human rights no matter how beneficial they might be. So, for example, crime would probably be reduced if the police were allowed very wide powers to arrest, detain and administer summary punishments, and if the courts were allowed to convict on a balance of probabilities rather than beyond reasonable doubt. The reduction in crime would enormously improve the lives of vast numbers of people and, furthermore, it is likely that some seriously unpleasant criminals would be removed from circulation. Why, the utilitarian might argue, should such a policy not be pursued so long as the suffering of the small number of genuinely innocent people who are wrongly convicted was outweighed by the benefits? The argument for human rights is opposed to this in principle (ie not just because the number of wrongful convictions might be high and the suffering of those convicted very intense). Human rights is an argument about individuals' entitlements which should be upheld even if the interests of the majority or society as a whole are thereby less well served.

But even the most dogmatic utilitarian is likely to be committed to at least a 'procedural' account of human rights. Utilitarians need to have some way of calculating how to maximise individual happiness. In making this calculation the interests of every individual must be taken into account and given equal weighting. This creates individual entitlements to vote, for example, or to be able to express preferences in other ways such as by speech or association. These are human rights.

1.2.3 **Legal theory**

As noted at section 1.1.3, essential to the concept of human rights is the idea that they should be expressed as 'law', rules involving enforceable obligations which are binding on states. This takes us to the interface between the two dominant ways of thinking about the nature of law.

- 'Positivism' refers to a complex body of legal theory which identifies law as the willed actions of states. The law, in this sense, is identified in terms of legal sources such as legislation, case law, international treaties, etc. The law is known from these sources alone and, the point is, it can be identified without any need for an evaluation of whether it is good or bad, right or wrong, moral or immoral. Such questions (what common purposes should we follow by means of the law, what behaviour should the law prohibit, etc.) are essentially 'moral' or 'political' matters, distinguished from law.

- 'Natural law' identifies the law not in terms of the content of a range of sources, whatever that happens to be, but in terms of the real, the true, obligations that we have towards others and towards society. The task of the natural lawyer is to try and identify such true obligations on the basis, for example, of the will of God or the necessary inferences from the use of reason.

The point about human rights law is to get human rights values, expressed as enforceable rules, accepted as part of the 'positive law' of the countries of the world. But human rights law also seems to involve a 'natural law' claim that human rights values express a truth from which a series of genuine, objectively true obligations derive. These are obligations which exist whatever states choose to do. They are objective legal standards against which the positive law of states can be measured.

1.2.4 **Constitutional theory**

Human rights law, because it is pre-eminently aimed at states, raises a number of constitutional issues involving the general power of a state and the relations between its component parts.

Sovereignty

The world is made up of sovereign states claiming freedom to act as they see fit, particularly as regards their own population. Human rights law asserts that there are limits to the freedom of action of the governments of these states, particularly over their own people, and so it undermines the basic idea of sovereignty.

Majority rule

Human rights law claims that some form of democracy is the only acceptable form of government. However, it does not mean democracy as majority rule. Majorities can only rule subject to the rights of minorities and individuals: no matter how popular a cause, it cannot be supported by the law and the state if it violates individuals' rights.

The judiciary

Perhaps the most difficult constitutional issue arising from human rights law is the enhanced role within the constitution that it gives to judges. Human rights are to be enforced by the courts. On some view of human rights, judges should have the power to strike down legislation and declare it invalid (that it is not law at all). This power is not available in the United Kingdom nor in many other states. Even without this power, it remains the case that, in deciding human rights cases, judges may have to deny the view of the public interest and the common good chosen by government and parliament. The constitutional problem, of course, is that judges are not elected nor are they accountable to elected representatives. Nevertheless, human rights are expressed in general 'open-textured' terms which require interpretation if they are to be applied to particular cases. This job of interpretation and application falls on the judges and will often involve 'political' judgments of, for example, what specific restraints on freedom of speech are needed for the proper workings of a democratic society.

Deference and the constitutional balance

In fact human rights law tends not to involve out and out assertions by judges that they know better than government or legislature how to square the pursuit of the common good with protecting human rights. Human rights law tends, instead, to involve what has been called a form of constitutional discourse, between the different branches of the state—the courts, Parliament and the government. This is well illustrated under the Human Rights Act 1998 in the United Kingdom where, even if the courts adjudge legislation to be incompatible with human rights, they still cannot refuse to put it into effect. Rather, they may make a 'declaration of incompatibility'. The consequence is that the issue returns to government, which may propose alterations to the law which Parliament, subject to its normal pressures, accepts or rejects. Issues such as whether a policy has been approved by Parliament, or whether a policy has been decided by a public body expressly established to take decisions that impact on human rights (issues about privacy and the media, for example) are clearly significant in the way judges are likely to assess and understand their role. On some issues, like fair trials, judges may feel especially competent to make judgments, whilst on others, involving national security, for example, judges may be more willing to defer to the view of government. The point is that the role of the judges in human rights matters is complex, involving questions about the nature and importance of the right in question, the circumstances of the case and the proper role of Parliament and government. In the end, however, under human rights law, the proper understanding of the constitutional role of judges includes their responsibility for protecting individuals from serious human rights abuses.

Democratic politics

One important form of doubt and criticism about human rights is concerned that human rights law narrows the scope for a society to debate and decide issues in democratic and participative ways. Proponents of this view support the idea of human rights but doubt whether legal–judicial mechanisms are the best way forward. They tend to see human rights law as undermining other forms of political participation and democratic decision-taking. Important issues, like what can be published, where the border between the public and the private lies, what forms of sexual behaviour are acceptable, and so on, are removed from processes of democratic debate, persuasion and choice. Instead, in human rights discourse, they become recast into arguments of abstract principle which are decided by judges or other bodies of the great and good. The objection is not to the idea of human rights as such, but to human rights in its judicialised, judge-based form. On this view there should be greater trust in the democratic, participative, institutions in which such issues can be decided through the arguments and debates of representatives.

1.3 What rights do we have?

1.3.1 Civil and political rights

Nothing has so far been said about the nature and content of the rights that human beings enjoy. It is reasonable to identify a core list of human rights whilst recognising that the exact expression of the items on the list depends upon the treaty or other legal instrument in which they are laid down. It is also important to remember that our conception of what is fundamental to the dignity of an individual and necessary for an effective democracy can, whilst building on some basics, develop with time and depend upon cultural factors.

A standard list, derived from the United Nations Declaration on Human Rights of 1948 (UNDHR) includes the following: whoever they are, a person has a right that their life should be protected; they not be tortured or enslaved, nor be subject to arbitrary, lawless treatment by those in authority; they should be given fair trials; enjoy basic privacy and basic freedoms such as freedom of religion, speech, association and assembly, and the right to voluntary marriage, rights to vote and stand for election, and rights not to suffer discrimination on racial, sexual and other grounds.

These rights are articulated and specified in a range of instruments built on the UNDHR, including the European Convention on Human Rights. They tend to be thought of as civil and political rights.

Civil rights

Civil rights aim at individual liberty and at securing (in the United States' phrase) 'equal protection of the laws'. All men and women are to have equal legal status and equal rights to pursue their own way of life in society free of state oppression. Such civil rights are 'private' in the sense that they protect the liberty of individuals in their personal, economic, familial, religious and social lives. The list tends also to include rights to property. The latter can be controversial since large, commercial corporations have massive property interests which clearly involve the exercise of social power. The extent to which the exercise of such power needs protection through human rights law is controversial.

Political rights

'Political' rights are those which protect the freedoms necessary for a democracy in which there is participation in political processes: freedom of speech and association, the right to vote and stand in elections, and so on.

1.3.2 Social and 'third generation' rights

The conventional list of civil and political rights excludes 'social' rights. These are, for example, rights to housing, health, education and welfare support. Without these, human beings are bound by the necessities of staying alive and are unable to exercise any of the freedoms human rights seek to protect, and which are essential to autonomy and flourishing. At issue is the question of what is so fundamental to being human that it needs the special protection offered by human rights. Obviously this changes over time. Although there is little express recognition of social rights in the UNDHR or the European Convention, they have been increasingly accepted at the international level during the second half of the twentieth century.

What entitlements are considered fundamental in the early years of the twenty-first century? So-called 'third generation' rights are being promoted and developed (civil and political rights are 'first generation', social rights are 'second generation' in this taxonomy). Third generation rights include issues such as rights to a safe and sustainable environment, rights of peoples to self-development and to the protection of their cultural heritage. Of these, it is probably environmental rights which are best developed in terms of 'hard law'—court-enforceable rules. Other aspects of third generation rights tend to be more 'soft law'—policy aspirations to which states agree but to which they are not firmly bound.

1.3.3 Discrimination

Human rights also include the need for laws outlawing 'discrimination'. A person should be protected from general disadvantage or from less favourable treatment based on irrelevant criteria such as skin colour, race, sex, religion, etc. The types of forbidden reason for treating someone less favourably than another change over time (it is now widely accepted, for example, that discrimination based on sexual orientation should be made unlawful). The second half of the twentieth century saw a widespread recognition at national and international levels that people have a right to legal protection from discrimination. This is embodied in particular treaties and is established as a general principle of interpretation of all legal instruments.

1.3.4 **Negative and positive obligations**

A distinction is made between negative and positive obligations. Negative obligations require a state, through the government, not to commit wrongs (e.g. not to torture its prisoners). Positive obligations require states, through their governments, to undertake actions, usually involving the expenditure of resources. These might be, for example, to provide a system of police and courts in order to deter crime and ensure fair trials. In fact, the positive/negative distinction is often not very illuminating since the securing of most rights involves states in a combination of doing and not doing which cannot be easily separated.

1.3.5 **Human rights and the distribution of wealth**

As mentioned in section 1.2.4, under 'Democratic politics', some critics of human rights law are concerned that it takes too much away from Parliament and the democratic forum and gives too much power to the judiciary.

Such a view has greatest force where human rights require states to make large expenditures from scarce resources. These matters involve choices between different desirable goals and should be taken democratically. For this reason, distributive justice, the question of 'who gets what, when and where', the question of how resources and wealth are to be distributed, tend, above a basic minimum, to be excluded from the domain of human rights law. Lord Hoffmann put the point in this way:

> Human rights are the rights essential to the life and dignity of the individual in a democratic society. The exact limits of such rights are debatable and, although there is not much trace of economic rights in the 50-year-old Convention, I think it is well arguable that human rights include the right to a minimum standard of living, without which many of the other rights would be a mockery. But they certainly do not include the right to a fair distribution of resources or fair treatment in economic terms—in other words, distributive justice. Of course distributive justice is a good thing. But it is not a fundamental human right.

> (*Matthews* v *Ministry of Defence* [2003] UKHL 4, para 26)

1.4 **Human rights movement**

1.4.1 **Some historical roots**

The core idea behind human rights, that government is limited by a need to respect minimum entitlements of individuals, has a long history. It can probably be traced back to aspects of classical political thought such as that of the Roman jurist Cicero (106–43BC). Modern manifestations of the idea are found in the work of seventeenth-century political philosophers, particularly John Locke. At the level of practical politics, the revolutions in the American colonies and France, at the end of the eighteenth century, both resulted in new regimes founded on the basis of written constitutions which included statements of what are in effect (though not necessarily called as such) human rights. Of course, European history in the nineteenth century and the first half of the twentieth century is, to a great extent, a history of imperial autocracy giving way to dictatorship. Under neither did human rights flourish, and under both autocracy and dictatorship constitutionally based rights were set aside or ignored and the population oppressed.

In Britain, legal restraints on government can be traced back to the Magna Carta (when, in 1215, King John accepted certain restraints imposed upon him by the feudal lords) and to the English idea of Kingship, which is that the King's authority is derived from the law so that he rules on the basis of law and not on the basis of his will alone (this idea is associated, in particular, with Henry Bracton, whose major work on legal theory was written, probably by a number of scholars, in the mid-thirteenth century). In the absence of a written constitution (except during the time of the Cromwellian Protectorate between 1653 and 1660), the common law developed on the basis of the idea that a person is free to do whatever is not forbidden by law (by statutes, rules of common law and the decisions of juries).

The system in Britain has been complicated. The eighteenth century, through legal writers such as Blackstone, proclaimed the virtues of the common law as embodying liberty and basic rights, especially to property, which the law would protect. Bentham, at the end of the century, was, however, appalled at the arbitrary, cruel and uncertain way in which the common law, so dependant on the will of judges, was applied. Equally, however, he rejected the grand statements of human rights associated with the French and American revolutions. Bentham regarded these lists of rights as being so general and abstract as to be meaningless 'nonsense on stilts'. His solution was for rational reforms, on utilitarian principles, to be achieved by statute.

The nineteenth century saw the common law continuing to give legal force and recognition to many of the freedoms that today are expressed as civil and political rights. Dicey's conception of the rule of law expresses the common law's presumption of liberty and the need for restrictions to be focused and specifically justified. Like Bentham, he thought the grand lists of rights found in continental constitutions problematic—they were not linked to remedies and were often suspended by autocratic governments. Where liberty derived from the constitution (rather than being a simple presumption of law) such suspensions left the population vulnerable. Dicey, of course, also recognised the supremacy of Parliament. The common law could not provide some important entitlements. A number of important basic rights, such as the right to vote, depended upon Parliament responding to popular political movements. Likewise it is only Parliament that could provide for education etc. and other social conditions under which basic rights can flourish.

Though Britain was not invaded and did not suffer dictatorship, the nineteenth century and the first half of the twentieth century saw times of intense political oppression and, in the context of class politics, the application of laws in a far from even-handed manner.

1.4.2 The development of international human rights law

This book is about the Human Rights Act and the European Convention on Human Rights to which the Act gives effect in United Kingdom law. The Convention (which is discussed in Chapter 2) is a part of the international human rights movement. This movement is itself part of a broader expansion of public international law which has origins in the Middle Ages and came to its current maturity through a range of international agreements entered into in the nineteenth and twentieth centuries. The central idea is that sovereign states have obligations, as states operating in the international community, not only to respect the sovereignty of other states (the traditional focus of international law), but also to act with proper restraint towards their own populations and others, including their enemies.

This context includes the following:

- Laws of war. International, legal restraints on the conduct of war go back at least to Pope Innocent II's ban on the use of crossbows against Christians in 1139. Hugo Grotius codified these laws in *De Juri Belli ac Pacis*, 1625. Binding international agreements came later. By the Hague Convention 1907, states agreed to instruct their armed forces to obey the restatement of the laws and customs of war annexed to the Convention. This restatement is still in force as the basis of the legal regulations of the conduct of war by states and their forces.

- Humanitarian law. The Geneva Conventions (the first dates from 1864) are international agreements dealing with the treatment of wounded members of the armed forces, prisoners and civilians during wartime. Today there are four Conventions, which have been added to by three protocols. The Fourth Geneva Convention relates to the protection of civilians in time of war, and the first two Protocols thereto relate to the protection of the victims of international and non-international 'armed conflict' (e.g. conflicts involving non-state groups). These are of particular relevance to terrorist violence and states' responses to it in the twenty-first century.

- The League of Nations was established at the end of the First World War. Under its auspices, the laws of war and laws against slavery were enhanced and there was an attempt to give international protection to the rights of minorities. With the rise of European and Japanese fascism in the 1930s, the weakness of the League in the face of aggressive sovereign states was exposed.

The League ceased to exist at the end of the Second World War. It was replaced by the United Nations. It is under the auspices of the latter organisation that what we call the international human rights movement has developed and expanded.

1.4.3 **United Nations**

The founding document of the United Nations is its Charter. This expresses the chief aims of the organisation. These are to secure peace and security throughout the world and 'to reaffirm faith in fundamental human rights, in the dignity and worth of the human person, in the equal rights of men and women and of nations large and small'. Under the auspices of the UN a network of treaties, commissions and monitoring committees has been established. In particular the Human Rights Council (which replaced the Human Rights Commission in 2011) has a major role in promoting human rights and reviewing their protection amongst member states. A range of other human rights focused organizations report to the Council.

further study

For the functions and organisation of the United Nations, in respect of human rights, see Smith, chapters 3–5.

1.4.4 The international bill of rights

At the heart of the United Nations, commitment to human rights is the 'International Bill of Rights'.

Universal Declaration of Human Rights

The Universal Declaration of Human Rights (UDHR) was adopted as an international standard by the General Assembly in 1948. It is the basic list of fundamental rights and freedoms, identified and accepted by the nations of the world. It is the inspiration and moral authority for the human rights movement. It does not, however, directly create legally binding duties and obligations on states. Nevertheless it is referred to in the constitutions of some states. There is also judicial opinion that the Declaration, or at least some of its most fundamental terms such as the bans on torture and slavery, can be considered to be part of customary international law (see the 'Customary international law and the common law' box text in this section) and thus binding on states. In any event, like other UN Declarations, it has great persuasive and inspirational authority on national and regional courts. It stands behind a number of regional systems of human rights, including the European Convention on Human Rights.

International Covenant on Civil and Political Rights

Through the International Covenant on Civil and Political Rights (ICCPR) the rights and freedoms in Articles 1 to 21 of the UDHR are made into binding obligations on states. States agree to ensure that the rights and freedoms listed in the Covenant are effectively protected in their national laws (Article 2 ICCPR). Articles 1 to 21 contain the fundamental civil and political rights derived from the principle of autonomy (rights to life, not to be tortured, to physical liberty, to freedom of expression, etc.) mentioned at 1.3.1.

The period after the Second World War was characterised by international tensions and fundamental ideological divisions. This meant that it was not until 1966 that a majority (but not all) UN states accepted such obligations and signed the Covenant; it then took a further ten years for the Covenant to be brought into effect. Most countries in the world are 'parties' to the Covenant and accept its obligations (167 in June 2012).

The main mechanism for enforcement is through five-yearly reports from the states on the measures they have taken to ensure compatibility with the Covenant. The reports are sent to the Human Rights Committee (established by the Covenant and to be distinguished from the Human Rights Council, mentioned in section 1.4.3), which is supervised by the Economic and Social Council of the UN and, ultimately, the UN's General Assembly. The reports from states can be commented upon by interested non-governmental organisations (NGOs) such as Amnesty. The Committee then makes its own comments on the state reports. Ultimate enforcement is through the publicity given to the Committee's comments through the annual report of the Committee to the General Assembly. The Committee also produces General Comments which involve a detailed examination on how particular articles of the Covenant should be implemented. There is a system allowing one state to bring a case before the Committee against another state, but this tends to be ineffective because it depends upon the agreement of both states involved and, for diplomatic reasons, states are reluctant to challenge each other.

The First Optional Protocol to the Covenant introduces a system for individuals to petition the Committee on violations of the Covenant of which they have been the victim and which have not been remedied by their national law. The Committee presents its 'views' on the case to the state involved and to the complainant, and summarises these individual cases in its annual report. Individual application is an important element in the enforcement of the Covenant. The First

Protocol is, however, optional for states. In June 2012, of the 167 parties only 114 were parties to the First Protocol (the United Kingdom, like the United States, has not agreed to the Protocol).

International Covenant of Economic, Social and Cultural Rights

Signatory states to the International Covenant of Economic, Social and Cultural Rights (ICESCR) agree to the progressive realisation, relative to their resources, of a range of rights such as a right to work and earn a living, rights to health, education and welfare, and rights to a cultural life. The Covenant is based on Articles 22 to 29 of the UN Declaration. Enforcement is by reporting alone and, it is generally agreed, the Covenant is predominantly aspirational (identifying policy goals which it is the hope and intention of a state to achieve, rather than setting out specific legal obligations.) Such second generation social rights are resource intensive and so it is hard to require states to accept full legal obligations in these areas.

There are many other instruments of international law, many based on the authority of the United Nations, which bear on human rights. Examples include

- International Convention on the Elimination of All Forms of Racial Discrimination (1966);
- Convention on the Elimination of All Forms of Discrimination against Women (1979);
- Convention against Torture and Other Cruel, Inhuman or Degrading Treatment or Punishment (1984);
- Convention on the Rights of the Child (1989);
- Convention against Transnational Organised Crime (2003) and its Protocol to Prevent, Suppress and Punish Trafficking of Persons, Especially Women and Children (2003).

Each Convention has its own methods of enforcement. It must be remembered that, at international law, a country is only bound by the treaties and obligations it has accepted. Some Conventions have additional protocols which can be important for making the protection effective (e.g. by allowing individuals to complain). But these may be voluntary and agreed to by a small number of states who may, in any case, be the states that have the least to fear.

International Criminal Court

The role of the International Criminal Court (ICC) is to prosecute individuals, including state officials, for the crimes (as defined in the statute) of genocide, crimes against humanity and war crimes. Its authority is based on the Rome Statute. It is linked to but independent of the United Nations. In 2012 it delivered its first judgment in the case of *Lubanga* ICC-01/04-01/06-2842.

Individual actions

Cross reference
See, for example, R (Al-Jedda) v Secretary of State for Defence [2007] UKHL 58, discussed in Chapter 4, 4.3.2.

The UN, acting through its institutions such as the Security Council, can require states to act, including requiring steps to be taken against particular individuals. For example, the Security Council's Al-Qaida and Taliban Sanctions Committee can authorise the freezing of assets of named persons. Likewise actions taken (in Iraq for instance) based on UN authority, can involve the detention of individuals. These actions can raise difficult questions about whether the procedures are fair to the individuals and whether their other human rights, especially the right to liberty, are properly protected.

Customary international law and the common law

There are some rules and practices that are universally recognised by states as being part of their general legal obligations as states; not just things they do voluntarily and in their own interests, but things they do as requirements of their status as civilised states recognising the rule of law.

These obligations apply generally and irrespective of any treaty obligations. Such obligations are part of the so-called compelling law of nations (*jus cogens*) and apply *erga omnes* (they are enforceable by all states against all states). As an overriding, non-voluntary obligation on states, it seems that an action based on a breach of the *jus cogens* can be heard in national courts, including those of the United Kingdom.

1.4.5 **Regional**

The United Nations has inspired a number of 'regional' developments. The Organization of American States, the African Union and the League of Arab States are regional international organisations which have developed institutions for the securing of human rights in ways that those organisations consider reflect the societies and cultures of the region, the problems they have to deal with and the power structures that apply. Thus there is the American Convention on Human Rights (1969), the African Charter on Human and People's Rights and the Arab Charter on Human Rights (2004). Linked to these Conventions and Charters are a range of other instruments and systems for enforcement.

The European Convention on Human Rights was created by the Council of Europe after the Second World War. In terms particularly of enforcement and authority it is probably the most effective of all the regional systems for protecting human rights. It is the substance of the rights and freedoms contained in this Convention that have been given further effect in the law of the United Kingdom by means of the Human Rights Act 1998 and which forms the subject matter of the rest of this book.

Summary

To make sense of the European Convention on Human Rights and the Human Rights Act 1998, it is helpful to

- understand some of the basic issues about human rights—what they are in philosophical and theoretical terms and what general issues of a political, legal and constitutional kind the enforcement of human rights is likely to give rise to;

- know the traditional content of human rights, and the question of how, if at all, that content should develop to reflect a modern political agenda; and

- understand in basic outline the development of the international human rights movement of which the European Convention is a part.

On the basis of this understanding, it is possible to move on to consider the Act and the Convention in more detail. Many of the issues addressed in this chapter underlie legal problems about the interpretation and application of the Act that are developed later.

Further reading

INTRODUCTIONS TO INTERNATIONAL HUMAN RIGHTS LAW

Smith, R. *Textbook on International Human Rights* 5th edn (2011) Oxford: OUP

ON THE CONCEPT OF HUMAN RIGHTS

Dworkin, R. *Taking Rights Seriously* (1977) London: Duckworth, esp Chapter 4

Finnis, J. *Natural Law and Natural Rights* (1980) (2011) Oxford: Clarendon Press

Gearty, C. A. *Principles of Human Rights Adjudication* (2004) Oxford: OUP

Griffin, J. *On Human Rights* (2008) Oxford: OUP

Rawls, J. *The Law of Peoples* (1992) Cambridge, Mass.: Harvard UP

Raz, J. 'Human Rights without Foundations' (2007) Oxford Legal Studies Research Paper No 14/2007

CRITICAL DISCUSSION ON HUMAN RIGHTS CAN BE FOUND IN

Campbell, T. et al (eds) *The Legal Protection of Human Rights Sceptical Essays* (2011) Oxford: OUP

Waldron, J. (ed) *Theories of Rights* (1984) Oxford: OUP

FOR DISCUSSION OF DIFFERENT CONSTITUTIONAL THEORIES SEE

Allan, T. R. S. *Constitutional Justice* (2001) Oxford: OUP

Hickman, T. 'Constitutional Dialogue, Constitutional Theories and the Human Rights Act 1998' [2005] *Public Law* 306

Tomkins, A. *Our Republican Constitution* (2005) Oxford: Hart Publishing

Waldron, J. *Law and Disagreement* (1999) Oxford: OUP

The European Convention on Human Rights

Chapter overview

- The creation of the European Convention and the European Court of Human Rights (ECtHR) by the Council of Europe (not the European Union).
- The rights and freedoms in the Convention and the obligation on the states to secure them.
- The right of an individual to apply to the ECtHR where states have failed in this duty.
- The make-up and functions of the ECtHR.
- The issue of reform.

Introduction

It is very important to distinguish the Human Rights Act 1998 (HRA) from the European Convention for the Protection of Human Rights and Fundamental Freedoms, usually known as the European Convention on Human Rights (ECHR). The Act is an ordinary Act of Parliament and is part of the law of the United Kingdom. The Convention is a legal instrument of the Council of Europe (the Council is identified and explained later in the chapter). The Convention is not, in itself, part of UK law. However, its content, the rights and freedoms contained in it, are given effect in the law of England and Wales, Scotland and Northern Ireland by the Act. The Convention is interpreted and applied by the ECtHR. Its judgments are not directly binding as legal judgments in the United Kingdom; however, the principles developed by the ECtHR in interpreting the Convention must be taken into account (and are usually followed) by UK courts dealing with HRA cases.

By the twenty-first century the ECtHR had developed a huge backlog of cases. In this context there is an on-going process of reform.

2.1 The history and development of the Convention system

convention

The term 'convention', in this context, simply means an international agreement between sovereign states by which they agree to be bound by the terms of the convention; it means broadly the same thing as a 'treaty'. The term 'convention' can also mean an unwritten rule based on practice, and this is the sense in which we talk of 'constitutional conventions' in Constitutional Law. It is important to distinguish between these two meanings.

As mentioned in Chapter 1, the general idea of legally protected human rights began to gather force at the end of the Second World War. The inspiration was the emergence of the United Nations, whose Charter came into force in October 1945 and which adopted the Universal Declaration on Human Rights in December 1948. The context was the appalling devastation, disruption and state of turmoil of large parts of the world when hostilities ceased in 1945. Europe, at the end of the war, had to deal with massive social and economic problems and the legacies of the Holocaust, widespread atrocities, racism and all the deadly corruption of public life associated with totalitarian dictatorships. The need after 1945 was not only to deal with these problems by reconstruction, but also to try to create institutions which would help to remove the causes of war for the future and provide protection from any threat that totalitarian government might revive. Two principal solutions were adopted: the European Union (as it has now become), and the Council of Europe. These need to be distinguished.

2.1.1 **The European Union**

The European Union, as it is now known, had its origins in the Treaty of Rome 1956. Its principal aim was to encourage European economic integration in order to eliminate the causes of war. Its aim now is to 'promote peace, its values and the well-being of its peoples', and its values include 'respect for human rights' (Articles 3 and 2 Treaty on European Union (TEU)). The original six members have now expanded to twenty-seven. The European Union has, of course, developed into one of the major economic and trading blocs in the world. Economic integration implies wider social and political linking, and the extent to which economic unity (through a free internal market) requires common laws and rules in other areas such as taxation, employment law, welfare policy, criminal law, health and safety, and even foreign policy is, of course, one of the most delicate and controversial matters of twenty-first century European politics.

The European Union has committed itself to the protection of human rights, and this is discussed in Chapter 3, section 3.4.

Full discussion of the European Union is outside the scope of this book.

KEY POINT A common mistake is to believe that the Human Rights Act and the ECHR are linked directly to the European Union. This is wrong. The Convention comes from the Council of Europe, which is separate from the European Union and has a different history, aims, organisation, etc. Many countries are members of the Council of Europe without being members of the European Union. However, the Convention is part of the 'general principles of the Union's law' and, following the Lisbon Treaty, the EU is committed to acceding to the Convention (Article 6 TEU).

2.1.2 **The Council of Europe**

A second solution was the Council of Europe. Since the principal instrument by which the Council achieves its aims is the ECHR, the Council needs to be considered in some detail.

2.2 **The Council of Europe**

2.2.1 **Introduction**

cross reference

The international context of the development of human rights is discussed in Chapter 1, sections 1.4.2. and 1.4.3

The Council of Europe was established by the Treaty of London in 1949. There were originally ten members: Belgium, Denmark, France, Italy, Luxembourg, the Netherlands, Ireland, Norway, Sweden and the United Kingdom. Where the European Union (as it now is) sought greater unity by predominantly economic means, the Council of Europe had and has a much wider aim, which embraces social, political and cultural development and the protection of human rights.

The Council of Europe is perhaps the most successful of the regionally based international organisations that take their inspiration from the United Nations and its Declaration of Human Rights.

2.2.2 Membership

The 'Cold War' created a divided Europe and, until the early 1990s, membership of the Council of Europe increased but was confined to western European states. Such states enjoyed broadly common interests: they had capitalist or 'mixed' economies, were Christian in heritage (with the major exception of Turkey, which joined in 1950) and had liberal democratic political institutions based, for example, on elected governments and the rule of law. There were few big disagreements between the members (the main exception being the dispute between Turkey and Greece over Cyprus). This common culture made the creation and development of the Council of Europe easier than if it was trying to establish itself amongst nation states that were fundamentally hostile to each other. With the ending of the Cold War, east European countries, Russia and other nations created out of the Soviet Union have joined. Members must be European states that are pluralist democracies which respect both the rule of law and human rights. In June 2012 there were forty-seven full member states.

2.2.3 Aims of the Council of Europe

The Statute of the Council of Europe is its constitution. Article 1(a) defines its basic purposes:

> The aim of the Council of Europe is to achieve a greater unity between its members for the purpose of safeguarding and realising the ideals and principles which are their common heritage and facilitating their economic and social progress.

The principal means to achieve this is defined in Article 1(b):

> This aim shall be pursued through the organs of the Council by discussion of questions of common concern and by agreements and common action in economic, social, cultural, scientific, legal and administrative matters and in the maintenance and further realisation of human rights and fundamental freedoms.

The most important way of promoting these aims has been the production, in 1950, of the ECHR and the creation, in 1959, of the ECtHR to enforce the Convention. But the aims of the Council go beyond securing human rights. It has, for example, a significant role in promoting amongst member states high common standards in relation to social cohesion, education, sport and culture; it also pursues 'integrated projects' on themes such as democracy or domestic violence. The Council has an important position in promoting and investigating human rights compliance by member states. It is also concerned in a huge variety of issues, not just human rights. These include (to name but a few): childrens' rights, migration in Europe, health care, media freedom and the internet, and violence in sport. It takes positions on international issues, such as (in 2012) the 'Arab Spring' and the violence in Syria.

The Council has also adopted many other conventions on human rights issues that go beyond the terms of the ECHR. These include

- the European Social Charter 1961, dealing with social and economic rights;
- the European Convention for the Prevention of Torture and Inhuman and Degrading Punishment 1987, which enhances state responsibilities on the treatment of prisoners and others;
- the European Convention on the Adoption of Children (revised) 2011, which updates principles dealing with adoption, for example requiring paternal consent.

2.2.4 Institutions of the Council of Europe

The principal institutions created by the statute

The Statute of the Council of Europe created two controlling 'organs':

The Committee of Ministers is the Council's decision-making body responsible for determining policy and putting the aims into effect. As a 'guardian of the Council's fundamental values', it also has the principal role in enforcing and monitoring the way in which member states comply with their Council of Europe obligations. This includes ensuring that states respond fully to adverse judgments by the ECtHR. The members of the Committee are the foreign ministers of the member states or their representatives. States may also appoint a Permanent Representative, usually a senior diplomat, who keeps continual contact between the state and the Council. The Committee represents the interests of the governments of the member states as they struggle both to protect their national interests but also to pursue the collective aims of the Council of Europe.

The Parliamentary Assembly (originally known as the Consultative Assembly) is the chief deliberative organ of the Council of Europe which debates issues and makes recommendations to the Committee of Ministers. It consists of delegations chosen from and by the national legislatures; the size of the delegation relates to the population of the country. The United Kingdom is allowed a delegation of eighteen, chosen from the House of Commons and House of Lords.

Institutions created by the Council of Europe

The Committee of Ministers, exercising its powers under the statute, and acting on recommendations from the Parliamentary Assembly, has created a number of 'institutions' and bodies such as

- the ECtHR, which is described later in this chapter and whose judgments form an important part of this book;
- the Congress of Local and Regional Authorities, which provides a forum for the promotion and monitoring of democracy as embodied in the local and regional government in member states.

Of particular importance in the human rights context is the Human Rights Commissioner.

- The Office of the Human Rights Commissioner was established by the Council of Europe in 1999. The Commissioner's role is to promote education, awareness and effective protection of human rights amongst the member states of the Council so that there is full enjoyment of these rights for all. Under Article 36(3) the Commissioner has standing to submit comments and take part in the hearings of cases before the Court.

- The Commissioner also identifies and comments on shortcomings of the law and practice of the member states in respect of human rights. To this end, the Commissioner visits member states and reports on the human rights protection in those states in general terms or in respect of particular issues (but not individual cases). During these visits he meets not only with government officials but also with non-government organisations (e.g. organisations promoting prison reform or the interests of asylum seekers) and others. These reports provide a very valuable means of measuring the success of member states in securing human rights for all persons in their territories; they also indicate the kinds of issues that are currently creating difficulties and problems for human rights protection. There have been general visits to all forty-seven countries. The current Commissioner (Nils Muiznieks) is now more concerned with focusing on particular issues.

further study

The Commissioner visited the United Kingdom in 2004 (which focused on anti-terrorism law, the detention of asylum seekers and anti-social behaviour orders) and again in 2008 (which focused on child custody). His concerns in 2012 related to juvenile justice and travellers' rights. The reports are a valuable source for critical evaluation of the state of human rights in the United Kingdom. See the Council of Europe Portal http://www.coe.int, follow the links to 'Commissioner for Human Rights' then 'Activities' then 'Country Monitoring'. These can be searched by country or by year.

Secretariat

The statute also establishes a Secretariat, led by the Secretary General. The Secretariat provides administrative and secretarial services to the Committee of Ministers and to the Parliamentary Assembly and to the institutions they have created, including the ECtHR.

Council of Europe and European Union

It is easy to confuse some of the offices and institutions of the Council of Europe with similar-sounding institutions of the European Union. Thus:

- The Council of Europe must be distinguished from the 'European Council' (where the heads of government of the member states of the European Union meet to decide basic policy) and 'the Council' (which has important legislative and executive functions in the EU and consists of ministers from member states).

- The Parliamentary Assembly must be distinguished from the 'European Parliament' (which is the directly elected assembly with various advisory and law-making powers of the European Union).

- The ECtHR, which sits in Strasbourg, must be distinguished from the Court of Justice of the European Union (which sits in Luxembourg and is the court which interprets and applies the treaties of the European Union).

- The European Commission of Human Rights, which, until it was abolished in 1998, decided which cases could be heard by the ECtHR (a role now performed by the Court itself) must be distinguished from the 'European Commission' (which is the chief executive body of the European Union).

- The flags and anthems of the Council of Europe and of the European Union are the same: a blue flag with a circle of twelve yellow stars, and Beethoven's tune from his setting of Schiller's 'Ode to Joy' in the Ninth Symphony.

2.3

European Convention on Human Rights: the rights and freedoms

2.3.1 Introduction

In fulfilment of its aims, the Council of Europe sought to create an effective means, legally enforced, for the protection of the human rights of the people living in the member states. The essential features of the system are

- a list of fundamental rights and freedoms;
- an obligation on member states to secure these rights and freedoms for all the people in their territory;
- a system for enforcement and remedies based on a court of human rights whose decisions should be accepted by member states: failure to accept the decision can lead to political or diplomatic pressure from the Committee of Ministers;
- a 'right of individual application' by which individuals can take their own governments before the ECtHR alleging they have been the victim of a violation of one or more of the rights or freedoms.

2.3.2 The drafting of the Convention

The Convention was adopted (signed and ratified by ten member states of the Council of Europe, the number needed to bring it into effect) in 1950 and came into force in 1953. In 1954 three rights (property, education and elections), which were not agreed in time, were added by the First Protocol to the Convention. Since then, there have been fourteen Protocols, some adding to the list of rights and freedoms and others dealing with the structure of the Court and procedural matters. Protocol 14 introduced important procedural reforms and came into effect in June 2010.

. . . .

Protocol

A Protocol is a further agreement which develops, amends or modifies the main Convention and has the same legal force as the main Convention. Some Protocols are voluntary and so states can have obligations under the main Convention without having to agree to the new Protocol (the United Kingdom, for example, has not agreed to Protocol 4 on freedom of movement and other matters). Other Protocols, such as Protocol 14, are compulsory in the sense that all signatories of the main Convention must agree to them.

. . . .

2.3.3 Rights and freedoms (the 'substantive rights')

The rights guaranteed by the Convention are:

The original Convention (section 1 of the Convention)

The right to life (Article 2); the right not to suffer torture or inhuman or degrading treatment or punishment (Article 3); the right not to suffer slavery or forced labour (Article 4); the right to liberty and security (Article 5); the right to a fair trial (Article 6); the right not to be punished other than on the basis of law (Article 7); the right to respect for private and family life, home and correspondence (Article 8); the right to freedom of thought, conscience and religion (Article 9); the right to freedom of expression (Article 10); the right to freedom of assembly and association (Article 11); the right to marry (Article 12).

cross reference

See Chapter 5, section 5.1 for Article 13 and Chapter 7 for the other ancillary rights.

Section 1 also includes ancillary rights, which qualify the way the other rights are secured: the right to a remedy (Article 13), the right not to suffer discrimination (Article 14, see section 2.3.3 and Chapter 7, section 7.1), the power of states to 'derogate' from (to suspend) parts of the Convention (Article 15), the power of states to restrict the political activities of aliens (Article 16) and the prohibition on the abuse of rights (Article 17).

The First Protocol

The right to the peaceful enjoyment of possessions (Article 1), the right to education (Article 2), the right to free elections (Article 3).

The Fourth Protocol

The right not to be imprisoned for debt (Article 1), the right to freedom of movement (Article 2), the right not to be expelled from the territory of one's nation state (Article 3), the right of aliens (foreigners) not to suffer collective expulsion (Article 4).

The Seventh Protocol

The right of an alien not to be arbitrarily expelled (Article 1), the right to an appeal in criminal cases (Article 2), the right to compensation for wrongful conviction of a crime (Article 3), the right not to be tried or punished twice (Article 4), the right of spouses to equality (Article 5).

The Thirteenth Protocol (replacing the Sixth Protocol)

The right not to suffer the death penalty even in time of war (Article 1).

Discrimination (Article 14 and the Twelfth Protocol)

Article 14 of the original Convention provides the right not to suffer discrimination, but it is confined to discrimination in the way the other rights in the Convention and Protocols are secured; Article 1 of the Twelfth Protocol creates a general right not to suffer discrimination which is not restricted to the context of a Convention right.

Section 2 of the original Convention and the other Protocols

These deal with the ECtHR and with procedural matters.

2.3.4 Types of rights

The Convention secures different freedoms in different ways:

- Absolute rights. The Convention aims to secure some freedoms by imposing duties on states that must be performed in all circumstances. In particular, the freedom must be secured even in times of national emergency and if there are strong public interests or rights of others that would be served or protected if the duty was not performed. The right not to be tortured, in Article 3, is the best example.

- Limited rights. Some Convention Articles seek to secure a particular freedom by asserting it in general terms and then identifying the only circumstances in which it can be limited. Thus Article 5 asserts the right to personal liberty and then goes on to itemise the only circumstances in which it is legitimate to limit it, for example by imprisonment after conviction for an offence.

- 'Qualified' or restrictable rights. Articles 8, 9, 10 and 11 provide rights to private life, freedom of belief, freedom of expression and freedom of association and assembly. In all four instances, it is easy to think of examples in which, in order to protect the rights of others or to protect a public interest, it is perfectly proper and legitimate to use the law to restrict the exercise of these freedoms. This is recognised in the Convention. For example, there is no serious objection in principle to restricting freedom of speech (especially of the media) in order to protect the fairness of trials. There is, though, likely to be disagreement on precisely how extensive these restrictions should be. As we shall see, each of these Articles allows the freedom they deal with to be restricted if it is done lawfully, if the restriction serves a legitimate purpose and if the restriction is necessary and is no more than a proportionate burden on the individual affected.

2.3.5 The Convention and the modern political agenda

cross reference
Civil and political rights are defined in Chapter 1, section 1.3.1.

As a reading of the list given at section 2.3.3 shows, the Convention expresses predominantly civil and political rights.

Some critics argue that, despite its capacity to evolve, the Convention fails to embody rights that reflect the political priorities and assumptions of the twenty-first century.

discussion topic

Has the 'human rights agenda' moved on and left the Convention looking rather old-fashioned and limited?

Consider

(a) Whether the Convention really does establish basic rights protecting the most important interests of individuals. For example, it is not strong on social rights (rights to health, education, housing, welfare, etc.) which, for most people, might be much more important than various civil and political rights that are never in issue for them.

(b) Whether there are 'new' interests and concerns that have come to the top of the political agenda in Europe and which ought to be considered for protection as human rights in the Convention. For example, the Convention gives no express protection to the environment (though some environmental rights are implied from Article 8); no special recognition of children's vulnerabilities and their need for rights protection; though committed to pluralism, there is little in the Convention that imposes duties on states to protect and empower women, ethnic or religious minorities, etc.; nothing in the Convention protects animals.

(c) Arguments against expanding Convention rights in this way might include considering

- whether widening the scope of court-enforceable human rights undermines democracy by taking too much away from political representatives and giving too much influence to judges;

- whether legal protection for welfare etc. is best achieved by particular, tailor-made conventions, rather than being grafted onto the European Convention. This, in fact, is what is happening with international conventions of an ever-widening range of matters, including the rights of children and the environment.

cross reference
Consider, on this point, the discussion in Chapter 1, section 1.2.4, (Democratic politics).

2.3.6 Comparisons with the International Covenant on Civil and Political Rights

Though the Convention was inspired by the United Nations, there are a number of rights in the International Covenant on Civil and Political Rights that are not in the Convention. The Fourth and Seventh Protocols of the Convention (see section 2.3.3) added rights from the Covenant that were left out of the original Convention.

In some areas the Covenant continues to give wider or more particular protection than the Convention appears to:

- The Covenant contains specific rights relating to the treatment of prisoners, such as the need to separate remand from convicted prisoners and to treat prisoners humanely.
- The Covenant expressly recognises, to some extent, the particular situation of children.
- The Covenant expressly gives a wider right to participate in public affairs than does the Convention.
- The Covenant gives a right not to suffer discrimination which is more extensive in its effects than the same right in the Convention.
- The Covenant expressly guarantees rights for minorities.
- The Covenant expressly outlaws propaganda for war.

cross reference

The International Covenant on Civil and Political Rights is discussed in Chapter 1, section 1.4.4.

2.4 The states' obligations and the impact of the Convention in domestic law

2.4.1 Sovereign states and international law

The Convention, produced by the Council of Europe, is part of the system of international law. International law operates on the basis of sovereign states who control their own affairs and should not interfere in the affairs of other states. There is no system of 'World government'; the authority of the United Nations comes solely from the agreement of sovereign states. It follows that the primary responsibility to protect individuals from human rights abuses lies with the states. The irony is obvious, since the states are also the perpetrators of human rights abuses. The Convention, therefore, is, ultimately, a voluntary system by which the member states agree to uphold human rights in their territories. To emphasise the 'voluntary' nature of the obligation is, however, slightly misleading. Of course European states can choose not to sign the Convention or to leave the Council of Europe. States are entitled to 'denounce' the Convention and no longer be bound by it, though Article 58 requires a minimum period of five years from signing before this can be done. But such steps are likely to be politically embarrassing and damaging, and considerable costs may flow from the loss of reputation that will follow.

2.4.2 The obligation of the states

cross reference

The 'positive duties' of states are discussed in Chapter 6, section 6.6.

Under the Convention and the Protocols, the 'High Contracting Parties' (the nation states that have signed and ratified the Convention) agree to the following:

- **Secure the rights for everyone.** By Article 1 the states agree 'to secure to everyone within their jurisdiction the rights and freedoms defined in section 1 of this Convention'. This is the basic, general obligation that the states enter into. It obliges states to alter and amend their laws if necessary and also the practices of their government, police and other public authorities in order to ensure that the Convention rights and freedoms are secured. It may also impose 'positive duties' which require states to introduce new laws or new government practices, perhaps even to spend large sums of money on so doing.

States must do what is required to secure human rights; though, in contexts where money may have to be spent, what is required may be no more than is reasonable in the circumstances.

KEY POINT A state's duty under Article 1 is owed to 'everyone'. What this means is that the state must protect the human rights not only of 'citizens' but of all human beings, including, for example, foreigners or people who are in the country illegally. In particular, it means that states cannot do what, for example, the Nazis did in respect of Jews, and identify a group for discrimination and simply declare that they are not citizens.

cross reference
Article 13 is discussed in Chapter 5, section 5.1. Exhausting domestic remedies is discussed in detail later in this chapter (section 2.7.1).

- **Provide effective remedy in national courts.** By Article 13 the states agree to provide an effective remedy in their courts for violations of the Convention. This demonstrates that the first and primary responsibility for human rights protection, the first line of defence for victims, lies with the national courts, not the ECtHR. The latter should only be called upon following a failure or inability of the national courts to put the Convention properly into effect. It follows that applicants to the ECtHR must have 'exhausted their domestic (national) remedies' before their case can be 'admissible' and heard by the Court.
- **Allow access to the ECtHR.** States must ensure that a person who is unable to get satisfaction from the national courts is able to exercise their right under Article 34 of the Convention and go to the ECtHR in Strasbourg. Article 34 requires that states do not 'hinder in any way the exercise of that right'.
- **Accept judgments of the ECtHR.** Where a case goes to the ECtHR the signatory states, under Article 46, agree to 'abide by the final judgment of the Court in any case to which they are parties'. Thus, if the Court orders the payment of money as 'just satisfaction' for the violation, then the states agree to pay it.

2.4.3 'The state'

These obligations are on the state in all its forms: a 'government', which makes policy and puts it into effect using the resources of the state (in the United Kingdom: the Prime Minister, Cabinet, ministers and civil service, etc.); a 'legislature' that make the laws for society, laws which apply to both the population and the government (in the United Kingdom: the House of Commons and the House of Lords); and the 'courts' or 'judiciary' who interpret and apply the laws in particular cases (in the United Kingdom: the courts and tribunals). Under the Convention the state as a whole (represented at Strasbourg by the government) has responsibility to ensure that all these bodies comply with the Convention. As can be seen in Chapter 4, however, the situation is different under UK law. In particular, Parliament, under the Human Rights Act, is not required only to legislate compatibly with the Convention, and the courts must apply national law even if it is incompatible.

A whole range of other public bodies also exercise state power in the sense that the state, through the government, is responsible for them to Strasbourg. These include regional and local government and the huge range of so-called 'non-departmental public bodies' or 'quangos' which characterise the 'multi-layered' character of modern administrative life. Indeed, the ECtHR has even insisted that, in some circumstances, 'the state' can be responsible for the activities of private companies or organisations (e.g. independent schools in respect of punishments which may violate Article 3).

2.4.4 **Reservations**

When signing the Convention and accepting its general obligations, states may, nevertheless, choose to exempt particular laws from the provisions of the Convention. This is called 'making a reservation'. A reservation can be made in respect of any provision in the Convention. Reservations are controversial and undesirable since they enable states to choose the Convention rights they will protect.

. . . .

reservations and derogations

Making a reservation can be contrasted with the power to 'derogate' under Article 15. A derogation is a suspension of agreed Convention obligations. States can only derogate in times of war or national emergency and cannot derogate in respect of the most fundamental rights, such as the right not to be tortured. Derogation is discussed in Chapter 7, section 7.2.

. . . .

Article 57   Reservations

1. Any state may, when signing this Convention or when depositing its instrument of ratification, make a reservation in respect of any particular provision of the Convention to the extent that any law then in force in its territory is not in conformity with the provision. Reservations of a general character shall not be permitted under this article.

2. Any reservation made under this article shall contain a brief statement of the law concerned.

The scope of this power was discussed by the ECtHR in *Belilos* v *Switzerland* (1988) 10 EHRR 466 (paras 52–59). Reservations must be interpreted restrictively. The ECtHR stressed that a reservation cannot be general in scope. It must identify, clearly and precisely, a specific legal provision or provisions to which it applies and the kinds of disputes and issues which are thereby likely to be exempted from Convention control. The brief statement of the law that is to be exempted, which is required by Article 57(2), is necessary for legal certainty and so its absence makes any purported reservation invalid. This provision must be fulfilled even if the nature of the legal system makes this difficult (as was the case in *Belilos* dealing with criminal procedure in a federal system). Reservations apply to the statutes etc. they specify. They do not automatically apply to similar laws enacted later (*Dacosta Silva* v *Spain* App 6996/01, judgment of 2 February 2007). Where, however, a reservation meets the requirements of Article 57, it will be given effect by the Court (see, for example, *Jecius* v *Lithuania* (2002) 35 EHRR 16).

KEY POINT The United Kingdom has a reservation in respect of Article 2 of the First Protocol, the right to education. It is maintained under the terms of the Human Rights Act 1998. The reservation, and possible problems with it, are discussed in Chapter 24, section 24.5.

2.4.5 **Extra-territorial application of the Convention**

There is an important question as to whether a state can have obligations under the Convention in respect of actions it undertakes outside its territory. In particular, the end of the Cold War has seen an increasing willingness of European powers (particularly the United Kingdom as an ally of the United States), and not always with the support of the international community, to take military action against states and governments that it believes threaten world peace. The bombing by NATO in Kosovo and Serbia (former Yugoslavia) and the wars in Afghanistan and Iraq are the well-known examples. The approach of the ECtHR to applications brought against signatory states in respect of such 'extra-territorial' actions is a developing jurisprudence.

The starting point is that states are obliged to secure Convention rights to everyone within their 'jurisdiction' (Article 1 ECHR). Jurisdiction is defined, primarily, in terms of a state's internationally recognised national territory. There are, however, recognised exceptions to this principle. These are discussed, for example, in *Hirsi Jamaa v Italy* App 27765/09, Grand Chamber judgment of 23 February 2012, paras 71–76.

Effective control

Where a signatory state exercises 'effective control' over an area outside its territory then, for Convention purposes, the area is part of its jurisdiction. Such control can be based on the consent of the state with normal jurisdiction over the area. But it can also be based on military invasion by the signatory state.

In *Loizidou v Turkey* (1997) 23 EHRR 513 the ECtHR held that Turkey was responsible for the actions of its armed forces in Northern Cyprus. Responsibility was based on the fact that Turkey exercised effective control over the area that it had invaded in 1973.

case close-up

Al-Skeini v UK (2011) 53 EHRR 18

The Grand Chamber considered whether the UK had a duty under Article 2 to investigate deaths of civilians caused by British troops on active service in Iraq. UK courts had held that Article 2 only applied to a detainee who died in a British army prison. Following *Bankovic* (discussed later in this section) it held that Article 1 'jurisdiction' was normally based on a state's territory. There were exceptions and these included where the state exercised effective, overall, administrative control over a state as a consequence of invasion, lawful or otherwise. Effective control was a matter of fact, though the strength of the military presence was a primary factor. On the facts, the UK had a duty, under Article 2, to fully investigate the deaths.

In *Al Jedda v UK* (2011) 53 EHRR 23, a Grand Chamber held that the UK had responsibilities under Article 5 (the right to liberty) in respect of an individual detained by the British Army in Iraq. In *Al-Saadoon v UK* (2009) 49 EHRR SE11, the UK owed duties under Article 3 (the prohibition on torture) in respect of another Iraqi detainee. In both cases the UK's Convention liability was based on its effective control, based on military action, of parts of Iraq following the invasion in 2003. It was clear from an examination of the facts that *de facto* control was retained by the UK even after UN involvement.

The control must be effective. *Bankovic v Belgium* (2007) 44 EHRR SE5 involved alleged breaches of the Convention by NATO-member signatory states in respect of the bombing of a broadcasting station in Belgrade. The Grand Chamber held that bombing from the air did not have the degree of continuity necessary for effective control over former Yugoslavia.

Embassies and other diplomatic and consular buildings

Actions taken within overseas embassies etc. are considered to be within the jurisdiction of the state. This is consistent with international law, which the ECtHR has adopted.

Vessels and aircraft

Actions on board vessels or aircraft flying the flag of a signatory state or registered in the signatory state are taken to be within its jurisdiction.

In *Hirsi Jamaa v Italy* App 27765/09, Grand Chamber judgment of 23 February 2012, would-be migrants were picked up on the high seas by Italian navy ships and forcibly returned to Libya.

These actions were within Italy's jurisdiction. Similarly, France was responsible for actions by its Navy in boarding an alleged drug-running ship on the high seas (*Medvedyev* v *France* App 3394/03, Grand Chamber judgment of 29 March 2010).

There are, therefore, a number of circumstances in which a signatory state acting outside its territory, in particular acting outside Europe, must adhere to the Convention. It seems, though, that the ECtHR now accepts that the state only has duties to secure those rights that are relevant to the situation of the applicant, not the full gamut of negative and positive obligations expressly found or implied in the Convention. Thus the Convention can be 'divided and tailored' in respect of its extra-territorial jurisdiction (*Hirsi Jamaa* v *Italy*, para 74).

KEY POINT This case law is important in respect of the question whether the Human Rights Act applies to the actions of UK soldiers overseas, in Afghanistan, for instance. The issue is addressed in Chapter 4, section 4.12.3.

2.4.6 The Convention and UN measures

Article 103 of the UN Charter states that obligations deriving from a state's membership of the UN are to prevail over any other international obligations they may have entered into. As mentioned in Chapter 1, the UN can require states to take actions which directly affect the rights and freedoms of individuals, and Article 103 appears to remove from such individuals the protection of the ECHR. Thus *Al-Jedda* v *United Kingdom* (2011) 53 EHRR 23 involved an individual interned (detained indefinitely without a fair hearing) by British forces in Iraq. Internment is incompatible with the right to liberty in Article 5 ECHR. The question was whether this right was displaced by the UN Security Council Resolution under which British forces were acting.

Courts have adopted three kinds of answer to this problem.

One is to accept the priority of UNSC resolutions but to minimize the impact on human rights. Thus the UK House of Lords in *R (Al-Jedda)* v *SSD* [2007] UKHL 58 accepted that the applicant could be detained (in breach of Article 5(1)) but he retained rights under other features of Article 5 (such as, perhaps, access to a court under Article 5(4)).

A second approach is to apply human rights norms in disregard of Article 103. In *Kadi* v *Council of the European Union* [2009] 1 AC 1225, the European Court of Justice held that anti-terrorism measures, authorised by the UN, which froze Kadi's financial assets, were illegal under EU law. These orders were incompatible with the EU's commitment to the rule of law, which included respect for human rights as found in the ECHR. Kadi's rights to a fair hearing (Article 6 ECHR) and to the peaceful enjoyment of his possessions (Article 1 of the First Protocol) were violated. The trouble with this position is that it has the danger of placing the states and organisations which do this in what appears to be a deliberate disregard of their obligations under international law.

The third approach is for a national or international court to interpret UN measures in a way that avoids incompatibility with human rights. This was the approach of the Grand Chamber in *Al-Jedda v UK*. UNSC Resolutions and other instruments have to be read in the light of the purposes and principles of the UN. These include respect for human rights. It must be presumed, therefore, that UNSC Resolutions do not authorise actions which violate international human rights (such as in the ECHR) unless a clear contrary intention can be discerned. Ambiguities in the language must be resolved in a way that protects human rights (see *Al-Jedda*, paras 102–105). On the facts in *Al-Jedda* no such unambiguous contrary intention could be found and so Article 5 applied and the applicant's internment was found to be a violation. This interpretative approach, however, leaves unanswered the question of what to do if human rights are expressly excluded by the UN measure.

Enforcing the Convention

2.5

Rights without remedies and means of enforcement are pointless. Convention rights are enforced either

• by a state bringing a case against another state (state action) or, more usually,

• by an individual bringing a case against his or her own state (the right of individual application).

2.5.1 State actions (Article 33)

Article 33   Inter-State cases

Any High Contracting Party may refer to the Court any alleged breach of the provisions of the Convention and the protocols thereto by another High Contracting Party.

By signing the Convention each state agrees to be part of a collective system of human rights protection. States are well resourced and able to bring actions, and human rights protection should not be left to the victims, who are the most vulnerable and perhaps least able to proceed. Article 33 does not require the state bringing the action to be acting on behalf of its own nationals. In reality the inter-state procedure has been little used (as of 1 January 2004 there had only been twenty cases and only two dealt with by the ECtHR).

further study

For fuller discussion of state actions, see Steiner, H. and Alston, P. *International Human Rights in Context* 3rd edn (2007) Oxford: OUP, Chapter 11B, section 5.

There have been two important inter-state cases dealt with by the ECtHR.

In a case brought by Ireland against the United Kingdom, the ECtHR held that various interrogation techniques used against suspected members of the IRA violated Article 3 (the case, *Ireland* v *United Kingdom* (1979–80) 2 EHRR 25, is discussed in Chapter 9, section 9.2).

The long-standing dispute between Cyprus and Turkey, over the invasion by Turkey in 1974 and the resulting division of the island, has come before the ECtHR. (The Commission had reported large-scale violations in three cases brought in the 1970s.) In *Cyprus* v *Turkey* (2002) 35 EHRR 30, the Court found that there were serious and continuing violations of the Convention in respect of missing and displaced persons.

2.5.2 The right of individual application (Article 34)

The vast majority of cases brought before the Strasbourg institutions are brought by individuals (people, companies or non-governmental organisations) who allege that they have been the victims of a violation of one or more Convention rights and that the courts of their own country have, for whatever reason, been unable to recognise this and to provide an effective remedy.

Individual application is unusual in international law, though, perhaps, becoming less so. Usually international law depends upon inter-state actions or goes little further than a reporting process by which an international body reports on the extent to which individual countries have fulfilled their obligations. Under the European system an individual, by his or her own motion, can bring their case to the ECtHR and, if the Court rules there has been a violation, obtain a ruling that the Convention has been violated. Consequently the state has an obligation to change the law or its practices for the future. In some cases the Court requires the states to pay financial compensation by way of 'just satisfaction'.

KEY POINT Originally the right of individual application only existed when states made declarations allowing their population this right (see the old Article 25). Under the current system, introduced by Protocol 11 (see section 2.6.1), individual application must be allowed by all member states.

2.5.3 **Implementation**

The system of implementation

The strength of the Convention lies in the system of enforcement. Enforcement has two stages.

First, application must be made to the ECtHR (discussed in section 2.6), which decides whether or not there has been a violation of the Convention in particular cases. If there has been a violation, the Court declares this and may, if it thinks it appropriate, award just satisfaction (damages).

cross reference
Admissibility is discussed at section 2.7.1.

Second, it is the obligation of the state against which the violation has been found to implement the ECtHR's judgment (Articles 1 and 45). The Committee of Ministers has the responsibility of ensuring that the judgments are put into effect both in terms of the individual applicant (the payment of just satisfaction, for example) and in terms of any changes to national law or administrative practice that should follow. The Committee can exert political and diplomatic pressure on states if they are reluctant to execute the judgment. The Committee's ultimate sanction is expulsion from the Council of Europe. Expulsion would have very serious consequences for the reputation of a state and might also have detrimental political, economic and social effects. Furthermore, expulsion leaves the victim and future victims defenceless. States can also denounce the Convention (as Greece did in 1969).

Friendly settlements

Article 39 requires the ECtHR to 'place itself at the disposal of the parties' with a view to obtaining a 'friendly settlement'. If such a settlement is obtained, the case is then to be struck out of the list. The negotiations and terms of any settlement are secret. There is a danger that a friendly settlement could be a compromise or a pay-off by which a significant breach of human rights is, in secrecy, brushed under the carpet. The Court must be satisfied that any settlement is consistent with respect for human rights and a settlement can be refused if it means that an important issue remains unresolved.

Pilot judgment procedure

Since 2004 the ECtHR has developed a 'pilot' procedure. This is where the Court identifies a 'structural or systemic' problem, or 'similar dysfunction' in the law or practice of a state which causes a large number of similar cases to come before it. In a pilot judgment the Court can identify the problem, specify the remedial action that needs to be taken and the time scale. It can then adjourn any individual cases whilst the reforms are being made (these can be resumed if the state fails to act). The Committee of Ministers is informed and, retaining its Convention role of supervising implementation, can seek to ensure the remedial action is taken. The Committee can refer the state's proposals for change back to the Court for final evaluation.

further study

Pilot procedures are discussed in, for example, *Broniowski* v *Poland* (2006) 43 EHRR 1, paras 189–194, and formalised in Rule 61 of the Court's Rules.

case close-up

Greens **v** *United Kingdom* **[2011] 53 EHRR 21**

cross reference
There is further discussion of the prisoner voting issue in Chapter 26, section 25.3.2.

The UK's total ban on prisoners' voting had been held to violate Article 3 of the First Protocol in an earlier case (*Hirst* v *UK*). The UK did not change the law and, five years later, *Greens*, a prisoner, was denied the right to vote in UK European Parliament elections. The case illustrates the Court dealing with a continuing violation of a Convention right which gives rise to a large number of pending or potential applications.

1. The Court reaffirmed that even in situations where states are refusing to remedy a situation, it will not award punitive damages (i.e. a financial penalty which aims at punishment and therefore goes beyond compensation for what has been lost or suffered).

2. The Court then adopted a pilot judgment procedure (see earlier in this section).

3. As part of the pilot judgment

   (a) it imposed a timetable, six months, on the UK to come up with appropriate remedial measures;

   (b) struck out pending cases from individual prisoners and refused to accept any new ones but with the threat of resumption if the UK failed to adopt suitable measures;

   (c) urged the UK to adopt general measures but also to consider other solutions, such as friendly settlements, of the outstanding cases.

The case illustrates the increasing importance of the Court's role in implementation. This complements the political and diplomatic role of the Committee of Ministers and gives implementation a more judicial quality, which is easier to reconcile with the rule of law.

2.6 The European Court of Human Rights (ECtHR)

KEY POINT The ECtHR must be distinguished from the Court of Justice of the European Union, the highest court of the European Union, which sits in Luxembourg.

2.6.1 History

The ECtHR sits in Strasbourg in France. It was established in 1959 and decided its first case (*Lawless* v *Ireland*) in 1960.

Under the original Convention (signed in 1950) the Court was envisaged as a part-time institution. Then, the assumption was that, since member states were democratic, pluralist and committed to the rule of law, cases that needed to go to the Court would be few and far between. Originally, the Court was assisted by another part-time institution, the European Commission of Human Rights. The Commission had a principal role in deciding whether applications made to the Court were admissible (i.e. were the kind of case the Court was able to hear). Then, as now, the majority of applications were not: they were inadmissible. The Commission would then forward most admissible cases to the Court for a decision on the merits; it would make its own assessment of the merits which the Court would consider. The Commission also had a role in organising or undertaking fact-finding.

Protocol 11

The European Convention on Human Rights has been one of the most (if not the most) successful systems for the international protection of human rights. The success has been particularly based on the right of individual petition and the general willingness of signatory states to accept and respond to adverse decisions of the Court.

The enormous (and continuing) expansion in the number of cases could not be dealt with under the part-time two-tier system of Commission and Court. The system became chronically overloaded, with resulting delays. The Council of Europe eventually responded with the Eleventh Protocol, which introduced major reforms in 1998. The most important of these was the abolition of the Commission and the old part-time court. A new full-time court was created in its place. The new court, assisted by the Registry and the Secretariat, took over admissibility decisions and other functions of the Commission.

KEY POINT Continued importance of the Commission. The Commission's reports on both admissibility and merits continue to be referred to by the ECtHR. They must also be 'taken into account' by United Kingdom judges deciding cases under the Human Rights Act 1998, section 2.

Many other important changes to procedure and to the powers of the Court were made by Protocol 11. This led to considerable rewriting of Part 2 of the Convention (which deals with those matters). Provisions which were retained often needed to be renumbered. For example, the right of individual application, originally Article 25, was renumbered as Article 34.

Protocol 11 did not solve the problem of the backlog of cases, and further changes to the procedures and powers of the Court were made by Protocol 14, which came into force in June 2010.

2.6.2 **Functions**

The principal function of the Court is to declare whether or not, in particular cases, there has been a violation of the Convention. Virtually all the cases brought before it are from individuals bringing cases in their own interest against their own state.

- The Court receives an application from the person who alleges they are a victim of a violation or from the state that alleges a violation by another state.
- It considers whether or not the case is admissible (before 1998 this was done by the Commission), see section 2.7.1.
- If a case is admissible the Court can then seek further details and receive further submissions from the parties.

- The Court makes a judgment on whether there has been a violation of the Convention. If so, it rules on whether the finding of a violation is a sufficient remedy or whether damages, just satisfaction, should be paid by the state involved and whether the state should also pay the applicant's costs.

- The Court submits its findings, on whether there has been a violation and what the remedy should be, to the Committee of Ministers, which has the responsibility to supervise the judgment and ensure it is put into effect by the government of the state involved.

- Under Article 47 the Court can be asked by the Committee of Ministers to give an advisory opinion. These cannot concern any matter involving the content or scope of the substantive rights, otherwise the opinion might prejudge a later case to be decided by the Court. A request to advise on the compatibility of the Convention with a human rights instrument applying to post-Soviet Union states was rejected on this ground in 2004. Issues about the election of judges to the Court were the subject of advisory opinions in 2008 and 2010.

2.6.3 **Publicity and openness**

The ECtHR does most of its work in private, on the basis of forms and other paperwork. The Court holds public hearings, under Article 40, when deciding the merits of a case, but many of its admissibility decisions, especially those taken by a Committee, are done in private and cannot be appealed. The Court must give reasons for its decisions. Reasoned dissenting judgments are permitted. Court documents should be public unless the Court decides otherwise. However, under the oath taken by the judges, the actual deliberations of the judges are secret.

2.6.4 **Organisation and procedure**

The organisation and procedure of the Court is based on Part 2 of the Convention (as amended by Protocols 11 and 14) and on the Rules of the Court. These Rules are made by the Court on the authority of the Convention. The current Rules were brought into effect on 1 May 2012. In all it does, the Court is assisted by a Registry and by legal secretaries.

further study

The Rules of the Court can be found at the website of the ECtHR http://www.echr.coe.int/ECHR/, accessed via 'Basic Texts'.

Plenary Court, President and Vice-Presidents, Sections, Committees and Chambers

- The full Court is the 'Plenary Court'. It has forty-seven positions, allowing for one judge from each country. In June 2012 there were forty-four judges and three vacancies. The function of the Plenary Court, under Article 25, is to elect the President and Vice-Presidents and set up the Chambers. The Plenary Court adopts the Rules and elects the Registrar.

- There is a President of the Court and two Vice-Presidents.

- The Court is organised, for administrative purposes, into at least four (currently five) Sections presided over by a President (Rule 25). These Sections have a balance of male and female judges and reflect the geography of Europe. Importantly they also reflect the different legal systems in Europe (e.g. common law or civilian).

The Court can act in the following ways (Article 26):

- Single judge formation. Straightforward admissibility decisions can be taken by a single judge appointed by the President. A single judge can declare an application inadmissible, or strike it out, and his or her decision is final—there is no procedure for appeal. If the application is not straightforwardly inadmissible, the single judge must forward it to a Committee or Chamber for further consideration of admissibility. The single judge formation was introduced under Protocol 14 to try and shorten the Court's backlog by dealing swiftly with the large number of obviously inadmissible applications that are received.

- Committee. Committees are set up within each section. They consist of three judges of the section and their tasks include decisions on the admissibility of cases brought by individuals (Article 28 and Rule 27). If the Committee disagrees on an admissibility issue, it is then decided by a Chamber. Importantly, a Committee also has jurisdiction to decide the merits of a case it finds admissible (i.e. it can decide whether there has been a violation or not). This is confined to cases which involve well-established principles of Convention law. These decisions, since they do not involve difficult issues of law, are final and not open to re-examination by a Chamber or Grand Chamber.

- Chambers. Chambers are made up of seven judges chosen from within a Section. They are judicial formations within each section. The Chambers decide the admissibility of cases which a Committee is unable to decide. Most importantly it is the Chambers that decide the merits of the case—whether there has been a violation of a Convention right. The President of the Section sits in each Chamber. A Chamber deciding a case should have on it the judge elected from the state concerned. If not a member of the Section involved, then he or she is appointed ad hoc (for that case only) to the Chamber. The other members of the Chamber are appointed by rotation from the members of the Section (Article 29 and Rule 26).

The Grand Chamber

The Court can also sit as a Grand Chamber and is then at its most authoritative. A Grand Chamber consists of seventeen judges who represent the Court as a whole. Most of the judges who form a Grand Chamber are chosen by lot, but a Grand Chamber must include the President and Vice-Presidents of the Court and the Presidents of the Sections.

Article 30 allows a Chamber to 'relinquish' (hand over) a case to a Grand Chamber if the case raises serious issues about the interpretation of one or more Convention rights or if the case is one which might require an outcome which is inconsistent with a previously delivered judgment by the Court (the Court is not strictly bound by its own earlier decisions and allows the substance of Convention rights to evolve in line with developments in legal, political and social opinion in Europe). The agreement of both parties is required.

Under Article 43, a Grand Chamber can decide (on the basis of a recommendation by a panel of five of its members) to accept a case referred to it by either party. This is the nearest there is to an appeal under the Convention. To be heard, the panel must accept that the case is exceptional and that it raises a serious question about the interpretation or application of the Convention or a 'serious issue of general importance'. The Grand Chamber rehears the case as it was when declared admissible in the first instance (though it can examine aspects of the admissibility decision if it so wishes). It is concerned with the case as a whole, not just with the particular issues in dispute—see *Yumak and Sadak v Turkey* (2009) 48 EHRR 4, Grand Chamber, paras 71–72. It takes into account the decision of the Chamber but is not bound to agree with that decision. Article 43 allows this right to a rehearing not only to the applicant but also to the defendant state. Though some cases have been controversial (e.g. the decision by the Grand Chamber in *Hatton* v *United Kingdom* (2003) 37 EHRR 28, which reversed a Chamber's decision that night flying regulations for Heathrow Airport violated the rights of residents to respect for their private and family lives), there is no evidence that the Grand Chamber is any more 'state friendly' than a Chamber.

A Grand Chamber can also consider requests for 'advisory opinions' under Article 47 (see Rule 87), see section 2.6.2.

2.6.5 The judges

At full compliment there are as many judges as there are High Contracting Parties (signatories of the Convention)—forty-seven in 2012.

further study

For an up-to-date list of judges, including any vacancies, see the Court's website and follow links to 'The Court' and 'Judges of the Court'.

The judges are elected. They are chosen by the Parliamentary Assembly, which votes for one name out of a list of three provided by the government of each state. The judges do not need to be nationals of the state that puts their name forward (though they usually are) and it must be stressed that they do not sit as representatives of the states that nominate them. They sit in their individual capacity and are expected to be impartial and to display the judicial virtues.

Independence and impartiality

Judges of the ECtHR must be of 'high moral character' and must be qualified in their own country for high judicial office or similar (Article 21(1)). They are required to desist from activities which are incompatible with the demands of a full-time judicial role or with the requirements of independence or impartiality. Political activity, such as being a minister, a member of a legislature or a prominent activist, is likely to be barred to them on these grounds (see Rule 4). They are elected for a period of nine years and may not be re-elected (Article 23). This was a change introduced under Protocol 14 in June 2010. The obvious danger of re-election was that it required renomination by the state and might undermine independence and influence judgments. They cannot be dismissed unless two-thirds of the other judges, in a vote, so decide.

2.7 Taking a case to Europe

A person wishing to take a case to Strasbourg must make a written application to the Court on the form provided (the form is on the Court's website). Applicants need to state (sensibly, but not necessarily, with the help of a legal representative) the facts, the respondent state, the Convention Articles that are alleged to have been violated, the fulfilment of admissibility criteria, the remedy sought, and so on. It should be accompanied by any relevant documentation. The form is submitted to the Registry.

2.7.1 **Admissibility**

Applications must be admissible—they must relate to issues which are within the jurisdiction of the Court to deal with and must disclose a possible violation. The overwhelming majority of applications are not admissible (about 90 per cent). As already mentioned, straightforward admissibility decisions (usually rejections) are taken by a single judge or a Committee and more complex decisions go to a Chamber. There is no direct appeal against a refusal to admit, though both the Chamber and Grand Chamber may deal with issues relating to admissibility if, for instance, these are interlinked with the merits (*Yumak*, para 72). The role of the Registry and the legal secretaries in preparing and advising the Committees on admissibility decisions is very important.

Article 35 lays down the basic admissibility criteria.

Exhaustion of domestic remedies, Article 35(1)

First responsibility for securing human rights lies with the states and they must be given the opportunity to discharge this obligation and remedy any defects in their national laws and practices. Therefore, as is normal in international law, a person who feels that he or she is a victim of a violation must first pursue their case in the national courts. The burden is on the applicant to show that he or she has pursued the issue to the highest level of national court capable of giving a definitive ruling on the national law. In the United Kingdom, for example, this will normally be the Supreme Court.

If the respondent state alleges that domestic remedies have not been exhausted, the burden is on it to show that such remedies exist.

The ECtHR accepts that the rules relating to exhaustion of remedies must be applied

> with some degree of flexibility and without excessive formalism [and] with regard to the object and purpose of those rules and of the Convention generally, which, as a treaty for the collective enforcement of human rights and fundamental freedoms, must be interpreted and applied so as to make its safeguards practical and effective.
>
> (*Ilhan* v *Turkey* (2002) 34 EHRR 36, para 51)

The available remedies must be effective and 'sufficient in theory and practice'. There may be special reasons which absolve the applicant of the need to exhaust domestic remedies. If, for example, going to the national courts would be futile because remedies are merely theoretical rather than real, or evidence suggests that the state and the courts seem incapable of action in the face of serious allegations of official misconduct, then the requirement may be waived.

In *Ocalan* v *Turkey* (2005) 41 EHRR 45, the applicant, a leader of the Turkish Kurds, was wanted on terrorism charges and he was effectively 'kidnapped' by Turkish security police whilst travelling abroad. He was held in detention. He had not sought judicial review of his detention. There was evidence indicating that applications to the Turkish courts in such situations was pointless. Detainees did not have a fair hearing and, even if the court found irregularities, release was never ordered. The ECtHR held that there were special reasons justifying Ocalan's failure to exhaust domestic remedies.

The exhaustion principle does not mean that an applicant must seek an ineffective remedy. In the United Kingdom, for instance, there is currently no need to take a case to the Supreme Court if the best that can be obtained is a 'declaration of incompatability' under section 4 HRA 1998.

However, if there is established a regular practice by which declarations of incompatibility regularly lead to appropriate changes in UK law or administrative practice, the situation may change: see *Burden* v *United Kingdom* (2008) 47 EHRR 38, Grand Chamber, paras 40–44.

cross reference

See Chapter 4, section 4.4.3 on 'declarations of incompatibility'.

further study

A summary of the general principles dealing with exhaustion of domestic remedies is in *Akdivar v Turkey* (1997) 23 EHRR 143, paras 65–69.

The need to exhaust domestic remedies applies to both state and individual applications. The other admissibility rules, now discussed, only apply to individual applications submitted under Article 34.

Application within six months, Article 35(1)

Individual applications will be inadmissible if they are submitted to the Court later than six months from the date that the applicant was aware or should have been aware of the decision by which domestic remedies were exhausted. The initial application letter or form must be sent to the Secretariat by that time. Where the alleged violation is a continuing situation (e.g. a legal rule which violates a Convention right) and not a specific action taken against the applicant, the six-month rule is irrelevant.

Anonymous applications, Article 35(2)(a)

The Court cannot admit individual applications that are anonymous, though, under Rule 47(3), the President can, if requested, take steps to ensure anonymity, and it is clear from the number of cases where the applicant is designated by a letter (e.g. *X* v *a country*) that this is often done.

Substantial similarity, Article 35(2)(b)

The Court will not admit an individual application that is dealing with the same factual situation that it has already examined in an earlier Convention case nor one where the same issue has been submitted to some other form of international investigation (an application to the United Nations Human Rights Committee under the optional protocol to the ICCPR, for example).

Incompatible with the Convention or a Protocol, Article 35(3)(a)

cross reference

The rules relating to who is allowed to bring a human rights case are discussed in Chapter 5, section 5.4.5.

The Court must reject an individual application if it relates to matters that are outside the scope of the Convention's protection. This can be for various reasons such as

- the Convention or Protocol relied on was not in force in the applicant's country at the time of the incident complained about ('*ratione temporis*' (for a reason relating to time)), or
- the applicant is complaining about an alleged wrong not dealt with by the Convention or Protocols ('*ratione materiae*' (for a reason relating to substance)), or
- the applicant was not a victim of the violation ('*ratione personae*' (for a reason relating to the legal person)).

Manifestly ill-founded, Article 35(3)(a)

The majority of individual applications are rejected because they do not disclose an arguable breach of the Convention. The Section Committee or Chamber may consider the merits of the case and report that, on examination, no likely breach is disclosed. The application is then rejected as inadmissible. Merits reviews in the context of admissibility proceedings are an important source of interpretation and understanding of the Convention.

Abuse of the right of application, Article 35(3)(a)

The Court will not admit an application that involves an abuse of the Convention system. Rejections on this ground are rare and the mere fact of an improper motive will not be sufficient to cause an otherwise good case to be rejected. There may be an abuse where the applicant persists with pointless applications or conducts him or herself in insulting or threatening ways.

Applicant has not suffered a significant disadvantage

Where an applicant's losses or sufferings are trivial, he or she may find their case is inadmissible. This provision, introduced by Protocol 14, reflects the fundamental nature of human rights. It also assists with reducing the backlog of cases. A case should attain a minimum level of severity, though this is relative. A court should consider both the importance of the matter for the applicant and what is objectively at stake in the case (see *Diaceno* v *Romania* App 124/04, judgment of 7 February 2012, para 41).

In *Ionescu* v *Romania* (2010) 51 EHRR SE7, the applicant had lost a breach of contract case worth €90. Since this was, for him, a small sum the Court found the application inadmissible.

However, a matter with trivial consequences may still be admissible if so required by proper respect for human rights. Likewise, an issue which has not been adjudicated by a national court cannot be rejected on the no significant disadvantage ground.

2.7.2 **Interim measures**

Rule 39 of the Court's Rules permits the Court to take interim measures which it considers appropriate and which prevent a state from taking actions, such as deportation, whilst the full hearing and judgment by the Court is awaited. These are binding on the state concerned and are appropriate where the Court considers the applicant otherwise faces a 'real risk of serious, irreversible harm' (see the Practice Direction first issued in 2003). Such measures are particularly relevant to deportation and extradition cases.

The deportation of Omar Othman (Abu Qatada) from the United Kingdom was prevented for about three years until the Court's final decision (which, anyway, held that it would violate Article 6). In 2012 the issue returned to the domestic courts.

2.7.3 **Fact-finding**

When a case is declared admissible it is the duty of the Court (under Article 38) to continue to examine the case. This usually involves seeking further information from either party and seeking agreement as to the facts. The Court's resources are such that for most situations it must rely on the representations of the parties. However, Article 38 authorises the Court to 'undertake an investigation'. Under Rule A1 a Chamber may adopt 'any' investigative measures, and these can include appointing one or more of its members to conduct an on-site investigation. The respondent state, as well as the applicant, must assist the implementation of these measures.

2.7.4 Evidence and proof

The Court is aware of its role as a protector of the human rights of, often, very vulnerable people. As such there are no procedural barriers to evidence. 'The Court adopts the conclusions that are, in its view, supported by the free evaluation of all evidence, including such inferences as may flow from the facts and the parties' submissions' (*DH v Czech Republic* (2008) 47 EHRR 3). Likewise it does not always insist that the burden of proof must lie with the applicant.

2.8 Reform

The ECtHR remains in need of reform. Much of the problem has been based on the huge backlog of cases. Following Protocols 11 and 14, considerable inroads have been made into this, based on innovations such as the single judge formation (dealing with the many inadmissible applications that are received), the pilot judgment procedure (dealing with single issues which generate multiple applications), toughening the admissibility criteria (the need for 'significant disadvantage'), and a system for identifying and dealing with priority cases. The hope is that the backlog will be removed by 2015.

For some states (including the UK under the Conservative-led coalition government of 2010) the backlog is a symptom of a wider problem. The Court, it is alleged, has allowed the Convention to evolve beyond anything that was anticipated in 1950. Under the spur of individual application, the Convention has developed into something approaching a European bill of rights, aiming to establish a common basis of human rights throughout Europe, irrespective of the existence of genuine threats of totalitarianism. Many of its cases are against countries and governments which have strong, democratic institutions, albeit imperfect ones, and a clear commitment to pluralism and the rule of law. Some countries feel that the independence and authority of their own courts, Parliaments and governments are being challenged.

Some of these points, as well as the backlog, are reflected in a reform process that began at Interlaken in 2010 and will continue until 2015. The agenda of these reforms, as demonstrated by the Brighton Declaration 2012, includes

- placing the focus on national implementation by raising the profile and awareness of human rights before national courts, Parliaments and governments;
- emphasising 'subsidiarity' and 'margin of appreciation' as principles which should guide the Court (these principles, discussed in Chapter 6, guide the Court to accept, within limits, the approaches to human rights adopted by national institutions);
- reforming the admissibility criteria (see section 2.7.1) to make it less likely that, where Convention rights have been fully and carefully applied by national courts to an issue, it can then be re-examined by the Court. This provision is controversial since it tends to weaken the 'backstop', supervisory, role of the Court and the Court is likely to retain the power to admit issues which, nevertheless, raise serious human rights questions;
- enhancing the quality of the judges elected to the Court.

In the long term the aim is a European court dealing with a smaller number of cases; being those where the facts suggest 'serious and widespread violations' and 'systematic and structural problems'.

The issue of reform, particularly from a UK perspective, is discussed more fully in Chapter 27.

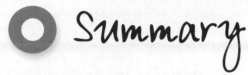 # Summary

- The Convention and the ECtHR are the creation of the Council of Europe (not the European Union) and grew out of the devastation of Europe at the end of the Second World War.

- Under the Convention, member states of the Council of Europe agree to secure for everyone in their territories the rights and freedoms listed in the Convention and agree to abide by the judgments of the ECtHR, a court created by the Council.

- The great strength of the Convention system lies in the right of individual application by which individual victims of a violation of Convention rights can take their own government to the Court.

- Court procedure and organisation is important. About 90 per cent of all applications to the Court are 'inadmissible' and do not go forward to judgment. The grounds of admissibility include the need to 'exhaust domestic remedies', which gives effect to the point that the primary duty to secure human rights for all lies with the nation states.

- The system has been the victim of its own success and is in danger of being overloaded. Significant reforms have already been made and the reform process is continuing.

 # Questions

For suggested approaches, please visit the Online Resource Centre.

1 Do you agree that the ECtHR is a constitutional court for Europe rather than a final back stop aimed at preventing the rise of undemocratic and oppressive governments? Does this matter? Is it, for example, inconsistent with democracy because it removes some difficult questions about the public good out of the hands of politicians into the hands of judges?

2 Josephine Bloggs, an English woman, alleges that she has been a victim of a violation of her rights under the Convention. Are her claims admissible?

(a) She complains that her privacy has been invaded when she was photographed in the street, violating Article 8. The photographer immediately destroyed the film, but Josephine feels there is an important principle at stake.

(b) She complains that, under a court order relating to anti-social behaviour, she is prevented from visiting the town where her friends live and this violates Article 2 of the Fourth Protocol.

(c) Her lawyer advises her that taking her cases through the UK courts is pointless because of clear Court of Appeal decisions, so she goes straight to Strasbourg.

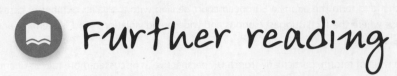
Further reading

SPECIALIST WORKS ON THE CONVENTION INCLUDE

Lester, A., Pannick, D. and Herberg, J. (see Preface) Chapter 1, D

Ovey, C. and White, R. *The European Convention on Human Rights (Jacobs and White)* 5th edn (2010) Oxford: OUP, Chapters 1 and 2

ON THE GRAND CHAMBER

Mowbray, A. 'An Examination of the Work of the Grand Chamber of the Court of Human Rights' [2007] *Public Law* (Autumn) 507–528

ON REFORM AND REMEDIES

Suchkova, M. 'An Analysis of the Institutional Arrangements within the Council of Europe and within Certain Member States for Securing the Enforcement of Judgments' [2011] 4 *EHRLR* 448–463

The European Convention and the law of the United Kingdom

Chapter overview

- The Convention as an obligation in international law on the United Kingdom.
- The inability of individuals to enforce their Convention rights directly in UK courts.
- Changes to law and administrative practice following from adverse judgments by the ECtHR.
- The persuasive influence of the Convention on UK law.

Introduction

The European Convention on Human Rights (ECHR, discussed in Chapter 2) was never part of UK law (and still is not). Its provisions were not and are not applied directly by UK courts. The Convention was, and remains, part of international law and international law is not directly enforceable in UK courts. The Human Rights Act 1998 (HRA) brings the substance of the rights and freedoms in the ECHR into UK law in particular ways. These are discussed in Chapters 4 and 5. However, prior to the Act coming into force, the ECHR had a significant and increasing influence on UK law and it is this influence which is discussed in this chapter.

3.1 Putting the Article 1 obligation into effect

The UK signed the Convention in 1950. In doing so it accepted the obligation under Article 1 of the Convention to 'secure for everyone within [its] jurisdiction the rights and freedoms in Section 1 of this Convention' (and the Protocols signed up to). This means

- ensuring that not only the laws, but also the policies and conduct of government and administration under the law, are compatible with the Convention;
- accepting and putting into effect adverse judgments of the European Court of Human Rights (ECtHR).

cross reference
For further detail on state obligations under the Convention see Chapter 2, section 2.4.2.

The right to individual application was granted in 1966. As a consequence, there was an increasing flow of cases taken to the ECtHR alleging breaches of the Convention and, in a significant number of cases, that Court found the United Kingdom to be in violation of the Convention.

KEY POINT Nothing in the HRA prevents people from continuing to take their cases to Strasbourg. Thus

cross reference
The right of individual application is explained in Chapter 2, section 2.5.2.

- in 1999 (a year before the HRA came into effect) 1,054 applications were received by the Court, though only 32 were admissible;
- in 2011 (eleven years after the HRA came into force) the total number of applications was 3,663. Of these 2,110 were rejected by the Registry but 1,553 had admissibility considered by judges. Of these only 1 per cent (30) eventually resulted in a judgment. Thus the vast majority were inadmissible. The United Kingdom has one of the lowest application levels as a proportion of the population.

further study

For a statistical survey of the UK and the Convention see: Equality and Human Rights Commission, 'The UK and the European Court of Human Rights' (2012) Research Report 82.

Generally the United Kingdom has fulfilled its obligations under the Convention and made changes to law or administrative practice where required. This has involved, in particular:

- creating a legal framework to regulate matters that relate to Convention rights and which were previously unregulated,
- amending Acts of Parliament,
- changing administrative practices.

Examples are given in what follows.

3.1.1 Matter previously unregulated by 'law'

The Convention is based on the rule of law. Any exercise of government power which affects a Convention right must be adequately regulated by law. In the United Kingdom, this will usually mean an Act of Parliament, but not always. Government authority can also be based on the Royal Prerogative (the residue of the traditional, absolute authority of the Crown that does not require the authority of an Act of Parliament); or on the common law assumption that something that is neither permitted nor forbidden by law is taken to be lawful. In both cases it can be hard to know what specific rules, if any, regulate the conduct in issue. The absence of clear rules leaves too much to the discretion of officials, which can be difficult to challenge in the courts. As a result of the Convention, it has been necessary for government to persuade Parliament to enact statutes that give some degree of regulation to various government activities which have an effect on people's Convention rights but which, previously, were not effectively regulated on the basis of law.

- Telephone tapping. In *Malone* v *United Kingdom* (1985) 7 EHRR 14, the ECtHR held that the absence of effective legal regulation of telephone tapping was a violation of Article 8, the right to respect for private life. As a result, the Interception of Communications Act 1987 was enacted. This created an offence of telephone tapping but also introduced a system by which the authorities could obtain interception warrants. By the beginning of the century, however, it became clear that the new law was inadequate and unable to create effective legal control over wider forms of surveillance as these were developing using new technology. With Article 8 very much in mind, the Regulation of Investigatory Powers Act 2000 was passed, which creates a complex structure of regulation over a number of forms of surveillance.
- The security and intelligence services. In 1989 (the Security Service Act) and 1994 (the Intelligence Services Act) the secret services were, for the first time, identified by Act of Parliament. Their functions were described (albeit in very general terms) and, in particular, a legal structure was created to give some degree of control over their surveillance activities. In 2012, for example, the Security Service was sued over its alleged complicity in torture (this tendency to give organisations a definite, public, legal identity is inspired by the Convention).

3.1.2 Amending or repealing Acts of Parliament

An adverse judgment may require the United Kingdom to change the terms of an Act of Parliament which is regulating some activity.

The law on sexual offences, such as buggery and indecency between males, was reformed by the Sexual Offences (Amendment) Act 2000 (now replaced by the Sexual Offences Act 2003).

In part this was a response to the decision of the ECtHR in *ADT* v *United Kingdom* [2001] 31 EHRR 33, which held that the previous law, the Sexual Offences Act 1956, failed to secure the right to private life of homosexual men.

Such changes are not necessarily narrow, mechanistic responses to an adverse judgment. They may also be explained by a range of other political and social pressures. The Sexual Offences Act 2003, for example, was a wide-ranging, comprehensive reform of the law involving much more than putting Convention rights into effect.

3.1.3 Administrative policies

The state must ensure that not only the law but also the policies it pursues within the law and the activities of its agents (its civil servants, police, prison officers and others) are compatible with the Convention. The Convention has had some of its most significant effects in this area. Examples include:

- The rights of prisoners. A large number of cases involving the United Kingdom have been to do with prisoners' rights. The Convention has been a significant influence for the reform not only of the law but also the practices of the Prison Service on issues like prisoners' rights to correspond with lawyers, to be subject to fair disciplinary procedures, to effective health care, to have the length of their sentence determined by the judiciary rather than the executive and to political rights, including the right to vote. Prisoners' cases can be found throughout this book, but are considered especially in Chapter 21.

- Homosexuals in the military. The general ban on gay men and lesbian women in the British armed forces was ended as a result of an adverse decision of the ECtHR (*Smith and Grady* v *United Kingdom* (2000) 29 EHRR 493).

3.2 The status of international law

3.2.1 The dual system: no direct enforceability

Changes like those just mentioned were derived from the UK's obligations under international law that flowed from its signature to the ECHR. What was not possible was for a person to take a case to a UK court and to have a right or freedom found in the Convention directly enforced as a matter of UK law: the point of the HRA is to make this possible. The rights and freedoms in the Convention, therefore, were not and are not part of UK law.

The Convention is an instance of treaty-based international law. It is one of the many international treaties the United Kingdom has entered into. Many such treaties deal with general issues, such as the environment, and do not aim to create rights for individuals. Others aim at creating international rights, in the sense of rights recognised and enforced at the international level. An example of this is the Rome Statute of the International Criminal Court, which creates internationally recognised crimes, an international court in which they can be prosecuted and some specific procedural rights for victims. But there are other treaties which oblige the states that agree to them to secure various rights and freedoms in their own national law. An example, mentioned in Chapter 1, is the International Covenant on Civil and Political Rights (ICCPR).

cross reference
For the ICCPR, see Chapter 1, section 1.4.4 and Chapter 2, section 2.3.6.

The problem is that under the legal system in the United Kingdom the individual rights and freedoms in such treaties cannot be directly enforced in United Kingdom courts. The United

Kingdom operates a 'dual' system, which distinguishes between international and national law, and it is national law that is enforced in the courts.

- International law, found in treaties and other sources, remains as obligations on the United Kingdom as a whole and is enforced by whatever mechanisms the treaties, in their separate ways, make available (e.g. the reporting obligation in the ICCPR).
- National law, the law enforced by the courts, consists of Acts of Parliament, including subordinate legislation, and rules of common law.

It follows, therefore, that for individual rights in international treaties to be enforced there needs to be an Act of Parliament bringing them into effect.

KEY POINT The European Union provides a good example.

- EU treaties provide for various individual rights, such as the rights of women to equal pay (Article 157 of the Treaty on the Functioning of the European Union (TFEU)).
- These rights can be directly enforced in UK courts. This is because of two necessary and complementary facts:
  o the United Kingdom is a signatory of the Treaty, *and*
  o the United Kingdom has enacted legislation (section 2 of the European Communities Act 1972) which requires that individual rights found in the EU treaties should be part of the law of the United Kingdom and enforced in the national courts.

cross reference

Jus cogens is defined in Chapter 9, section 9.4.1.

It should be noted, though, that whilst treaty-based international law is not directly enforced in the United Kingdom, *jus cogens* (the compulsory, customary law of nations) is treated as an enforceable part of the common law of the United Kingdom. In *A v Secretary of State for the Home Department* [2005] UKHL 71, the House of Lords recognised that the prohibition of torture was part of the *jus cogens* (see para 33). The case is discussed in Chapter 9, section 9.4.

3.2.2 A 'persuasive and pervasive influence'

Even though they are not directly enforced, individual rights founded in international law, such as those in the ECHR, are not merely ignored. They cannot have priority over clear national law, but can be taken into account by the courts and can influence the decisions they make in various ways.

The point was made by Lord Bingham in *R v Lyons* [2002] UKHL 44, which was a case dealing with the impact of the ECHR prior to the HRA; but what his lordship says of the Convention applies to all other international treaties.

> rules of international law not incorporated into national law confer no rights on individuals directly enforceable in national courts. But although international and national law differ in their content and their fields of application they should be seen as complementary and not as alien or antagonistic systems. Even before the Human Rights Act 1998 the Convention exerted a persuasive and pervasive influence on judicial decision-making in this country, affecting the interpretation of ambiguous statutory provisions, guiding the exercise of discretions, bearing on the development of the common law. I would further accept . . . that the efficacy of the Convention depends on the loyal observance by member states of the obligations they have undertaken and on the readiness of all exercising authority (whether legislative, executive or judicial) within member states to seek to act consistently with the Convention so far as they are free to do so.   (para 13, Lord Bingham)

Examples of the 'persuasive and pervasive' influence of the Convention, prior to the HRA, are given in what follows in this chapter.

3.3 The impact of the Convention on the development of the law

The Convention has influenced the way courts have

- interpreted ambiguous statutory provisions,
- developed public law rights in order to control the exercise by ministers and others of discretionary powers, and
- developed the common law.

3.3.1 The interpretation of statutes

An important influence of the Convention prior to October 2000 was on the way 'ambiguous' **statutory provisions were interpreted**. The basic constitutional position is that Parliament is 'supreme' and free of constitutional restraint as to content. No court can invalidate an Act of Parliament on the grounds that it is unconstitutional or incompatible with human rights. Nevertheless, the words in an Act of Parliament need to be interpreted (made sense of) and applied to the facts of particular cases. This is the constitutional role of the courts.

. . . .

statutory interpretation

The general rule is that the courts aim to give effect to the intention of Parliament and this intention is best found by a 'literal' reading of the words (using their ordinary, dictionary definitions). Where the meanings of the words are uncertain, where, for example, they may be ambiguous (capable of more than one meaning) or where they lead to an absurd result that Parliament would not have intended, the courts have to decide what the intention of Parliament was. In doing this they

- 'have recourse to recognised principles of interpretation [such as the principle that Parliament intends to legislate compatibly with the UK's international obligations, mentioned later at 'Parliament intends to legislate compatibly with international law']
- and also a variety of aids, some internal, found within the statute itself [such as the 'long title' to the Act or section headings,
- some external, found outside the statute' [such as Royal Commissions or other reports to which the Act is a response and which therefore indicate the problem (the 'mischief') the Act aims to resolve].

The quotation comes from *Wilson* v *Secretary of State for Trade and Industry* [2003] UKHL 40, para 56.

. . . .

Parliament intends to legislate compatibly with international law

One of the recognised principles of statutory interpretation is that the courts will apply unclear or ambiguous words (words capable of more than one meaning) in an Act of Parliament by using various assumptions. One of these is an assumption that Parliament intends to legislate in a manner that is compatible with the UK's international obligations (such as the ECHR).

In a case involving European Union law, the House of Lords said

> it is a principle of construction of United Kingdom statutes, now too well established to call for citation of authority, that the words of a statute passed after the Treaty has been signed and dealing with the subject-matter of the international obligations of the United Kingdom, are to be construed, if they are reasonably capable of bearing such a meaning, as intended to carry out the obligation and not to be inconsistent with it.

> (*Garland* v *British Rail Engineering* [1983] 2 AC 751, 771 (Lord Diplock))

If the legislation is clear, however, it needs to be given full effect by the courts even if to do so is to violate an international obligation of the United Kingdom. This point was clearly made in *R* v *Lyons* involving the Convention prior to the HRA.

case close-up

R v *Lyons* [2002] UKHL 44

Criminal defendants (who were company directors accused of fraud) alleged that their trial, which took place before the HRA came into effect, was in breach of Article 6 ECHR. They had been required to incriminate themselves because they were convicted on the basis of answers to questions that, under company law, they had been compelled to give. The House of Lords accepted the general principle that uncertainties in legislation (here companies legislation which made refusal to answer companies inspectors' questions an offence) should be resolved by reference to international law. On the facts, however, there was no such uncertainty. It was clearly Parliament's intention that the prosecution should be able to rely on the compelled evidence, and, under UK law, this intention should be followed.

53

General words in Acts of Parliament

Acts of Parliament often confer wide, general powers on ministers or others. Such general powers grant a wide discretion (area of judgment and choice) to a minister or other official to make decisions, enact rules, etc. as he or she thinks is appropriate. However, it is a general rule of administrative law in the United Kingdom that such discretion is never unlimited and must be properly exercised. Under the influence of international law, particularly human rights law, the courts have developed the principle that general words in an Act of Parliament cannot authorise actions that violate fundamental human rights. If Parliament does intend that such a discretion might be exercised in a way that violates human rights, then it must make this clear. Lord Hoffmann expressed the general point in a case involving the free speech rights of prisoners (*R* v *Home Secretary ex parte Sims* [1999] 3 All ER 400). He acknowledged the point that the legislative supremacy of Parliament meant it could enact legislation which is contrary to human rights. But, he went on:

> the principle of 'legality' means that Parliament must squarely confront what it is doing and accept the political cost. Fundamental rights cannot be overridden by general or ambiguous words. This is because there is too great a risk that the full implications of their unqualified meaning may have passed unnoticed in the democratic process. In the absence of express language or necessary implication to the contrary, the courts therefore presume that even the most general words were intended to be subject to the basic rights of the individual. In this way the courts of the United Kingdom, though acknowledging the sovereignty of Parliament, apply principles of constitutionality little different from those which exist in countries where the power of the legislature is expressly limited by a constitutional document. (p 412).

This principle applies to the interpretation of statutes generally and does not depend on the HRA.

Secondary or subordinate legislation

The UK courts, again acting independently of the HRA, have developed the legal rule that subordinate legislation is void if it is incompatible with fundamental rights, such as those in the Convention.

secondary or subordinate legislation

These are regulations of various kinds which are enacted not by Parliament but by a minister, a department, a governmental body, etc. The authority to enact these rules is found in an Act of Parliament. The Act identifies the point and purposes of the regulations and any regulation that goes beyond that which the Act allows can be challenged in court and declared to be invalid (without legal effect). The courts say it has been enacted *ultra vires* (beyond the powers in the Act). (See also Chapter 4, for further discussion.)

The ultimate supremacy of Parliament is accepted since subordinate legislation which is required, by the clear words of its authorising Act, to disregard fundamental rights will be applied.

In *R* v *Secretary of State for Social Services ex parte Joint Council for the Welfare of Immigrants* [1996] 4 All ER 385, the government, on the basis of a general power to make social security regulations, introduced regulations that denied asylum seekers benefits unless they applied instantly on arrival in the United Kingdom. In the view of the Court of Appeal the regulations meant that genuine asylum seekers were placed in a dilemma between pursuing their fundamental right to seek asylum but starving whilst doing so, or giving up their claim and being deported but probably fed. The regulations were void: such a policy needed express, unambiguous primary legislation.

Why the Human Rights Act?

Given these existing influences on the way legislation is interpreted and applied by the courts, why was the HRA necessary? As can be seen in Chapter 4, the Act still does not allow the courts to invalidate an Act of Parliament. But the Act does

- place a legal (statutory) duty on the courts to continue what they were previously doing on a discretionary basis;
- allow them, as we shall see, much more scope to give effect to statutes in ways which are compatible with the Convention. The interpretative moves, illustrated earlier in this section, are confined to places where the meaning of an Act is uncertain or unclear. As we shall see, the HRA allows the courts to give effect to legislation in Convention-compliant ways, even when the words of the Act are clearly not compliant, so long as this does not undermine the basic policies the Act is putting into effect. This goes much further than what was permissible prior to the Act.

3.3.2 **Development of public law rights and judicial review**

The law has recognised public law rights at least since the time of Queen Elizabeth I. Today these rights are normally asserted through a procedure called 'judicial review'. An individual, company or organisation can challenge a decision or action of a public authority, including a minister, on the grounds that the decision or action was, in outline terms, unlawful (done outside the authority's powers), unreasonable or unfair.

Judicial review and human rights

Judicial review involves the High Court reviewing the lawfulness of an official's decision, not retaking the decision in place of the official. The issue, prior to the HRA, was whether the court could require an official (including a minister) to take a person's human rights into account or even require the official to protect human rights as determined by the court. Perhaps the most important case is *Smith*, the 'gays in the military' case. An earlier case, involving the Northern Ireland broadcasting ban (*Brind* v *Secretary of State for the Home Department* [1991] 1 AC 696), is also relevant.

case close-up

R v *Ministry of Defence ex parte Smith* [1996] 1 All ER 257

A number of gay men and lesbian women were dismissed from the armed forces. This was done on the basis of a rule, made under the Royal prerogative, that homosexuals were to be administratively discharged from the armed forces irrespective of their service record or behaviour. The ban was based on the simple fact of a person's sexual orientation. The ban was challenged in the courts on the basis that it was an unreasonable exercise of power, by the Ministry of Defence, because it violated the right to respect for private life (Article 8 ECHR). The Court of Appeal upheld the ban.

- Under ordinary judicial review the issue was whether the ban was within the range of decisions and policies that were open to a reasonable decision-maker.

- Where human rights are involved, it is not necessary to prove bad faith or an abuse of power by the minister. It was accepted (by Lord Bingham) that 'the more substantial the interference with human rights, the more the court will require by way of justification before it is satisfied that the decision is reasonable [in the public law sense of the term]'.

- However, the Convention could not be directly enforced in the courts: it is no more than part of the 'background' to the case and (said Lord Bingham) 'The fact that a decision-maker failed to take account of Convention obligations when exercising an administrative discretion is not of itself a ground for impugning that exercise of discretion'.

- The primary decision-maker was the Ministry of Defence. The ministry had grounds for the ban (e.g. the efficiency of the armed forces), which, it judged, outweighed whatever rights the individuals might have.

- There were clearly issues relevant to the question whether the Convention had been complied with, but these were not for the Court of Appeal.

- Under ordinary principles of judicial review, there was no basis to set the decision aside as being unreasonable.

The principle in *Smith* requiring compelling justification for a decision that interferes with Convention rights was followed, and strengthened, in later cases (e.g. *R* v *Lord Saville of Newdigate ex parte A* [1999] 4 All ER 860).

In *Doherty v Birmingham CC* [2008] UKHL 57 the House of Lords dealt with an unqualified statutory power of a public authority landlord to evict. They thought that the 'reasonableness' of the eviction could be challenged, by the tenant, through ordinary judicial review proceedings. The similarity of judicial review grounds with those based on human rights was emphasised (see paras 108–109 and 135, in particular).

But the basic problem remained: under the principles of judicial review the particular balance that the public authority (minister or official) made, between a Convention right and the public interest, could not be set aside by a UK court so long as the authority had acted in good faith and had taken the Convention right fully into consideration. In other words, a court could not adjudicate directly on whether or not a Convention right had been violated but only on whether it had been properly taken into consideration.

The issue came to a head when the *Smith* case went to Strasbourg. In *Smith and Grady* v *United Kingdom* (2000) 29 EHRR 493, the ECtHR held that there had been a violation of Article 8 (the right to respect for private life) and (more importantly in the context of this chapter) of Article 13, the right to a remedy. Judicial review proceedings did not allow UK courts to give proper consideration to Convention rights. The ECtHR said

> the threshold at which the High Court and the Court of Appeal could find the Ministry of Defence policy irrational was placed so high that it effectively excluded any consideration by the domestic courts of the question of whether the interference with the applicants' rights answered a pressing social need or was proportionate to the national security and public order aims pursued, principles which lie at the heart of the Court's analysis of complaints under Article 8 of the Convention.   (para 138)

Why the Human Rights Act?

The HRA places a clear duty on the UK's courts to ensure that, unless legislation requires otherwise, ministers, officials and public authorities protect the Convention rights of the people they deal with when exercising their powers. The courts now have the job of deciding whether the Convention rights have been secured (this matter is explained in Chapter 4, particularly section 4.6.1). Previously this could not be done directly and the courts had to accept decisions that might not have been compatible with the Convention but which were within the range of 'reasonable' decisions the authorities could take. The situation remains that, in cases not involving the HRA, there was and is no enforceable legal duty on officials to exercise statutory discretions in line with the ECHR (confirmed by *Hurst* v *London Northern District Coroner* [2007] UKHL 13, para 56).

3.3.3 **Development of private law**

The Convention, of course, is primarily to do with the relations between state and individual (though it sometimes requires the states to make changes to private law to ensure that the Convention rights and freedoms are properly secured). Nevertheless, even when developing private law principles, English courts have taken fundamental rights into account.

Defamation and political bodies

cross reference

For freedom of expression see Chapter 17; the celebrity cases are discussed in Chapter 22.

The law of defamation allows a person to seek damages from another on the grounds that the other has published something that lowers his reputation. Commercial companies can protect their reputations in this way but the courts have held that political and public bodies, including local councils, cannot. The reason is to protect freedom of expression and to ensure that the right to criticise and oppose public bodies is not curtailed. In *Derbyshire County Council* v *Times Newspapers Ltd* [1993] AC 534, the House of Lords, disagreeing with the Court of Appeal, made it clear that this recognition of freedom of speech was based on fundamental principles in the common law and was not the direct enforcement of Convention rights.

Confidentiality and privacy

The common law and equity have long provided remedies to protect certain sorts of confidential information, such as medical records or matrimonial intimacies. Under the influence of the right to respect for private life in the Convention, the protection of 'confidentiality' has become the protection of 'privacy' (a wider notion altogether). The point is illustrated by a number of celebrity cases, such as litigation in which Michael Douglas and Catherine Zeta-Jones sued *Hello!* magazine for publishing unauthorised photographs of their wedding. What has happened is that a well-established legal principle allowing a person to protect matters which are 'confidential' (e.g. medical history, commercial secrets) has been developed to include matters which are merely 'private' (the Douglas–Zeta-Jones wedding, publicised and attended by many guests, could not be said to be 'confidential'; but it was intended to be private). The right to 'private life' in Article 8 of the Convention clearly influenced the way the courts approached the matter.

cross reference
This so-called 'horizontal effect' of the Convention on private law is discussed in Chapter 4, section 4.7

Why the Human Rights Act?

The HRA further strengthens this approach by the courts and makes a consideration of the Convention a duty, not just judicial discretion. The Act does not directly impose the Convention on private law; however, it does put a general duty on courts to act in line with the Convention, including when dealing with private law.

3.4 The European Union

European Union (EU) law recognises and gives effect to human rights. Since its early cases the European Court of Justice ((ECJ) now the Court of Justice of the European Union (CJEU)) insisted that EU law should uphold fundamental rights. These rights were found in the ECHR but also reflected the legal and constitutional traditions of member states. Member states wished to give this commitment to fundamental rights the authority of a treaty. To this end the EU's Charter of Fundamental Rights was proclaimed in 2000 and annexed to the Nice Treaty but it did not have direct legal force. It was not until the Lisbon Treaty (in force from 2009) that the Charter was given binding effect, and so equal to a treaty.

The Charter of Fundamental Rights codifies and makes more 'visible' the fundamental rights already recognized by the EU. By Article 6 of the Treaty of European Union (TEU), the EU 'recognises' the Charter—though it also continues to recognise fundamental rights in its general law. The Charter's terms are binding on EU institutions (such as the EU Commission); but they are also binding on member states (acting through their Parliaments, court, executives and administrative systems) when implementing EU law. The Charter has the same legal value as an EU Treaty.

The Charter lists individual rights and freedoms found in the ECHR (such as the right to liberty, Article 6), but also rights and freedoms from other sources (such as the right to asylum, Article 18, or access to documents, Article 42). It also contains a number of principles, which are not expressed as rights, but which must be given weight by courts applying the Charter (e.g. that the EU should respect the rights of the elderly, Article 25). It includes, therefore, but goes way beyond the civil and political rights in the ECHR. Title IV on 'solidarity', for instance, contains a number of employment, social and environmental rights.

The rights, freedoms and principles are to be interpreted in line with general provisions in Title VII. Article 52 allows rights etc. to be limited in their application, but only so long as the 'essence' of the right is guaranteed and the limitations are lawful and subject to tests of proportionality and necessity. Where Charter rights correspond with ECHR rights their meaning is the same as under the ECHR, although the EU can give 'more extensive' protection.

The point of the Charter is to codify and give formal expression to existing EU fundamental rights. Article 6(1) makes it clear that the Charter does not 'in any way' extend the competences (areas of activity) of the EU. An explanatory document sets out the sources of the rights (in treaties, ECJ/CJEU case law, etc.), and this document must be given 'due regard' in applying the Charter. These restraints are unlikely to undermine the evolutionary nature of rights, particularly those originating in the ECHR and subject to the jurisdiction of the ECtHR.

EU law, of course, applies in the UK by virtue of the European Communities Act 1972. Individual rights are directly enforced on the authority of section 2(1), and this will include the fundamental rights found in the 'general law' of the Union. Any conflicts with UK law are resolved in favour of EU law by virtue of section 2(4). By Protocol 30 TEU, however, the UK (along with Poland) seemed to opt out of the Charter. But the impact of the Protocol is not clear. It does not in any general way limit the impact of the Charter's civil and political rights in the UK. This is made clear by the CJEU in *NS* v *SSHD* C-411/10. The Protocol, perhaps, will have more of an opt-out effect in respect of the Charter's social, employment and economic rights. But even this can be doubted given that such rights may already be part of EU law, independent of the Charter, and hence already applying in the UK.

Article 6 TEU commits the EU to accede to the ECHR. When this happens, Union institutions will be subject to the jurisdiction of the ECtHR. In *Bosphorous v Ireland* (2006) 42 EHRR 1, the ECtHR accepted a rebuttable presumption that reasoned decisions of the CJEU, based on EU fundamental rights, were also compatible with the ECHR. Such a presumption is not given for signatory states subject to the ECHR. After accession the ECtHR may be less 'deferential' to EU institutions and member states implementing EU law.

3.5 'Human rights' protection in the United Kingdom before the Human Rights Act: a mixed story

Any idea that, prior to the HRA, the United Kingdom was a land in which civil and political rights were unrecognised, is false. It fails to take into account the recognition, development and protection of such rights through the activities of both Parliament and the courts. It is, of course, a mixed story, but the UK's record on these matters was better than most European countries in the nineteenth and twentieth centuries.

3.5.1 Parliament

Some of the most important principles upon which human rights law is based are expressed, and thereby given legal recognition, in Acts of Parliament which remain on the statute book.

- Magna Carta ('the Great Charter of the Liberties of England') was first granted by King John to the nobles in 1215 but was renewed with the authority of a statute in 1297, of which Chapter 29 is still in force. From a human rights perspective, it represents one of the first attempts to express, in specific terms, a range of limits on the powers of the King. Though much of it is to do with the privileges of the landed nobility, the principle of the rule of law and opposition to arbitrary government are famously expressed and can still be cited in court today.

Chapter 29. No freeman shall be taken or imprisoned, or be disseised of his freehold, or liberties, or free customs, or be outlawed, or exiled, or any other wise destroyed; nor will we not pass upon him, nor condemn him [deal with him] but by lawful judgment of his peers, or by the law of the land. We will sell to no man, we will not deny or defer to any man either justice or right.

- The Bill of Rights 1688. The great constitutional struggles of the seventeenth century ended with the forced abdication of James II (brother of the restored monarch Charles II) and the accession to the throne of William and Mary. From a human rights point of view, the importance of this is that the new monarchs reigned on terms established by Parliament. Under the Bill of Rights Parliament is strengthened and protected (e.g. by securing the right to 'freedom of speech and debates' in Parliament); also it is clearly made unlawful for the Crown to seek to set the laws aside. The Bill of Rights also contains the famous ban on 'cruel and unusual punishments'.

- Habeas Corpus Acts 1640, 1679, 1803, 1804, 1816 and 1862. The prerogative writ of habeas corpus enables a detained person to challenge the legality of his or her detention. It is still available today, though other procedures are often preferred. In the past it has been an important weapon to be used against the threat of arbitrary arrest and detention on the order of the King (as in the seventeenth century). The Acts regulate the procedure, usually, though not always, making the writ easier to obtain.

Some of the most important developments in the recognition and protection of human rights have involved Parliament and legislation. Through political activity, particularly in political parties, but also through pressure groups, protest and demonstration, the great social and economic struggles of history have forced their attentions on Parliament, which has brought about major reforms bearing on human rights. For example:

- the expansion of the franchise (the right to vote) first for all adult men and then, later, for all adult women;
- the equal rights of women;
- the rights of workers to organise into trade unions.

In particular, of course, the HRA itself should be recognised as Parliament's insistence that the governance of the United Kingdom should be consistent with human rights.

Parliamentary history is, of course, a mixed story. Parliament tends to reflect the interests and concerns of the socially and economically dominant classes; it is also under the sway of the government, and it will react to the issues and threats of the day as these are perceived by its members and by government. Just as there is legislation, such as indicated in this chapter, which enhances human rights protection, so Parliament has enacted legislation which threatens and diminishes it. Particularly in times of war or national emergency, the government has had Parliament enact emergency powers which, for example, allow detention without trial, increase the powers of the police and restrict speech. Statutes such as these were enacted at the end of the eighteenth century, when the government feared French revolutionary ideas would cross the channel; notoriously wide-ranging Defence of the Realm Acts were enacted during both the First and Second World Wars, and, since the Second World War, we have seen a succession of anti-terrorism statutes which have given wide, discretionary powers to police and government. These were first aimed at terrorism in the context of Northern Ireland, they are now aimed at international Islamist terrorism and may be thought to be as draconian as any emergency laws have ever been.

3.5.2 **The common law**

The history of the common law's protection of human rights is, likewise, a mixed story.

In *Entick* v *Carrington* (1765) 19 Howell's State Trials 1030, 95 ER 807, the judges upheld the rule of law by denying that the Crown, the government, could enter and search the premises of a political opponent on the basis of a general warrant for which there was no legal authority.

On the other hand, in *Duncan* v *Jones* [1936] 1 KB 218, the High Court accepted that police officers had acted within their duty when they arrested Mrs Duncan. She had refused to cooperate with police, who wanted to stop her making a speech in a public place. The police acted because they said they feared that the speech, though lawful in itself, might provoke others to violence. In upholding the police view, the High Court denied that Mrs Duncan had any 'right' to speak which should be weighed against the alleged threat to public order.

These are just two examples from a myriad of cases that indicate that the history of the common law in protecting what we now call human rights is complex.

In the last few decades judges have expressly recognised fundamental rights as inherent in the common law (e.g. *Morris* v *Beardmore* [1981] AC 446, especially p. 464, per Lord Scarman). This development (which may be no more than a continuation of the older commitments to 'liberty' by using new 'human rights' terminology) is partly inspired by the Convention, though it does not involve the direct application of Convention rights. Common law rights in this sense cover much the same content as Convention rights and, according to the judges, enjoy much the same flexibility. For some judges there is little, if anything, in the ECHR which does not enjoy equivalent protection through the common law. In particular, both common law and the Convention embody the need to seek a fair and proper balance between the rights and freedoms of individuals and the public interest whose proper protection may require some limits to individual liberty.

The weakness of the common law is, in particular, in its subordination to Parliament. The issues are well illustrated by the following, notorious case.

case close-up

Liversidge v *Anderson* [1942] AC 206

During the Second World War, L was detained under regulation 18B of the Defence (General) Regulations 1939. This was subordinate legislation made under the Emergency Powers (Defence) Act 1939. Under the regulations the Home Secretary could detain any person he had 'reasonable cause to believe' was of 'hostile origin' (e.g. a German living in Britain). The question for the court was whether the Home Secretary could be compelled to disclose his reasons for the detention order and thus challenge the detention before a court on the grounds of an absence of a reasonable cause to detain. The House of Lords held that the Secretary of State did not need to disclose his reasons. L remained in detention without a remedy.

Lord Wright expressed the common law position as follows (pp 260–261):

- The courts will uphold personal liberty, they are 'as jealous as they have ever been in upholding the liberty of the subject'.

- Parliament is supreme and 'can enact extraordinary powers of interfering with personal liberty'.

- If there is a valid Act of Parliament it will be enforced by the courts. Likewise, the courts will scrutinise subordinate legislation (such as the regulations in the case) to see if they are properly made, in particular, that they are within the law-making powers granted by the Act. If they are (as was not disputed in the case) then they are valid and will be enforced.

- There are 'no guaranteed or absolute rights' recognised in the British Constitution which the courts can, as it were, assert against the clear words of an Act of Parliament. 'The safeguard of British liberty is in the good sense of the people and in the system of representative and responsible government which has been evolved'.

- The only issue for the courts is to determine, from the language, what is the precise scope of the powers given to the government in the Act.

Liversidge v *Anderson* was a Second World War case dealing with an emergency situation and decided long before the HRA came into force. It expresses, in stark form, both the strength and the weakness of the common law in respect of the protection of human rights prior to the HRA. In contrast, there have been a number of important House of Lords decisions involving the 'war on terrorism' of the early twenty-first century. Such decisions still accept the supremacy of the clear words of Acts of Parliament; nevertheless they show a much more demanding, less deferential attitude towards the government even in times of so-called 'war'. They are decisions applying the HRA but demonstrate, too, the willingness of judges to define their constitutional role in terms of upholding the rights of individuals. This is illustrated by *A* v *Secretary of State for the Home Office (1)* [2004] UKHL 56 and *(2)* [2005] UKHL 71 discussed in Chapter 7, section 7.2.5, and Chapter 9, section 9.4, respectively. Modern judges are concerned not only with whether a minister has the 'power' to act but whether what was done was a 'reasonable' exercise of that power—see, for example, *R (Bancoult)* v *Secretary of State for the Foreign and Commonwealth Office* [2008] UKHL 61.

Summary

- Prior to the coming into force of the HRA, the Convention was already having an impact on UK law: the UK government and Parliament were responding to adverse judgments from Strasbourg and the courts were influenced by the Convention in the way they developed the law.

- The recognition of what, today, are called 'human rights' is not something new in UK law. Important rights were already secured by Acts of Parliament and also by the common law. It is, however, a mixed story, with both Parliament and the courts capable of actions which are hardly compatible with human rights.

- Membership of the European Union is an increasingly important influence on UK law, which requires respect for human rights.

Questions

For suggested approaches, please visit the Online Resource Centre.

1   Although the United Kingdom was among the first states to sign up to the European Convention on Human Rights in 1950, British citizens could not directly enforce anywhere the rights and freedoms the Convention aimed to grant them, neither in national courts nor at Strasbourg. Explain this and explain how, after 1966, the situation changed.

2   In interpreting statutes, English courts have been able to give effect to Convention rights, independently of the HRA. Explain this process, consider its limits and give examples.

Further reading

Lester, A., Pannick, D. and Herberg, J. (see Preface) Chapter 1F and 1G

CIVIL LIBERTIES BOOKS

Fenwick, H. *Civil Liberties and Human Rights* 4th edn (2007) Oxford: Routledge-Cavendish, Chapter 3

Stone, R. *Textbook on Civil Liberties and Human Rights* 8th edn (2010) Oxford: OUP, Chapter 1.4

HISTORICAL PERSPECTIVE

Ewing, K. and Gearty, C. *The Struggle for Civil Liberties* (2000) Oxford: Clarendon Press

DETAILED ANALYSIS OF THE LEGAL FORCE OF HUMAN RIGHTS ARGUMENTS IS FOUND IN

Hunt, M. *Using Human Rights Law in English Courts* (1998) Oxford: Hart Publishing

STANDARD WORKS ON JUDICIAL REVIEW ARE

Wade, Sir William and Forsyth, C. *Administrative Law* 10th edn (2009) Oxford: OUP

Craig, P. *Administrative Law* 6th edn (2008) London: Sweet & Maxwell

ON EUROPEAN UNION LAW AND HUMAN RIGHTS

Mock, W. (ed) *Human Rights in Europe: Commentary on the Charter of Fundamental Rights of the EU* (2010) Durham, N.C.: Carolina Academic Press

Denman, D. 'The Charter of Fundamental Rights' [2010] 4 *EHRLR* 349–359

The Human Rights Act 1998 (1): rights and duties

Chapter overview

- The main provisions of the Human Rights Act 1998 (HRA), including
  - interpretation of statutes (sections 3, 4 and 10),
  - the duty on public authorities and the definition of 'public authority' (section 6),
  - the role of the courts under the HRA,
  - the role of ministers and Parliament.
- Bringing the HRA into effect.
- The territorial application of the HRA.

Introduction

The Human Rights Act 1998 (HRA) gives 'further effect' in UK law to the content of the rights in the European Convention on Human Rights (ECHR).

It has two main ways of doing this:

- it requires the UK courts to interpret Acts of Parliament in a way that makes them compatible with rights in the Convention, but only if it is 'possible to do so';
- it places a legally enforceable duty on government bodies and other 'public authorities' to act in a way that is compatible with the rights in the Convention unless a statute which cannot be interpreted for compatibility requires otherwise.

Section 11 of the Act makes it clear that the point of the HRA is to add to existing rights that are enjoyed under UK law. So the HRA does not in any way diminish an individual's right to pursue a case against the United Kingdom in Strasbourg; nor does it prevent human rights arguments being raised in 'ordinary' judicial review, as discussed in Chapter 3, section 3.3.2.

'Articles' and 'sections'

The ECHR, which is an Act of the Council of Europe (see Chapter 2, section 2.2), is divided into 'Articles'. The HRA, which is an act of the UK Parliament, is divided into 'sections'. The HRA provides the legal means by which the rights in the ECHR can be enforced in UK courts. Schedule 1 HRA (a schedule is like an appendix) has the text of the ECHR rights.

(4.1) Origins of the Human Rights Act

The United Kingdom was a signatory of the ECHR from the beginning in 1950 and it granted its population the right of individual petition in 1966. However, the ECHR is international law. As such it was not part of the law of the United Kingdom and could not be directly enforced before the UK's courts.

cross reference
The impact of the ECHR in the United Kingdom is the topic of Chapter 3.

Pressure for making Convention rights directly enforceable in the courts of the United Kingdom dates at least from lectures delivered by Sir Leslie Scarman, then Law Commissioner, later a Law Lord, in 1974. In the 1980s and 1990s, other senior judges followed suit in arguing for incorporation in one way or another (but it should not be thought that all members of the senior judiciary were in favour). There was also support from some Parliamentarians resulting in Private Members' Bills being introduced in both the Commons (1987) and the Lords (1994 and 1996), though without success. It was the adoption of the policy of incorporation of the European Convention by the Labour Party in 1996 that gave the required political impetus. After Labour's victory in 1997, a White Paper, *Rights Brought Home: the Human Rights Bill* Cm 3782, was produced and the Human Rights Act was enacted in 1998 and brought into effect in October 2000.

further study

Articles by senior judges favouring 'incorporation' include Sir Nicolas Browne-Wilkinson, 'The Infiltration of a Bill of Rights' [1992] *Public Law* 397–410 The Hon Sir Stephen Sedley, 'Human Rights: A Twenty-First Century Agenda' [1995] *Public Law* 386–400 and Sir John Laws, 'Law and Democracy' [1995] *Public Law* 72–93. A general acceptance of some form of incorporation masks very different views about human rights and the role of the judges in these articles.

For judicial opposition to giving effect to the ECHR in national law, see Lord McCluskey, *Law, Justice and Democracy* (1986).

4.1.1 **Arguments for the Act**

The content of UK law

There was a growing sense that in certain areas UK law was failing to secure and keep pace with emerging international standards of human rights protection such as the ECHR or the International Covenant on Civil and Political Rights (ICCPR) (discussed in Chapter 1, section 1.4.4). The flexibility of the common law and its subordination to Parliament meant that, in times of political emergency (as in Northern Ireland in the 1970s) legislation could be passed which gave the security forces wide powers and the individuals affected little protection. Nor was it possible to argue in any direct way that human rights had been violated in areas such as the laws on political meetings, marches and demonstrations. These, it was argued, authorised wide police discretion and the priority of maintaining public order rather than a recognition of political rights. Advocates of some form of incorporation hoped for significant changes in these and other areas.

cross reference

The effectiveness of the HRA in the context of anti-terrorism laws in the early twenty-first century remains a matter of debate—see Chapter 26.

Another group of reasons for introducing human rights protection related to the ability of UK law to control effectively the exercise of state power. In the 1980s, serious political disturbance (e.g. the miners' strike, the peace movement, race riots and racial tension) was met by significant legislative responses, such as the Police and Criminal Evidence Act 1984, the Public Order Act 1986, the Official Secrets Act 1989 and the Criminal Justice and Public Order Act 1994. This created a significant body of opinion concerned that traditional civil liberties were under threat and that some form of legally enforceable protection for human rights was necessary.

65

further study

For an examination of the extent to which UK law in the mid-1990s complied with the ICCPR, see Klug, F., Starmer, K. and Weir, S. *The Three Pillars of Liberty* (1996) London: Routledge.

It was not the case that all those concerned about political liberty in the 1980s thought that a bill of rights was the right answer—compare, for example, Dworkin, R. *A Bill of Rights for Britain* (1990) London: Chatto & Windus, with Ewing, K. and Gearty, C. *Freedom under Thatcher: Civil Liberties in Modern Britain* (1990) Oxford: Clarendon Press.

The unfairness of 'the road to Strasbourg'

The most widely accepted argument was procedural. The UK, by signing the ECHR, had an obligation under international law to secure the Convention rights and freedoms for all within its jurisdiction. Yet (as we saw in Chapter 3) it was unable to provide a remedy for violations of those rights in the courts. An aggrieved person had to take his or her case to

Strasbourg and, in the mid-1990s, this could take about five years and cost about £30,000. For example, it was unjust for a person to be convicted for a criminal offence in a UK court fully aware that an adverse judgment from the European Court of Human Rights (ECtHR) was the likely result.

In *R* v *Morrisey* [1997] 2 Cr App Rep 426 the Court of Appeal upheld the conviction of a company director. His conviction was on the basis of evidence the admissibility of which was almost certainly a violation of Article 6 ECHR, but which was clearly lawful under UK statutes. The Court of Appeal accepted that the situation was 'very unsatisfactory' (pp 433–434; see also *R* v *Lyons* [2002] UKHL 44, Chapter 3, section 3.3.1).

In addition (as noted in the White Paper) some form of incorporation would enable human rights to be more 'subtly and powerfully woven into our law' and enable UK judges to make a distinct, British contribution to the developing standards of human rights protection. Direct enforcement of human rights would also enable closer and more effective scrutiny of government actions by the courts.

4.1.2 The form the 'Bill of Rights' should take

Once the principle of bringing human rights into the law of the United Kingdom was accepted, the next question was, what specific form should this take? The government rejected a strong form in which the courts would be able to invalidate (set aside) an Act of Parliament. Lord Scarman's proposal, made back in the 1970s, was for such a measure which would embody what was, for him, the basic point: that human rights are a form of higher law binding on states, including their legislatures. For the British government such a view was a step too far. It was incompatible with British traditions and, in particular, with the sovereignty of Parliament and the ultimate deference of the judiciary to Parliament.

The solution, as we shall see, was one in which the courts have a widely drawn obligation to interpret existing and future legislation for compatibility with the Convention, but, if that is impossible, the legislation remains valid, though the courts can make a 'declaration of incompatibility'. The Act also places a duty on public authorities to act compatibly with Convention rights and this is enforceable in the courts subject, again, to legislation which requires the public authority to act in the way it does. The Act does not otherwise impose duties on private individuals or companies, though, as we shall see, it is likely to have some impact of that kind.

4.2 Identification of Convention rights

cross reference

For discussion of this point, see Chapter 2, section 2.3.5.

The purpose of the Act is to give 'further effect' to the rights and freedoms in the ECHR. It makes no attempt to add to or modify the provisions of the Convention. Nothing in the Act, for example, strengthens what little human rights protection there is in the Convention for the environment or for basic social welfare. Nor is there a stronger anti-discrimination provision than in the Convention, nor unambiguous duties to take positive steps to advance the interests of under-represented groups defined by gender, ethnicity, etc. In other words, the rather traditional human rights protection of the Convention is adopted into UK law (albeit that the evolving nature of the Convention needs to be recognised).

4.2.1 The Convention rights and ancillary rights

Section 1 identifies the rights and freedoms in the ECHR whose content is to be given further effect by the Act. They are listed in Schedule 1 and are properly to be referred to as 'the Convention rights'. These are

- Articles 2–12 and Article 14 (i.e. not Article 1 or Article 13),
- Articles 1, 2 and 3 of the First Protocol,
- Article 1 of the Thirteenth Protocol (which requires the complete abolition of the death penalty in all circumstances).

These rights are to be 'read with' Articles 16 to 18 of the Convention. (Article 16 allows certain restrictions on the political activities of foreigners, Article 17 prohibits the use of Convention rights in order to abuse the rights of others and Article 18 prohibits states from restricting a right or freedom other than on the grounds allowed for in the Convention.)

4.2.2 Rights not included in Schedule 1: Articles 1 and 13

Article 1 and Article 13 are not included in the Convention rights in Schedule 1. Article 1 is the general duty on states to secure human rights for 'everyone within their jurisdiction'. Article 13 is the duty on states to provide an effective remedy in national courts for breaches of the Convention. The government's position is that the HRA is itself giving effect to these Articles and so their inclusion would be pointless. We shall see that, under section 2 HRA, UK courts are required to take the rulings of the ECtHR into account when interpreting Convention rights. These rulings deal with Articles 1 and 13 and so may influence UK courts indirectly. For example, in *R (Al Skeini)* v *Secretary of State for Defence* [2007] UKHL 26, the House of Lords, following section 2, took into account the ECtHR's understanding of the term 'jurisdiction' found in Article 1. They did this in order to determine whether the HRA applies to British troops operating in Iraq (see section 4.12.3).

4.2.3 Rights not included in Schedule 1: Protocols 4 and 7

cross reference
'Protocols' are defined in Chapter 2, section 2.3.2.

Protocol 4 ECHR creates a qualified right to 'freedom of movement'. Protocol 7 creates a range of rights found in the ICCPR but not in the original Convention. Protocol 4 has been signed but not ratified by the UK; Protocol 7 has neither been signed nor ratified. Neither is, therefore, listed in Schedule 1. The absence of Protocol 4 has significance for anti-terrorism law in the United Kingdom (see Chapter 26).

4.2.4 Derogations and reservations: Article 15

Article 15 ECHR, which allows states to 'derogate' from the Convention (suspend their duties), is not in Schedule 1 HRA. Section 1(2) HRA, however, makes it clear that the Convention rights in Schedule 1 are to have effect subject to any derogations or reservations made by the United Kingdom. Section 14 HRA allows existing derogations to be continued and new derogations to be made. Under section 16, derogations need the approval of Parliament and they lapse after five years unless renewed for an extra five years.

Despite Article 15 not being in Schedule 1, the House of Lords held that an anti-terrorist derogation was not compatible with the requirements of Article 15 in *A (FC)* v *Secretary of State for the Home Department* [2004] UKHL 56.

Article 57 of the Convention allows states to make reservations—to choose, at the time of signature or ratification, not to be bound by specific provisions of the Convention. The United Kingdom made one reservation, in respect of parental choice in education (discussed in Chapter 24, section 24.5) and this is expressly referred to in section 15 of the Act. New reservations can be made (in respect of new Protocols, for example). Under section 17 of the Act the government must keep any reservations under review.

Derogations are discussed in more detail in Chapter 7, section 7.2. The derogation from Article 5, now lapsed, made in the context of anti-terrorism law, is mentioned in Chapter 26, section 26.3.2. Reservations are discussed in Chapter 2, section 2.4.4.

4.3 Section 2 HRA: the ECHR and 'Convention rights'

4.3.1 Following Strasbourg jurisprudence: the principle and its exceptions

As made clear in Chapter 3, the HRA does not make the ECHR directly part of UK law nor does it mean that the judgments of the ECtHR are enforceable in UK courts. This difference between the ECHR (international law) and the 'Convention rights' under HRA Schedule 1 (UK law) is insisted on by UK courts: see *R (Hurst)* v *London Northern District Coroner* [2007] UKHL 13.

What the HRA does is to bring the content of the ECHR (the rights and freedoms listed therein) into UK law. The ECHR (as itself, a part of international law) remains of great importance. It is the basic source for UK courts to use when interpreting the rights listed in Schedule 1 HRA. This is because section 2 HRA requires that the interpretations of the Convention made by the Strasbourg institutions (the ECtHR, the Commission of Human Rights (until 1998) and the Committee of Ministers) to be 'taken into account' by any UK 'court or tribunal determining a question that has arisen in connection with a Convention right'. Thus the full case law developed by the Strasbourg institutions can be cited in UK courts when Convention rights and freedoms in Schedule 1 HRA are in issue.

Section 2 only requires the Strasbourg case law to be 'taken into account', not to be always followed.

KEY FACT Section 2 HRA can be compared with section 3 of the European Communities Act 1972, which, in respect of EU law, requires UK courts to follow the rulings of the Court of Justice of the European Union. Unlike the European Union, the Convention is not designed to be the basis of a common, integrated legal system.

UK courts, specifically the House of Lords (UKHL) or the Supreme Court (UKSC) have always accepted that there can be circumstances, albeit exceptional, in which Strasbourg rulings can be departed from (see *R (Ullah)* v *Special Adjudicator* [2004] UKHL 26, [2004] 2 AC 323, para 20).

In *Pinnock v Manchester CC* [2011] UKSC 6, the Supreme Court, unanimously and authoritatively, summarised the position:

> where . . . there is a clear and consistent line of decisions whose effect is not inconsistent with some fundamental substance or procedural aspect of our law, and whose reasoning does not appear to overlook or misunderstand some argument or point of principle, we consider that it would be wrong for this court not to follow that line
>
> *(Pinnock v Manchester CC*, para 48)

It follows that, first, UK courts are not bound by specific applications of the Convention to UK institutions. In *SSHD v JJ* [2007] UKHL 45, Lord Bingham said that Strasbourg is 'laying down principles and not mandating solutions to particular cases' (para 13). Where, for example, the ECtHR has not been fully appraised of the factual context of a situation, its applications of Convention rights in specific situations (as distinct from its enunciation of general principles) will not need to be followed. An example is *R (Brooke) v Parole Board* [2008] EWCA Civ 29 involving different views on the independence and impartiality of the Parole Board.

Second, and much more significantly, UK courts are not always required to follow principles laid down by the Strasbourg court even when these are clear and consistently expressed statements of the scope and meaning of a Convention article. If such principles are incompatible with important aspects of UK law and procedure or are based on misunderstandings of facts, reasoning or principle, they need not be followed. In *R v Horncastle* [2009] UKSC 14, for example, the UKSC refused to follow a consistently reiterated Strasbourg principle that a criminal conviction could not be 'solely or decisively' based on hearsay evidence if it was to be compatible with Article 6. In the UK such a conviction was, by Act of Parliament, possible, subject to the full range of protections common law and statute allowed for the defence. The UKSC carefully analysed the Strasbourg jurisprudence and held it to be not well grounded in principle or properly reasoned, and it was not appropriate to common law systems. The Grand Chamber, taking *Horncastle* into account, reformulated the Strasbourg principles to the effect that the 'solely or decisively' rule (in the criminal trial context) was not absolute and could be departed from if there were sufficient safeguards in the trial process (*Al-Khawaja* v *UK* (2012) 54 EHRR 23). These cases represent a good example of how section 2 HRA permits a form of 'dialogue' between the UKSC and Strasbourg over difficult questions of human rights law. Indeed the possibility of such dialogue is the main reason why even clear and consistent Strasbourg principles need not always be followed (*Pinnock*, para 48).

Pinnock makes it clear that even principles enunciated by the Grand Chamber of the ECtHR (i.e. the Court speaking with its fullest authority) do not 'in theory' have to be followed by the UKSC. The 'in theory' qualification is important. So far, Grand Chamber judgments have been followed as the final authority. In *A v UK* (2009) 49 EHRR 29, for example, the Grand Chamber expressed a principle concerning the fairness of procedures followed in the UK in respect of terrorist suspects. This principle was contrary to the somewhat more flexible approach of the UKHL in an earlier case on a related issue (*MB/AF v UK* [2007] UKHL 46). Nevertheless the UKHL, in later proceedings, felt obliged to change its position and adopt the Strasbourg approach (*Secretary of State for the Home Department v AF* [2009] UKHL 28). Lord Rodger said: 'in reality, we have no choice: Argentoratum locutum, iudicium finitum—Strasbourg has spoken, the case is closed' (para 98). *Pinnock*, however, suggests it is not quite as final as that. The decision in *Al-Khawaja* meant that the UKSC did not have to consider how to respond when the Grand Chamber, with its full authority, upholds a principle at odds with an important principle of substantive or procedural UK law. That issue, at least 'in theory', remains open.

Inherent in *Horncastle* is an assertion of the continuing significance of the common law and a desire that this should not be subordinated to Convention principles. In a speech in 2010, the Lord Chief Justice went even further and insisted that section 2 even allowed a reasoned Grand Chamber decision to be departed from so long as it had been shown proper and detailed

cross reference

The terrorism cases are discussed in the context of anti-terrorism law in Chapter 26, 26.9.1.

respect. He felt there was an over-focus on Strasbourg cases and not enough on the common law, and that section 2 'ensures that the final word does not rest with Strasbourg, but with our Supreme Court'.

further study

- Lord Judge, LCJ, 'The Judicial Studies Board Lecture 2010' 17 March 2010 (available on the website of the Judiciary of England and Wales http://www.judiciary.gov.uk/ (follow Media > speeches > 2010 > March)).
- Contrast: Lord Irvine, 'A British Interpretation of Convention Rights' [2012] *Public Law* 237–252, who argues against an over-rigid following of Strasbourg, especially in the context of UK courts developing a more generous account of human rights, with Sir Philip Sales, 'Strasbourg Jurisprudence and the Human Rights Act: A Response to Lord Irvine' [2012] *Public Law* 253–267, who argues that legal certainty requires an authoritative legal hierarchy with the ECtHR, speaking through the Grand Chamber, at its peak.
- Bratza, N. (President of the ECtHR) 'The Relationship between the UK Courts and Strasbourg' [2011] 5 *EHRLR* 505–512.

It needs to be noted that this 'dialogue' with Strasbourg is for the Supreme Court. As already mentioned, the Convention is part of international law. Nothing in the HRA undermines the basic structures of UK law: the domestic system of precedent should be upheld and followed. So the Court of Appeal is not entitled to depart from a UKHL/UKSC precedent on the grounds that it is inconsistent with Convention law laid down by the Strasbourg court (e.g. where Convention law has evolved since the UKHL/UKSC ruling involved). The Court of Appeal should follow the UKHL/UKSC (other than in wholly exceptional circumstances). It is then up to the UKSC to reconsider its position in the light of the Strasbourg judgment (*Kay* v *Lambeth* [2006] UKHL 10, paras 40–45). Where, however, there is no ruling of the UKHL/UKSC to follow, the Court of Appeal (Civil Division) may, if it thinks appropriate, depart from its own earlier decision (Convention compatibility is, therefore, another exception to the general rule in *Young* v *Bristol Aeroplane* [1946] AC 163). These positions are confirmed in *R (RJM)* v *Secretary of State for Work and Pensions* [2008] UKHL 63.

4.3.2 How far can UK courts go?—the 'mirror' principle

The judicial justification for interpreting section 2 in the way described in the previous section is the 'mirror' principle. This is that the underlying policy of the HRA is to provide the means for enforcing Convention rights in the UK. Therefore it authorises the courts to give remedies in the UK only when such remedies could also be available from the Strasbourg court.

This principle, that UK law, generally, should mirror Strasbourg law, is relatively uncontroversial in so far as UK courts might otherwise give readings of Convention rights which are less 'generous' to applicants than those of the ECtHR. If UK courts began to diverge too far in this direction, disappointed applicants would still have recourse to the ECtHR, and the point of the HRA would be lost.

There is more concern when UK courts are asked to adopt more 'generous' approaches to rights, approaches in which public authorities are required to respect rights in new situations which the Strasbourg jurisprudence has not clearly identified. Lord Brown, in *Rabone* v *Pennine Care NHS Foundation Trust* [2012] UKSC 12, summarised the position:

- If the domestic court is inclined to uphold a Convention challenge against a public authority in a new situation it should not refuse so to do merely because there is no Strasbourg decision on the point.

- However, the domestic court needs to be satisfied that what it is doing is applying Convention rights in a way that 'flow[s] naturally' from existing Strasbourg case law.
- Domestic courts may provide common law rights which are more generous than those in the Convention, but if these purport to be based on the Convention (and not on some other common law source) they must not go beyond what is 'recognized by or reasonably envisaged within, existing Strasbourg jurisprudence'.

Baroness Hale, for instance, would have happily read into Article 2 (the right to life) a duty on states not to send troops to fight in unlawful wars. But this would be a new significant interpretation of the article which only the Strasbourg court could do: 'We are not free to foist upon Parliament or upon public authorities an interpretation of a Convention right which goes way beyond anything we can reasonably foresee that Strasbourg might do', *R (Gentle)* v *Prime Minister* [2008] UKHL 20, para 56.

As Lord Brown said, 'It is for Strasbourg alone definitively to interpret the Convention and determine what rights are guaranteed by it' (*Rabone*, 113). The Supreme Court, in *Pinnock* left open the possibility of divergence even from Strasbourg at its most authoritative. But this was only 'in theory' and, probably, will have little practical significance.

further study

An argument for a more 'generous' UK approach, see Lewis, J. 'The European Ceiling on Human Rights' [2007] *Public Law* 720–747.

The significance of the mirror principle is also relevant to the broader issue of a distinctly British 'bill of rights'. This matter is discussed in Chapter 27.

71

4.4 Legislation and the Human Rights Act: sections 3, 4, 5 and 10

4.4.1 Introduction

Sections 3, 4, 5 and 10 HRA concern the first of the two principal ways in which the Act gives further effect to Convention rights in UK law. These sections deal with Acts of Parliament and the way they are to be interpreted and given effect by the courts. In summary:

- Acts of Parliament should be read and given effect, if they can be, in a way that is compatible with the Convention rights in Schedule 1.
- If this is not possible then the offending legislation remains valid but the courts may issue a 'declaration of incompatibility'.
- Although such a declaration does not affect the validity and effect of the law, a minister may choose to take 'remedial action' and change the law by an order made under the Act.

These points will now be looked at in more detail.

KEY POINT Whether the HRA itself is subject to interpretation under section 3 is uncertain. In *R (Al Skeini)* v *Secretary of State for Defence* [2007] UKHL 26, for example, the Law Lords who discussed the issue disagreed (compare para 15(2) (Lord Bingham) with paras 145–146 (Lord Brown)).

4.4.2 The duty to interpret legislation for compatibility with scheduled Convention rights (section 3 HRA)

3 Interpretation of legislation

(1) So far as it is possible to do so, primary legislation and subordinate legislation must be read and given effect in a way which is compatible with the Convention rights.

(2) This section—

(a) applies to primary legislation and subordinate legislation whenever enacted;

(b) does not affect the validity, continuing operation or enforcement of any incompatible primary legislation; and

(c) does not affect the validity, continuing operation or enforcement of any incompatible subordinate legislation if (disregarding any possibility of revocation) primary legislation prevents removal of the incompatibility.

There are a number of important points to note.

An interpretative duty

Section 3 HRA imposes an interpretative duty on the courts. Acts of Parliament are to be interpreted ('read and given effect') for compatibility with Convention rights if this is possible. They are to be interpreted so that the rights, duties, powers and liberties that they establish can only be exercised in ways that are compatible with, and do not lead to breaches of, Convention rights.

No power to invalidate a statute

But the interpretative duty only applies 'so far as it is possible to do so'. Under section 3, no court, not even the Supreme Court, has the authority to invalidate an Act of Parliament. Section 3(2)(b) makes it clear that legislation which cannot be read or given effect in a way that is compatible with Convention rights remains valid and the courts are required to enforce it. Parliament retains its 'sovereignty' and remains free to enact legislation that clearly and intentionally permits or requires violations of Convention rights. This approach to human rights protection can be compared with, for example, the systems in the United States or in Germany. In those countries rights and freedoms are listed in a written constitution and a constitutional court (the US Supreme Court or the German Constitutional Court respectively) has the power to invalidate acts of the legislature on the grounds that they are unconstitutional.

Applies to legislation 'whenever enacted': enactments made before October 2000

Section 3(2)(a) means that in-force legislation that was enacted prior to October 2000 (when the HRA came into effect) is subject to the interpretative duty. In this way, the HRA empowers the courts to undertake a form of ad hoc law reform resolving incompatibilities between existing legislation and human rights on a case-by-case basis. This is, no doubt, a more efficient approach than trying to perform the same task by a massive Act which identifies and amends all such incompatible legislation in the abstract.

Applies to legislation 'whenever enacted': enactments made after October 2000

The interpretative duty applies to all legislation enacted after the HRA was brought into effect. It should be noted that post-October 2000 legislation which is apparently incompatible with Convention rights does not implicitly repeal the HRA. Rather, it is dealt with under that Act's terms: the new legislation is either capable of being read and given effect in a Convention-compatible manner or it is put into effect as legislation which is incompatible but still valid.

Subordinate legislation

'Subordinate legislation' (which can also be called 'secondary' or 'delegated' legislation) refers to rules, which are enacted under the authority of an Act of Parliament (primary legislation). These rules have the full force of law. Typically primary legislation empowers someone, such as a government minister, a government department, a 'quango' (e.g. the Health and Safety Executive) or a local council, to produce legally enforceable rules and regulations. The Act identifies the general purpose which the regulations etc. are to achieve, but the specific rules are left to the minister etc. Examples include 'Orders in Council' or regulations made by ministers under statute (these are likely to be 'statutory instruments') and by-laws made by local councils. There are many other forms.

The duty under section 3 HRA to read and give effect to legislation in a way that is compatible with Convention rights applies to subordinate legislation.

Unlike primary legislation, subordinate legislation which cannot be interpreted for compatibility with Convention rights is invalid and not to be applied by the courts. This is implied by section 3(2)(c) HRA. It is already a general principle of law, independent of the HRA, that subordinate legislation which is incompatible with 'fundamental rights', as recognised by the common law, is invalid; it is *ultra vires* (outside the powers), which means that it has been enacted in a way or for a purpose which was not authorised by the primary Act of Parliament. In the court's view Parliament cannot have intended to authorise ministers etc. to make subordinate legislation which violates fundamental rights. If Parliament does so intend it must say so expressly. Apparently unlimited power to make regulations does not mean any regulations made can violate fundamental or human rights. Section 6 HRA, as we shall see, makes it unlawful for a minister etc., to make regulations which violate Convention rights.

cross reference

For examples of this see Chapter 3, section 3.3.1, secondary or subordinate legislation.

Subordinate legislation which is incompatible with Convention rights remains valid if the primary legislation under which it is made prevents the removal of incompatibility (section 3(2)(c) HRA). If primary legislation gives a minister etc. broad, general powers to make subordinate legislation, the courts will be unlikely to read these powers as preventing the removal of incompatible regulations. It is more likely that the courts will 'read down' the scope of such a broad and general law-making power in the primary legislation so as to exclude incompatible regulations.

KEY POINT The subordinate legislation covered by section 3 is identified in section 21 HRA, the interpretation section. It includes

- Orders in Council if made on the authority of an Act of Parliament;

- any 'order, rules, regulations, scheme, warrant, byelaw or other instrument made under primary legislation';

- Acts of the Scottish Parliament, Acts of the Northern Ireland Assembly and Executive, and Measures and Acts of the National Assembly for Wales.

It expressly excludes Orders in Council made under the Royal Prerogative and some provisions relating to Northern Ireland, which are therefore treated as primary legislation

4.4.3 Declarations of incompatibility, section 4 HRA

4 Declaration of incompatibility

(1) Subsection (2) applies in any proceedings in which a court determines whether a provision of primary legislation is compatible with a Convention right.

(2) If the court is satisfied that the provision is incompatible with a Convention right, it may make a declaration of that incompatibility.

If a court finds that it is not possible to read and give effect to primary legislation in a manner that is compatible with the Convention, it has the discretion to make a 'declaration of incompatibility'. Such a declaration can also be made in respect of subordinate legislation whose repeal is prevented by its authorising primary legislation. A declaration of incompatibility is discretionary: a court is not bound to issue one. Such a declaration does not affect the validity of the legislation involved, which remains valid and enforceable. Nor does it affect the parties to the case in which it was made—their legal position is determined by the valid, enforceable but incompatible law. Only the senior courts can make declarations of incompatibility. In England and Wales these are the High Court, Court of Appeal and Supreme Court.

further study

Section 4(5) HRA has a full list of all the UK courts with the power to make declarations of incompatibility.

Though such declarations do not affect the validity or enforceability of legislation, they are made with the authority of the senior judiciary and are not to be lightly disregarded by government. Before a declaration of incompatibility can be made, the government must be given the chance to make representations to the court (see section 5 HRA).

Magistrates' or Crown Courts hearing criminal trials, or a county court dealing with a civil matter, or a tribunal are unable to make declarations of incompatibility. Under section 3 they are required to interpret the legislation they are dealing with, if possible, for compatibility. If a compatible interpretation is impossible then they must apply the incompatible law (e.g. convict a defendant even though the conviction may be a violation of his or her Convention rights). The defendant may then appeal to the High Court (usually the Divisional Court of the Queen's Bench) or the Court of Appeal (Criminal Division). These appellate courts would have to uphold the conviction if they agree with the lower court that a compatible interpretation of the legislation is not possible, but they are able to complement that with a declaration of incompatibility if it is appropriate.

Examples of declarations of incompatibility include:

- In *International Transport Roth GmbH* v *Secretary of State for the Home Department* [2002] EWCA Civ 158 the Court of Appeal (Laws LJ dissenting), made a declaration of incompatibility in respect of primary legislation which penalised international road hauliers for bringing people into the country illegally hidden in their lorries. The legislation placed the burden of proof on the companies to disprove their liability and was incompatible with Article 6; other elements of the scheme were disproportionate and incompatible with Article 1 of the First Protocol (the protection of property).

cross reference

See section 4.4.4 for what happened next in these cases.

- In *R (H)* v *Mental Health Review Tribunal N&E London Region* [2001] EWCA Civ 415, the Court of Appeal made a declaration of incompatibility in respect of section 73 of the Mental Health Act 1983. This placed the burden of proving to a Mental Health Review Tribunal that the grounds for detaining a person for treatment in a mental hospital still existed, on the applicant rather than the hospital, and was incompatible with Article 5, the right to liberty and security.

cross reference

Examples of this prior to the HRA have been given in Chapter 3.

KEY POINT Declarations of incompatibility under section 4 HRA need to be distinguished from the ordinary 'declaratory' remedy.

4.4.4 **Consequences of incompatibility: section 10, remedial action**

If a UK court makes a declaration of incompatibility under section 4 HRA (or if the ECtHR in Strasbourg decides that the UK has violated the Convention) there are three courses open to the government.

1. Do nothing. Neither a declaration of incompatibility from a UK court nor an adverse finding from Strasbourg changes UK law. The government may decide to keep the incompatible law, or administrative practice it authorises, as it is. No court in the UK has the power to order a minister to introduce legislation to change the law (confirmed by section 6(6) HRA). If nothing is done a person directly affected may still take their case to Strasbourg and the UK could be faced with an adverse judgment from the ECtHR. Nevertheless the option of doing nothing is clearly one of the possibilities envisaged by the approach to human rights protection introduced by the Act. However, where a case is taken to Strasbourg following a declaration of incompatibility, the UK government is likely to seek a 'friendly settlement' (see Chapter 2, section 2.5.3); an example is *Kent* v *United Kingdom* App 21843/04, decision of 30 August 2005, following the *International Transport Roth* case in section 4.4.3.

2. Change the law or administrative practice. The usual practice (and the practice adopted prior to the Act coming into force in respect of Strasbourg judgments) is to change the law or administrative practice purportedly authorised under it. The government may, for example, introduce new legislation to Parliament or withdraw and redraft subordinate legislation.

3. Remedial orders.

10   Power to take remedial action

(1) This section applies if—

(d) a provision of legislation has been declared under section 4 to be incompatible with a Convention right and [any appeal process has been completed] or

(e) it appears to a Minister of the Crown . . . that [after an adverse finding by the ECtHR] a provision of legislation is incompatible with an obligation of the United Kingdom arising from the Convention.

(2) If a Minister of the Crown considers that there are compelling reasons for proceeding under this section, he may by order make such amendments to the legislation as he considers necessary to remove the incompatibility.

Section 10 HRA introduces an important innovation. Following a declaration of incompatibility, an adverse judgment from Strasbourg or the quashing of incompatible subordinate legislation, a minister may introduce changes to Acts of Parliament or to subordinate legislation in order to remedy the incompatibility. The normal way to amend primary legislation is by a second, amending, Act of Parliament. Under section 10, however, repeal or amendment to legislation can be made simply by an order made by the minister: an Act of Parliament is not required. The idea that the executive can change the law by making an order rather than by obtaining an Act of Parliament is seen as potentially oppressive (sections in Acts of Parliament which permit this, which are not uncommon, are sometimes known as 'Henry VIII clauses'). For this reason the provision was one of the most controversial features of the Act when it was enacted and the section 10 power can only be exercised subject to the following safeguards.

- The minister must have 'compelling reasons' for introducing a remedial order. There is no indication in the Act of what these could be. The need to make amendments speedily is an obvious reason. The decision by a minister to proceed or not to proceed under section 10 cannot be challenged in the courts (see section 6(6)(b) HRA).
- Any order is limited by what the minister considers is necessary to remove the incompatibility.
- The legal process in the UK has been exhausted. Thus all rights of appeal have either been given up by the parties (who must signify this in writing) or have been unsuccessfully pursued in the courts.
- Parliamentary approval. This is the most important safeguard. Orders made under section 10 are subject to Parliamentary approval. The detail of this is in Schedule 2 HRA. It should be remembered that Acts of Parliament, especially those concerned with emergencies and restricting human rights, have often had rather short and cursory examination in Parliament (especially by the House of Commons). It is possible that the kind of scrutiny remedial orders will get under Schedule 2 will be at least as careful, probably more careful, than the same terms would get in an Act of Parliament. During the approval process there are opportunities for representations to be made and for amendment to the draft order. Furthermore, since a remedial order is subordinate legislation, the Parliament Acts 1911 and 1949 do not apply and so the consent of the House of Lords cannot be dispensed with.

The consequences of the declarations of incompatibility in the two cases mentioned previously were as follows:

Following *International Transport Roth GmbH* v *Secretary of State for the Home Department* [2002] EWCA Civ 158, the Immigration and Asylum Act 1999 Part II was amended by the Nationality, Immigration and Asylum Act 2002. Schedule 8 introduced a Code of Practice to deal with the issues on which the declaration of incompatibility was based.

Following *R (H)* v *Mental Health Review Tribunal N&E London Region* [2001] EWCA Civ 415, the Mental Health Act 1983 was amended by a remedial order by which the burden of proof on whether grounds for detaining a person in a mental hospital existed was now placed on the hospital. (See Mental Health Act 1983 (Remedial) Order 2001 (SI 2001/3712).) The need to allow the tribunals to continue functioning, not to detain people longer than was necessary and to prevent a build-up of cases were 'compelling reasons' for such an order.

4.4.5 **The meaning of 'so far as it is possible to do so': general principles**

The House of Lords has decided a number of important cases on the meaning and impact of the courts' interpretative duty under section 3. In this section the general principles will be identified; in the next section some of the important, illustrative, cases will be discussed.

Three general techniques are open to the courts:

- 'reading down'—introducing limiting words or meanings to an Act of Parliament to ensure its possible effects are Convention compatible. Where, for example, an Act of Parliament seems to give a minister a widely drawn discretionary power, the scope of this power might be 'read down' by the courts inserting a provision restricting the discretion so it can only be exercised in a manner compatible with Convention rights.
- 'reading in'—introducing words or meanings into an Act of Parliament which create necessary safeguards to ensure that the Act is compatible with Convention rights.
- 'reading out'—in which courts remove or will not enforce provisions in an Act of Parliament which would otherwise make it incompatible with Convention rights.

What is unclear is when the use of such techniques is appropriate. Although some judges are unwilling to be too specific about what section 3 does or does not permit, certain broad principles concerning when it is appropriate to use such techniques can be identified.

Section 3 only applies when there is incompatibility under 'normal' canons of interpretation

Section 3 only applies when under 'normal' canons of statutory interpretation (i.e. the literal rule, the golden rule, the mischief rule, etc.) it is not possible to read the legislation as being compatible with Convention rights.

> Orthodox canons of statutory construction must give way to the strong obligation imposed by s3(1) of the 1998 Act. The role of the court is not (as in traditional statutory interpretation) to find the true meaning of the provision, but to find (if possible) the meaning which best accords with Convention rights.

> (*R (Wright)* v *SSH* [2007] EWCA Civ 999, para 112)

• •

'normal', 'orthodox' ways of interpreting statutes

The basic rule is to construct the intention of Parliament by giving the words of a statute their ordinary meaning (the 'literal rule'). If that meaning is ambiguous or unclear, the courts are allowed to use various principles of statutory interpretation and various internal and external aids to obtain what they take to be the intention of Parliament (the 'golden rule'); one important approach is to identify the problem the Act aims to resolve and interpret the Act to that effect (the 'mischief rule'). The courts seldom refer to these rules as such when seeking the meaning of a statute. Statutory interpretation is also discussed in Chapter 3, section 3.3.1.

• •

Section 3 overrides the literal rule

Under the literal rule the intention of Parliament is known through the ordinary meaning of the words used. Under section 3, however, the words of the statute are no longer ultimately decisive and so the intention of Parliament at the time is no longer followed. The House of Lords has said, for example:

> In accordance with the will of Parliament as reflected in section 3 it will sometimes be necessary to adopt an interpretation which linguistically may appear strained.

> (*R* v *A* [2001] UKHL 25, para 44)

In the ordinary course the interpretation of legislation involves seeking the intention reasonably to be attributed to Parliament in using the language in question. Section 3 may require the court to depart from this legislative intention, that is, depart from the intention of the Parliament which enacted the legislation.

(*Ghaidan* v *Godin-Mendoza* [2004] UKHL 30, para 30)

Ambiguity or uncertainty is not necessary

Thus, even when the words of an Act of Parliament are, on the literal rule, clear, they can still be departed from, added to or ignored under section 3 if it is necessary to do so in order to achieve compatibility with Convention rights.

Section 3 is only invoked where, to achieve compliance with the convention, the court must depart from the unambiguous meaning the legislation would otherwise bear.

(*R (Hurst)* v *Northern London District Coroner* [2007] UKHL 13, para 49, per Lord Brown)

cross reference
See Chapter 3, section 3.3.1.

One important reason for this 'downgrading' of the words is that, otherwise, section 3 would not add very much to the law. As discussed in Chapter 3, there is already a principle of statutory interpretation, independent of the HRA, that ambiguities in the language of an Act can be resolved on the principle that Parliament intended to legislate compatibly with the international obligations of the United Kingdom, including, of course, the ECHR.

Declarations of incompatibility: a last resort?

cross reference
For further discussion of the desirability of declarations of incompatibility, see the Discussion Topic, at section 4.4.7.

The implication of all this is that a court should try, first, to interpret the legislation so it is compatible with Convention rights. There is a consistent stream of judicial opinion that a declaration of incompatibility should be a 'last resort' (e.g. *R (L)* v *Commissioner of Police for the Metropolis* [2009] UKSC 3, para 74, per Lord Neuberger). This was the expressed hope of the government when promoting the bill. Section 3, with its reference to what is 'possible', requires the courts to do all they can to achieve compatibility. On this view, there is no point to section 3 if problems of compatibility with Convention rights are continually being put back to the government and Parliament. The purpose behind the HRA is to delegate to the courts the bulk of the work of creating Convention compatibility in the law. Of course, if the courts come up with an interpretation of an Act that Parliament dislikes, Parliament is free to amend the law and restore the incompatibility (though this would reopen the possibility of a further challenge before the ECtHR). But judges do not take an absolute, mechanical approach. A declaration may be chosen because it is the most appropriate solution even if, in strict terms, a section 3 reading is possible. An example is the views of the dissenting minority in *R (G)* v *Metropolitan Police Commissioner* [2011] UKSC 21. Some commentators see a virtue in the declaration precisely because it ensures Parliamentary responsibilities for human rights (see the Discussion Topic, at section 4.4.7).

4.4.6 What is not 'possible': interpretation not legislation

There are limits to what is 'possible' for the courts to do. Section 3 permits 'interpretation' not 'legislation' by the courts. As the House of Lords said in *Re S* [2002] UKHL 10:

In applying section 3 the courts must be ever mindful of this limit [not to go beyond interpreting legislation]. The 1989 Act reserves the amendment of primary legislation to Parliament. By this means the 1998 Act seeks to preserve Parliamentary sovereignty. The 1998 Act maintains the constitutional boundary. Interpretation of statutes is a matter for the courts; the enactment of statutes, and the amendment of statutes, are matters for Parliament.   (para 39)

What is not 'possible': maintain consistency with fundamental features of the Act in question

Any reading in, reading out or reading down must be consistent with the 'fundamental features' of the sections of the Act being interpreted. A section 3 interpretation is only possible if it goes 'with the grain' and is consistent with the 'underlying thrust' of the legislation (these terms are taken from Ghaidan v Godin-Mendoza, para 33). Behind the words lies the 'concept' of the statutory provisions in issue and any section 3 interpretation must not do violence to this concept.

What is not 'possible': maintain the proper balance between the courts and Parliament

Section 3 does not license the courts to rewrite legislation in a manner that usurps or undermines the relationship between the courts and Parliament. To some degree, section 3 has redefined this relationship in favour of the courts, but, even so, it does not make 'possible' a reading in, out or down that (a) is incompatible with a fundamental feature of the legislation or with the broad policy the legislation is putting into effect, (b) undermines a provision in an Act that has been expressly endorsed by Parliament or (c) involves the court in a complex policy judgment for which they are ill-equipped.

In this way the courts recognise and give effect to the primacy and proper role of Parliament. There are two intertwined reasons. The first is a constitutional reason. Under the constitution the legitimacy and authority of the courts stems from their ultimate subordination to Parliament. The second is a practical reason. The courts are ill-equipped to alter the underlying policy an Act pursues; or to alter an Act in a way that has significant implications for the policy of the law. The courts decide disputes between individuals based on their assessment of the legal rights of those individuals. This is very different from policy-making, when a range of options should be considered in the light of all relevant issues and all foreseeable consequences. This is for administrators and politicians, not judges.

Clarity and certainty

The courts understand section 3 as allowing them to depart from the clear and unambiguous meaning of a statute. The difficulty is that this may have increased uncertainty. It is not at all clear that the 'grain' or 'concept' or 'fundamental feature' of a statute, supposedly implicit in the Act, will be clear. In both the cases from which these general principles have been derived (Ghaidan v Godin-Mendoza and R v A) there were important doubts expressed and dissension over the application of the principles. It remains to be seen whether the distinction between 'interpretation' and 'legislation' under section 3 is one that can be convincingly applied by the courts in the cases that come before them.

KEY POINT Some Law Lords have compared the interpretative obligation under section 3 with the obligation in sections 2 and 3 of the European Communities Act 1972 (Ghaidan v Godin-Mendoza, paras 45–48). This requires UK courts to interpret UK law for compatibility with European Union law, specifically with 'directives' that should have been brought fully into effect. In Litster v Forth Dry Dock Engineering Co Ltd [1990] 1 AC 546, for example, the House of Lords read words into a UK regulation in order to ensure that it gave proper effect to an EC directive. Following the comparison, section 3 HRA case law has been used to determine the principles for interpreting UK law aimed at implementing EU directives (see Alstom v Eurostar International [2012] EWHC 28, paras 34–38).

Any such parallel with EU law does not have implications for the impact of the Convention on domestic law outside the HRA: see Chapter 3 and Hurst v Metropolitan Police Commissioner [2007] UKHL 13, para 52.

4.4.7 The meaning of 'so far as it is possible to do so': some leading cases

The principles discussed in previous sections have been identified and applied in a number of leading cases including these that follow.

case close-up

Ghaidan v *Godin-Mendoza* [2004] UKHL 30

The legislation to be interpreted

Schedule 1 Rent Act 1977:

2(1) The surviving spouse (if any) of the original tenant, if residing in the dwelling-house immediately before the death of the original tenant, shall after the death be the statutory tenant if and so long as he or she occupies the dwelling-house as his or her residence.

(2) For the purposes of this paragraph, a person who was living with the original tenant as his or her wife or husband shall be treated as the spouse of the original tenant.

Paragraph 3(1) of the Schedule went on to say that if paragraph 2 did not apply but the claimant was living as a 'family member' then they could continue to live in the dwelling house but only as an 'assured tenant', which gave them fewer rights and greater vulnerability to rent rises and changes in terms.

The issue: whether the surviving member of a same-sex relationship could succeed to a statutory tenancy despite words in the legislation ('spouse', 'wife' and 'husband'), which, if read literally, suggested that only those in heterosexual relations could benefit.

The Convention question: whether such a statutory provision discriminated against same-sex couples in violation of Article 14, the right not to suffer discrimination with respect to Convention rights, when read with Article 8, the right to private life.

The House of Lords held that it was 'possible' to read the schedule in a way that included same-sex couples. A declaration of incompatibility was not necessary.

The case illustrates a reading of a legislative provision which, though probably at odds with the unambiguous literal meaning of the words (which imply relationships only between men and women), is 'possible' in the sense that it 'goes with the grain', the 'underlying thrust', of the legislation. Paragraph 2(2) of the Schedule indicates an intention by Parliament to provide rights to unmarried persons and the social policy which explained that would also justify extending the right to same-sex couples. Otherwise the Act would discriminate against same-sex couples. Discrimination against same-sex couples was not required by the Act and, without such a requirement, could not be justified.

A word of caution must be noted, however. Lord Millett dissented in *Ghaidan*. He accepted the general approach adopted towards section 3, but felt that the underlying thrust of the statute, especially its extension under paragraph 2(2), was confined to heterosexual relations and that extending them to same-sex relations was to legislate, not interpret. Perhaps this is an illustration of uncertainties that may arise when judges depart from the words and claim to know the 'concept' or 'thrust' of the legislation they are dealing with.

On the basis of the approach summarised in *Ghaidan*, the courts have sometimes used section 3 for radical interventions. This is especially so in the context of protecting rights to a fair hearing (Article 6), which the courts see as their preserve.

- In *R* v *A* [2001] UKHL 25, an early decision under the HRA, the court restored the discretion of a judge in a rape trial to allow cross-examination of the victim about her sexual history. Parliament, in legislation, had quite deliberately sought to narrow this discretion as part of a

cross reference

Similar boldness, referring to Hammond, was used in an anti-terrorism case Secretary of State for the Home Department v MB/ AF [2007] UKHL 46, discussed in Chapter 26, section 26.9.1.

policy of encouraging victims to go to court. Some of the judges used section 3 HRA to read in the need to protect the defendant's Article 6 rights.

- *R (Hammond)* v *Secretary of State for the Home Department* [2005] UKHL 69 involved legislation which allowed life-sentence prisoners to apply to a judge for a reassessment of the minimum time they had to spend in jail. The legislation expressly said that the judge should decide the matter 'without an oral hearing'. The right to an oral hearing was, nevertheless, read into the legislation if necessary to protect prisoners' Article 6 rights.

The next case is an example of the courts accepting that the will of Parliament was clear and that to read a Convention-compliant meaning would be, in effect, to legislate.

---

case close-up

R (Anderson) v Secretary of State for the Home Department [2002] UKHL 46

Section 29 Crime Sentences Act 1997 (now repealed):

The legislation to be interpreted

(1) If recommended to do so by the Parole Board, the Secretary of State may, after consultation with the Lord Chief Justice together with the trial judge if available, release on licence a life prisoner who is not [a discretionary life prisoner].

(2) The Parole Board shall not make a recommendation under subsection (1) above unless the Secretary of State has referred the particular case, or the class of case to which that case belongs, to the Board for its advice.

The issue: judges have no discretion over the punishment of murderers. They must pass a life sentence. Most life sentences do not result in imprisonment for life. The words in the Act gave the Home Secretary the power to release those serving such a 'mandatory' life sentence on licence if recommended to do so by the Parole Board. The Parole Board could only make a recommendation if the Home Secretary chose to refer the matter to them. The Home Secretary had a well-established policy. Before a prisoner could be referred to the Parole Board he would have to serve what was then called the 'tariff', the period to be served for the purposes of punishment. After the 'tariff' had been served, the Parole Board could be asked to consider release on the basis of whether the prisoner was still dangerous. The Home Secretary set the tariff after consultation with the trial judge and the Lord Chief Justice. In Anderson's case the trial judge and Lord Chief Justice had recommended 15 years but the Home Secretary had set it at 20 years.

The Convention question: whether the setting of the tariff by the Home Secretary was in essence a sentencing exercise, which, under Article 6 of the Convention (the right to a fair trial), should be done by an 'independent and impartial tribunal', meeting a range of fair trial requirements. The Home Secretary was not such a tribunal.

The House of Lords held that the Home Secretary's powers were incompatible with Article 6 but it was not 'possible' to read section 29 compatibly with Article 6: a declaration of incompatibility was issued.

This case illustrates the limits to section 3. To have read into section 29 provisions establishing compatibility with Article 6 would have been to go against the clear and express policy of Parliament. It was clearly the intention of Parliament that the Home Secretary should have the final say in respect of the punishment of mandatory life sentence prisoners.

The declaration of incompatibility meant that the statute remained valid and in force. Following this case and a further adverse judgment in Strasbourg, the law has now been changed giving the Parole Board a greater role.

case close-up

Bellinger v *Bellinger* [2003] UKHL 21

The legislation to be interpreted

Section 11 Matrimonial Causes Act 1973:

> A marriage . . . shall be void on the following grounds . . .

> (c) That the parties are not respectively male and female.

The issue: a woman had been born a man but had gone through a process of gender reassignment and, physically and emotionally, she was a woman. She had gone through a ceremony of marriage with a man. She sought a declaration that her marriage was valid. The problem was that, in various ways, she remained a man in the eyes of the law; in particular, her birth certificate could not be changed.

The Convention question: whether section 11 of the Matrimonial Causes Act was compatible with Mrs Bellinger's rights under Article 8 (private life) and Article 12 (the right to marry).

The House of Lords held that her Convention rights had not been secured, however, it was not 'possible' to read section 11 in a compatible manner and so a declaration of incompatibility was issued.

This case illustrates the point that major policy changes ought not to be brought in under section 3. To have redefined 'male and female' in order to accommodate transsexual persons would involve a major change in the law which would have far-reaching ramifications. There would be significant issues of 'social policy and administrative feasibility' to be dealt with; perhaps there should be public consultation. These are matters for Parliament, both because that is the constitutionally proper place for changes of such significance to be made, but also because the courts are simply not equipped to deal with the full range of factors involved.

case close-up

The DNA database cases

The cases here (*Marper* in the House of Lords under the HRA, *Marper* at Strasbourg under the ECHR and *R(G)*, where the issue is returned to under the HRA) illustrate the working of the Act.

The underlying facts were that section 64 Police and Criminal Evidence Act (1984) PACE gave the police powers to retain DNA from suspects even if not convicted. DNA profiles, from the samples, were held on the national DNA database and regulated on the basis of Guidelines issued by the police. The police's refusal, following the Guidelines, to remove the applicants' profiles was challenged under the HRA as being incompatible with Article 8 (the right to private life).

1. *R (Marper)* v *Chief Constable of South Yorkshire* [2004] UKHL 39

The UK case under the HRA

The House of Lords held that retaining samples and profiles on the database did not breach Article 8.

2. *Marper* v *UK* (2009) 48 EHRR 50

The Strasbourg case

cross reference

The issues in the cases are discussed in Chapter 20, section 20.6.2.

Marper then applied to the ECtHR, which disagreed with the UKHL and held that the database did violate Marper's Article 8 rights.

3. *R (G)* v *Metropolitan Police Commissioner* [2011] UKSC 21

G brought a case in the UK courts after, and based on, the principles as laid down by the ECtHR in *Marper* v *UK*.

(a) Section 2 HRA means that UK courts must take into account the principles in *Marper* v *UK* and (given the way UK courts have interpreted this provision) should follow these principles unless there are exceptional reasons not to (see section 4.3).

(b) There were no exceptional reasons, so the principles in the UK case had to be replaced by those in the Strasbourg case. Therefore section 64 PACE and the Guidelines had to be interpreted with reference to those Strasbourg principles.

(c) The Supreme Court had two options:

   (i) To accept that it was not 'possible' to read section 64 PACE so that it only authorised actions (such as producing Guidelines) which were compatible with Article 8 (as interpreted in *Marper* v *UK*). Taking this option would mean that a declaration of incompatibility, under section 4 HRA, could be issued. Any further action designed to ensure compatibility with Article 8 would then be for the executive and Parliament.

   (ii) To use section 3 HRA and 'read down' section 64 PACE so that, as a matter of law, it could only authorise actions compatible with Article 8. In that case the Guidelines would be unlawful because they would have been made without statutory authority.

(d) The majority of the Supreme Court chose option (ii). In enacting the legislation, Parliament did not intend to authorise the police to make disproportionate interferences with private life that violated Article 8. Furthermore, there was no reason why Parliament should not delegate to the police the power to regulate the retention of DNA profiles, so a declaration of incompatibility was not constitutionally necessary: section 3 was not being taken beyond its interpretative purposes and being used to legislate. The minority, on the other hand, read section 64 PACE as requiring the retention of data in breach of Article 8, and so a declaration of incompatibility was the proper step for the court to take.

discussion topic

The balance between courts and Parliament in the Human Rights Act

The HRA creates a particular constitutional balance between Parliament (dominated by the government) and the courts. Has the right balance in terms of both effectiveness and legitimacy been achieved? Does the Act create foundations for proper mutual respect between Parliament and the courts? To consider this issue, it is necessary both to consider matters in this chapter but also the broader theoretical issues about 'bills of rights' raised in Chapter 1.

Issue 1: There is no full 'legislative review'. Incompatible legislation remains valid. If Parliament wishes to violate human rights it may do so, so long as it expresses that intention clearly.

Arguments such as the following can be considered:

• The absence of full legislative review is acceptable. It does not mean that Parliament can or will act oppressively (political culture, the House of Lords as 'watchdog of the constitution', the need for regular elections, will normally see to that). It recognises that human rights (or at least some of the rights) are not absolute but are subject to reasonable restrictions which reflect complex judgments about the public interest (see *R* v *A*, the rape shield case, discussed at section 4.4.7, as an example). Such judgments are best made by Parliament or by ministers accountable to Parliament.

- The absence of full legislative review is unacceptable. The essence of human rights, the point of their being valued, is that they represent a form of higher law which is binding on legislatures such as Parliament, as much as on governments. Reliance on political culture, the House of Lords and elections is insufficient. This will not give proper protection to unpopular minorities. Human rights protection requires institutions which are independent of government and the popular will: we call these courts.

Issue 2: The Act gives the courts too much influence on what are essentially political questions. These include identifying what may or may not be 'necessary in a democratic society' (a phrase found in the Convention when identifying the grounds on which rights such as the right to freedom of expression can be restricted by law). Section 3 HRA leaves the courts reluctant to issue declarations of incompatibility and thus return an issue to Parliament. On the contrary, they feel licensed to depart from the clear and unambiguous words of statutes in order to re-draft them to make them compatible with Convention rights. Arguments such as the following can be considered:

- The role of the courts in the Act is unacceptable. Difficult moral or political issues should be decided by the elected Parliament and the accountable government not by the unelected and unaccountable courts. Furthermore, interpreting section 3 as they have, the courts have increased legal uncertainty—we are now bound not by what an Act of Parliament says but by what the courts think the 'underlying thrust' of the policy of the Act is.

- The role of the courts is acceptable. Human rights express limits on the exercise of state power. To apply these limits, impartial bodies, independent of government, are necessary—we call these courts and tribunals. Otherwise, government becomes judge in its own cause. In any case, the courts are strongly aware of the need to respect the will of Parliament where appropriate and have developed the notion of 'deference' by which they give way to political judgment on issues like national security.

Issue 3: Some commentators believe the courts should be more willing to use declarations of incompatibility. They argue that declarations both allow the democratic will of Parliament to prevail but also allow the courts to register human rights concerns and return the matter to Parliament for reconsideration. There is thus a type of dialogue or debate between the courts and Parliament and the executive through which fruitful answers to the usually complex and controversial matters to which human rights law relates, may emerge.

- See, for example: Nicol, D. 'Law and Politics after the Human Rights Act' [2006] *Public Law* 722–751; cf Hickman, T. 'The Courts and Politics after the Human Rights Act' [2008] *Public Law* 84–100.

4.5 The duty on public authorities: sections 6, 7 and 8

4.5.1 Introduction

Sections 6, 7 and 8 concern the second of the two principal ways in which the HRA gives further effect to the Convention rights in UK law. These sections impose a duty on public authorities:

- section 6 makes it unlawful for a 'public authority' (as that term is understood in the Act) to act incompatibly with the Convention rights in Schedule 1 HRA, unless it is required to do so by a valid Act of Parliament;

- section 7 creates rights to bring proceedings against public authorities if they act unlawfully under section 6; and

- section 8 identifies the remedies that courts can order.

KEY POINT The HRA is but one of a number of statutes imposing particular duties on 'public authorities'. For example, the Freedom of Information Act 2000 requires public authorities to disclose non-personal information, and the Race Relations (Amendment) Act 2001 amends the Race Relations Act 1976 to require public authorities to take active measures to promote good race relations.

4.5.2 The identification of a public authority: UK responsibility at Strasbourg

With two important exceptions (Parliament and the courts) the Act does not define a public authority. Whether Convention rights apply to particular bodies and institutions is left to the courts. Other Acts, such as the Freedom of Information Act 2000, take a different approach and list by name or type all the public authorities that are covered (with a provision for the list to be amended).

The general idea of the HRA is that if a person could take a case to the ECtHR in Strasbourg they should, under the Act, be able to take the same case to UK courts. 'Public authorities', therefore, are those bodies for which the United Kingdom, as a state, would be responsible under the Convention.

> The purpose is that those bodies for whose acts the state is answerable before the European Court of Human Rights shall in future be subject to a domestic law obligation not to act incompatibly with convention rights.
>
> *(Aston Cantlow v Wallbank* [2003] UKHL 37, para 6)

cross reference

State responsibility under the Convention is discussed in Chapter 2, section 2.4.2.

Although the basic approach is to leave the identification of public authorities to the courts, the Act does specify the status of two institutions.

4.5.3 Parliament

Parliament, including both the House of Lords and House of Commons, is not a public authority, nor is any one exercising functions in connection with 'proceedings in Parliament' (other activities connected with Parliament over which Parliament has sole control) (section 6(3)(b) HRA). Excluding Parliament from the reach of section 6 is a necessary consequence of Parliamentary supremacy and of section 3 HRA, which clearly recognises that Parliament can make valid and effective law even though it is incompatible with Convention rights.

4.5.4 The courts

Courts and tribunals are specifically identified, in section 6(3)(a) HRA, as public authorities bound by the HRA. Included in this is the Supreme Court of the United Kingdom (and previously the House of Lords in its judicial capacity). The consequences of this are discussed in sections 4.6 and 4.7.

4.5.5 Defining and identifying 'public authorities'

Section 6(1) HRA says:

> It is unlawful for a public authority to act in a way which is incompatible with a Convention right.

The section does not define a public authority. This is left to the courts as they interpret those words. Though reference may be made to the type of body which is amenable to ordinary judicial review and to bodies which are 'emanations of the state' for the purposes of European Union law, the test for 'public authority' under the HRA is independent of both of these.

The leading case for identifying public authorities is *Aston Cantlow Parochial Church Council v Wallbank*.

case close-up

Aston Cantlow Parochial Church Council v *Wallbank* [2003] UKHL 37

Mr and Mrs Wallbank purchased a property that was subject to a traditional duty which required them to pay for the upkeep and repair of the chancel of the local parish church (the area of a church used by the clergy). This duty to repair was enforced by the local Parochial Church Council (PCC) exercising statutory powers. Mr and Mrs Wallbank argued that the enforcement of this duty was arbitrary and involved a violation of their right to the peaceful enjoyment of possessions under Article 1 of the First Protocol (a scheduled Convention right). The PCC would only be bound by the provisions of Article 1 if it was a public authority under section 6.

The House of Lords held that the PCC was not a public authority. They also held that even if Article 1 had been engaged, the enforcement of the duty to repair would not have been a violation.

The Law Lords said the central characteristic pointing towards a body being a public authority is that it is broadly 'governmental' in character and function. A public authority is

> a body whose nature is governmental in a broad sense of that expression.

(Aston Cantlow, para 7)

cross reference
This is an example of the mirror principle; see section 4.3.2.

The reason for this definition is that the HRA aims to provide a remedy in a UK court if, and only if, such a remedy would also be available from the ECtHR in Strasbourg. Article 34 ECHR says that 'non-governmental' bodies can bring cases before the ECtHR and so, by inference, governmental bodies cannot bring cases, they do not have 'human rights'. Governmental bodies, therefore, are those bodies for which the state (the UK) has responsibility and which have the duty, in their spheres, of putting the UK's obligations to secure human rights for all into effect.

'Intuitive' public authorities

But what are governmental bodies? Some bodies are obviously part of 'government' and are public authorities without argument. In *Aston Cantlow* the House of Lords identified government departments, local authorities, the police and the armed forces as being 'intuitively' governmental. HM Revenue and Customs can easily be added to this list. It needs to be recalled that the civil service is no longer organised in single bureaucratic departments of state but is structured as a number of relatively free-standing agencies, such as the Prison Service or the Immigration Service. Since these are the organisational structures adopted by government departments, they clearly come within the definition of governmental. Scottish ministers, exercising devolved powers based on the Scotland Act 1998 are 'public authorities' (*Somerville* v *Scottish Ministers* [2007] UKHL 44).

General characteristics

Many other bodies will be governmental and, therefore, public authorities. There is no definitive list but the House of Lords (adopting proposals by Professor Dawn Oliver) suggested features such as the following:

- the possession of special powers (i.e. powers given by an Act of Parliament which enable the body concerned to regulate, take decisions and in other ways exercise authority over others),
- democratic accountability (e.g. to Parliament or other representative assembly or its committees or to a minister responsible to Parliament),
- public funding in whole or in part,
- a statutory constitution (i.e. the body is established under statute for purposes given in the statute and for no other),
- an obligation to act only in the public interest (i.e. there are no additional or complementary private interests).

Two other factors were listed in a Scottish case, *Grampian University Hospitals NHS Trust* v *Procurator Fiscal* [2004] HRLR 18, at paras 9 and 19, which may have general relevance:

- a body established by the executive with functions specified by the executive, a legal duty to comply with directions given by the executive, and which is funded by the executive and dissolvable by the executive (it is not clear whether the reference to 'the executive' is confined to the Scottish Executive);
- bodies which are 'wholly under the supervision of the state' and 'very far from being an entity distinct from or independent of the State'.

Quangos or NDGOs

These general principles mean that public authorities will probably include 'quangos' or 'non-departmental governing organisations' (NDGOs). These are bodies, normally established by Act of Parliament, which perform a wide range of functions and duties. These can include, for example, regulating or inspecting a particular area of governmental, social or economic activity. They all have different characteristics from each other. They are, to varying degrees, independent of central government but are also, to varying degrees, subject to direction or supervision by central government. They are, however, wholly 'public' in the sense of not having a significant charitable or commercial side to their activities. Examples include the Commission for Equality and Human Rights, the Office of Communications (Ofcom), the Financial Conduct Authority the various Directors General responsible for regulating the utility companies (Ofgas, Ofwat, etc.) and the Chief Inspector of Prisons. Such bodies (and there are many of them) are likely to fit at least some of the criteria for being a public authority. If they do, it needs to be remembered that, whilst they are themselves bound to act compatibly with Convention rights, they do not themselves have Convention rights which they might otherwise use to challenge a minister's direction.

Service providers

What of service providers, for example the maintained education sector (from play school to university) and the National Health Service? These are governmental in the sense that the state, through the government, accepts responsibility for, and funds, the bulk of educational and health provision in the United Kingdom (universities less so). They also have special powers: school education in the UK is compulsory, universities have special authority to issue degrees and the distribution of health care involves the exercise of power.

- In *Ali* v *Head Teacher and Governors of Lord Grey School* [2006] UKHL 14, a state-maintained school (acting through the governors and the head teacher) was 'undoubtedly' a public authority under section 6(1) (see para 79).

- In *R (Munjaz)* v *Mersey Care NHS Trust* [2005] UKHL 58, there was 'no doubt' that the NHS Trust in question was a public authority under section 6(1) (see para 7).

In neither case was the issue subject to much discussion. A focus on the provision of services could lead to the conclusion that schools and hospitals are not governmental and so only bound by human rights when exercising their special powers, rather than in all they do. This would make them 'functional' authorities, see section 4.5.6. This does not seem to be the case. In *Copland* v *UK* (2007) 45 EHRR 37, the UK accepted that it had state responsibility for the actions of a further education college in respect of one of its administrative employees.

Where a body is defined as a public authority by section 6(1) alone it can be referred to as a 'core' or 'standard' authority.

4.5.6 **Any person exercising public functions**

Public functions

Some of the difficulties about whether a body is a public authority are resolved by section 6(3)(b) and (5) HRA. Section 6(3)(b) says that 'public authority' includes

> any person certain of whose functions are functions of a public nature.

Thus anyone, an individual, a business, a charity or a public organisation such as a university or the BBC, can be bound by Convention rights in so far as they are exercising public functions. These non-governmental bodies performing public functions can be referred to as 'functional' authorities. They are subject to the HRA in respect of their public functions but not in respect of any other commercial or charitable activities they may perform (section 6(5)). At least in respect of these non-public functions they have rights under the HRA.

There is no definitive test for a public function in this context. In *Aston Cantlow* the House of Lords said that the matter was to be decided on the facts of each case (a Parochial Church Council was not a 'functional authority'—though Lord Nicholls dissented on the point). Guidance on the matter in *Aston Cantlow* has been built on by the House of Lords in *YL* v *Birmingham City Council* [2007] UKHL 27—in which a majority of their Lordships decided that a private care home, providing care to elderly people under contract with a local authority, was not performing functions of a public nature. In *YL* Lord Neuberger suggested the following (paras 156–169):

- Applying section 6(3)(b) should not result in persons and organisations having human rights responsibilities under the HRA even though the United Kingdom does not have responsibility for such persons or organisations at Strasbourg.

- A pointer to functions being 'public' is that they are 'governmental' in character.

- The simple fact that the state has accepted responsibility for a service (such as health, education or pensions) does not mean that particular providers are necessarily performing public functions.

- Public funding of a service as a whole points to the provision of that service being a public function; this should be distinguished from particular payments to particular individuals.

- Of 'particular importance' is that a function is likely to be public when it involves the exercise of coercive or other particular and intrusive powers, based usually but not necessarily on statute.

- A function is unlikely to be 'public' if it is exercised on the basis of a private, contractual relationship rather than one arising from statute.

Section 6(3)(b) recognises one of the important features of the way public functions are dealt with in the modern state of the twenty-first century. Examples are:

- Commercial companies running public services, such as prisons or transportation of prisoners. These involve the exercise of special powers at the behest of a core authority. In *Yarl's Wood Immigration Ltd* v *Bedfordshire Police* [2009] EWCA Civ 1110, it was held that Group 4, running an immigration detention centre on behalf of the Home Office, was a functional authority 'in many circumstances'.

- Commercial companies exercising regulatory and supervisory powers. For example, commercial operators of airports and docks have some responsibilities for safety; airlines have duties as regards immigration.

- Charities when they have a specific statutory role (as the NSPCC does under the Children Act 1989). In *RSPCA* v *Attorney General* [2001] 3 All ER 530, on the other hand, it was held that the famous animal charity did not perform public functions (para 37).

- The professional regulatory bodies, such as the Solicitors Regulation Authority. Professional disciplinary decisions may be taken, ultimately, by a tribunal, which is expressly a public authority (see *Virdi* v *Law Society* [2010] EWCA Civ 100). In *Tehrani* v *United Kingdom Central Council for Nursing, Midwifery and Health Visiting* [2001] IRLR 208 (a Scottish case), the Professional Conduct Committee of the nurses' professional body was, when exercising its disciplinary function, performing functions of a public nature.

- Independent schools can be subject to the HRA since the UK has state responsibility over, for example, their use of punishment (this issue is discussed in section 4.7).

Sporting regulators such as the Football Association are normally not considered to be exercising public functions (*Stretford* v *FA* [2006] EWHC 479). Likewise informal systems of cooperation, such as a pub watch scheme, in which pub landlords cooperated over the banning of undesirable customers, are unlikely to involve the exercise of a public function (*R (Boyle)* v *Haverhill Pub Watch* [2009] EWHC 2441).

Private acts

> 6(5) In relation to a particular act, a person is not a public authority by virtue only of subsection (3)
> (b) if the nature of the act is private.

Persons and organisations discussed in the previous sections, i.e. those which are not governmental but that perform public functions, are not bound by Convention rights in respect of their 'private' acts. Private acts are likely to include matters connected with contracts of employment, property matters and matters relating to internal management (see the *RSPCA* case, this section). In particular, such non-governmental public authorities are likely to have extensive private functions (e.g. their commercial or charitable activities) and actions connected with these are likely to be private acts and, therefore, not subject to the HRA.

The issue of the private acts of a body performing public functions can be complex. In *R (Weaver)* v *London and Quadrant Housing Trust* [2009] EWCA Civ 587, it was conceded that a charitable housing trust, in receipt of large project grants and central to the chosen means by which government policy on affordable housing was pursued, was exercising public functions and was a public authority by virtue of section 6(3)(b). The issue was then whether the individual action of evicting W, a tenant, was a 'private act'. Taking into account the circumstances, the Court of Appeal decided that the eviction was part of the exercise of the public function and not a private act.

The position of a functional authority is different in principle from a core, governmental, public authority. The latter are taken to be subject to human rights in all they do. Their employment and property relations are at least arguably subject to the HRA. In a series of cases the UKHL/UKSC has, following Strasbourg principles, held that public landlords (e.g. local authorities) do not have the freedom of private landlords when exercising statutory powers of eviction.

4.5.7 Contracting out and the 'welfare gap'

These days it is normal for standard public authorities, such as local councils, to contract out the provision of services. A local council, exercising statutory powers and duties, will decide whether, for example, an elderly person is entitled to care, but the care itself will be provided by a commercial or charitable organisation on the basis of a contract. The nature and quality of care can raise issues under, for example, Article 8 of the Convention (the right to respect for a person's home) and the question arises whether the private or charitable organisation providing the service is a functional authority and so subject to the HRA.

YL (at section 4.5.6) indicates that a body that simply delivers a service on a contract with a core public authority, such as a local council, does not have obligations under the Convention. In the court's view the simple provision of a service to individuals (as distinct from the decision that they are entitled to it) is not within the concept of public function in section 6(3)(b) (see section 4.5.6). The provider's rights and duties are private: they are founded on a contract with the core authority rather than a statutory scheme. Convention rights may apply, however, if the provider is closely tied, institutionally and organisationally with the core authority (see *Poplar Housing and Regeneration Community Association Ltd* v *Donoghue* [2001] EWCA Civ 595).

This position is controversial. It seemed to leave vulnerable people (such as the old and the homeless) unable to bring human rights claims even though they may have suffered degrading treatment (raising issues under Article 3) or interferences with their sense of selfhood and autonomy (raising issues under Article 8); in particular they lose the chance to claim that their right to a home (in Article 8) has been violated if the accommodation they have grown used to is suddenly closed. Critics argue that it is arbitrary to make the rights of vulnerable people in such situations depend on issues of political fashion—whether services are provided directly (as they often were into the 1980s) or by being contracted out (as they normally are today). So far as care homes are concerned (the issue in *YL* at section 4.5.6), the matter has now been resolved by Parliament. Under section 145 Health and Social Care Act 2008, the provision of accommodation coupled with nursing or personal care in a care home involves exercising a public function. But the problem of a 'gap' in human rights protection for the vulnerable remains in others areas, such as provision for the homeless.

The courts have, however, made it clear that the public authority that contracts with the mere service provider retains its statutory obligations under the HRA and this may involve responsibilities for the human rights of the vulnerable to be secured through direct regulation or by the terms of the contract with the provider.

The definition of a 'public function'

· ·

At the heart of the matter is a deep-seated disagreement over what is a public function, and this, in turn, raises questions about the role of the state.

• On one view, public functions are to do with the exercise of coercive authority based on special powers: a public function is to do with the exercise of power, restricting people's liberty in the public interest, regulating, etc. The provision of services does not involve these things. Responsibility, including funding, should lie with public authorities properly so-called and they should ensure that service providers meet high standards. A particular advantage of this view, under the Act, is that it permits organisations, such as universities and care homes, to enjoy Convention rights. If they were public authorities they might not have standing to bring cases.

• Alternatively it is argued that the failure of families and of civil society to deal with a range of social problems, such as poverty, adequate education, care of the mentally ill, etc. has meant that (since the mid-nineteenth century if not before) these have increasingly become state responsibilities. Where programmes originate in legislation and government action they should be recognised as public functions. It is arbitrary to withhold Convention rights from people merely because of the current administrative fashions.

Leading texts on this debate include: House of Lords, House of Commons Joint Committee on Human Rights Seventh Report of the Session 2003–2004, *The Meaning of a Public Authority under the Human Rights Act* and Oliver, D. 'Functions of a Public Nature under the Human Rights Act' [2004] *Public Law* (Summer), 329. The debate is reflected in their Lordships' disagreements in *YL* v *Birmingham City Council* [2007] UKHL 27.

4.5.8 **Public authorities defence, section 6(2)**

Public authorities do not act unlawfully if statute requires them to act in a way which is incompatible with Convention rights (i.e. the statute cannot be read and given effect in a compatible way, see the discussion of section 3 HRA, at section 4.4.2). Section 6(2) says:

Subsection (1) does not apply if—

(a) as the result of one or more provisions of primary legislation the authority could not have acted differently; or

(b) in the case of one or more provisions of, or made under, primary legislation which cannot be read or given effect in a way which is compatible with the Convention rights, the authority was acting so as to give effect to or enforce those provisions.

Section 6(2) has been discussed by the House of Lords.

R (Hooper) v *Secretary of State for Work and Pensions* [2005] UKHL 29

· ·

Various welfare payments and pensions were, according to the Social Security Contributions and Benefits Act 1992 (now repealed), only available to widows and not widowers. This was sex discrimination in respect to property rights and incompatible with the Convention (see Chapter 7, section 7.1). The legislation could not, under section 3, be read for compatibility. The claimants had asked the Secretary of State (a public authority) to make equivalent non-statutory payments to widowers but the Secretary refused to do so. The House of Lords held that the Secretary was protected by section 6(2) and had not acted unlawfully.

Though in *Hooper* the Law Lords disagreed between themselves about the precise application of section 6(2), broadly it can be said that

- if the legislation prevents a Convention-compatible action (here the making of non-statutory payments) then section 6(2)(a) protects the public authority that does not act;
- if the legislation does not expressly prevent Convention-compatible actions but, to make them, involves a public authority going against the clear purpose of the legislation, then section 6(2)(b) protects the public authority.

Thus section 6(2) protects a public authority not only when it is acting in accordance with the express requirements of the statute (performing a duty), but also when it is acting compatibly with the statute even though it could, legally, act differently. In other words, the public authority has chosen to exercise a discretion which can only be exercised in a non-compatible way. In *Doherty* v *Birmingham City Council* [2008] UKHL 57, the House of Lords upheld the right of a local authority to evict tenants in breach of Convention rights. The local authority had the statutory power (discretion) to evict in breach of Article 8 and was protected by section 6(2)(b) when it chose to do so.

4.5.9 Actions against public authorities

Sections 7, 8 and 9 of the HRA deal with enforcement: with the way Convention rights can be asserted against public authorities in UK courts and the remedies that can be obtained from the courts. This important matter is dealt with in Chapter 5.

4.6 The courts and the Human Rights Act: proportionality and deference

The job of the UK courts is to apply Convention rights in cases involving statutes or the actions of public authorities. In doing so they will often have to assess the 'proportionality' of a public authority's actions. This is because proportionality pervades the way Convention rights are applied (see Chapter 6, section 6.5). Proportionality can involve the courts in assessing the relative importance of an individual's Convention rights measured against the rights of others or the general public interest.

4.6.1 Proportionality and the HRA

Based on Convention law, proportionality is now accepted by UK courts when dealing with human rights issues either under section 7 HRA or 'ordinary' judicial review.

Proportionality and 'ordinary' judicial review

In *R* v *Secretary of State for the Home Department ex parte Daly* [2001] UKHL 26, the House of Lords compared so-called '*Wednesbury*' principles of administrative law (named from *APPH* v *Wednesbury Corporation* (1948) 1 KB 223) with the requirements of the Convention. The

Wednesbury principles, broadly speaking, confined the job of a reviewing court to that of deciding whether an official, politician or administrator had made a reasonable decision. This meant asking whether the official had taken relevant matters into account and not acted on irrelevant considerations. If so, the decision was lawful: it was within the range of decisions the official was entitled to take. The court had no business in making its own assessment of the matter. *Daly* develops English administrative law and makes it compatible with Convention rights by requiring the courts (dealing with human rights issues) to judge not the 'reasonableness' but the 'proportionality' of an official action. Often the old reasonableness test and the new proportionality test will produce the same outcome. Nevertheless a focus on proportionality should require

- heightened scrutiny: a more precise, complex and intensive analysis by the courts structured around the specific terms of the Convention Articles; and
- judicial decision-making: the judge may have to assess for him or herself the balance of interests involved and their relative weight; rather than merely asking whether the official has struck a balance within the reasonable range. It is the court's job to decide whether Convention rights have been upheld. As Baroness Hale said: 'In human rights adjudication, the court is concerned with whether the human rights of the claimant have in fact been infringed, not with whether the administrative decision-maker properly took them into account' (*Miss Behavin' Ltd* v *Belfast City Council* [2007] UKHL 19, para 31).

cross reference
Judicial review and human rights is discussed in Chapter 3, section 3.3.2.

Depending on the context this will involve judges in assessing the proportionality of the public authority's actions.

The test for proportionality

In *Daly* (following *De Freitas* v *Permanent Secretary of Ministry of Agriculture, Lands and Housing* [1999] 1 AC 69 (PC)) proportionality was said to require a court in England and Wales to ask whether

(i) the legislative objective is sufficiently important to justify limiting a fundamental right?

(ii) the measures designed to meet the objective are rationally connected to it?

(iii) the means used which impair the right or freedom are no more than is necessary to achieve the objective?

In *Huang* v *Secretary of State for the Home Department* [2007] UKHL 11, however, the House of Lords held this formulation to be incomplete (para 19). In addition a court must be satisfied, an overriding requirement, that officials or Parliament have achieved a 'fair balance' between the interests of society or the rights of others, which purport to justify an interference with rights, and the interests of the individual's concerned. In *Bank Mellat* v *HM Treasury* [2011] EWCA Civ 1, considering the tension between these positions, it was pointed out that the 'no more than necessary' ('least intrusive means') test is not an overriding factor. Rather, the possibility of officials using less intrusive means is a factor that must be given proper consideration by the court (para 30).

4.6.2 Deference or the 'discretionary area of judgment'

As part of this process, a reviewing court must decide how much weight to give to the views of the Parliament or the public authority whose decisions are in issue. The basic tension is that a court must avoid 'merits' review in the sense of substituting its view of the underlying policy for that of Parliament or the officials. At the same time, though, the courts must give effect to their overriding duty, which is to protect individuals' rights: 'the court's role under the 1998 Act [the Human Rights Act] is as the guardian of human rights. It cannot abdicate this responsibility', Simon Brown LJ (as he then was) in *International Transport Roth GmbH* v *Secretary of State for the Home Department* [2003] QB 728, para 27; a statement endorsed by the House of Lords in other cases.

At least some weight must be given to the intention of Parliament or the views of officials on the balancing of interests (without that the basic respect owed by one power to another would be lost). However, the intensity and nature of the human rights review by the court will depend upon context and a range of factors. Matters such as the following are relevant:

- The nature and scope of the Convention right in issue. In particular, where a Convention right, such as Article 8, requires a balance to be struck between competing rights and interests there is, perhaps, more reason for a court to give greater weight to the reasoning of Parliament or the authorities.

- Expertise and knowledge. A reason for giving weight to Parliament or the authorities would be that they have a greater and more convincing access to relevant knowledge and expertise than is available to the court (the decisions of regulators might be relevant here).

- The subject matter of the right. On issues such as personal liberty and fair trials, the courts may claim a special responsibility based on their constitutional role, thus may give much less weight to the executive's view. On other issues, such as national security, there may be a temptation to defer to the expertise of the executive and its constitutional responsibility; likewise when social policy is in issue.

- The 'legitimacy' of the decision-taker—whether elected or not, for instance, or the extent to which the decision in issue is based on carefully chosen policy.

Some judges seem to have approached these issues as if it was a question of *a priori* principle—as if the process of adjudication required them to, first, identify the kind of issue in the case and then give it an appropriate degree of 'deference'. The position of Laws LJ in *International Transport Roth GmbH* v *Secretary of State for the Home Department* [2003] QB 728 is, perhaps, an example of this approach (see paras 83–87); likewise Lord Hoffmann expressly related deference to the separation of powers in *R (Pro-Life Alliance)* v *BBC* [2003] UKHL 23, paras 75–76. This requires a principled recognition of, and respect for, the particular functions of the legislature, executive and judiciary to be reflected in the approach of a reviewing court to proportionality. Its virtue is that it provides a constitutional framework for judgments of proportionality and a more rule-based practice which, perhaps, protects legal certainty. Critics suggest that this approach weakens the ability of the independent judiciary to protect human rights as individuals' entitlements which should be protected even against a democratically elected legislature. If rights are violated, the fact that the violator is or is responsible to an elected chamber is irrelevant. Democratic legitimacy is of no particular weight in assessing human rights.

The alternative view, which seems to be endorsed in *Huang*, stresses context and circumstance. The court that is reviewing a decision against the standard of proportionality must weigh factors such as those listed, but not introduce *a priori* rules, such as the executive should always be deferred to in a national security context or that because a policy is chosen by an elected Parliament it must trump all but the strongest human rights claims. In *Huang*, the House of Lords sought to demystify the process—the weighing of factors in seeking a fair balance is part of the ordinary judicial task (*Huang*, para 16); there are no special, *a priori* principles which must be followed.

The operation of proportionality, the when, why and to what extent the courts defer to Parliament of the authorities, is demonstrated in the discussion of the Convention and HRA case law in the rest of this book.

4.7 The courts and the Human Rights Act: the Convention and private law

Courts and tribunals are public authorities.

> 6(3)(b) In this section 'public authority' includes—
>> (a) a court or tribunal.

This means that courts and tribunals must ensure that in all they do in hearing cases and granting remedies, etc. they act compatibly with the Convention rights.

4.7.1 The impact on private parties

The main point of the ECHR is to provide rights against the state acting through its agents such as the police and civil service (thus section 6 HRA is confined to 'public authorities'). Treating courts and tribunals as public authorities and requiring them to act compatibly with Convention rights, raises the question of the impact of Convention rights on private law (the legal relations between private parties—individuals, commercial companies, charities, etc.). The courts deal with private law (contract, tort, etc.) and the duty under section 6(3)(b) must apply to this as much as to public law.

further study

> For authoritative discussion see Sir William Wade, 'Horizons of Horizontality' (2000) 116 *LQR* (April) 217–224 and criticised by The Rt Hon. Sir Richard Buxton, 'The Human Rights Act and Private Law' (2000) 116 *LQR* (January), 48–65.

Horizontal effect

'Horizontal effect' means the effect on the relations between private parties as distinct from 'vertical effect', which refers to the relationship of individual and the state.

No direct horizontal effect

The Act does not provide for 'direct' horizontal effect. Sections 6 and 7 only permit cases to be brought against public authorities and not against private companies and other bodies. For example, newspapers, which in the United Kingdom are owned by commercial companies, are not public authorities under section 6 and so cannot be directly sued under section 7. Nevertheless there are a number of ways in which Convention rights will apply to private parties. This is sometimes known as 'indirect horizontal effect'.

Section 3 applies in both a public and a private context

The duty under section 3 of the HRA to interpret statutes so far as possible for compatibility applies to all statutes, including those which govern private relations. Nothing in the Act suggests that it is only statutes governing public authorities that need to be so interpreted.

case close-up

X v Y [2004] EWCA Civ 662

X went to the lavatory in a transport café where he had a sexual encounter with another man. Police were undertaking surveillance and X was arrested and then cautioned for an offence under section 13 of the Sexual Offences Act 1956 (gross indecency between men, now repealed). As a consequence of the caution, X's name was placed on the sex offenders' register and this became known to his employer. He was dismissed because he had failed to disclose the offence to his employer. He brought an action for unfair dismissal under the Employment Rights Act 1996. Under section 98 the employer must (broadly speaking) prove that the dismissal was fair. X argued that fairness in relation to section 98 should be interpreted so as to secure his right to privacy.

The Court of Appeal held that section 98 of the Employment Rights Act should be interpreted for compatibility with Convention rights. It held that the encounter did not take place in a private place, and so, on the facts, Article 8 was not engaged (Brooke LJ dissented on this point).

Positive obligations/duties

These points, of course, raise the question of how Convention rights can affect the actions and decisions of private parties. Courts' duties under sections 3 and 6(3)(b) HRA are to seek compatibility with Convention rights. They do not imply that the courts should impose new kinds of duties and obligations which are not found in Convention rights.

cross reference
Positive duties are discussed in Chapter 6, section 6.6.

- The Convention does not directly place duties on individuals, private companies, etc. Rather, duties are imposed on the state to secure the rights for all (Article 1) and provide effective remedies (Article 13).

- Nevertheless the ECtHR has said many times that securing Convention rights and freedoms for all may involve the state in taking positive steps. These can include changing the law or regulatory regime that applies to private parties. For example, the law governing the relations between newspapers and the public must be capable of guaranteeing that a proper balance between freedom of expression and private life is struck. Similarly, employment law should enable a tribunal to balance employees' rights to freedom of expression against employers' interests when private sector employees are dismissed for things they have said or written (see *Sanchez* v *Spain* App 28955/06, Grand Chamber judgment of 12 September 2011, paras 57 and 60). As state institutions, the courts can be expected to give effect to these positive obligations in the way they develop the law.

cross reference
Ghaidan v Godin-Mendoza [2004] UKHL 30, discussed at section 4.4.7, involved applying Article 8 to legislating regulating private landlords and tenants.

- These positive obligations, however, remain obligations on the state, so they do not impose obligations on private bodies directly.

- The extent to which the language of positive obligations really does authorise the imposition of Convention rights on private parties should not be overstated. Under the Convention, states have a wide margin of appreciation on the way positive obligations are achieved.

Developing the common law

Convention rights have clearly influenced the way in which some aspects of the common law governing private relations has developed. Nothing in the HRA authorises courts directly to impose Convention duties on private parties or to create new remedies and causes of action. Nevertheless, as was expected during the Act's passage through Parliament, the Convention has influenced the way in which private law has developed. The values inherent in the Convention have, in some areas, been absorbed as values of the common law.

This was a process that occurred before the HRA came into effect: see Chapter 3, section 3.3.3. A good example of this process of absorption is found in cases where the courts have developed the common law concept of breach of confidence in order to protect celebrities' reasonable expectations of privacy against the press. Convention rights are not directly in issue, since newspapers are not public authorities and no Act of Parliament is being relied upon. Nevertheless, in *Campbell* v *MGN* [2004] UKHL 22, the House of Lords held that Convention rights provided 'values' and gave 'important guidance' for the common law and dealt with the issue in terms of a balancing of Articles 8 and 10.

cross reference

The 'celebrity' cases are discussed in Chapter 22.

But the issue is within the discretion of the courts. In *Smith* v *Chief Constable of Sussex Police* [2008] UKHL 50, for instance, a majority of the House of Lords expressly refused to strengthen the common law liability of the police for damages in a way that would have endorsed Article 2 (see paras 136–139).

cross reference

For section 12 see Chapter 17, section 17.3; for section 13 see Chapter 16, section 16.1.3.

4.8 Free speech and freedom of religion

During the passage through Parliament of the HRA, concern was expressed that there could be detrimental effects on freedom of expression and religious freedom. It was feared, for example, that freedom of the press would be unduly restricted by the need to respect private life (under Article 8) or that religious schools would be unable to defend themselves by dismissing teachers whose behaviour was incompatible with the school's ethos. Though these concerns were probably exaggerated, sections 12 and 13 of the Act require courts to have 'particular regard' to freedom of expression and freedom of religion.

4.9 Ministers and Parliament

4.9.1 Ministers and human rights culture

The HRA embodies a particular constitutional balance between the courts, Parliament and ministers over the proper way to protect human rights in the United Kingdom. Obviously the primary duties lie with the courts, specifically regarding the interpretation of statutes and the legally enforceable duty on public authorities. However, a significant role for Parliament and ministers is allowed for under the Act.

• Ministers of the Crown (and equivalents from the devolved assemblies) are entitled to be joined as a party to the proceedings if a court is considering whether or not to make a declaration of incompatibility (section 5 HRA).

• If the courts do award a declaration of incompatibility it is then up to ministers (and Parliament) to decide what is the best course of action (see section 4.4.4).

The 'Ministerial Code', in which Prime Ministers express the general standards which ministers should meet when performing their duties and obligations, refers to the 'overarching duty on Ministers to comply with the law, including international law and treaty obligations' (2010 version, para 1.2). This duty involves respecting human rights, including the ECHR.

But the matter is wider than this. The Act is an important part of an effort to develop a 'human rights culture' in government by which all actions and decisions are considered for compatibility with human rights.

further study

The 'Human Rights Inquiry' produced by the Equality and Human Rights Commission in 2012 contains a detailed exploration of the extent to which a human rights culture has been successfully embedded in public authorities.

4.9.2 **Section 19 HRA**

The Act requires ministers to consider compatibility with human rights when promoting legislation before Parliament.

Statement of compatibility

19(1) A Minister of the Crown in charge of a Bill in either House of Parliament must, before Second Reading of the Bill—

    (a) make a statement to the effect that in his view the provisions of the Bill are compatible with the Convention rights ('a statement of compatibility'); or

    (b) make a statement to the effect that although he is unable to make a statement of compatibility the government nevertheless wishes the House to proceed with the Bill.

  (2) The statement must be in writing and be published in such manner as the Minister making it considers appropriate.

These statements have no legal effect and are not binding on the courts. Section 19 does not require ministers to give reasons for their view. A typical statement is one or two lines long simply stating that, in the minister's view, the bill is compatible. Where a minister thinks the bill is not compatible he or she is legally required merely to say whether or not the bill should be proceeded with. The way section 19 is put into effect is left to the discretion of ministers.

It is, however, common, these days, for major bills to be accompanied by 'explanatory notes' produced by the department, which may contain explanations in some detail.

Section 19 only applies to the time prior to the second reading of a bill. Amendments made after that, such as in committee, do not, by law, have to have a statement of compatibility. It is perfectly possible for bills to be significantly amended after the second reading with provisions that raise human rights issues.

Most bills are stated to be compatible. An exception was the Communications Bill 2003. This was a vast bill which reorganised the regulations of broadcasting and telecommunications. The Secretary of State (the minister) made the following statement under section 19:

> I am unable (but only because of clause 309) to make a statement that, in my view, the provisions of the Communications Bill are compatible with the Convention rights. However, the government nevertheless wishes the House to proceed with the bill.

Clause 309 was a total ban on political advertising and may have been incompatible with Article 10 (but see *R (Animal Defenders International)* v *Secretary of State for Culture Media and Sport* [2008] UKHL 15, discussed in Chapter 17, section 17.8.3). No reason is given in the section 19 statement but the 'explanatory notes' accompanying the bill gave an explanation (see explanatory notes on the Communications Bill, paras 631–634, on clause 309).

4.9.3 *Pepper v Hart*

Ministerial statements made during the parliamentary process can be used to assist statutory interpretation under the rule in *Pepper* v *Hart*. On limited occasions, such statements can be used to determine the Convention compatibility of legislation under section 3 HRA. Such statements can only be used to provide background information (such as on the mischief the legislation aims to remedy) to assist the courts. However, it remains the job of the courts to make their own judgment on whether or not the legislation is compatible with Convention rights, see *Wilson* v *First County Trust (No 2)* [2003] UKHL 40, para 67.

4.9.4 Parliament and the Joint Select Committee on Human Rights

A human rights culture and proper adherence to human rights values should involve legislators. The HRA does not expressly require anything of legislators (indeed, as we have seen, it permits Parliament to legislate incompatibly with Convention rights). Nevertheless, Parliament responded to the Act by establishing a Joint Committee on Human Rights. This is a select committee of MPs and peers established under the rules and standing orders of both Houses. It has cross-party membership of six backbench MPs and six peers. The Committee has a staff and a legal advisor. The committee has a broad remit to 'consider matters relating to human rights in the United Kingdom'. It does not deal with individual cases. The Committee has the following duties:

- The Committee reports to Parliament on the compatibility of bills with Convention rights. The Committee examines all bills before Parliament and brings the attention of Parliament to any problems of compatibility there may be. The Committee's reports contain detailed examination of issues and are an impressive and authoritative source of information and ideas.

- The Committee examines any remedial orders made under section 10 of the Act.

- The Committee produces ad hoc reports on themes and issues relevant to human rights generally and the HRA in particular. It has, for example, conducted its own report into deaths in custody in the United Kingdom as well as producing an influential report on the definition of a public authority under the Act and whether this should include private and charitable bodies providing welfare services at the behest of local councils. As currently operating, the Committee provides a strong parliamentary voice contributing to the development and protection of human rights in the UK, often in opposition to the government.

further study

The reports of the Joint Committee are available on the internet via the Parliament website http://www.publications.parliament.uk/pa/jt/jtrights.htm (UK Parliament/Publications and Records/Committee Reports/Select Committee Publications/Joint Committee/Human Rights).

(4.10) Equality and Human Rights Commission

The HRA did not set up a public authority with a brief to promote human rights and, perhaps, to aid individuals in bringing human rights cases. Northern Ireland does have a Human Rights

Commission. In the rest of the United Kingdom such bodies had been set up only in the context of sex, race and disability discrimination. One of the reasons for not establishing a specific human rights commission at the time of the Act was opposition from these established bodies, coupled with the fear that there would be difficult 'turf wars' between them and the human rights body, and that difficult questions of priority between, say, racial discrimination and other human rights might occur.

Under the Equality Act 2006, the Equal Opportunities Commission, the Commission for Racial Equality and the Disability Rights Commission were abolished and replaced by a single agency, the Equality and Human Rights Commission. (Scotland and Wales have their own Commissions.) On the basis of its powers, the Commission works to eliminate discrimination in disability, age, gender, religion or belief, sexual orientation and race. The Commission has important powers to promote human rights (including rights not in the Convention) generally and, with public authorities, to monitor the effectiveness of the law and advise on change. It can, exceptionally and subject to the Lord Chancellor's order, assist some individual human rights claimants (section 28(7)(c)).

further study

For further detail on the Commission see http://www.equalityhumanrights.com.

4.11 Bringing the Act into effect

The HRA was brought into effect on 2 October 2000 (the need for judicial training was one of the reasons explaining why the Act was not brought into effect immediately after enactment). There have been a number of important issues concerning whether the Act applies to actions and events which took place before that date.

4.11.1 Retroactive application

Section 3 HRA applies the interpretive duty to legislation 'whenever enacted'. Legislation enacted *before* October 2000 but applied to actions and events which occurred *after* October 2000 must be interpreted for compatibility with Convention rights. However, the courts will not normally give the section 'retroactive' effect. This means section 3 does not require courts to interpret Acts of Parliament, enacted *before* 2000, in a way which alters the legality of actions undertaken or agreements entered into *before* the HRA was implemented. This was established in *Wilson* v *Secretary of State for Trade and Industry* [2003] UKHL 40, though the House of Lords accepted that there may be exceptions (such as the need to protect children by retroactive application of section 3).

• In *Commissioner of Police for the Metropolis* v *Hurst* [2007] UKHL 13, the House of Lords (overturning the Court of Appeal) held that a HRA challenge to a coroner based on Article 2 (the right to life) could not be in respect of a death that occurred before October 2000.

4.11.2 Public authorities

The situation may be different if it is the actions of a public authority under section 6 HRA which are in issue. Section 22(4) HRA makes it clear that the right, under section 7(1)(b) HRA, to rely on Convention rights in proceedings involving the acts and decisions of public authorities made after October 2000, does not apply in respect of any 'act' (i.e. any action or event) taking place before October 2000.

The Act says nothing about the right to initiate actions against public authorities for breach of Convention duties (section 7(1)(a) HRA 1998). Nevertheless, the House of Lords maintained the presumption against retroactive effect and has been reluctant to allow such action in so far as it relates to actions and decisions taken before October 2000.

In *Re McKerr* [2004] UKHL 12, for example, the House of Lords held that the duty on the state, under Article 2, to hold an investigation into a violent death, did not apply to deaths occurring long before October 2000 (but see now *Re McCaughey* [2011] UKSC 20).

There is one exception to section 22(4). It does not apply to 'proceedings brought by or at the instigation of a public authority'. The main impact of this is that a person subject to court action brought by a public authority *after* October 2000 in respect of actions or events occurring *before* October 2000 will be able to rely on his or her Convention rights in the trial. This applies, for example, to criminal prosecutions and other forms of action, such as enforcement notices of various kinds, brought by local councils or regulatory bodies. The House of Lords has held (reluctantly) that the exception in section 22(4) does not apply to an appeal held *after* 2000 against a conviction in a trial held *before* 2000 (*R v Kansal (No 2)* [2001] UKHL 62).

4.12 Where does the Human Rights Act apply?

The HRA is an Act of the United Kingdom, which applies, therefore, to the law in England, Wales, Scotland and Northern Ireland. The laws in these four countries can be very different. Scotland and Northern Ireland have their own legal systems.

4.12.1 Devolution

Devolution is the process through which political and legal powers have been transferred to Scotland, Northern Ireland and Wales.

cross reference

For an example see Napier v Scottish Ministers 2005 1 SC 229, discussed in Chapter 21, section 21.4.

The Scotland Act 1998 created a Scottish Parliament and Scottish Executive, which have primary law-making and governing authority over all matters relating to Scotland which have not been expressly held back for the UK Parliament and government. The Scottish Parliament and Executive are established by, and derive their power from, the Scotland Act 1998 and nowhere else. The Scotland Act 1998 makes it clear that it is unlawful for the Parliament or the executive to legislate or act incompatibly with Convention rights. If they do so, they can be challenged before the Scottish courts. Appeal is to the the United Kingdom's Supreme Court. Thus Acts of the Scottish Parliament can be held to be void if they are incompatible with Convention rights (unlike the Acts of the UK Parliament, which remain valid); and a minister of the Scottish Executive who violates Convention rights has acted *ultra vires*, outside his powers. Ministers of the Scottish Executive, as public authorities are also subject to actions under sections 6 and 7 of the HRA. This was confirmed in *Somerville* v *Scottish Ministers* [2007] UKHL 44. Human rights actions can be brought under either the Scotland Act 1998 or section 7 HRA—different remedies are available and this will determine an applicant's choice.

further study

For discussion of human rights law in the context of devolution, see Lord Hope, 'Devolution and Human Rights' [1998] 4 *EHRLR* 367–379.

In the past there was the possibility of inconsistency between the way human rights apply in Scotland and England because, in respect of Scotland, devolution matters (which include human rights) were decided by the Judicial Committee of the Privy Council, rather than the House of Lords. Inconsistency is now less likely since the Supreme Court has taken over jurisdiction on devolution matters. This has not lessened controversy, however, as it can lead to Scottish concern that matters of Scottish law are being decided south of the border. These arose, for example, in *Fraser* v *HM Advocate (Scotland)* [2011] UKSC, when the Supreme Court reversed the Scottish courts on a point of human rights relating to Scottish criminal law and procedure.

KEY POINT Devolution to Northern Ireland and Wales is different in detail and context from Scotland. Nevertheless, the basic principle that the devolved assemblies and executives cannot lawfully act incompatibly with Convention rights remains.

4.12.2 **Territories for which the United Kingdom is responsible**

The HRA applies to the United Kingdom. Here we have to distinguish between the UK's obligations under the ECHR (a matter of international law) and the obligations of the British government and public authorities under the HRA (a matter of national law). The United Kingdom has extended, under Article 56 ECHR, the protection of the Convention to many of its overseas territories (areas still under the ultimate control of the United Kingdom) and other places, like the Channel Islands for which the United Kingdom had accepted foreign policy responsibilities. Such places are not part of the United Kingdom and so their populations do not have rights under the HRA and cannot assert Convention rights in UK courts. Their populations can, however, take cases against the United Kingdom to the ECtHR in Strasbourg—so long as the Convention right or freedom they allege has been violated, has been extended to them. (For example, Protocol 1 has not been extended to all places outside the United Kingdom.)

further study

This position has been clarified by the House of Lords in *R (Quark Fishing Ltd)* v *Secretary of State for Foreign and Commonwealth Affairs* [2005] UKHL 57.

4.12.3 **UK actions overseas**

The question can arise whether the HRA applies in respect of the action of UK officials abroad. For example, are soldiers in Iraq or Afghanistan bound to act compatibly with Convention rights and do those foreigners affected by what the soldiers do have a right of action under the Act?

case close-up

R (Al Skeini) v Secretary of State for Defence [2007] UKHL 26

....

A number of Iraqis alleged a failure by the United Kingdom properly to investigate whether the deaths of six civilians killed by British forces occupying Basrah in southern Iraq was a breach of Article 2. The House of Lords held that the HRA applied but only in respect of Baha Mousa, who had died whilst in a British military prison in Basra.

The House of Lords held, first, that British public authorities (including the military) could have obligations under the HRA, even when they were operating outside the United Kingdom. The normal principle is that UK statutes do not, in the absence of express words, apply to actions done outside the jurisdiction of the United Kingdom. However, in order to ensure remedies that would be available in Strasbourg are also available under the HRA, the jurisdiction of the UK had to be interpreted in the same way as by the ECtHR. In *Bankovic v Belgium* (2007) 44 EHRR SE5, the ECtHR held that 'jurisdiction', a term found in Article 1 defining the scope of a state's responsibilities, was based on a state's territory but that there were exceptions (see Chapter 2, section 2.4.5). One of the exceptions was where the European state exercised effective control over the administration of a non-European state. The House of Lords applied its understanding of 'effective control'. One of the claimants, Baha Mousa, had been killed whist detained in a British-run prison. This involved effective control and Article 2 rights applied. The other claimants, however, had been killed in the towns and countryside, and Article 2 did not apply in their case: there was not effective control.

This decision may no longer be compatible with the ECHR. In *Al-Skeini v UK* (2011) 53 EHRR 18, a Grand Chamber found there was effective control in all cases (see Chapter 2, section 2.4.5). Effective control involves a factual judgment but it can be found where European forces are responsible for general, if not detailed, administration of a country.

In *R (Smith) v Oxfordshire Coroner* [2010] UKSC 29, the Supreme Court, following the House of Lords in *Al-Skeini*, applied the effective control principle to British troops and held that they did not have Article 2 rights in Iraq when outside their bases. This has been followed by the Court of Appeal in *Smith v MoD* [2012] EWCA Civ 1365, which is a case decided after, and in the light of, the Grand Chamber decision in *Al-Skeini v UK*. The Court of Appeal followed the *Oxfordshire Coroner* case not only because it accepted it as a binding precedent (see *Kay v Lambeth LBC* [2006] UKHL 10), but also because of doubts whether the effective control definition of jurisdiction, which was designed to protect the interests of civilians in the invaded and occupied country, would also apply to the control a state exercises over its own troops. The matter is pending before the ECtHR (*Pritchard v UK* App 157311).

R (Al-Saadoon) v Secretary of State for Defence [2009] EWCA Civ 7 was a judicial review, based on the HRA, of the Secretary of State's decision to transfer the applicant, who had been detained in Iraq by UK troops, to the Iraqi authorities. The Court of Appeal held that UK was not acting within its jurisdiction since the UK did not have civil legal authority. The ECtHR, in *Al-Saadoon v UK* (2009) 49 EHRR SE11, focused on the fact of control (rather than its legal basis) and held that Convention rights did apply.

In *R(B) v FCO* [2004] EWCA Civ 1344, the Court of Appeal held that the Act applied to consular officials in the British Embassy in Melbourne Australia (though there was no breach of Article 3 when consular officials returned asylum seekers, who had sought refuge in the embassy, to Australian officials).

UK troops themselves will still enjoy Convention rights relating to actions affecting them which originate in the United Kingdom. In *R (Gentle) v Prime Minister* [2008] UKHL 20, it was held that there was no duty owed by the UK government under the HRA and Article 2 not to send UK troops to war without reliable legal advice on the legality of the war. No such duty could be read into Article 2.

The HRA can be used to prevent a person being deported from the United Kingdom to a country in which their Convention rights might be violated. This matter is considered in Chapter 9, section 9.8; Chapter 15, section 15.10.7 and Chapter 12, section 12.17.

 Summary

- The HRA creates the legal framework in terms of which the content of the rights and freedoms in the ECHR are given further effect in UK law.

- There are two principal ways in which the Act does this: by imposing a duty on the courts to interpret legislation 'so far as it is possible to do so' for compatibility with Convention rights, and by putting a legally enforceable duty on 'public authorities' to act compatibly with the Convention rights.

- Anyone can be a public authority to the extent that they are performing public functions. Otherwise the Act does not impose duties on private individuals or companies directly.

- The courts are public authorities. They may be influenced by the Convention when developing the common law, including in areas that relate to the rights and obligations of private parties.

- The Act creates a particular constitutional balance between the courts, Parliament and the government. If its intention is quite clear, Parliament may enact legislation that violates human rights. In such circumstances the courts can make a 'declaration of incompatibility'. If so, ministers must decide whether to seek a change in the law from Parliament. Where there are 'compelling reasons', ministers may change the law themselves; although they need the consent of Parliament, there is no need for a full Act of Parliament. When introducing a bill to Parliament, ministers are required to certify that they have considered the impact of the bill on human rights.

 Questions

For suggested approaches, please visit the Online Resource Centre.

1   Parliament enacts new legislation which places the burden of proof on to those accused of terrorist offences to prove their innocence in certain circumstances. There are likely violations of Article 6 (the right to a fair trial) if the new Act is put fully into effect.

Choose one of the following: the courts will—

(a) not apply the Act or those parts of it which are incompatible with Convention rights;

(b) apply those parts of the Act which are unambiguous but interpret the ambiguous parts for compatibility;

(c) interpret and apply all the parts of the Act, whether ambiguous or not, for compatibility unless, in doing so, they offend against their understanding of the underlying policy of the Act.

2 The Ministry of Justice decides to introduce a new, severe regime into some of the nation's prisons. There are good grounds for thinking that aspects of this new regime are so tough that they may violate Article 8 (private life), perhaps even Article 3 (inhuman and degrading treatment).

Consider whether the courts would be able to hear the following cases:

(a) Prisoners in prisons directly operated by the Prison Service (an executive agency of the Ministry of Justice; in effect a part of the civil service) bring a case against the Prison Service and the Minister of Justice alleging a violation of Articles 3 and 8.

(b) Prisoners in prisons operated by Bars R Us, a (fictitious) security company which runs a number of prisons under contract from the Prison Service, bring a similar case.

(c) An employee of Bars R Us speaks to the press about the issues and is sacked for being in breach of a 'gagging' clause in his contract of employment. He claims that, because of Article 10 (the right to freedom of expression), his dismissal is unfair.

Further reading

Amos, M. (see Preface) Parts 1–5

Bamforth, N. 'The Application of the Human Rights Act 1998 to Public Authorities and Private Bodies' (1999) 58(1) *CLJ* (March) 159–170

Edwards, R. 'Judicial Deference under the Human Rights Act' (2002) 65 *MLR* 859–882

Gearty, C. *Principles of Human Rights Adjudication* (2004) Oxford: OUP

Hickman, T. *Public Law after the Human Rights Act* (2010) Oxford: Hart Publishing

Kavanagh, A. *Constitutional Review under the UK Human Rights Act* (2009) Cambridge: CUP

Lester, A., Pannick, D. and Herberg, J. (see Preface) Chapters 2 and 3

Oliver, D. 'The Frontiers of the State: Public Authorities and Public Functions under the Human Rights Act' [2000] *Public Law* 476–493

The Human Rights Act 1998 (2): proceedings and remedies

Chapter overview

- Article 13, the right to a remedy, and the Human Rights Act 1998 (HRA).
- Procedures and remedies under section 3 HRA (interpretation of statutes).
- Procedures and remedies against public authorities (sections 7, 8 and 9 HRA).
- Rules of 'standing' (who is entitled to bring a Human Rights Act case): section 7 HRA and Article 34 of the Convention.
- Damages ('just satisfaction') and the HRA.

Introduction

The ways the rights of the European Convention on Human Rights (ECHR) are given further effect in the law of the United Kingdom, by the Human Rights Act 1998 (HRA) are discussed in Chapter 4. In this chapter examination of the issue is continued by exploring how cases can be brought under the HRA and what remedies are available from the courts if a violation of a Convention right is found. The main issues are

- the importance of remedies and Article 13 ECHR—the right to a remedy,
- procedural issues for seeking remedies under the HRA (including the issue of who is entitled to bring a case against a public authority), and
- remedies available under the HRA (these mirror the remedies available from the European Court of Human Rights (ECtHR)).

5.1 Article 13 and the need for a remedy

Article 13   Right to an effective remedy

Everyone whose rights and freedoms as set forth in this Convention are violated shall have an effective remedy before a national authority notwithstanding that the violation has been committed by persons acting in an official capacity.

Rights need remedies to be effective. A mere list of rights which are then ignored by governments is pointless. In Chapter 2, on the ECHR itself, we saw that the major strength of the Strasbourg system lies in the opportunity it gives to individuals to take their case to the ECtHR and, if successful, to obtain a remedy which the states of the Council of Europe generally accept. People can do this if they feel that the political and legal system in their own country has failed to secure their ECHR rights and freedoms.

cross reference

The right of individual application is discussed in Chapter 2, section 2.5.2.

The Court's purpose is to provide a remedy when national systems have failed. By accepting Article 13, a state agrees to ensure that effective remedies for breaches of the Convention are available through its own legal system and from its own national courts. People should only have to go to Strasbourg if, after a full and proper examination of all the human rights issues by their national courts, they feel they still have good grounds for claiming that their Convention rights and freedoms have not been secured. There needs to be a full willingness of national governments to accept the judgments of their own courts on these issues.

5.1.1 Article 13 and the HRA

The need for a remedy from the national courts is recognised by Article 13 of the Convention. Article 13 is not one of the Convention rights in Schedule 1 HRA. The government's principal explanation for not allowing UK courts to ensure that there are adequate remedies, as Article 13 requires, was that it was unnecessary. The HRA itself provided effective remedies. This means that even if it appears to a court that the remedies available are inadequate, courts are not able directly to create a new, more effective remedy. If the ineffective remedy is embodied in statute the courts must accept it. If Article 13 had been included, a court in the UK would have been able to create a new remedy or, at least, issue a declaration of incompatibility, in certain areas where existing remedies might not be satisfactory. Remedies for people who think they have been the victim of unlawful surveillance by the Intelligence Services (who must use the Investigatory Powers Tribunal) or who are to be deported from the country in the public interest (who must use the Special Immigration Appeal Tribunal) are possible examples.

cross reference
Declaration of incompatibility is defined in Chapter 4, section 4.4.3.

KEY POINT Note that the courts are 'public authorities' under section 6 HRA and are bound to act compatibly with Convention rights unless compelled otherwise by primary legislation. In this regard, though they cannot create new remedies, they are able to adjust and develop existing remedies in order to secure Convention rights. See Chapter 4, section 4.7.

It is helpful, therefore, to consider the requirements of Article 13 in order to assess whether the HRA really does meet its requirements.

5.1.2 Article 13 in summary

Article 13 obliges states to provide:

- Adequate procedures. The national law must allow for access to a court or other appropriate forum which is properly independent and able to deal, under its rules of procedure and evidence, with all the points raised by a human rights claim.
- Adequate remedies. The court or other forum must have sufficient authority to provide an adequate remedy. For example, if an award of damages is necessary to compensate for the breach of human rights, then the court must be able to make such an award; if someone is deprived of their liberty in breach of Article 5 of the Convention, the court or tribunal must have the power to order his or her release.

The right to a remedy may be integrated into some of the substantive rights, with Article 13 adding little to what is already required. Article 5(4) ECHR already gives a person deprived of his or her liberty a right to challenge before a judicial body the basis of their detention and, as a requirement of Article 2 (right to life), the ECtHR has made it clear that deaths in custody should be properly investigated (see Chapter 8, section 8.5).

5.1.3 Arguable claim

Article 13 requires states to provide a procedure by which 'arguable claims' that the Convention has been violated can be tested in a national forum (a court etc.). In a surveillance case, *Klass* v *Germany* (1979–80) 2 EHRR 214, the ECtHR said:

> Article 13 requires that where an individual considers himself to have been prejudiced by a measure allegedly in breach of the Convention, he should have a remedy before a national authority in order both to have his claim decided and, if appropriate, to obtain redress.   (para 64)

cross reference
Admissibility is discussed in Chapter 2, section 2.7.1.

The test for 'arguable claim' is not clear. It is likely to be linked to the question of whether a matter is admissible before the ECtHR. The lack of such a procedure in the national courts to deal with cases that would be admissible before the Strasbourg court can mean that Article 13 has been violated. It is not necessary to show that the case would have succeeded and that some other Convention right has also been violated (e.g. *Hatton* v *UK* (2003) 37 EHRR 28, para 137).

5.1.4 **An effective remedy**

The remedy that a person with an arguable claim of a Convention violation is entitled to, need not be from a fully judicial body such as a 'court'. It can be from tribunals (such as First Tier Tribunal (Mental Health) hearing claims by the mentally ill that they should not be detained in hospital) and, in principle, any other body capable of meeting the requirements of Article 13. In particular

cross reference

Fairness is defined by reference to the requirements of Article 6 (right to a fair trial) and Article 5(4): see Chapters 12 and 11, section 11.8, respectively.

- the body providing the remedy needs to be properly independent of the government or other agency, such as the police, whose actions are being questioned;

- the procedure must be fair, giving proper opportunities to the alleged victim to put his or her case;

- the body must be able to give an effective remedy (e.g. to order the release of a person detained in violation of Article 5);

- the body must be able to hear evidence on, and deal with, all the issues of fact and law which relate to the alleged Convention violation.

An example of the United Kingdom being in breach of Article 13 is *Peck* v *United Kingdom*.

case close-up

> ### *Peck* v *United Kingdom* (2003) 36 EHRR 41
>
> P attempted suicide in part of a town centre. The attempt was caught on CCTV. The images were distributed by the local authority (which controlled the CCTV) to the local media and stories, illustrated by the images, were run on TV and in the local press. The attempts to blank out P's identity were unsuccessful. P made various attempts to obtain redress but these were only partially successful. The ECtHR held that there had been a breach of Articles 8 and 13.

The ECtHR noted that Article 13 did not require a particular form of remedy, and there is a margin of appreciation afforded the states on this matter. Legal systems, including in the United Kingdom, tend to have a complex range of institutions dealing with the redress of grievances against public bodies. In *Peck* the principal remedies for the applicant were complaint to a media regulator, a private law action or judicial review of the actions of the local authority. In the circumstances all were inadequate.

(5.2) **Redress of grievances in the United Kingdom**

As was made clear in *Peck*, securing human rights through legally enforceable remedies need not be confined to the courts. In the United Kingdom, like all other modern countries, a wide and variable range of institutions may be able to provide different forms of redress of grievances. These institutions all have an important part to play in ensuring that individuals' human rights are properly protected. Examples from the United Kingdom include the following.

5.2.1 The courts of law

These include both the civil courts dealing with private law matters and public law disputes (in the Administrative Court) and the criminal courts, such as the Crown Court and Magistrates' Courts.

Judicial review by the High Court (Administrative Court)

Judicial review, involving public law actions brought against public authorities, is outlined in Chapter 3. In some contexts it has been doubted whether judicial review can provide adequate remedies for violations of the Convention. This is because, put simply, judicial review is focused on the manner in which a public decision is taken rather than with the outcome of the decision. Again, put simply, the High Court, traditionally, would not interfere with a properly taken decision even if the result might have been a violation of the Convention. The court, in judicial review, is mainly concerned with issues of law rather than fact and so again, it can be difficult for all the issues bearing on whether Convention rights and freedoms have been secured, to be fully aired. These were the main reasons why judicial review was held to be an inadequate remedy by the ECtHR in *Peck*.

cross reference
For other examples see Chapter 3, section 3.3.2.

In fact, following adverse decisions from Strasbourg, but mainly in order for the High Court to perform its duties as a 'public authority' under the HRA (and thus put Article 13 into effect), judicial review tends now to be flexible. Depending on the facts and on the matters raised by the Convention right in issue in a case, judicial review is normally capable of allowing a full examination of all the issues, of fact and law, to enable a judicial judgment to be made on whether or not there has been a breach of a Convention right. This was the view taken by the House of Lords in *R (Alconbury Developments Ltd)* v *Secretary of State for the Environment, Transport and the Regions* [2001] UKHL 23 in respect of challenges to the planning system based on the requirements of a fair hearing in Article 6. The moving together of the grounds of judicial review and Convention rights was noticed and discussed by the House of Lords in *Doherty* v *Birmingham City Council* [2008] UKHL 57, e.g. para 135.

Private law

cross reference
See Chapter 4, section 4.7.1 for the impact of the HRA on private law.

Private law actions (breach of contract or tort) can be brought against both private and public parties. These will not necessarily provide adequate remedies. In *Peck* an action for breach of confidentiality was thought, by the ECtHR, to be inadequate since it was not (reliably) available for a simple invasion of privacy. There have been significant legal developments in this area (see Chapters 15 and 22).

5.2.2 Tribunals

Tribunals are court-like bodies that have statutory powers to provide remedies in specific areas. Matters dealt with by tribunals can involve both basically private law (such as Employment Tribunals, which deal with disputes over employment rights) or public law (such as First Tier Tribunals (Mental Health), which have powers to release patients who are detained in mental hospitals).

5.2.3 Inspectorates, regulators and commissions of various kinds

These bodies can perform a range of functions such as investigating problems, regulating activities and adjudicating disputes. They may provide a suitable remedy themselves. The media regulator, Ofcom, has a range of remedies which might, in some circumstances, be adequate for a violation of the right to respect for private life under Article 8 (though in *Peck* the ECtHR held that the inability of the predecessors of Ofcom to award financial compensation meant that they did not satisfy Article 13). The Independent Police Complaints Commission (IPCC) investigates, for example, police killings, which are possible violations of Article 2. The investigation is a requirement of Article 2. The Commission can also instigate other remedies by, for example, sending reports to the prosecuting authorities and so be a part of what is necessary for Article 13. One of the reasons for creating the Commission was to satisfy Article 13 by creating a body that was (unlike its predecessor) properly independent of the police and the executive.

5.2.4 **Ombudsman systems**

There are a number of Ombudsmen dealing with, for example, central government, local government and prisons. They can investigate and suggest ways of remedying so-called 'maladministration'. The Ombudsman's inability to make a binding order (the Ombudsman makes findings and recommendations) can mean that it may not be an adequate remedy, see, for example, *E v United Kingdom* (2003) 36 EHRR 31, a case involving compensation for victims of violent crime.

5.2.5 **Access to the courts**

Inspectorates, regulators, commissions and Ombudsmen are just some of a complex range of different bodies operating in different areas of social, economic and political life in the United Kingdom. They can offer a wide range of remedies, specific to the area they deal with. Not all the remedies will, in all situations, be sufficient to satisfy Article 13 or other Convention requirements. Where this is so, access to the courts, often to the High Court for judicial review, becomes important. It may be only because the decisions of such bodies can be challenged in the courts that there is no violation of the Convention.

Interpreting legislation: remedies and section 3

5.3.1 **The duty under section 3**

cross reference
For discussion of section 3 see Chapter 4, section 4.4.

The duty under section 3 HRA to interpret legislation, so far as it is possible to do so, to make its meaning compatible with Convention rights applies not only to courts and tribunals but also to any other institutions or organisations whose powers and functions depend upon Acts of Parliament. These may be government, police, public bodies, commercial organisations, charities, private individuals, etc. The duty applies in both public law and private law.

There is no direct remedy provided by section 3 HRA. The point is that everyone who is affected by an Act of Parliament has a right that the Act be interpreted, if it is possible to do so, for compatibility with Convention rights. If the matter goes to a court or tribunal, whether it is private law (e.g. an action for breach of contract) or public law (e.g. a judicial review or a complaint to the IPCC) there is a duty on the court, tribunal, etc. hearing the case to interpret the legislation in a manner that it thinks is required by the Convention. Failure to do this is a basis on which an appeal could be made.

5.3.2 **Declaration of incompatibility**

cross reference

For declaration of incompatibility see Chapter 4, section 4.4.3.

As discussed in Chapter 4, section 4 HRA authorises senior courts to make a 'declaration of incompatibility' if it is not 'possible' to read and give effect to legislation in a way that is compatible with Convention rights.

The fact that a UK court cannot invalidate (make of no legal effect) an Act of Parliament that it is not possible to interpret for compatibility, is not, as such, a violation of Article 13. The ECtHR has held that Article 13 does not require US-style procedures through which national courts can set aside primary legislation on the grounds that it violates the Convention (*James* v *United Kingdom* (1986) 8 EHRR 123, para 85).

cross reference

The identification of a 'victim' for the purposes of the HRA and the Convention is discussed at section 5.4.5.

Normally only a person who alleges they are a victim of a human rights violation (directly and detrimentally affected by the legislation in question) can seek a declaration of incompatibility. In *Re S* [2002] UKHL 10, a case involving child care, the House of Lords said: 'Ordinarily the court will grant such relief [a declaration of incompatibility] only to a person who is a victim of an actual or proposed breach of a Convention right' (para 88); and this has been followed by the Court of Appeal in *Taylor* v *Lancashire* [2005] EWCA Civ 284. There may be exceptions. In *R (Rusbridger)* v *Attorney General* [2003] UKHL 38, the editor of *The Guardian* alleged that the Treason Felony Act 1848 might make it an offence to publish stories advocating a republic and that this would be incompatible with Article 10 ECHR, the right to freedom of expression. Both an 'ordinary' declaration was sought and a declaration under section 4 HRA. In either event a majority agreed with Lord Steyn that there was no need for the applicant to prove that he had been a 'victim' of the legislation in order to seek a declaration (see para 21).

The courts, it seems, are currently taking a flexible, context-dependent view on the issue. They decline to make a clear rule which might prevent important cases getting to court, but they are also reluctant to allow themselves to be used as part of an abstract political battle or to provide pointless remedies for individuals.

5.4

Actions against public authorities

cross reference

Section 6 HRA is discussed in Chapter 4, section 4.5.

Section 6 of the HRA requires public authorities to act compatibly with Convention rights unless required otherwise by primary legislation.

Sections 7 and 8 provide statutory procedures and remedies in order to enable a person to uphold his or her Convention rights against the actions of a public authority.

Under section 7(1):

a person who claims that a public authority has acted (or proposes to act) in a way which is made unlawful by section 6(1) may—

(a) bring proceedings against the authority under this Act in the appropriate court or tribunal, or

(b) rely on the Convention right or rights concerned in any legal proceedings

Thus remedies for breach of the Convention by a public authority can be sought in one of two ways:

- in an action originated by the person alleging the breach (section 7(1)(a)); or
- in any legal proceedings of any kind in which the victim is involved—whether as claimant or defendant (section 7(1)(b)). This could be, for example, alleging Convention violations by the police as part of a defence in criminal proceedings; using Convention rights as a defence to eviction proceedings brought, in the County Court, by a local authority; or using Convention rights as part of tribunal proceedings against a public authority.

5.4.1 *Ex turpi causa*

Some common law rules can mean that a trial or action does not proceed and a victim loses the right of access to a court to have a human rights case determined. An example is *ex turpi causa non oritur actio* (no claim arises from a dishonourable cause of action). This was held not to apply to HRA cases in *Al Hassan-Daniel* v *Revenue and Customs Commissioners* [2010] EWCA Civ 1443. AH-D was a drug smuggler who died from cocaine poisoning whilst in the custody of HM Customs. His relatives brought a case alleging a breach of Article 2. The Court of Appeal rejected, as a matter of policy, the application of *ex turpi causa* in human rights cases. Such rules would prevent proper examination of the case; and 'victims' could include close relatives who themselves had not done wrong. Criminality would be relevant in determining who really caused the alleged breach. The Court of Appeal strongly hinted that the case should not proceed.

5.4.2 **Appropriate court or tribunal**

In respect of section 7(1)(a), where the alleged victim brings the case him or herself, the Act stipulates that the case must be brought before the 'appropriate tribunal'. The appropriate tribunal is identified by 'rules' made by a Secretary of State or the Lord Chancellor (section 7(9)). For England and Wales judicial review (see section 5.2.1) is the normal procedure. The Civil Procedure Rules (CPR) (the rules governing all aspects of civil procedure) have been amended to facilitate actions brought under section 7 (see CPR Part 7).

KEY POINT Scotland has its own particular code of rules dealing with HRA cases.

In some situations there are special rules which identify a particular court or tribunal which, alone, can hear human rights claims. For example:

- Allegations that the Secretary of State has breached the Convention in banning a political party or organisation under powers in the Terrorism Act 2000 can only be heard by the Proscribed Organisations Appeals Commission (a body established by the Terrorism Act). This is required by rules made under section 7 (SI 2006/2290).
- Allegations that Convention rights have been breached in respect of surveillance by the security services are determined only by the Investigatory Powers Tribunal established by Part IV of the Regulation of Investigatory Powers Act 2000 (RIPA). This is required by section 65(2) RIPA.

5.4.3 Judicial actions and decisions

Often what is complained about as a violation of the Convention will be a judicial act (e.g. a magistrate committing a person to prison allegedly in breach of Article 5 (right to liberty and security)). Here the appropriate way of pursuing a human rights case is by exercising any existing right of appeal (section 9(1) HRA). For example, an appeal against a criminal conviction from Crown Court to the Court of Appeal (Criminal Division), an appeal from most statutory tribunals to the Upper Tribunal, by judicial review (this can be the way to challenge some decisions of magistrates and also other tribunals, particularly those such as the Parole Board for which there is no other form of appeal) or by any other form of appeal allowed by law. There are specific provisions which apply to whether damages can be awarded in respect of judicial decisions, which are discussed below.

5.4.4 Time limits

Section 7 requires a person to bring an action within one year unless rules require a shorter period or fairness requires a longer period (section 7(5)). Under the Civil Procedure Rules relating to judicial review, cases must be brought 'promptly' and, at most, not more than three months from the time of the decision or action complained about. If a person is seeking a remedy that is only available through judicial review (e.g. a 'prerogative order' quashing (i.e. cancelling) a public authority's decision) then the case must be brought according to the judicial review rules. Where, on the other hand, the human rights case is made directly under section 7, the one year with possible extension for fairness rule applies.

case close-up

Rabone v _Pennine Care NHS Foundation Trust_ [2012] UKSC 2

R brought proceedings based on section 7(1)(a) HRA alleging a breach of Article 2 (the right to life) by the defendant hospital in respect of the death of his daughter. The proceedings were issued nearly sixteen months after the daughter's death. The Supreme Court, exercising discretion under section 7(5), allowed the case to be brought. Issues to be weighed by a court included the degree of prejudice likely to the suffered by the public authority; the length and reasons for the delay. However, the 'most important' reason was the merit of the case—that there had been a violation.

The Supreme Court confirmed the view in _Dunn_ v _Parole Board_ [2008] EWCA Civ 374 that factors relating to extensions of time in ordinary civil proceedings (in section 33(3) Limitation Act 1980) can be taken into account but are not decisive as regards section 7(5) HRA.

The one-year rule under the HRA can be compared with the position at Strasbourg. Article 35 of the Convention requires an application to be made within six months of domestic remedies being exhausted.

5.4.5 Standing: the victim test

Under section 7 HRA only a person who would be able to bring a case before the ECtHR can bring a case in the UK courts alleging a breach by a public authority of its duty under section 6 HRA to act compatibly with Convention rights.

standing or locus standi

These are the rules developed by the law which define who is entitled to bring cases in various types of procedure. To bring an action for breach of contract, for instance, you normally have to be a party to the contract; to bring a judicial review against a public body the law requires you to have 'sufficient interest' in the case.

To bring a case before the ECtHR a person must be a 'victim' as defined in respect of Article 34 ECHR (section 7(7) HRA).

5.4.6 **Article 34**

Because Article 34 controls who can bring a case not only to Strasbourg but also before the UK courts under the HRA, it needs to be carefully examined.

Article 34

The Court may receive applications from any person, non-governmental organisation or group of individuals claiming to be the victim of a violation by one of the High Contracting Parties of the rights set forth in the Convention or the protocols thereto. The High Contracting Parties undertake not to hinder in any way the effective exercise of this right.

Directly affected

Cases can only be brought by a 'victim', as this is defined by the ECtHR. A victim is a 'person directly affected by the act or omission which is in issue' (*Eckle* v *Germany* (1983) 5 EHRR 1, para 66). Thus a person can only bring a case (to Strasbourg or under the HRA) if they, themselves, have been directly affected by the alleged breach of the Convention.

Potentially, if not actually, affected

A person can be 'directly affected' and a victim even if they have not actually suffered from a breach of a Convention right but they are in a group or class who might potentially suffer. Article 34 does not require a victim to have suffered from a 'measure of implementation'. The ECtHR has said that a law can violate the Convention rights of a person who 'runs the risk of being directly affected by it'.

In *Open Door Counselling* v *Ireland* (1993) 15 EHRR 244, the issue was whether a ban on counselling on the availability of abortions in the United Kingdom, given the illegality of abortions in Ireland, violated Article 10 (right to freedom of expression). Some of the applicants were individual women, none of whom were pregnant but who were women of child-bearing age who could potentially be affected by the ban. The ECtHR held that they were victims (see paras 41–44).

Indirect victims

In order to maintain the effectiveness of the Convention in protecting human rights, 'indirect' victims have to be recognised in certain situations. This is particularly where the direct victim is dead or there is some other compelling reason why the direct victim cannot bring the case. In such circumstances the Court allows cases to be brought by close relatives such as parents and siblings. This is particularly the case in respect of the most fundamental articles, such as Article 2 (right to life) and Article 3 (the prohibition on torture) where Convention protection against state oppression needs to be most insistent.

Quoting cases such as *Yasa* v *Turkey* (1999) 28 EHRR 408, the Supreme Court in *Rabone* (section 5.4.4) allowed parents to mount an Article 2 challenge in respect of the death of their child.

Corporations (companies)

'Person' can include an artificial legal person and so commercial corporations, no matter how vast and powerful they may be, can have legally recognised human rights. Company rights are expressly recognised in the Convention in respect of the right to property in Article 1 of the First Protocol, but the Strasbourg institutions have accepted that companies also have other rights, such as the right to a fair trial (Article 6) or a right to freedom of expression (media companies, for instance, enjoy Article 10 rights). Some Articles, such as the right to life, the prohibition on torture, the right to liberty or the right to marry (Articles 2, 3, 5 and 12) require a physical body and so are irrelevant to companies. Companies have at least some Article 8 rights, such as a right to respect for their correspondence and for their offices (their 'home') if searched. This matter is discussed in Chapter 15, section 15.1.4.

Shareholders are not usually victims of an alleged violation affecting their company. They are not directly affected by a wrong done to the company. In *Agrotexim* v *Greece* (1996) 21 EHRR 250, shareholders in a brewery challenged a range of planning restrictions coupled with inaction by Athens council. The council's actions affected the ability of the brewery to develop its site and hence the value of the applicant's shares. The ECtHR held that it was the company, not the shareholders, which was directly affected. The company, as a legal entity, chose not to bring a case.

KEY POINT *Agrotexim* was followed by the High Court in *Weir* v *Secretary of State for Transport* [2005] EWHC 2192 (Ch), when shareholders of Railtrack failed in their bid to argue that the forced liquidation of their company violated Article 1 of the First Protocol (paras 294–298).

Political parties, trade unions and other 'non-governmental' groups

Other organisations, such as political parties, trade unions and pressure groups, can also have standing under Article 34 (and also, therefore, before UK courts under the HRA) but only in respect of wrongs done to them as organisations. Trade unions can bring cases in their own name when their complaint is a matter of trade union law and political parties on issues which affect them organisationally. In *United Communist Party* v *Turkey* (1998) 26 EHRR 121, a political party had no difficulty in showing that they were directly affected by a banning order.

No 'actio popularis'

The ECtHR does not allow **actio popularis**.

actio popularis

Cases brought by pressure groups or individuals on behalf of the public or some section of the public. Most legal systems restrict them to some extent, since the courts do not like to be used for what might be thought of as political disputes; Parliament being the correct forum for those. The public interest is represented in the courts by an official such as, in England and Wales, the Attorney General.

Likewise it does not allow 'abstract' cases: where a law or state action is challenged in general terms rather than in terms of its particular effects on particular individuals. Associations, pressure groups, political parties, etc. can bring cases which affect them as associations; but they are normally not able to bring cases on behalf of the population generally, a section of the public or their members. The issue can be complex: are political parties who put forward candidates at elections directly affected by the electoral system, or is it only the voters?

In *Liberal Party* v *United Kingdom* (1982) 4 EHRR 106, the Commission left open the question whether the Liberal Party was a victim of the first-past-the-post electoral system for Parliamentary elections in Britain. There were other applicants who, as voters, were directly affected and, anyway, the case was lost on the merits.

Underlying this approach is the traditional dislike of the courts to be a forum for the resolution of general disputes regarding the public interest. These should be decided by 'political' institutions such as an elected Parliament rather than an unelected court.

In *Norris and the Gay Federation of Ireland* v *Ireland* (1986) 8 EHRR CD 75, the Commission (which in those days had primary responsibility for deciding admissibility), decided the admissibility of an allegation that Irish laws criminalising homosexual activity were in breach of Article 8. The application by N, a gay man, was admissible as he was a potential victim of the laws. The application by the Federation was not admissible since the laws in question could not be applied to them. They were a group campaigning for a change in the law.

Article 34 can be compared with ordinary judicial review in English law. Here the statutory rule is that a person must have a sufficient interest in a matter to be able to bring a case. The courts have interpreted this broadly to allow pressure groups to bring cases on behalf of others who may be too poor or under-resourced to bring their own case, or in environmental cases where the immediate victim, the environment, has no voice of its own. Under section 7 HRA, it will be the Convention approach which is followed.

further study

An example from ordinary judicial review is *R* v *Secretary of State for the Foreign and Commonwealth Office ex parte World Development Movement* [1995] 1 All ER 611, where the WDM, a pressure group, was allowed to challenge the legality of a decision by the Secretary of State to finance a dam in Malaysia.

Representative actions

Actions brought by one person on behalf of others (representative actions) are only permitted where those who are represented have been directly affected by the alleged violation, can be individually identified and have given express consent to be represented.

> It is essential for the applicant association to identify the individuals represented by it and to show that it has received specific instructions from each of them.

> (*Zentralrat DSRR* v *Germany* (1997) 23 EHRR 7 CD 209)

A 'class action', brought on behalf of a group or category of claimants who are not necessarily identified as individuals and may not have given their express consent, is not permitted by the Strasbourg rules.

The 'pilot judgment procedure' (which is discussed in Chapter 2, section 2.5.3) provides a means for dealing with a single issue affecting a large number of people. In essence, the Court stops hearing individual claims and invites the respondent state to introduce reforms.

Governmental bodies

Government bodies, however, do not have human rights. Under the Convention, it is the state and its agencies which have primary responsibility to protect human rights. Public bodies should not, therefore, be bearers of human rights themselves. Given that 'non-governmental' bodies can be victims, it follows that 'governmental' bodies cannot be. Governmental bodies are organisations which 'participate in the exercise of governmental powers or run a public service under government control' (*Radio France* v *France* App 53984/00, admissibility decision of 23 September 2003). In *Danderyds Kommun* v *Sweden* App 52559/99, admissibility decision of 7 June 2001, the ECtHR held that a Swedish 'municipality', a local council, was exercising public functions and could not claim Convention rights.

The argument has been accepted by United Kingdom courts and claims to Convention rights under the HRA by, for example, English local authorities and Scottish NHS Trusts, have been rejected (see *R (Mayor of the City of Westminster)* v *Mayor of London* [2002] EWHC 2440 (Admin) and *Grampian University Hospitals NHS Trust* v *Procurator Fiscal* [2004] HRLR 18 Appeal Court, High Court of Justiciary, respectively).

5.5 Remedies, sections 8 and 9

5.5.1 General

Sections 8 and 9 HRA deal with the remedies that can be given when a court in the United Kingdom finds that a public authority has violated a Convention right. The sections indicate what orders can be made and when financial compensation can be awarded.

Section 8(1) allows a court or tribunal to grant whatever remedy it considers 'just and appropriate', provided that the remedy proposed is one it is authorised to impose.

Section 8 does not, therefore, allow courts and tribunals to create new remedies that they do not have the power to grant (a Crown Court, for example, still cannot award damages). UK courts can, however, fashion the remedies they are allowed to grant in ways that are appropriate to the Convention violation. Financial compensation (discussed at section 5.5.2) can be awarded, but only by a civil court which already has the power to award damages (section 8(2)).

Since sections 6, 7 and 8 HRA involve actions against public authorities, the remedy will often be sought by way of judicial review (see section 5.2.1). The High Court can issue certain remedies (known as 'prerogative orders') which are only available by way of judicial review:

- a quashing order cancels a decision made by a public body and may require that decision to be taken again on a proper legal basis;
- a mandatory order requires a public body to perform a legal duty;
- a prohibitory order requires that a public body desist from a proposed action;
- the High Court, in judicial review proceedings, can also award private law remedies such as injunctions and, but only if there is a legal basis, damages. In particular the High Court can make a 'declaration' which does not order anyone to do anything but declares what the law is; public bodies characteristically obey the law.

Public authorities can also be the subject of private law actions (e.g. against the police for false imprisonment) and the section 6 duty can be relevant to these. Examples of remedies based on section 7 include:

- In *R (Amin)* v *Secretary of State for the Home Department* [2003] UKHL 51, the House of Lords held that there had been a breach of Article 2 (right to life) in respect of the investigation carried out by the Home Office into the death of a prisoner. The remedy was an order requiring a proper investigation that met the standards of Article 2.

- In *A* v *Secretary of State for the Home Department* [2004] UKHL 56, the House of Lords first quashed a government order purporting to derogate from Article 5 in order to allow the detention without trial of foreign terrorist suspects; then, second, made a declaration of incompatibility regarding the legislation under which the detentions had been authorised.

- In *R (K)* v *Secretary of State for the Home Department* [2009] EWCA Civ 219, the Court of Appeal issued a declaration that the Home Secretary should have investigated alleged violations of Article 3 regarding a privately run immigration detention centre.

cross reference

The private law ('horizontal') impact of the HRA is discussed in Chapter 4, section 4.7.

Courts and tribunals, being public authorities, are themselves subject to the section 6 HRA duty. When dealing with, for example, private, common law matters (like contract and tort) they are required, by section 6, to act compatibly with Convention rights and this can have an impact not only on the way the law develops but also on the way the remedies and the situations in which they are available are developed.

5.5.2 **Damages**

General

Damages can be awarded against a public authority for breach of its duty under section 6 HRA by a UK court. Damages can only be awarded if

- the court is one with powers to award damages or compensation in civil proceedings. This can include, for example, the High Court but excludes the Crown Court (which tries serious criminal cases);

- in all the circumstances the award of damages is necessary to afford 'just satisfaction' to the applicant.

In deciding whether or not to award damages and, if so, how much, section 8(4) HRA requires the UK to take into account the Strasbourg case law on just satisfaction under Article 41 of the Convention.

further study

A full and detailed summary of the Convention position has been produced by the Law Commission: *Damages under the Human Rights Act 1998* Report 266.

Article 41 allows the ECtHR to compensate for the failure of national courts to provide an adequate remedy by affording, if necessary, 'just satisfaction to the injured party'. The following principles, derived from the Strasbourg case law, were accepted by the House of Lords as guiding the way in which section 8 HRA should be applied by UK courts (see *R (Greenfield)* v *Secretary of State for the Home Department* [2005] UKHL 14).

Finding of a violation often sufficient

The principal aim is to remedy violations rather than focus on the financial compensation of the victim. The ECtHR frequently holds that a finding in favour of the applicant is sufficient satisfaction and no further remedy is required.

Restorative principle

If a financial payment is necessary, the underlying principle of Article 41 is *restitutio in integrum* (restored in full)—the principle of returning the person, as far as possible, to the situation he or she would have been in had his or her Convention rights not been violated. Primary responsibility for this lies with the state. The ECtHR may make an award if the state has not remedied the situation or its purported remedy is inadequate.

Causative link

Compensation is confined to those losses attributable to the public authority's breach of the Convention. Unlike under the common law, the ECtHR does not award 'exemplary' or 'punitive' damages. These recognise particularly reprehensible behaviour by the respondent authority by imposing a higher award than restitution strictly requires. Nevertheless, it is clear that the ECtHR does take context into account and this can include the conduct of the parties. The Court awards non-pecuniary damages on an 'equitable basis' without going into detail on how the equity is assessed. There are often considerable gaps between amounts claimed by applicants and the amount the Court is prepared to award.

Pecuniary losses

Convention breaches directly causing monetary loss, such as loss of income, welfare benefits or valuable property, can be compensated under Article 41. Violations of Article 1 of the First Protocol (the right to peaceful enjoyment of possessions) can commonly lead to significant awards. In *Scordino* v *Italy* (2007) 45 EHRR 7, for example, there was a violation of Article 1 of the First Protocol when the applicant's land was lawfully expropriated but with inadequate compensation. The ECtHR awarded €580,000. In *Smith and Grady* v *United Kingdom* [2001] 31 EHRR 24, £59,000 and £40,000 respectively were awarded for loss of salary due to being dismissed from the armed forces in breach of Article 8.

Non-pecuniary losses

These cover intangible matters such as distress, anxiety and psychological trauma. Thus the applicants in *Smith and Grady* also received £19,000 each to compensate for the distress and destabilisation caused by the investigation into their sexual lives, which then triggered their dismissal (see Chapter 15, section 15.10.3). Awards for breaches of Article 2 have been between €5,000 and €60,000 (*Rabone*, at section 5.4.4, para 85). The award of non-pecuniary damages does seem to be based partly on an unstated ethical assessment of the case. Thus those convicted of criminal offences or who are terrorist suspects may find that a finding in their favour is sufficient just satisfaction and an award for non-pecuniary damages is denied. The graver the violation, the more likely it is that significant non-pecuniary losses will be recognised and compensated. Underlying the Convention jurisprudence is, as always, the need to establish a 'fair balance' between individual interests and public good.

Costs and expenses

These are legal costs and expenses incurred in bringing the case to Strasbourg. They do not normally cover costs incurred whilst exhausting domestic remedies in the national courts though they might include extra costs incurred in trying to persuade a national court not to act incompatibly with the Convention. It is common to find that an applicant is not awarded any financial just satisfaction but is awarded a considerable sum to cover actual costs and expenses. Perhaps the most controversial instance is *McCann* v *United Kingdom* [1996] 21 EHRR 97. The ECtHR found a violation of Article 2 in the case of the shooting by British forces of members of an IRA active service unit in Gibraltar. No damages were awarded in 'just satisfaction' but the relatives who brought the case received £38,700 (from which legal aid of about £4,000 already received was deducted) in costs and expenses.

Damages and the HRA

Damages under section 8 HRA are discretionary, not a matter of right. The principles governing the exercise of this discretion for the law of England and Wales have been discussed by the House of Lords in *R (Greenfield)* v *Secretary of State for the Home Office* [2005] UKHL 14 (see section 5.5.4). This case relates to just satisfaction for a breach of Article 6, but it also deals with just satisfaction more generally. The overall requirement is that UK principles mirror those of the ECtHR and, perhaps, to lessen expectations and opportunities for major financial awards following a breach of Convention rights.

The House of Lords made clear that UK courts needed to follow the general principles of the Strasbourg court (outlined earlier in this section) when considering just satisfaction. Their lordships disapproved of deciding amounts of just satisfaction by reference to domestic law, such as the principles on which the quantum of damages was assessed in tort or awards were made by, for example, Ombudsmen or the Criminal Injuries Compensation Board (see *Greenfield*, para 19). UK courts should look to Strasbourg for guidance (*Rabone*, section 5.4.4, para 82).

In particular:

- The priority under the HRA is the protection of human rights rather than compensation for harm caused. Even where a finding of a violation is not sufficient it is still a matter of weight whose value needs to be subtracted, as it were, from the amount of damages that would be awarded under tort principles.
- In *Anufrijeva* v *Southwark* LBC [2003] EWCA Civ 1406 it was also pointed out that in human rights cases the need is often to balance personal and public interests, a task that is much less relevant in a tort context.
- The point of the HRA, enshrined in section 8(4), is to enable victims to obtain from UK courts what they could get from Strasbourg—no less but also no more.

There are, therefore, a range of issues that are relevant to determine whether just satisfaction should be awarded and, if so, how much to award. Factors to be weighed include the Article in issue; the nature and seriousness of the violation; the conduct of both the applicant and the behaviour of the respondent state; and also, perhaps, the impact the award may have on the public service which must fund it.

In *Rabone* (section 5.4.4) the High Court considered there was no breach of Article 2 but would have awarded £1,500 to each parent. The Court of Appeal, agreeing there was no breach, would have increased this to £5,000. The Supreme Court found there was a breach. It retained the award of £5,000 (there had been no appeal of the point) but thought there was 'real force' in the contention that this was too low.

5.5.3 **Just satisfaction and Article 5**

Article 5(5) creates a right to compensation for anyone arrested or detained in contravention of Article 5 (the right to liberty). It is likely that the applicant will also have been a victim of 'false imprisonment' (a tort) and so the award will be based on common law principles (e.g. *R (Kambadzi)* v *Secretary of State for the Home Department* [2011] UKSC 23). Remedies must, obviously, be available against judges and other judicial officers such as magistrates and tribunals. Generally, under English law, there is absolute immunity for members of the senior judiciary; legal protection against claims for damages in respect of good faith decisions of magistrates is found in sections 31 and 32 of the Courts Act 2003. These principles are found in section 9(3) HRA, which does not allow an action for damages in respect of a 'judicial act done in good faith' by a judge, magistrate or tribunal member. An express exception is made for the purposes of Article 5(5). Awards for damages against judges etc. for breach of Article 5(5) are paid from public funds.

case close-up

A v United Kingdom (2009) 49 EHRR 29

A number of foreign terrorist suspects were detained, without trial and in breach of Article 5, in UK prisons. Since no terrorist activities had been proved against the applicants, the ECtHR would not refuse any compensatory award (as it had done in the case of *McCann* v *UK*). Nor would the award be large (as in *Assanidze v Georgia* (2004) 39 EHRR 32) because the UK had acted in good faith in a time of public emergency (the aftermath of '9/11'). It made awards (combining pecuniary and non-pecuniary factors) of between €1,700 and €3,900.

This, of course, is a case decided by the ECtHR, but it indicates approaches that UK courts should follow. *Assanidze* indicates that awards for breaches of Article 5(5) can be large. The applicant was acquitted of various offences but not released. The pecuniary and non-pecuniary damages combined were assessed at €150,000.

5.5.4 Just satisfaction and Article 6

The issue of just satisfaction if there has been a violation of Article 6, the right to a fair trial, raises a particular problem. If, as a result of the breach, the claimant was denied a full and proper opportunity to make his or her case, should the court, in considering whether to award just satisfaction, speculate on what the outcome of the original trial would have been had it been conducted in line with Article 6? The issue has been discussed in *Greenfield*.

case close-up

R (Greenfield) v *Secretary of State for the Home Office* [2005] UKHL 14

G, a serving prisoner, was sentenced to 21 additional days in prison as a result of a disciplinary process in which, in breach of Article 6, he was denied representation. The House of Lords held that the finding of a violation was sufficient and that no financial award should be made.

The House of Lords reviewed the general principles governing awards for just satisfaction (see section 5.5.2). The judgment is, however, focused on a breach of Article 6. Regarding such breaches the House of Lords noted that:

- The ECtHR does not normally speculate on what the outcome of a trial would have been (see, for example, *Ezeh and Connors* v *United Kingdom* (2004) 39 EHRR 1, para 141 of the Grand Chamber's judgment adopting paras 112–114 of the Chamber's judgment). The exception is where a national court has itself indicated that a different outcome would have been likely had the trial been fair. In that situation, damages might be awarded. An example is *Perks* v *United Kingdom* (2000) 30 EHRR 33, where the ECtHR accepted that the applicant would

> probably not have been imprisoned if, as fair trial procedures dictated, they were told about his personal circumstances (he was awarded £5,500).
>
> • Non-pecuniary damages for physical and mental suffering caused by failures in the fairness of a trial are sometimes awarded under Article 42, and this is done without reference to the likely outcome of the trial. Such damages are invariably of small amounts (see, for example, *Stephen Jordan* v *United Kingdom (No 2)* (2002) App 49771/99, judgment of 10 December 2002).

Delay in a criminal or civil trial can be a violation of Article 6. Here an additional question arises: should the delayed trial proceed? There is now clear authority from the House of Lords that the delayed trial should proceed unless, for additional reasons, it would be unjust to continue. The violation of Article 6 can be recognised by appropriate measures such as release on bail (if delay is recognised before the trial) or a lesser sentence or payment of compensation (if recognised during or after the trial) (*Attorney General's Reference (No 2 of 2001)* [2003] UKHL 68 (before a panel of nine Law Lords)).

Summary

- Effective human rights require effective remedies.

- Under the HRA, people can seek the protection of their human rights either by persuading a court or tribunal to interpret a relevant Act of Parliament in the way that protects their human rights or by bringing or defending cases on the grounds that a public authority has acted in a way that violates Convention rights.

- Various procedural issues have to be borne in mind—particularly that, in cases involving public authorities, a person must show that he or she was a 'victim' and could, therefore, have brought a case to the ECtHR.

- Remedies available under the HRA are English law remedies fashioned to reflect the remedies available in Strasbourg. In particular, these are a finding that the Convention has been violated and 'just satisfaction' in terms of financial compensation (damages) for pecuniary and non-pecuniary losses. The principles for awarding damages are complex but need to be distinguished from ordinary tort actions.

123

? Questions

For suggested approaches, please visit the Online Resource Centre.

1 The BBC is subject to government action that involves a clear and unambiguous violation of Article 10. What principles will decide whether the BBC can bring a case against the government under section 7 HRA?

2 The ECtHR makes financial awards in 'just satisfaction' on the basis of the overall equity of the case. What factors are taken into account by the Court? How are these adapted by UK courts for the purposes of the HRA?

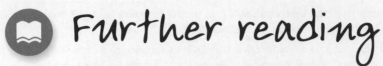

Further reading

Amos, M. (see Preface) Part 1, Chapter 6

Lester, A., Pannick, D. and Herberg, J. (see Preface) Chapter 2, Chapter 4, Article 13

STANDING AND THE 'VICTIM' TEST

Miles, J. 'Standing under the Human Rights Act 1998: Theories of Public Rights Enforcement and the Nature of Public Law Adjudication' (2000) 59(1) *CLJ* 133–167

JUST SATISFACTION

Law Commission, *Damages under the Human Rights Act 1998* Report 266

Mowbray, A. 'The European Court of Human Right's Approach to Just Satisfaction' [1997] *Public Law* (Winter) 647–659

Convention law: pervasive themes

Chapter overview

- Concepts and background values which apply generally and pervade the Convention and the way it is interpreted.

- These include legality and the rule of law, 'margin of appreciation', democracy, proportionality.

- The obligation of states to take positive steps to secure Convention rights for all.

Introduction

The European Convention on Human Rights (ECHR) is a constitutional document. The words and phrases in it are written in highly abstract and general terms which need interpretation if they are to be applied to the particular facts and situations of individual cases. There are a number of general principles, concepts and values which pervade the Convention (that is, they are relevant to all or most of the Convention's Articles). Some of these principles, concepts and values are derived from the text of the Convention (e.g. the importance of 'democracy') others derive from international law generally. Whatever the source, the pervasive principles originate in the European Court of Human Rights' (ECtHR) own conception of its duty—it is an international court, so it must respect the sovereignty of states; yet it is applying an international instrument whose purpose is to give effective, individual protection to human rights, usually when these are threatened by the actions or inactivity of states.

cross reference
On section 2 HRA, see Chapter 4, section 4.3.

These pervasive principles, concepts and values are also part of the law of the United Kingdom. Section 2 of the Human Rights Act 1998 (HRA) requires UK courts to take into account the judgments of the ECtHR, judgments, which embody, explain and apply the pervasive principles.

Of particular importance are the ideas of

- legality and the rule of law,
- margin of appreciation,
- democracy,
- proportionality,
- positive duties.

6.1 International law

The Convention is an international treaty and the ECtHR is an international court.

6.1.1 The Vienna Convention

The United Nations Vienna Convention on the Law of Treaties 1969 is a treaty about treaties. It contains a range of general principles, agreed by states, on how the treaties they enter into should be interpreted. From the earliest cases the ECtHR accepted that it should be guided by the Vienna Convention (*Golder* v *United Kingdom* (1979–80) 1 EHRR 524, para 29). Article 31 of the Vienna Treaty, for instance, requires that treaties should be interpreted by reference to their 'context' and 'object and purposes'. Time and again the ECtHR emphasises that it interprets and applies the ECHR in a way that recognises its purpose as being to give effective human rights protection to individuals.

6.1.2 **Other UN treaties etc.**

Other treaties bearing on human rights issues can influence the way in which the ECtHR interprets the Convention (both the Vienna Convention and the Preamble to the ECHR itself authorise this). General human rights treaties, such as the International Covenant on Civil and Political Rights (ICCPR) (Chapter 1, section 1.4.4) assist the ECtHR, as do more focused treaties such as the UN Convention against Torture (see *Selmouni* v *France* (2000) 29 EHRR 403, Chapter 9, section 9.2.2).

6.1.3 **Subsequent documents from Council of Europe**

The Council of Europe (of which the ECtHR is part) produces a vast range of documents relating to human rights issues. These include other Conventions (which have the force of law) and a range of 'Recommendations' and 'Resolutions' which have persuasive authority.

6.1.4 **Convention materials**

Travaux préparatoires

The *travaux préparatoires* are the records of the process of writing and agreeing the Convention in 1950. The Court may refer to the *travaux préparatoires*. However, the ECtHR reads the Convention as a 'living instrument', evolving with the times, which means that the influence of these early documents can be limited.

6.1.5 **Preamble and Article 1**

These are both part of the Convention. Neither can be the basis of a decision but both can influence the way the Convention is interpreted.

The Preamble

The Vienna Convention allows courts to refer to the Preamble of a treaty for interpretative purposes. The Preamble of the ECHR is a significant source of guidance for the Court. It guides the Court and allows it, for example, to

- refer to international law,
- insist on the importance of democracy and the rule of law, and
- invoke the 'common heritage' of European political traditions.

Article 1

Article 1 (along with Article 46) expresses the basic duties undertaken by states when they sign the Convention. They are discussed in Chapter 2, section 2.4.2.

6.1.6 **The evolutive approach and precedent**

The evolutive principle

The ECtHR treats the ECHR as a 'living instrument' and not as something whose meaning was set in stone for all time by the drafters in 1950. The aim is to ensure that the application of the Convention can evolve as European society, culture and values change.

The evolutive approach means that the Court has only a weak idea of precedent. The Court tends to follow the principles and decisions found in its earlier decisions, but is perfectly willing to depart from these in order to provide an effective protection of human rights in the modern age.

further study

A good discussion of the evolutive approach is in *Stafford* v *United Kingdom* (see especially paras 68–80). Examples, found in this book, include *Goodwin* v *United Kingdom* (2002) 35 EHRR 18 (transsexuals: see Chapter 19, section 19.4) and *Stec* v *United Kingdom* (2005) 41 EHRR SE 18 ECHR (possessions and welfare: see Chapter 23, sections 23.2.3).

6.2 Legality and the rule of law

6.2.1 The idea of the rule of law

The duties and responsibilities the ECHR imposes on its signatory states must be exercised only on the basis of law. The 'rule of law' is a golden thread that runs through the Convention.

The rule of law is a foundation principle of modern national constitutional law, though its origins lie back in classical times. As an abstract principle it is fully recognised in the constitutional law of the United Kingdom (see *R* v *Goldstein* [2005] UKHL 63, para 32, for quotations). It is a principle found in international law and in 'liberal' political theory.

The general idea of the rule of law is that state power should only be exercised on the basis of laws—general rules for the regulation of conduct, both of individuals and the state's own agents. The rule of law is usually contrasted with 'arbitrary' or 'tyrannical' government found in dictatorships of various kinds. Under such systems individuals have no security: the activities of government are not controlled by rules and it is not possible to predict what actions are going to be penalised.

The problem is that there is nothing in the nature of rules which prevents their being used for oppressive purposes. Historically, therefore, the rule of law has come to be associated with certain values believed to underlie good government. In particular, it has come to embody certain 'procedural' values—such as the need for rules to be publicised; not to be applied retrospectively; to be sufficiently clear and certain so that they can be put into effect and, above all, the right of access to the courts. Other accounts equate the rule of law with part or all of the full range of human rights. Two English cases illustrate the application of the principle.

In *R (Anufrijeva)* v *Secretary of State for the Home Department* [2003] UKHL 36, the House of Lords held that the refusal to communicate administrative decisions to asylum seekers who were thus prevented from going to court to challenge those decisions went against 'fundamental principles of our law' (para 26). In *R* v *Secretary of State for the Home Department ex parte Simms* [2000] 2 AC 115, Lord Hoffmann, in a much-quoted passage, equated the principle of 'legality' with the protection of fundamental rights (see Chapter 3, section 3.3.1).

Binding officials to obey rules may mean, in some situations, they are unable to do the right and best thing in any particular situation. The tension between rule following and exercising 'discretion' (choice of action) is one of the ongoing issues about the rule of law and is demonstrated in the understanding of that concept developed by the ECtHR.

6.2.2 The place of law in the Convention

References to 'law' are found throughout the Convention.

- The Preamble describes the rule of law as part of the common heritage of Europe.
- Restrictions on personal liberty and other freedoms can only be compatible with the Convention if authorised by law (see, for example, Articles 5 and 9–11).
- Rights and freedoms, such as the right to life, must be secured by law (see, for example, Articles 2 and 6).
- The requirement that criminal punishment must be based on the rule of law is expressly found in Article 7.

6.2.3 The autonomous Convention concept of law

Law and legality has an 'autonomous' meaning in the Convention.

• •

autonomous concepts

A number of concepts found in the Convention have a particular meaning given to them by the ECtHR for Convention purposes. This meaning is autonomous in the sense that it does not depend on the way concepts are defined in national laws.

• •

The leading ECHR case is *Sunday Times* v *United Kingdom* (1979–80) 2 EHRR 245, para 49. The principles have been referred to by the ECtHR in countless cases and they have been summarised for the purposes of English law under the HRA in *R* v *Shayler* [2002] UKHL 11 (Lord Hope, para 56).

- There must be a legal basis for the state's action in the domestic law.
- Accessibility—the law or rule in question must be sufficiently accessible to the individuals who are affected by the restriction.
- Foreseeability—the law or rule in question must be sufficiently precise to enable the individuals affected to understand its scope and foresee the consequences of their actions so that they can regulate their conduct without breaking the law.
- The law must not have been applied in an arbitrary way.

Legal basis

Lawless action by a state in an area covered by human rights is likely to be a violation.

Accessibility—identifying the law

First, the law must be adequately accessible: the citizen must be able to have an indication that is adequate in the circumstances of the legal rules applicable to a given case.

(*Sunday Times*, para 49)

An individual, or at least her or his legal advisor, must be able to identify the legal rules on the basis of which the state has allegedly interfered with their Convention rights.

In *R (Gillan)* v *Commissioner of Police for the Metropolis* [2006] UKHL 12, the Terrorism Act 2000 allowed police to stop and search people even though there was no reasonable suspicion against those people. This could only be done if an 'authorisation' had been made in respect of the locality where the stops and searches are made. Such an authorisation was made in respect of the London area, but its existence was not made known to the public. The House of Lords held that the use of stop and search powers, given the context of the terrorist threat, satisfied the legality provision in Article 5.

Accessibility—what counts as 'law'

What counts as a 'law' depends on the particular legal system. In the *Sunday Times* case, the Court had to deal with the judge-made common law (the rules on contempt of court). The ECtHR had no difficulty in holding that 'unwritten', non-statutory law, such as English case law, was properly thought of as law. Enactment in a statute or code of law is not a requirement. Sources of law, therefore, include any rules which have the rule-like quality of generality and are accepted as such by the national courts. In the United Kingdom, for example, as well as case law, Acts of Parliament and delegated legislation, there are also 'codes of practice', 'rules', 'regulations', 'guidelines' of various kinds and many other forms in which general rules applying in different places and contexts are expressed. The legal force of such documents are a matter of domestic law and the ECtHR, it seems, will accept these as sources of law in so far as they are so accepted by the national courts. 'In sum, the "law" is the provision in force as the competent courts have interpreted it', *Sahin* v *Turkey* (2007) 44 EHRR 5, para 88, Grand Chamber.

A so-called law which does not have general application but which only applies to a particular, individual or purpose does not meet the Convention test of law. 'Such an act is valid for one specific purpose only and is not intended to prescribe a general rule of conduct for recurrent applications', *Amat-G* v *Georgia* (2007) 45 EHRR 35, para 61.

Foreseeability, the absence of regulation

Secondly, a norm cannot be regarded as a 'law' unless it is formulated with sufficient precision to enable the citizen to regulate his conduct: he must be able—if need be with appropriate advice—to foresee, to a degree that is reasonable in the circumstances, the consequences which a given action may entail.

(*Sunday Times*, para 49)

In order for individuals to foresee (or predict) the circumstances in which the might of the state may be used against them, it is sometimes necessary for there to be a proper, sufficiently detailed body of law and regulations dealing with a particular matter. The absence of this in a matter touching on human rights can be a violation.

In *Malone* v *United Kingdom* (1985) 7 EHRR 14, the ECtHR held there was a breach of Article 8 (the right to private life) in a phone tapping case. In the United Kingdom, at the time, there was no statute-based regulatory regime dealing with phone tapping by the police. Surveillance seemed to be predominantly a matter of official discretion, a position which had been accepted by the UK courts (see, in particular, para 67).

Foreseeability and discretion

In many areas, officials need 'discretion', the freedom to decide policies and take decisions. The more precise and demanding the rules, the less discretion officials enjoy. The advantage of discretion is that it enables officials to take actions appropriate to the particular situation; the disadvantage, of course, is that it lessens certainty about what is acceptable or unacceptable under the law. There is no simple answer to this issue, which goes to the heart of questions about the nature of legitimate government.

The ECtHR takes a view which is circumstance and context dependent.

> The Court reiterates that the scope of the notion of foreseeability depends to a considerable degree on the content of the instrument in question, the field it is designed to cover and the number and status of those to whom it is addressed.

> (*Sahin* v *Turkey* (2007) 44 EHRR 5, para 91)

Laws drafted with too much precision may be too rigid and be unable to keep pace with changing circumstances. For this reason laws are 'inevitably couched in terms which, to a greater or lesser extent, are vague' (*Kokkinakis* v *Greece* (1994) 17 EHRR 397, para 40).

In *R (Purdy)* v *DPP* [2009] UKHL 45, the House of Lords (in its last judgment) held that guidelines, produced by the Director of Public Prosecutions, provided a proper legal basis for general prosecution decisions. In the context of assisted suicide, however, these guidelines did not differentiate clearly enough between different situations and motives. They failed, therefore, the 'foreseeability' test.

cross reference
See Chapter 15, section 15.4.8, for a discussion of surveillance.

Laws which confer a discretion must indicate the scope of that discretion. Even in matters of national security and surveillance, some sense of the circumstances and reasons for state action must be given.

6.2.4 States themselves must obey legal orders

The rule of law requires governments to follow the law and obey court orders. In a number of cases the national courts have, for example, ordered the state to pay compensation. The response of simply refusing to pay (as in *Amat-G Ltd* v *Georgia*, above), or of enacting legislation which retrospectively alters a court judgment (as in *Pressos Compania Naviera SA* v *Belgium* (1996) 21 EHRR 301) or refusing to release a person from custody despite a court order (as in *Goral* v *Poland* App 38654/97, judgment of 30 October 2003) are all likely to be violations.

6.3 Margin of appreciation

KEY POINT The margin of appreciation is a concept relevant only to an international court. It is not, directly, appropriate for domestic courts. These, though, may have reason to 'defer' to the judgments of the legislature or executive on the 'fair balance' of interests in a case (see Chapter 4, section 4.6; *Evans* v *Amicus Healthcare* [2003] EWHC 2161, at 90).

The ECtHR has recognised, from its earliest cases, the need to take into account the different conditions and standards that apply in different countries. States have the primary duty to secure human rights and they are allowed a degree of freedom of choice over the measures they take regarding the issues that are the subject matter of the different articles in the Convention. The term given to this degree of freedom for states in the way Convention rights and freedoms are secured is 'margin of appreciation'.

A margin of appreciation is often recognised in respect of the power of states to restrict the exercise of freedoms found in the second paragraphs of Articles 8–11 (private life; thought, conscience and religion; expression; assembly and association). It is not, however, confined to these Articles.

The margin of appreciation doctrine has been recognised from the earliest cases (see, in particular, *Handyside* v *United Kingdom* (1979–80) 1 EHRR 737, para 48). The basic points are:

• primary duty to protect human rights lies with the nation states;

• the role of the ECtHR is subsidiary and supervisory;

- the national authorities are in principle better placed than an international court to evaluate local needs and conditions. They have 'direct democratic legitimation' (*Hatton* v *United Kingdom* (2003) 37 EHRR 28, para 97) and so it is for the national authorities to make the initial assessment of the 'necessity' for an interference with a Convention right or freedom;

- this applies both to the laws and to the particular measure of implementation complained about;

- however, although a margin of appreciation is thereby left to the national authorities, their decision remains subject to review by the Court for conformity with the requirements of the Convention. Even a wide margin of appreciation is subject to limits based on the Court's assessment of the minimum required to uphold a right (its 'essence' or core).

The existence and extent of a margin of appreciation is variable. It is a matter for the ECtHR based on a range of relevant matters such as

- the importance and nature of the right guaranteed—there is less room for a margin of appreciation in respect of absolute or unqualified rights like Article 3, than in respect of those rights, like Articles 8–11, which expressly require a balance to be struck between competing interests;

- the importance of the matter for the individual—where what is at stake is the effective enjoyment of 'intimate or key' rights, such as sexuality (*Dudgeon* v *UK* (1982) 4 EHRR 149, para 52), the margin will be less; likewise where a particularly important 'facet of an individuals existence or identity' is at stake;

- the nature of the activities which have been restricted—factors such as 'the circumstances, the subject matter and its background' (*Fretté* v *France* (2004) 38 EHRR 21, para 40);

- the nature of the interference and the purpose being pursued by the state;

- the lack of any consensus between the states on the importance of the issue or the best means of protecting it, indicates a wide margin of appreciation.

further study

A recent Grand Chamber restatement of the basic principles is *Marper/S* v *United Kingdom* (2009) 48 EHRR 50, para 102.

6.3.1 Matters over which states have little or no margin of appreciation

Convention relevant matters which indicate no margin of appreciation or only a very narrow one, include the following:

cross reference
Goodwin is discussed in Chapter 19, section 19.4.

- Where the Convention standard is 'objective', and its application more straightforward than one which is open to debate and disagreement. Torture and inhuman treatment, prohibited by Article 3 is an example.

- Where the Court feels able to identify a clear European consensus. In *Goodwin* v *United Kingdom* (2002) 35 EHRR 18, the Court decided that a general European cultural and medical consensus on the rights of transsexuals had developed and so, where before there had been a margin of appreciation, this was now greatly reduced.

- Where an important Convention principle needs to be upheld. For example, the importance of political democracy means that there is very little margin of appreciation for states to restrict political speech (protected by Article 10).

6.3.2 **Matters over which states have a wide margin of appreciation**

Issues over which the states are likely to have a wide margin of appreciation include:

- Matters of controversy and diverging views, particularly in respect of 'moral' issues. In cases involving, for example, sadomasochism (*Laskey, Jaggard and Brown* v *United Kingdom* (1997) 24 EHRR 39) or obscenity (*Muller* v *Switzerland* (1991) 13 EHRR 212), a wide margin of appreciation is allowed. But even the most profound moral views may sometimes be outweighed by the need to protect individual rights. See, for example, *Open Door Counselling and Dublin Well Woman* v *Ireland* (1993) 15 EHRR 244, Chapter 17, section 17.6.3.

- Matters of social policy, such as housing, health care or the environment. These are issues that are very dependant on the social, economic and political factors prevailing in a country and are the sorts of matter over which there is reasonable disagreement between people, often expressed in the differences between political parties and going to the very heart of democratic debate. See, for example, *James* v *United Kingdom* 1986 8 EHRR 123 (housing policy, Chapter 23, section 23.6.1) or *Hatton* v *United Kingdom* (2003) 37 EHRR 28 (night flying at Heathrow, Chapter 15, section 15.10.1).

- Matters over which states are assumed to have special, exclusive knowledge. This can involve the existence and seriousness of threats to national security and the methods needed to deal with them. Even here, though, the ECtHR expects states to protect the core of the individual rights in issue (e.g. an early surveillance case: *Klass* v *Germany* (1979–80) 2 EHRR 214, paras 49–50).

6.3.3 **Criticisms of the doctrine**

The margin of appreciation can be a controversial doctrine because it appears to undermine the universal nature of human rights and, in the name of diversity, may allow oppressive government actions to go unchallenged. In particular it introduces an unwarranted level of flexibility into a Convention which already, in its express terms, is highly flexible.

Defenders of the margin of appreciation see it as recognising the reality of the existence of different cultural and political standards in different countries. Such recognition is necessary to ensure the continuing support of the Convention amongst governments and people. It also supports the Convention value of democracy by ensuring that, where appropriate, decisions are taken by elected or accountable political bodies rather than handed over to judges.

In any event it must be recalled that the ECtHR retains its reviewing role and, even where the margin is at its widest, has a duty to ensure that the 'essence' of a right is not undermined.

6.4 **Democracy**

6.4.1 **The importance of democracy**

Under the Convention, protecting human rights means upholding political democracy. As the ECtHR has said on more than one occasion:

> democracy is the only political model contemplated by the Convention and, accordingly, the only one compatible with it.

> (*United Communist Party of Turkey* v *Turkey* (1998) 26 EHRR 121, para 45)

This central importance of political democracy is affirmed by the Court in, for example, cases involving the banning of political parties (as in *United Communist Party of Turkey,* see para 45) or the imposition of restrictions on political participation such as refusing to allow a person to stand in an election (as in *Zdanoka* v *Latvia* (2007) 45 EHRR 17, Grand Chamber, see para 98).

The importance of democracy for the Convention flows, first, from the Preamble, which asserts that human rights are best protected in a democratic society.

The Preamble also refers to the European 'common heritage of political traditions': these the ECtHR takes as embodying democracy. There is, of course, a problem with the 'common heritage' argument. Until the last decade of the twentieth century, Europe was divided. States in Eastern Europe were not members of the Council of Europe and their governments were not 'democratic' or respectful of human rights in the Convention sense. In reality it is the concept of democracy, as developed by liberalism as a political theory and justified by abstract principles, that is maintained by the Convention. These principles may have been widely adopted in Western Europe after the Second World War, but they have hardly been 'common' to Europe as a whole.

'Democracy' is specifically referred to in Articles 8 to 11. These deal with respecting private life and protecting the freedoms of thought, conscience and religion; expression; and assembly and association.

These freedoms can be restricted by the state but only on certain conditions, and one of these conditions is that the restriction be 'necessary in a democratic society'. In other words, restrictions on a person's private life, religion, expression, etc. are only justified if they spring from the needs of a democratic society (see, for example, *Gorzelik* v *Poland* (2005) 40 EHRR 4, Grand Chamber, para 89).

6.4.2 **The Convention concept of democracy**

Democracy has many meanings. Virtually all states claim in one sense or other to be democratic. The ECtHR, interpreting the Convention, has developed a general sense of democracy.

No particular political system

cross reference

Political participation is, of course, secured by the rights to freedom of belief (Article 9), freedom of expression (Article 10) and freedom of association and assembly (Article 11). See Chapters 15–18.

The Convention does not specify any particular form of government. The only specific reference to the political system is in Article 3 of the First Protocol. This places a duty on states to hold elections and, as interpreted by the ECtHR, gives individuals rights to vote, to stand in elections and to take their seats in the legislature if elected. From this can be inferred that the Convention requires some system of representative democracy based upon an elected legislature; but little else.

There is little, if any, requirement in the Convention that would support a conception of democracy based on participation in the public life of the nation. The Convention appears to be narrower on this than international law generally. Article 25 ICCPR, in particular, refers to direct or indirect participation in 'the conduct of public affairs'. Systems of direct democracy, by which citizens have rights to be directly involved in the political decisions that affect them, gain no support from the ECHR. A passive democracy, based on no more than the peoples' choices, from time to time, of representative legislators, is all that the Convention requires by way of the political system.

The limits to majority rule—pluralism, tolerance and broadmindedness

A concept of democracy based solely on majority rule or on the decisions of representative and accountable institutions is incompatible with the Convention. Human rights are to be enjoyed by all, including unpopular minorities and individuals. It is not permissible, for example, to deprive someone of his or her liberty or to stop someone exercising freedom of speech just because it is the wish of the majority that this be so. This can, for majoritarians (those who believe the essence of democracy is majority rule) make human rights themselves seem undemocratic.

The idea of democracy developed by the ECtHR involves a number of non-majoritarian elements. In particular democracy requires society to be pluralist, tolerant and broadminded. This issue is discussed further in Chapter 1, section 1.1.

cross reference
The idea of pluralism is discussed further in Chapter 18, on Article 11. See in particular, section 18.7.1.

Pluralism means that the legal and constitutional system must accept and allow for the existence of different groups based, for example, on ethnic, religious, social, political or other differences. This applies even if such groups are unpopular with the majority in society and their representatives. In particular:

- The state and legal system cannot impose a particular religious, ideological or other belief system on society as a whole.

- The state and legal system must allow people to express and further their different ways of life through associations and groups. In particular people must be free to form and join political parties which can compete effectively for state power.

cross reference
Issues of tolerance and broadmindedness are discussed further in Chapter 15 (Article 8 private life) and Chapter 17 (Article 10 freedom of expression).

On tolerance and broadmindedness, the Convention requires society to tolerate minorities of whom the majority may disapprove, in particular, where the minority's behaviour is (to use an often repeated phrase) 'offensive, shocking or disturbing'. This is true especially in the context of freedom of expression (Article 10) but is also relevant to other Articles such as the right to private life in Article 8. Speech or behaviour which is opposed solely because it shocks, offends or disturbs ought to be protected under the Convention. If, however, the expression or behaviour not only shocks, offends and disturbs but also interferes with the lives of others or with the legitimate interests of state and society, then legal restriction may be necessary and acceptable under the Convention.

Democracy

135

6.4.3 **Protecting democracy**

Political democracy sometimes needs defending against political groups seeking to undermine its institutions and values. The ECtHR, from its earliest cases, has accepted that it can be compatible with the Convention for governments to ban or restrict the activities of groups which pose credible threats to the democratic quality of their society. In particular:

- Restrictions on political activity, such as racist or anti-democratic groups, can be 'necessary in a democratic society' and so are acceptable under the terms of the second paragraphs of Article 10 or 11 ECHR and not violations of the Convention.

cross reference
Article 17 is the topic of Chapter 7, section 7.3.

- The claims by the anti-democratic or racist groups or individuals to have their rights to freedom of expression or assembly protected may, in fact, be claims to use Convention rights in order to undermine the rights of others. Such claims can be barred under the terms of Article 17 ECHR, which prohibits the abuse of rights in this way.

discussion topic

Conception of democracy

In an age in which the power of states is increasingly subordinated to the demands of global capitalism and corporate power, is there a need for a more effective and active conception of democracy to be protected by human rights?

Four articles may be helpful as further reading:

- Gearty, C. 'Democracy and Human Rights in the European Court of Human Rights: A Critical Appraisal' 51(3) *Northern Ireland Legal Quarterly* 381–396.
- Harvey, P. 'Militant Democracy and the European Convention on Human Rights' (2004) 29(3) *European Law Review* 407–420.
- Mowbray, A. 'The Role of the European Court of Human Rights in the Promotion of Democracy' [1999] *Public Law* (Winter) 703–725.
- O'Connell, R. 'Towards a Stronger Conception of Democracy in the Strasbourg Convention' [2006] 3 *EHRLR* 281–293.

6.5 Proportionality

6.5.1 The idea of proportionality

In applying the text of the Convention to individual cases, the ECtHR seeks 'proportionality'. The basic question is whether or not the interference with an individual's rights in the case can be justified by the social good or gain to others that the interference aims at. This depends on a balancing assessment between, on the one hand, the importance of the human right in question and, on the other hand, the benefit that the interference is likely to achieve. The point has been made emphatically and continuously by the Court, from some of its earliest cases:

> the Court must determine whether a fair balance was struck between the demands of the general interest of the community and the requirements of the protection of the individual's fundamental rights . . . The search for this balance is inherent in the whole of the Convention.

> (*Sporrong and Lönnroth v Sweden* (1983) 5 EHRR 35, para 61)

The term 'proportionality' does not appear in the text of the Convention. It is a principle developed by the ECtHR for the purpose of interpreting and applying the Convention. It is a concept with a long history both in public international law and in some European national jurisdictions (German administrative law, for example), but not English common law.

Proportionality applies to all the Convention articles. For example, a balancing judgment of proportionality is needed in situations such as the following:

- whether restrictions on various freedoms guaranteed by Articles 8 to 11 ECHR are 'necessary in a democratic society' to achieve certain purposes,
- whether a use of lethal force by police or military was 'no more than absolutely necessary'. If so there will have been no violation of Article 2 ECHR (right to life),
- whether a deprivation of liberty is arbitrary or not (this judgment goes to the heart of Article 5 ECHR),
- whether 'treatment' of a person by the state meets a threshold of seriousness so that it is 'inhuman or degrading' and thus a violation of Article 3 ECHR.

6.5.2 Fair balance

What is or is not proportionate and a fair balance will depend on the facts of the case. A range of considerations, such as those listed in this section, have been taken into account by the ECtHR when determining proportionality.

State actions may be held disproportionate in situations including the following:

- Less restrictive alternatives. If there were alternative, less restrictive ways of achieving a legitimate purpose (see, for example, *Hentrich* v *France* (1994) 18 EHRR 440).

- Absolute rules. If rights were restricted by putting into effect an absolute rule, one which does not allow for the exercise of individual discretion (see, for example, *Hirst* v *United Kingdom* (2006) 42 EHRR 41).

- Inappropriate reasons. If the reasons given for an action by the state do not properly justify what is done (see, for example, *Stafford* v *United Kingdom* (2002) 35 EHRR 32).

- Flawed or inadequate procedural protections and safeguards. Whether or not qualifications or restrictions on rights and freedoms are proportionate may depend on whether there are reasonable procedural protections by which the legality of actions can be challenged or other safeguards by which the burden and effects of a restriction are minimised. These include rights of access to independent and impartial courts and fair trials. The nature of such protections can depend on the context and the justifications for the restriction (see, for example, *Klass* v *Germany* (1979–80) 2 EHRR 214).

- Maintaining the 'essence' of a right. In some circumstances the ECtHR will allow restrictions and qualifications of rights so long as the essence of the right is maintained: it must still be possible to exercise the right even though the restrictions and qualifications may make it harder or less effective in individual cases. Qualifications on the right to vote (Article 3 of the First Protocol) are examples (see Chapter 25).

cross reference
The impact of proportionality on the UK courts under the HRA is discussed in Chapter 4, section 4.6.

6.6   **Positive duties**

'Securing' Convention rights and freedoms places on the state parties both negative and positive duties.

6.6.1 **Negative duty**

A negative duty obliges a state not to do certain things. Examples of negative duties on states include not to torture people or subject them to inhuman treatment (Article 3); not to use deadly force intentionally, save in certain situations (Article 2); not to detain people other than in the circumstances laid down in Article 5; and not to restrict freedom of expression other than in the circumstances laid down in Article 10. The negative approach tends to dominate human rights thinking: the point of classical human rights is to protect individuals from oppressive and arbitrary actions by those in political power.

6.6.2 **Positive duties**

cross reference
See Chapter 8, section 8.3, for example.

A positive duty obliges a state to take the necessary steps to secure the Convention rights and freedoms. The point is that Convention rights and freedoms cannot be effectively secured unless such steps are taken. These 'positive duties' can involve significant expenditure of money, official time and resources.

Some Articles, by their very nature, require positive steps and expenditure. Under Article 6, for example, states have to establish a system of courts, judges, a regulated legal profession, etc. in order to satisfy even the most minimum requirements of a 'fair trial'; similarly securing the right to life under Article 2 requires states to have an effective criminal justice system with an organised police force, a prosecution service, a system of criminal courts and a prison service, and so on. Furthermore, none of that would be effective unless there was also a positive duty to investigate deaths.

Positive duties can also be owed to individuals. Thus if a state agency (e.g. the police) know of a specific threat to an individual's Convention rights, such as the right to life, there may be a positive obligation to take appropriate steps to protect that person.

cross reference
See Chapter 15, section 15.2.2 and Chapter 4, section 4.7.

Positive duties can also require states to alter private law, the law dealing with the relations between private persons (such as contract and tort in England and Wales). This duty is particularly relevant in respect of the right to respect for private and family life under Article 8.

Positive duties, particularly where implied, tend not to impose absolute obligations on states. Depending on the circumstances, and because states have limited resources and must decide their priorities, the burden on the state is only to do what is reasonable in the circumstances. Sometimes positive duties give rise to strict obligations, such as the duty to provide an effective investigation of deaths of prisoners and others who died under the control of the state.

Increasingly the ECtHR recognises that distinguishing positive from negative actions can be quite unreal. Rather the approach is to ask whether the position the applicant is in engages state responsibility under the Convention. If it does, the principles which govern the question whether the interference is compatible with the Convention are the same whether state responsibility is couched in negative or positive terms, or both:

> In both contexts regard must be had to the fair balance to be struck between the competing interests of the individual and of the community as a whole.

(*Broniowski* v *Poland* (2005) 40 EHRR 21, para 144, a case involving the right to possessions)

 # Summary

- A number of concepts pervade the Convention and are used by the ECtHR in interpreting the Convention (and so will be adopted by UK courts under the HRA).
- They are relevant to the way all the Articles are understood, either as interpretive devices (e.g. 'margin of appreciation') or as background values (e.g. 'democracy'). Their direct influence varies according to the Convention right in issue and the particular facts and circumstances of a case.

 # Questions

 For suggested approaches, please visit the Online Resource Centre.

1   How does 'proportionality' affect the way Convention rights and freedoms are applied?

2   How does the recognition of a 'margin of appreciation' affect the way Convention rights and freedoms are applied?

Further reading

Bingham, T. *The Rule of Law* (2010) London: Allen Lane.

Kavanaugh, K. 'Policing the Margins: Rights Protection and the European Court of Human Rights' [2006] 4 *EHRLR* 422–444

Lester, A., Pannick, D. and Herberg, J. (see Preface) Chapter 3

Rivers, J. 'Proportionality and Variable Intensity of Review' (2006) 65(1) *CLJ* 174–207

See also reading on 'Conception of democracy', Discussion Topic, section 6.4.3

Fredman, S. 'Human Rights Transformed: Positive Duties and Positive Rights' [2006] *Public Law* 498–520

Part 2

Substantive rights and their application in the United Kingdom

Ancillary rights

Chapter overview

- Important 'ancillary' rights in Part 1 of the Convention which affect the way the main rights are put into effect. These are:

    – Article 14 (discrimination),

    – Article 15 (derogation),

    – Article 17 (abuse of rights),

    – Article 16 (restraints on aliens), and

    – Article 18 (limiting restriction on rights).

Introduction

Part One of the European Convention on Human Rights (ECHR) includes the substantive Articles which secure the human rights to life: the prohibition on torture, the right to a fair trial, etc. Part One also contains a number of Articles which are ancillary in the sense that they do not in themselves establish any human rights but are relevant to the way the substantive Articles are put into effect. In particular, the rights in the Convention must be applied without discrimination (Article 14) and not in a way which allows a person to undermine the rights of others (Article 17). Article 15 allows states, when under threat, to suspend some of the substantive rights (Article 15).

7.1 Article 14

Article 14   Prohibition of discrimination

The enjoyment of the rights and freedoms set forth in this Convention shall be secured without discrimination on any ground such as sex, race, colour, language, religion, political or other opinion, national or social origin, association with a national minority, property, birth or other status.

7.1.1 Introduction

Article 14 is the anti-discrimination provision in the ECHR. As will be shown, its scope is limited: it only deals with discrimination in the way a state gives effect to its obligations under the Convention.

It needs, therefore, to be placed in the context of anti-discrimination law more generally. In its modern form this can be traced back, in the UK, to the Sex Discrimination Act 1975 and the Race Relations Acts from 1975. These sought to prohibit both direct discrimination (not justifiable) and indirect discrimination (which could be justified) on the grounds of sex and race in the contexts of employment and the provision of services. Since then there has been a great expansion. The coverage of the law has widened (e.g. to people with disabilities, or on the grounds of religion or sexual orientation), as has the context of legal enforcement (e.g. beyond employment and services to include education and other public services). Likewise concern with anti-discrimination (dealing with comparatively less favourable treatment) has been complemented with a more general concern with equality (e.g. ensuring the opportunity to participate on equal terms in employment). The European Community, now European Union, is, and has been, a major driving force behind this. UK law gives effect to Treaty provisions and, in particular, EU directives in this field.

The Equality Act 2010 is the major UK legislation dealing with anti-discrimination and the promotion of equality. It repeals most of the existing legislation (Acts of Parliament like the Sex Discrimination Act 1975 and Regulations like the Equality Act 2006 (Sexual Orientation) Regulations 2007) and restates them in a single Act. It also enacts new provisions which extend equality law in various ways.

- It stipulates age, disability, gender reassignment, marriage and civil partnership, pregnancy and maternity, race, religion or belief, sex and sexual orientation as 'protected characteristics' to which equality law applies.

- It defines different ways in which it is unlawful to treat someone unequally—by discriminating against them (treating them less favourably, this can be done directly or indirectly), harassing or victimising them, or failing to make, in respect of a person with a disability, a reasonable adjustment.

- It defines the areas in which such prohibitions, differently, apply (e.g. in employment, the provision of goods and services, in schools and in private associations);

- It extends the law in various ways such as by stipulating situations in which equality must be promoted. Of particular importance is the duty, in Part 11, on public authorities and those exercising public functions, to have 'due regard' to the need to eliminate discrimination and advance equality of opportunity and in other ways to seek to overcome disadvantage suffered by persons who share a protected characteristic.

- It defines the circumstances in which positive action may, lawfully, be taken to eliminate disadvantages or recognise different needs of those who share a protected characteristic (i.e. where that might otherwise be discrimination against those who do not share the protected characteristic).

- It deals with enforcement of these provisions, mainly, though not exclusively, in an Employment Tribunal or County Court.

There are other provisions which deal with equality and discrimination in various ways. It is a massive and highly complex piece of legislation and it is outside the scope of this book to deal with it in any detail. It is subject to any directly effective EU rights enjoyed by individuals and, like any UK legislation, must, under the Human Rights Act 1998 (HRA), be interpreted compatibly with Convention rights.

The Equality Act 2006 created and empowered the Equality and Human Rights Commission. This took over the roles of the Equal Opportunities Commission and the Commission for Racial Equality. Its job is to promote anti-discrimination, equality and human rights in various ways.

further study

On the Equality Act 2010 see Wadham, J. (ed) et al *Blackstones Guide to the Equality Act 2010* 2nd edn (2012) Oxford: OUP.

On the Equality and Human Rights Commission see http://www.equalityhumanrights.com

7.1.2 **Article 14: general principles**

The general principles of Article 14 were laid down by the ECtHR in the so-called '*Belgian Linguistics*' case.

case close-up

Case Relating to Certain Aspects of the Laws on the Use of Languages in Education in Belgium (Belgian Linguistics Case (No 2)) (1979–80) 1 EHRR 252

Under Belgian education laws, the language of publicly funded education provision depended on the dominant language of the area. French-speaking parents, some living in Dutch-speaking areas and some in an area where no language predominated, challenged these laws because they meant that their children would not be taught in French. The case was argued on the basis of language discrimination in the way the right to education (in Article 2 of the First Protocol) was put into effect. The European Court of Human Rights (ECtHR) (in this important early case) upheld the laws regarding their impact on the predominantly Dutch-speaking areas but, in the case of an area where no language predominated, held that there was a breach.

The principles discussed in the next section derive from the ECtHR's reasoning in this case.

7.1.3 Article 14 relates solely to the 'rights and freedoms set forth in this Convention'

Article 14 applies only to discrimination in the way Convention rights and freedoms are secured. For this reason there cannot be a violation of Article 14 in isolation. Any alleged violation must be of Article 14, linked to one of the other Articles. In the case law of the Court, Article 14 tends to play a subordinate role and normally will only be considered separately if 'a clear inequality of treatment in the enjoyment of the right in question is a fundamental aspect of the case' (*Chassagnou* v *France* (2000) 29 EHRR 615, para 89).

KEY POINTS

- Article 14 can be compared with Protocol 12 ECHR, which prohibits discrimination in respect of 'any right set forth in law'. The Protocol came into force on 1 April 2005 but the United Kingdom is not a signatory.

- The EU Charter of Fundamental Rights also has an unqualified anti-discrimination provision (Article 21)—see Chapter 3, section 3.4.

7.1.4 No need for a breach of the linked Article

It is not, however, necessary for there to have been a breach of the substantive Article to which Article 14 is linked. What is necessary is that the discriminatory actions must have fallen 'within the ambit' of one of the Convention rights. It must relate to a matter that is covered by a substantive Article (be 'linked to the exercise of a right guaranteed' by the Convention). So, even if there is no breach of the substantive Article, there can still be a breach of Article 14.

The Convention

In *Abdulaziz, Cabales and Balkandali* v *United Kingdom* (1985) 7 EHRR 471, the ECtHR held that part of British immigration law was in breach of Article 14. Women were treated less favourably than men on the issue of the rights of spouses to enter the country. This touched on Article 8 ECHR (right to family life). There was no breach of Article 8 since the United Kingdom was entitled to regulate immigration. Only Article 14 was violated; but Article 14 was only in issue because the matter related to Article 8.

A matter can be within the ambit of a Convention right even if it is the provision of a service by the state that it has no Convention duty to provide. Examples given in *Belgian Linguistics* were the provision of a particular kind of educational provision (e.g. grammar schools) and a system of appeal courts (not required by Article 6). If states do choose to provide such services, Article 14 can still be violated if they are provided in a discriminatory way.

In *Stec* v *United Kingdom* (2006) 43 EHRR 47, a Grand Chamber held that although the Convention does not require states to provide welfare payments and pensions, if they are provided, they are 'possessions' within the ambit of Article 1 of the First Protocol and Article 14 means they must be provided without discrimination.

The HRA

In giving effect to anti-discrimination for UK law under the HRA, the House of Lords has expressed concern at the uncertainty of the scope of Article 14.

M v Secretary of State for Work and Pensions [2006] UKHL 11

M lived in a homosexual relationship with another woman. She was separated from her husband. Her children were looked after by her husband. Her contributions to the maintenance of her children under the Child Support Act 1991 were greater than they would have been had she been living in a heterosexual relationship. The House of Lords rejected the argument that there was a violation of Article 14 linked to Article 8.

The House of Lords held that 'ambit' was a very loose expression. For Article 14 to be engaged, there has to be something more than a tenuous (weak) link. The difference in treatment must be such as to undermine the core, underlying values inherent in the article in issue (here Article 8). Here the difference in treatment meant that M was financially worse off but it did not affect her ability to have and enjoy a family life.

7.1.5 What is 'discrimination': objective and reasonable justification

The Convention

As *Belgian Linguistics* made clear, Article 14 is not violated if a state can show that treating someone differently for a reason based on their sex, race, nationality, etc. is a legitimate way of solving a particular problem or of correcting 'factual inequalities' between groups. In *DH v Czech Republic* (2008) 47 EHRR 3, a Grand Chamber summarised the core meaning of discrimination in Article 14: 'discrimination means treating differently, without an objective and reasonable justification, persons in relevantly similar situations' (para 175).

All forms of different treatment are in principle capable of justification. In some situations, indeed, a state may be under a positive duty to treat people differently on 'status' grounds where this is necessary to correct an unjust inequality.

In *Thlimmenos v Greece* (2001) 31 EHRR 15, the ECtHR held that the failure of Greek law to distinguish between convicted conscientious objectors and ordinary criminals when it came to the rules governing entrance to the professions, violated Article 14 linked to Article 9 (freedom of thought, conscience and religion).

The existence of an 'objective and reasonable justification' depends upon two factors:

- Does the difference in treatment have a legitimate aim?
- Is there a relationship of proportionality between the aim and the discriminatory means used?

Intensity of justification

The depth and degree of justification depends upon the nature of the issue. In its case law the ECtHR has indicated that whilst some differences in treatment may only require a rational explanation, other differences in treatment require enhanced, 'very weighty' justification. In *AL (Serbia)* v *Secretary of State for the Home Department* [2008] UKHL 42, Baroness Hale identified differences based on the following characteristics as requiring, according to Strasbourg, such increased justification:

- race, colour or ethnic origin (*DH* v *Czech* (2008) 47 EHRR 3, Grand Chamber, para 196);
- sex (*Abdulaziz*, para 78);
- sexual orientation (*EB* v *France* App 43546/02, para 91);
- birth or adopted status (*Inze* v *Austria* (1987) 10 EHRR 394);
- nationality (*Gaygusuz* v *Austria* (1996) 23 EHRR 364).

Partly these reflect grounds of long-standing historical subordination and contempt which human rights law must seek to overcome. But the Strasbourg jurisprudence seems to go further. Weighty justification is required for differences in treatment based upon 'personal characteristics of an individual which he cannot or should not be asked to change' (*AL (Serbia)*, para 31).

On the other hand, differences in treatment which relate to measures of 'economic or social strategy' (involving social and economic policies whose impact may depend on a person's status) require a less demanding scrutiny by the Court. A rational justification (that the means used are likely to achieve a legitimate purpose) is likely to be accepted: Strasbourg allows a wide margin of appreciation.

case close-up

Stec v *United Kingdom* (2006) 43 EHRR 47, Grand Chamber

A number of applicants, some men, some women, received welfare benefits that were lower than would have been received by the opposite sex. The underlying reason for all the claims was the difference in the retirement age between men and women at the relevant time. A Grand Chamber dealt with the case by applying Article 14 linked to Article 1 of the First Protocol. It held that there was no violation of Article 14 because there was an objective and reasonable justification for the different pension age enjoyed by men and women.

It was held (para 66) that

- at the time it was introduced a difference in pension age had an objective and reasonable justification which recognised the 'traditional' economically inactive role of women which the pension system sought to compensate for;
- the economic role of women has, of course, changed greatly over the years. At some point the justification for differential pension ages no longer applied (indeed they have been held to be incompatible with EU law) and change was necessary. States, however, have a wide margin of appreciation over the pace and nature of that change, which the United Kingdom had not exceeded.

The HRA

In adopting the need for objective and reasonable justification for differences in treatment into UK law, the House of Lords/Supreme Court has recognised the distinction, made earlier in this section, between differences based on social policy and those requiring more intense scrutiny. In *AI (Serbia)*, Baroness Hale summarised Article 14 (see paras 20–29). She noted that Article 14 focuses on justification for differences in treatment and, unlike domestic anti-discrimination law, is less concerned with the precise identification of some other group or individual for comparison; though the argument for discrimination is often supported by the identification of a general comparator.

R (Carson) (Reynolds) v Secretary of State for Work and Pensions [2005] UKHL 37

C objected to the fact that, as an overseas resident, she was not entitled to cost of living increases to her pension. S objected to the fact that the job seekers' allowance was lower for persons under 25 years old. The House of Lords applied Article 14 linked to Article 1 of the First Protocol and held that the differences in treatment were justified. Differences in the impact of social policy based on residence or age did not require close scrutiny by the courts.

It was important for their Lordships to ensure that Article 14 embodies something more than just an objection to differences in treatment. The point of Article 14 is to uphold (in Lord Hoffmann's words) the 'Enlightenment value that every human being is entitled to equal respect and to be treated as an end and not a means' (para 15). Article 14 requires that differences in treatment that offend our sense of equal respect must be justified by the state and the justification subjected to intense scrutiny by the courts. *AL (Serbia)*, mentioned earlier, clarifies the issue by focusing the court's attention on differences of treatment based on personal characteristics and lessening the parallel drawn in *Carson* with the so-called 'suspect classifications' based on historical subordination. In *Humphreys v HM Revenue and Customs* [2012] UKSC 18 following *Stec* (see section 7.1.5), the Supreme Court accepted that justifications even for differences based on personal characteristics (such as, in the case, sex) could be subject to the less intense degree of scrutiny in respect of state benefits.

In *A v Secretary of State for the Home Department* [2004] UKHL 56, the House of Lords had no difficulty in finding incompatibility with Article 14 linked to Article 5. Foreign-born terrorist suspects were deprived of their liberty whilst suspects who were UK nationals were not. The matter was subjected to intense review.

7.1.6 **The victims of discrimination: 'status'**

Unlike many anti-discrimination provisions found in national and international law, Article 14 is not restricted to a specific range of types of victim. The given list includes many of the main victim groups whose suffering of discrimination has disfigured European history in the twentieth century and beyond. But the term 'or other status' means that the list is not closed. Other forms of discrimination that have only affected the public conscience after the Convention came into effect or which reflect new ways of living, can be included. Sexual orientation is an obvious example (see *Salgueiro da Silva Mouta v Portugal* (2001) 31 EHRR 47, para 28).

In *Kjeldsen v Denmark* (1979–80) 1 EHRR 711, the ECtHR sought to limit 'other status' to a personal characteristic. In *Clift v UK* App 7205/07, judgment of 13 July 2010, the Court made it clear that this term is to be given a broad and inclusive meaning that was not necessarily *ejusdem generis* the list in Article 14 and not confined to characteristics which are innate or inherent (paras 54–59). In the case, it held that differences in the treatment of long-term prisoners was a difference based on status.

Examples of matters accepted as going to status for the purposes of Article 14 by UK courts include

- being a resident in a foreign country: *Carson* (see section 7.1.5),
- being an unmarried couple treated differently from a married couple in the context of adoption law: *Re G (Adoption: Unmarried Couple)* [2008] UKHL 38,

- being homeless and therefore denied benefits available to others (*R (RJM)* v *Secretary of State for Work and Pensions* [2008] UKHL 63 (their Lordships rejected the view that if a state of affairs had been voluntarily chosen it was less likely to be a personal characteristic, para 47)).

An example of a characteristic which was not accepted:

- being innocent but involved in a criminal investigation and, in respect of the retention of DNA samples taken, treated differently from those not so involved: *R (Marper)* v *Chief Constable of South Yorkshire* [2004] UKHL 39.

For the future, the issue of discrimination based on caste may come into question. Caste, for instance, is not one of the 'protected characteristics' on which the Equality Act 2010 is based, so a human rights case may be appropriate.

7.1.7 The Human Rights Act and Article 14

The UK courts have moved away from an over-structured approach (found in *Wandsworth London BC* v *Michalak* [2002] EWCA Civ 271) to Article 14 issues and the issues for UK courts may be summarised as follows:

- Is the alleged discrimination within the ambit of a Convention right? This means does it undermine the core values inherent in the right?
- Is the status of those disadvantaged by the differences in treatment listed in Article 14? If not it must be based on a personal characteristic.
- The essential question is whether the reasons for the difference in treatment can withstand scrutiny by the court. If there is a 'suspect classification' then the scrutiny will be intense. At the heart of Article 14 are differences in treatment indicating lack of respect. The state must prove that the restriction is a proportionate way of meeting a legitimate purpose.

7.2 Article 15

Article 15   Derogation in time of emergency

(1) In time of war or other public emergency threatening the life of the nation any High Contracting Party may take measures derogating from its obligations under this Convention to the extent strictly required by the exigencies of the situation, provided that such measures are not inconsistent with its other obligations under international law.

(2) No derogation from Article 2, except in respect of deaths resulting from lawful acts of war, or from Articles 3, 4 (paragraph 1) and 7 shall be made under this paragraph.

(3) Any High Contracting Party availing itself of this right of derogation shall keep the Secretary General of the Council of Europe fully informed of the measures which it has taken and the reasons therefore. It shall also inform the Secretary General of the Council of Europe when such measures have ceased to operate and the provisions of the Convention are again being fully executed.

7.2.1 Derogation

States can be faced with political movements who believe the end justifies the means and who are prepared to use violence, including the kind of violence aimed at civilians that, today, we call 'terrorism'. Because such movements are likely to hold the existing laws in contempt and because they are intentionally and deliberately seeking to undermine the established order, states can feel vulnerable and in need of special powers. These are powers that make it easier for the police and security services to operate—to do things like enter property and search it, arrest and detain suspects, ban organisations, make it easier to secure convictions, and so on.

Such powers are likely to be incompatible with some of the rights and freedoms in the Convention. Article 15, therefore, allows states to 'derogate' from (or suspend) most, though not all, of the articles. For example, suspending the operation of all or parts of Article 5 (the right to liberty), a state may detain people on suspicion, without their being suspected, or convicted, of a criminal offence and without full judicial supervision of the grounds on which they are detained (as happened in the United Kingdom between 2002 and 2005).

Derogation is, of course, highly controversial. It means that at precisely the time when suspects need greatest protection of their basic rights, that protection is removed. The alternative to derogation is the position that tends to be adopted by international bodies such as the Council of Europe (e.g. in various documents it has produced in the context of anti-terrorism laws). This position recognises that states may need to deal with genuine threats by the use of special measures but that such special measures should be compatible with Convention rights. Convention rights are not inflexible. Their application usually involves seeking a 'fair balance' between the rights of individuals and the legitimate requirements of society. They can then be given effect in ways that recognise the problems faced by states dealing with terrorism, insurrection, etc. The need is to ensure that the minimum, or the 'essence' of the right is preserved.

7.2.2 Derogations and the HRA

Under the HRA, Convention rights are to take effect subject to any derogations made by the United Kingdom (section 1(2): see Chapter 4, section 4.2.4).

7.2.3 Main points of Article 15

Article 15 allows derogation

- only if there is a 'war or other emergency facing the life of the nation';
- only if the measures which require derogation are strictly necessary to deal with the emergency and are not more extensive than is necessary for that purpose;
- where the measures taken are not incompatible with other international obligations;
- where the Council of Europe, through its Secretary General, is informed of the measures taken and why they are necessary, and is told when the measures are no longer in effect and the derogation is ended.

7.2.4 **Limits to derogation**

States cannot derogate from the following Articles:

- Article 2, the right to life. The claim that there is an emergency cannot be used to allow a loosening of the rules regarding the use of deadly force. Even at such a time, the use of deadly force by the police etc. needs to be justified under the terms of Article 2(2) (e.g. that the force is 'strictly necessary' to quell a riot or insurrection). There is an exception: Article 2 can be disregarded in the context of 'lawful war'. The war needs to be 'lawful' (today this probably means that it is sanctioned in some way by the United Nations). Furthermore, the measures taken need to be compatible with other international obligations, and so any actions must be compatible with the Geneva Convention and other international 'laws of war'.

- Article 3, the prohibition of torture. The existence of a war or emergency does not provide justification for the use of torture or inhuman or degrading treatment or punishment. The ban on torture etc. is 'absolute' in the sense that it must not be done no matter how strong the justification in any particular instance. The likelihood of saving the lives of others is not a factor that can be weighed against the prohibition on torture.

- Article 4(1), prohibition of slavery and forced labour. The necessities of war or public emergency cannot justify the enslavement of captives or a population. The ban on forced or compulsory labour in Article 4(2) can, however, be suspended under Article 15. It should be noted that military service is not considered as forced or compulsory labour.

- Article 7, no punishment without law. The criminal law cannot be changed and used retrospectively against those alleged to be involved in war, insurrection, terrorism, etc. It should be noted that nothing in Article 7 prevents the prosecution and conviction of people for war crimes and crimes against humanity.

7.2.5 **'War or other public emergency facing the life of the nation'**

There can be no derogation unless there is a 'war or other public emergency facing the life of the nation'. This means that there is

> an exceptional situation of crisis or emergency which affects the whole population and constitutes a threat to the organised life of the community of which the State is composed.
>
> (*Lawless v Ireland No 3* (1979–80) 1 EHRR 15, para 28)

In the *Greek Case* (1969) 12 YB 1, the Court identified the following characteristics of a public emergency:

> (1) It must be actual or imminent. (2) Its effects must involve the whole nation. (3) The continuance of the organised life of the community must be threatened. (4) The crisis or danger must be exceptional, in that the normal measures or restrictions, permitted by the Convention for the maintenance of public safety, health and order, are plainly inadequate.

The ECtHR allows states a wide margin of appreciation on the question of the existence of the threat. The IRA campaign against the British in Northern Ireland was recognised as such an emergency (see *Lawless v Ireland* and, for the period 1968–98, *Brannigan and McBride v United Kingdom* (1994) 17 EHRR 539); similarly the Kurdish insurrection against Turkey in the late twentieth century (*Aksoy v Turkey* (1997) 23 EHRR 553).

The HRA

Article 15 was given full consideration by the House of Lords in a landmark case involving the detention, without conviction, of a number of foreign terrorist suspects.

case close-up

A v Secretary of State for the Home Department [2004] UKHL 56

Part IV of the Anti-terrorism, Crime and Security Act 2001, enacted in the aftermath of the '9/11' attacks in New York and Washington, allowed the Home Secretary to certify a foreigner (someone without permanent rights of residence in the United Kingdom) as a terrorist suspect. Normally such a person would be deported. Article 3 of the Convention prohibits deportation if there are grounds for thinking that the person would be tortured or treated inhumanely in the country to which he or she is deported. Article 3 cannot be derogated from. Rather than release terrorist suspects, the government decided that they should be detained in prison, and some were sent to Belmarsh Prison, a maximum security prison in London. Detention for this reason involves a breach of Article 5. Article 5, however, can be derogated from. This the British government did, using Article 15. The grounds of the derogation were challenged by the detainees. The House of Lords held that the derogation was not 'strictly necessary' and so it was not lawful. In particular, it involved discrimination against foreigners in breach of Article 14. Therefore the detentions were incompatible with Article 5. The derogation was quashed (cancelled) and a 'declaration of incompatibility' under the HRA was made in respect of Articles 5 and 14. The detainees were released about three months later and made subject to **control orders**. Part IV was repealed.

153

'control orders'

These were restraints on personal freedom imposed on unconvicted terrorist suspects under the Prevention of Terrorism Act 2005. The Act has been repealed and the orders replaced by 'terrorism prevention and investigation measures' (see Chapter 26, sections 26.3.6 and 26.7.2).

cross reference

Declarations of incompatibility and their effects are explained in Chapter 4, section 4.4.3.

On the issue of the existence of a threat (international jihadist terrorism), Lord Bingham applied the *Greek Case* criteria but, with the majority of Law Lords, he accepted that the courts could not easily interfere with the government's assessment of the risk. Deference to the government by UK courts (see Chapter 4, section 4.6.2) mirrors the margin of appreciation states have under the Convention.

Lord Hoffmann's dissent

In the *Belmarsh* case, Lord Hoffmann dissented on the issue of the existence of a public emergency. In an eloquent passage (paras 91–96) he argued that a 'public emergency facing the life of the nation' must involve a threat to the democratic institutions and way of life of the country. Jihadist terrorism of the twenty-first century might lead to a significant number of deaths but does not threaten the life of the nation or its institutions (though an over-reaction by government might begin to do just that).

> I do not underestimate the ability of fanatical groups of terrorists to kill and destroy, but they do not threaten the life of the nation. Whether we would survive Hitler hung in the balance, but there is no doubt that we shall survive Al-Qa'ida. (para 96)

7.2.6 'to the extent strictly required by the exigencies of the situation'

Though a wide margin of appreciation is left to the states on the issue of the existence of an emergency, the question whether the measures taken, measures which require derogation, are 'strictly required' is treated differently. Article 15 requires that these measures are no more than what is strictly required to deal with the emergency. Any derogation is incompatible with Article 15 in so far as it purports to authorise measures which are not needed or which are not reasonable means of dealing with the emergency. On this issue the states still have a margin of appreciation but that must be subject, first, to effective supervision by national bodies (e.g. individuals must be able to test the legality of the way they are applied in the national courts) and second, to supervision by the ECtHR (see *Aksoy* v *Turkey* (1997) 23 EHRR 553 para 68).

In *Aksoy* v *Turkey* (1997) 23 EHRR 553 the ECtHR stressed the need for proper procedures. The detention of an individual, in that case for 14 days, without access to lawyers or courts, was disproportionate, even in the circumstances of deadly terrorism, and so was not covered by any purported derogation. In *A* (see section 7.2.5) the House of Lords found that the measures were more than 'strictly required' because they treated dangerous foreign terrorist suspects (subject to detention without trial) differently from equally dangerous British nationals (who were not subjected to control). The government's justifications for this difference in treatment (based on immigration law) were not accepted by the court. Since it was not necessary to detain British nationals, there was no reason for detaining equally dangerous foreigners and so the derogation did more than was necessary.

7.2.7 International law

The derogation must be compatible with international law. It must not authorise behaviour which is inconsistent with other international obligations of a state. United Nations conventions against discrimination on sexual or racial grounds, for example, must be adhered to; likewise the International Covenant on Civil and Political Rights whose provisions are similar to the European Convention. Like the Convention, Article 4 of the Covenant allows derogation on similar terms to Article 15 supplemented by the Siracusa Principles of 1984.

7.2.8 Information

The Council of Europe must be kept informed by the state seeking to derogate of the measures being taken which are incompatible with the Convention and the reasons which explain and justify them. Although not expressly in Article 15, it seems that some form of announcement or proclamation of the existence of an emergency may be necessary.

7.3 Article 17

Article 17   Prohibition of abuse of rights

Nothing in this Convention may be interpreted as implying for any State, group or person any right to engage in any activity or perform any act aimed at the destruction of any of the rights and freedoms set forth herein or at their limitation to a greater extent than is provided for in the Convention.

Article 17 expresses the great dilemma of a liberal society. A liberal society is one in which pluralism, tolerance and political freedom are fundamental values. How can such a society defend itself against intolerance and various types of political extremism without, at the same time, fatally undermining these values?

The need for a provision such as Article 17 seemed very clear to the drafters of the Convention. It underscored the point that one of the Convention's main purposes was (and is) to prevent totalitarianism ever again scarring Europe's governments and politics.

From its inception the ECtHR has had to deal with cases in which states have taken steps to ban or restrict political parties or individuals. For example:

- bans after the Second World War of Nazi and fascist parties and their successors: the ban on successors to Mussolini's fascist party in Italy was upheld (on the basis of Articles 10(2) and 11(2)) in *X* v *Italy* (1976) DR 5, 83;

- bans, during the 'Cold War', on Communist parties, on the grounds that they sought to impose dictatorship (see *German Communist Party (KPD)* v *Germany* (1957) App 250/57, 1 YB 222). There were also bans on individual communists working in the public sector, which the Court upheld in *Glasenapp* v *Germany* (1987) 9 EHRR 25, but then took a more tolerant position in later cases such as *Vogt* v *Germany* (1996) 21 EHRR 205 (both cases were decided on the basis of Article 10(2) rather than Article 17).

In fact (as these examples indicate) Article 17 has been little used. Usually cases can be dealt with under Article 11 (freedom of association), Article 10 (freedom of expression) or Article 3 of Protocol 1 (free elections). These three Articles allow proportionate restrictions on political freedom which are normally sufficient for the effective protection of political democracy.

The HRA

Under the HRA, UK courts must read the Convention rights in the light of Article 17 (see Chapter 4, section 4.2.1). In cases where it has arisen, the attitude of UK courts is that Article 17 adds little to what is already allowed by Article 10 etc. (see, for example, the Scottish case of *Whaley* v *Lord Advocate* 2004 SC 78, paras 46–47.

General principles

A Grand Chamber of the ECtHR affirmed the following principles as regards Article 17 in *Zdanoka* v *Latvia* (paras 98–101). They represent what has been called 'militant democracy'.

case close-up

Zdanoka v Latvia (2007) 45 EHRR 17, Grand Chamber
. . . .
Latvia obtained independence from the Soviet Union in 1991. Just before, there was (it was alleged) an unsuccessful, pro-Soviet, attempted *coup d'etat*. Latvian election law banned ex-communists and pro-Soviet sympathisers who may have been implicated in the coup, from standing for the independent Latvian Parliament. Z was banned under this provision. The party she would have sat for won 19% of the vote and had 25% of the seats. The ECtHR (a Grand Chamber reversing the previous Chamber decision) held that there had not been a violation of Article 3 of the First Protocol (which includes a right to stand in elections for the legislature).

- Democracy is the only political system acceptable to the Convention.

- The danger that individuals, groups or parties may seek to use their Convention rights in order to undermine the rights of others cannot be ruled out and Article 17 is designed to deal with this: the Convention concept of democracy is one that is 'capable of defending itself'.

- There are two aspects to the protection of Article 17:

  – protecting the Convention rights of others, but also

  – protecting 'the ideals and values of a democratic society'.

- The state is entitled to take special measures in order to safeguard its democratic values. In the context of genuine threats to a democratic society individuals may have to accept restraints on their political or other freedoms in order to uphold common interest in effective democracy.

- A proper balance will need to be achieved between such restraints and the social good. Restrictions on political freedom in the name of the greater good need the most careful evaluation (which is ultimately under the supervision of the ECtHR).

- Pre-emption: a state is entitled to take pre-emptive measures to prevent an established threat to democratic institutions from occurring. Subject to rigorous European supervision, a state may 'reasonably forestall the execution of such a policy which is incompatible with the Convention's provisions, before an attempt is made to implement it through concrete steps that might prejudice civil peace and the country's democratic regime'.

Current issues

Early twenty-first-century issues which involve the defence of democracy include:

- Racist political parties. In *Glimmerveen and Hagenbeek* v *The Netherlands* (1982) 4 EHRR 260, the Commission applied Article 17 in accepting that a ban on racist politicians from standing in an election did not violate the Convention. The applicants would have used their candidatures to propagate racist views.

- Holocaust denial. In *Garaudy* v *France* App 65831/01, admissibility decision of 24 June 2003, the ECtHR said that the denial of clearly established political facts, specifically denial that the Holocaust occurred, would be speech which, because of Article 17, would not be protected by the right to freedom of speech in Article 10 (see also *Lehideux* v *France* (2000) 30 EHRR 665).

- The 'emerging democracies' of eastern Europe and issues about the continuing political activities of those associated with the displaced Communist regime of the past (as in *Zdanoka*, mentioned earlier).

cross reference
Refah Partisi v Turkey is fully discussed in Chapter 18, section 18.7.2.

Applying the general idea behind Article 17, militant democracy, the idea of democracy defending itself by measures which are, on their face, undemocratic, is fraught with danger. For this reason, as suggested earlier, the ECtHR prefers analysing a restraint on political freedom by exploring its justification in terms of the more specific and particular language of the second paragraphs of Articles 10 and 11. Because this expressly requires the Court to address directly issues of legality, purpose and proportionality, it is, it seems, preferred to applying the more general words in Article 17. An example is the important case, *Refah Partisi v Turkey* (2003) 37 EHRR 1 (which involves the tension between Islamic Sharia law and the Convention concept of a democratic society), the Grand Chamber upheld a ban by the Turkish state of an Islamist party which was the elected, majority party in the Turkish Parliament and the party which was likely to form the next government. The party intended to impose Sharia law (Islamic private law), important elements of which would be incompatible with the Convention.

Two issues about Article 17 are particularly important:

First, the underpinning values of the Convention, particularly 'democracy', are open-textured and uncertain. In particular there is no clear and uncontested conception of democracy available. There is a danger, therefore, that Article 17 allows the suppression of political views on the grounds of being undemocratic when, in fact, they are simply inconsistent with one conception of democracy but consistent with another. A communist, for example, could perhaps argue that the dominant form of democracy in Western capitalist countries is no more than, in effect, rule by global corporations; and that communism gives hope of a more participative form of politics based on advancing the interests of the working class.

Second, Article 17 also raises the danger that states can silence their more radical critics simply by labelling them anti-democratic. This is, for example, an allegation made in respect of the *Refah Partisi* case, where some critics claimed there was no real evidence of anti-democratic intentions by the Islamist party.

7.4 Article 18

Article 18   Limitation on use of restrictions on rights

The restrictions permitted under this Convention to the said rights and freedoms shall not be applied for any purpose other than those for which they have been prescribed.

Many of the Convention articles permit limits, qualifications and restrictions on an individual's freedom. The point of Article 18 is to ensure that rights and freedoms are only restricted for the purposes allowed for in the Articles and not for other purposes that the state may consider important. Article 18 reinforces the other, substantive Articles. Like Article 14 it requires a link to the other Article to be established, but, also like Article 14, there does not need to be a breach of that other Article for there to be a breach of Article 18. Article 18 is not widely used (although see *Gusinskiy* v *Russia* App 70276/01, judgment of 19 May 2004, para 73).

7.5 Article 16

Article 16   Restrictions on political activity of aliens

Nothing in Articles 10, 11 and 14 shall be regarded as preventing the High Contracting Parties from imposing restrictions on the political activity of aliens.

Article 16 is an anomaly whose continued presence in the Convention is widely criticised. It allows restrictions on the political freedom of aliens (foreigners) and, as such, is at odds with Article 1 of the Convention, which insists that the rights and freedoms in it are to be secured for 'everyone' (not just citizens); and it seems to contradict Article 14, which requires that the Convention Articles should be applied to everyone without discrimination on various grounds including 'national...origin'. In the few cases in which the Article has been considered, both the ECtHR and UK courts have avoided basing their judgments on Article 16 (see *Piermont* v *France* (1995) 20 EHRR 301 and *R (Farrakhan)* v *Secretary of State for the Home Department* [2002] EWCA Civ 606).

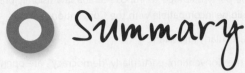

Summary

- Article 14 prohibits discrimination in the way Convention rights and freedoms are secured. Differences in treatment can be justified if there is an objective and reasonable justification but intense scrutiny is required of certain suspect classifications such as race and sex.

- Article 15 allows states to derogate from their responsibilities under the Convention in times of 'war or other public emergency facing the life of the nation'. Any derogation must only be to the extent strictly required by the emergency (a matter over which courts have an important scrutinising role). Some Convention rights cannot be derogated from.

- Article 16 allows states to restrict the political activities of aliens. It is incompatible with the spirit of the Convention and is little used.

- Article 17 authorises the ECtHR and national courts to refuse to uphold the rights of those, like racists, who would use their rights to undermine the rights of others. It does not mean that such people have no Convention rights at all.

- Article 18 insists that rights and freedoms in the Convention can be restricted and qualified but only for the purposes allowed by the Convention.

Questions

 For suggested approaches, please visit the Online Resource Centre.

1   Is it possible, compatibly with the Convention, to have laws which restrict the political activities of groups and individuals whose aim is to impose an authoritarian government on a country?

2   Proposals are made under which only women candidates can be chosen for at least half of the seats contested by a political party. Men candidates will be barred. Men who lose out complain that they have been discriminated against in respect of their rights to stand for election found in Article 3 of the First Protocol. How would a court deal with this issue under Article 14?

Further reading

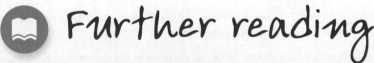

Amos, M. (see Preface) Chapter 15

Lester, A, Pannick, D. and Herberg, J. (see Preface) Chapter 4, Articles 14–18

ON ARTICLE 14

Baker, A. 'The Enjoyment of Rights and Freedoms: A New Conception of the "Ambit" under Article 14 ECHR' (2006) 69(5) *Modern Law Review* 714–737.

Article 2: right to life

Article 2   Right to Life

(1) Everyone's right to life shall be protected by law. No one shall be deprived of his life intentionally save in the execution of a sentence of a court following his conviction of a crime for which the penalty is provided by law.

(2) Deprivation of life shall not be regarded as inflicted in contravention of this Article when it results from the use of force which is no more than absolutely necessary

(a) in defence of any person from unlawful violence;

(b) in order to effect a lawful arrest or to prevent the escape of a person lawfully detained;

(c) in action lawfully taken for the purpose of quelling a riot or insurrection.

Introduction

Article 2(1) imposes a general duty on the state to protect 'everyone's right to life'. The right to have the death penalty is retained in Article 2, although it has now been made unlawful under the European Convention on Human Rights (ECHR), for all purposes including in time of war, by Protocol 13. Article 2(2) describes the only purposes for which failures to protect life, including where there are deaths resulting from the intentional use of force, can be lawfully justified. Under Article 2(2) force can only be used for these purposes so long as the amount used is 'no more than absolutely necessary' and, in all the circumstances, meets the test of proportionality.

The right to life is morally fundamental. Respect for life is the condition, the basic presumption, of moral thinking and belief—without respect for life the idea of individual human autonomy and dignity is meaningless. Article 2 does not establish the right to life but imposes on states the duty to protect life. It makes specific what non-totalitarian political theories require: that the first duty on states is to protect the physical security of all those within their jurisdiction. A government that fails to protect the lives of its citizens has no justification and so no authority over the citizens.

The need to respect life is fully recognised in the common law. In *Airedale NHS Trust* v *Bland* [1993] AC 789 (concerning whether the law would allow the switching off of life support to a young man in a 'persistent vegetative state') Lord Hoffmann said: 'We have a strong feeling that there is an intrinsic value in human life, irrespective of whether it is valuable to the person concerned or indeed to anyone else', a feeling shared equally by 'those who adhere to religious faiths' and 'those without any religious belief' (p 826).

Legal protection for 'life' is also common to international human rights instruments. Article 6 of the International Covenant on Civil and Political Rights establishes the right to life, as well as requiring its legal protection:

Every human being has the inherent right to life. This right shall be protected by law. No one shall be arbitrarily deprived of his life.

General principles

In interpreting and applying Article 2, the European Court of Human Rights (ECtHR) has identified and developed a number of general principles to which the domestic laws of signatory states must adhere.

- **A fundamental duty.** Securing the right to life is a fundamental, primary duty on states. It enshrines one of the basic values of a democratic society. It cannot be derogated from under Article 15 (except in times of lawful war) and it applies 'absolutely' in the sense that the terms of Article 2 do not permit a balancing with the public interest.

  > It must also be borne in mind that, as a provision which not only safeguards the right to life but sets out the circumstances when the deprivation of life may be justified, Article 2 ranks as one of the most fundamental provisions in the Convention—indeed one which, in peacetime, admits of no derogation under Article 15. Together with Article 3 of the Convention, it also enshrines one of the basic values of the democratic societies making up the Council of Europe.
  >
  > (*McCann v United Kingdom* (1996) 21 EHRR 97, para 147)

- **Effectiveness.** Article 2 must be interpreted and applied by the courts to ensure that its safeguards are made practical and effective.

- **The 'negative' duty.** States must refrain from the intentional taking of life except under the conditions in Article 2(2).

- **The 'positive' duties.** In order to ensure that 'everyone's life is protected by law' states must take positive measures of various kinds. Thus the impact of Article 2 goes beyond the deliberate use of force by the state and it can include duties, of various degrees of specificity, in areas such as environmental protection and medical practice. The ECtHR has been careful, however, to describe a positive duty in terms of what is reasonable in the circumstances and to allow a wide margin of appreciation to states. The positive duties can be summarised as:

  (a) **Provision of an adequate legal and administrative framework.** There must be an adequate system of criminal law with appropriate offences such as murder and manslaughter, and with an adequate police force and court structure through which the criminal laws are made effective. The specific nature of the national offences, and the structures and powers of the police, prosecution and court system are not matters for the Court so long as they meet the requirements of Article 2. In some circumstances the availability of a civil remedy may be sufficient. The absence of an effective civil remedy for damages against the police etc. can be the basis of a breach of Article 13 (see *Bubbins v United Kingdom* (2005) 41 EHRR 24; see Chapter 5, section 5.1 on Article 13).

  (b) **Operational duty.** The need to take appropriate, protective, action in respect of particular individuals or groups who are in danger.

  (c) **Investigation.** States must undertake full and adequate investigations into deaths that are within the scope of the Article. This applies not only to deaths caused by state agents but also to the deaths of persons, such as prisoners, for whom the state has assumed responsibility; likewise the duty to investigate relates not only to intentional killing but also to unintended deaths.

further study

These general principles have been asserted by the ECtHR in important cases such as *McCann v United Kingdom* (1996) 21 EHRR 97, paras 146–150 and *Giuliani v Italy* (2012) 54 EHRR 10, paras 174–182, 208–210, 244–251 and 298–306 (a Grand Chamber judgment).

KEY POINT The ECtHR refers to the 'substantive' and 'procedural' limbs of Article 2. The substantive limb relates to the duty to secure life and prevent the disproportionate use of force; the procedural limb refers to the provision of adequate remedies and, in particular, the duty to investigate.

8.1.1 The scope of Article 2 and other Convention rights

Article 2 can be invoked in situations such as the use of lethal force by police and other state agencies, the treatment of prisoners and others in the custody of the state, and respecting medical issues such as consent to treatment. Other Articles, such as Article 3 (prohibition of torture etc.) or Article 8 (respect for private life) are also applicable to such situations. As will become plain, a frequent problem is to identify the relative significance or weight of the right to life when measured against these other rights or against state imperatives concerning the maintenance of order and the suppression of crime.

8.1.2 Standing (who can bring a case)

cross reference
See Chapter 5, section 5.4.5 on standing: the victim test.

Usually (though not always) the person whose right to life has been allegedly violated will be dead. Under general rules relating to standing before the ECtHR, close relatives can bring and sustain cases of deceased victims, and this rule applies all the stronger in respect of the right to life. Claims by spouses, parents or siblings are normal; claims by those with a somewhat more distant relationship, such as nephews, are also accepted.

8.1.3 United Kingdom law

The general principles, discussed earlier, have been recognised and adopted into the law of England and Wales, and UK law generally. Under the Human Rights Act 1998 (HRA) the various UK statutes and principles of common law dealing with matters of life and death will need to be interpreted for compatibility with Article 2. Supreme Court authority includes *Rabone* v *Pennine Care NHS Foundation Trust* [2012] UKSC 2—a case focused on hospital duties reflecting the right to life of potentially suicidal mental patients: see section 8.4.4.

8.2 The intentional use of force by police, military and other state agents

8.2.1 General principles

Article 2 deals with the intentional use of lethal force (though it is not confined to this). From Article 2(1) it can be inferred that states must have adequate laws, police forces and systems for investigation, prosecution, trial and punishment of anyone, civilians or officials, who might have used force in a manner likely to result in death. Article 2(2), however, defines the exclusive circumstances in which these laws and practices may permit the intentional use of lethal force. Issues involving the legal justification for the use of force characteristically focus on actions taken by state agents: the police, the military and other security forces.

The leading case in which the ECtHR first laid down the general principles that apply to the use of lethal force by the military, police and security forces is *McCann* v *United Kingdom* (1996) 21 EHRR 97. The ECtHR found, by a majority of 10–9, that there had been a violation of Article 2 when members of the SAS shot three members of an IRA active service unit as they were leaving Gibraltar. The case was one of the most controversial ever decided by the Court and it led to a degree of tension between the British government of the time and the Court.

case close-up

McCann v *United Kingdom* (1996) 21 EHRR 97

British security officials had intelligence indicating a possible IRA attack on the British army in Gibraltar. Three members of an active service unit of the IRA, two with convictions for explosives offences and one believed to be an explosives expert, were identified at Malaga and followed through Spain and not stopped from entering Gibraltar. Military intelligence officers were convinced that a remote control device was a likely form of attack and one of the suspects was seen parking a car in the area in Gibraltar where the attack was likely; this was reported back to the military commanders as a 'suspect car bomb'. The three IRA members were shot dead by soldiers from the SAS as they were walking towards the Spanish border well away from the area of attack. The evidence of the soldiers was that they believed their actions were necessary to avoid the suspects detonating what they believed to be a car bomb. Other witnesses, however, suggested that the suspects were shot whilst attempting to surrender and that the geographical circumstances of the shooting made it impossible for a remote control bomb to be detonated. After the shooting it was found that, in fact, the suspects were unarmed and there was no bomb in the parked car.

   The ECtHR held there was a violation of Article 2, not in respect of the decision to shoot taken by the soldiers but in respect of the decision to allow the suspects to continue their journey into Gibraltar, the certainty with which intelligence assessments were communicated to the soldiers and the fact that the soldiers automatically shot to kill rather than disable. These factors, for the majority, meant that the killings were more than was 'absolutely necessary' in the circumstances. The large minority of judges entered a strong dissenting judgment in which they dissected and criticised the reasoning of the majority. In particular the minority insisted on the need for a court to avoid the benefits of hindsight and to discount the tactical advantage of the suspects: that the security forces were required to operate within the rule of law whilst the suspects operated outside such constraints with no need to take steps to preserve innocent lives.

case close-up

Giuliani and Gaggio v *Italy* (2012) 54 EHRR 10

Police shot dead a demonstrator who appeared to be attacking them with lethal intent in the context of a violent political protest (the G8 summit, in 2001 in Genoa). A majority of a Grand Chamber held that there was no violation of Article 2 in its various aspects.

The following principles from *McCann* have been developed and applied in later cases, such as *Giuliani*, which involve the use of lethal force by agents of the state.

Not confined to intentional killing

Article 2, read as a whole, includes but is not confined to intentional killing by the state. It is in issue whenever force is used which 'may result, as an unintended outcome', in a person's death. This includes the use of force which is not intended to be lethal but does result in a killing; it also can include the use of force that puts a person's life at risk even if no death actually results.

In *Makaratzis* v *Greece* (2005) 41 EHRR 49, the applicant had broken through a police road block and was pursued by police who fired at him many times. Though wounded, he survived. The ECtHR held that Article 2 was applicable (para 55).

Allegations of brutality and abuse against the police and security services which, even though serious and life threatening, did not result in death will normally be approached in terms of Article 3 ('No one shall be subjected to torture or to inhuman or degrading treatment or punishment').

cross reference
Article 3 and ill-treatment is discussed in Chapter 9, section 9.5.

In *Ilhan* v *Turkey* (2002) 34 EHRR 36, the applicant's brother had been detained by Turkish police. He suffered serious brain damage as a consequence, at least, of being struck on the head by a rifle butt. The ECtHR held that there had been no violation of Article 2; there had been a violation of Article 3.

The reason why Article 2 was relevant in *Makaratzis* but not in *Ilhan* is, presumably, to do with the nature and intentions behind the violence; guns were fired in *Makaratzis* and so there is, perhaps, more reason to suppose an intention to kill and a likelihood of death.

Strict test for absolute necessity

cross reference
Justification in respect of Articles 8–11 is discussed in Chapter 14, section 14.4.

The force used must be no more than is absolutely necessary. This is a demanding requirement. It is harder for the state to justify the use of lethal force by showing its absolute necessity than it is for the state to justify an interference with one of the freedoms in Articles 8–11 by showing the interference was 'necessary in a democratic society'. It is easier to justify the latter in terms of balancing an individual's freedom with the public good.

Strict scrutiny of justifications

The absolute necessity test means that the justifications for the use of force in Article 2(2) must be subjected to the strictest scrutiny. Article 2(2) will only justify a use of lethal force, or non-lethal force which nevertheless threatens a person's right to life, if it was 'strictly proportionate' in all the circumstances. A non-proportionate use of force, even if done for one of the purposes in Article 2(2), will not be justifiable under Article 2(2).

Planning and control

The strict scrutiny required must include not only a consideration of the particular actions and decisions taken by those directly responsible for the use of force but also the 'surrounding circumstances including such matters as the planning and control of the actions under examination'. It was failures in the planning and control of the operation, not the actions of the SAS soldiers, that was the basis of the finding of a violation in *McCann*. Issues that arise can include, for example:

- Allowing a situation to develop in which lethal force might be necessary. In *McCann* one of the reasons for finding a violation of Article 2 was the decision taken by the British authorities to allow the suspects to enter Gibraltar and plant what was believed to be a bomb. A reason for not arresting the suspects at the border was that there was, at the time, insufficient evidence on which 'reasonable suspicion' of an offence (the basis of a lawful arrest) could be based and so the suspects would have had to be released. In the Court's view this problem was not sufficient to outweigh the threat to the lives of people in Gibraltar, which was, after all, the threat which justified the decision of the soldiers to shoot and kill.

- Inadequacies in the intelligence and information given to the police or soldiers on the ground. In *McCann*, for example, all sorts of assumptions about the intentions of the suspects were communicated to the soldiers as factual certainties.

- Training and techniques used by security forces. The soldiers in *McCann* had been trained to shoot to kill rather than disable and this inflexibility in response pointed to a violation. In *Giuliani*, on the other hand, the training, in the circumstances of a mass protest, was adequate (para 255).

- The planning and control of the incident. The decisions taken by the authorities on using force, the nature of the operation, the type of force that is used, the timing, the existence of effective alternatives and so on are all matters that can be in issue. The legal basis for the exercise of force is also relevant. In *Giuliani*, the Court examined the relevant legislation and found that, since it only authorised lethal force as a last resort, it was compatible with Article 2. In *Makaratzis v Greece* (2005) 41 EHRR 49, by contrast, there was an unplanned and uncoordinated chase, involving the firing by the chasing police of many shots at a driver who had driven through a number of road blocks. Greek law and police practice had not, at the time, developed an adequate set of rules and systems for control and management of situations in which lethal force might be used and this was an important reason for the finding of a violation of Article 2.

Honest but mistaken belief

Where the particular decision to use force is based on a mistaken but honest belief that, in the circumstances, lethal force is necessary, there will not be a violation of Article 2. Lethal force used on the basis of a mistaken belief that it is necessary in self-defence or to save the lives of others, for example, is not necessarily a breach of Article 2. The belief must not only be honestly held (a subjective matter relating to the state of mind of the officer involved) but there must also have been 'good reasons' for the officer, at the time, to have believed the circumstances to be what he or she thought they were (a more objective matter). The Court in *McCann* said

the use of force by agents of the State in pursuit of one of the aims delineated in paragraph 2 of Article 2 (art. 2–2) of the Convention may be justified under this provision (art. 2–2) where it is based on an honest belief which is perceived, for good reasons, to be valid at the time but which subsequently turns out to be mistaken. To hold otherwise would be to impose an unrealistic burden on the State and its law-enforcement personnel in the execution of their duty, perhaps to the detriment of their lives and those of others. (para 200)

This is confirmed in *Giuliani*, para 178.

In *Bubbins v United Kingdom* (2005) 41 EHRR 24, police shot dead the applicant's brother in the belief that he was armed and holding a woman hostage. In fact it turned out that the gun was only a replica. The ECtHR held that, given the honest but mistaken belief about the gun, and given the circumstances of being confronted by an apparently armed man, the use of force was not disproportionate (paras 138–140).

Proving responsibility

In a number of instances, too often involving Turkish forces in Cyprus or the Kurdish area of South East Turkey, troops or police have arrived at a village, people have been stopped and questioned, perhaps arrested and taken away. Sometimes people have disappeared and never been seen again; other times they have turned up later dead or badly injured. In such circumstances the facts are often disputed, with the state denying responsibility. Prior to 1998 the Commission of Human Rights investigated and determined the facts of a case. Although the

Court was not required to accept the Commission's findings, it would do so in all but exceptional circumstances. Since then the facts are agreed by the Court. Given the importance of Article 2, the facts must be proved by the applicant 'beyond a reasonable doubt'. However, the Court will accept proof to that standard on the basis of 'sufficiently strong, clear and concordant inferences or of similar unrebutted presumptions of fact'. The Court will also take into account the conduct of the parties when evidence is being obtained. The position is summarised in *Giuliani*, paras 180–182, from where the quotation comes.

Where it is established beyond a reasonable doubt (based on inferences from the evidence of witnesses, for example) that the deceased or disappeared person was in the custody of the authorities, the Court may act on the presumption of state responsibility for what eventually happens. In *Ikincisoy* v *Turkey* App 26144/95, judgment of 15 December 2004, the applicant's son was arrested by police after a violent episode in which a police officer had been killed. The applicant's son was never seen again. The Turkish authorities claimed he had been in an armed clash. The ECtHR held that, since there was clear evidence that the son had been taken into custody, there was a strong, resulting presumption that he had been killed whilst in custody. The presumption could only be rebutted by proof to the contrary, which the state, Turkey, had failed to provide (see para 69).

cross reference
The duty to investigate deaths (which is not confined to the use of lethal force by state agents) is discussed at section 8.5.

Where there is this presumption, the ECtHR, characteristically, will find a violation of Article 2 on the grounds of the state's failure adequately to investigate the killings. The duty to investigate deaths is, in terms of practical impact, perhaps the most important duty required of states under Article 2(2). The fact that the state alleges that it was not responsible for the killings does not assist since the duty to investigate applies to all suspicious deaths.

8.2.2 Justifications for the intentional use of force, Article 2(2)

Use of force by police or security forces which causes death or is likely to do so, will not be a violation of Article 2 if it is justified under the terms of Article 2(2). However, the fact that the use of lethal force is for one of the purposes listed in Article 2(2) is not sufficient. Measured by the relevant circumstances, the use of force for the purpose must be no more than is absolutely necessary.

Article 2(2)(a): 'in defence of any person from unlawful violence'

This includes both actions taken in self-defence, and actions taken to prevent a person causing death or injury to others. As *McCann* and *Giuliani* make clear, in both situations the principle that police or military can act on the basis of an honest but reasonable mistake as to the need to exercise force is accepted. The absolute necessity for the amount of force used is to be judged in respect of the situation as understood, albeit mistakenly, at the time. Nevertheless the force used must be proportionate (absolutely necessary) to the situation as understood at the time.

In *Giuliani*, video evidence showed an 'unlawful and very violent attack' on the police vehicle which was trying to leave the scene and which posed no threat to the demonstrators. In these circumstances the officers inside could reasonably fear they might be lynched (para 187). Their use of force was justified.

Article 2(2)(b): 'in order to effect a lawful arrest or to prevent the escape of a person lawfully detained'

The requirement of absolute necessity is very important here. Article 2(2)(b) cannot justify the use of lethal force to enforce a lawful arrest where, if the arrest was not made or the person was allowed to escape, no serious danger to others will result. This view has been confirmed by a Grand Chamber of the ECtHR in *Nachova* v *Bulgaria*.

***Nachova* v *Bulgaria* (2006) 42 EHRR 43, Grand Chamber**

Bulgarian military police shot and killed two conscripts who had gone absent without leave and, on being discovered by the police hiding out in a barn, had tried to escape. The men presented no threat and were not violent. The ECtHR held there had been a violation of Article 2. The conscripts were of Roma origin and the Court also found a violation of Article 14 (discrimination) linked to Article 2, regarding failures of investigation.

In *Nachova* the Grand Chamber said (at para 95):

> Accordingly, and with reference to Art. 2(2)(b) of the Convention, the legitimate aim of effecting a lawful arrest can only justify putting human life at risk in circumstances of absolute necessity. The Court considers that in principle there can be no such necessity where it is known that the person to be arrested poses no threat to life or limb and is not suspected of having committed a violent offence, even if a failure to use lethal force may result in the opportunity to arrest the fugitive being lost.

In *Wolfgram* v *Germany* (1987) 9 EHRR CD 548, the Commission of Human Rights accepted that the use of lethal force by police was justified when they opened fire on a group of heavily armed bank robbers after one of the robbers had detonated a grenade whilst the police were trying to effect an arrest.

In *Streletz, Kessler and Krenz* v *Germany* (2001) 33 EHRR 31, and *K-HW* v *Germany* (2003) 36 EHRR 59, the ECtHR made it clear that the shooting by border guards of people trying to escape from (what was then) East Germany (German Democratic Republic) to West Germany (German Federal Republic) could not be justified by reference to Article 2(2) (see paras 96 and 98 respectively).

Article 2(2)(c): 'in action lawfully taken for the purpose of quelling a riot or insurrection'

The use of potentially lethal force by police and security forces in the context of quelling a riot or insurrection must meet the test of being absolutely necessary. The ECtHR will take into account the general difficulties of the authorities in such situations, such as their need to act on the basis of the situation as they reasonably understand it to be at the time, even if that belief is mistaken, and their need to use the weapons and equipment available to them, even if it increases the likelihood of death. The latter point, though perhaps justifying the use of lethal force by those directly responsible, is relevant to an assessment of whether the actions involved were properly planned and organised.

In *Stewart* v *United Kingdom* App 10044/82 (1984) 39 DR 162 the Commission of Human Rights reported that, on the particular facts, there was no violation of Article 2 when troops used 'plastic bullets' in the course of quelling a riot which resulted in the death of the applicant's 13-year-old son. The case turned on the Commission's assessment of the facts both relating to the circumstances in which the bullets were fired and the Commission's view that the statistical evidence indicated that the weapon was less dangerous than alleged.

In *Gülec* v *Turkey* (1999) 28 EHRR 121 Turkish security forces used a machine gun to disperse a crowd of demonstrators. The bullets were not deliberately aimed at the demonstrators but the applicant's son was killed by a ricochet. The ECtHR held that Article 2 had been violated.

8.2.3 **Lawfulness**

For the use of force to be justified under Article 2(2) it must be 'lawful'. This term is specifically mentioned in Article 2(2) but is also pervasive through the Convention.

cross reference
The Convention concept of law and legality is introduced in Chapter 6, section 6.2.

Under the Convention, state actions are only lawful if they are not only compatible with national law but also meet the Convention tests of being 'accessible' and 'foreseeable'.

If the security services can use potentially lethal force on the basis of national law which appears to provide a near unlimited and unchallengeable discretion to the authorities, the necessary legal basis may not be compatible with the Convention.

In *Makaratzis* v *Greece* (2005) 41 EHRR 49, mentioned earlier, the Greek law on the use of firearms by the police had been enacted by the Nazis in 1943. It enabled state officials to use firearms, for example, in order 'to enforce the laws, decrees and decisions of the relevant authorities or to disperse public gatherings or suppress mutinies'. The ECtHR held that this (even after later changes to the law requiring any use of force to meet the test of necessity) did not create an adequate legal framework.

8.2.4 **The duty to hold a full and adequate investigation**

Under Article 2 the intentional use of force by state agents that results in death requires a full investigation. This important requirement, because it applies to other situations in which deaths may occur, is discussed later in the chapter.

8.2.5 **The law of England and Wales**

Compatibly with Article 2, nothing in the law of England and Wales prevents the full weight of the criminal law from being used against officials such as the police. Police and civilians alike are protected in so far as the law permits the use of 'reasonable force' in order to prevent crime or to effect or assist in the lawful arrest of offenders, suspected offenders or persons unlawfully at large (section 3 Criminal Law Act 1967). Reasonable force includes the right of self-defence against unlawful attack (the prevention of crime) and this right is recognised in the permitted defences to murder and manslaughter in English law. Police officers ('constables') may also use 'reasonable force, if necessary' when exercising their powers under the Police and Criminal Evidence Act 1984, such as stop and search, arrest and entry into premises (section 117 of the **Police and Criminal Evidence Act 1984**).

....

Police and Criminal Evidence Act 1984

This is the major, basic legislation that defines the general powers of the police. The impact of the HRA on police powers is considered in more detail in Chapter 20.

....

cross reference
Section 3 HRA is discussed in Chapter 4, section 4.4.

Section 3 HRA requires that these statutory references to 'reasonable' force should be 'read and given effect' to be compatible with the Convention standard of force that is 'no more than is absolutely necessary'. Following *McCann* v *United Kingdom* the courts of England and Wales accept that there is no difference between the two standards (see *R (Bennet)* v *HM Coroner* [2007] EWCA Civ 617, para 3, quoting Collins J in [2006] EWHC 196, para 25).

For the purposes of criminal law (including murder) reasonableness is measured in terms of how the defendant (e.g. a police officer) honestly understood the situation he or she was in at the time. Honest mistakes of fact, even if unreasonable, do not alter this (see *R v Williams (Gladstone)* [1987] 3 All ER 411. This has been given statutory force by section 76 Criminal Justice and Immigration Act 2008). The full compatibility of this with Article 2 needs to be tested since, as mentioned previously, *McCann* requires mistakes of fact to be based on 'good reasons' if there is not to be a violation of Article 2.

Civil actions (e.g. for damages) which arise out of the use of lethal force, are treated differently from criminal prosecutions. Any mistake of fact must also have been a reasonable one to have made if it is to succeed as a defence (*Ashley* v *Chief Constable of Sussex Police* [2008] UKHL 25). This may be enough to satisfy Article 2.

The 'procedural' aspect to Article 2 (the duty to ensure proper management and control of actions by armed forces and police and the duty to establish an effective investigation) is not always explicitly or even implicitly found in UK law. Under the HRA it is now a requirement of the law.

discussion topic

The use of lethal force by police and army

Is the view that police and security forces are merely civilians in uniform who are able to use lethal force, on the basis of the same general principles of law that apply to civilians, a sound position? At the moment differences between civilians and police and military are recognised only in the judgments of fact that, for example, juries make when assessing the 'reasonableness' of or 'necessity' for an act of force. Is this enough or should the law be developed to accommodate not only the special difficulties and dangers that the police and security forces face but also the special responsibilities they have given their licence to use force?

Issues such as the following are relevant:

- Should police and security forces be able to rely on an honest mistake as to the facts even if the mistake was not based on reasonable grounds (section 76(4)(b)(ii) Criminal Justice and Immigration Act 2008)?

- Is it reasonable that the proportionality of the use of force can depend upon the nature of the weapons that the security forces have available to them? Is it acceptable that standard issue, high velocity rifles should be used by the military when dealing with civil disorder (see the *Gülec* case)?

- The planning of operations must be taken into account in any assessment of whether a use of force was absolutely necessary (e.g. *McCann*; see also *Andronicou* v *Cyprus* (1997) 25 EHRR 491); ought this to mean that an officer responsible for inadequacies in the planning etc. of an operation that results in death could be held personally criminally liable? Should it mean at least civil liability either for individuals or for their forces? This issue was central in the case of Jean Charles de Menezes. He was an innocent man, mistaken for a suicide bomber, who (in the immediate aftermath of the London tube bombings of July 2005) was deliberately shot by police in an underground train on his way to work. The investigation disclosed a degree of confusion among those controlling the police operation and the Metropolitan Police Service was convicted under the Health and Safety at Work etc. Act; a jury which heard the evidence expressly recommended that the officer in charge should not be censored. The results of this case are discussed at section 8.5.1 (Key Point).

- Should the common law's famous refusal to acknowledge a defence of obedience to 'superior orders' (see *R v Clegg* [1995] 1 AC 482) still apply? The Rome Statute, which creates the International Criminal Court with jurisdiction over 'crimes against humanity', 'war crimes' and 'genocide' limits the defence, under Article 33, to occasions where a soldier had a legal obligation to obey orders, did not know that the order was unlawful and the order was not obviously unlawful.

8.3 The duty on states to take adequate steps to protect life (positive duty)

8.3.1 Introduction

cross reference
For positive duties in general, see Chapter 6, section 6.6.

Article 2 is not confined to situations in which force has been deliberately used by state agents such as police and military. On the basis of the first sentence of Article 2, that 'everyone's life shall be protected by law', the ECtHR has applied the Article in such a way as to impose on states 'positive duties' to take 'appropriate steps' to safeguard peoples lives in various circumstances. There can, therefore, be an issue, which will be considered in terms of Article 2, if states fail to develop laws and practices by which people are protected from various risks of death. These positive duties apply particularly, but not only, when people are under the direct responsibility of the state.

The scope of these positive duties and the burden they place upon the authorities is not precisely determined, and a 'margin of appreciation' (see Chapter 6, section 6.3) is accorded the states. The duties include, depending on the situation, the need for

* a system of criminal law and procedures (police, prosecutors, courts, prisons, etc.): 'putting in place effective criminal law provisions to deter the commission of offences against the person backed up by law enforcement machinery' (*Osman*, para 115, see section 8.3.2);

* civil procedures to provide remedies resulting from carelessness and errors of judgment;

* criminal penalties in more serious situations such as where officials know of dangers and their powers to act, but do nothing;

* ensuring the provision of adequate information to the public;

* ensuring there is adequate investigation of deaths so that proper responsibility can be identified and attributed, and the criminal, civil and administrative remedies made effective.

The duty is not absolute. It is to take appropriate and reasonable measures in the circumstances and the ECtHR gives a wide margin of appreciation to states on the issue of what is reasonable.

case close-up

R (Silva) v Director of Public Prosecutions [2006] EWHC 3204 (Admin)

The investigation into the police shooting of Jean Charles de Menezes (mentioned in the Discussion Topic, section 8.2.5) was followed by a decision not to prosecute any individual police officer. This decision, made by the Crown Prosecution Service (CPS) and the DPP, was subject to a judicial review. The decision was upheld. The High Court held that there was no breach of Article 2. The Code of Practice followed by the CPS was compatible with the positive duties under Article 2. For a prosecution the Code required there to be a 'realistic prospect' of conviction. On the facts, the decision not to prosecute had been carefully taken at a senior level and was reasonable.

8.3.2 **Specific threat to individuals: the *Osman* duty**

> **case close-up**
>
> ***Osman v United Kingdom* (2000) 29 EHRR 245**
>
> Ahmet Osman, a school pupil, became an object of obsession of one of his teachers, Paget-Lewis. The problem was recognised by the school authorities and reported to the police who interviewed some of the parties but did not take action directly against Paget-Lewis. The obsession manifested itself in increasingly violent incidents. Eventually Paget-Lewis, armed with a shotgun, went to Ahmet Osman's home and seriously wounded him and killed his father, going on to injure the deputy headmaster of the school and kill his son. The Court of Appeal, following earlier authority of the House of Lords, held that the police did not, as a matter of law, owe a duty of care to the Osman family. Thus the family had no legal remedy available to them against the police. The family took the case to the ECtHR alleging a violation of Articles 2, 8 and 6.
>
> The ECtHR held that there had not been a violation of Article 2. Although the state had positive obligations to protect the right to life, these had been discharged since the police had done all that could be reasonably expected of them and there was no evidence that the police knew or ought to have known that the lives of the Osman family were at real and immediate risk from Paget-Lewis. On similar grounds it was held that there was no violation of Article 8.

In *Osman,* the Court (at paras 115 and 116) established the existence of positive duties in general terms. It went on to develop a specific duty on the authorities, in 'certain well-defined circumstances',

> to take preventative operational measures to protect an individual whose life is at risk from the criminal acts of another individual. (para 115)

This duty arises when

> the authorities knew or ought to have known at the time of the existence of a real and immediate risk to the life of an identified individual or individuals from the criminal acts of a third party.

The duty is to

> take measures within the scope of their powers which, judged reasonably, might have been expected to avoid that risk. (para 116)

This duty involves a higher standard than the avoidance of gross negligence but is a long way from being absolute:

> such an obligation must be interpreted in a way that does not impose an impossible or disproportionate burden on the authorities.

On the facts in *Osman*, there was no breach of the duty.

8.3.3 **The *Osman* duty and the HRA**

The positive duty on the authorities to take reasonable steps to protect the lives of specific individuals has, through the HRA, been utilised and amended for the purposes of English law.

case close-up

Re Officer L [2007] UKHL 36

The Robert Hamill Inquiry was investigating allegations of police involvement in the alleged sectarian killing of Robert Hamill in Northern Ireland in 1997. The Court of Appeal had allowed a claim by the police officers involved that they were entitled to anonymity and to be screened from view when giving evidence. The Inquiry appealed this decision to the House of Lords. The House of Lords allowed the appeal and established the basic principles on which the Article 2 duty applied.

- When is the duty triggered? Following *Osman* the House of Lords in *Re L* held that there must be a 'real and immediate' risk to life. The risk must be 'real' in the sense of being based on verifiable circumstances and not just on the subjective fears of the person involved. It must be 'immediate' in the sense of being present and continuing. Most importantly, this risk must be one created or increased by the matter in hand (e.g. giving evidence). In *Re L* the risk was already there and was not increased by involvement in the Inquiry.

- The evidence must be strong: proving a real and immediate risk is not easily done. Furthermore the House of Lords disapproved of the idea (found in some earlier UK cases) that the degree of proof should be lower in respect of activities the authorities are themselves contemplating (removing a prisoner from solitary confinement, for example).

- The duty of the authorities is to do what is reasonable and proportionate and they are not expected to undertake obligations that are unduly burdensome in proportion to the risk. Circumstances, resources and the ease of taking protective measures are all relevant to compatibility with Article 2. In *Van Colle* v *Chief Constable of Hertforshire Police* [2008] UKHL 50, the House of Lords held that assessment of the *Osman* duty must be based on the knowledge and understanding of the risk to the applicant that the police had or ought to have had at the time; there is no breach of the duty if the facts as the police reasonably understood them at the time did not disclose a real and immediate risk.

In *Venables* v *News Group Newspapers* [2001] All ER 908 (Family Division), an injunction was issued to protect the anonymity of two men who, as 10-year-old children, had murdered a two-year-old child. The case had created considerable controversy with some portions of the public, led by elements of the press, forming the view that the punishment had not been sufficient and there had been credible threats that the lives of the two men might be threatened after their release. Awarding an injunction, such as in *Venables*, involves the court in seeking a balance between Article 2 and the right, under Article 10, to freedom of expression enjoyed by both the media and the population at large. Where the threat is real and serious, an injunction may be a proportionate restriction on freedom of expression, which is done to protect the rights, under Article 2, of the potential victims. Section 12 HRA requires the UK courts to have 'particular regard to the Convention right of freedom of expression' when considering the issuing of injunctions.

cross reference
Section 12 HRA is discussed further in Chapter 17, section 17.3.

In *Savage* v *South Essex NHS Trust* [2008] UKHL 74, the *Osman* duty was discussed and applied in the context of the duty of hospitals towards potentially suicidal patients (see section 8.4.4).

8.3.4 Prisoners and others under direct state control

Prisoners, both convicted and remand, and others who are under the direct control of the state authorities, are in a particularly vulnerable position, being subject to the decisions made about them over which they have little if any control. The ECtHR has recognised that it follows that the state has special responsibilities to provide appropriate care to protect prisoners' lives.

This matter is discussed in Chapter 21, section 21.7.

8.3.5 Dangerous activities and environments

The state may have positive duties to secure the safety and right to life of individuals who may be affected by hazardous activities that it undertakes. For a duty to exist there will need to be clear evidence that the state knew or should have known of a serious risk to the health and life of the applicant.

In *LCB* v *United Kingdom* (1999) 27 EHRR 212 the applicant was diagnosed with leukaemia as a child. She attributed this to the fact that her father may have been exposed to radiation through being involved with the UK's nuclear testing programme in 1957–58, about eight years before she was born. She alleged that, under Article 2, the state had a duty to warn her parents of the possible dangers and that, had this been done, her illness would have been diagnosed earlier. The ECtHR held that the state had discharged its duty to prevent the applicant's life from being avoidably put at risk. There was no evidence that her father had been exposed to radiation and there was no reason, given the state of knowledge at the time, for the state to fear that the effects of possible radiation of the father might involve a threat to the life of the daughter which should have been communicated to the family.

cross reference
The application of Article 8 to environmental issues is discussed in Chapter 15, sections 15.8 and 15.10.1.

Thus there will be no breach of any such duty so long as the state acts reasonably given the state of knowledge and understanding available to it at the time. Even when the danger is known, the duty may be no more than a duty to communicate risks to those involved rather than a duty to stop the dangerous activities.

A broader question is whether, under Article 2, the state has positive duties towards the population at large regarding environmental dangers caused by private and commercial activities. Environmental issues are usually dealt with under Article 8 ECHR (private life), which involves the Court in seeking a fair balance between the impact on individuals and the public good.

Article 2 can be relevant where there has been a death consequent to the behaviour of the authorities; usually their lack of action.

case close-up

Oneryildiz v *Turkey* (2005) 41 EHRR 20

Local authorities were responsible for and used a rubbish tip. After the authorities started using the tip, slum dwellings, involving illegal occupancy, had developed in the vicinity of the tip. An expert's report indicated that the tip was not in conformity with safety regulations and there was a potential danger to the slum dwellers. No action was taken. There was a methane gas explosion on the site which killed members of the applicant's family who were in occupation of one of the slum dwellings. Though there was an investigation, resulting in criminal prosecutions of two mayors, a report attributed official responsibility more widely. Furthermore judgment in the applicant's favour for compensation was never paid.

Held, by a Grand Chamber, that there had been a violation of Article 2.

In *Oneryildiz*, in the context of the regulation of dangerous activities, the Grand Chamber emphasised (see paras 89–96):

- The need for a proper regulatory system which is geared to the particular dangers, including procedures for making information available to the public.

- Where the threat to life involves officials knowing of the dangers but disregarding the powers they have to take remedial action, then the situation is akin to the unjustified use of lethal force. National courts must be willing and able to impose, if justified, a criminal penalty on those responsible. This is necessary in order to maintain public confidence, ensure the maintenance of the rule of law and prevent any official collusion in unlawful actions.

- A lesser degree of official culpability (blameworthiness) may only require a civil remedy against the authority.

- A proper investigation, capable of identifying, attributing and measuring fault and responsibility is vital.

If the system fails to meet these essential requirements, there will be a violation of Article 2.

8.4 Medical treatment

Article 2 applies in the context of health care; this includes both the substantive and procedural aspects and the positive and negative duties. States, for example, have positive duties to ensure that both public (e.g. NHS) and private hospitals 'adopt appropriate measures for the protection of patient's lives' (see *Vo v France* (2005) 40 EHRR 12, para 89). This objective is to be pursued through appropriate regulations and the availability of civil remedies and, in proper cases, criminal remedies (see, for example, *Calvelli v Italy* App 32967/96, judgment of 17 January 2002, concerning allegations of negligence against Italian doctors). Article 2, therefore, is relevant to the law that applies to morally complex issues such as withdrawal of treatment from the terminally ill or voluntary euthanasia.

8.4.1 Medical treatment and the HRA

Medical treatment in England and Wales must be compatible with Convention rights.

- NHS Trusts are 'public authorities' for the purposes of section 6 HRA (*R (Munjaz)* v *Mersey Care NHS Trust* [2005] UKHL 58, para 7). States have positive duties in the medical context which may apply to private treatment, too.

- Relevant statutes must be interpreted with regard to section 3 HRA.

- Courts are public authorities under the Act and they are involved in some of the most pressing issues, such as the extent of the duty of care owed by a doctor to his or her patients or whether the withdrawal of treatment is lawful.

cross reference
For Article 3 see Chapter 9, section 9.7.2 and Article 8 see Chapter 15, section 15.4.1.

Medical professionals in making decisions must, therefore, act compatibly with their patients' rights to life under Article 2 (which, amongst other things, imposes a positive duty to protect life) and Article 3 (which prohibits treatment causing a person to suffer inhuman or degrading treatment). However, in the medical context, even these rights may have to give ground to the principle, found in Article 8, of patient autonomy (the right of a **competent** patient to consent or refuse consent to treatment). This is also a fundamental principle of common law. Autonomy is so important it can outweigh concerns, under Article 2, that a patient's decisions will lead to his or her death or to their being left in a condition that violates Article 3 (see, for example, *NHS Trust A* [2001] 1 All ER 801, paras 25–26). It must be remembered, however, that interferences with Article 8(1) rights, including the right to autonomy, can be justified under the terms of Article 8(2). No such justification is possible if the complaint is of a violation of Article 3.

competent

A competent patient is one who knows his or her situation, understands the consequences of treatment and can make a reasonable, independent judgment about whether to start or continue with such treatment. Adults are assumed to be competent; children can consent to treatment once they reach 16 or earlier if they are, in fact, competent.

8.4.2 **Normal treatment**

Normal, therapeutically sensible treatment administered to a consenting patient in good faith is unlikely to raise Convention issues. Even where treatment is administered negligently, it is likely that the state will have discharged its duties under the Convention if there is an adequate system of civil remedies—an action for negligence, for example.

8.4.3 **Resources**

The possibilities but also the costs of medical treatments are ever expanding and very hard questions about the affordability of treatments, especially in the context of a publicly funded health service, can arise. Article 2 imposes positive duties on states to secure the right to life and this must involve a burden on resources. However, in *Keenan* v *United Kingdom* (2001) 33 EHRR 38, the ECtHR said, in relation to Article 2:

> the scope of the positive obligation must be interpreted in a way which does not impose an impossible or disproportionate burden on the authorities.

Where treatments have significant resource implications it is unlikely that Article 2 will compel health authorities to fund treatments whatever the impact this may have on their budgets generally (see, for example a pre-HRA case: *R* v *Cambridge Health Authority ex parte B* [1995] 2 All ER 129).

In *R (Rogers)* v *Swindon Primary Health Care Trust* [2006] EWCA Civ 392, a health authority refused to fund Herceptin, an expensive breast cancer drug, which had been prescribed for R by her doctor. The Administrative Court had held that the claimant's Article 2 rights had not been violated. On appeal, the Court of Appeal did not consider the impact of Article 2 but subjected the health authority's decision to intense scrutiny on ordinary public law grounds. It held that the authority's policy was unlawful and needed to be reconsidered, but it did not order the drug to be funded.

8.4.4 **Operational duty to particular patients**

The *Osman* duty (mentioned in section 8.3.3) has been applied, under the HRA, in respect of the duty of hospitals to their patients.

case close-up

Rabone v Pennine Care NHS Foundation Trust **[2012] UKSC 2**

Melanie Rabone, 24, agreed to voluntary admission to a mental hospital. The hospital agreed to her request to go on home leave, despite the concerns of her parents. Whilst on home leave she committed suicide. The hospital admitted negligence.

The Supreme Court took the view that M's situation was one of those 'circumstances' which gave rise to the *Osman* ('operational') duty, mentioned in section 8.3.3. Her situation was different from 'ordinary' medical situations in which mere negligence leading to death will not violate Article 2 (assuming that civil remedies are available). In *Savage* v *South Essex Partnership NHS Trust* [2008] UKHL 74 the House of Lords had imposed the duty in the circumstances of a non-voluntary patient detained under the Mental Health Act 1983 who had been able to leave and who had committed suicide. The Supreme Court extended the circumstances in which the duty arises to voluntary patients, being persuaded that the differences with non-voluntary patients were not decisive. Both types are vulnerable and require the special protection of the authorities. There was a real and immediate risk to M's life which the hospital should have appreciated and sought to prevent by taking appropriate measures.

8.4.5 Refusal of medical treatment by a competent patient

The general situation of competent patients regarding their Convention rights has been summarised by the Court of Appeal in *R (Burke)* v *General Medical Council* [2005] EWCA Civ 1003, paras 32–34.

- Patients are owed a duty of care by medical staff to take 'such steps as are reasonable' to keep them alive.

- However, a competent patient can refuse such treatment on the grounds of his or her autonomy.

- Withdrawal of treatment from a consenting competent patient does not violate Article 2 and may even be required, for a competent patient, in order to prevent inhuman or degrading treatment, prohibited by Article 3 (paras 38–39)—an example is *Re JT (Adult: Refusal of Medical Treatment)* [1998] 1 FLR 48 (refusal of renal treatment).

- Article 2 ECHR would be violated, however, if doctors withdrew life-prolonging treatment from a competent patient who did not consent, even if it meant the patient would suffer degrading treatment etc. (*Burke* para 39).

8.4.6 Withdrawal of medical treatment from an incompetent patient

Article 2 may be in issue when what is proposed is the withdrawal of treatment from an incompetent patient. For English law the 'best interests' test was established in *Airedale NHS Trust* v *Bland* [1993] AC 789, and this has been confirmed in post-HRA cases.

case close-up

NHS Trust A v M; NHS Trust B v H [2001] 1 All ER 801

Two NHS hospital trusts sought declarations that they could lawfully withdraw treatment from two patients in a 'permanent vegetative state'—a clinical condition defined by a complete lack of awareness of self and of the environment. Withdrawal of treatment would result in death.

The Family Division of the High Court issued the declarations.

A responsible medical decision that withdrawal of treatment was in the best interests of an incompetent patient was not an intentional deprivation of life prohibited by Article 2: death was a consequence of the patient's condition, not of the withdrawal of treatment.

> The positive obligations of the state under Article 2 were discharged when a responsible medical decision was taken that continuance of treatment was not in the patient's best interests.

Article 2 may be of little assistance when appalling choices have to be made between lives. Nothing in Article 2 suggests that one life can be of lesser value than another.

case close-up

Re A (Children) (Conjoined Twins: Surgical Separation) [2000] 4 All ER 961

The Court of Appeal had to decide whether, against the wishes of parents, doctors could proceed to separate conjoined twins. With no separation both twins would die within a few months. With the operation the stronger twin would live with a reasonable expectation of length and quality of life, but the weaker twin would inevitably die. The court permitted the separation. Their decision was taken in the light of Article 2. The decision (essentially a decision that one twin should die to enable the other to live) was not made on the basis that one life was worth less than the other, but because separation was the lesser of two evils: the doctrine of necessity applied when a choice had to be made between two equal claims to life.

The decision was mainly founded on common law principles. Article 2 was understood to be compatible with such a decision. Specifically rejected was the idea that the negative duty to protect life (of the weaker twin) outweighed the positive duty to preserve life (of the stronger twin). This was not intentional killing, and so Article 2(2) was not relevant. The uniqueness of the case was stressed.

8.4.7 Deaths in hospital

Deaths in hospital may, depending on the circumstances, require an investigation under the procedural aspect of Article 2: see section 8.5.

8.4.8 Assisted suicide

Euthanasia, in the sense of allowing one person to assist another in the latter's voluntary decision to die, is controversial and, in many countries (including the United Kingdom) would involve a crime, perhaps murder, by the person assisting.

case close-up

Pretty v United Kingdom (2002) 35 EHRR 1

The applicant, Diane Pretty, suffered from Motor Neurone Disease, which involved progressive muscular deterioration and would lead inevitably to a death that would be distressing and undignified. Pretty's mental faculties were unimpaired. She was frightened by the prospect of her death and wanted, instead, to die at a time and in a manner of her own choosing. For this she needed the assistance of another and her husband was willing to assist her. Such action would, however, be likely to involve the husband in committing the crime of assisting another's suicide (section

2(1) Suicide Act 1961). The Director of Public Prosecutions refused to give any undertaking that her husband would not be prosecuted. The House of Lords refused to hold that the DPP had acted unlawfully.

It was held by the ECtHR that the right to life in Article 2 does not imply its opposite, a right to die—states are not under a duty to have laws permitting voluntary euthanasia (though the Court did not say that states had a duty not to have such laws).

In *Nicklinson* v *Ministry of Justice* [2012] HRLR 16, the High Court held that a man with 'locked in syndrome', who was seeking the right to die, had no realistic prospect of succeeding on the basis that Article 2 required a reconsideration of the law by Parliament (though his case was heard on other grounds).

Article 2 imposes a duty to protect life; it does not indicate a minimum standard of the quality of life that is to be protected.

Issues relating to the quality of the life a person leads are dealt with under Article 3 (prohibiting inhuman or degrading treatment) or Article 8 (requiring personal autonomy).

The Director's refusal to give the assurance did engage Article 8 because of the principle of autonomy. However, the inclusion of assisted suicide within the definition of 'murder' was justified under Article 8(2). It was necessary to protect the rights of others, in particular ill people who might be pressurised by relatives to choose to die.

These principles endorsed the position adopted into English law, under the HRA, by the House of Lords in *R (Pretty)* v *DPP* [2001] UKHL 61 (see paras 3–10) except that the House of Lords, deciding the case under the HRA, strongly doubted whether Article 8 was engaged at all.

8.4.9 **Abortion**

Abortion is a profoundly controversial issue on which, in its moral aspect, irreconcilable positions are adopted. In its barest essentials there is, on the one hand, the claim that a foetus, from conception, is a life, equivalent to post-natal life, and should be protected by Article 2 to the same extent as a post-natal life. On the other hand, there is the claim that a foetus is clearly distinguishable from a post-natal life and has no claims that can legitimately interfere with a woman's right to autonomy over her body and reproductive activity. There is, of course, a full range of more modulated intermediate positions.

cross reference
For Article 8 and 'autonomy' see Chapter 15, section 15.4.6.

The ECtHR has consistently refused to rule that a foetus is directly protected by Article 2. Article 2 does not define when 'life' begins. There is no legal, moral or scientific consensus in Europe on these matters. A wide margin of appreciation is to be allowed to the states (see, in particular, *Vo* v *France* (2005) 40 EHRR 12, paras 75–82 and, in particular paras 80 and 82).

KEY POINT The position in English law, under the HRA, is similar—a foetus is not recognised as having a 'life' (*Evans* v *Amicus Healthcare* [2004] EWCA Civ 727, paras 174–179).

Likewise, an absolute ban on abortion would be incompatible with the right to life of the mother (para 75). Where access to abortion is limited, a mother's right to respect for her private life, under Article 8, is engaged. The 'rights' of the foetus, such as they are, are recognised in this context: the Convention does not give a mother an absolute right to choose to terminate her pregnancy. The issue is discussed in Chapter 15, section 15.10.4.

8.5 Article 2 and the need for a full investigation—the procedural obligation

Since *McCann* v *United Kingdom* (see section 8.2.1), the ECtHR has insisted that states have a duty to provide an effective official investigation into deaths covered by Article 2, particularly, but not exclusively, when these result from the use of force. This is the 'procedural' aspect of Article 2 (see Key Point in section 8.1) and is implied from the text of Article 2. A full Grand Chamber summary of the obligation, confirming the points made in this section, is in *Giuliani* (section 8.2.1) paras 298–306. The duty has been adopted into UK law: *R (Amin)* v *Secretary of State for the Home Department* [2003] UKHL 51, see, in particular, paras 20–21.

- An investigation is necessary to ensure that the national laws and procedures dealing with the right to life can be effectively implemented. In *R (Amin)* v *Secretary of State for the Home Department* [2003] UKHL 51, Lord Bingham described the purposes of an investigation as:

  > To ensure as far as possible that the full facts are brought to light; that culpable and discreditable conduct is exposed and brought to public notice; that suspicion of deliberate wrongdoing (if unjustified) is allayed; that dangerous practices and procedures are rectified; and that those who have lost their relative may at least have the satisfaction of knowing that lessons learned from his death may save the lives of others. (para 31)

- An investigation is necessary to ensure that there is proper accountability by officials for their actions including, if necessary, criminal prosecution.

- An investigation is necessary to learn lessons for the future (*R (JL)* v *Secretary of State for Justice* [2008] UKHL 68).

- An investigation must be adequate to this purpose and so the precise nature and scope of the duty to investigate will depend upon the circumstances of different cases. Regarding 'ordinary' murder (intentional killing), a police investigation followed by prosecution and a proper criminal trial is likely to be sufficient to discharge the duty. Where death results from alleged negligence (failing to guard against risks) the existence of a system of civil courts and remedies may be sufficient (see *R (Goodson)* v *Bedfordshire and Luton Coroner* [2004] EWHC 2931).

- The main issues concerning the duty to investigate arise where the authorities have, themselves, some degree of responsibility for the death. In this context the requirement for an effective investigation may require more specific action.

8.5.1 The existence of the duty

The duty of investigation is not confined to intentional killing by security forces: it includes all deaths covered by the positive duty to secure life. Furthermore it exists even in times of war and emergency; states cannot avoid their duties on the grounds of the difficult times they are experiencing.

It is now clear that the procedural obligation is 'detached' from the substantive duties in Article 2. The procedural obligation may be breached in relation to deaths which raise the question of state responsibility, even if it turns out that there was no breach of the state's substantive obligations. But it is not an open-ended obligation to reopen old issues. The procedural obligation arises where, after the Convention has come into force, investigative steps have been taken in respect of an earlier death. Those steps must conform to the procedural limb of Article 2 (*Silih* v *Slovenia* (2009) 49 EHRR 37, paras 153–163). This principle has been accepted by the Supreme Court in respect of the application of the HRA. It applies to post-HRA investigations undertaken by UK authorities of deaths which occurred before the entry into force of the HRA (*Re McCaughey* [2011] UKSC 20).

The use of force by police, army or other state agents

- **The use of lethal force.** The duty to investigate applies when deaths occur following the deliberate use of force by state agencies. In *McCann* v *United Kingdom* (1996) 21 EHRR 97, for instance, the ECtHR held that the duty had been discharged by the coroner's hearing in Gibraltar in which all relevant matters had been fully dealt with (see paras 157–163).

- **Unexplained deaths.** The duty to investigate can be very important where the precise facts about a person's death are unclear and disputed but there are well founded allegations that the person was in the custody of the police or security forces at the time. In such circumstances an effective investigation to establish the facts and responsibilities is essential. As *Ikincisoy* v *Turkey* (discussed in section 8.2.1) indicates, the ECtHR has been prepared to presume state responsibility for the death from the fact of the deceased being in custody, which only a sufficient investigation leading to a convincing alternative explanation, can rebut.

- **Allegations of security forces' involvement in deaths.** The duty to investigate applies to unexplained killings where there are allegations of direct or indirect involvement of the security forces. The mere denial of responsibility by the state is not enough. There will be a breach of Article 2 if the allegations are not fully and effectively investigated as part of the investigation of the death. This principle has been important in the context of allegations made of unofficial collusion between security forces and armed groups.

KEY POINT The shooting by police of Jean Charles de Menezes in July 2005 (mistaken for a suicide bomber) clearly engaged state responsibility. It led to an investigation and report from the Independent Police Complaints Commission (IPCC) ('Stockwell 1'), which identified issues for the Crown Prosecution Service to examine when considering the need for criminal prosecutions against the police. The Crown Prosecution Service decided that there was insufficient evidence for criminal prosecutions against police officers involved (a decision upheld by the High Court in *R (Silva)* v *DPP* [2006] EWHC 3204 (Admin)). The Metropolitan Police, as an organisation, was prosecuted and convicted under the Health and Safety at Work etc. Act 1974 for endangering the public and fined £175,000. The IPCC did not require any officers to face internal disciplinary proceedings. The inquest, the first public examination of the case, opened in September 2008. For inquests to be compatible with Article 2 they must be able to explore the circumstances surrounding the death (see section 8.5.3). The jury returned an 'open verdict' (they were not allowed to consider 'unlawful killing'). The IPCC also investigated early inaccuracies in the information released by the police and criticised a named police officer ('Stockwell 2').

Deaths of persons for whom the state is directly responsible

The duty to investigate under Article 2 ECHR extends to deaths of those, such as prisoners, who are under the care of the state. There must be an adequate investigation where, for example, prisoners die whilst in custody, either intentionally killed by other prisoners (see *Edwards v United Kingdom* (2002) 35 EHRR 19) or by committing suicide (such as *Keenan v United Kingdom* (2001) 33 EHRR 38).

The matter has been of great importance under the HRA.

case close-up

> ### R (Amin) v Secretary of State for the Home Department [2003] UKHL 51
>
> ....
>
> A British Asian man, serving a sentence in a young offender's institution, was placed by the Prison Service in the same cell as a prisoner with known racist tendencies, who subsequently murdered him. The House of Lords held that there was a duty under Article 2 of a proper investigation, which the state had not discharged (the inadequacies are identified at section 8.5.2).

The duty to undertake an enhanced investigation as required by Article 2 can apply to deaths in custody without, first, proving state liability for the death, though the extent and nature of the investigation will depend on the circumstances, including the degree of state responsibility (*R (JL) v Secretary of State for Justice* [2008] UKHL 68).

Deaths in hospital

Deaths in hospital must be properly investigated (see *Calvelli v Italy*, section 8.4, paras 49–51). As we have seen, the substantive limb of Article 2 will not be violated by mere hospital negligence—unless special circumstances give rise to the *Osman*/'operational' duty (see *Rabone*, discussed at section 8.4.4). Under the HRA, the issue has been considered by the Court of Appeal in *R (Takoushis) v Inner London North Coroner* [2005] EWCA Civ 1440, paras 70–109. The case involved a mental patient who was not stopped by a hospital from leaving its Accident and Emergency department and who then killed himself. The Court of Appeal found:

- Article 2 required an effective investigation into hospital deaths.
- This does not necessarily require a particular, state initiated investigation. In normal situations the availability of an inquest (whose conduct, as here, can be challenged in the courts) and the availability of a civil action for negligence, is likely to satisfy this duty (see, for example, *R (Goodson) v Bedfordshire and Luton Coroner* [2004] EWHC 2931.
- In other circumstances a more demanding investigation may be required (such as where the operational duty has arisen).

Death in a safe-environment context

As mentioned previously (see section 8.3.5) the 'substantive' aspect of Article 2 includes a duty on states to take reasonable steps to protect against dangerous environmental conditions. The duty to investigate also applies in such circumstances. In *Oneryildiz v Turkey* (see section 8.3.5), where death was caused by an explosion at a rubbish tip, the ECtHR said (at para 94):

> Where lives are lost as a result of a dangerous activity...the competent authorities must act with exemplary diligence and promptness and must of their own motion initiate investigations capable of, firstly, ascertaining the circumstances in which the incident took place and any shortcomings in the operation of the regulatory system and, secondly, identifying the state officials or authorities involved in whatever capacity in the chain of events in issue.

181

8.5.2 **The nature of the duty: an effective investigation**

The investigation must be effective. What this requires will depend on the circumstances. Where the state is not directly responsible for a death, the requirements of Article 2 may be significantly less onerous (see, in relation to rail safety, *R (Main)* v *Minister for Legal Aid* [2007] EWCA Civ 1147). Where there is direct state responsibility for the death, or the death is of a prisoner or person under state control, the investigation must be able to determine, in detail, how the deceased died and to allocate responsibility, including amongst officials. Any special, official investigations are in addition to the availability of more general legal proceedings such as criminal trials, if necessary, or civil actions in the courts. The official investigation should provide facts on which such other proceedings can be based.

case close-up

Jordan v *United Kingdom* (2003) 37 EHRR 2

....

PJ, the applicant's son who was, it later transpired, treated by the IRA as an active member, was shot dead by members of the Northern Ireland police (then called the Royal Ulster Constabulary). The police account of the death referred to their shooting in self-defence a man they believed to be dangerous who, in attempting to resist arrest, appeared to threaten deadly violence to the arresting officers. The account of a number of witnesses, however, suggested something closer to the execution of a man by police after his car had been deliberately rammed and stopped. The ECtHR held that there had been a violation of Article 2.

In *Jordan* the general requirements for an adequate investigation have been identified by the ECtHR, see paras 105–109 (see also *Giuliani* at section 8.2.1, paras 300–306). The case involves the use of force by security forces but the principles apply, with necessary changes, more generally.

- **Initiation.** The authorities must initiate the investigation and not leave it to others, such as next of kin (in England and Wales this includes through the system of coroners and inquests).

- **Independence.** The investigators must be fully independent of those officials who are implicated in the investigation.

- **Authority.** To be effective, the investigation must have sufficient authority to be able to do its job of determining the facts, considering justification and allocating responsibility. To that end it must be able to obtain the evidence and the appearance of witnesses, for example, and be able to cross-examine witnesses.

- **Promptness.** The investigation must be conducted with reasonable promptness.

- **Public scrutiny.** Public confidence requires that there should be an element of openness in the investigation process. The degree of openness will depend on the circumstances and the ECtHR recognises that there can be exceptional reasons for limiting scrutiny. In *Taylor* v *UK* (1994) 79-A DR 127, for example, there was no breach of Article 2 when the government refused to set up a public inquiry into killings of patients by a hospital nurse.

- **Family involvement.** States have a duty to involve the close family (next of kin) in the investigation, by making information available and by giving full reasons for decisions taken. Involvement of the family must be 'to the extent necessary to safeguard his or her legitimate interests' (para 109). In some circumstances this may require publicly funded representation (see, for example, *R (Khan)* v *Secretary of State for Health* [2003] EWCA 1129).

In *Amin* (see section 8.5.1) the House of Lords found that the investigation into the prisoner's murder was inadequate: there was no inquest, the police investigation (properly) did not involve the family, the advice not to prosecute prison officers was not made available, the Prison Service's own inquiry was not independent, it was conducted in private and was not published and an inquiry by the Commission for Racial Equality only focused on race issues (paras 33–37).

further study

Following *Amin* a public inquiry was held which identified major failings by named individuals in the Prison Service, see *Report of the Zahid Mubarak Inquiry* (2006) HC 1082-I.

What counts as an adequate investigation depends on the circumstances.

- In *R (D)* v *Secretary of State for the Home Department* [2006] EWCA Civ143, D, a prisoner, had attempted suicide. The Court of Appeal held that an adequate investigation under Article 2 required evidence to be taken in public: an inquiry by the Prison Ombudsman was not sufficient. The involvement of D was required but this did not give him a right to cross-examine witnesses. (See further *R (JL)* v *Secretary of State for Justice* [2008] UKHL 68.)

- In *Ramsahai* v *Netherlands* (2008) 46 EHRR 43, a Grand Chamber found that the investigation of a controversial police shooting had not been effective. For example, police officers involved had not been separated from each other, not properly tested, there were no photographs of the body and the setting up of the independent investigation was delayed.

The purpose of the investigation remains that of exploring the reasons for the death. Courts are likely to resist using Article 2 to require a wider exploration of, for example, the background political policies that formed the context in which the death took place. In *R (Gentle)* v *Prime Minister* [2008] UKHL 20, mothers of two soldiers killed in Iraq argued that Article 2 required the government to take reasonable steps to be satisfied that the war was lawful. The House of Lords rejected the argument on various grounds. In particular, that an effective investigation was an implied, not an express, duty and so it should not be given a scope beyond what the draftsmen and governments of the time (at the end of the Second World War) would have had in mind. States would not have obligated themselves to the possibility of such a wide-ranging investigation that would both second-guess the United Nations and also hand over matters of high politics to an investigation that was neither representative nor accountable to Parliament. (Baroness Hale adopted this position but with reluctance: see paras 55–57.)

8.5.3 **Coroners in England and Wales**

The duty to investigate is one of the areas in which the Convention has had a significant impact on UK law. In particular, cases brought before the English courts have cast doubt on whether the **coroner** system for investigating deaths satisfies Article 2.

· ·

coroner

A coroner in England and Wales has the statutory duty to investigate sudden and unexplained deaths, and other deaths which are referred to the coroner for various legal reasons. About one-third of all deaths are currently referred.

· ·

A coroner's court, because of the limitations on juries in the Coroner's Rules, may not have sufficient authority to allocate responsibility for deaths. The House of Lords found that such inadequacies existed in *R (Middleton)* v *West Somerset Coroner* [2004] UKHL 10 and *R (Sacker)* v *West Yorkshire Coroner* [2004] UKHL 11. Both cases involved prisoners who had committed suicide. In both cases the coroner's jury formed the view that neglect by the Prison Service was a contributory factor. Under the Coroners Act 1988, such findings could not be accepted or, if accepted, could not be included in the coroner's findings. The House of Lords held that this was incompatible with the investigative duty in Article 2 in respect of a death that occurred after October 2000 and engaged state responsibility. For these deaths the Coroners Act could be read and given effect to make it compatible with Article 2.

KEY POINT This is an example of the court exercising its interpretative obligation under section 3 HRA. Section 11(5)(b)(ii) of the Coroners Act 1988 (now repealed) required coroners to determine 'how, when and where the deceased came by his death'. In *Middleton* and *Sacker,* the House of Lords read 'how' to mean not only 'by what means' the deceased died (a narrow meaning given in earlier cases) but also 'in what circumstances' (giving the term a wider meaning in order to accommodate the Article 2 duty of investigation and allow, for example, consideration of allegations of negligence by public authorities).

8.6 Death penalty

Article 2(1) expressly reserves the possibility that states may have the death penalty. However, Protocol 13 of the European Convention, which is a scheduled right under the HRA, requires abolition in all circumstances including time of war. In the United Kingdom the death penalty has been progressively abolished, for murder in 1965, piracy and treason in 1998 and for military offences in the face of the enemy by section 21 HRA.

8.7 War

Article 2 does not give an exemption to states for acts of war, which involve intentional killing. It will apply, therefore, to acts of war which are within a state's 'jurisdiction' (as required by Article 1 ECHR).

Derogation from Article 2 in respect of 'deaths resulting from lawful acts of war' is allowed under Article 15 ECHR. This places great emphasis on the legality of the war, a matter determined by the principles of international law and is outside the scope of this book.

If the Convention does not apply, the armed forces involved will still be subject to the laws of war and also, if their nations, like the United Kingdom, are signatories to the Rome Statute, they will be subject to the jurisdiction of the International Criminal Court. Both these issues are outside the scope of this book.

The application of the Convention outside the territory of a signatory state is discussed in Chapter 2, section 2.4.5 and the application outside the United Kingdom of the HRA is discussed in Chapter 4, section 4.12.3.

For Article 15 in general, see Chapter 7, section 7.2.

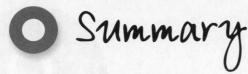 # Summary

- Article 2 expresses one of the most fundamental of the Convention rights, one that is not subject to derogation, in peacetime, under Article 15.

- Article 2 requires states to ensure that the use of intentional force that causes death is unlawful except under the specific circumstances allowed for under Article 2(2).

- Article 2(1) requires that everyone's right to life shall be protected and this has led the ECtHR to impose 'positive duties' on states to provide a proper framework of law, regulation and administrative practice. These duties include the provision of a proper system of criminal law, enforced by a system of police, prosecutors and courts; access to civil remedies may be enough in some circumstances.

- Positive duties apply to dangerous activities generally, including, for example, medical treatments in hospitals and environmental dangers.

- Perhaps the most important duty on states is to ensure that deaths are properly investigated.

- However, the duty on states is not absolute but subject to what is reasonable and, on that issue, to a wide margin of appreciation.

Questions

For suggested approaches, please visit the Online Resource Centre.

1 An armed man is holding a woman hostage. The police end the siege violently, causing the death of both the armed man and his victim. What principles found in Article 2 should govern the way the issue is handled by the authorities?

2 How effective is the doctrine of positive duties under Article 2 in bringing about a safe environment; or is it merely confined to providing remedies after the event?

 # Further reading

Chevalier-Watts, J. 'Effective Investigation under Article 2 ECHR: Securing the Right to Life or an Onerous Burden on a State?' (2010) 21(3) *EJIL* 701–721

Lester, A., Pannick, D. and Herberg, J. (see Preface) Chapter 4, Article 2

Leverick, F. 'Is English Self-defence Law Incompatible with Article 2 ECHR?' [2002] *Crim LR* 347–362

Tettenborn, A. 'Wrongful Death, Human Rights, and the Fatal Accidents Act' (2012) 128(Jul) *LQR* 327–331

9

Article 3: prohibition of torture

Chapter overview

- The absolute nature of Article 3.
- The definitions of torture and inhuman and degrading treatment and punishment.
- State responsibility to secure Article 3 rights.
- The unlawfulness of torture.
- Article 3 and punishment.
- Article 3 and unintended suffering.

Article 3   Prohibition of Torture

No one shall be subjected to torture or to inhuman or degrading treatment or punishment.

Introduction

The ban on torture and on inhuman and degrading treatment and punishment is the most absolute and fundamental Convention right. In this chapter the fundamental nature of Article 3 is considered and the main terms of the Article ('torture', 'inhuman', 'degrading') are defined in general terms. The broad nature of state responsibility to prevent suffering which is severe enough to violate Article 3 is discussed. This involves the legal ban on torture and other forms of deliberate ill-treatment by officials. But Article 3 also creates limits to what is acceptable as punishment (whether administered by the state or otherwise) and, importantly, applies in a wide range of situations for which the state has responsibility in respect of otherwise lawful activity not involving an intention to harm—hospital treatment or the treatment of asylum seekers, for example.

Article 3 has had an important impact on the treatment of prisoners, which is discussed separately in Chapter 21.

9.1 The fundamental nature of Article 3

cross reference

Derogation (suspending rights) is discussed in Chapter 7, section 7.2.

Article 3 of the European Convention on Human Rights (ECHR) is expressed in absolute terms. There are no qualifying terms (as there are in the second paragraph of Article 8, for example) which would allow torture or inhuman or degrading treatment if it was a proportionate way of achieving a pressing social need, such as public safety (see *Ahmed* v *Austria* (1997) 24 EHRR 278, para 40) or saving the lives of others (see *Gäfgen*, section 9.1.1). Likewise the text of Article 3 does not identify any general purposes for which torture etc. can be justified (unlike, for example, Article 2, the right to life, which permits intentional killing in the circumstances defined in its second paragraph: see Chapter 8, section 8.2.2). If the treatment comes within the definitions in Article 3, it is illegal under the Convention.

The fundamental nature of Article 3 is confirmed by its being an Article from which states may not, under Article 15, derogate from even in times of war and public emergency. Again, it can be contrasted with Article 2, which does allow derogation in respect of deaths occurring as a result of 'lawful acts of war' (see Chapter 8, section 8.7).

The European Court of Human Rights (ECtHR) has emphasised that treatment which violates Article 3 cannot be justified in terms of public benefit. In *Balogh* v *Hungary* App 47940/99, judgment of 20 July 2004, at para 44, for example, the Court said:

> Even in the most difficult of circumstances, such as the fight against terrorism or crime, the Convention prohibits in absolute terms torture or inhuman or degrading treatment or punishment. Unlike most of the substantive clauses of the Convention and of Protocols Nos 1 and 4, Article 3 makes no provision for exceptions and no derogation from it is permissible under Article 15 even in the event of a public emergency threatening the life of the nation.

Ill treating a suspect on the basis of a well-founded likelihood of obtaining information which will save, in a proximate way, the lives of identifiable people, is banned under Article 3. Likewise winning the 'wars' on crime or terrorism do not justify raising the threshold of severity for what counts as a breach of Article 3 so that states can use tough methods of interrogation without violating Article 3 (see *Tomasi* v *France* (1993) 15 EHRR 1, para 115). Nor can a 'noble purpose' be a matter of weight in deciding whether treatment prohibited by Article 3 is 'torture' or something less.

9.1.1 Article 3 and the rights of others

The absolute nature of Article 3 means it cannot be violated even in order to secure the Convention rights of others. The argument that torture should be used against a terrorist suspect, for example, to secure the right to life of others (even if convincing) is not acceptable.

In *Gäfgen* v *Germany* (2011) 52 EHRR 1, police threatened a suspect with physical harm in order to get him to disclose the whereabouts of a kidnapped and murdered child, which he did. A breach of Article 3 was not disputed, however the Grand Chamber held that the small suspended fine imposed by the German courts was an insufficient response to the breach, whatever its motive.

In hospital cases, it may be wrong to continue with treatments which might prolong life but which would be inhuman or degrading for the patient (subject to patient autonomy). Likewise other rights: the claim by a defendant that, in order to obtain a fair trial under Article 6, it is necessary for a witness to suffer humiliating cross-examination (a claim that has arisen in rape trials) could be challenged on Article 3 grounds, for example.

9.1.2 Minimum level of severity

Treatment can only violate Article 3 if it reaches a minimum level of severity. This is a matter for a court to assess.

case close-up

Costello-Roberts v United Kingdom (1995) 19 EHRR 112

A seven-year-old boy had been 'slippered' three times by his headmaster as a punishment under school rules. In the view of the ECtHR, the punishment did not cross the threshold of severity necessary for a violation of Article 3.

In *Costello-Roberts,* the Court held that the 'threshold of severity' necessary for a violation of Article 3 cannot be determined in the abstract. It depends on all the circumstances of the case. A range of contextual factors were identified as illustrating the kinds of issue that are relevant:

> Factors such as the nature and context of the punishment, the manner and method of its execution, its duration, its physical and mental effects and, in some instances, the sex, age and state of health of the victim must all be taken into account. (para 30)

In *E* v *Chief Constable of the RUC* [2008] UKHL 66, Baroness Hale, following *Mayeka* v *Belgium* (2006) 46 EHRR 449, held that the 'special vulnerability of children' is relevant to whether treatment they are subjected to reaches this minimum level of security (see para 8). Clearly, considering the 'context' of treatment may involve the Court in some degree of balancing the treatment with its purpose (to promote a public interest or protect the rights of others, for example) and so, even in respect of Article 3, some need to weigh competing interests may be required of a court.

9.1.3 **Article 3 and Article 8**

There is overlap between Article 3 and Article 8, the right to respect for private and family life. Treatment of a person that is within Article 3 is also likely to involve a failure to respect a person's physical or psychological integrity and thus give rise to an alternative action under Article 8.

Where treatment does not meet the minimum level of severity needed for Article 3 it may, nevertheless, come within the scope of Article 8. There is, however, an important difference between the two Articles. Treatment that comes within the scope of Article 3 is, as we have seen, incapable of legal justification in terms of the Convention. Treatment or action which involves an interference with a person's private life, however, is capable of justification by the state under the terms of Article 8(2). The state has to prove that the interference was in accordance with the law, for one of the purposes listed in Article 8(2) and necessary in a democratic society in the sense of being a proportionate way of achieving a pressing social need. Consequently, if only an Article 8 case is available, the applicant is vulnerable to the state successfully justifying the interference—which is not possible under Article 3. Thus in *Pretty* v *United Kingdom* (2002) 35 EHRR 1 (the facts are given in section 9.2.3) the failure of English law to allow assisted suicide was not 'treatment' that violated Article 3. On the other hand the ECtHR accepted that it might be an interference with the applicant's private life; however, if so, it was a justified interference in terms of the second paragraph of Article 8 as it was a proportionate way of protecting the vulnerable from possible abuse (see paras 61–78).

9.2 Definitions: 'torture', 'inhuman', and 'degrading treatment' and 'punishment'

The ECtHR has given general defining descriptions of 'torture' and of what makes treatment or punishment 'inhuman' or 'degrading'. The leading case is *Ireland* v *United Kingdom*.

case close-up

***Ireland* v *United Kingdom* (1979–80) 2 EHRR 25**

Security services in Northern Ireland, as a matter of policy, used five techniques when interrogating Republican terrorist suspects. These techniques were hooding; subjection to continuous loud, hissing noises; sleep deprivation; reduced diet; and being made to stand against a wall in a painful posture for a long period of time. They were applied with premeditation and for hours at a stretch. The ECtHR held that these techniques, in context, did not amount to torture but to inhuman treatment.

> The five techniques were applied in combination, with premeditation and for hours at a stretch; they caused, if not actual bodily injury, at least intense physical and mental suffering to the persons subjected thereto and also led to acute psychiatric disturbances during interrogation. They accordingly fell into the category of inhuman treatment within the meaning of Article 3. The techniques were also degrading since they were such as to arouse in their victims feelings of fear, anguish and inferiority capable of humiliating and debasing them and possibly breaking their physical or moral resistance. (para 167)

KEY POINT The report into the death of Baha Mousa (an Iraqi detainee who, in 2003, was beaten to death by members of the Queen's Lancashire Regiment—see *R (Al-Skeini)* v *Secretary of State for Defence* [2007] UKHL 26) showed that, although these 'conditioning' techniques were illegal, the MOD had failed to take proper, effective and publicised steps to ban them in the armed forces (see, *The Baha Mousa Public Inquiry Report* at http://www.bahamousainquiry.org, Report, Volume III, Summary, para 270).

9.2.1 **Torture and inhuman treatment**

In *Ireland* v *United Kingdom* torture is defined as 'deliberate inhuman treatment causing very serious and cruel suffering' (para 167). Inhuman treatment, the case suggests, is treatment or punishment that is

• likely to cause actual bodily injury or intense physical and mental suffering including acute psychiatric disturbance (the causing of bodily injury is not necessary) (see also *Pretty* v *United Kingdom* (2002) 35 EHRR 1, para 52),

• premeditated and intentional,

• applied for long periods at a time.

KEY POINT Given that Article 3 can apply to inhuman treatment which is unintended (see section 9.7) the last two bullet points are not necessary to every application of Article 3.

9.2.2 **The special case of torture**

In *Ireland*, the Court's view was that Article 3 expressly distinguishes 'torture' from other forms of inhuman and degrading treatment. Torture is a particularly serious form of inhuman treatment, distinguished by the degree of suffering caused and the deliberateness with which it is applied. Consequently it is behaviour to which a special stigma is attached. An example is given below.

case close-up

Aksoy v *Turkey* (1997) 23 EHRR 553
. . . .

The applicant was subjected to 'Palestinian hanging' by Turkish security forces. He was stripped naked, with his arms tied together behind his back, and suspended by his arms. The ECtHR found this to be torture because

• it was deliberately inflicted and must have involved preparation and exertion on the part of the torturers,

• it was administered in order to obtain information or admissions from the victim,

• it caused severe pain with some long lasting consequences.

The Court considers that this treatment was of such a serious and cruel nature that it can only be described as torture.

There is a special UN Convention dealing with torture, the UN Convention against Torture and Other Cruel, Inhuman or Degrading Treatment or Punishment (UNCAT). UNCAT has been used by the ECtHR to determine the border between 'torture' and 'inhuman treatment' (as in *Selmouni* v *France* (2000) 29 EHRR 403).

Article 1 UNCAT defines 'torture' in relation to

- the degree and nature of suffering: torture involves the infliction of severe physical or mental pain

- intentional acts of public officials: the pain and suffering is intentionally inflicted by a public official or with, at least, the acquiescence of a public official;

- purpose: the pain or suffering is inflicted for a purpose such as obtaining information or a confession; for purposes of punishment, intimidation or coercion; or for a reason based on some form of discrimination.

Whether some form of brutal treatment by officials has attached to it the particular stigma of being torture is a matter of judgment for a court. It can depend on context and circumstances and the sense of changing values.

cross reference
The illegal nature of torture is discussed at section 9.4.

> **case close-up**
>
> **El-Masri v The Former Yugoslav Republic of Macedonia App 39630/09, Grand Chamber judgment of 13 December 2012**
>
> As a suspect in the 'war on terror', E-M was detained in Macedonia, handed over to the CIA and taken to Afghanistan. The Grand Chamber held that he had been subjected to 'extraordinary rendition' (transfer of an individual outside the rule of law) (para 221). The Macedonian authorities held and interrogated him, incommunicado, in a hotel room for 23 days. The Court found this was 'inhuman and degrading treatment'.
>
> He was handed over to the USA at the airport where he was physically beaten and 'stripped and sodomised with an object. He was placed in a nappy and dressed in a dark blue short-sleeved tracksuit. Shackled and hooded, and subjected to total sensory deprivation, the applicant was forcibly marched to a CIA aircraft where he was forcibly tranquilised and chained to the floor' (para 205). This treatment, the Court held, amounted, in the circumstances, to 'torture' (para 211).

9.2.3 'Degrading treatment'

Article 3 prohibits 'degrading' treatment or punishment. The meaning of 'degrading' has been discussed in general terms in *Pretty* v *UK*.

> **case close-up**
>
> **Pretty v United Kingdom (2002) 35 EHRR 1**
>
> Diane Pretty suffered from motor neurone disease. Under English law it was unlawful for her husband to assist her in dying at a time and in a manner of her choice. She sought a finding from the ECtHR that this was incompatible with the Convention. Her argument, in relation to Article 3, was that being able to die at a time and in a manner of her choosing would enable her to die with some dignity and less suffering. By refusing her this right she was condemned to suffer in a way that was inhuman and degrading.
>
> The ECtHR found no violation of Article 3 and held that the refusal of the state to sanction assisted suicide did not amount to 'treatment' nor could there be a positive duty on the state to assist a person's suicide by a change in the law.

In *Pretty*, degrading treatment was defined as follows:

Where treatment humiliates or debases an individual showing a lack of respect for, or diminishing, his or her human dignity or arouses feelings of fear, anguish or inferiority capable of breaking an individual's moral and physical resistance, it may be characterised as degrading and also fall within the prohibition of Article 3. (para 52)

Thus treatment or punishment is degrading if it is likely to

- arouse in victims feelings of fear, anguish and inferiority which is humiliating and debasing and is capable of breaking physical and moral resistance;

- in considering whether treatment is degrading, the Court will consider the motive behind the treatment, but a motive to degrade or humiliate is not a necessary requirement;

- discrimination on certain grounds is capable of being degrading. This has been recognised as a possibility by the ECtHR in respect of racial discrimination and discrimination based on sexual orientation.

cross reference
Pretty v United Kingdom is also discussed in Chapter 15, the right to private life.

9.3 State responsibility and positive duties

9.3.1 The scope of Article 3

The definitions of 'torture' and 'inhuman or degrading treatment or punishment' include but are not confined to treatment meted out or supervised by state officials such as police or members of the security services. Unlike under UNCAT (which requires at least the acquiescence of officials, see section 9.2.1) the definition of torture in Article 3 ECHR does not expressly require official involvement. Likewise, the definition of inhuman and degrading treatment or punishment extends to actions by private individuals such as a parent beating his child (as in *A v United Kingdom* (1999) 27 EHRR 611) or a teacher beating one of his pupils (see *Costello-Roberts v United Kingdom* (1995) 19 EHRR 112). *Pretty*, in particular, makes it clear that Article 3 has an important role outside the torture chamber. Article 3 can apply to treatment which is not intended to cause suffering and is not aimed at obtaining information or punishment or intimidation, etc. but is, nevertheless, treatment for which the state can be made responsible: hospital treatment, treatment of prisoners and state responsibility for welfare are examples. Article 3 bases liability on a general approach to state responsibility. It is violated if the state has failed to produce an adequate framework of laws and procedures to protect individuals from behaviour by anyone that causes them to suffer in ways that are incompatible with Article 3. In the context of welfare provision the *Pretty* definition has been adopted into the law of England and Wales, under the Human Rights Act 1998 (HRA), in *R (Limbuela) v Secretary of State for the Home Department* [2005] UKHL 66, see paras 7 and 54 (see section 9.7.1).

9.3.2 Deliberate brutality by officials

Where officials, such as police, military, security officials, or prison officers torture people or intentionally subject them to other degrees of ill-treatment, the state is responsible under Article 3. States must ensure that there are proper laws and effective administrative and judicial processes and sufficient punishments (see *Gäfgen*, at section 9.1.1) by which the perpetrators, even though officials, can be brought to justice by the criminal law. Both Article 1 and, in particular, Article 13, which requires effective remedies 'notwithstanding that the violation has been committed by persons acting in an official capacity' will otherwise be violated. If effective legal remedies against officials are not available, the requirement that a victim must exhaust his or her domestic remedies (see Chapter 2, section 2.7.1) can be waived.

9.3.3 Deliberate brutality by others

Such duties also extend to the deliberate infliction of torture and inhuman treatment by rogue officials acting outside their duty or by others such as terrorists or ordinary criminals. In *E v United Kingdom* (2003) 36 EHRR 31, the ECtHR said that Article 1 taken with Article 3

> requires states to take measures designed to ensure that individuals within their jurisdiction are not subjected to torture or inhuman or degrading treatment, including such ill-treatment administered by private individuals. (para 88)

9.3.4 Article 3 outside the torture chamber

The Article 3 case law has imposed positive duties on states to take reasonable steps to avoid the non-deliberate infliction of suffering that is sufficiently severe to cross the Article 3 threshold. Such duties under Article 3 apply, for instance, in respect of people in the care of the state or who are affected by decisions taken by the state. Examples include prisoners, those treated in public funded hospitals or those subject to deportation (see section 9.8) The main authority is *Pretty v United Kingdom* (2002) 35 EHRR 1:

> The suffering which flows from naturally occurring illness, physical or mental, may be covered by Article 3, where it is, or risks being, exacerbated by treatment, whether flowing from conditions of detention, expulsion or other measures, for which the authorities can be held responsible. (para 52)

Such responsibility is based on an unexpressed political theory that states have general responsibilities over areas such as education and health or the safety of children. In *Costello-Roberts* (1995) 19 EHRR 112 (see section 9.1.2) the ECtHR held that in both domestic and international law the state had responsibility for education including the punishment of children. This responsibility had to be directly accepted and could not be 'delegated' to independent schools. There was, therefore, state responsibility in respect of the punishment of a child by his headmaster in a private school (though, on the facts, the punishment did not meet the Article 3 threshold of seriousness). The same principle is likely to apply in other areas, such as medicine, and so the giving or withdrawing of treatment resulting in suffering in breach of Article 3 is a state responsibility whether or not the hospital is publicly or privately funded.

9.3.5 The nature of the duty

The principal duty of the state is to give effect to its responsibilities by providing effective institutions and systems for preventing and remedying violations of Article 3. The existence of reasonably well-resourced systems of police and criminal justice, health care, child protection and so on, will go a long way towards discharging the duty. In particular there must be an effective system of criminal and civil law so that remedies, such as punishment or compensation, are available against those responsible (including police and other officials) for causing suffering covered by Article 3.

In *E v Chief Constable of the RUC* [2008] UKHL 66, children going to a Catholic primary school in Belfast were subjected to hostile and violent abuse by Loyalists. The House of Lords held that the police's positive duty to protect children from treatment by others that violated Article 3 was not absolute. The positive duty was to do all that could be reasonably expected of them, in the circumstances; this the police had done.

State responsibility under Article 3 can also be based on the *Osman* duty, discussed in Chapter 8, section 8.3.2. The duty is owed where the state is aware or ought to have been aware that someone in the jurisdiction is in danger of suffering above the Article 3 threshold. The duty is to take preventive actions but the extent of these actions is not required to be such as would 'impose an impossible or disproportionate burden on the authorities'. Nevertheless, the duty is context dependent. Failure to give adequate protection to children, for example, may give rise to a violation, as in *Z* v *United Kingdom* (2002) 34 EHRR 3 (failure by local authority social workers to protect the applicant children from abuse and neglect).

9.3.6 **Investigation**

State responsibility requires an effective official investigation into allegations that Article 3 has been violated so that legal responsibility, including criminal responsibility, can be identified and acted upon. In principle the duty to investigate includes, but is not confined to, allegations of abuse by police and other officials (see *Secic* v *Croatia* App 40116/02, judgment of 31 May 2007, paras 53–54). The requirements of an effective investigation are discussed in Chapter 8, section 8.5.2 (in the context of Article 2).

Such a duty can often arise where a person is injured whilst in the custody of the authorities.

In *Toteva* v *Bulgaria* App 42027/98, judgment of 19 May 2004, the evidence showed that the applicant went to the police station in good health and when she left, a few hours later, she had visible bruises and swellings to her head and shoulders. The Court held that the applicant, a 67-year-old woman, had suffered ill-treatment prohibited by Article 3 and the state was responsible since it had failed to rebut the presumption that the applicant had been beaten up by the police.

The duty to investigate under Article 3 has been accepted by UK courts in *R (Green)* v *Police Complaints Authority* [2004] UKHL 6 (para 59). In *R (AM)* v *SSHD* [2009] EWCA Civ 219, a breach of Article 3 was declared because the Home Secretary, alerted to possible breaches of Article 3 in a commercially run immigration detention centre, failed to hold an effective investigation.

9.3.7 **Proof of state responsibility**

cross reference
The powers of the ECtHR to undertake its own investigation are mentioned in Chapter 2, section 2.7.3.

Torture and ill-treatment cases often involve disputes over the facts; in particular the state may deny that its agents were responsible for a victim's suffering. The state's duty in such situations is to hold an effective inquiry. The ECtHR must be satisfied beyond a reasonable doubt that the state was responsible. In the absence of an effective inquiry by the state, the ECtHR may make certain presumptions of state responsibility, which the state must then rebut. Presumptions of responsibility may be made, for example, from the fact that the applicant was arrested in a good physical state but emerged from state custody injured.

9.4　**The illegality of torture**

Torture has come in for the special condemnation of mankind. As the ECtHR recognises, there is a particular shame for a state shown to conduct torture. Most, if not all, states condemn it and make it unlawful. However, most states have officials who have practised, and continue to practice, torture.

case close-up

A v Secretary of State for the Home Department [2005] UKHL 71

. . . .

The Special Immigration Appeals Commission (SIAC) hears appeals from deportations by the Home Secretary on public interest grounds; they also heard appeals from decisions made under Part IV of the Anti-Terrorism, Crime and Security Act 2001 that certified foreign terrorist suspects should be detained indefinitely when it was legally impossible to deport them (this power has now been repealed). The House of Lords held that SIAC could not admit evidence that may have been procured by torture, 'torture evidence'.

In its judgment the House of Lords surveyed the law in terms of general international law, law of the Council of Europe and domestic law of England and Wales.

9.4.1 **International law**

Jus cogens erga omnes

Prohibition of torture is a 'peremptory norm' of international law. It is **jus cogens** (compelling law) and imposes a general obligation on states to act against torture wherever it is found (**erga omnes**). It represents perhaps the highest and most universally recognised obligation on states.

. . . .

jus cogens erga omnes

Some international obligations on states are compulsory. They are not derived directly from an agreed text in a convention or treaty the state has voluntarily chosen to sign. Rather the obligation is imposed on states whether they like it or not, and cannot be avoided. For some lawyers (natural lawyers) the obligations are derived from universal morality; for others (positivists) the obligations are inferred from the constant practices of and public positions adopted by civilised states throughout the world. As well as torture, the prohibition on slavery and genocide are other accepted examples of *jus cogens*. Compulsory law not only requires states to desist from torture themselves but also empowers them (if they wish) to act lawfully against it wherever committed (*erga omnes*—in relation to everyone).

. . . .

further study

A full discussion of the implications of this is in *Prosecutor v Furundzija* [1998] ICTY 3, paras 147–157 (a case of the International Criminal Tribunal for the Former Yugoslavia) quoted in *A*, para 33 (section 9.4).

General Conventions (see *A*, section 9.4, paras 30–33)

cross reference
See Chapter 1 for a general discussion of the ICCPR and enforcement mechanisms, section 1.4.4.

The outlawing of torture and inhuman and degrading treatment and punishment is found widely in international law, not just in Article 3. Article 5 of the Universal Declaration of Human Rights (UDHR) said that 'No one shall be subjected to torture or to cruel, inhuman or degrading treatment or punishment'. These words are reproduced in Article 7 of the International Covenant on Civil and Political Rights (ICCPR), which adds, 'In particular, no one shall be subjected without his free consent to medical or scientific experimentation.'

UN Convention against Torture (see *A*, section 9.4, para 32)

The special UN Convention dealing with torture, the UN Convention against Torture and other Cruel, Inhuman or Degrading Treatment or Punishment (UNCAT), has been mentioned previously. The obligations on signatory states include

- establishing effective laws and procedures so that torture is outlawed as a crime in their jurisdiction in all circumstances;
- not expelling persons to countries where they might be tortured;
- investigating and, if necessary, prosecuting persons in their territory against whom well founded allegations of involvement in torture have been made.

Torture has a severity and also a link to official sanction that distinguishes it from 'ordinary' brutality and ill-treatment (see *A*, section 9.4, para 53). The problem is that making this distinction may enable states to treat suspects in inhuman or degrading ways without attracting full legal condemnation. The routine hooding of detainees in Iraq in 2003 may be an instance of this.

9.4.2 European Convention for the Prevention of Torture and Inhuman or Degrading Treatment or Punishment

The Council of Europe has strengthened its measures against torture in the European Convention for the Prevention of Torture and Inhuman or Degrading Treatment or Punishment. This creates the European Committee for the Prevention of Torture and Inhuman of Degrading Treatment or Punishment. The Committee makes regular visits to the signatory states and reports on a range of matters, such as prison conditions.

9.4.3 Law of the United Kingdom (see *A*, section 9.4 paras 11–13; 103–111)

Torture has been illegal in England since 1640 (when the King's claim to use torture under the prerogative was ended) and, in Scotland, by section 5 of the Treason Act 1708.

The UK's obligations under UNCAT are given effect by section 134 of the Criminal Justice Act 1988, which makes 'torture', as defined by UNCAT, a crime under UK law wherever in the world it is committed and by whoever it is committed, including officials and including an ex-head of state (see *R* v *Bow Street Metropolitan Stipendiary Magistrate ex parte Pinochet Ugarte (No 3)* [2000] 1 AC 147). Torture will also involve a range of ordinary offences for which anyone, including officials, can be prosecuted.

9.4.4 Using the product of torture in courts

Prohibition of torture is one thing, the use of evidence obtained by torture performed by others, raises different issues. Article 15 of UNCAT expressly bans the use of evidence obtained by torture in any proceedings.

The issue in *A* v *Secretary of State for the Home Department* (section 9.4) was whether evidence that might have been obtained by torture, conducted in foreign countries, could be admissible before courts in the United Kingdom dealing with anti-terrorism cases.

The House of Lords made it clear that the use of torture evidence in UK courts is illegal. The reasons for this are, in part, the unreliability of torture. More importantly, it is that the use of torture evidence would shock the conscience of the court. Torture, even where effective and productive of reliable information, is unlawful: it is incompatible with the dignity of the law. The only exception (in recognition of Parliamentary supremacy) would be if an Act of Parliament expressly provided for the use of torture—any such statute would violate international law.

In *A*, the Law Lords disagreed on the burden of proof. All judges agreed that a prisoner alleging torture did not have to prove his or her case. This would be impossible to do. If the applicant could raise a reasonable suspicion that there was torture evidence being relied upon, then the court (in *A* the court was the SIAC) had a duty to investigate.

- The minority view. The evidence allegedly obtained by torture should be rejected unless the court was satisfied, on a balance of probabilities, that the evidence was not the product of torture.

- The majority view. The evidence allegedly obtained by torture should be accepted (so long as it was thought reliable and otherwise admissible) unless, on a balance of probabilities, the court was satisfied that torture had been used.

In other words, the majority took the view that where doubt persisted on whether there had been torture, the evidence should be admitted, if reliable.

KEY POINT The difficulty with the majority view on the burden of proof is that it allows the evidence to be admitted where torture cannot be established because, for example, the allegations are answered by silence from the security services of the states concerned. In *Mamatkulov* v *Turkey* (2005) 41 EHRR 25, a Grand Chamber found no violation of Article 3 when it could 'not conclude' (i.e. it was not proved) that the applicant faced a real risk of torture if extradited.

A refers to evidence admissible in courts. The House of Lords accepted that the Secretary of State can use torture evidence in his or her executive role, in deciding whether a person should be arrested, whether to take action to protect individuals or the public, etc.

cross reference

Whether a person can, compatibly with the Convention, be deported if there is a real risk their trial in the receiving country will be based on torture evidence, is discussed in Chapter 12, section 12.17.

---

discussion topic

Can torture ever be justified?

- The arguments against torture are clear. Persons under the absolute control of others must be treated properly and without abuse and oppression. To torture someone is to deny their very humanity: they are not treated as a 'person' but merely as an object. Even the most dangerous or most unpleasant persons must be accorded this basic respect. The ban on torture is, perhaps, the strongest principle of both international and common law.

- Opposition to torture is partly a 'deontological' argument (an argument about what is 'right' rather than what is useful). It is based on the conception of the person and 'trumps' all other arguments, i.e. you can achieve outcomes that are in the public interests (e.g. public safety) but only if, in doing so, you also safeguard the basic rights of individuals not to be tortured etc. A 'consequentialist' argument, on the other hand, is one that weighs the full range of arguments for and against and looks at the overall outcome.

- There are arguments that might concede the legitimacy of torture in some circumstances (though some argue that even to raise the issue is to concede too much).

– Giving an absolute priority of one right over another may lead to serious consequences for others. In particular can states fulfil their obligations under Article 2 to protect life if they cannot torture, for example, the alleged bomber (consider *Gäfgen*, section 9.1.1)?

– States always claim not to engage in torture. Nevertheless intelligence services throughout the world seem to find inflicting pain and fear on their prisoners an effective way of obtaining information. It is better to accept this and put it on a legal basis. Torture would still be barred but lesser, still serious, forms of physical treatment of detainees could then be undertaken on the basis of a regulated legal structure with defined limits. It is better to regulate dangerous activities that are going to happen anyway: they are more dangerous if unregulated.

For a summary of the arguments see: Rumney, P. and O'Boyle, M. 'The Torture Debate' (2007) 157 *NLJ* 1566.

 ## 9.5 Deliberate ill-treatment by officials

Allegations of abuse of prisoners detained by police, military or other security forces are normally to be considered in the light of Article 3. This is so even if the use of force alleged also threatened the right to life (as in *Ilhan* v *Turkey* (2002) 34 EHRR 36, mentioned in Chapter 8, section 8.2.1).

The ECtHR has made the position very clear. Persons detained by the police etc. must be treated properly and not be subjected to treatment which violates Article 3 (see *Ribitsch* v *Austria* (1996) 21 EHRR 573). Suspects are entirely within the control of the state, they have little autonomy (few choices) and they are vulnerable to the will and the prejudices of their captors. The use of force against detainees is limited to that required by the suspect's own behaviour and that which is 'strictly necessary' to keep him or her under proper control in custody. The threshold of severity is low in respect of detainees since even a minor beating is incompatible with a prisoner's basic dignity. The duty to hold an effective investigation is particularly pressing in respect of people who are apparently injured whilst in the custody of the police or other officials.

Not all physical treatment of suspects will meet the threshold of severity. The normal use of handcuffs and other forms of restraint, for example, can be compatible with Article 3. Such restraints are both below the threshold of severity and for a legitimate purpose consequent on arrest and detention (see *Raninen* v *Sweden* (1998) 26 EHRR 563). Similarly, such restraints are also unlikely to violate Article 8. It needs to be stressed, however, that Article 3 may be breached if, for example, the aim of a particular use of restraining devices is to humiliate or degrade or if the person is young or otherwise vulnerable and such restraint is, given the circumstances, above the minimal level of severity necessary to engage Article 3.

In *FGP* v *Serco* [2012] EWHC 1804, the claimant was detained at an immigration removal centre. When taken to hospital for examination and treatment he was handcuffed and restrained by long chains at all times. The High Court held that the continual use of restraint, in particular whilst he was being treated, was unnecessary, disproportionate and violated Article 3 (*Mouisel* v *France* (2004) 38 EHRR 34 was followed).

9.6 Punishment

Lawful punishment must be compatible with Article 3.

9.6.1 Corporal punishment

The Convention sets its face against corporal punishments (beating etc.) and has had a significant influence on the law in England and Wales.

As a judicial punishment

In 1948 the UK abolished physical punishments (specifically birching) as a judicial punishment for criminal convictions. It was retained by the Isle of Man but in *Tyrer* v *United Kingdom* (1979–80) 2 EHRR 1, the ECtHR held that this was a degrading punishment whose use was incompatible with Article 3 of the Convention (it was then abolished). Judicial corporal punishment, anywhere, cannot survive the general thrust of *Tyrer*. It is specifically the institutional character of the punishment, 'institutionalised violence', carried out impersonally by police officers in a police station with complete physical control over the victim, which is the basis of the Court's finding that the punishment was degrading.

Schools and other institutions

Corporal punishment in schools has tended to be distinguished from judicial birching on the grounds that it is not likely to reach the threshold of severity to violate Article 3 ECHR (see, for example, *Costello-Roberts* v *United Kingdom* (1993) 19 EHRR 112 and *Campbell and Cosans* v *United Kingdom* (1982) 4 EHRR 293). Nevertheless there have been indications of a lack of approval by Strasbourg institutions of corporal punishment in schools (see *Warwick* v *United Kingdom* (1989) 60 DR 5 and *Y* v *United Kingdom* (1994) 17 EHRR 238). Corporal punishment is now unlawful in all schools, state or independent, in the United Kingdom (section 548 Education Act 1996).

KEY POINT School punishment also raises issues under Article 2 of the First Protocol, which gives parents a right that their children be educated in line with their broad philosophical and religious beliefs: see Chapter 24, section 24.4.1.

Parents and carers

The state is responsible for ensuring that punishment imposed on children and others, even by their parents and carers, does not go beyond the level of severity permitted under Articles 3 and 8. The Convention imposes a positive duty on the state to ensure that the criminal law is available to deter and punish those, including private individuals, who inflict such punishment.

case close-up

***A* v *United Kingdom* (1999) 27 EHRR 611**

Between the ages of six and nine years A was frequently punished by his stepfather who beat him with a garden cane, causing bodily marks indicative of serious injury. The stepfather was prosecuted for assault occasioning actual bodily harm but was acquitted. The jury accepted his defence, available to him under English law, that he had done no more than administer 'reasonable chastisement' of a child.

The ECtHR held that, in the circumstances, the punishment reached the level of severity required for a breach of Article 3 and that the state had failed to provide an adequate legal framework for protecting A's Article 3 rights.

Though the judgment in *A* is not clear on the point, the failure of the United Kingdom seems to have been that the law left it to the prejudices of a jury to decide whether or not a punishment was reasonable. The Court also mentioned the fact that the burden of proof was on the prosecution to prove that the beating went beyond what was reasonable. Partly as a consequence of this case, section 58 of the Children Act 2004 removes the defence of reasonable punishment from those accused of offences involving the causing of various degrees of bodily harm or of cruelty to children. The defence remains available for lesser forms of physical punishment of children (such as a common assault or battery not causing bodily harm). This means there is (in England) no outright ban on 'smacking' children; nor, as *Costello-Roberts* indicates, is such an outright ban required under the Convention.

9.6.2 Prisoners' rights under Article 3

Article 3 has a significant impact on the rights of prisoners, particularly in regard to the general conditions they experience, their medical treatment and the types of punishment and security measures they can be subjected to. Since prisoners' rights also involve other Convention rights and are usefully considered in the context of domestic law, they are discussed further in Chapter 21.

9.7 Unintended suffering and hardship

The ban in Article 3 extends to 'inhuman and degrading treatment'. This means that the effect of Article 3 extends beyond the torture chamber and the prison. It applies to action taken where suffering is not intended but is a consequence of entirely lawful decisions and actions which have nothing to do with punishment or with extracting information. Civil servants, for example, may take welfare decisions affecting individuals. If, as a consequence of such otherwise legitimate activity, a person ends up in a situation in which they suffer bodily injury, intense physical or mental suffering, or a situation in which they are humiliated or debased or in which feelings of fear, anguish or inferiority are aroused so that their moral or physical resistance is broken, they may have a right under Article 3. Likewise, the state has positive duties under Article 3 to ensure that the activities of others for which it has responsibilities (e.g. health care and education) are conducted in ways which avoid causing suffering which, in context, goes above the Article 3 threshold of severity. As is made clear below, the 'threshold of severity' in cases that do not involve the deliberate infliction of suffering, can be high.

cross reference
For authority see section 9.3 (the discussion on 'positive duties' above, especially section 9.3.4).

9.7.1 Asylum seekers and welfare under the HRA

The duty on states not to treat people in a way that, unintentionally, may cause suffering which, in context, is above the Article 3 threshold, has become an important issue in English law, particularly in respect of what duties the state has towards people seeking political asylum (foreigners seeking refuge in the United Kingdom on the grounds of a well-grounded fear, which they have yet to prove, of persecution in their own country).

Citizens, and those entitled to reside in the United Kingdom, have access to the welfare state. Other people, such as asylum seekers, who are in the country may have no such right and so the question arises whether there is any duty under the HRA on the state to provide at least a minimum level of subsistence to prevent destitution. Article 3 is not the only Convention right potentially involved: Article 2 can be invoked if the state's refusal to provide accommodation and subsistence is likely to lead to death. Article 8 can be invoked if the state's refusal will lead to circumstances in which a person could be said no longer to be an autonomous person (though the Court of Appeal has suggested that there is no positive duty on the states to provide welfare in respect only of a possible a breach of Article 8 by itself (*Anufrijeva* v *Southwark LBC* [2003] EWCA Civ 1406, para 43)).

Although Article 3 does not require states to provide welfare to a certain level, being left in extremely poor conditions could violate Article 3, especially where domestic legal entitlements are not made available (*MSS* v *Greece and Belgium* (2011) 53 EHRR 2). The issue of the extent of the duty under Article 3 of the state towards asylum seekers has come before the UK courts.

case close-up

R (Limbuela) v Secretary of State for the Home Department [2005] UKHL 66

Asylum seekers are not entitled to the ordinary range of welfare benefits. Nor are they permitted to work. It is also accepted that charitable provision, though available, can be hard to come by.

Section 95 of the Immigration and Asylum Act 1999 permits the Secretary of State to provide welfare support to 'destitute' asylum seekers. However, section 55(1) of the Nationality, Immigration and Asylum Act 2002 prevents the provision of welfare to late applicants, defined as those who had not claimed asylum 'as soon as reasonably practicable after arriving in the United Kingdom'. Nevertheless, the Act gives the Secretary of State the power to grant welfare payments to late applicants if this is necessary to avoid a breach of an applicant's Convention rights, including those under Article 3. Cases were brought by three late applying asylum seekers who had been denied benefits. The question was whether the Home Office's understanding of the threshold of severity, when Article 3 would require some form of welfare support, was, in the three cases, correct. The House of Lords approached the matter on these principles:

- In the context of treatment that does not involve the deliberate infliction of pain, the threshold of severity of the suffering involved is high (though their Lordships rejected the Court of Appeal's analysis in so far as it had suggested that a higher degree of suffering needed to be shown than for deliberately inflicted suffering).

- 'Treatment' means that Article 3 is only involved when the state has taken specific action. Article 3 does not provide a general duty to house the homeless or provide for the destitute. However, there can be 'treatment' where the state takes a decision about an individual, the consequences of which are suffering above the Article 3 threshold. In *R* v *Altham* [2006] EWCA Crim 7, the defendant had used cannabis to alleviate severe pain consequent to a road accident. The Court of Appeal held that the authorities had done nothing to cause the defendant's pain and so had no positive duty under Article 3 to take steps (such as making the defence of necessity available to him) to alleviate it.

- Treatment is inhuman or degrading if 'to a seriously detrimental extent, it denies the most basic needs of any human being'. The threshold of severity may be crossed if a person with no alternative means available to him is 'by the deliberate action of the state, denied shelter, food or the most basic necessities of life'.

On these principles the House of Lords held that there had been a violation of Article 3 in all three cases.

Adam: He claimed to have sought asylum the day after he arrived in the United Kingdom. He was denied benefits. He had to sleep rough in a car park though he had access to Refugee Council premises during the day and could wash himself and his clothes. He was eventually recognised as a genuine refugee.

Limbuela: He claimed to have sought asylum on the day he arrived in the United Kingdom but not at the place of entry. He was denied benefits and had to sleep rough and beg for food (unsuccessfully). He had no access to washing facilities and became ill. His asylum claim failed.

Tesema: He claimed asylum the day after his arrival in the United Kingdom. He was denied benefits. He lived in a hostel but if evicted would have had to sleep rough. He was eventually recognised as a genuine refugee.

(See paras 18–33 for each individual's situation.)

The House of Lords was careful not to lay down a general rule, nevertheless, these cases suggest that an official would violate the duty under section 6 HRA if he or she made a decision which left a person with no food, shelter or means of subsistence.

KEY POINT Article 3 can be relevant in other 'welfare' contexts, such as the care of the elderly and other vulnerable groups. The House of Lords, House of Commons Joint Committee on Human Rights in one of its reports (*The Meaning of Public Authority under the Human Rights Act,* Seventh Report of Session 2003–4, HL Paper 39, HC 382) described a range of abusive treatments allegedly used against old people in care homes which could be violations of Article 3. The main issue in the report is a discussion of whether such treatment, if occurring in privately run homes, engages state responsibility at all (on the latter issue see Chapter 4 on the meaning of 'public authority' under the HRA, section 4.5.5–4.5.8).

9.7.2 **Medical treatment**

State duties

cross reference
On the application of the HRA in a medical context see Chapter 8, section 8.4.

States have responsibilities under the Convention to ensure that medical treatment is given in ways which are compatible with Article 3. Likewise the HRA applies to lawfulness of medical treatment in the UK.

States have positive duties under Article 3 to ensure that the suffering that flows from illness etc. is not made worse by measures taken which engage state responsibility (*Pretty* v UK (2002) 35 EHRR 1, para 52). State responsibility can be engaged in acute situations, situations involving vulnerable people or where the state's monopoly over legitimate force is in issue (such as imprisonment, deportation or forcible treatment).

Normal, therapeutic treatment, aimed at curing the disease or curing the symptoms, administered by competent professionals who are supported by a well-resourced health system is unlikely to violate Article 3. The ECtHR said in *Herczegfalvy* v *Austria* (1993) 15 EHRR 437 'as a general rule, a measure which is a therapeutic necessity cannot be regarded as inhuman or degrading' (para 82).

Medical treatment is also likely to engage Article 8 (respect for private life etc.). It must be remembered that whilst an interference with, say, a patient's private life can be justified under the terms of Article 8(2), treating someone in an inhuman or degrading way which crosses the threshold of severity will violate Article 3 irrespective of any alleged justification. Article 3, therefore, is likely to apply in the most serious cases (though, as said previously, the threshold of severity depends on a range of contextual factors).

A competent patient, of course, can refuse treatment even against his or her acknowledged best interests. Patient autonomy is overriding even if, it may appear, the patient is left in a degrading position. Conversely, a withdrawal, consented to by the patient, of highly invasive treatment may be justified by Article 3 (death being preferred to the severe, degrading, consequences of the treatment)—see *R (Burke)* v *GMC* [2005] EWCA Civ 1003, paras 38–39.

cross reference

Withdrawal of treatment leading to death is discussed in Chapter 8, section 8.4.

Decisions relating to incompetent patients are based on an assessment of the patient's best interests. Such patients are to be treated with dignity. A properly taken medical decision, taking into account all the factors from which a patient's best interests are indicated, including a decision to withdraw life-saving treatment, will not give rise to a breach of Article 3 (*Re M, (Adult Treatment)* [2011] EWHC 2443, para 92.

Forcible treatment

Forcible treatment is treatment imposed, against his or her will, on a patient who is competent enough to give consent for medical treatment. Clearly, this engages the state's monopoly of legitimate force. In England and Wales, for instance, such treatment is permitted under the Mental Health Act 1983 where the treatment is for the patient's mental condition (see section 63, read with sections 57, 58 and 58A). In *Herczegfalvy* v *Austria* (1992) 15 EHRR 437 (the forced feeding of a mental patient on hunger strike), the Court required that the need for the forced treatment must be demonstrated and must relate to convincing therapeutic grounds not, for example, just the desire to maintain physical dominance and control over a patient. The position of inferiority and powerlessness of patients in psychiatric hospital calls for particular vigilance and the patients retain the protection of Article 3. Since the Court did not insist that forced treatment must be for the mental condition, the Convention, perhaps, has a lower standard than under English law.

Whether treatment is 'forced' may depend upon the degree that consent was freely given on the basis of full information; the lack of such full and free consent to a sterilization procedure was the basis of a violation of Article 3 in *VC* v *Slovakia* App 18968/07, judgment of 8 November 2011.

Under the HRA courts will examine with 'increased vigilance' proposals for non-voluntary treatment under the Mental Health Act 1983.

case close-up

R (Wilkinson) v Responsible Medical Officer, Broadmoor Hospital [2001] EWCA Civ 1545

The applicant was a convicted mental patient, compulsorily detained under the Mental Health Act. His doctors wished to give him anti-psychotic drugs despite his refusal to consent. He argued, among other things, that compulsory treatment would violate his rights under Article 3 ECHR. It was held by the Court of Appeal that the importance of Article 3 meant that the strict therapeutic necessity for the treatment needed to be proved to the satisfaction of the court, through an adversarial procedure.

Article 8 can also be engaged by forcible treatment. In *YF* v *Turkey* (2004) 39 EHRR 34, a forced gynaecological examination done, apparently, to forestall allegations of rape, was a violation of Article 8.

9.8 Deportations—'foreign cases'

9.8.1 The legal basis of deportation etc.

People who are not British Citizens may, on various grounds, be removed from the UK.

Persons who are in the UK lawfully may be 'deported'. This can be done under the Immigration Act 1971 and other legislation. There are two principal grounds of deportation: as a consequence of conviction and punishment for a serious offence (section 3(6) Immigration Act 1971); or where in the view of the government the presence of the person (and family members) in the UK is not 'conducive to the public good' because they represent a threat to national security, for example, (section 3(5) Immigration Act 1971).

Persons who are not in the UK lawfully may be 'removed'. Overstayers, illegal entrants, former refugees, etc. are subject to summary removal by immigration officials exercising powers under section 10 Immigration and Asylum Act 1999.

Persons, including British citizens, can be 'extradited'. This is where they are sent to another country that is seeking to try them for a serious criminal offence. Extradition is based on treaty arrangements between the UK and other states and is brought into effect through the Extradition Act 2003; within the EU the European Arrest Warrant applies.

9.8.2 Real risk of a violation of Article 2 or 3 in the receiving state

The fundamental nature of Articles 2 and 3 means that it is a violation of the Convention to deport, extradite or otherwise remove a person to a country in which there is a 'real risk' that they might be killed, tortured or suffer other ill-treatment prohibited by Articles 2 and 3. This applies even though the receiving country is not a member of the Council of Europe. The principle was first developed in *Soering v United Kingdom* (1989) 11 EHRR 439. It was held that the proposed extradition of a West German national to the United States to face a murder charge would be a violation of Article 3. If he was sentenced to death, the intensity and duration of suffering associated with being on 'death row' was such that it crossed the Article 3 threshold of severity. The violation stems not from actions of the United States (which is not a signatory to the Convention) but from actions by the United Kingdom in complying with the extradition request.

case close-up

Chahal v United Kingdom (1997) 23 EHRR 413

Chahal was an Indian citizen resident in the United Kingdom. He was politically involved in the movement for a separate Sikh state in Indian Punjab and was suspected by UK authorities of involvement in terrorism in India and violence in the United Kingdom. The Home Secretary sought to deport him back to India on public interest grounds. The ECtHR found, on the facts (particularly Amnesty International reports), that there was a real risk that Chahal would suffer torture at the hands of Punjab security forces and others and that deportation would, therefore, violate Article 3.

In coming to this decision the Court established a number of important general principles:

- States have the right to control the entry, residence and expulsion of aliens (para 73).

- However, the right must be exercised in full recognition of the absolute and fundamental requirements of Article 3.

- Under Article 3 there was an unqualified duty on states not to remove a person who would face 'a real risk of being subjected to treatment contrary to Article 3 in the receiving country' (para 74).

- The obligation is absolute in the sense that it applies where the risk of torture etc. is 'real'. There is no balance to be struck between the public interest served by the removal and the degree of likelihood that the real risk will materialise (para 76): 'the national interests of the State could not be invoked to override the interests of the individual where substantial grounds had been shown for believing that he would be subjected to ill-treatment if expelled' (para 78).

The absolute ban on capital punishment (by Protocol 13) means that a deportation or extradition in circumstances where the death penalty may be imposed in the receiving state will violate the Convention. The fear of execution in the receiving state will cross the threshold of severity and breach Article 3 (*Saadoon* v *UK* (2010) 51 EHRR 9; by implication such a deportation etc. could breach Protocol 13, para 123).

It is the illegitimacy of the death penalty that is crucial; fear of or experience of lesser punishments is less likely to cause a breach. The suffering must go beyond that inevitably associated with imprisonment. Whether there would be a breach will depend upon individual circumstances. In *Babar Ahmed* v *UK* App 24027/07, judgment of 10 April 2012, the 'highly restrictive' conditions in a particular Federal US prison did not cross the threshold of severity so as to prevent extradition. A real risk of a life sentence with no hope of parole might violate Article 3 unless some other procedure, such as executive clemency, was, even though unlikely, available (*R (Wellington)* v *Secretary of State for the Home Department* [2008] UKHL 72).

Reform

The position adopted by the European Court is highly controversial. It means that people who, in the judgment of the judiciary or executive, are dangerous, threatening or undesirable cannot be removed from the country. As the Court made clear in *Ahmed* v *Austria* (1997) 24 EHRR 278, 'the activities of the individual in question, however undesirable or dangerous, cannot be a material consideration' (para 40). Various attempts, by the UK and other states, to introduce an element of proportionality (balancing the degree of risk of torture etc. with the degree of danger posed by the individual) have failed (*Saadi* v *Italy* (2009) 49 EHRR 30).

KEY POINT Deportation and other forms of removal raise issues under other Articles of the Convention. These are considered in the appropriate chapters. Thus the effect of family ties in the UK is considered in Chapter 15, section 15.10.7 (Article 8) and the issue of the fairness of a trial in the receiving country is considered in Chapter 12, section 12.17 (Article 6). Important issues respecting the deportation of terrorist suspects, including reliance on diplomatic assurances, are addressed in Chapter 26, section 26.7.3.

205

Summary

- Article 3 is perhaps the most fundamental of the Convention rights. It applies absolutely in the sense that torture and inhuman and degrading treatment or punishment is prohibited no matter how strong the public interests are which purport to justify it.

- Treatment prohibited by Article 3 must, however, meet a threshold of severity. This threshold is context dependent so what counts as a violation of Article 3 depends upon a range of factors.

- Torture is defined in terms of the deliberate infliction of severe suffering in order to obtain information or a confession, or to punish, or simply to abuse. Characteristically it is imposed by state agents but the Convention does not require this.

- Inhuman and degrading treatment and punishment involves suffering that is less severe than torture and not necessarily for the purposes of torture.

- Of great importance is the way the jurisprudence of the ECtHR has extended the notion of 'treatment' for which the state is responsible into fields such as education, health care, prisons and deportation. Suffering which meets the Article 3 threshold but which is not imposed deliberately and for which the state agents may not be the direct cause (it being imposed by a private individual, for example) may still engage state responsibility and lead to violations of Article 3.

Questions

 For suggested approaches, please visit the Online Resource Centre.

1 The family of an old lady living in a private care home complain that she is being abused. The UK courts refuse to consider whether there has been a breach of Article 3 (they say, the care home is not a 'public authority' under section 6 HRA). The family take their case to the ECtHR alleging a breach of Article 3. What are the main arguments they will have to make? Note: whether or not the care home is a public authority under the HRA, is not the issue here (see Chapter 4, section 4.5.6).

2 A suspected child kidnapper is detained by police. On good grounds they believe he has an accomplice who is holding the child and that the suspect knows where the child is. They believe the child to be in serious danger. The police subject the suspect to loud noise, he is denied food and sleep and made to stand for hours on end in an uncomfortable posture. On what principles would the application of Article 3 to these matters be considered?

Further reading

GENERAL

Amos, M. (see Preface) Chapter 8

Lester, A., Pannick, D. and Herberg, J. (see Preface) Chapter 4, Article 3

ARTICLES DEALING WITH ISSUES UNDER ARTICLE 3

Grief, N. and Addo, M. 'Does Article 3 ECHR Enshrine Absolute Rights?' (1998) 9(3) *European Journal of International Law* 510–524

Kenny, J. 'European Convention on Human Rights and Social Welfare' [2010] 5 *EHRLR* 495–503

Lawson, A. 'Disability, Degradation and Dignity: The Role of Article 3 ECHR' (2005) 56(4) *Northern Ireland Legal Quarterly* 462–491

Palmer, S. 'A Wrong Turning: Article 3 ECHR and Proportionality' (2006) 65(2) *Cambridge Law Journal* 438–451

ON TORTURE

Articles in [2006] 2 *EHRLR* (special issue on torture)

Evans, M.D. and Morgan, R. *Preventing Torture* (1998) Oxford: OUP, especially Chapters 1 and 2

Sands, P. *Lawless World* (2005) London: Penguin, Chapter V

Article 4: prohibition of slavery and forced labour

Chapter overview

- The absolute ban on 'slavery' and 'servitude' (Article 4(1)).
- The prohibition of 'forced or compulsory labour' (Article 4(2)).
- Exceptions to the prohibition on forced or compulsory labour in respect of various forms of work that people may be required to do (Article 4(3)).

Article 4   Prohibition of slavery and forced labour

(1) No one shall be held in slavery or servitude.

(2) No one shall be required to perform forced or compulsory labour.

(3) For the purpose of this article the term 'forced or compulsory labour' shall not include:

(a) any work required to be done in the ordinary course of detention imposed according to the provisions of Article 5 of this Convention or during conditional release from such detention;

(b) any service of a military character or, in case of conscientious objectors in countries where they are recognised, service exacted instead of compulsory military service;

(c) any service exacted in case of an emergency or calamity threatening the life or well-being of the community;

(d) any work or service which forms part of normal civic obligations.

Introduction

'Slavery' and 'servitude' imply the ownership or total control of one person by another. A slave has no freedom or autonomy and so is denied the minimum dignity that is essential for any human being. Article 4(1), like all international conventions on the subject, imposes an absolute ban on the holding of persons as slaves or serfs.

'Forced labour' implies being forced to work for another under threat of punishment or death. The lack of freedom and, as demonstrated by experience, the likelihood that the conditions of work are likely to be atrocious, means that the forced labourer is denied autonomy and dignity. Forced labour is banned under Article 4(2).

There are circumstances in which requiring someone to work can be a reasonable and proportionate part of punishment. Similarly, certain types of work can be worthy and honourable expressions of the duties and obligations that follow from membership of society and the enjoyment of its benefits. If done in a proportionate manner, requiring work in such circumstances is not necessarily incompatible with human dignity and is allowed for under the terms of Article 4(3).

 ## 10.1 The ban on slavery and servitude

Slavery implies ownership by one person of another, and ownership is always a matter of law. In this strictly legal sense there are few, if any, slaves left in the world because slavery is illegal under most, if not all, legal systems. But that is not the point. Millions of men, women and children throughout the world are treated like slaves or reduced to the condition of slavery. Anti-Slavery International defines slavery in terms of working under threat and coercion, being 'controlled' by abuse or threatened abuse, being treated as a commodity and being physically restrained in various ways. In this sense slavery is as great a problem throughout the world as it ever was.

further study

See the website of Anti-Slavery International http://www.antislavery.org/

10.1.1 **The illegality of slavery**

Slavery in Britain, in the sense of a claim by one person to have absolute control over the life of another, seems to have been illegal at common law since at least the sixteenth century. However, where the law of other countries, including British colonies, permitted slavery, English law would uphold contractual and property rights (for example, between buyer and seller of slaves). The rights of the master over the slave, once in England, were a different matter. The famous words: 'the air of England is too pure for a slave to breath' may have originated in a decision of the Court of Star Chamber in the time of Queen Elizabeth 1st in which the claim of a slave owner to beat his Russian slave with impunity, was denied (see *Oxford Dictionary of Quotations*, 4th edn, p 17; Sedley J. 'Human Rights: A Twenty-First Century Agenda' [1995] *Public Law* (Autumn) 386–400, 392–393).

Somerset's case 1772, was understood to confirm that slavery in England was illegal (exactly what Lord Mansfield said or meant remains unclear).

case close-up

> ***Somerset* v *Stewart* (1772) Lofft 1; 98 ER 499**
> . . . .
> The court was concerned with the liberty of a runaway slave (James Somerset) who had been recaptured and was being held on board ship in London awaiting transport to Jamaica. Lord Mansfield ordered his release. No clear rule of law permitted the detention of Somerset and, because slavery was 'so odious that nothing can be suffered to support it but positive law', the detention was illegal and his release was ordered.

But, as the quotation makes clear, slavery can still be legal if expressly allowed by 'positive law' (definite rules of law such as are laid down in statute). Slavery in the West Indian colonies was recognised by English courts who denied, for example, that the presence of a slave in England meant that he or she remained free on returning to their home country (see *The Slave Grace* (1827) 2 St Tr (NS) 273). It was up to nation states and, later, the international community, to make slavery illegal by 'positive law'. Important dates include:

- 1807—Parliament made British involvement in the slave trade illegal.

- 1833—slavery in the British colonies ended.

- 1863—ending of slavery of African-Americans in the United States by constitutional amendment after the civil war.

- Second half of the nineteenth century—increasingly, European courts would free slaves brought within their jurisdiction and bilateral treaties between states were made aimed at suppression of the slave trade.

- 1885—the Treaty of Berlin made the slave trade illegal at international law.

- 1926—the Slavery Convention committed the international community to 'prevent and suppress the slave trade' and 'to bring about, progressively and as soon as possible, the complete abolition of slavery in all its forms'.

- 1936–45—the use of slave labour under the Nazi and Japanese dictatorships (Russian also) before and during the Second World War was a spur to further international action. In 1953 the Slavery Convention was extended to seek the abolition of 'practices similar to slavery' such as serfdom and debt bondage.

10.1.2 The Prohibition of Slavery and servitude, Article 4(1)

Slavery and servitude are not defined in the Convention.

Slavery

In *Siliadin* v *France* (2006) 43 EHRR 16, the European Court of Human Rights (ECtHR) accepted the 'classic' definition of slavery found in the 1926 Convention:

> Slavery is the status or condition of a person over whom any or all of the powers attaching to the right of ownership are exercised. (Article 1(1))

In the strict sense, based on legally recognised ownership, slavery is not found in Europe and is unlikely to reappear.

There is, of course, plenty of evidence from Europe, including the United Kingdom, pointing to widespread trafficking in children and women and of the slave-like use (being treated as a possession to be used, abused and destroyed at will) that is made of these victims; similarly it seems that domestic servants who accompany some visitors to the United Kingdom may be little better than slaves. Such conditions may be dealt with as forced or compulsory labour under Article 4(2). If not the Court might be persuaded to consider a definition of slavery that looks more to the factual circumstances (subordination and control by another) rather than legal status.

States have positive duties to ensure that there are adequate criminal penalties to punish the practices prohibited by Article 4 (*Siliadin*, para 89). In England, section 71 Coroners and Justice Act 2009 creates offences dealing with slavery, servitude and forced labour. Likewise, section 4 Asylum and Immigration (Treatment of Claimants, etc.) Act 2004 (amended by the Protection of Freedoms Act 2012) creates an offence of trafficking people for exploitation and its terms have been held to contain the core elements of Article 4 (*R* v *K* [2011] EWCA Crim 1691).

Servitude

Unlike 'slavery', 'servitude' does not imply ownership. In *Van Droogenbroeck* v *Belgium* (1982) 4 EHRR 443 the Commission of Human Rights identified the central point of servitude as including 'the obligation on the part of the "serf" to live on another's property and the impossibility of changing his condition'.

The utility of such a concept, in dealing with modern conditions of trafficking and exploitation, depends upon a realistic rather than legal understanding of the nature of the 'obligation' a person is under. Work is 'servitude' if it is imposed on another in a way that involves a 'particularly serious…violation of freedom' (*Van Droogenbroeck*, para 58). Under Article 4(3), as discussed in section 10.3, it is acceptable under the ECHR to require work from prisoners, soldiers and others. But such work must be 'normal' in the context. If the work is normal it is unlikely to be servitude: see *W, X, Y and Z* v *United Kingdom* App 3435/67, Commission decision of 19 July 1968 (military service) and *Van Droogenbroeck* v *Belgium* (1982) 4 EHRR 443 (prison work).

10.2 Forced or compulsory labour, Article 4(2)

The concept of forced or compulsory labour was discussed by the ECtHR in *Van der Mussele* v *Belgium*.

case close-up

Van der Mussele v *Belgium* (1984) 6 EHRR 163

The Belgium legal profession, putting into effect requirements of Belgian law for a form of legal aid, required some trainees (pupil 'avocats') to act for poor clients without payment. The ECtHR held that there was not a violation of Article 4. The obligation on trainees had to be considered in context: the trainee gained the valuable right of membership of the profession with exclusive rights of audience in the courts; the required work enabled the trainee to add to his or her experience and professional reputation. Given also that the trainees had opportunities for paid work, the obligation was a proportionate requirement imposed on those who were voluntarily seeking professional membership.

The ECtHR took as its starting point the definition of forced labour in the International Labour Organization Convention of 1930:

 all work or service which is exacted from any person under the menace of any penalty and for which he has not offered himself voluntarily.

The ECtHR went on to refine the meaning of these terms for the purposes of Article 4 ECHR.

- 'Labour' means all kinds of work or service and is not confined to physical work (para 33).
- 'Forced' implies a 'physical or mental constraint' (para 34).
- 'Compulsory' means 'work exacted…under the menace of a penalty' and 'performed against the will of the person concerned'. Labour is not 'compulsory' just because it is based on a contract freely entered into and breach of the contract would have legal consequences.

KEY POINT Article 1 of Protocol 4 ECHR, which follows Article 11 of the International Covenant on Civil and Political Rights (ICCPR), prohibits depriving a person of his or her liberty 'merely on the ground of inability to fulfil a contractual obligation'. (The UK has not ratified Protocol 4 and so is not bound by it either at Strasbourg or under the Human Rights Act 1998 (HRA).)

- Voluntary. The ECtHR does not accept that the fact that a person has consented to the obligation necessarily makes it voluntary. *Van der Mussele* illustrates the situation where an organisation has monopolistic control over the provision of a benefit (e.g. a professional body controlling entry to a profession) and the body imposes costs and burdens on a person seeking the benefit. The fact that the person, after weighing the advantages against the burdens, chooses to obtain the benefit and accept the burden, does not mean that the burden is accepted voluntarily: in the Court's view there is no real choice (para 36).
- Need not be 'unjust' etc. In *Van der Mussele* the ECtHR rejected the argument that forced or compulsory labour needed to be 'unjust', 'oppressive', 'an avoidable hardship',

'needlessly distressing' or 'somewhat harassing' (para 37). The Commission had considered this in *Iversen v Norway* (as *X v Austria*) App 1452/62 Commission decision of 18 December 1963.

There is no simple test for forced or compulsory labour. Its existence depends on a range of circumstances, in particular:

- the nature of the work involved,
- the existence of a penalty or of a burden comparable to a penalty,
- the fact of consent (lack of consent does not, alone, mean the labour was forced or compelled),
- the benefits that may accrue to the individual,
- the degree of oppression and hardship involved, and
- the general circumstances.

The legal test is proportionality: whether, in the circumstances, the burden is excessive and disproportionate in relation to any benefit or advantage enjoyed (see *Van der Mussele*, para 38). Article 4(3) (discussed at section 10.3) stipulates that certain obligations to work are not 'forced or compulsory labour'. The principles underlying these exceptions help to identify what is or is not a disproportionate obligation to work.

The 'work' (arduous physical labour, domestic service, prostitution, etc.) that is done by persons 'trafficked' into the United Kingdom from overseas is capable of being brought within the prohibitions of Article 4(2). However, the issue is best dealt with by specific, focused, international conventions which impose particular positive obligations on states. Both the United Nations and the Council of Europe have produced such agreements (see the following Further reading section).

KEY POINT Article 4(2) is unlikely to be relevant in respect of claims about poor conditions for those working under contracts of employment in the United Kingdom. Such matters are more likely to raise issues under health and safety and employment protection legislation (including from the European Union); or be dealt with by trade unions and collective bargaining. Nor does non-payment of lawfully due wages engage Article 4 (*Vorana v Ukraine* App 44372/02, judgment of 9 November 2006).

10.3 Article 4(3) exclusions

Article 4(3) is said to 'delimit' (specify) the scope of the ban on forced or compulsory labour. Article 4(3) guides the interpretation of Article 4(2). It identifies certain types of work which are not prohibited under Article 4(2) merely because they are compulsory. Conscripts, for example, are compelled into the armed forces but are not thereby the victims of compulsory labour under Article 4(2). It is, however, only the normal kinds and degrees of labour expected of such groups that is exempted from the ban in Article 4(2). If conscripts, for example, were subject to burdens of work unlike those normally expected of military service, there could be a violation of Article 4(2), or of Article 4(1) if abnormal work so restricted freedom that it amounted to servitude.

The principles underlying the exemptions under Article 4(3) are said to be 'general interest, social solidarity and what is in the normal or ordinary course of affairs' (see *Van der Mussele*, para 38). They embody the sense that, in some circumstances, an obligation to work can be a reasonable expression of social membership.

10.3.1 **Prison work**

It is common in European penal systems, including that of the United Kingdom, for prisoners to be required to work. Work can be part of the punishment or it can be aimed at rehabilitation and reintegration into the community. Under Article 4(3)(a) normal prison work is not 'forced or compulsory' labour. This extends, it seems, to work demanded of anyone lawfully detained under Article 5(1) and so can extend to work demanded of those detained in a mental hospital, for example. It also extends to those released from prison under licence who are subject to recall. In the United Kingdom convicted criminals can be punished by being required to do unpaid community work. In *R* v *Clarke* [2008] EWCA Crim 893 such punishment was said to be justified under Article 4(3)(a).

What is normal prison work will depend upon different national customs and develop over time. Thus working unpaid for private companies was considered normal and so not a violation of Article 4 in the late 1960s (*21 Detained Persons* v *Germany* App 3134/67, Commission decision of 6 April 1968). In *Stummer* v *Austria* (2012) 54 EHRR 11, it was held that, in the early twenty-first century, states were not required to allow prison work to count towards entitlement to the old age pension.

10.3.2 **Military service and conscientious objection**

cross reference

Conscientious objection may involve Article 9 and is discussed in Chapter 16, section 16.4.6.

Article 4(3)(b) exempts military service from being challenged under Article 4(2) as forced or compulsory labour. It includes conscription (found in some European countries though ended in the United Kingdom in 1960), but is not confined to it. The normal demands of military life, even if compulsorily imposed, are not, in themselves, a form of servitude (*W, X, Y, Z* v *United Kingdom* App 3435/67, admissibility decision of 19 July 1968).

Article 4 does not require states to grant rights of conscientious objection to citizens. If, however, conscientious objection to military conscription is recognised by law, any alternative service that may be required cannot be regarded as forced or compulsory labour unless wholly disproportionate and unusual in its demands, or sufficiently oppressive to count as servitude.

10.3.3 **Emergency service**

The principle of social solidarity means that proportionate, though compulsory, demands on individuals can be made as a means of dealing with 'an emergency or calamity threatening the life or well-being of the community', Article 4(3)(c).

In *Iversen* v *Norway* (as *X* v *Austria*) App 1452/62, Commission decision of 18 December 1963, the Commission declared a claim by newly qualified dentists to be inadmissible. The dentists were required to work in the public dental service in order to deal with a crisis shortage of dentists in parts of Norway. Some of the Commissioners focused on the fact that the work was not 'oppressive', and others held that the requirement was a reasonable response to the crisis.

10.3.4 **Normal civic obligations**

On the principle of 'solidarity', Article 4(3)(d) exempts compulsory work which is part of 'normal civic obligations' from being forced or compulsory labour. What counts as a 'normal' civic obligation will depend on the circumstances and the context. Such obligations may be required in order for society, through the state, to discharge its duties to the least well-off and those in need: *Van Mussele* and *Iversen* (mentioned at section 10.2) concerned, respectively, legal aid and free dentistry. Compulsory jury service is a normal civic obligation (*Adami* v *Malta* (2007) 44 EHRR 3).

In the United Kingdom, under the HRA, it has been held that procedures and penalties connected with the payment of taxes do not disclose a violation of Article 4 (*Murat v Inland Revenue Commissioners* [2004] EWHC 3123).

discussion topic

Compulsory labour and the modern world

Do the exceptions to the concepts of forced or compulsory labour found in Article 4(3) continue to reflect the reasonable demands which a state can make on its citizens or has our understanding of individual freedom and respect for persons developed in such a way as to make these seem outdated survivals from the 1950s which ought to be interpreted away in the more individualistic twenty-first century? Is it right that a state should fulfil its obligations to its least well-off citizens by compelling the young and recently qualified to work for free?

Summary

- Article 4 requires a total ban on slavery and servitude.

- There is also a total ban on forced or compulsory labour, but the meaning of these two terms excludes any work a person is legally obliged to do as a lawful prisoner, as a member of the armed forces, to assist in an emergency or as part of established civic obligations, so long as such work is normal in the context.

Question

@ For suggested approaches, please visit the Online Resource Centre.

How have the Commission and ECtHR defined 'slavery', 'servitude' and 'forced or compulsory labour'? Are these concepts sufficient to be the legal basis for dealing with the exploitation of men, women and children associated with 'people trafficking' in the twenty-first century?

Further reading

THE UN AND COUNCIL OF EUROPE CONVENTIONS ON PEOPLE TRAFFICKING ARE

The Protocol to Suppress and Punish Trafficking in Persons Especially Women and Children (the UN Convention against Transnational Organized Crime)

The Council of Europe Convention on Action against Trafficking in Human Beings (in force in the UK from 1 April 2009)

GENERAL TEXTS

Lester, A., Pannick, D. and Herberg, J. (see Preface) Chapter 4, Article 4

Article 5: right to liberty and security

Chapter overview

- The basic idea: that no one should be arbitrarily detained by the authorities.

- The meaning of 'deprivation of liberty'.

- The particular, exclusive purposes for which a person can be detained (Article 5(1)).

- The requirement that deprivations of liberty be subject to proper, independent and impartial judicial supervision (Article 5(3) and (4)).

Article 5   Right to liberty and security

(1) Everyone has the right to liberty and security of person. No one shall be deprived of his liberty save in the following cases and in accordance with a procedure prescribed by law:

(a) the lawful detention of a person after conviction by a competent court;

(b) the lawful arrest or detention of a person for non-compliance with the lawful order of a court or in order to secure the fulfilment of any obligation prescribed by law;

(c) the lawful arrest or detention of a person effected for the purpose of bringing him before the competent legal authority on reasonable suspicion of having committed an offence or when it is reasonably considered necessary to prevent his committing an offence or fleeing after having done so;

(d) the detention of a minor by lawful order for the purpose of educational supervision or his lawful detention for the purpose of bringing him before the competent legal authority;

(e) the lawful detention of persons for the prevention of the spreading of infectious diseases, of persons of unsound mind, alcoholics or drug addicts or vagrants;

(f) the lawful arrest or detention of a person to prevent his effecting unauthorised entry into the country or of a person against whom action is being taken with a view to deportation or extradition.

(2) Everyone who is arrested shall be informed promptly, in a language which he understands, of the reasons for his arrest and of any charge against him.

(3) Everyone arrested or detained in accordance with the provisions of paragraph 1(c) of this article shall be brought promptly before a judge or other officer authorised by law to exercise judicial power and shall be entitled to trial within a reasonable time or to release pending trial. Release may be conditioned by guarantees to appear for trial.

(4) Everyone who is deprived of his liberty by arrest or detention shall be entitled to take proceedings by which the lawfulness of his detention shall be decided speedily by a court and his release ordered if the detention is not lawful.

(5) Everyone who has been the victim of arrest or detention in contravention of the provisions of this article shall have an enforceable right to compensation.

217

Introduction

Article 5 deals with freedom of the person, with 'liberty' in the sense of not to be under the direct physical control of another. As the European Court of Human Rights (ECtHR) said in *Engel* v *The Netherlands* (1979–80) 1 EHRR 647, para 58, Article 5 deals with 'individual liberty in its classic sense, that is to say the physical liberty of the person'. It is not to do with broader ideas of liberty, such as the sense of personal autonomy and the lack of individual or social subordination. The core examples of restriction of liberty in this sense are arrest and detention by the police, imprisonment after conviction, detention of the mentally ill in hospitals and the detention of foreigners in the context of immigration and asylum.

States are entitled to exercise their 'monopoly of legitimate force' by imposing (given the ending of the death penalty) the ultimate sanction of taking away liberty. The point of Article 5 is to protect individuals from the 'arbitrary' (unprincipled or oppressive) exercise of such power. It does this

- **by identifying the only, exclusive, reasons for which physical liberty can be restricted (the reasons listed in Article 5(1)(a)–(f));**

- **by requiring any restriction on liberty to be 'lawful' in the Convention sense (lawful under national law but, also, national law must not permit arbitrary detention) by requiring that states have procedural protections in place to ensure that interferences with physical liberty are subject to proper judicial supervision (see Article 5(2)–(5)).**

cross reference
See Chapter 6, section 6.2 for the Convention conception of law.

further study

These general principles are recognised in *R (Wardle)* v *Crown Court at Leeds* [2001] UKHL 12, see paras 83–84.

11.1 The right to liberty and the law of England and Wales

The importance of physical liberty has been long recognised in English law. Lord Bingham has referred to

> the long libertarian tradition of English law, dating back to chapter 39 of Magna Carta 1215, given effect in the ancient remedy of habeas corpus, declared in the Petition of Right 1628, upheld in a series of landmark decisions down the centuries and embodied in the substance and procedure of the law to our own day.
>
> (*A* v *Secretary of State for the Home Department* [2004] UKHL 56, para 36)

cross reference
Section 7 HRA is discussed in Chapter 5, section 5.4.

Article 5 can be enforced directly against a public authority in the UK (e.g. the Home Secretary or a prison governor) by using section 7 of the Human Rights Act 1998 (HRA). But this is in addition to a number of long-standing remedies, protecting liberty, already recognised in the law of England and Wales (and also, differently, in Scotland and Northern Ireland). Many Acts of Parliament permit restrictions on liberty (e.g. the Police and Criminal Evidence Act 1984); under section 3 HRA, such Acts must be interpreted, as far as possible, for compatibility with Article 5. In English law the right to liberty can be given effect in various ways such as:

- *Habeas corpus.* By means of the writ a person alleging they have been unlawfully detained can seek from the High Court an order for their immediate release by whoever is detaining them. The Court has no discretion and must issue the writ if it finds that the detention is unlawful. The writ can be issued against state agents such as the police or immigration officers as well as private parties. Though developed by the judges, the availability of the writ has been strengthened by Habeas Corpus Acts dating back to 1679.

cross reference
Judicial review is outlined in Chapter 5, section 5.2.1.

- Courts, tribunals and judicial review. *Habeas corpus* tends to be a back-stop remedy. It is rarely going to be appropriate where a person is detained on the basis of detailed rules in an Act of Parliament (such as being detained by the police under the Police and Criminal Evidence Act 1984, or in a mental hospital under the Mental Health Act 1983). In such contexts legal challenge is most likely to be based, first, on the procedures for challenge provided for in the Act (such as magistrates supervising suspects' detentions in police stations or First Tier Tribunals (Mental Health) hearing claims that the grounds for detention in a mental hospital no longer exist). Second, the legality of the decisions of such officials and tribunals can themselves be challenged through judicial review or, in the case of tribunals, by appeal within the tribunal system itself to the 'Upper Tribunal'. There is a legal presumption in favour of liberty so any intention by Parliament that a statute will allow a deprivation of liberty must be clear and unambiguous (*R (Kelly)* v *Secretary of State for Justice* [2008] EWCA Civ 177, para 26).

- A civil action for damages in the tort of false imprisonment. The claimant needs to prove that he or she was directly and intentionally imprisoned by the defendant; the tort is proved unless the defendant can show lawful justification. There is no need to prove other loss (*Lumba* v *Secretary of State for the Home Department* [2012] UKSC 12, paras 64–65).

The implication in *Austin* v *Commissioner of Police of the Metropolis* [2009] UKHL 5, is that the tort and the Convention right are linked: a justified false imprisonment cannot also be a violation of Article 5, and vice versa.

cross reference
On the validity of incompatible statutes see Chapter 4, section 4.4.2.

KEY POINT No court in England and Wales can order release or award damages if the deprivation of liberty is permitted by the law. Under the HRA, if the clear policy of legislation is to permit detention on grounds which are incompatible with Article 5, then nothing in the Act or *habeas corpus* or any of the other remedies outlined above will require a person's release. An example is the detention without trial of foreign terrorist suspects between 2001 and 2005. The House of Lords declared that this was incompatible with Article 5 but had no power to order release because the detention was clearly allowed for by legislation (see Chapter 26, section 26.3.2 and Chapter 7, section 7.1.5).

International Covenant on Civil and Political Rights

The United Kingdom is also bound by the right to liberty in Article 9 of the International Covenant on Civil and Political Rights (ICCPR). In addition Article 10 ICCPR places obligations on states regarding the way they treat the people they detain (see Chapter 21, section 21.4). The ICCPR is discussed in Chapter 1, section 1.4.4.

11.2 Deprivation of liberty

11.2.1 Deprivation of liberty or restriction on movement

Article 5 applies where there is a 'deprivation of liberty'. This is a legal term. Not all restrictions imposed by the state on individuals' movements are within the ambit of Article 5. Deprivation of liberty, in Article 5, needs to be distinguished from general restrictions on movement such as when a person is banned from entering a geographically defined area but whose freedom of movement is otherwise not restricted.

KEY POINT 'Restrictions on movement' which are not 'deprivations of liberty' are within the ambit of Article 2(1) of Protocol 4 ECHR (freedom of movement). Since the United Kingdom has signed but not ratified this Protocol it is not in Schedule 1 HRA. In any case, Article 2(3) of the Protocol allows proportionate restrictions on movement where the state can show these are necessary.

Though imprisonment is the obvious example of a deprivation of liberty, the ECtHR has made it clear that the term has a wider meaning. The existence of a deprivation of liberty is a matter of judgment based on all the circumstances. The leading case on the distinction between deprivation of liberty and restrictions on movement is *Guzzardi* v *Italy* (1980) 3 EHRR 333.

case close-up

Guzzardi v Italy (1981) 3 EHRR 333

A mafiosi suspect was required to live and be supervised in a small village on a small island off Sardinia. The village had an area of about 2.5 square kilometres. The ECtHR held that Article 5 was engaged. A range of factors, such as being under a curfew, being unable to mingle with the bulk of the island's population and being subject to punishment for breach of these and other conditions were, when taken together, sufficient to amount to a deprivation of liberty.

The ECtHR held (in paras 93 and 95) that:

- 'The difference between deprivation of and restriction upon liberty is nonetheless merely one of degree of intensity, and not one of nature or substance'.

- Deprivation of liberty is not confined to 'classic detention in prison' but may take 'numerous other forms' which cannot be identified in abstract.

- The Court is required to take 'account…of the whole range of criteria such as the type, duration, effects and manner of implementation of the measure in question' in determining whether or not a deprivation of liberty has occurred.

further study

See also *Engel* v *Netherlands* (1979–80) 1 EHRR 647 where the ECtHR distinguished between military punishments which involved a deprivation of liberty and those which did not.

The *Guzzardi* approach has been adopted by the UK courts. There is some disagreement on the extent to which factors involving restrictions on normal life but not confinement, are to be taken into account.

case close-up

cross reference
See Chapter 26, section 26.7.2 for Terrorism Prevention and Investigation orders.

Secretary of State for the Home Department v JJ [2007] UKHL 45

JJ (a terrorist suspect) was made subject to a 'control order' (now repealed and replaced by Terrorist Investigation and Prevention Measures) that required him to remain in his flat for 18 hours a day and subjected him to a range of restrictions over the remaining six hours. The House of Lords, interpreting *Guzzardi*, held, by a majority, that JJ was 'deprived of his liberty'. All five Law Lords seemed to agree that, for a deprivation of liberty, there must be a core element of physical confinement (JJ's 18 hours' house arrest). But they gave different significance to the effect of the other restrictions, on movement, sociability, etc., which, under *Guzzardi*, can be taken into account. For Lord Bingham the other restrictions indicated there had been a deprivation of liberty because they left JJ in a position similar to imprisonment in an open prison (without the opportunities for association). For Baroness Hale they indicated a deprivation of liberty because of the extent to which JJ was unable to lead a normal life in his six free hours. Lord Brown, on the other hand, insisted that there could only be a deprivation of liberty if there was a core period of confinement (he suggested at least 16 hours) and without it no amount of restriction over non-confined hours could be significant. Lords Carswell and Hoffmann dissented. They held there was no deprivation of liberty because confinement was the defining idea. JJ had six hours of freedom and was, therefore, not in a prison-like situation. The restrictions on his ability to lead a normal life in those six unconfined hours could not change this.

In *Austin* police 'kettled' (confined) demonstrators, some of whom were violent, in a small area in order to control them. The House of Lords, *Austin v Commissioner of Police of the Metropolis* [2009] UKHL 5, held that whether there was a deprivation of liberty depended not on the circumstances in which the demonstrators found themselves but on the police's purpose. A measure of crowd control done in good faith and which was a proportionate response to the threat would not be a deprivation of liberty.

The position was, in substance though not terminology, accepted by the ECtHR (*Austin v United Kingdom* (2012) 55 EHRR 14). *Guzzardi*, as noted earlier, requires a range of factors, including the 'type' of measure imposed and its 'manner of implementation', to be taken into account when deciding whether there had been a deprivation of liberty. A necessary police response, in circumstances such as occurred in *Austin*, could be of a type that meant it merely restricted movement rather than deprived persons of their liberty. However, a similar police response that was not proportionate to the danger could be of a type that was sufficiently restrictive to be a deprivation of liberty and engage Article 5 (it would then have to be shown that the deprivation of liberty was for one of the purposes in Article 5(1)(a)–(f)).

further study

The question whether a police stop and search involves a deprivation of liberty is discussed in Chapter 20, section 20.2.

discussion topic

Should the United Kingdom ratify Protocol 4? If it did so, would it make any difference? Note that, in England, persons can be subject to restrictions on their ability to live a normal life (such as ASBOs or football banning orders).

11.2.2 **Voluntary detention**

Persons who choose to give themselves into the hands of the authorities or who choose to stay under confinement when they are free to leave, will still enjoy the protection of Article 5. This is especially true where there are significant non-voluntary aspects to their circumstances. The ECtHR has recognised that 'temporary distress or misery' may cause a person to give themselves up to the authorities but that the importance of the right to liberty is such that a detained person should not lose the protection of Article 5 simply because he or she voluntarily surrendered to the authorities (see the 'vagrants' case, *De Wilde, Ooms and Versyp v Belgium* (1979–80) 1 EHRR 373). The point is particularly important in respect of asylum seekers. They should not (and do not) lose the protection of Article 5 just because they are free to accept the risk of leaving the host country.

In *Amuur v France* (1996) 22 EHRR 533 the applicants were kept in the transit lounge of an airport for 20 days whilst their application for asylum was being considered. They were free to leave France but not to enter the country during that period. The ECtHR held that they had suffered a deprivation of liberty under Article 5.

Procedure prescribed by law: non-arbitrariness

Time and again the ECtHR has emphasised that the point of Article 5 is to ensure that any deprivation of liberty must not be arbitrary and a court dealing with detention must satisfy itself that this is so. The general principles are summarised in *Saadi* v *United Kingdom* (2008) 47 EHRR 17, where a Grand Chamber made it clear that, whilst there is no definitive list of what makes a decision 'arbitrary', the case law indicates a number of factors including the following (see paras 67–70).

11.3.1 Lawfulness

A main protection from 'arbitrariness' is the requirement that any deprivation of liberty must be 'in accordance with a procedure prescribed by law'.

cross reference
The Convention concept of law is introduced and discussed in Chapter 6, section 6.2.

The authorities (police etc.) need to act lawfully in terms of their own national law. It is normal for the ECtHR to accept the determination of the national law that is made by the national courts. If there is compelling evidence that a deprivation of liberty was not consistent with national law or lacked the continuing authority of the national law, the Court will find a violation. For example, the detention of a person for a psychiatric examination despite the absence of legal power to detain for that purpose in the national law violated Article 5 (*Kepenerov* v *Bulgaria* (2004) 38 EHRR 33).

But conformity with national law is not 'decisive'. The law authorising detention must also meet the Convention's concept of law: it must meet the standards of 'accessibility', 'certainty' and 'foreseeability' that are at the heart of the Convention concept of the rule of law and the avoidance of arbitrary power.

> It is therefore essential that the conditions for deprivation of liberty under domestic law be clearly defined and that the law itself be foreseeable in its application, so that it meets the standard of 'lawfulness' set by the Convention, a standard which requires that all law be sufficiently precise to allow the person—if need be, with appropriate advice—to foresee, to a degree that is reasonable in the circumstances, the consequences which a given action may entail.
>
> (*Jecius* v *Lithuania* (2002) 35 EHRR 16)

In *R (Lumba)* v *Secretary of State for the Home Department* [2011] UKSC 12, the claimants, on completion of a prison sentence, were due to be deported. They were detained on the basis of an unpublished policy which required the blanket detention of all such persons. This was inconsistent with the published policy, which required detention only in certain circumstances. The Supreme Court held that the detention was unlawful both at common law and for violating the 'prescribed by law' requirement of Article 5.

11.3.2 Illegal acts by the authorities

Arbitrariness is also found where the authorities detain people on a basis of dubious legality or a breach of good faith and so deny the persons involved the substantive and procedural rights that the law provides. For example, in *Conka* v *Belgium* (2002) 34 EHRR 54, the police persuaded a group of Slovakians of Romany origin to attend a police station in order to complete the formalities of their asylum application. In fact the Belgium authorities had turned down their application. They were then arrested and deported. The ECtHR held that there had been a violation of Article 5: they had been subject to an 'administrative ruse' and thereby treated in an arbitrary fashion.

11.3.3 **Purpose and conditions**

The deprivation of liberty must genuinely relate to one of the purposes listed in Article 5(1)(a)–(f), which are the only purposes for which the state may deprive a person of his or her liberty. Also, the conditions under which a person is detained must be governed by the purpose to be served (it would be wrong to detain a harmless mentally ill person in a maximum security prison, for example).

11.3.4 **Necessity**

Deprivation of liberty is so serious that, for most purposes, it can only be justified as a last resort where other, less severe, measures have been considered and rejected. (This does not apply when someone is detained with a view to their deportation: see Article 5(1)(f), below.)

11.3.5 **Records**

cross reference
Disappearances may engage Articles 2 and 3. For discussion see Chapter 8, section 8.2.1, 'Proving responsibility'.

The requirement that a deprivation of liberty must not be arbitrary and must be in accordance with a 'procedure prescribed by law' places a positive duty on states to ensure that all deprivations of liberty are properly acknowledged and that adequate records are kept. Adequate records assist states in their duty to conduct proper investigations into alleged disappearances. In *Cyprus* v *Turkey* (2002) 35 EHRR 30, the ECtHR held that the continuing refusal of Turkey to investigate alleged disappearances of men last seen in the custody of its troops following their invasion of Cyprus in 1974 (which, in 1992, had been held to be a violation of Article 5) was a further violation of Article 5.

11.3.6 **Legal supervision**

Deprivations of liberty must be properly supervised by the national courts. This principle is enshrined in Article 5(3) and (4), and is discussed below.

11.4 The purposes of lawful deprivation of liberty

Even if prescribed by law a deprivation of liberty can only be compatible with the Convention if it is for one of the six purposes listed in Article 5(1)(a)–(e). These are exclusive: depriving a person of their liberty for some other purpose violates Article 5.

11.4.1 Article 5(1)(a)

> the lawful detention of a person after conviction by a competent court.

Normal imprisonment following conviction for a criminal offence is a deprivation of liberty that does not violate Article 5. A court is 'competent' if it is able to provide the procedural protections of a fair trial. The lawfulness of the conviction is normally a matter for the national courts, though if the ECtHR finds that there has been a blatant disregard of the national law by the convicting court, it may find a violation of the Convention on that ground (see *Tsirlis* v *Greece* (1998) 25 EHRR 198, for example).

Release on appeal

A person who is convicted, imprisoned, and then released after a successful appeal has not thereby been a victim of a violation of Article 5 since all those stages are lawful. If, however, the ground of appeal is that the court had no legal jurisdiction to imprison, for example the person was imprisoned for an offence that did not carry a prison sentence as a possible punishment, then a violation of Article 5 can be argued.

The proportionality of the punishment

The 'detention' must be 'lawful'. Lawfulness includes the requirement that a period of imprisonment must be proportionate to the offence. Specifically, there needs to be a 'causal relationship' between the nature of the offence, the sentence passed and the purpose for which a convicted person is actually kept in prison.

Under UK law, a convicted murderer is sentenced to 'life imprisonment'. This used to mean that, after he or she had served a set period in jail for punishment, he or she could be released on licence, subject to recall by the Home Secretary, who was advised by the Parole Board. In *Stafford* v *United Kingdom* (2002) 35 EHRR 32 the Home Secretary had refused to release the prisoner for fear that he would commit non-violent offences such as theft and fraud. The ECtHR held that there had been a violation of Article 5. There was no causal connection between Stafford's continued detention for fear of non-violent offences and the purpose of the original life sentence, which was a punishment for a murder, a violent offence.

11.4.2 Article 5(1)(b)

> non-compliance with the lawful order of a court or in order to secure the fulfilment of any obligation prescribed by law.

Non-compliance with the lawful order of a court

Article 5 also allows lawful deprivation of liberty for breach of a court order requiring certain behaviour or some event to occur. For example, a court might order that a person pay a tax demand or require a person to undergo a blood test to establish paternity. If, under the national law, such orders can be enforced by the threat of prison (or some other form of deprivation of liberty) then, so long as any sentence is proportionate, enforcing the order will not be a violation of Article 5 (see, for example, *Harkman* v *Estonia* App 2192/03, judgment of 11 July 2006). Where breaching a court order is itself a distinct offence (as, under English law, with the breaching of an Anti-Social Behaviour Order) then Article 5(1)(a) is engaged and recourse to Article 5(1)(b) is unnecessary.

Secure the fulfilment of any obligation prescribed by law

The ECtHR has made it clear that this part of Article 5(1)(b) needs to be interpreted narrowly. Any national law which permits someone to be detained in order to obtain from them the performance of a legal duty must

- relate to a 'specific and concrete' legal obligation and not be just a way of compelling general obedience to the law,
- have as its purpose the obtaining of the performance of the obligation and not the punishment of a person for failing to perform the obligation.

further study

See *Engel* v *The Netherlands* (1979–80) 1 EHRR 647, para 69.

There must also be specific reasons why detention is, in the circumstances, a proportionate way of securing compliance. A disproportionate detention will be a violation of Article 5(1): see, for example, *Vasileva* v *Denmark* (2005) 40 EHRR 27.

In most cases a deprivation of liberty should follow a deliberate or neglectful failure to perform the obligation. The person under the obligation should know of the duty and have had an opportunity to perform it in his or her own time. However, this is not an absolute requirement. In special circumstances the ECtHR has accepted the compatibility with Article 5(1)(b) of national laws which permit the detention of a person so that the obligation can be performed in the first place. Rules aimed at the prevention of terrorism provide such circumstances.

case close-up

McVeigh v *United Kingdom* (1983) 5 EHRR 71, in particular, paras 188–196

McVeigh and two others were detained at the port of Liverpool under Prevention of Terrorism Act 1989 regulations. They were detained for 45 hours, searched, questioned, photographed, and their fingerprints taken. They were not detained on the grounds of evidence of a criminal offence (this could have brought their detention within Article 5(1)(c)). They were not charged with any offence. The regulations imposed a duty on everybody to submit to a security examination on entering the United Kingdom from Northern Ireland and permitted detention for that purpose. The Commission of Human Rights held that this was a specific and concrete obligation done for a legitimate purpose and, if the authorities needed to carry out more extensive checks on individuals than was usual, the performance of the obligation could be secured by detention. There was, therefore, no breach of Article 5(1).

In *Gillan* v *Commissioner of Police for the Metropolis* [2006] UKHL 12, the House of Lords said that if a person was detained in the context of a stop and search and if there were special circumstances (such as the person being handcuffed or taken away to be searched) then the stop and search might involve a deprivation of liberty but it would probably be lawful by virtue of Article 5(1)(b).

11.4.3 Article 5(1)(c)

the lawful arrest or detention of a person effected for the purpose of bringing him before the competent legal authority on reasonable suspicion of having committed an offence or when it is reasonably considered necessary to prevent his committing an offence or fleeing after having done so.

Any legal system must permit its police force to arrest and detain those who are suspected of a crime. Equally important is that such powers are only exercised under careful legal control and that those who are so detained enjoy certain basic rights and protections reflecting the presumption of their innocence.

KEY POINT Article 5(3), discussed at section 11.7, provides additional, express rights for persons arrested for the purposes of Article 5(1)(c).

'the lawful arrest'

Any arrest must be on the basis of the national law. The question of lawfulness is for the national courts in the first place but, as stated previously, the ECtHR can review the national law and find a breach of the Convention if that law fails to meet the Convention standard of legality or fails to prevent arbitrary arrest.

KEY POINT Arrest under the law of England and Wales is generally thought to be compatible with Article 5(1)(c). This is discussed in Chapter 20, section 20.3.

'reasonable suspicion'

Any otherwise lawful arrest is only compatible with Article 5 if it is based on 'reasonable suspicion'. The ECtHR has identified the main requirements of a reasonable suspicion and emphasised the importance of this requirement as part of the general protection against arbitrary arrest afforded by Article 5.

- The suspicion must be honestly held: an arrest in bad faith would be incompatible with the Convention.
- But an honest belief is not enough. For a suspicion to be 'reasonable' there must be in existence 'facts or information which would satisfy an objective observer that the person concerned may have committed the offence in question' (see *Fox, Campbell and Hartley* v *United Kingdom* (1991) 13 EHRR 157, para 32). What is sufficient to satisfy this test will depend on the circumstances, and reasonableness depends on the facts or information as understood by the arresting officer at the time of the arrest. The reasonableness of an arrest cannot be retrospectively validated by new facts or information unknown at the time (see *Stogmuller* v *Austria* (1979–80) 1 EHRR 155).
- Furthermore, the state must be prepared to disclose sufficient facts and information on which the arrest was based so that a court (or at least the ECtHR) can be satisfied that the reasonable suspicion test has been met (see *O'Hara* v *United Kingdom* (2002) 34 EHRR 32, para 35).
- Nevertheless, so long as the evidence suggests the suspect 'may have' committed the offence, he or she can be arrested. Reasonable suspicion does not require that there is, at the time of arrest, enough evidence on which to bring charges (see *O'Hara* v *United Kingdom* (2002) 34 EHRR 32, para 36).

further study

A full summary by the ECtHR of the relevant principles is in *O'Hara* v *United Kingdom* (2002) 34 EHRR 32, paras 34–36.

Proportionality

It is not enough for there to exist a reasonable suspicion: the decision to arrest and detain must be a proportionate response to that suspicion (see, for example, *Shishkov* v *Bulgaria* App 38822/97, judgment of 9 January 2003).

'of an offence'

The person who is deprived of his or her liberty must be reasonably suspected of having committed an 'offence' under the state's domestic law. Classification of the matter as a crime under domestic law is an important indicator, however, even if a matter is not so classified, it may, nevertheless, be accepted as an offence for the purpose of Article 5(1)(c).

In *Brogan* v *United Kingdom* (1989) 11 EHRR 117 the applicants had been arrested on suspicion of 'terrorism' related to Northern Ireland. There is no offence of terrorism as such; however, the term implies suspicion of criminal activities of various kinds and, in fact, the applicants, after being detained, had been questioned about particular offences. The ECtHR held that, in the circumstances, they had been arrested for an offence.

In *Steel* v *United Kingdom* (1999) 28 EHRR 603 Steel was arrested (and detained for 44 hours) for a breach of the peace when she walked in front of a 'gun' during a grouse shoot and so prevented him from enjoying his lawful sport. Breach of the peace is not an offence. The facts to which it relates may be offences for which the person may be subsequently charged (Steel was charged under section 5 of the Public Order Act 1986) or, as also happened to Steel, a person can be 'bound over' to keep the peace for a period of time on the security of a sum of money. For the ECtHR, arrest for breach of the peace had all the characteristics of arrest for an offence.

'bringing him before the competent legal authority'

An arrest or other deprivation of liberty which does not have as its purpose the bringing of a person to court, is likely to be incompatible with Article 5(1)(c).

Arresting someone merely to question them is incompatible with the Article (as well as English law). If, in the *Brogan* case, the applicants were arrested on suspicion of terrorism (not in itself an offence) and then questioned on general, background matters, rather than specific offences in which they might have been involved, it is arguable that there would be a breach of Article 5. This point is clearly relevant to the long periods of pre-charge detention allowed under the UK's anti-terrorism laws, which are discussed in Chapter 26, section 26.8.2.

'when it is reasonably considered necessary to prevent him committing an offence'

From earliest cases (*Lawless* v *Ireland* (1979–80) 1 EHRR 15, paras 13–14) the ECtHR has held that this provision permits neither internment (executive detention of persons considered to threaten national security) nor preventive detention directed against those with a propensity to crime (*Guzzardi* v *Italy* (1981) 3 EHRR 333, para 102): see also *Al-Jedda* v *UK* (2011) 53 EHRR 23, para 100. This also follows from the lack of an intention to bring the person to trial.

Legality and proportionality suggest that arrest to prevent conduct that might take place in the future is compatible with Article 5(1)(c) only when the apprehended offence is immediately likely or at least the likely and proximate outcome of an already existing chain of events. In the United Kingdom a person can be detained because it is feared they may, in the future, commit a breach of the peace. In *R (Laporte)* v *Chief Constable of Gloucester Constabulary* [2006] UKHL 55, the House of Lords restated the law to require not just that the police (or civilian) doing the detaining have reasonable grounds to fear a future breach of the peace but that their fear is that disorder or violence is immediate or imminent. The decision is compatible with Article 5 even though that article was not the basis of the decision.

KEY POINT A preventive element in a criminal punishment following conviction, such as indeterminate sentences where prisoners serve a period for punishment but are only subsequently released if the Parole Board consider them no longer a threat, are compatible with Article 5(1)(a).

11.4.4 **Article 5(1)(d)**

> the detention of a minor by lawful order for the purpose of educational supervision or his lawful detention for the purpose of bringing him before the competent legal authority.

Parental rights of custody over children are recognised so that, for example, parents may decide, compatibly with national law, that the best interests of their children require treatment in a hospital or other establishment and, given a fair balance in the law between parental rights and the autonomy of children, it is unlikely that the ECtHR will find that there has been a deprivation of the child's liberty (see, for example, *Nielsen* v *Denmark* (1989) 11 EHRR 175 regarding the placing of a child in a child psychiatric ward by his mother).

Nothing in Article 5(1)(a)–(c) prevents the detention of children after conviction of a crime or after arrest on reasonable suspicion. Article 5(1)(d) identifies extra grounds on which children can be lawfully deprived of their liberty: educational supervision or being brought before the competent legal authority.

'educational supervision'

case close-up

DG v *Ireland* (2002) 35 EHRR 33

DG was a child with a serious personality disorder who was made subject to a court order requiring 'high support therapeutic care'. He had not been convicted of an offence. The Irish authorities were unable to find a place where appropriate intensive and educational care could be given. As the 'least offensive' alternative, the High Court ordered DG to be detained in a prison environment whilst a proper placement was found. The prison did not provide the 'high support' required or, indeed, much by way of even basic education. DG absconded and was returned to the prison environment. He was held in the prison for just over a month.

The ECtHR in *DG* held that there had been a violation of Article 5(1).

- The ECtHR insists that 'educational supervision' must mean more than providing just 'class room teaching'. It must 'embrace many aspects of the exercise, by the authority, of parental rights for the benefit and protection of the person concerned'. (*DG*, para 80; *Ichin* v *Ukraine* App 28189/04, judgment of 21 December 2011, para 38)
- Appropriate care may not be immediately available and the Court accepted that temporary accommodation in an unsuitable environment does not in itself violate Article 5. If this happens the state must act with diligence to provide an appropriate placement.

- The Court is not sympathetic to a lack of resources argument. The states are required to fund and resource the system of child protection they have chosen to adopt:

> [The Irish state] was obliged to put in place appropriate institutional facilities which met the security and educational demands of [the system chosen to deal with juvenile delinquency]. (*DG*, para 79)

(See also *Bouamar* v *Belgium* (1988) 11 EHRR 1)

English law and children in care

In England and Wales, section 25 of the Children Act 1989 authorises local authorities to place children whom they are looking after into 'secure accommodation' so long as certain conditions apply. Any detention beyond a specified period (currently 72 hours) requires a court order.

In *Re K (A Child) (Secure Accommodation Order)* [2001] 2 All ER 719 the Court of Appeal held that the exercise of this power was not in principle incompatible with the requirements of Article 5(1)(d). Although section 25 does not, in its terms, refer to educational provision, the general duties to educate children under the Education Acts still apply.

The wide meaning of 'educational provision' means that the detention of a child in local authority care who is over school leaving age (e.g. a 17-year-old) will be compatible with Article 5(1)(d) so long as there is beneficial, broadly educational, provision, such as a life-skills course (see *Koniarska* v *United Kingdom* App 33670/96, admissibility decision of 12 October 2000).

Re K does not mean that any deprivation of liberty made under section 25 will, necessarily, be compatible with Article 5(1)(d). A court making a section 25 order must be satisfied that the particular terms of the court order contain appropriate educational provision. *Re K* means that section 25 can no longer authorise secure accommodation, other than interim, which does not have educational supervision, broadly defined, as its purpose.

'the purpose of bringing him before the competent legal authority'

Article 5(1)(d) also permits the remanding of a minor in custody in the context of legal proceedings. These might be on remand awaiting criminal trial or after sentence awaiting social reports, for example. The usual Convention principles, such as the need for lawfulness and for proportionality, apply. The educational requirement, however, does not apply.

11.4.5 Article 5(1)(e)

> the lawful detention of persons for the prevention of the spreading of infectious diseases, of persons of unsound mind, alcoholics or drug addicts or vagrants.

General principles

Depriving a person with a mental disability of his or her liberty must be compatible with Article 5(1)(e). In *Hutchison Reid* v *United Kingdom* (2003) 37 EHRR 9, paras 46–48, the ECtHR summarised the general principles; these are discussed in the following paragraphs.

Lawfulness

Any detention must be 'lawful' as that term is understood in Convention terms (see section 11.3). The national law must not permit arbitrary detentions of the mentally ill (see, for example, *Kepenerov* v *Bulgaria* (2004) 38 EHRR 33).

In England and Wales, the Mental Health Act 1983, as amended by the Mental Health Act 2007, permits persons to be detained for assessment or in order to receive 'appropriate medical treatment' (it no longer needs to be treatment that can cure or ameliorate their condition). Persons unfit to stand trial for serious criminal offences because of mental incapacity can also be detained under other measures. These provisions are likely to meet the 'lawfulness' requirement of Article 5.

Persons who lack mental capacity (who are unable to make decisions for themselves because of mental impairment) can also (independently of the Mental Health Act) be cared for in conditions that may deprive them of their liberty. This is allowed under common law if necessary for the patient's 'best interests'. In *HL* v *United Kingdom* (2005) 40 EHRR 32, the ECtHR held that the lack of a formalised admission system, the total reliance on professional judgment as to the patient's best interests and the lack of adequate safeguards and remedies violated Article 5. The Mental Capacity Act 2005 (as amended by the Mental Health Act 2007) now forbids deprivation of liberty except as allowed for in the Act (section 4A) (the 'deprivation of liberty safeguards'). Specifically, Schedule A1 authorises the managing authority of a hospital or care home to deprive a person of his or her liberty under specific conditions and if this is in the patient's 'best interests' (the Act lays down procedures and criteria for determining these). It provides a detailed procedure for hospitals and care homes to follow. A system of review is created, with the Court of Protection having ultimate supervisory authority. The Court of Protection itself has the power to order a deprivation of liberty if necessary for a person's welfare (section 16).

The *Winterwerp* conditions

Any detention must satisfy the three conditions laid down in *Winterwerp* v *The Netherlands* (1979–80) 2 EHRR 387, at para 39.

- The person must be shown to be of 'unsound mind'. There is no Convention definition of this term. It implies some form of mental disorder. States are allowed a margin of appreciation over the forms this might take. However, depriving a person of his or her liberty on the basis of behaviour which is merely 'deviant' cannot be permitted under Article 5(1)(d).

- The mental disorder must be sufficiently serious in its effects to 'warrant' compulsory confinement in hospital. Later case law suggests that this understates the position: any detention must be necessary, in the sense that less severe alternatives have been considered and found to be inadequate.

- The validity of continuing detention requires the persistence of the mental disorder.

Need for a therapeutic environment

A person detained in relation to Article 5(1)(e) must be provided with a suitable therapeutic environment (i.e. one which is aimed at providing treatment rather than punishment). However, so long as the treatment is therapeutic, Article 5 does not require anything more regarding the suitability of the treatment for the patient.

case close-up

Ashingdane v *United Kingdom* (1985) 7 EHRR 528

A (who had been convicted of various offences) was placed in a high security special hospital. His condition improved but, for administrative reasons, the Home Secretary would not authorise his transfer to a local mental hospital. The ECtHR held that Article 5 had not been violated.

The ECtHR said (para 44):

> The Court would further accept that there must be some relationship between the ground of permitted deprivation of liberty relied on and the place and conditions of detention. In principle, the 'detention' of a person as a mental health patient will only be 'lawful' for the purposes of sub-paragraph (e) of paragraph 1 if effected in a hospital, clinic or other appropriate institution authorised for that purpose. However, subject to the foregoing, Article 5(1)(e) is not in principle concerned with suitable treatment or conditions.

In *Aerts v Belgium* (2000) 29 EHRR 50, for example, the applicant was detained in a prison rather than a social protection centre. There was a breach of Article 5(1)(e).

This position has been confirmed for English law under the HRA.

case close-up

R (B) v Ashworth Hospital Authority [2005] UKHL 20 (see para 34)

B was a compulsorily detained mental patient. He sought to prevent the hospital transferring him from a ward in which he was being successfully treated for schizophrenia to one specialising in psychotic personality disorders. The House of Lords allowed the transfer. It made it clear that there was no breach of Article 5(1)(e). (The case was mainly about whether the Mental Health Act 1983 allowed a person detained for one type of illness to be treated, whilst detained, for another.)

Need for treatment

The Convention does not require a lawful deprivation of liberty to have the treatment of a treatable mental illness as its purpose. National laws may authorise detention of persons of unsound mind for other purposes which can be compatible with the Convention.

case close-up

Hutchison Reid v *United Kingdom* (2003) 37 EHRR 9

HR was convicted of homicide but detained in a mental hospital. He continued to be detained even though it became clear that he was suffering from an untreatable psychopathic disorder. His applications for discharge from mental hospital were turned down. The ECtHR held that his detention was compatible with Article 5(1)(e). (There was a breach of Article 5(4).)

The ECtHR held that there could be a deprivation of liberty under Article 5(1)(e) even if a person cannot be treated for a cure but 'needs control and supervision to prevent him, for example, causing harm to himself or other persons' (para 51).

Immediate release

A person no longer needing to be detained (e.g. because no longer suffering from a mental disorder) should be released. However, sensible transitional and rehabilitative arrangements, which delay release, are not necessarily incompatible with Article 5 (see, for example, *Johnson v United Kingdom* (1999) 27 EHRR 296, paras 61–63).

If a tribunal thinks that a patient should be released but only subject to conditions (e.g. effective care in the community) and these conditions cannot be met, he or she can continue to be detained. If the conditions are not met, the grounds justifying detention remain. This approach was adopted in English law in *R (IH) v Secretary of State for Health* [2003] UKHL 59. The House of Lords did, however, find a breach of Article 5(4) (see section 11.8) because IH had no right to effective legal review of the possibility of meeting the conditions.

The basic approach in *IH*, to both Article 5(1)(e) and 5(4), was agreed with by the ECtHR in a similar case: *Kolanis v United Kingdom* (2006) 42 EHRR 12.

11.4.6 'spreading of infectious diseases…alcoholics or drug addicts or vagrants'

There is little case law on these issues. The most important point is their range—to what kinds and conditions of persons do they apply. The Court has held that the term 'alcoholics' in Article 5 is not confined to persons in a 'clinical state of "alcoholism" '. It extends to laws which permit the taking into custody of persons who, under the influence of drink, pose, through their behaviour, a threat to public order, or to themselves. What is not permitted is the taking into custody of a person merely because of being drunk rather than because of their behaviour (see *Litwa v Poland* (2001) 33 EHRR 53, paras 60–61).

As regards the term 'vagrants', the ECtHR accepted the definition in Belgium national law: 'persons who have no fixed abode, no means of subsistence and no regular trade or profession' (*De Wilde, Ooms and Versyp v Belgium* (1979–80) 1 EHRR 373, para 33: see section 11.2).

11.4.7 Article 5(1)(f)

> the lawful arrest or detention of a person to prevent his effecting unauthorised entry into the country or of a person against whom action is being taken with a view to deportation or extradition.

Detention of persons trying to enter a country illegally or who are liable to deportation is permitted by the Convention.

case close-up

Saadi v United Kingdom (2008) 47 EHRR 17, Grand Chamber

In *R (Saadi) v Secretary of State for the Home Department* [2002] UKHL 41, the House of Lords had held that the detention of asylum seekers whose applications could be speedily dealt with was lawful. A Grand Chamber of the ECtHR found this to be compatible with Article 5(1)(f) (though there was a violation of Article 5(2): see section 11.5).

In particular the Grand Chamber held that:

- Article 5(1)(f) allows states to detain people who are lawfully seeking entry to a country; it is not confined to those seeking to evade entry requirements.

- So long as done in good faith with a view to lawful deportation, there is no need to show detention is otherwise necessary (e.g. as the only means available to prevent the detainees absconding). Thus the normal Article 5 requirement that any deprivation of liberty should be necessary is less stringently applied in the immigration context than under, in particular, Article 5(1)(b), (d) and (e).

- The place and conditions of detention should be appropriate (i.e. to detainees who were innocent of any crime and may have been the victims of horrific experiences).

discussion topic

Was *Saadi* v *United Kingdom* correctly decided? Is it an executive-friendly decision which fails to recognise the position and difficulties of asylum seekers who are some of the most vulnerable people in the world (see a strong dissent supported by a minority of judges in the Grand Chamber)?

cross reference

The grounds of deportation in UK law and the ban if there is a real risk of torture is discussed in Chapter 9, section 9.8.

Detention should only be allowed if deportation is being actively undertaken. As the ECtHR said in *Chahal* v *United Kingdom* (1997) 23 EHRR 413, at para 113:

> any deprivation of liberty under art 5(1)(f) will be justified only for as long as deportation proceedings are in progress. If such proceedings are not pursued with due diligence, the detention will cease to be permissible under art 5(1)(f) of the Convention.

When deportation is legally impossible (because, for example, it would breach the Convention), detention under Article 5(1)(f) is not possible.

case close-up

A v *United Kingdom* (2009) 49 EHRR 29

After '9/11' the applicants, all foreign nationals, were suspected of involvement in terrorism. The Home Secretary sought to deport them but was legally barred because of a real risk of torture in any likely receiving country. The solution was to detain them in prison, indefinitely, under the Anti-Terrorism Crime and Security Act 2001. For three detainees there was no realistic chance that they could be deported. The ECtHR held that there was a breach of Article 5(1)(f). Merely keeping the situation under review did not mean that deportation proceedings were in progress.

233

11.5 The right to be informed, Article 5(2)

Article 5(1)(a)–(f) specifies the purposes of legitimate deprivation of liberty. The remaining provisions of Article 5 identify basic rights of those deprived of their liberty.

11.5.1 Article 5(2)

> Everyone who is arrested shall be informed promptly, in a language which he understands, of the reasons for his arrest and of any charge against him.

The right to be informed applies only where there has been an 'arrest' (usually a deprivation of liberty justified under Article 5(1)(c)). It will not necessarily apply to other deprivations of liberty allowed by Article 5 which are not based on an arrest, such as some detentions for treatment of persons with mental incapacity.

Knowledge of why they have been arrested enables the detained person to realise the degree of seriousness of his or her situation and to take practical steps, such as obtaining appropriate legal advice, if the situation warrants it. Precise details of the offence need not be given nor need the full information be given at the time of arrest. The test for the nature of the requirement was laid out in *Fox, Campbell and Hartley* v *United Kingdom* (1991) 13 EHRR 157, para 40:

> any person arrested must be told, in simple, non-technical language that he can understand, the essential legal and factual grounds for his arrest, so as to be able, if he sees fit, to apply to a court to

challenge its lawfulness in accordance with paragraph 4...Whilst this information must be conveyed 'promptly'...it need not be related in its entirety by the arresting officer at the very moment of arrest. Whether the content and promptness of the information conveyed were sufficient is to be assessed in each case according to its special features.

In *Saadi* v *United Kingdom* (see section 11.4.7) a Grand Chamber held that Article 5(2) had been violated because it took 76 hours to inform the applicant why he, as an individual, was being detained. The fact that general statements about the detention of some asylum seekers had been made in Parliament was insufficient.

Article 5(2) also requires that the information is given in a language the arrested person understands and this may require the speedy presence of interpreters at police stations (see, as an example, *Ladent* v *Poland* App 11036/03, judgment of 18 March 2008).

cross reference
The law of England and Wales on the right to be informed is discussed in Chapter 20, section 20.3.5.

11.6 Judicial supervision of deprivation of liberty: introduction

Deprivation of liberty must be compatible with the rule of law. Article 5 requires adequate and proper judicial supervision of decisions taken by the authorities to detain a person.

Article 5(3) applies only to persons arrested and detained on reasonable suspicion of having committed an offence as allowed by Article 5(1)(c). It applies mainly to people held by the police prior to being charged, for example someone who has been lawfully arrested and detained by the police for questioning.

Article 5(4) applies to all deprivations of liberty allowed by Article 5(1)(a)–(f). For example, those held on remand awaiting trial or people detained for long periods (e.g. in mental hospitals) when the circumstances justifying their original detention may change.

The specific way these provisions are put into effect varies according to the nature and provisions of the different legal systems in Council of Europe countries.

11.7 Judicial supervision prior to trial, Article 5(3)

11.7.1 Article 5(3)

Everyone arrested or detained in accordance with the provisions of paragraph 1(c) of this article shall be brought promptly before a judge or other officer authorised by law to exercise judicial power and shall be entitled to trial within a reasonable time or to release pending trial. Release may be conditioned by guarantees to appear for trial.

'Shall be brought promptly'

The idea that a person should languish for days in police cells being subject to questioning, perhaps torture, with no access to the courts, is anathema. In the ECtHR's language, it is 'arbitrary' detention. Where someone has been detained by the police following arrest on reasonable suspicion, Article 5(3) requires prompt judicial supervision as a safeguard against abuse of power. This must be automatic and not require an application by the detained person (*McKay* v *United Kingdom* [2007] 44 EHRR 41, para 32).

The ECtHR has always been very reluctant to determine in advance any specific time limits. It prefers to judge matters according to the particular circumstances of the case. Nevertheless the word 'promptly', which, in the French text ('aussitôt') is more like 'immediately', does not permit flexibility.

case close-up

Brogan v *United Kingdom* (1989) 11 EHRR 117

Brogan and three others were arrested under the Prevention of Terrorism (Temporary Provisions) Act 1984 (now repealed) on suspicion of terrorist activities and detained for between four days and six hours, and six days and 16 hours. Under the Act police could detain individuals, for up to a week, with the authority of the Home Secretary (a member of the executive, not a magistrate or judge) being required for any period beyond two days. The applicants were questioned about terrorist offences and were then all released without charge.

The ECtHR held that there had been a violation of Article 5(3) in all the cases.

cross reference
The law of England and Wales on police detention is discussed in Chapter 20, section 20.5.

The significance of *Brogan* is that it concerns a terrorist investigation and, as discussed in Chapter 26, section 26.2.1, the ECtHR permits states a certain leeway in that context. In a non-terrorist context, four days' detention without being brought before a court is likely to be beyond what is permitted unless there are extraordinary circumstances that explain a longer period. A period of 10 days before being brought before a judge, even in a terrorist context, is clearly a breach (see *Yildirim* v *Turkey* App 40518/98, judgment of 29 July 2004).

11.7.2 Bail or remand in custody?

Article 5(3) also relates to the situation following a suspect being charged with a criminal offence, which raises different issues from pre-charge detention. The authorities must decide whether a person who has been arrested on reasonable suspicion and then charged with a criminal offence should be released pending the trial (released on bail) or kept in custody (held on remand). Under Article 5(3):

• A person who is remanded in custody is entitled to trial within a 'reasonable time'.

• Under Article 6(1) those who are released on bail are also entitled to trial within a 'reasonable time' (see Chapter 12, section 12.11).

• Article 5(3) creates a presumption in favour of release after a person has been charged.

A person charged with an offence must always be released unless the State can show that there are 'relevant and sufficient' reasons to justify the continued detention (see *Wemhoff* v *Germany* (1979–80) 1 EHRR 55, para 12).

Relevant reasons

The ECtHR has identified the 'relevant' reasons for refusing bail. There must be evidence that:

• The accused might abscond and not appear for trial. Personal factors of the accused, such as the 'character of the person involved, his morals, his assets, his links with the State in which he is being prosecuted and his international contacts', are relevant (*Smirnova* v *Russia* (2004) 39 EHRR 22, para 60).

• If released, the accused will take action which prejudices the administration of justice. For example, intimidate witnesses or destroy evidence.

• If released, the accused is likely to commit further offences.

• The release of the accused could create a danger to public order. This reason applies only in exceptional circumstances where release of an unpopular accused person might trigger an adverse public reaction.

These reasons must be properly established, on evidence, produced by the state (it should not be up to the accused to prove the absence of these factors). The seriousness of the offence or of the likely sentence is not, of itself, a basis for justifying pre-trial detention.

Sufficient reasons

The relevant reasons must also be 'sufficient' to justify remand in custody in the individual case. To justify remand the national courts must be satisfied that there is a genuine reason, found in the particular circumstances of the case, which outweighs the force of the presumption of innocence and the respect for the individual liberty of the suspect. It follows from this that the courts must make their decisions on the basis of the individual circumstances of the case. Laws which require the automatic refusal of bail because of the severity of the offence or the previous record of the accused person, are likely to breach the Convention.

further study

The basic principles regarding custody or bail have been summarised by the ECtHR in, for example, *Smirnova* v *Russia* (2004) 39 EHRR 22, at paras 56–64.

Review

The situation of a person who is detained rather than released on bail must be kept under review by the authorities. It is not up to the detained person to seek such reviews although he or she should be entitled to do this under the provisions of Article 5(4): discussed at section 11.8. If the reasons which had previously justified detention no longer exist or if the grounds for reasonable suspicion on which the original arrest was made have also diminished, it may be necessary to bail the accused. Failure to do this will be a breach of Article 5(3).

In *Labita* v *Italy* (2008) 46 EHRR 50, Grand Chamber, a mafia suspect was held in custody on remand for two years and seven months. There was a breach of Article 5(3) because the initial grounds on which reasonable suspicion was based had faded away and were never very strong in the first place. Labita's arrest had been based on the hearsay of 'pentiti' (mafia members now cooperating with the authorities), at least one of whom was dead.

Diligence

The ECtHR refuses to lay down, '*in abstracto*' (in general terms) the periods of detention, prior to trial, that the national authorities must abide by. It does insist that the prosecution authorities display 'special diligence' in preparing the case and bringing it to trial.

**case
close-up**

Erdem v *Germany* (2002) 35 EHRR 15

. . . .

The German authorities detained Erdem, a leading member of the PKK (the leading Kurdish separatist organisation). Erdem was detained awaiting trial for five years and 11 months. The ECtHR held that there had been a breach of Article 5(3). It stressed

- the need for individual assessment of the necessity for remand in custody,
- the need for significant reasons why the public interest requires detention,
- these reasons must relate to the specific situation of the individual (i.e. not just because he or she is a particular type of defendant),
- these reasons must persist throughout the time of the detention and the state must realise the likelihood that they will lessen over time.

The Court found that although many of the reasons which explained the delay in the trial—involving the complexity of the case and the actions of the defendant—were reasonable, there was a violation of Article 5(3) because the authorities failed to show 'special diligence' in the way they pursued the case.

Judicial supervision

Article 5(3) requires that the decisions taken authorising detention by the police during investigation or in prison or house arrest whilst awaiting trial, must be taken by a 'judge or other officer authorised by law to exercise judicial power'—a court or similar body having a judicial character. The court must have sufficient authority in law, be properly independent and impartial and conduct itself with proper procedural safeguards for the defendant. In England and Wales such decisions are taken, in respect of regular offences, by magistrates. In the context of anti-terrorism, specially designated District Judges are involved (see Chapter 26, section 26.8.2). As *Brogan* (section 11.7.1) demonstrates, detention authorised for more than a few days solely by the executive (e.g. police or Home Secretary) will violate Article 5(3).

Authority—the power to order release

The court supervising the custody decisions must have the power to order the release of the suspect. Merely being able to recommend release or make declarations as to the lawfulness of detention is not enough (see *Sabeur Ben Ali* v *Malta* (2002) 34 EHRR 26, for instance).

Impartiality and independence

The court supervising the custody decisions must be independent and impartial. Effective independence from the executive and from the parties to the criminal process is essential.

In *Boyle* v *United Kingdom* (2008) 47 EHRR 19, there was a breach of Article 5(3) when a commanding officer ordered the detention of a suspect soldier prior to trial by court martial. The commanding officer was not sufficiently impartial and independent because of his general responsibilities for discipline at the base.

Fair procedure

The court supervising custody decisions must have a fair procedure. In particular the procedure must allow 'equality of arms' and proper participation by the accused. Decisions about bail, which are taken in the absence of defendants or their representatives, or decisions based on evidence that the accused has been unable to challenge, are likely to be breaches of Article 5(3).

Further detail on fair procedures, relevant to Article 5(3), is given below, in respect of Article 5(4).

further study

These requirements for judicial supervision under Article 5(3), in respect of both pre- and post-charge detention, have been summarised by a Grand Chamber of the ECtHR in *McKay* v *United Kingdom* (2007) 44 EHRR 41, paras 30–47. See Chapter 20, section 20.5.2.

11.8 Judicial supervision of persons deprived of their liberty, Article 5(4)

> Article 5(4)   Everyone who is deprived of his liberty by arrest or detention shall be entitled to take proceedings by which the lawfulness of his detention shall be decided speedily by a court and his release ordered if the detention is not lawful.

11.8.1 Introduction

The principles of non-arbitrariness and the rule of law require that anyone deprived of their liberty is entitled to go to a court or tribunal to challenge the lawfulness of his or her detention and be released if continued detention is unlawful or incompatible with Article 5. This right applies to those detained for any of the purposes in Article 5(1)(a)–(f) (including mental patients and deportees, for instance). This is a judicial function—it must be performed by a court or, if not, by a body which has proper independence from government and a fair procedure. As indicated in some of the cases discussed in section 11.8.4, the adoption of this principle into the law of England and Wales has had some important effects.

11.8.2 The remedy must be real and effective

Article 5(4) requires access to court to be effective and not just a right that is never enforced.

In *Ocalan* v *Turkey* (2005) 41 EHRR 45, O was taken to Turkey and held incommunicado for 10 days in police custody. Under Turkish law there was a legal right of access to the court by persons detained by the police but no evidence that the remedy was effective in practice. One of the findings of a Grand Chamber in this complicated and important case was that there was a violation of Article 5(4) (paras 68–72).

cross reference
The situation of prisoners with an indeterminate sentence in England and Wales is discussed further in Chapter 21, section 21.3.2.

11.8.3 Criminal sentences

For normal criminal sentences the requirements of Article 5(4) are satisfied by the decision of the convicting and sentencing court; continual review of determinate prison sentences (where the prisoner is released after a certain term) is not required. Where a court passes an indeterminate sentence (where a prisoner may only be released if it is safe to do so) the processes for determining the time of release must be compatible with Article 5(4).

11.8.4 A 'court' and its authority

The body to which the detained person can apply must have the authority, under the national law, to deal with all the issues that bear on the question of the deprivation of liberty, including the merits of the decision to detain and its compatibility with Article 5. Above all the body must be able to order the detained person's release.

The law of England Wales has been significantly amended to ensure compatibility with Article 5(4). *Habeas corpus* and judicial review (discussed at section 11.1) provide generally available procedures for determining the legality of a deprivation of liberty and ordering release. (The availability of a civil action for damages based on, for instance, false imprisonment or negligence, may provide compensation but does not meet the Article 5(4) requirement for ordering release.) However, *habeas corpus* and judicial review may not always be enough to satisfy Article 5(4).

In *HL v United Kingdom* (2005) EHRR 32, the applicant had been detained in a mental hospital, but not on the basis of the Mental Health Act 1983. Consequently he had no access to a tribunal which could have ordered his release. The ECtHR held that there were inadequate remedies available to HL and so there had been a breach of Article 5(4). Following this decision, under the Mental Capacity Act 2005, such patients now have access to a review procedure and can challenge the deprivation decision in the Court of Protection.

HL suggests that general remedies in English law, such as *habeas corpus* or judicial review may sometimes be inadequate. Neither remedy may give the High Court sufficient scope to consider all the factual issues bearing on the merits of the decision to detain. Furthermore, the test for proving the lawfulness of a detention may be too easy to satisfy and not allow the court to make its own, rigorous, evaluation of the need to detain. *Habeas corpus* was also found, by the ECtHR, to be inadequate for dealing with deprivations of liberty based on national security concerns (see *Chahal* v *United Kingdom* (1997) 23 EHRR 413).

Under the HRA these remedies are either adjusted to meet the requirements of the Convention (see Chapter 3, section 3.3.2) or detained persons can pursue the remedies available to them directly under section 7 HRA (see Chapter 5, section 5.4).

There are other judicial (court-like) bodies which deal with deprivations of liberty and whose procedures must be compatible with Article 5(4). For example:

- The Parole Board determines the release date for prisoners serving a life sentence an other indeterminate sentences (the situation of the Parole Board is discussed further at section 11.8.5).

- The First Tier Tribunal (Mental Health) hears cases brought by persons detained for treatment under the Mental Health Act 1983 in England and Wales. Following an adverse decision from the ECtHR, this tribunal (whose power used to be only advisory) has the power to order a person's release from detention.

- The position of persons detained under immigration legislation is complex. Detentions are subject to *habeas corpus* and judicial review; some detainees have a right to seek bail from the Asylum and Immigration Tribunal.

11.8.5 Procedure

A court which meets the requirements of Article 5(4) must have a proper judicial procedure. It is not necessary to provide the full range of procedural guarantees found in Article 6 for criminal trials (see Chapter 12, section 12.16), since the purpose of a trial is different from the issues raised by Article 5(4) (see the discussion in *DPP* v *Havering Magistrates Court* (2001) 3 All ER 997, para 35). Nevertheless the basic requirements of access to the courts, independence, impartiality, and fairness must be secured. The precise nature of the procedural requirements required under Article 5(4) depends upon the facts and circumstances of the case. As some of the cases in the following illustrate, English courts, under the HRA, are prepared to accept that procedural rights are context-dependent and flexible (see, for example, *Roberts* v *Parole Board* [2005] UKHL 45, below, 'Equality of arms').

Access to court

The law must enable detained people to take their case to court. States have positive duties to make this possible.

- Under the Mental Health Act 1983 mental patients who are challenging certain aspects of their situation cannot, whilst the issue is being resolved, apply to the First Tier Tribunal. In *R (H)* v *Secretary of State for Health* [2005] UKHL 60, the House of Lords declined to issue a declaration of incompatibility. Aspects of the law, particularly the power enjoyed by the Secretary of State to refer a matter to a tribunal on his or her own motion, satisfied Article 5(4).

- In *Allen* v *UK* (2010) 51 EHRR 22, the ECtHR held that the normal practice of denying a remand prisoner the right to be present whilst a prosecution appeal against bail is heard, violates Article 5(4).

Delay

The importance of liberty means that the hearings should not be delayed. In *R (Johnson)* v *Secretary of State for the Home Department* [2007] EWCA Civ 427, delays in Parole Board hearings involved violations of Article 5(4). In *R (KB)* v *Mental Health Review Tribunal* [2002] EWHC 639, delays and postponements in hearing mental health cases involved violations of Article 5(4).

'Equality of arms'

Both parties must be in the same position as regards access to the court and access to the materials on which the court will decide. *R (Roberts)* v *Parole Board* raised the question whether the Parole Board could, in principle, make a decision on the basis of a prejudicial letter about a prisoner seeking parole, which was neither known about nor disclosed to the prisoner or to his lawyers. A majority of the House of Lords, illustrating the flexibility of procedural rights, agreed that this course of action could be compatible with Article 5(4) in certain circumstances, such as the existence of a credible threat against the writer of the letter. The use of a 'special advocate' (who would represent the prisoner without consulting him) was also, in principle, compatible.

Oral hearing

The importance of liberty means that an oral hearing will often be necessary (as for life sentence prisoners recalled to prison by the Parole Board, in *R (Smith)* v *Parole Board* [2005] UKHL 1).

cross reference
For remedial action, see Chapter 4, section 4.4.4.

Burden of proof

The state or public agency (such as a mental hospital) must prove the need to detain. Original provisions in the Mental Health Act 1983 put the burden of proof on the applicant appearing before a Mental Health Review Tribunal (as then called). This was the subject of a 'declaration of incompatibility' under section 4 HRA by the House of Lords and the rules were changed by 'remedial action' under section 10 HRA.

11.8.6 Remedy by appeal: 'decided speedily'?

Failures by a court or tribunal hearing to meet Article 5 standards can, in principle, be remedied by an appeal court. However, this may not be sufficient to satisfy Article 5(4) if the process of appeal takes too long and so the issue is not decided 'speedily'.

further study

The general principles dealing with procedure have been summarised in *Megyeri* v *Germany* (1993) 15 EHRR 584, paras 22 and 23.

11.9 Article 5(5) compensation

cross reference
Article 5(5) is considered in Chapter 5, section 5.5.3.

Article 5(5) requires national laws to make provision for the compensation of someone who has been deprived of their liberty in contravention of Article 5(5). Compensation is for breach of Article 5, not just for any wrongful conviction leading to a jail sentence. In England and Wales compensation can be awarded: as damages for false imprisonment, against the police, for example, and under section 133 Criminal Justice Act 1988 for miscarriages of justice (miscarriage of justice is defined in *R (Adams)* v *SSJ* [2011] UKSC 18).

241

Summary

- Article 5 gives effect to the right to physical liberty; specifically the right not to be detained ('deprived of liberty') in an arbitrary manner.

- Article 5(1)(a)–(e) identifies the exclusive purposes for which a person can be deprived of his or her liberty.

- Article 5(2) requires a proper explanation to be given to arrested persons.

- Of great importance is that the grounds on which a person is detained, and on which he or she continues to be detained, must be judicially supervised by a court with full powers (see Article 5(3) and (4)).

Questions

For suggested approaches, please visit the Online Resource Centre.

1 Does the power of 'stop and search' raise issues under Article 5?

2 What are the main requirements for judicial supervision of a deprivation of liberty?

Further reading

GENERAL TEXTS

Amos, M. (see Preface) Chapter 9

Baros, M. 'A Developing Gap in the Application of Articles 5 and 8 of the ECHR in the Immigration Context—the Shifting Nature of Humanity' (2009) 23(3) *JIANL* 264–280

Lester, A., Pannick, D. and Herberg, J. (see Preface) Chapter 4, Article 5

Stone, R. 'Deprivation of Liberty: The Scope of Article 5 of the European Convention on Human Rights' [2012] *EHRLR* 46–58.

Article 6: right to a fair trial

Chapter overview

- The importance of fair trials and the rule of law.
- The scope of Article 6: trials 'determining' 'civil rights and obligations' or a 'criminal charge'.
- The general right to a fair trial: express and implied rights found in Article 6(1) which apply to both civil and criminal trials (e.g. equality of arms and access to the courts).
- Fair trial rights that are specific to criminal trials (Article 6(2) and (3)).
- The general character of Article 6 rights: flexibility and the importance of context.

Article 6   Right to a Fair Trial

(1) In the determination of his civil rights and obligations or of any criminal charge against him, everyone is entitled to a fair and public hearing within a reasonable time by an independent and impartial tribunal established by law. Judgment shall be pronounced publicly but the press and public may be excluded from all or part of the trial in the interests of morals, public order or national security in a democratic society, where the interests of juveniles or the protection of the private life of the parties so requires, or to the extent strictly necessary in the opinion of the court in special circumstances where publicity would prejudice the interests of justice.

(2) Everyone charged with a criminal offence shall be presumed innocent until proved guilty according to law.

(3) Everyone charged with a criminal offence has the following minimum rights:

(a) to be informed promptly, in a language which he understands and in detail, of the nature and cause of the accusation against him;

(b) to have adequate time and facilities for the preparation of his defence;

(c) to defend himself in person or through legal assistance of his own choosing or, if he has not sufficient means to pay for legal assistance, to be given it free when the interests of justice so require;

(d) to examine or have examined witnesses against him and to obtain the attendance and examination of witnesses on his behalf under the same conditions as witnesses against him;

(e) to have the free assistance of an interpreter if he cannot understand or speak the language used in court.

Introduction

Article 6

- **Article 6 requires the signatory states to provide fair trials for both civil and criminal proceedings.**

- **All trials governed by Article 6, criminal and civil, must meet the general requirement of fairness, independence, etc., identified in Article 6(1).**

- **Those charged with a criminal offence have the right to be presumed innocent (Article 6(2) and the other rights listed in Article 6(3)).**

- **Fairness is not defined in Article 6. A range of particular rights have been implied, by the European Court of Human Rights (ECtHR), from the general concept of a fair trial.**

- **The right to a fair trial is absolute. This is a matter for the courts (there is little deference owed to the executive or legislature). However, the requirements of fairness, as understood by the courts, can be context dependent and subject to qualification.**

The significance of Article 6

Article 6 might be thought dry and procedural. This is misleading. In some areas, such as terrorism (dealt with in Chapter 26), serious crime, drug dealing, even drink

driving and speed cameras, the prosecution of alleged offenders can be difficult because of the nature of the evidence, intimidation, the wish to protect police and security service procedures, issues of national security, and so on. These difficulties can lead to a tension with the need for trials to be fair and public. The question arises: should a trial be stopped if the ordinary legal requirements of fairness cannot be met? If so, it may be that dangerous people are released or laws promoting important social interests become unenforceable. The alternative is to adjust the concept of 'fairness' to the circumstances with the equal and opposite danger that the innocent are at greater danger of conviction. These problems are at the heart of the Article 6 case law.

What counts as 'fair' is likely to be controversial and open to reasonable disagreement in a society. The fairness of a criminal trial, for instance, can depend upon changing and contestable views on what is the appropriate and fair balance between the twin goals of convicting the guilty and protecting the innocent. In England and Wales the tendency is increasingly in favour of obtaining convictions. Changes in the law have, for example, restricted the 'right of silence' and have permitted a greater use of presumptions on which guilt can be based. Pressure to restrict the use of juries in complex fraud trials continues. Such changes do not necessarily mean that the trials cease to be fair, rather they point to the contestable nature of the concept of fairness.

The role of the European Court of Human Rights (ECtHR)

cross reference
For margin of appreciation see Chapter 6, section 6.3.

The Convention does not require fair trials to take a particular form. In Europe there are major differences between different legal systems and court procedures. How the fairness of trials is obtained is, principally, up to the national governments and judiciary. The ECtHR, therefore, accepts a wide margin of appreciation on the issue of what makes a fair trial. Its role is to judge the overall fairness of individual trials by measuring the application of national laws and procedures, whatever they happen to be, in the particular case against the terms of Article 6.

United Kingdom courts and deference

cross reference
For deference see Chapter 4, section 4.6.2.

Fair trials and procedures are at the heart of the traditional role of the courts under the separation of powers. Article 6 cases, therefore, are likely to be decided by the courts acting, on judicial principles, without much, if any, deference to the views of the executive. To say this, however, is not to suggest that the courts do not accept that the needs of social policy (see *Sheldrake* at section 12.14.2) or national security (see *R v A* at section 12.9.2) may require, in context, qualifications and limitations in the application of Article 6.

12.1 English law and fair trials

In England, irrational forms of trial, such as trial by ordeal, were abolished in the thirteenth century (though aspects, including 'dunking for witches', seem to have survived into the seventeenth century).

Fundamental requirements of a fair trial, such as the presumption of innocence in criminal trials, have been practised under English law for centuries. However, some fundamentally important rules were not introduced until comparatively recently. The rule which prevented a defendant from giving evidence on oath was not altered until the late nineteenth century, for example.

12.1.1 English law and fair trials

Today the fairness of trials (both criminal and civil) is protected by rules such as the following:

- Laws of evidence. These include important statutory rules such as, for criminal trials, sections 76 and 78 of the Police and Criminal Evidence Act 1984 (PACE), which impose on judges the duty to exclude confessions obtained by oppression and give judges the discretion to exclude any evidence which is likely to have 'an adverse effect on the fairness of the proceedings'.

- The law on contempt of court. This prevents the publication of stories and other actions which might undermine fair trials.

- Rules of 'natural justice'. These are rules of fairness which apply to criminal trials (such as those in magistrates' courts) and to non-criminal procedures in courts, tribunals and administrative and professional bodies.

- Civil Procedure Rules. These are the detailed rules of procedure governing the conduct of civil trials and procedures. The Rules have an 'overriding objective', which is to ensure that cases are dealt with 'justly'.

12.1.2 The Human Rights Act 1998

Under the Human Rights Act 1998 (HRA), such laws and procedures need to be applied in a way that is compatible with Article 6 of the European Convention on Human Rights (ECHR). Generally there is a high level of compatibility, although, as we shall see, there are a number of important and controversial areas where compatibility is, to say the least, strained.

12.2 International Covenant on Civil and Political Rights (ICCPR)

The right to a fair trial in Article 14 of the ICCPR (see Chapter 1, section 1.4.4) contains a number of provisions that are not found, at least as express rights, in Article 6. These include the right not to be compelled to confess guilt, the right of appeal in criminal cases and the right to compensation for a miscarriage of justice.

The substance of these rights is already recognised in the domestic law of the United Kingdom. They are also found in Protocol 7 ECHR but the United Kingdom has neither signed nor ratified this and so it is not in the HRA. It can be taken into account by UK courts, as in *R (Mullen)* v *Secretary of State for the Home Department* [2004] UKHL 18.

For England and Wales, the Criminal Justice Act 2003 (CJA 2003) allows for the retrial of someone previously acquitted of murder if there is 'new' and 'compelling' evidence. This is in tension with the traditional principle against 'double jeopardy' (being tried twice for the same offence), a principle which is not in Article 6 ECHR but is in Article 14 ICCPR; it is in Protocol 7 ECHR but with exceptions that would allow CJA 2003 (see *R v Dunlop* [2006] EWCA Crim 1354).

12.3 The application of Article 6: introduction

12.3.1 Article 6 does not apply to all types of trial

For Article 6 to apply the 'trial' must be one which 'determines' either

- 'civil rights and obligations', or a
- 'criminal charge'.

Therefore, not all trial-like procedures are covered by Article 6 (see section 12.4.4).

If Article 6 does apply it is a matter of significance whether it is a 'criminal charge' or 'civil rights and obligations' that are being determined. Both criminal and civil trials have the rights based on Article 6(1) but only criminal trials must accord with the rights listed in Article 6(2) and (3). Deciding whether a matter is 'criminal' or 'civil' can be difficult (see, for example, *International Transport Roth GmbH* v *Secretary of State for the Home Department* [2002] EWCA Civ 158 where the Court of Appeal divided on the matter).

12.3.2 Other fair trial articles

Even if Article 6 does not apply, a person may have other fair trial rights under the Convention. In particular there are rights under Article 5(3) and (4) (testing the legality of a deprivation of liberty) and Article 13 (the right to a remedy). In both contexts fair procedures appropriate to the different contexts are required. In *R (Smith)* v *Parole Board* [2005] UKHL 1, for example, the House of Lords held that Article 6 did not apply to decisions of the Parole Board but that Article 5(4) did (see paras 40–41; 37).

cross reference
For Article 5(4), see Chapter 11, section 11.8; for Article 13, see Chapter 5, section 5.1.

There is a lot of common ground between what is required by Article 6 and by Article 5(4). Nevertheless the two rights are not necessarily the same. The purposes of a trial subject to Article 6 (e.g. to determine guilt or innocence) and a hearing subject to Article 5(4) (e.g. to determine whether it is safe to release a person into the community) are very different and the content of the rights that each Article secures relates to that purpose (for discussion see *R (DPP)* v *Havering Magistrates Court* [2001] 3 All ER 997).

12.4 The application of Article 6: 'civil rights and obligations'

The term 'civil rights and obligations' is not defined in Article 6. It has an 'autonomous' meaning (see Chapter 6, section 6.2.3) and is not dependant on whether a right or obligation is categorised as civil in the domestic law. The person claiming fair trial rights under Article 6 must have a substantive legal right, recognised by national law, which the trial is determining (see *R (Kehoe)* v *Secretary of State for Work and Pensions* [2005] UKHL 48).

12.4.1 'Private law' rights

The core meaning of civil rights and obligations relates to trials dealing with ordinary 'private law' rights. Thus, in terms of the law of England and Wales, trials determining contracts, torts, real and personal property, etc. come within the core meaning of civil rights and obligations.

Employment law and professional discipline

The rights under a contract of employment, and the right to practise a profession or remain employable are also 'civil rights' (*Le Compte* v *Belgium* (1982) 4 EHRR 1; *R (Wright)* v *Secretary of State for Health* [2009] UKHL 3). Generally, however, an employer's internal disciplinary processes, which result in dismissal, will not engage Article 6 and so those processes need not be fully independent or grant rights, such as representation, to the employee. Such proceedings are seen (by UK courts following *Le Compte* and other cases) to be just the exercise by the employer of an alleged contractual right to dismiss. The civil right involved is not being 'determined' by these proceedings (though see the next paragraph). This 'determination' takes place in an Employment Tribunal or County Court if the employee chooses to challenge the lawfulness of the employer's actions. Article 6 rights must be available in the tribunal or court (*Mattu* v *University Hospitals* [2012] EWCA Civ 641, paras 76 and 102).

Decisions taken by disciplinary bodies (e.g. of the professions) that prevent a person working in their chosen profession, 'determine' the right to remain employable and will engage Article 6(1) (*Le Compte*; *Wright*). Where the internal, employer's, procedures, referred to earlier, also have a 'substantial influence or effect' on the disciplinary body's decision, then, contrary to what has been said earlier, Article 6 rights may also be required of the employer's procedures. Usually, though, a disciplinary body will make its own, fully independent, assessment. If so the employer is not bound by Article 6 (*R (G)* v *Governors of X School* [2011] UKSC 30); and if the employer's decision merely makes it harder for an employee to be employed by someone else, then Article 6 is probably not engaged for the reasons given in the previous paragraph (*Mattu*).

12.4.2 The determination of Convention rights

Some, but not all, Convention rights are likely to be civil rights and so courts and tribunals deciding them have to meet Article 6 standards. The House of Lords has suggested that disputes about Article 8 (private and family life) and Articles 10 and 11 (freedom of expression and freedom of assembly and association) involve civil rights, see *R (McCann)* v *Crown Court at Manchester* [2002] UKHL 39, paras 78–79. Trials relating to serious restrictions on liberty, whether or not they engage Article 5, are likely to involve civil rights and so come within the scope of Article 6 (*Aerts* v *Belgium* (2000) 29 EHRR 50 and, under HRA, *R (MB)* v *Secretary of State for the Home Department* [2007] UKHL 46, para 24). Some Convention rights certainly are not civil rights, e.g. the right to free and fair elections under Article 3 of Protocol 1.

12.4.3 **The individual and the state**

The notion of 'civil rights and obligations' is based on a distinction found in Continental legal systems (such as in France) between 'private' and 'public' law. Public law, dealing with the relationship of individual and state, raises complex policy questions which cannot be dealt with on the same basis as private law. Disputes may be dealt with by administrative courts or tribunals on the basis of principles of public law. The intention of the Convention's drafters in 1950 was to introduce a separate body of fair procedure rights to deal with the individual–state relationship, but this has not happened (see *Begum* v *Tower Hamlets LBC* [2003] UKHL 5, para 28).

12.4.4 **Public law rights**

Article 6(1) does not apply to public law rights in the absence of any direct implication for private rights.

Political rights

Determination of rights which are 'political', in the narrow sense that they are concerned with rights of political participation, such as rights under election laws and other laws dealing with direct participation in the political processes, are outside the scope of Article 6 (even though these rights may engage Article 3 of Protocol 1) (see *Pierre-Bloch* v *France* (1998) 26 EHRR 202).

Civic status and duties

Disputes over status and basic civic obligations may not engage Article 6(1). Two examples are immigration and taxation.

- In *Maaouia* v *France* (2001) 33 EHRR 42, the ECtHR confirmed that decisions about 'entry, stay or deportation', are not determinations of a person's civil rights and obligations. This has been followed under the HRA in *R (Ullah)* v *Immigration Appeal Tribunal* [2003] EWCA Civ 1366, para 20.
- In *Ferrazzini* v *Italy* (2002) 34 EHRR 45, the ECtHR confirmed that disputes about tax demands were outside the scope of Article 6: 'tax matters still form part of the hard core of public-authority prerogatives, with the public nature of the relationship between the taxpayer and the community remaining predominant'.

12.4.5 **Public law decisions decisive of private rights**

State officials and agencies exercise a vast range of regulatory powers involving economic and social life. They take decisions which directly affect the significance and value of individual's private rights such as rights under contract or property. These may, for example, be decisions about planning applications for permission to build or the granting of economically valuable licences to sell products. Such decisions should be taken on the basis of fair trial rights in Article 6(1) or, at least, be subject to effective review by courts or tribunals that provide Article 6(1) rights (e.g. *Tre Traktörer Aktiebolag* v *Sweden* (1991) 13 EHRR 309, licence to sell alcohol).

12.4.6 **Welfare state benefits**

Article 6(1) is now applied to disputes with government agencies about social welfare provision. In the past the ECtHR would only grant Article 6 rights where the welfare scheme was contributory and so had features similar to private insurance (e.g. *Feldbrugge* v *The Netherlands* (1986) 8 EHRR 425). However, this position is now changed. In *Schuler-Zgraggen* v *Switzerland* (1993) 16 EHRR 405 the Court held that 'the general rule is that Article 6(1) does apply in the field of social insurance, including even welfare assistance' (para 46) and in *Salesi* v *Italy* (1998) 26 EHRR 187 (involving a state disability pension) the ECtHR held that similarity with private insurance may not be necessary. Article 6(1) can apply to any dispute over 'a specific economic right flowing from a statute'. Disputes over entirely non-contributory benefits, especially if they are discretionary, may still be outside the scope of Article 6(1).

12.4.7 **Administrative decisions**

Decisions, like those mentioned in sections 12.4.4, 12.4.5 and 12.4.6, are amongst the thousands taken all the time by civil servants, local council officers and other officials. These decisions may give public money and extend public services to individuals. They involve the application of complex legislation, both primary and secondary, to individuals. They give effect to government policy often in the general context of the welfare state. They are made on the basis of complex factual assessments, in the light of policy objectives, and take into account resources and the public interest. They are the ultimate responsibility of elected bodies. Obviously such decisions are of great importance to the individuals involved. However, they are rarely taken on the basis of a full hearing, with full procedural rights presided over by fully independent officers. They are 'administrative' not 'judicial' decisions. The question is whether such decisions need to be taken in line with Article 6.

Two issues need to be determined.

The first is whether the decision is one which determines civil rights and obligations. This is a context-sensitive matter. In *Bryan* v *UK* (1996) 21 EHRR 342, the ECtHR held that planning decisions may well determine civil rights since they affect property interests. In *Tsfayo* v *United Kingdom* (2009) 48 EHRR 18, a welfare dispute about the amount of housing benefit owed to the applicant also came within the scope of Article 6.

British courts, working with decisions such as these, have explored the underlying principles.

case close-up

Ali v *Birmingham City Council* [2012] UKSC 8

The case involved the decisions made by local authority housing departments. The legal issue was whether the decision of a local authority that it has discharged its duty to secure accommodation for homeless persons, is a decision which determines the homeless person's civil rights and so needs be taken independently and otherwise in accordance with Article 6.

The Supreme Court noted that, whilst Convention case law has accepted that welfare state decisions can involve civil rights (see sections 12.4.5 and 12.4.6), it has never been proposed that all administrative decisions affecting individuals should be covered by Article 6. This is partly a matter of principle: the public/private distinction inherent in Article 6 (referred to at section 12.4.3); it is also a recognition of the practical problems and costs which would result if welfare administration was 'judicialised' and had to be reorganised to allow hearings, rehearings and appeals to conform to Article 6.

The Justices made a distinction between

- benefits to which the claimant has a specific entitlement based upon the clear words of a statute; here Article 6 is likely to apply, and

- benefits which are more discretionary—they are 'dependent upon a series of evaluative judgements by the provider as to whether statutory criteria are satisfied and how best to meet the claimant's needs; here Article 6 is unlikely to apply.

Determinations of planning applications can be examples in the first category (see *Bryan*, at section 12.4.7, followed by *R (Alconbury) v Secretary of State for the Environment* [2001] UKHL 23. Decisions about the housing by local authorities of children in need are examples of the second, see *R (A) v Croydon LBC* [2009] UKSC 8. The decision in *Ali* is likely to reduce significantly the extent to which Article 6 rights can intrude into administrative decision taking.

If, however, a decision does relate to a specified right (it is in the first category and Article 6 is engaged) then the second issue arises: whether Article 6 has been violated. Internal reviews and appeals of the decision, in particular, are unlikely to be properly 'independent' and 'impartial' as required by Article 6. If internal processes do not satisfy Article 6, the approach of the ECtHR is that Article 6 is not violated so long as the claimant has a right of appeal or review to a court or tribunal that does satisfy Article 6 and has 'full jurisdiction' to hear all the matters of fact and law that are in dispute (*Albert v Belgium* (1983) 5 EHRR 533, para 29). Whether such a court or tribunal has full jurisdiction will depend on context. The High Court, through 'judicial review', for example, may not be able to deal with predominantly factual disputes (as in *Tsfayo*, at section 12.4.7).

In *Alconbury*, mentioned earlier in this section, on the other hand, the dispute was more a matter of fact and law and the High Court, through judicial review, did have full jurisdiction. In a housing case, *Begum v Tower Hamlets LBC* [2003] UKHL 5, the right of the applicant to appeal the housing department's decision to the County Court was held, by the House of Lords, to satisfy Article 6 (the application of Article 6 was presumed).

cross reference
Judicial review is summarised in Chapter 5, section 5.2.1.

(12.5) The application of Article 6: 'criminal charge'

12.5.1 Criminal charge

A trial which determines a 'criminal charge' must accord not only with the fair trial rights in Article 6(1) but also those additional and more specific rights in Article 6(2) and (3). As with civil rights and obligations, the concept of a 'criminal charge' is autonomous to the Convention (see Chapter 6, section 6.2.3).

case close-up

Engel v The Netherlands (1979–80) 1 EHRR 647

. . . .

E and others were Dutch conscripts subjected to a range of military disciplinary measures of varying degrees of severity. One issue was whether these measures were criminal charges that had been imposed in breach of Article 6.

The ECtHR identified three principal criteria for deciding whether or not a legal procedure involved the determination of a criminal charge (see paras 82–83).

- National classification. If the matter is classified as 'criminal' under national law, this is conclusive that the full range of Article 6 rights apply.

What matters are the realities of the situation. Where a matter is not classified as criminal (but is, for example, called a disciplinary or administrative offence) there may still be a criminal charge for Convention purposes. This depends on two things:

- The nature of the offence. Does it have criminal characteristics such as a whether there is a requirement for **mens rea** or whether the process results in a finding of guilt. How other countries deal with the problem can also be relevant.

....

mens rea, strict liability

This is the requirement that, for most criminal offences, there must be both a guilty act (*actus reus*) but also a guilty mind or intention (*mens rea*). Offences which are defined in statute as not to require *mens rea* are known as offences of 'strict liability'.

....

- The point of proceedings is punishment. This is the most important matter. If the point of the proceedings is to punish (retribution or deterrence) in non-trivial ways, then there is a strong inference that a criminal charge is being determined.

KEY POINT These principles have been discussed and adopted under the HRA by the House of Lords in *R (McCann)* v *Manchester Crown Court* [2002] UKHL 39: see section 12.5.3.

12.5.2 **Example of 'criminal charges'**

Applying these principles, the ECtHR has held that a criminal charge is being determined in relation to, for example, 'administrative offences': regulations enforced by penalties applied in contexts such as road traffic, food quality, the environment (e.g. *Mauer* v *Austria* (1998) 25 EHRR 91, involving minor traffic offences); military discipline: trials by courts martial of members of the armed forces for serious military offences are likely to involve a criminal charge (e.g. *Findlay* v *United Kingdom* (1997) 24 EHRR 221, discussed at section 12.8.2); and prison discipline: prisoners who break Prison Rules can be disciplined by the Prison Service. Where such hearings can lead to significant punishment, including extra days in prison, the matter is likely to involve the determination of a criminal charge (e.g. *Ezeh* v *United Kingdom* (2004) 39 EHRR 1).

12.5.3 **Non-punitive procedures—not 'criminal charges'**

In the United Kingdom, as in other societies, there are legal procedures that can result in significant detriment for the individuals affected but which do not have punishment as their aim. They have some other purpose such as the protection of the public. Such procedures are likely not to involve the determination of a criminal charge. Examples include:

- Professional bodies, working through independent tribunals such as the Solicitors Disciplinary Tribunal or the Medical Practitioners Tribunal Service, holding disciplinary hearings. These hearings aim to protect the public from incompetent or wicked practitioners, and not at punishment. (Their decisions, which may lead to 'striking off', are likely to be determining civil rights and obligations (see *Le Compte*, at section 12.4.1).

- Disqualification from public office, such as in *Pierre-Bloch* v *France* (section 12.4.4).

- Forfeiture of goods etc. under tax laws, money laundering legislation, obscenity laws, etc. (there may be rights under Article 1 of the First Protocol).

Measures of public protection

States may have laws and procedures which aim at protecting the public from dangerous or anti-social persons. For example, in the United Kingdom, the Parole Board decides whether certain prisoners (e.g. murderers serving a life sentence) who have served the punishment part of their sentence, are safe to release. The Board is concerned not with punishment but public safety, *R (Smith)* v *Parole Board* [2005] UKHL 1. Prisoners enjoy the procedural protection of Article 5(4) (see Chapter 11, section 11.8) and they may have civil rights, see *Smith*, para 44.

Entry on the Sex Offenders' Register may, in some circumstances, be an alternative to punishment or it may be a consequence of a criminal conviction, but its purpose is to enhance the safety of the public, not to punish (see *Jones* v *Greater Manchester Police Authority* [2001] EWHC 189 (Admin) and *R (R)* v *Durham Constabulary* [2005] UKHL 21).

discussion topic

Should those threatened with anti-social behaviour orders (ASBOs) have full rights to a fair trial guaranteed in Article 6?

. . . .

The Crime and Disorder Act 1998 permits magistrates to impose ASBOs. These orders, subject to proportionality, can be whatever is necessary to prevent the behaviour that has been deemed to be anti-social (there is no definition of anti-social behaviour in the Act, though the Home Office has produced indicative guidelines). The orders may have a significant impact on an individual such as restricting where they may go and whom they may associate with. ASBOs do not involve 'deprivation of liberty' so as to engage Article 5.

The question is whether it is fair to impose such orders on the basis of, for example, hearsay evidence (admissible in civil but not criminal proceedings), which cannot be directly challenged in court.

Arguments in favour of avoiding full criminal trial procedures include the following:

- Victims of anti-social behaviour need to feel safe from possible retribution before they will come forward.

- ASBOs do not involve punishment; all they do is to require a person to stop behaving in an anti-social way.

- Perpetrators are often young and may themselves have had difficult lives. ASBOs do not involve a criminal record.

Arguments in favour of requiring the full range of criminal trial safeguards include the following:

- An ASBO can restrict a person's freedom in a way that, to him or her at least, seems like punishment.

- Breach of an ASBO is a crime and the punishment can involve imprisonment.

- The lack of precision in the definition of anti-social behaviour and on the orders that may be imposed creates the possibility that ASBOs will be used disproportionately: a risk that full criminal procedures would reduce.

ASBOs have been considered by the House of Lords in *McCann* (above) which held that:

- ASBOs do not have punishment as their purpose and so do not involve the determination of a criminal charge. Article 6(2)–(3) is not, therefore, engaged and so hearsay evidence (e.g. the views of anonymous people reported to the court by the police) can be used. (They may involve civil rights.)

- However, the court issuing the ASBO must be satisfied to the criminal standard of proof (beyond reasonable doubt) that the person was responsible for anti-social behaviour (para 37).

further study

A White Paper, *Putting Victims First*, was published by the Home Office in May 2012 (Cm 8367). A general reform of law, practice and remedies dealing with anti-social behaviour is proposed, including the replacement of ASBOs by a new 'Criminal Behaviour Order'.

12.6 Express rights, implied rights and qualifications

Sections 12.3–12.5 deal with the circumstances in which a person is able to claim rights based on Article 6. The next issue is to identify what rights Article 6 secures. It is important to stress that the substance of criminal law and of trial procedures are primarily matters for the states. The ECtHR's role is to ensure that, whatever system is adopted in a country, the essence of a fair trial is assured.

- Pervasive fairness. The concept of a 'fair trial' in Article 6(1) is the governing idea in Article 6. This idea must influence the way the express and implied rights in Article 6 are given effect.

- Express rights. Particular rights are expressed in Article 6(1) (e.g. the right to an independent tribunal) and, for those facing criminal charges, express rights are also found in Article 6(2) and (3).

- Inherent rights. Various rights have been identified by the ECtHR as inherent in, or implied by, the concept of a fair trial, e.g. the right of access to a court. These are not expressed as such in Article 6 but will apply, in context, to both civil and criminal trials.

- Qualifications and context dependency. What counts as 'fair' will depend upon circumstances and context and upon the particular system adopted in the state. Article 6 rights, especially inherent rights, have a certain flexibility. What is fair can depend upon a range of factors including, given the situation, the need to balance fairness to individuals with the rights and interests of others and even with the general public interest. As Lord Bingham said in *Brown v Stott (Procurator Fiscal)* [2003] 1 AC 681, 704:

> The jurisprudence of the European Court very clearly establishes that while the overall fairness of a criminal trial cannot be compromised, the constituent rights comprised, whether expressly or implicitly, within art 6 are not themselves absolute. Limited qualification of these rights is acceptable if reasonably directed by national authorities towards a clear and proper public objective and if representing no greater qualification than the situation calls for... The case law shows that the court has paid very close attention to the facts of particular cases coming before it, giving effect to factual differences and recognising differences of degree... The court has also recognised the

need for a fair balance between the general interest of the community and the personal rights of the individual, the search for which balance has been described as inherent in the whole of the convention.

- Overall fairness. Any limitations or qualifications must, nevertheless, be compatible with the overall fairness of a trial, otherwise there will be a breach of Article 6. There is little, if any, 'deference' by the courts to the views of Parliament or the government on fairness.

12.7 Article 6(1): access to court

Perhaps the most important right in Article 6 is the right of a person to be able to take his or her case to court for a fair hearing. This right is inherent in the concept of a fair trial in Article 6(1). It is recognised as 'fundamental' by English common law, to be departed from only by clear statutory words—*Pyx Granite Co* v *Ministry of Housing and Local Government* [1960] AC 260.

12.7.1 Criminal law and the right of appeal

Since the state initiates proceedings the right of access to court is of lesser significance in respect of criminal charges. The Convention itself does not give a person convicted after a fair trial a right to appeal. Such a right is found in Article 2 of the Seventh Protocol; but this has not been signed or ratified by the United Kingdom.

12.7.2 Civil rights and obligations

The general principle

The right of access to the court has greatest impact in civil law.

> ### *Golder* v *United Kingdom* (1979–80) 1 EHRR 524
>
> G was accused by a prison officer of participation in a prison disturbance. The allegation was later withdrawn but not removed from his record. G's letters to his MP concerning his circumstances and his attempt to consult a solicitor with a view to an action for defamation against the officer were stopped by the governor exercising powers under the prison rules.
>
> The ECtHR held that there had been a breach of Article 6(1).

For the Court, the right of a person to go to court in order both to assert or defend his or her civil rights and obligations was fundamental. It was rooted in the commitment of the signatory states to the rule of law and it also follows from the general requirement that Convention rights need to be effective:

> And in civil matters one can scarcely conceive of the rule of law without there being the possibility of having access to the courts. (para. 35).

A qualified right

As with all implied rights, the right of access to the courts is not absolute and may be subject to qualifications over which states have a considerable margin of appreciation. Any restrictions must pursue a legitimate aim, have a proportionate effect in particular cases and not under-mine the very essence of the right (see, for example, *Fayed* v *United Kingdom* (1994) 18 EHRR 393, para 65). Examples of accepted restrictions include those on children, persons of unsound mind, 'vexatious litigants', bankrupts and those defamed by Members of Parliament speaking with the protection of Parliamentary privilege.

In *Ashingdane* v *United Kingdom* (1985) 7 EHRR 528, the ECtHR upheld a statutory restriction which prevented mental patients suing their carers. The Court accepted that preventing unfair harassment of staff by patients was a legitimate aim (paras 56–59).

In *Seal* v *Chief Constable of South Wales Police* [2007] UKHL 31, the House of Lords upheld a clear statutory requirement that mental patients must obtain the leave of the High Court before they could bring a legal challenge to contest certain decisions made about them. Article 6 was not mentioned. The ECtHR then held, on margin of appreciation grounds, that there was no violation of Article 6 (*Seal* v *UK* (2012) 54 EHRR 6.)

Procedural bars

A right of access to court can be in issue if procedural rules or rules of evidence are such as to make any court action pointless. If, for example, national security considerations prevent crucial evidence from being admitted or challenged, then a person may have no effective access to court (e.g. *Tinnelly* v *United Kingdom* (1998) 27 EHRR 249).

Traditionally, under international law, states and their senior officials, enjoy a wide immunity from being sued in the domestic courts of other countries. This immunity has been generally accepted by the ECtHR as serving a legitimate purpose, even in the context of allegations of torture.

case close-up

Al-Adsani v *United Kingdom* (2002) 34 EHRR 11

The applicant came into possession of sex videos involving Sheik Al-Sabah. He alleged that, fol-lowing the videos getting into public circulation, he had been abducted, beaten and tortured by the Sheik and by agents of the state of Kuwait (the Sheik was allegedly related to the Emir of Kuwait). He brought a tort action for damages in the English courts against the Sheik and the state of Kuwait. The English courts dismissed the claim on the grounds that, under English and international law, Kuwait enjoyed state immunity. The ECtHR held that there had been no breach of Article 6. State immunity pursued a legitimate purpose (promoting good relations between states by respecting sovereignty) and that there was no developed legal consensus that state immunity did not apply to allegations of torture (the Court accepted that torture was now generally forbidden at international law but that whilst there was a tendency to remove immunity from individual officials, the state itself continued to enjoy immunity). There were powerful dissenting judgments.

In *Jones* v *Ministry of the Interior* [2006] UKHL 26, the House of Lords upheld this immunity in respect of a tort action brought, in English courts, against Saudi Arabian officials. The claim-ants had alleged they had been systematically tortured whilst imprisoned in Saudi Arabia. The House of Lords followed *Al-Adsani* and accepted that the immunity of Saudi Arabia and its officials did not violate the claimants' rights of access to the courts.

Procedural bars or substantive rights?

Procedural bars need to be distinguished from substantive rights. Under English law, for example, a person can only sue for negligence if the person being sued owes them a 'duty of care'. The existence of a duty of care is a matter of law to be decided by the courts. In a number of areas the English courts have denied that various public officials owe duties of care to the people they deal with. Is this a matter of substantive law (a person does not have a civil right to damages flowing from the actions of certain public officials) or is it a procedural barrier seeking to immunise public officials from what would otherwise be a cause of action?

In *Osman* v *United Kingdom* (2000) 29 EHRR 245, the ECtHR held that the denial that police owed a duty of care to those they knew might be at risk of a criminal attack, was a procedural barrier which violated Article 6(1). This view is no longer held (see *Z* v *United Kingdom* (2002) 34 EHRR 3) and it is now clear that Article 6(1) is not concerned with substance (what rights people have) but with the procedure for dealing with disputes about these rights (*R* v *G* [2008] UKHL 37, para 4).

Legal aid

In criminal cases, the provision of free legal aid is virtually a requirement of the Convention, based on Article 6(3)(c) (see section 12.16.3). In civil cases, the situation is much less clear. How the right to a fair trial is achieved is a matter, in the first instance, for the national authorities: it is not for the ECtHR to insist on the provision of legal aid in all circumstances. In some cases, for example, the right of a litigant to appear in person may satisfy the requirements of a fair trial; in others it will not (see *Airey* v *Ireland* (1979–80) 2 EHRR 305).

In *Steel and Morris* v *United Kingdom* (2005) 41 EHRR 22, the applicants had distributed leaflets that made a number of allegations against McDonalds, including allegations that the fast food was unhealthy and environmentally unfriendly. McDonalds sued them for libel. Under English law, legal aid was not available. At stake in the case were complex issues of fact and interpretation (the trial turned into the longest ever in English legal history, civil or criminal). The ECtHR held that, given the complexity of the case, legal aid should have been available and that there was a breach of Article 6. The case can be contrasted with *McVicar* v *United Kingdom* (2002) 35 EHRR 22 where, because the case was relatively straightforward, the lack of legal aid did not violate Article 6.

12.8 Article 6(1): an 'independent and impartial tribunal'

12.8.1 Introduction

The judicial function

A court, tribunal, etc. determining civil rights and obligations or a criminal charge must be and must appear to be 'independent and impartial'. These values are, of course, at the heart of any known conception of judicial procedure and decision taking. They imply that the proper application of the law in individual cases excludes reasons such as the personal advancement of the judge, the promotion of political policies or discrimination against particular groups represented by a litigant. Independence and impartiality embody the constitutional principle of the **separation of powers**: that the application of the laws in individual cases (the judicial function) needs to be separated from the making of the laws (the legislative function) and policy making and enforcement (the executive function).

separation of powers

This is a widely found constitutional doctrine requiring the mutual independence ('separation') of the executive, legislature and judiciary (the constitutional 'powers'). Such separation helps to prevent tyranny by ensuring that each of the powers can act as a check on the others. No system has complete separation of powers. In the UK the Parliamentary system means that there is considerable fusion between executive and legislature. The independence of the judiciary is now embodied in statute: sections 1 and 3 of the Constitutional Reform Act 2005.

. . . .

A matter of appearance

There is no need to prove that a court or tribunal has been biased or prejudiced in the way it actually decided the case. Appearance of lack of independence or impartiality is enough.

Natural justice

cross reference
See Chapter 5, section 5.2.1 for a description of judicial review.

Under English law, the principle that courts, tribunals and other bodies should appear to be unbiased is part of general administrative law. There are rules of natural justice which can be given effect through judicial review and other proceedings. Natural justice has a strong and effective rule against the appearance of bias.

For the ECtHR, independence and impartiality are closely linked ideas. Nevertheless it is possible to identify distinct general features of each concept.

12.8.2 **Independence**

General features of independence

The general idea of independence is that bodies determining civil and criminal cases should do so on the basis of their own judgment and not act under the influence of the executive or other outside pressures. Independence is a matter of fact. The ECtHR has suggested that independence can be measured by factors such as the following (see *Findlay* v *United Kingdom* (1997) 24 EHRR 221, para 73):

- the manner of appointment of the members of a court or tribunal,
- their term of office,
- the existence of guarantees against outside pressures, and
- whether it presents an appearance of independence.

Independence and the United Kingdom

As discussed at section 12.4.7, those administrative procedures which also determine civil rights and obligations, such as executive involvement in the planning process, are unlikely to be independent (e.g. *Alconbury*). But, so long as the applicant has access to an Article 6 compliant court or tribunal which has 'full jurisdiction' to deal with disputed issues of law and fact that arise, there will be no violation of Article 6.

Difficulties about independence, therefore, tend to arise in respect of courts and tribunals that perform judicial, not administrative, functions.

case close-up

Findlay v *United Kingdom* (1997) 24 EHRR 221

F, a soldier, was charged with a number of offences arising out of a shooting incident in his barracks. His defence was that, as a result of his participation in the Falklands War he was suffering post-traumatic stress disorder. He was tried and convicted by a Court Martial, which was held properly according to the rules and procedures then in place. The applicant alleged he had been denied a fair hearing before an independent tribunal.

The ECtHR held that there had been a violation of Article 6. Under the rules, the decision on the charges to be brought, the type of court martial, the membership of the court and the choice of the prosecuting and defending officers were the responsibility of the 'convening officer'. This officer also had other links with the prosecution (his consent was necessary if the prosecution were to accept a lesser charge, for example) and it was the convening officer who confirmed the sentence. The convening officer, therefore, played a major organising role but it was one linked to the prosecution. The members of the court were subordinate in rank to the convening officer and were within his chain of command. For this reason the ECtHR held that F had grounds to fear a lack of independence in the court.

KEY POINT Following *Findlay*, the court martial system was reformed to meet the requirements of Article 6. UK courts and the ECtHR have accepted the compatibility of the new system (*R* v *Spear* [2002] UKHL 31 and *Cooper* v *United Kingdom* (2004) 39 EHRR 8).

The concept of independence has had a practical impact in a number of UK cases such as:

- *Starrs* v *Ruxton* 2000 SLT 42, where the Scottish High Court of Justiciary held that the system of using temporary sheriffs in the Scottish summary justice system was incompatible with Article 6. The Lord Advocate played an important role in the appointment of these sheriffs and their make-up to a full-time position was subject to his judgment. The Lord Advocate, however, was also ultimately responsible for criminal prosecutions.

- *Scanfuture UK* v *Secretary of State for Trade and Industry* [2001] IRLR 416 where the independence of employment tribunals was successfully challenged before the English courts regarding cases where the Secretary of State was a party. The Secretary of State was responsible for appointing the tribunal members (the system has now been changed).

12.8.3 **Impartiality**

The general approach under the Convention

Impartiality is linked to independence but shows its own distinctive focus of concerns. The ECtHR considers impartiality in terms of an objective and subjective test (see, for example, *Hauschildt* v *Denmark* (1980) 12 EHRR 266, paras 45–48).

The subjective test considers reasons relating to characteristics of a judge and whether these are sufficient both to set aside the presumption of judicial impartiality and, also, to render the trial unfair. Matters such as political prejudices and personal links with the prosecution are relevant here.

The objective test focuses on external factors which may undermine public confidence in the impartiality of the trial. Objective factors can lead to a violation of Article 6 even in the absence of evidence of subjective bias. On the objective test the question of 'appearances' is important.

Objective bias must itself be decided objectively, from the standpoint of an impartial and informed observer: the standpoint of the defendant is not enough.

The HRA

The rules of natural justice, in the law of England and Wales, recognise two tests for bias by a judicial body.

- **Direct personal interests**. Where a judge or tribunal member has a personal interest in the outcome of the trial, he or she should be automatically removed from the case. This was originally focused on the judge having a 'pecuniary' (financial) interest in the case.

case close-up

R v Bow Street Magistrates ex parte Pinochet (No 2) [2000] 1 AC 119

Lord Hoffmann's decision decided the outcome of a case concerning whether General Pinochet, the former dictator of Chile, should be extradited to Spain to face charges of torture. Lord Hoffmann was a director of a charitable wing of Amnesty International who were interveners in the case. This was not known at the time of the case. A different House of Lords held that the decision should be set aside and reheard by a different committee of Law Lords.

The House of Lords, determining English law in a manner consistent with Article 6, extended the need for automatic removal to cases in which a judge's other political, moral, intellectual, etc. interests might be in issue. Later cases, however, have made it clear that the barrier to prove the appearance of bias on these grounds is very high (see *Locabail* v *Bayfield* [2000] 1 All ER 65).

Bias cannot, for example, be based on the fact that judge and defendant are of different faiths (*Seer Technologies* v *Abbas* The Times, 16 March 2000; *Helow* v *Advocate General for Scotland* [2008] UKHL 62 provides a clear affirmation of judicial detachment).

In *Hoekstra* v *HM Advocate* 2000 JC 391, a case involving HRA issues was set aside because of the appearance of bias. One of the judges (Lord McCluskey, a very senior judge and author on legal affairs) had published an article in a Sunday newspaper that was highly critical of the Convention and its incorporation into Scots law.

- **Objective factors**

case close-up

Porter v Magill [2001] UKHL 67

The Leader and Deputy Leader of Westminster Council had been removed from office by the District Auditor and surcharged for wilful misconduct in office. They challenged the auditor's impartiality. The House of Lords held that the auditor had not breached Article 6(1).

In *Porter* the House of Lords confirmed the test, based on objective factors, for the appearance of bias:

> The question is whether the fair-minded and informed observer, having considered the facts [the facts relating, for and against, to the issue of bias] would conclude there was a real possibility that the tribunal was biased. (para 100)

Factors such as links to those previously involved in the case (*R (Chief Constable of Lancashire Constabulary)* v *Crown Court at Preston* [2001] EWHC 928 (Admin)), or friendship with witnesses (*AWG Group* v *Morrison* [2006] EWCA Civ 6) can be grounds for finding bias.

Particular difficulties in England and Wales arise in respect of tribunals. These are often chaired by a lawyer who is assisted by two experts in the area the tribunal deals with. Expert members of the tribunal may also, in different cases, appear before the tribunal as an expert witness. Depending on the facts, there may be bias (as in *SSWP* v *Cunningham* 2004 SLT 1007). The matter has been discussed by the House of Lords in *Gillies* v *SSW&P* [2006] UKHL 2.

Juries

Juries do not give reasons for their decisions. Under the Contempt of Court Act 1981, their deliberations must be kept secret. Allegations are sometimes made that the jury has been racist or has used irrational ways of deciding cases, like the use of an ouija board (*R* v *Young* (1995) QB 324). The ECtHR requires allegations of racism to be taken seriously by the judge and action taken which is sufficient to deal with the allegations (compare *Gregory* v *United Kingdom* (1998) 25 EHRR 577 with *Sander* v *United Kingdom* (2001) 31 EHRR 44). In *R* v *Mirza* [2004] UKHL 2, the House of Lords upheld the approach of the ECtHR but insisted that action taken in the face of well-founded allegations must not compromise the underlying secrecy of jury deliberations.

discussion topic

Should police officers, prosecutors and other public officials associated with the criminal justice system be allowed to sit on juries? The law of England and Wales has been altered to allow this. However, the House of Lords, in *R* v *Abdroikov* [2007] UKHL 37, has imposed considerable limits to the application of this law because of the fear that police, prosecutors, etc. would show unconscious bias in favour of the prosecution (the case did not directly involve Article 6). A strongly dissenting minority (in particular Lord Rodger, paras 31–42) thought that such officials would have the ability to be objective and that the collective wisdom of the jury would negate bias.

12.9 **Public hearing**

12.9.1 **Introduction**

Trials that are covered by Article 6 must generally be held in public. But a public hearing is by no means an absolute right and the second sentence of Article 6(1) permits the exclusion of press and public in a wide range of circumstances, discussed below.

A public hearing protects litigants and defendants against secret trials: one of the evils of a totalitarian system. It helps to maintain public confidence in the courts. Publicity also deters inappropriate behaviour by the court, maintains public confidence that the courts are impartial and can result in evidence being available which would otherwise not be known. See *Diennet* v *France* (1996) 21 EHRR 554, para 33 and *R* v *Legal Aid Board ex parte Kaim Todner* [1998] 3 All ER 541, 549–50.

12.9.2 **Exceptions**

Article 6(1) permits exceptions to the principle of public trials

- where the exclusion of the press or public serves the interests of morals, public order or national security as these terms are understood in a democratic society;
- where the exclusion is necessary to protect the interests of juveniles or the private life of the parties;
- where publicity would, in the opinion of the court, prejudice the interests of justice.

These exclusions have had an important impact on the development of English law under the HRA.

Juveniles and private life

Restrictions on public access to court and on media publicity are found in the law of England and Wales (both statute and common law) in respect of juvenile justice, both civil and criminal. They are also found in respect of many issues of family and matrimonial law. Such restrictions are likely to be consistent with Article 6(1).

Difficulties can arise when the principle of public trials and the protection of private life under Article 8 ECHR come into tension.

case close-up

Re S [2004] UKHL 47

S was charged with the murder of one of her children. An order was made prohibiting the publication of information and photographs that might lead to the identification of her other child. At the behest of newspapers the order was varied to allow the publication of the names and photographs of the parents and the deceased child. The other child challenged the variation. The House of Lords held that, weighing Article 8 and Article 10 in the facts of the case, the variation of the order should stay.

cross reference
See Chapter 8, section 8.3.3.

Although Article 6 was not directly involved (the other child was not on trial) the principle of open justice in Article 6(1) was the starting point. The House of Lords held that neither media freedom nor respect for private life had priority over the other. The court undertook a 'balancing' exercise (see para 17) of those rights in the context of open justice. Where there are good grounds for thinking that publicity might lead to a witness or defendant being killed or otherwise threatened, their rights under Article 2 may override the presumption in favour of publicity.

Prisoners and detainees

Prison disciplinary hearings have been accepted as exceptions to the rule in favour of open justice. Privacy can be justified as a proportionate means of securing 'public order' and security (see *Campbell and Fell* v *United Kingdom* (1985) 7 EHRR 165, paras 86–88).

In *AH* v *West London MHT* [2010] UKUT 264, the Upper Tribunal accepted that the claimant (who had been detained in a special hospital for 23 years) had a right to a public hearing before a mental health tribunal. The 'interests of justice', interpreted in the light of Article 6, meant that the norm of private hearings should be departed from.

National security

Article 6 permits restrictions on the public nature of trials in the context of national security. In the UK, courts have discretion to hear matters in private ('*in camera*') with a right of appeal to the Court of Appeal.

In *R* v *A* [2006] EWCA Crim 4, the applicant was charged with conspiracy to cause explosions in the UK. He alleged he had been tortured before being brought to the UK. The trial judge held that evidence about torture which the prosecution might have to disclose would be heard *in camera*. The Court of Appeal accepted that *in camera* orders in this criminal law context did not violate Article 6(1). Questions of disclosure in a civil context are discussed at section 12.12.3.

Contempt of court

The law on contempt of court permits restrictions on media publicity in order to protect the fairness of a trial. In England and Wales the law is found in the Contempt of Court Act 1981 and also in common law. Such rules are not only compatible with Article 6(1) but are likely to be compatible with Article 10, the right to freedom of expression, as being a proportionate way of protecting the rights of defendants and of maintaining the 'authority and impartiality of the judiciary'. Legal rules aimed at restricting the publication of articles that might prejudice the outcome of a trial were upheld as being compatible with both Article 6 and Article 10 in *Worm v Austria* (1998) 25 EHRR 454.

12.10 Pronounced publicly

Even where the trial itself has been conducted in private or secretly, there is a strong presumption that judgment should be given in open court or at least be available to public knowledge. Otherwise the fact that there has been a trial at all could be withheld. The Court, therefore, takes a strict view of the grounds on which the judgment itself can be withheld from the public (see *Campbell and Fell v United Kingdom* (1985) 7 EHRR 165). The parties themselves have a right to the full judgment (not just a summary) in order to consider whether there are grounds for appeal (e.g. *Ryakib Biryukov v Russia* App 14810/02, judgment of 17 January 2008).

The need for publicity can lead to tensions between Article 6 and other Convention articles, particularly Articles 8 (private life) and Article 10 (freedom of expression, including media freedom).

In *Blunkett v Quinn* [2004] EWHC 2816, the judge, in family proceedings involving David Blunkett, the former Home Secretary, decided that the proportionate balance between Articles 6, 8 and 10 was to pronounce judgment in open court if only to correct inaccuracies in the massive press coverage that the case had generated.

12.11 Trial within a reasonable time

cross reference
For Article 5(3) see Chapter 11, section 11.7.

It is a denial of justice to allow unreasonable delays in the judicial processes by which civil rights and obligations and criminal charges are determined. Article 6 requires a trial within a 'reasonable time'. A complementary provision is found in Article 5(3), which provides, in effect, that everyone charged with a criminal offence must be released on bail or, if they need to be remanded in custody, must be tried within a reasonable time. What is a reasonable time to await trial is likely (depending on all the circumstances) to be shortest in respect of a person on remand and is primarily dealt with under Article 5(3); trials of such prisoners should be a priority for the state, which must display 'special diligence'.

Longer periods are acceptable under Article 6 for defendants on bail and for civil litigation.

12.11.1 Starting and finishing the process

The reasonableness of the time in criminal cases is measured from the time of the 'charge'. This has an autonomous Convention meaning and was defined in *Corigliano v Italy* (1983) 5 EHRR

334 as 'the official notification given to an individual by the competent authority of an allegation that he has committed a criminal offence'.

In England and Wales 'official notification' runs from the time of being charged or summonsed (*Attorney General's Reference (No 2 of 2001)* [2003] UKHL 68, para 29). For civil actions official notification is likely to be from the time that proceedings are instituted, for example the issuing of a writ.

For both criminal and civil cases the period of time in issue ends with the final determination of the case, which will usually be after all appeal procedures have been exhausted. Delay concerns 'the entirety of the proceedings in issue, including any appeals' (*Poiss* v *Austria* (1988) 10 EHRR 231, para 50).

12.11.2 **Reasonableness**

The reasonableness of the time the authorities take to complete a trial process depends upon the particular facts and circumstances of the case. In assessing this, matters such as the following are taken into account (see *Philis* v *Greece (No 2)* (1998) 25 EHRR 417):

- the complexity of the case,
- the conduct of the applicant,
- the conduct of the authorities, and
- the importance of the case for the applicant.

Examples of unreasonable delay in Convention cases include:

- Over four years to determine a straightforward dispute on costs: *Robins* v *United Kingdom* (1998) 26 EHRR 527.
- Eight years, 11 months in a complex fraud case. The applicant bore considerable responsibility for the delay but the authorities had not pursued the matter diligently: *Eastaway* v *United Kingdom* (2005) 40 EHRR 17.
- Periods of up to seven years in determining claims for compensation brought by haemophiliacs infected with HIV from blood transfusions with contaminated blood; the authorities had not been sufficiently diligent and the issue was of life and death importance to the applicants: *A* v *Denmark* (1996) 22 EHRR 458.

In the United Kingdom, the Privy Council, applying the HRA in Scottish devolution cases, held that two years, four months' delay in the trial of a 13-year-old boy for serious sexual offences was too long, the need for particular diligence where children are concerned had not been met. On the other hand, a period of one year and 10 months to deal with a trial of police officers for perjury was not unreasonable (*Dyer* v *Watson* [2002] UKPC D1).

12.11.3 **The consequences of delay**

In *Dyer*, dealing with Scots law, it was held that delay created a 'continuing breach' of Article 6(1) that could only be remedied by a 'stay' (stopping the trial and acquitting the defendant). For the law of England and Wales, the view was that a breach of Article 6(1) based solely on delay could be remedied by other means such as public recognition of the delay, a lowering of sentence or compensation (*Attorney General's Reference (No 2 of 2001)* [2003] UKHL 68). Following a review of Convention law, the latter position has now been adopted in the United Kingdom (*Spiers* v *Ruddy* [2007] UKPC D2).

Article 6(1): the nature of a fair hearing

12.12.1 Introduction

Under Article 6 criminal and civil trials must be fair overall. This, as we have seen, includes their being conducted without unreasonable delay, usually conducted in public and decided by judges who are independent and impartial.

Article 6 says nothing particular about what makes the hearing itself, criminal or civil, a fair one. A number of general rights and characteristics of a fair hearing have been identified by the ECtHR as being inherent in the idea of a fair trail. These 'inherent' or 'implied' rights of a fair hearing may be subject to context-related qualifications, though any such qualifications are limited by the overriding principle that the trial be fair overall (see section 12.6). These general characteristics of a fair hearing are discussed in this section.

KEY POINT The general right to a fair hearing in Article 6(1) applies to both civil and criminal trials. Article 6(2) and (3) gives additional more specific rights to criminal defendants.

12.12.2 Participation

vThere is a general right to effective participation in a trial. This applies to both civil and criminal trials, though in relation to the latter the right is enhanced by various, more specific entitlements in Article 6(3). In criminal trials especially there is a strong presumption that the defendant should attend the trial (though a trial *in absentia* is not necessarily a violation).

Effective participation can, depending on context, mean a right to an oral hearing.

case close-up

R (Wright) v Secretary of State for Health [2009] UKHL 3

. . . .

Under the Care Standards Act 2000, care workers, against whom allegations of abuse had been made, could be put, immediately, on an interim list which prevented them from working with vulnerable adults. After being on the list for nine months, the care worker could apply to an independent tribunal. Listing was by the Secretary of State who allowed care workers to be put on the list without the opportunity to be heard. The House of Lords held that civil rights were engaged and the lack of an opportunity to make representations prior to listing violated Article 6. A declaration of incompatibility was made.

cross reference
'Civil rights' are defined at section 12.4; 'declarations of incompatibility' are discussed in Chapter 4, section 4.4.3.

See also *R (Hammond) v Secretary of State for the Home Department* [2005] UKHL 69, in Chapter 4, section 4.4.7.

Participation means not only being present but also being able to follow the proceedings, at least in general terms. What is required for effective participation must be appropriate to the person concerned.

> **case close-up**
>
> **T v United Kingdom (2000) 30 EHRR 121**
>
> An 11-year-old boy was, along with another boy, V, accused of murder. The victim was two years old, the murder was brutal and shocking and, as a result, there was intense national and international media attention. T and V were tried in an adult court, which retained adult procedures and formalities. Various measures were taken to assist T and V to understand the trial process. The ECtHR held that there had been a violation of Article 6(1).

In this famous case the ECtHR made it clear that the right to participate in the trial means, in the case of a child,

> that it is essential that a child charged with an offence is dealt with in a manner which takes full account of his age, level of maturity and intellectual and emotional capacities, and that steps are taken to promote his ability to understand and participate in the proceedings.

Although a number of things had been done to assist T in understanding the proceedings, the ECtHR held that these were was not enough (indeed some, such as the placing of the defendant on a raised platform so he could better see the proceedings, may have contributed to his feeling of discomfort and being under pressure) and that in all the circumstances, including the intense and sometimes hostile media scrutiny, there had been a breach of Article 6(1) (see paras 84–85).

12.12.3 Equality of arms

The concept of equality of arms

Hearings involving civil rights and obligations and criminal charges must be adversarial. The principle of equality of arms is an aspect of an adversarial hearing which applies to both civil and criminal trials. The idea is that, both in reality and appearance, the parties should be treated equally and have equal rights in the trial process. In particular this can require

- equal access to the evidence;
- equal participation in the procedures through which the matter is determined by the court;
- the equal treatment of witnesses (see *Dombo Beheer* v *The Netherlands* (1994) 18 EHRR 213);
- the right of a person to see and comment upon all the evidence on which the court or tribunal's decision will be made. Thus in *McMichael* v *United Kingdom* (1995) 20 EHRR 205, there was a breach of Article 6(1) in respect of a mother denied access to various social reports about her on which her ability to have the care of her child was determined;
- if an official advises the court, like a magistrate's clerk or as advocate general, their advice, if it may influence the way the court decides, must be open to challenge by the defence (see *Borgers* v *Belgium* (1993) 15 EHRR 92 and *Clark (Procurator Fiscal, Kirkcaldy)* v *Kelly* [2003] UKPC D1).

Disclosure and public interest immunity

The general principle in a criminal trial is that the prosecution must disclose evidence to the defence which is likely to undermine the prosecution or assist the defence. In civil cases the court can order the disclosure of evidence if one of the parties is reluctant. There may, however, be reasons why, in the 'public interest', evidence which should otherwise be disclosed, should be kept secret; for example, to protect the usefulness and, perhaps, physical safety of a police informant, or to maintain the operational effectiveness of surveillance devices. Of particular importance is the government's duty to maintain national security (such as defence matters or the mode of operation of the security services) or other government secrets.

If important evidence cannot be disclosed, can the trial, especially a criminal trial which may result in a long prison term, go ahead without violating Article 6(1)? A number of cases on this point have come before the ECtHR.

> **case close-up**
>
> ### *Rowe and Davis* v *United Kingdom* (2000) 30 EHRR 1
>
> R and D were convicted of a series of brutal attacks known as the 'M25 murders'. Crucial evidence, that the main allegation against R and D came from a police informer who had been paid £10,300 and who had himself been a suspect, was not disclosed even to the trial judge, let alone the defence; though it was made available at the appeal. The ECtHR held that there had been a violation of Article 6.

The main principles are (see paras 60–62):

- A fair trial is the over-arching requirement. Subject to this, rights securing a fair trial can be subject to reasonable and proportionate qualification.
- An adversarial trial, based on equality of arms, requires full disclosure and an opportunity for both parties (prosecution as much as defence) to know of and comment on the evidence on which the other party relies.
- However, the right to disclosure is not absolute but can be qualified in the light of important competing interests. It may be necessary in order to preserve, for example, the fundamental rights of third parties who are involved (such as the right to life of a witness) or to protect important public interests involving, for example, national security.
- However, the law can only permit those restrictions on the basic rights of the defence which are 'strictly necessary' (i.e. disclosure can be restricted for legitimate purposes, proportionately and in a manner consistent with the overall fairness of the trial).
- The judicial authorities must develop adequate safeguards aimed at reducing the impact on the defendant and which 'counterbalance' the difficulties caused by the restriction on rights.

As in the *Rowe and Davis* case, where no adequate safeguards are in place there will be a violation of Article 6(1).

Following cases such as *Rowe and Davis*, safeguards for the defence have been introduced into English law, specifically:

- Disclosure to the judge in chambers who decides whether to proceed. The proceeding may be *ex parte* (without the defence being present or even knowing of the hearing).
- If the defence are not present when the evidence is disclosed to the judge, **'special advocates'** may attend.

Special advocates

These are security cleared advocates. They represent the defendant, but once they have seen the 'closed material' concerning the defendant they may no longer discuss the case or take instructions from the defendant or his or her lawyers. They are also used outside the sphere of the criminal law: deportations on national security grounds and sensitive decisions by the Parole Board (see Chapter 11, section 11.8.5), for example. Their use in the counter-terrorism context has been highly controversial and is discussed further in Chapter 26, section 26.9.1.

The principles in *Rowe* were endorsed by the House of Lords in *R* v *H* [2004] UKHL 3. In particular the issue was whether it was compatible with Article 6, in a criminal case, for the judge to rule on public interest immunity without a full adversarial hearing and if the defendant's interests were represented by special advocates. The House of Lords held that ways of protecting the interests of the defendant need to be explored. The use of special advocates had huge disadvantages for the defendant and should only be considered as a last resort. Indeed special advocates, given their inability to take instructions, might be unable to make a difference in terms of redressing the balance in favour of the defendant. The judge would have to consider staying the trial.

Increasingly the problem operates in a civil context. Under the current system, evidence is disclosed in open court unless the judge, who may review the evidence, agrees to a public interest immunity request from the government. If the request is agreed, the trial may have to stop if to proceed would be unfair to the claimant or if the government withdraws.

case close-up

R (Mohamed) v Secretary of State for Foreign and Commonwealth Affairs [2010] EWCA Civ 65

. . . .

Denying a public interest immunity request by the foreign secretary, the Court of Appeal ordered the disclosure of evidence that might have proved the use of torture against M. M then sought to use this evidence in a civil action for damages against the Security Services. The government then sought to have important sections of the trial heard in secret. This was denied by the Supreme Court (*Al Rawi* v *Security Services* [2011] UKSC 24). As a consequence the government reached an out-of-court settlement with M.

In the government's view this is unsatisfactory. Justice is not done. An out-of-court settlement is unfair to the claimant (who receives too much or too little) and to officials who are stigmatised without being able to defend themselves. Under the Justice and Security Bill 'closed material procedures' will be required in civil cases involving national security. Cases will be heard in secret with the claimant represented by special advocates. This allows the case to proceed. Critics point to the way this institutionalises the unfairness of secret procedures.

12.12.4 Representation

The value of legal representation is that the relevant points of a case are properly understood by the court, the evidence is properly tested and, as a result, a just outcome emerges. Many people, through lacking legal knowledge, being inarticulate or lacking other skills, will be unable to present their case with its due strength without professional assistance. Defendants and civil litigants may also believe, with good reason, that their chances of winning are greater if they are represented.

Criminal trials

Defendants in criminal trials have a strong right to representation under Article 6(3)(c), which is discussed below, section 12.16.3.

Civil trials

There is no equivalent right for civil litigants. Representation may be an inherent right, required in order to achieve a fair trial in the circumstances.

case close-up

P, C and S v United Kingdom (2002) 35 EHRR 31

P and C were involved in complex and emotionally charged family proceedings involving the fate of their youngest child, S. During the care proceedings P and C's legal representatives withdrew because they felt they were being asked to conduct the case unreasonably, and P and C represented themselves. P and C lost the care proceedings and, consequently, an action to free S for adoption was begun by the local authority. P and C were denied legal representation in these adoption proceedings. Subsequently S was adopted and all contact with P and C was ended. The ECtHR held that the lack of legal representation was a breach of Article 6(1).

The ECtHR said that under Article 6(1) (see paras 88–91):

- There is no automatic right, under the Convention, to representation in civil proceedings.

- However, representation might be necessary to ensure access to court and the fact and appearance of a fair trial.

- A range of relevant factors include: whether representation is compulsory (under some legal systems representation is necessary before the higher courts); the complexity of the case; and the degree of emotional involvement, which might undermine the degree of objectivity necessary for effective representation and the seriousness of the matter for the applicant (see also *Airey* v *United Kingdom* (1979–80) 2 EHRR 305, paras 26–28 for examples).

- Like all rights implied from the overarching right in Article 6(1), representation and access to the court is subject to proportionate restrictions and these can be justified by a range of factors relating to the administration of justice including costs and the need to expedite some kinds of hearing.

Under the law in England and Wales, a right to representation will be found in the rules of courts and tribunals. Inferior courts, tribunals or other bodies which, consistent with their rules, deny a right of representation can be challenged by judicial review. The High Court denies a general legal rule requiring representation but it is unlawful (a breach of natural justice) for a tribunal to refuse representation if it is needed because of circumstances, such as the seriousness and complexity of the case, the capabilities of the parties or the consequences for the litigants.

further study

See, Craig, P. *Administrative* Law 6th edn (2008) London: Sweet & Maxwell.

In *Perotti* v *Collyer-Bristow* [2003] EWCA Civ 1521, the Court of Appeal recognised that Article 6 imposed a lesser requirement in civil cases than criminal cases. The test for whether representation was necessary was whether, without representation, a court would be unable to do justice in the case. The mere fact that a case might be poorly presented was not sufficient.

12.12.5 Illegally or improperly obtained evidence

General principles

As has been said before, the law on criminal procedure, including the admissibility of evidence, is a matter for the national authorities. The law of England and Wales, like most legal systems, does not have a rule of law banning the admissibility of illegally or improperly obtained evidence.

Section 78 PACE gives judges discretion to exclude evidence it would be unfair to admit and this includes on grounds relating to 'the circumstances in which the evidence was obtained'.

Nothing in Article 6(1) requires an absolute exclusion rule. The ECtHR accepts the existence of discretion under national laws to admit illegally obtained evidence so long as the overall trial remains fair. Of particular importance is the need to maintain the rights of the defence. In *Khan* v *United Kingdom* (2000) 31 EHRR 45 even evidence obtained in breach of a Convention right (Article 8) was accepted in the circumstances. What is important is that there should be adequate remedies to deal with illegal or oppressive actions by the police. These principles have been followed by English courts, in relation to the HRA, in *R* v *P* [2001] 2 All ER 58 (see pp 67–70).

discussion topic

Should unlawfully obtained evidence always be inadmissible?

In favour of general inadmissibility is the deterrent effect this would have on police and other officials who might, often from public interest motives, break the law in order to convict alleged criminals.

In favour of allowing admissibility is that the unlawfully obtained evidence may be true or have a high value in helping to convict dangerous criminals. Law breaking by the police, from this point of view, should be dealt with in other ways such as by police complaints, disciplinary actions or civil actions.

Oppressive confessions

Confessions obtained by oppression should be inadmissible as a matter of law (indeed section 76 PACE gives judges no discretion: once a judge has decided there has been oppression he or she must exclude the evidence). Article 6(1) rights would be violated if it was left to a jury to consider whether or not there had been oppression (see *R* v *Mushtaq* [2005] UKHL 25).

KEY POINT Evidence obtained in breach of Article 3, i.e. by torture or inhuman treatment, must be excluded both under international law (Article 15 of the UN Convention against Torture) and English law (section 76 PACE 1984). On 'torture' evidence see *A* v *Secretary of State for the Home Department* [2005] UKHL 71, discussed in Chapter 9, section 9.4.4.

Entrapment

Despite the absence of a general rule banning illegally or improperly obtained evidence, the ECtHR has held in a number of cases that the way in which evidence is obtained can effect the overall fairness of a trial (see, for example, *Ludi* v *Switzerland* (1993) 15 EHRR 173).

KEY POINT This illustrates that Article 6 rights are not confined to the hearing itself but can relate to pre-trial happenings.

The use of surveillance and undercover officers does not in itself violate Article 6. However, if the undercover officers do more than merely conduct surveillance and make reports, a violation of Article 6 can occur. In particular there may be a violation of Article 6 where there has been 'entrapment'. This is where police or other authorities act in a way which incites the commission of a crime. The principles of the leading Convention case, *Teixeira de Castro* v *Portugal* (1999) 28 EHRR 101, have been adopted by the House of Lords.

case close-up

R v Looseley; Attorney General's Reference (No 3 of 2000) [2001] UKHL 53

One defendant (L) was convicted of supplying drugs. He alleged entrapment. The other defendant's trial was stayed (stopped) by the judge on the grounds of entrapment. In L's case the House of Lords held there was no entrapment because undercover officers had merely presented themselves to him as ideal customers. In the other case the judge was right to stay proceedings because the police had encouraged the defendant to commit a crime he would not otherwise have committed.

The House of Lords made a strongly worded attack on entrapment.

- The law must set its face against 'state created crime'. This is an abuse of process and an affront to the public conscience.
- Police are not required only to be passive observers of crime. They can play a 'proactive' role but must not overstep the boundary and behave in a way which brings the administration of justice into disrepute.
- Issues for a court to consider are the nature of the offence, the reasons for the police operation and the nature and extent of police participation.
- It will not be unlawful for the police to behave as an ordinary customer of an illegal trade, nor to give the defendant an unexceptional opportunity to commit a crime. In *R* v *Jones* [2007] EWCA Crim 1118, for example, a police officer pretended, on the internet, to be a child to whom J willingly made unlawful sexual overtures. There was no entrapment.
- There must be evidence to support police suspicion of the defendant, more than a criminal record and a disposition to commit crimes.

These basic principles reflect the Convention law and represent a toughening of English law. Judicial disapproval means that, where there has been entrapment a trial should normally be stayed, rather than the evidence considered for exclusion under section 78 PACE.

271

12.13 Additional rights relating only to criminal trials

Criminal defendants enjoy the full range of rights under Article 6(1). Article 6(2) and (3) provides them with an additional range of rights. Frequently the same issue in a case can be dealt with under the general idea of fair trial involving Article 6(1) or under one of the more specific rights found in Article 6(2) or (3). The ECtHR characteristically resolves the case under Article 6(1) unless there are additional issues that can only be dealt with in terms of Article 6(2) or (3). The rights expressed in Article 6(2) and (3) are subject to reasonable restrictions and limitations, which serve legitimate purposes and which are proportionate in respect of the individual and the particular context.

Article 6(2): the presumption of innocence

The presumption of innocence is perhaps the most fundamental principle governing a criminal trial and it has a long history, certainly in European legal systems, as the principal idea in terms of which the fairness of a trial is recognised. The state, in whose name the prosecution is brought, has the burden of proving the guilt of the accused. The accused should not be required to prove his or her innocence and should, therefore, not be compelled to give evidence and cannot be compelled to incriminate him or herself. The principle is so important that it warrants an express section in Article 6 (though the presumption of innocence is also inherent in Article 6(1)).

12.14.1 Strict liability and reverse burdens of proof

Most European legal systems, including that of the United Kingdom, have offences in which guilt is fully or partially based on a finding of fact rather having to go further and prove the defendant's 'guilty mind' or a particular intention or state of knowledge. It is sometimes alleged that such offences violate Article 6(2). The ECtHR has not taken a strict, absolutist approach to such cases. The Court outlined its position in *Salabiaku v France* (1991) 13 EHRR 379 (see paras 27–28):

- Subject to not violating other Convention rights, the content of the criminal law is up to the states.

- Presumptions of fact or law, in the way crimes are defined, are not, in themselves, prohibited under the Convention (they are commonly found in European legal systems).

- But these presumptions must be kept within reasonable limits 'which take into account the importance of what is at stake and maintain the rights of the defence'.

12.14.2 Reverse burden defences: evidential and legal burdens

The most serious cases have involved so-called 'reverse burden' or 'reverse onus' defences. This is where guilt can be based on a presumption which the defendant is then left to disprove. For example, a person occupying premises in which terrorist articles are found may be presumed to be in 'possession' of the article and, therefore, can be convicted of an offence unless they can prove that they did not know the articles were on the premises (as in *R v DPP ex parte Kebilene* [1994] 4 All ER 801; see now section 57 Terrorism Act 2000). On the basis of the *Salabiaku* principles, such reverse burden defences are not in principle incompatible with Article 6(2) so long as they are justifiable.

Following *Kebilene*, UK law distinguishes between reverse burden offences which impose an 'evidential burden' and those which impose a 'legal burden' of proof on the defendant. Whether it is an evidential or legal burden is either expressly stipulated in the Act (as is the case with some of the anti-terrorism offences) or is a matter of statutory interpretation for the courts. Since the HRA, of course, such interpretation must seek compatibility with Article 6(2).

- 'Evidential burdens' do not alter the burden of proof and so do not violate Article 6(2). An evidential burden merely requires the defendant to raise a matter which, because of the statutory defence, it is relevant for the court to consider. For example, it can be an offence under anti-terrorism legislation not to disclose certain information to the police and some such offences have a 'reasonable excuse' defence. A journalist, for example, might raise the fact that he or she is investigating terrorist groups as a reasonable excuse. If, on a literal reading of the statute, the burden is 'evidential', simply raising the issue establishes the defence. There should be an acquittal unless the prosecution, to whom the burden of proof now returns, can prove, beyond reasonable doubt, that in the circumstances the matter raised does not assist the defendant (e.g. that being a journalist is no defence). Article 6(2) is not in issue.

- A 'legal burden' requires the defendant to prove, at least on a balance of probabilities, one of the matters specified in the defence. This does reverse the burden of proof and so raises an Article 6(2) issue.

- If on 'ordinary' principles of statutory interpretation, it is a legal burden, section 3 HRA requires the courts, if possible, to 'read down' the defence to turn it into an evidential burden. If this is not 'possible' the court must consider whether Article 6(2) is violated. *Salabiaku* is taken to mean that departures from a strict application of the presumption of innocence are compatible with Article 6(2) if they can be justified (*R v Lambert* [2002] 2 AC 545, para 88). Proportionality is at the heart of the matter. It requires a fair balance between the fundamental rights of the individual and the social interest in the suppression of crime. Issues such as the seriousness of the punishment, the extent and nature of the issues that the defendant must prove (e.g. whether they are matters over which he has personal knowledge) are relevant to proportionality (see, in particular, *Sheldrake* v *DPP* [2004] UKHL 43, para 21).

case close-up

Sheldrake v DPP; Attorney General's Reference (No 4 of 2002) [2004] UKHL 43

Sheldrake: S was convicted, under the Road Traffic Act 1988, of being drunk and in charge of a motor vehicle, which, at the time, was parked. There was a defence for him to prove that there was no likelihood of his actually driving the car whilst over the statutory limit. The House of Lords held that the defence imposed a legal burden on the defendant. The burden was reasonable and not a violation of Article 6(2) since the offence served a reasonable purpose (road safety) and it was not unfair to expect the defendant to discharge the burden since he or she would be well placed to provide the necessary evidence.

AG's Reference: the defendant had been prosecuted for membership of a part of Hamas, a proscribed (banned) terrorist organisation. The legislation allowed a defence if the defendant could prove that the organisation was not banned when he joined and that he had not taken part in any of its activities since it was banned. The House of Lords held that, on ordinary statutory construction, the defence imposed a legal burden on the accused. This could be unfair, however, since the defence would be difficult to prove and a wholly innocent person might be put in an impossible position. Therefore, 'reading down' the statute on the basis of section 3 of the HRA, the defence would be interpreted as requiring only an evidential burden and thus potential conflicts with Article 6(2) would be avoided.

further study

UK law on reverse defences is summarised by Lord Philips in *R* v *Keogh* [2007] EWCA Crim 528, paras 4–12 (concerning the Official Secrets Act 1989); see also *R* v *Johnstone* [2003] UKHL 28 (concerning selling bootleg CDs).

12.15 Article 6(2): the right to silence

The right to silence is considered here in relation to Article 6(2). It involves the general right to a fair trial and so cases may relate to Article 6(1) alone or Article 6(1) read in the light of Article 6(2).

The presumption of innocence means that the prosecution should have the burden of proving the guilt of the accused who need say or do nothing and, specifically, who cannot be required to incriminate him or herself. There are two aspects to the right.

- Compelled evidence. The accused should not be required, on pain of punishment, to answer questions whose answers are used to convict.

- Drawing inferences. The courts should not be able to infer guilt from the accused person's silence either when being questioned by the police or at his or her trial.

The general position under the Convention (reflecting the ECtHR's unwillingness to adopt absolutist positions) is: the right to silence is at the heart of the protection offered by Article 6, however, the rule is not absolute and qualifications are acceptable so long as they do not undermine the essence of a fair trial.

12.15.1 Compelled evidence

A fair trial issue under Article 6(1) (read with Article 6(2)) is raised if a person is prosecuted for a criminal offence on the basis of evidence which, through other legally based procedures, he or she was required by law to provide.

> **case close-up**
>
> ### *Saunders v United Kingdom* (1997) 23 EHRR 313
>
> Statute required S to answer questions from government inspectors inquiring into a city takeover battle. Failure to answer could lead to contempt of court proceedings and punishment. S was later prosecuted and convicted for theft, false accounting and conspiracy, and transcripts of evidence given by S to the inspectors was used by the prosecution in the criminal case. The ECtHR, following its decision in *Funke* v *France* I1993) 16 EHRR 297, held that there had been a breach of Article 6(1).

The Court asserted:

- The importance of the right to silence and the right not to incriminate oneself as inherent in the idea of a fair trial and as closely linked to Article 6(2) and the presumption of innocence.

- Its justification is to prevent the use by the authorities of improper compulsion. The argument is that this is likely to increase the likelihood of a fair trial.

- The right does not extend to material whose existence is independent of the accused person's will—nothing in Article 6 restricts the powers of the state to compel the production of documents, blood samples, etc. and for these to be used in court.

- The violation of Article 6 results from the use in a criminal trial of the compelled evidence: the legal duty to answer investigator's questions does not of itself violate Article 6 (see *IJL* v *United Kingdom* (2001) 33 EHRR 11, paragraph 100).

However, *Saunders* should not be read as imposing an absolute right not to incriminate oneself. The right is implied and subject to proportionate and reasonable restrictions serving a legitimate purpose which is compatible with the overall fairness of the trial.

In *O'Halloran and Francis v United Kingdom* (2008) 46 EHRR 21, a Grand Chamber dealt with speeding convictions based on speed camera evidence. Section 172 of the Road Traffic Act 1988 compelled a motorist to admit whether he or she was driving a car caught in a speed camera. That admission, if made, could then be used in criminal proceedings to prosecute the driver for speeding. The Grand Chamber held that there was no violation of Article 6(1) (Article 6(2) raised no separate issues). In particular the interferences with the rights of the defence were relatively slight and, it was noted, drivers of cars accept certain responsibilities as part of the regulatory regime governing motor cars (para 57).

12.15.2 Drawing inferences

The right to silence is also protected by forbidding the court from drawing inferences of guilt from the fact that an accused person chooses to remain silent. In Northern Ireland since 1988 and England and Wales since 1994, magistrates and juries (and judges in special courts in Northern Ireland) have been able to draw such inferences in certain circumstances. This has been tested against Article 6.

case close-up

> *Murray v United Kingdom* (1996) 22 EHRR 29
>
> . . . .
>
> M had been arrested in the house where the IRA had held an informer captive. M remained silent under police questioning. He was convicted of aiding and abetting the false imprisonment of the informer and sentenced to eight years' imprisonment. The judge (who determined guilt) made adverse inferences from M's silence. The ECtHR held that there was no violation of Article 6.

In *Murray* the ECtHR stated that the right to silence was not absolute. All the circumstances of the case needed to be taken into account. In particular in a situation which 'clearly calls for an explanation' the drawing of an adverse inference was reasonable. However, it was essential that the basis of a fair trial is not displaced. A system, for example, in which guilt could be based on silence alone, i.e. with no other evidence, would violate Article 6. Preventing improper inferences was strongest in respect of jury trial.

In *Condron v United Kingdom* (2001) 31 EHRR 1, two heroin addicts remained silent in interviews on the advice of their solicitor. The ECtHR held that there had been a violation of Article 6(1).

Condron suggests that the proportionality of any restriction on the right to silence includes consideration of the plausibility of the reasons for silence. This has been followed in English Law in *R v Betts* [2001] EWCA Crim 224. The Court of Appeal held that it was incompatible with Article 6 to allow a jury to draw an adverse inference even though they found the explanation for silence to be plausible.

discussion topic

The right to silence is not necessary to a fair trial?
. . . .

The right to silence is controversial and, as indicated previously, has been restricted.
The right to silence is defended on grounds that include:

- The best way to maintain the fundamental dimensions of a fair trial is by a simple rule placing, unambiguously, the burden of proof onto the prosecution.

- It discourages improper compulsion of defendants and so helps to avoid miscarriages of justice.

- There may be many legitimate reasons why a person would be best advised to keep silent.

The arguments of critics of the right include:

- There is no need for such a rule since 'innocence proclaims itself'.

- The rule is abused by skilled criminals and their advisors and so, by increasing the likelihood of a wrongful acquittal, it fails to serve the ends of justice.

- So long as a conviction cannot be based solely on silence, the real burden of proof remains with the prosecution.

- In respect of compelled evidence, some defendants are in a special situation. People such as company directors are in legally defined positions of power and responsibility on which others rely. They should be expected to answer truthfully questions relating to their responsibility; there is no reason why answers given should not also be used in related criminal proceedings. See further: Sedley, S. *Ashes and Sparks* (2011) Cambridge: CUP, Chapter 9.

12.16 Article 6(3): the rights of the defence

Article 6(3) contains a number of specific rights that the defence in a criminal trial should enjoy in order to secure a fair trial. These are free-standing rights but they may also be aspects of the overarching right to a fair trial in Article 6(1). (Some of the issues raised have already been discussed earlier in the chapter.) Though express rights, they are not absolute and may be subject to reasonable and proportionate restriction so long as the overall fairness of the trial is not compromised.

12.16.1 The right to be informed, Article 6(3)(a)

cross reference
Article 5(2)—an arrested person must be informed of the charge against them, discussed in Chapter 11, section 11.5 and Chapter 20, section 20.3.5.

Persons charged with criminal offences have the right to be informed of the nature and cause of the accusations against them. It is impossible to answer an unknown charge or one which is imprecisely formulated. The information must be precise enough for the accused to be able to formulate a relevant defence.

UK laws on arrest and court procedures normally meet these information requirements. Note that they only apply to a person 'charged with a criminal offence'. In relation to other coercive actions the state may take, Article 6 does not, expressly at least, require states to provide information, though, if detained, such information might be required under Article 5(2).

12.16.2 Time and facilities for the defence, Article 6(3)(b)

Article 6(3)(b) requires that the national law and procedures give the defendant an adequate opportunity to prepare his or her defence. Too swift a trial, for example, would violate this provision. In some circumstances the state may be under a positive duty to delay a trial or allow an adjournment if, for example, there is new evidence to be assessed or late changes in legal representation (as in *Goddi* v *Italy* (1984) 6 EHRR 457).

As ever, the ECtHR refuses to lay down as rules any specific time periods. Whether time and facilities are adequate will depend upon the circumstances of the case, such as its legal complexity, the length of documents to be considered and changes in personnel.

12.16.3 The right to defend oneself, Article 6(3)(c)

Article 6(3)(c) requires states to ensure that any defendant in a criminal trial is able to defend him or herself either in person or on the basis of legal representation. Such a general right is, of course, part of the overall right to a fair trial but, again, a criminal defendant has a specific and express right to rely on whilst a civil litigant must argue in terms of rights inherent in a 'fair hearing'. The terms of the express rights in Article 6(3)(c) are open to interpretation and exactly what they do or do not require will, typically of Article 6, be subject to proportionate, context-based, restriction.

A number of specific issues have arisen in the context of Article 6(3)(c) either standing alone or read in tandem with Article 6(1).

The right to attend

In the ECtHR's view it is difficult to make sense of the various rights of the defence in Article 6(1) and (3) without the defendant's presence (*Sejdovic* v *Italy* App 56581/00, Grand Chamber judgment of 1 March 2006). States have positive duties to ensure that a defendant is able to attend and failure to allow prisoners to come to court or have adequate facilities to participate, can lead to a violation of Article 6 (see *Brozicek* v Italy (1990) 12 EHRR 371).

A trial in the absence of the defendant (*in absentia*) can be compatible with Article 6, especially when this is due to the intentional actions of the defendant. In such a situation the court must ensure that the defendant is treated as fairly as possible (a second trial with the defendant may be necessary, see *Sejdovic*, mentioned earlier in this section).

In *R* v *Jones (Anthony)* [2002] UKHL 5, the House of Lords held that the holding of J's trial, despite his having absconded and, also, despite his not being represented at the trial, was compatible with Article 6 so long as the court acted with great caution and ensured that the trial was as fair as the circumstances allowed.

Access to a lawyer and legal advice

Criminal punishment must be based on the breach of a legal rule which is accessible and foreseeable in its application (see Article 7, Chapter 13). Legal advice must be available so that this principle, inherent in the rule of law, can be effective. The presence of lawyers helps accused persons understand their situation, what rights they have and what issues are relevant to any defence they may have. It also helps to ensure that, both at the trial and before, the proper procedures necessary to fairness are followed. Where the right to silence has been limited, as in the United Kingdom, access to a lawyer is particularly important (see *Murray* v *United Kingdom* (1996) 22 EHRR 29). The right to legal advice (as distinct from legal representation) is an implied right that is, like all implied rights, subject to restrictions for a legitimate purpose ('a good cause') so long as the overall objective of a fair trial is maintained (see, for example, *Brennan* v *United Kingdom* (2002) 34 EHRR 18, para 45). The right to legal advice can apply to pre-trial events, such as the questioning of the accused by the police (as in *Murray*, earlier in this section).

Under English law, section 58 PACE (exercised in line with Code C) provides a right of persons detained for questioning to have access to a solicitor, but the exercise of this right can be postponed for up to 36 hours in respect of serious crimes and on the authority of a senior police officer.

Legal representation

Article 6(3)(c) gives a criminal defendant

cross reference
The right to representation in civil cases is discussed in section 12.12.4.

- the right to defend him or herself in person if they wish, or
- the right to legal assistance of his or her own choosing, and
- the right to legal aid 'when the interests of justice so require'.

(See *Pakelli* v *Germany* (1984) 6 EHRR 1, para 31.)

There is, therefore, an unqualified right to representation in criminal cases. This is much stronger than the right to representation regarding civil cases. If, in the law of England and Wales, civil proceedings might result in a person being committed to prison for breach of a court order, representation is likely to be necessary, as in *Hammerton* v *Hammerton* [2007] EWCA Civ 248.

The right of prisoners to representation at disciplinary hearings which could result in a longer stay in prison, has been strongly upheld by the ECtHR in *Ezeh* v *United Kingdom* (2004) 39 EHRR 1, and is discussed in Chapter 21, section 21.8.4.

Legal aid

cross reference
For legal aid in civil cases see section 12.7.2.

In order to meet the representation requirements of Article 6, the state may be under a positive duty to provide free legal assistance including representation. This will be so if the defendant lacks means (there is no requirement for legal aid of a defendant who can afford his own lawyers) and 'if the interests of justice so require'. It represents a much stronger right to legal aid than is required in respect of civil cases.

Benham v *United Kingdom* (1996) 22 EHRR 293 suggests that legal aid, along with representation, is necessary in cases involving a person's liberty (the case was followed in *Hammerton*, section 12.16.3).

12.16.4 Examination of witnesses, Article 6(3)(d)

Article 6(3)(d) provides a right of the defence to be able to test, usually by cross-examination, the prosecution's evidence. Conviction on the basis of evidence that the court can rely on, but that the defendant cannot test, is likely to be a breach of Article 6(3)(d) and also of Article 6(1) (the principle of 'equality of arms').

There may be circumstances in which restrictions on the right to examine witnesses may be legitimate. It may be necessary to use evidence statements by deceased witnesses, witnesses may be intimidated and need protection (indeed their Convention rights may need protection), the prosecution may wish to protect the identity of an informer and the identity of a security service witness may need to be withheld for reasons of national security. Thus rules of evidence may allow criminal trials to be conducted using anonymous witnesses or on the basis of hearsay (where someone, such as a police officer, gives a third party's evidence against the defendant).

The basic approach of the ECtHR, found in numerous cases (a good example is *Doorson* v *Netherlands* (1996) 22 EHRR 330, paras 68–76) is:

- Rules of evidence are primarily for the domestic law to determine; the role of the ECtHR is supervisory, not to insist on particular procedures.

- Article 6 requires, normally, that evidence must be produced in open court, in the presence of the accused and be fully testable.

- However, there can be exceptions based on the need to protect victims, witnesses and also public interests.

- Restrictions on the capacity of the defence fully to test the evidence must be proportionate. There need to be effective counter-balancing procedures aimed at protecting the rights of the defence so far as possible. The job of the ECtHR is to evaluate the overall fairness of the trial.

cross reference
The 'sole or deci-sive' rule in the context of counter-terrorism measures is discussed in Chapter 26, section 26.9.1.

The 'sole or decisive' rule

In this criminal context the ECtHR has also said, in a number of cases, that a decision based 'solely or decisively' on evidence the defendant cannot test will, for that reason, violate Article 6. This led to a 'dialogue' between the UK Supreme Court and the ECtHR.

> **case close-up**
>
> ### *R* v *Horncastle* [2009] UKSC 14; *Al-Khawaja and T* v *UK* (2012) 54 EHRR 23
>
> Criminal convictions were secured on the basis of the statements by witnesses who had died prior to the trial or who were too frightened to attend the trial. The Chamber judgment in *Al-Khawaja* held that the convictions of A-K and T violated Article 6. They were solely or decisively based on the untested evidence, and Article 6 imposed an absolute ban on convictions in those circumstances. In *Horncastle*, a later case with different defendants, the Supreme Court disputed the jurisprudential basis of the absolute nature of the 'sole or decisive' rule. It ruled that English law provided sufficient safeguards, in statute and in judicial discretion, to protect the defendant and ensure the overall fairness of the trial. *Al-Khawaja* went to a Grand Chamber, which upheld the sole or decisive rule but not as an absolute provision (para 147). If there is careful scrutiny and strong procedural safeguards there will not, necessarily, be a breach of Article 6. In *Al-Khawaja* there was some corroborating evidence so no breach of Article 6; in *T*, however, there was little corroborating evidence and insufficient safeguards—the breach of Article 6 remained.

In *R* v *Davis* [2008] UKHL 36, the House of Lords held that in England and Wales, the admission of hearsay evidence and anonymous witnesses must be done by statute: the tradition of open justice is too rooted in the common law to allow such radical departures. But legislation that allows convictions solely or decisively based on such evidence can be compatible with Article 6 if there are sufficient safeguards (per Lord Mance, para 88).

The evidence of vulnerable people

These principles are relevant when court procedures, which inhibit the rights of the defence, are aimed at protecting children and vulnerable persons. The ECtHR accepts such restrictions subject to the need for adequate balancing of the rights of the defence. In *R (D) v Camberwell Green Youth Court* [2005] UKHL 4, the House of Lords upheld, as compatible with Article 6, the use of video-link when evidence is given by child witnesses in cases of a sexual nature or those involving violence.

12.16.5 **Interpreter**

Article 6(3)(e) imposes a positive duty on a criminal court to provide an interpreter for any defend ant who cannot understand the language of the court. The duty is, of course, subject to proportionality, and so the extent to which this duty requires translating all the materials of the case or whether it is enough for most purposes to rely on defence lawyers giving the main points, will depend upon the circumstances of particular cases.

12.17 **Deportation and Article 6**

We have seen that there is an absolute ban on deporting someone where there is a real risk that they will be killed or suffer torture or inhuman treatment, in violation of Articles 2 and 3 respectively.

cross reference
The grounds of deportation are discussed in Chapter 9, section 9.8.1.

In *R (Ullah) v Special Adjudicator* [2004] UKHL 26, the House of Lords held (following Strasbourg case law) that there was a real risk that other Convention rights might be violated if the violation would be 'flagrant'. So a person should not be deported to face a trial in a foreign country if there is a real risk not just that the trial, if held in a European country, would violate Article 6, but that the trial would be flagrantly unfair.

case close-up

> **Othman v United Kingdom** (2012) 55 EHRR 1
>
> The British government sought to deport O to Jordan on the grounds that his presence in the UK was inconsistent with the public interest. O alleged he would be tried on the basis of torture evidence.
>
> The ECtHR held:
>
> - A 'flagrant' denial of justice went beyond mere irregularities: it meant the nullification or destruction of the essence of the rights protected by Article 6 (para 260).
>
> - The admission of torture evidence would be a flagrant denial of justice (para 267).
>
> - Evidence of a 'real risk' was sufficient to refuse deportation given the difficulties of proof to a higher standard such as balance of probabilities.
>
> Therefore the deportation of O by the United Kingdom would violate Article 6.

cross reference
Othman raises other points about deportation in a counter-terrorist context which are discussed in Chapter 26, section 26.7.3.

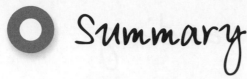

Summary

- The right to a fair trial is an essential element in ensuring people's effective protection of their legal rights, including their human rights.

- Article 6 establishes rights to a fair trial which apply only where a civil right or obligation, or a criminal charge is being determined. These are autonomous terms not dependant on national laws. Limiting fair trial rights to these kinds of trials means that some legal processes are not subject to its terms.

- Article 6(1) applies to both civil and criminal trials. It lays down a generic right to a fair trial, from which more specific rights can be implied and it makes specific requirements concerning speed, publicity, independence and impartiality.

- Article 6(2) and (3) applies only to criminal trials and preserves the presumption of innocence and a range of other rights of the defence.

- The rights implied from the general concept of a 'fair trial' and also the more specific rights found in Article 6, are subject to qualifications and restrictions which are related to context; these restrictions should not undermine the essence of a fair trial and should protect the rights of the defence as appropriate.

Questions

For suggested approaches, please visit the Online Resource Centre.

1 After finishing his final exams, Charles is expelled from university for a disciplinary offence and he also fails his degree. Under the university regulations neither the disciplinary board (which has the power of expulsion) nor the examinations board (which determines his degree), gives him a right to be heard. Comment on his allegation that his right to a fair trial has been violated.

2 The Prison Service is creating an entirely new set of procedures dealing with prison discipline and you have been charged with ensuring compliance with Article 6 for the system to be used in the prisons housing the most dangerous prisoners. You are asked to advise on (a) whether Article 6 is involved and, if so, in which situations; (b) what specific rights Article 6 provides; and (c) whether those rights can be restricted to prevent, for example, the intimidation of one prisoner by another.

Further reading

LEADING TEXTS ON ARTICLE 6

Amos, M. (see Preface) Chapter 10

Jacobs, F. 'The Right to a Fair Trial in European Law' [1999] 2 *EHRLR* 141–156

Lester, A., Pannick, D. and Herberg, J. (see Preface) Chapter 4, Article 6

CRITICAL ANALYSIS

Craig, P. 'The Human Rights Act, Article 6 and Procedural Rights' [2003] *Public Law* (Winter) 753–773

Masterman, R. 'Determinative in the Abstract? Article 6(1) and the Separation of Powers' [2005] 6 *EHRLR* 628–648

Article 7: no punishment without law

Article 7   No punishment without law

(1) No one shall be held guilty of any criminal offence on account of any act or omission which did not constitute a criminal offence under national or international law at the time when it was committed. Nor shall a heavier penalty be imposed than the one that was applicable at the time the criminal offence was committed.

(2) This article shall not prejudice the trial and punishment of any person for any act or omission which, at the time when it was committed, was criminal according to the general principles of law recognised by civilised nations.

Introduction

Article 7(1) requires states to ensure that their criminal law is not applied retrospectively. This means:

- **A person should not be convicted and punished for actions which were not criminal at the time they were performed.**

- **Punishments should not be heavier than the punishment available to the courts at the time the actions were taken.**

- **There is nothing to stop states changing their criminal law but this must not be done so that someone who acted lawfully at the time is later punished.**

- **There is an exception in respect of crimes against humanity.**

13.1 *Nullum crimen, nulla poena sine lege*

Article 7 embodies a general principle of law, found in most legal systems and in international law: this is the principle of *'nullum crimen, nulla poena sine lege'* (no crime, no punishment without law). It means that there should be no crimes and no punishments other than on the basis of law. States act in an arbitrary manner, and will be caught by Article 7, if they impose a penalty on a person which has no effective legal basis. The Convention standard of legality must be met: any legal rule on which a criminal penalty is based should be sufficiently clear and precise in its potential application so that individuals can know in advance whether any proposed action is likely to be criminal or not.

cross reference
See Chapter 6, section 6.2, for the Convention concept of 'law'.

The justification for the *nullum crimen, nulla poena sine lege* principle is that the rule of law requires that people be able to know and follow (or choose to break) the law that applies to them at the time they act. Otherwise states act arbitrarily and people suffer unjustly. Historically it is clear that majorities, or those in power, can create laws and apply them retrospectively as a way of discriminating against, and subordinating, minorities and powerless groups, who are often the defeated in a civil war or conflict.

13.1.1 Common law

Nullum crimen, nulla poena sine lege is a long-established principle of English common law.

English courts will interpret criminal legislation on the presumption that it is not intended to apply retrospectively. In *Waddington* v *Miah* (1974) 59 Cr App Rep 149, 151 and 152, Lord Reid said:

> There has for a very long time been a strong feeling against making legislation, and particularly criminal legislation, retrospective...I use retrospective in the sense of authorising people being punished for what they did before the Act came into force.

Of course Parliament can, in constitutional theory, enact criminal legislation with retrospective effect. To do so, it must express itself with sufficient clarity and precision on the point not only to displace the presumption but also to escape the interpretative obligation placed on the courts by section 3 Human Rights Act 1998 (HRA) (see Chapter 4, section 4.4)

The courts no longer allow themselves to create new criminal offences. Under the system of judicial precedent, such offences apply retrospectively, at least the first time they are pronounced (see *R* v *Withers* [1975] AC 842).

There is a strong steer from the courts against the expansion of existing common law offences into new areas and applications.

In *R* v *Goldstein*; *R* v *Rimmington* [2005] UKHL 63, the House of Lords refused to allow the common law offence of public nuisance to be redefined so that it was no longer necessary for the prosecution to prove that the defendant had acted in a way which interfered with the public at large and so the offence could be used against a person who harassed particular, identifiable individuals rather than the general public. The House of Lord's refusal was based on the *nullum crimen* principle and Article 7.

further study

R v *Goldstein*; *R* v *Rimmington*, is a rich source of quotations on the common law principle: see in particular para 33.

There are, therefore, unlikely to be many difficulties of achieving compatibility of English and Convention law on this issue. As is indicated later in the chapter, the main issues have arisen over retrospective changes to burdens placed on persons convicted of offences (e.g. whether they can be made to pay compensation) and whether such burdens amount to a punishment or not.

13.1.2 **International Covenant on Civil and Political Rights (ICCPR)**

cross reference
The ICCPR is discussed in Chapter 1, section 1.4.4.

The *nullum crimen* principle is found in other international human rights instruments. Article 15 ICCPR contains similar provisions to Article 7 of the European Convention on Human Rights (ECHR). It has one additional provision that may be implicit but is not explicit in Article 7 ECHR: that lighter penalties for an offence should be retrospectively applied so that convicted persons should be allowed to benefit from such changes if they take place after the events in question and before the trial.

(13.2) **General principles governing Article 7(1)**

The general principles guiding the application of Article 7 are discussed in sections 13.2.1–13.2.6. They have been recently confirmed by a Grand Chamber in *Kononov* v *Latvia* (2011) 52 EHRR 21 (paras 185–186).

13.2.1 Article 7 is an important feature of the rule of law

The guarantees in Article 7 are an essential element of the rule of law and, as such they occupy a prominent place in the Convention system of protection.

13.2.2 'Law' means the same in Article 7 as in other Articles

The concept of legality and law pervades the Convention. This is the same notion of 'law' as is applied through Article 7. As discussed in Chapter 6, section 6.2, to be a law, for Convention purposes, a rule must

- be accepted as law by the national courts (in England, for instance, it must be a rule found in an Act of Parliament, in the common law or equity and occasionally in custom);
- be 'accessible' (the laws which apply can be identified) and 'foreseeable' (the applicable laws are sufficiently clear and precise to be able to guide a person's conduct).

Conviction and punishment on the basis of criminal laws that do not meet this test will be a violation of Article 7.

13.2.3 A safeguard against arbitrary action

Article 7 should be construed and applied so as to provide an effective safeguard against arbitrary prosecution, conviction and punishment. This is, in any case, part of how the European Court of Human Rights (ECtHR) understands the rule of law. That this is the underlying point of Article 7 is shown by the fact that the ECtHR will not allow its guarantees to be used in a way which contradicts the rule of law and which gives protection to lawless, oppressive state actions.

case close-up

***Streletz, Kessler and Krenz v Germany* (2001) 33 EHRR 31**

The unification of Germany after 1989 led to some prosecutions in Germany of officials of the former German Democratic Republic (GDR). S and others (political leaders of the GDR) were prosecuted in 1993 for authorising shoot to kill policies and practices against East German civilians who were trying to cross the border into west Germany (the Federal Republic of Germany)—the policies called for the 'annihilation' of escapers if they could not be arrested. S was prosecuted for breaking laws of the GDR which were in force at the time (1971–89) but which, partly at S's behest, were disregarded by, and not enforced against, the border police. S argued that a prosecution in the 1970s and 1980s was not foreseeable; therefore his later prosecution, in 1993, violated Article 7. The ECtHR rejected this argument. S was claiming that the policies and practices were the relevant law of the time; yet they were the opposite of law, they emptied the enacted law of all meaning. Article 7(1) seeks to uphold the rule of law; the applicants, on the other hand, were seeking to uphold lawless and brutal practices.

In *Kononov* v *Latvia* (2011) 52 EHRR 21, a Grand Chamber, disagreeing with the Chamber, held that the prosecution by Latvia (now independent; formerly part of the USSR) of the commander of a Red Army Partisan (fighting the Nazis) group did not violate Article 7. The defendant was found guilty of allowing the ill-treatment and killing of villagers in Latvia who, allegedly, had been cooperating with the Nazis. The Court reviewed the state of international law as it was in 1944 and found that attacks on civilians who were not engaged in combat were clearly defined, in a range of treaties, as war crimes. These international war crimes applied to the individual responsibility of a commander, and, although they had not been promulgated in the Soviet Union, a 'cursory reflection' by the commander would have alerted him at least to the possibility that not forbidding the attacks might be a war crime.

cross reference

Derogation under Article 15 is discussed in Chapter 7, section 7.2.

13.2.4 Article 7 is non-derogable

The central place of the rule of law in the Convention system means that Article 7 is one of the rights which cannot be derogated from by states in time of 'war or other public emergency facing the life of the nation'.

13.2.5 Article 7 prohibits retrospective criminal law and punishment

The express words of Article 7 bar the retrospective application of the criminal law to the disadvantage of an accused person. In *Coëme* v *Belgium* App 32492/96, judgment of 22 June 2000, the ECtHR said:

> The Court must therefore verify that at the time when the accused person performed the act which led to his being prosecuted and convicted there was in force a legal provision which made that act punishable and that the punishment imposed did not exceed the limits fixed by that provision. (para 145)

It is important to note that Article 7 only prohibits retrospective criminal law. Retrospective provisions in civil law, such as private or administrative law, are not barred by Article 7. They might be barred by the application of other provisions such as the right to peaceful enjoyment of property in Article 1 of the First Protocol. This could happen, for example, if the legislature enacts legislation which retrospectively changes the effects of a court decision (as in *Pressos Compania Naviera SA* v *Belgium* (1996) 21 EHRR 301, discussed in Chapter 23, section 23.7.4).

13.2.6 Article 7 guarantees go beyond just retrospective criminal law

Article 7's place as one of the guarantors of the rule of law means that it has a wider application than just a bar to retrospective criminal prosecutions. As noted previously, it is taken as embodying the *nullum crimen* principle, which clearly includes something more than just a ban on retrospective law. Article 7 also includes the following principles:

- There can be no crimes and no punishments unless these are found in the law.
- The criminal law must not be construed to the accused's detriment.
- Offences must be clearly defined in the law.

Such principles are found being applied in some of the Convention case law discussed at sections 13.3 and 13.4.

13.3 Article 7(1) and offences (the first sentence)

The first sentence of Article 7(1) requires that, if a person is convicted of a criminal offence, there must be

- a clearly defined criminal offence, that was
- in force at the time the alleged crime was committed, and which
- covered, within its terms, the actions for which the defendant was convicted.

The essence of this is that changes to the criminal law and procedure cannot be used to prosecute people in respect of their actions performed before the changes came into effect (as in, for example, *Veeber* v *Estonia* (2004) 39 EHRR 6).

13.3.1 What counts as a criminal offence?

cross reference
See Chapter 12, section 12.5.

Article 7(1) only applies to the application of the rules of criminal law. Whether legal rules are 'criminal' or not for Article 7 purposes, is a matter of autonomous Convention law (i.e. it is not solely dependent on the way the matter is classified under national law). The obvious link would be to the concept of a 'criminal charge' found in Article 6, but the ECtHR has not had occasion to make this clear. In most cases the fact that there has been a criminal conviction under the national law is sufficient, and without it, Article 7 may not apply.

The need for a criminal conviction means that the retrospective application of laws in the area of, for example, immigration or deportation may not raise Article 7 issues. Despite the seriousness of the matter for the individuals involved, they do not involve a criminal conviction.

case close-up

> ***Lawless* v *United Kingdom (No 3)* (1979–80) 1 EHRR 15**
>
> L was interned under an Irish law brought into force in 1957. His internment was based on his activities before that date. The ECtHR held that Article 7 did not apply (para 19).

Limiting Article 7 to criminal offences makes sense given the article's wording. But it might be thought to weaken the protection for the rule of law that is the essence of Article 7. It allows the retrospective application of laws and procedures in a wide range of issues, like internment, which have a severe impact on the lives of the individuals and which might embody state oppression of political opponents or unpopular minorities.

13.3.2 Clarity with flexibility

Clarity

Article 7 requires that the criminal offence for which a person is prosecuted and convicted must be clearly defined in the national law. This means that

> the individual can know from the wording of the relevant provision and, if need be, with the assistance of the court's interpretation of it, what acts and omissions will make him criminally liable.

> (*Cantoni* v *France* App 17862/91, Grand Chamber judgment of 22 October 1996, para 29)

The ECtHR accepts that the offence may be found in unwritten law, though the requirement for certainty may be all the more demanding.

Flexibility

The notion of a law implies a rule of general application—laws regulate the conduct of the public or a class of the public and do so over a period of time. Laws, in this sense, are different from judicial decisions, which apply the law to individuals. Under the separation of powers, legislatures are not normally permitted to enact legislation which relates only to an individual or to a specific event.

Characteristically laws are couched in general terms. This implies some degree of vagueness and imprecision which requires interpretation before being applied to particular circumstances. The ECtHR accepts this, not only in the context of Article 7 but also in respect of its pervasive concept of law. This 'open-textured' nature of law (as the British legal philosopher H.L.A. Hart called it) is necessary to ensure that laws are not over-rigid and unable to develop with time and changing contexts. The danger, of course, is that individuals will end up being convicted on the basis of new developments or applications of the law which could not be foreseen.

Where general words in a statute have been interpreted by courts and a settled body of case law created, the ECtHR is likely to find that the certainty requirement has been satisfied. This acceptance of the necessary flexibility in legal rules is illustrated in the matrimonial rape case: *SW* v *United Kingdom* (see also *CR* v *United Kingdom*).

case close-up

SW v *United Kingdom* (1996) 21 EHRR 363

In 1990 SW was convicted of the rape (having sexual intercourse without consent) of his wife. At that time there was an accepted common law rule that a husband could not be convicted of the rape of his wife since, by agreeing to marriage, the wife was held to have agreed, once and for all, to sexual intercourse with her husband. In *R* v *R* [1991] 2 All ER 257, decided in 1991, the House of Lords held that the common law rule was no longer the law of England. SW argued, unsuccessfully, that he should be tried under the law of rape as it stood at the time of the alleged offence (prior to *R* v *R*) and that to apply *R* v *R* would be to impose a change in the law retrospectively. After conviction, SW applied to the ECtHR, which held there had not been a violation of Article 7.

The Court said:

> There will always be need for elucidation [clarification] of doubtful points and for adaptation to changing circumstances . . . Article 7 of the Convention cannot be read as outlawing the gradual clarification of the rules of criminal liability through judicial interpretation from case to case, provided that the resultant development is consistent with the essence of the offence and could reasonably be foreseen. (para 36/34)

- In *R* v *R* the House of Lords had not created a new offence but extended an existing offence to new circumstances (husbands having sex with their wives) without changing the essence of the offence (lack of consent to sex).
- This legal development was foreseeable because it continued an identifiable line of case law (e.g. that the immunity of husbands did not apply when the parties were separated).
- Given the debasing nature of rape, to have allowed the husband to succeed would be using Article 7 against its own purpose and that of the Convention as a whole: to uphold human dignity.

In *Jorgic* v *Germany* (2008) 47 EHRR 6, the ECtHR upheld the use by the German courts of a wide definition of genocide in order to convict the applicant. This interpretation was reasonably foreseeable.

13.3.3 **UK cases**

UK courts have applied Article 7, or at least referred to it as a complement to domestic law, in a number of cases dealing with the question whether crimes are defined with adequate clarity. For example:

- In *Webster (Procurator Fiscal)* v *Dominick* 2003 SCCR 525, Scottish courts held that the Scottish common law offence of 'shameless indecency' had not been defined with sufficient clarity to meet the test in Article 7.

- In *R* v *Remington*; *R* v *Goldstein* [2005] UKHL 63, the House of Lords held that the offence of public nuisance was, in its traditional definition, defined with adequate clarity (but rejected its extension in the way outlined earlier in this chapter).

- In *R* v *Misra* [2004] EWCA Crim 2375, the Court of Appeal accepted that the offence of gross negligence manslaughter had been defined with sufficient clarity to meet the test of common law and Article 7.

13.3.4 **International law**

The first sentence of Article 7(1) makes it clear that a conviction can be compatible with Article 7 if the crime in issue is defined under international law. International offences are crimes that have been defined by the international community and which states may (or, in some cases, must) prosecute if an alleged offender is in their custody, even if the crimes were committed elsewhere. Such offences include torture, drug trafficking and aircraft sabotage. The Rome Statute of the International Criminal Court 1998, gives detailed definitions of the offences of 'genocide', 'crimes against humanity' and 'war crimes' (the definition of the offence of 'aggression' has been postponed).

cross reference
Jus cogens is defined in Chapter 9, section 9.4.1.

Some international crimes, such as torture, are part of the compulsory law of nations ('*jus cogens*') and apply irrespective of specific agreements.

Other offences (such as those under the Rome Statute) only apply where a country has expressly signed a treaty recognising the offence. A prosecution might be brought by a new regime against officials of the predecessor regime (as in *Streletz, Kessler and Krenz* v *Germany* (2001) 33 EHRR 31, mentioned at section 13.2.3). In such a situation Article 7 allows prosecutions based on *jus cogens*, because this contains general duties applicable to all states independent of their wills. It is not clear whether a prosecution could be based on the retrospective application of a treaty-defined offence which the predecessor state had not signed up to.

13.4 Article 7(1) and punishment (the second sentence)

The courts must not impose a heavier sentence on a convicted criminal than was available to the courts at the time the offences were committed. A clear case of this is *Ecer* v *Turkey* (2002)

35 EHRR 26, in which the applicant was convicted of national security offences committed between 1988 and 1989 but given a punishment that was not introduced until 1991.

13.4.1 Changes within the range of possible sentences

The problem is that most legal systems give the courts considerable discretion over punishment. The general approach under English law is for the judges to decide the appropriate sentence up to a maximum penalty. This maximum has been laid down by Parliament and will be appropriate only for the most serious instances of the offence. The question is then raised whether Article 7 can be invoked if, by retrospective changes in practice, a person is given a more severe punishment than he or she might have expected at the time they committed the crimes, even though this more severe punishment is still within the range laid down in the statute which applied at that time. In *Coëme* v *Belgium* (section 13.2.5), the ECtHR defined the task of a court dealing with an Article 7 challenge as to

> verify that at the time when an accused person performed the act which led to his being prosecuted and convicted there was in force a legal provision which made that act punishable, and that the punishment imposed did not exceed the limits fixed by that provision. (para 145)

In the United Kingdom, the House of Lords has interpreted these words to mean that (in the words of the Article) the 'penalty . . . that was applicable at the time the criminal offence was committed' is the maximum which under the law could have been imposed as distinct from that which was, at the time, normally imposed.

case close-up

R (Uttley) v Secretary of State for the Home Department [2004] UKHL 38

U committed three rapes in a period ending in 1983. He was not convicted until 1995. In 1983 the maximum sentence for rape was life imprisonment. U was sentenced to 12 years' imprisonment. If given 12 years in 1983 he would, subject to good behaviour, have been unconditionally released after eight years. Under changes introduced in 1991, he was still entitled (with good behaviour) to be released after eight years but his release was subject to various conditions which put him at risk of being recalled to prison if he breached them. The House of Lords held that there had not been a breach of Article 7(1) since it was clearly the case that the sentence imposed, though more severe than the sentence that would have been expected in 1983, was still less severe than the maximum (life imprisonment with a longer jail term than 12 years) that could have been imposed in 1983. Uttley's application to the ECtHR was inadmissible .

Thus *Uttley* permits retrospective, even detrimental, changes in sentence, so long as they are within the statutory range applicable at the time of the offence. The principle in *Uttley* has, for example, been applied to the sentencing for offences committed many years previously. Such sentences can be based on current principles so long as they are within the maximum allowed at the time of the offence (*R* v *H* [2011] EWCA Crim 2753).

13.4.2 What is a 'penalty'?

Convention principles

The second sentence of Article 7(1) only applies to the retrospective application of a 'penalty'. Measures which are not penalties may be applied retrospectively to the detriment of a convicted person, without coming within Article 7. Such other measures can include, for example, orders for compensation or orders aimed at prevention of crime and the protection of the public.

The concept of 'penalty' is autonomous, it has a particular meaning for the purpose of the Convention and does not depend on how the matter is defined in national law.

> **case close-up**
>
> ### Welch v United Kingdom (1995) 20 EHRR 247
>
> W was convicted in 1988 for drug offences committed prior to 1987. He was sentenced to 22 years' imprisonment and made subject to a confiscation of property order. This required him to surrender to the state a high proportion of his property on the grounds that it was the proceeds of selling drugs. Failure to hand over the property could be punished by extra years in prison. Confiscation orders were introduced in 1987 (after W had committed the offences) but their application was expressly made retrospective (see the Drug Trafficking Offences Act 1986). W alleged a breach of Article 7. It was agreed that the confiscation orders had been retrospectively introduced; the issue for the ECtHR was whether these orders were a penalty. The Court held that they were a penalty and that there had been a violation of Article 7.

cross reference
Note similarities with the definition of a 'criminal charge' for Article 6 purposes. See Chapter 12, section 12.5.1.

In *Welch* the ECtHR suggested five criteria for identifying whether a measure is a penalty. The essential point is whether or not it is, in reality, a punishment.

(1) A penalty is imposed following a conviction for a crime. However:

- Just because a measure is imposed following criminal conviction, it does not follow that this is a penalty. The other matters, identified in this section must be taken into account.
- If a measure is imposed without there being a criminal conviction, it is unlikely that Article 7 will be of assistance. This is so even if the measure is imposed retrospectively or on the basis of a vague legal rule and even if its impact is as severe as a penalty might be. For example, in *De Wilde, Ooms and Versyp v Belgium* (1979–80) 1 EHRR 373, Belgian law allowed a so-called 'vagrant' to be detained under powers that did not require a criminal conviction. Though Article 5 was violated, the ECtHR held that Article 7 was irrelevant.

(2) A penalty aims at punishment. A measure imposed on a convicted criminal might be imposed for purposes of prevention or compensation. However, as the Court itself pointed out, the fact that a measure is aimed at the prevention of crime does not mean that it is not a penalty—'deterrence' (the prevention of crime) is, after all, one of the main justifications for punishment.

(3) A penalty need not be defined as such in national law. The way a measure is defined in national law is of weight, but is not decisive.

(4) Penalties are imposed by procedures recognising the rights of the defence. The fact that a measure can only be imposed on the basis of trial procedures that recognise the rights of the defence is evidence pointing to the fact that it is a penalty.

(5) Penalties are relatively severe. The more severe the measure the more likely it is that it will be a penalty.

English law under the HRA

Courts in England and Wales, following *Welch* v *United Kingdom* (section 13.4.2), have found that measures such as those noted later in this section are not subject to the provisions of Article 7(1). This means they can be imposed retrospectively and cannot be challenged on the basis of lack of clarity etc. They are preventative: aimed at the protection of the public rather than punishment and they do not necessarily require conviction for a criminal offence. For example:

cross reference

See Chapter 12, section 12.5.3, for other examples of preventative, non-punitive, measures.

- football banning orders (by which an individual can be banned from football grounds or from travelling abroad to watch football): see *Gough and Smith* v *Chief Constable of Derbyshire* [2002] EWCA Civ 351:

- disqualification orders (now replaced) which prevented people from working with children): see *R* v *Field* [2002] EWCA Crim 2913.

13.5 Article 7(2) war crimes exception

The Nuremburg trials of the Nazi leaders at the end of the Second World War involved, in a sense, retrospective justice. Herman Goring and others were tried for actions that, probably, were 'lawful' under German law at the time they were committed. However, the justification for these Nuremburg trials was that the Nazis were tried for crimes already established in international law either in custom or treaty. The great advance made at Nuremberg was the codification of these war crimes, their application to the political leaders as well as to lesser figures and the principle of individual responsibility.

With the ending of the 'Cold War' the Nuremberg principles could be revived. Under UN auspices, specific tribunals have been established for the trials of persons involved in atrocities committed in, for example, the former Yugoslavia and in Rwanda. The International Criminal Court has also been established with a more general jurisdiction, but it can only deal with crimes committed after 2002. Of equal, if not greater, importance is the gradual acceptance by many states, including European states, that they have a duty to try and punish alleged war criminals and perpetrators of crimes against humanity who may be within their control—the national law is applying internationally defined crimes. In the UK, for instance, section 51 of the International Criminal Court Act 2001 makes it an offence, under the domestic law of England and Wales to commit 'genocide, a crime against humanity or a war crime'.

Article 7(2), therefore, exempts such international and national proceedings from the ban on retrospective law. This is not the endorsement of 'victor's justice'. The claim is that such trials do not really involve retrospective law because all that is done is to try people according to norms and standards which had already been recognised internationally before the deeds in question were committed.

There has been little serious discussion by the ECtHR on the impact of Article 7(2). *Streletz, Kessler and Krenz* v *Germany* (see section 13.2.3) and *Kononov* (see section 13.2.3) were both decided on the basis of Article 7(1) alone. The question for the court was whether, in the circumstances of the cases, there was applicable law, domestic or national, which was accessible and foreseeable and which meant the perpetrator could be held criminally responsible for his actions. Given the positive answers to these questions the prosecutions did not involve arbitrary, retrospective applications of the criminal law. Hence the provisions of Article 7(2) did not need to be considered.

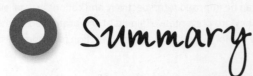

Summary

- Article 7(1) prohibits the retrospective application of criminal laws: a person should not be convicted for an offence that did not exist at the time he or she committed the acts in question, nor should any punishment they receive be one that was not available to the courts at that time.

- Article 7 also embodies the principle of legal certainty at least in the context of criminal law. People must be able to know the laws that apply to them and be able to foresee the circumstances in which laws will be applied. They can then adjust their conduct accordingly.

- As the case law indicates, Article 7 permits considerable flexibility in the way these principles are applied.

- As an aspect of the 'rule of law', Article 7 embodies the idea that the law should not be used arbitrarily.

Questions

 For suggested approaches, please visit the Online Resource Centre.

1 Prisoner 1234 killed his wife in 2003 and was convicted of murder in 2004 and sentenced to life imprisonment. In 2003 he might have expected to serve eight years in prison before being considered for release. By changes in 2006 to the parole and early release schemes he is now expected to serve at least 15 years in prison before being considered for release (these facts are made up and do not reflect the situation under English law).

(a) Has prisoner 1234 been a victim of a violation of Article 7?

(b) Does your answer indicate that the application of Article 7 may be too narrow to cover all situations in which changes to laws are applied retrospectively?

Further reading

Atrill, S. 'Nulla Poena Sine Lege' in Comparative Perspective: Retrospectivity under the ECHR and the US Constitution' [2005] Public Law 107–131

Lester, A., Pannick, D. and Herberg, J. (see Preface) Chapter 4, Article 7

Introduction to Articles 8–11

Chapter overview

- The common features of Articles 8, 9, 10 and 11.
- Identifying the basic right (first paragraphs).
- Identifying the exclusive circumstances under which states can restrict those rights (second paragraphs).

Introduction

This is a brief summary chapter in which the main terms of Articles 8–11 are introduced.

Articles 8, 9, 10 and 11 deal with individual freedom: freedom to live a private and family life (Article 8); freedom to hold and 'manifest' (demonstrate) religious and other beliefs (Article 9); freedom of expression, including the freedom of the media (Article 10); and the freedom to 'assemble' (to hold meetings, to march, to protest, etc.) and to 'associate' (to form, join and participate in pressure groups, political parties and other types of organisation) (Article 11).

The way a person or group exercises these freedoms can have a significant impact on the lives and freedoms of others, or can undermine important public interests or general concerns of one kind or another. There is, for example, widespread agreement that freedom of speech is not absolute and there are many circumstances in which any reasonable society is entitled to restrict expression: the protection of military and defence secrets, preventing the publication of matter which could prejudice a fair trial and allowing people to take legal action against those who have said things that unfairly damage their reputations are examples. Whilst there may be agreement on this as a general principle there can be deep disagreement over how this works in practice. A particular restriction on the freedom of the press on national security grounds, for example, is often criticised as just a government attempt to forestall criticism.

14.1 The structure of Articles 8–11

Articles 8–11 embody these types of dilemmas in their two-paragraph structure.

- First paragraph: the articles establish the freedoms (private life, religious belief, expression, etc.) as rights that the states which have signed the Convention must secure for everyone.
- Second paragraph: the articles state the conditions which must be satisfied if these freedoms are to be restricted. The freedoms can only be restricted, or interfered with, if these conditions are satisfied.

14.2 The scope of the first paragraph

A court must, first, decide whether the facts of the case disclose that the applicant has been exercising a freedom which is protected by the first paragraph of Article 8, 9, 10 or 11. This is often obvious, but not always. For example, is 'private life' (protected by Article 8) in issue when a person is photographed in the street, are political demonstrations covered by Article 10, does the right of association in Article 11 include a right not to be legally or economically compelled to join a trade association or union?

14.3 Whether there has been an interference for which the state is responsible

Next, a court must decide whether the exercise of a freedom protected by Articles 8–11 has been interfered with. Again, this is generally obvious. The principal issue for a court, including the European Court of Human Rights (ECtHR), is whether the interference is one for which the state has responsibility.

Frequently a person will be complaining about some interference with his or her freedom (of private life, belief, speech, etc.) which has been imposed by a state official putting into effect a legal rule. Thus demonstrators may have been arrested by the police, a political party refused registration by an election official or a group of religious believers prevented from building a church by a planning decision taken by a local council. In such circumstances, the responsibility of the state is direct and the question of whether it can justify its action under the terms of the second paragraph must then be considered.

cross reference
Positive duties are discussed in Chapter 6, section 6.6.

At other times a person will be complaining about an interference with his or her freedom which has been directly brought about not by a state official but by some private person or organisation (an individual, a commercial body or a charity, for example). Here the question is whether the state has responsibility for what has happened. Only if it does is it necessary then to consider its possible liability for a breach of one of the articles. The ECtHR refers to the state having 'positive duties' to regulate, to take official action or to change the law, in order to prevent the type of interference with a person's freedom that is in issue.

14.4 Justification (the second paragraph)

Once state responsibility for an interference with one of the freedoms protected by Articles 8–11 is established, the next issue is whether the state is able to justify the interference. It can only do this by reference to the terms in the second paragraphs of these Articles. Interferences must be

- on the basis of 'law',
- for a legitimate purpose, and they must
- be 'necessary in a democratic society'.

cross reference
For the Convention concept of 'law' see Chapter 6, section 6.2.

14.4.1 'Law'

Any interference must be 'in accordance with the law' (Article 8) or 'prescribed by law' (Articles 9, 10 and 11). The Convention concept of 'law' means not only that the interference

Justification (the second paragraph)

297

must be lawful in terms of the national law but the national law has to be 'accessible' (capable of being identified) and 'foreseeable' (people subject to the law can know or be advised on the likely application of the law); it must also be non-arbitrary and consistent with rule of law values.

14.4.2 Legitimate purpose

cross reference
For Article 18 see Chapter 7, section 7.4.

Restrictions on the freedoms protected by Articles 8–11 can only be compatible with the Convention if they pursue one of the purposes listed in the relevant second paragraph. Article 18 ECHR makes it clear that any restrictions on rights and freedoms that are allowed under the Convention can only be for the purposes allowed by the Convention.

Each of the Articles has its own particular list of purposes. Some purposes are common to all four Articles: all of the freedoms can be restricted to protect the 'rights of others'.

cross reference
'Rights of others' can include background rights not established precisely in the law. See Chapter 17, section 17.6.3 for examples involving freedom of expression.

Other purposes are only found in respect of one or some but not all of the four Articles. Thus it is possible to interfere with private and family life (Article 8) if this is in the interests of the 'economic well being of the country', but such a trade-off between economic wealth and individual rights and freedoms is not permitted under Article 9, 10 or 11. Similarly, 'national security' can justify restrictions on private and family life, expression, assembly and association, but not interferences with the way a person manifests his or her religion.

States normally find it relatively easy to show that a restriction on a freedom serves one of the listed purposes. The purposes are expressed in very open-textured language and it is easy to establish some kind of instrumental link between the interference and the purpose.

14.4.3 Necessary in a democratic society

Many cases involving Articles 8–11 are resolved in relation to the third requirement of the second paragraph: that any interference must be 'necessary in a democratic society'.

A judicial assessment of whether an interference is necessary in a democratic society involves factors such as the following:

cross reference
Ideas of 'democracy' and 'proportionality' pervade the Convention. See Chapter 6, sections 6.4 and 6.5 respectively.

- Whether, as well as serving one of the purposes listed in the second paragraph of the Article concerned, there is also a 'pressing social need' for the particular action taken.
- Whether there is clear evidence that the state has made a careful assessment of the situation and arrived at reasonable conclusions which take into account the impact of its decisions on the parties concerned. At the heart of the issue is 'proportionality'. There must be a 'fair balance' between the various private and public interests affected by the issue.

Of great importance in this context is to distinguish the role of the ECtHR from a national court, such as a court in England and Wales dealing with a case under the Human Rights Act 1998 (HRA).

cross reference
'Margin of appreciation' is discussed in Chapter 6, section 6.3. Deference by UK courts is discussed in Chapter 4, section 4.6.2.

The role of the ECtHR is a reviewing one. What is 'necessary' in a democratic society is likely to involve questions about what is for the good of the public and society. In this context, the ECtHR may accept, depending on context, that states enjoy a 'margin of appreciation', which, as an international court, it must respect. National courts, such as courts in the United Kingdom, acting under the HRA, will have to consider whether and to what extent the 'necessary in a democratic society' issue requires them to 'defer' to Parliament or to executive bodies on what is proportional, or whether the issues of fair balance and proportionality are ones they must answer for themselves. It is clear that necessary in a democratic society is dependent on context.

Summary

Articles 8–11 have a similar, two-paragraph structure which requires the courts to decide, first, whether some action for which the state is responsible interferes with a protected freedom and, if it does, whether the state has shown that the interference is justified in terms of the second paragraph of the Article involved.

In the chapters that follow each Article will be looked at in detail.

Question

For suggested approaches, please visit the Online Resource Centre.

A court order restrains the media from publishing a story. What general questions will an appeal court judge have to ask him or herself when deciding whether the order is compatible with the Convention?

Further reading

See Further Reading in Chapters 15–18

Article 8: right to respect for private and family life

Article 8   Right to respect for private and family life

(1) Everyone has the right to respect for his private and family life, his home and his correspondence.

(2) There shall be no interference by a public authority with the exercise of this right except such as is in accordance with the law and is necessary in a democratic society in the interests of national security, public safety or the economic well-being of the country, for the prevention of disorder or crime, for the protection of health or morals, or for the protection of the rights and freedoms of others.

Introduction

Any non-totalitarian society must recognise there are some matters which are personal, over which individuals are sovereign, and with which the state should not interfere. 'Autonomy' (self-directedness) is at the heart of human rights. Most people accept the general idea that there exists a sphere that is personal and to be protected. What is controversial is where the border is to be drawn. Moralists, for example, tend to argue that certain forms of sexual activity should be illegal on moral grounds even if they do not harm others; libertarians, in reply, argue that only sexual activity which harms others should be banned.

Article 8, in its first paragraph, identifies 'private life', 'family life', 'home' and 'correspondence' as the general concepts in terms of which this sphere of the personal is to be protected under the European Convention on Human Rights (ECHR). However, it is easy to think of circumstances in which the state is justified in interfering with the private sphere. Article 8(2), therefore, lays down the general legal conditions which must be satisfied before such interference is justified and compatible with the Convention.

301

Article 8: general issues

15.1.1 Article 8 and the two-paragraph structure

Respect for private and family life is a qualified right.

Thus the job of a court dealing with an Article 8 claim is

cross reference
The general principles governing qualified rights have been discussed in Chapter 14.

- first, to determine whether the matter in issue (i.e. the particular freedom of action claimed by the applicant) is covered by the concepts of 'private and family life', 'home' and 'correspondence' in Article 8(1);

- second, if the matter is covered by Article 8(1), to decide whether there has been an interference with that right by a public authority; and

- third, whether this interference by a public authority can be justified in the terms of Article 8(2): is the interference in accordance with the law, is it for one of the listed purposes and is it 'necessary in a democratic society', i.e. is it a proportionate response to a pressing social need?

15.1.2 **A right to privacy in English law**

No general right to privacy has been developed by English common law. Different aspects of privacy are protected in a number of different ways. Thus 'home' and property can be protected by laws of property and the tort of trespass to land; bodily integrity is protected by the criminal law and the tort of trespass to the person; confidences by an action for breach of confidence; reputation by an action for defamation, and so on. In *Wainwright* v *Home Office* [2003] UKHL 53, the House of Lords refused to develop a general tort (a civil wrong not directly based on a breach of contract) of privacy. It saw this as a pointless abstraction. The existing remedies gave specific and effective remedies. Any 'gaps' could be met by the Human Rights Act 1998 (HRA) (see Lord Hoffmann's analysis, paras 15–51).

15.1.3 **Article 8 and other rights**

Issues involving Article 8 often also raise issues under other articles of the Convention such as Article 12, the right to marry (see Chapter 19) and Article 1 of the First Protocol, protection of property (see Chapter 23).

Furthermore, issues about discrimination (e.g. on grounds of sexuality) frequently involve Article 14 (prohibition of discrimination) linked to Article 8 (see, on Article 14, Chapter 7, section 7.1).

It can also be necessary to weigh the importance to an individual of his or her rights under Article 8 with the importance to others of their rights under a different Convention article. This is common in respect of invasions of privacy by the media (the media have rights to freedom of expression under Article 10).

cross reference
On Article 3, see Chapter 9, particularly, section 9.1.3.

Particularly difficult questions involve the relations between Article 8 and Article 3, the prohibition of torture and inhuman and degrading treatment, and punishment. Treatment which reaches the threshold of severity to violate Article 3 cannot be justified no matter how compelling are the gains to the common good or to the rights of others. Treatment which is not so severe can violate Article 8 but, in that case, it is open to the state to justify the treatment in the terms allowed by Article 8(2).

15.1.4 **Companies**

Commercial **companies** may be able to enjoy rights under Article 8.

- -

companies

Companies (corporations) are, in law, independent legal persons. They exist legally separately from their owners (shareholders), managers and employees. They are said to have 'artificial' legal personality. No matter how vast and wealthy they may be, no matter how much economic power they may exercise, they are treated as a 'person' with at least some 'human' rights.

- -

- Companies can be 'victims' under Article 34 ECHR (see Chapter 5, section 5.4.6).
- Article 8 rights can be asserted in a commercial context.

It is now established that respect for a home can (in circumstances such as official raids and searches) include respect for a company's premises such as its head office (see *Société Colas Est* v *France* (2004) 39 EHRR 17, para 41).

KEY POINT Searches of company premises may also engage EU law and its own protection of fundamental rights (e.g. *National Panasonic* v *Commission* [1980] ECR 2033).

- Companies may even have some kind of 'private life'. The Convention position is uncertain. The Court of Appeal has accepted that companies may, under statute, assert their privacy against broadcasters and that doubt about the Convention position should not be used to restrict the application of this right (*R v Broadcasting Standards Commission ex parte BBC* [2000] 3 WLR 1327).

The states' obligations and positive duties

15.2.1 Respect

Article 8 requires states to 'respect' private and family life etc. There is no obligation on states to provide these things in the first place. For example, states are not required to ensure that everyone has a home, rather to respect what rights to a home people have (this is discussed later in the chapter). Respect may also imply a threshold of seriousness. Non-serious interferences or interferences which do not imply a lack of respect, may be outside the ambit of Article 8(1) altogether (see Lord Walker's discussion of the case law in *M* v *Secretary of State for Work and Pensions* [2006] UKHL 11, paras 62–83).

15.2.2 Positive duties

Under the Convention

In *Belgian Linguistics Case (No 2)* (1979–80) 1 EHRR 252 the European Court of Human Rights (ECtHR) stated that the 'essential' purpose of Article 8 is negative, it requires the state to desist from arbitrary interferences with private life etc. However, since that case, the Court has frequently said that Article 8 may require states to take positive steps to ensure that private life etc. is respected. States must not only desist from interfering unreasonably in private life, but also they may have a legal duty to do things, like change the laws or take particular administrative steps.

cross reference

Positive duties are found throughout the Convention, see Chapter 6, section 6.6.

The classic statement by the ECtHR is from *X and Y* v *The Netherlands* (1986) 8 EHRR 235, para 23:

> The Court recalls that although the object of Article 8 is essentially that of protecting the individual against arbitrary interference by the public authorities, it does not merely compel the State to abstain from such interference: in addition to this primarily negative undertaking, there may be positive obligations inherent in an effective respect for private or family life. These obligations may involve the adoption of measures designed to secure respect for private life even in the sphere of the relations of individuals between themselves.

In the context of Article 8 positive duties have been found in contexts such as the following:

- To ensure that there are adequate legal remedies. *X and Y* v *The Netherlands* (above) involved the failure by the Netherlands authorities to bring a criminal prosecution in a rape case. Under Netherlands law a prosecution required a complaint by the victim. The victim in this case was a 16-year-old girl who, because of her mental disability, was unable to make a complaint that was acceptable to the authorities. The ECtHR held that the availability of civil remedies, for damages, was insufficient to make the protection of Article 8 effective. Criminal processes, aimed at punishment, needed to be available.

- To provide information and ensure proper access to personal information.
- To undertake a proper investigation of allegations of a breach of Article 8.

Interferences by private companies and individuals

As the quote from *X and Y* v *The Netherlands* indicates, Article 8 requires states to ensure that private and family life etc. is respected even where the intrusions come from non-state sources. The ECtHR, therefore, reads Article 8, as meaning

- there is to be proper respect for private life, and that
- the only acceptable interferences with private life are those by public authorities which can be justified under Article 8(2). Other interferences are not acceptable.

cross reference
For 'horizontal effect' see Chapter 4, section 4.7.1.

To secure this, the state may have to prevent or regulate interferences with private life etc. that come from non-state sources (part of the 'horizontal effect' of the Convention).

The obvious example is the media. Under the Convention, the media must be independent of the government. Media intrusions into the personal lives of individuals, such as celebrities, may need to be regulated in order to ensure that press and TV give proper respect to their private and family lives. The national courts must be able to balance the media's rights to freedom of expression with a person's right to respect for private life. The law of England and Wales has done this by extending the common law remedy for breach of confidence to give effect to a right to privacy that embodies the provisions of Article 8 (see, in particular, Chapter 22).

KEY POINT In the United Kingdom the law is complemented by the role of media regulators such as Ofcom (for commercial television) and the Press Complaints Commission (PCC). They are 'public authorities' under section 6 HRA, and so must act in accordance with Convention rights, including Article 8. Under the Convention a state must be prepared to act if these regulators fail to secure adequate respect for Article 8 rights. There are doubts whether the regulators are able to provide adequate remedies for a breach of Convention rights, as is required by Article 13 (see *Peck* v *United Kingdom* (2003) 36 EHRR 41, para 108; discussed in Chapter 5, section 5.1.4). Despite reforms, the Leveson Report on press ethics (2012) exposed continuing, serious concerns about the effectiveness of the PCC , which will be replaced.

Positive duties and the HRA

The issue of positive duties has arisen under the HRA.

One issue is whether the Convention requires ministers to provide welfare payments in order to prevent people living in such poverty that their right to private and family life is not respected.

In *Anufrijeva* v *Southwark LBC* [2003] EWCA Civ 1406, the Court of Appeal accepted that Article 8 could impose positive obligations on the state; this would not mean a duty to provide welfare support to an asylum seeker unless his situation was so severe that, without welfare support there might be a breach of Article 3. Where children are involved, however, welfare support may be necessary to enable 'family life' to continue (see para 43).

In *R (B)* v *Crown Court at Stafford* [2006] EWHC 1645, it was held that Article 8 required courts to consider procedures and decision taking processes (here in a child abuse case) to ensure that Article 8 rights (here of the child witness) had been secured.

15.3 The approach of courts to Article 8

Scope and interference

The first issue for a court dealing with an Article 8 claim is to decide whether there has been an interference with a person's 'private' life, 'family life', 'home' or 'correspondence'. These are open-textured and controversial terms which need interpretation by the courts. Are you 'private' when in a public place, does 'family' include unmarried or same-sex couples? It is only if the courts, interpreting the Convention, answer 'yes' that Article 8 is relevant (these matters are discussed in the next section). If the issue is one which falls outside private and family life etc., then Article 8 is not engaged at all.

The second issue is whether there has been an 'interference'. Again, judgment by the courts is called for. Does taking photographs or keeping records amount to an interference? The interference must be by the state (directly) or indirectly through a failure to perform a positive duty.

Justification

If there is an issue within the scope of Article 8(1) and an interference, it still does not follow that the complainant's rights under Article 8 have been violated. Courts dealing with Article 8 must go on to consider whether the interference can be justified under the terms of Article 8(2). There is only a breach of the Convention if the answer to the latter question is 'no'.

cross reference

Proportionality is discussed in Chapter 6, section 6.5.

Where the state has interfered with a person's private or family life etc., the approach of the courts to justification is to check through Article 8(2) in order and form a judgment on whether the interference is justified. Where the issue is the failure to perform a positive duty the approach has to be different (there has been no interference to be justified). The ECtHR, in such circumstances, approaches the matter in terms of proportionality: has there been a 'fair balance' between the interests of individuals and those of society. The Court dislikes overly formal distinctions and the difference between positive and negative duties may not always be clear. The overriding concern, in either context, is to ensure the fair balance.

Margin of appreciation and deference

cross reference

Deference by UK courts is discussed in Chapter 4, section 4.6.2. 'Margin of appreciation' is discussed in Chapter 6, section 6.3.

Striking a fair balance between individual entitlements and legitimate social values and benefits can involve complex questions of policy and controversial questions of what common goods are valuable and worthwhile. The ECtHR acknowledges that, depending on the issue, nation states enjoy a wide margin of appreciation on many issues. The margin is focused on the issue of justification under Article 8(2), especially on the need for an interference in a democratic society. Under the HRA, for the same types of reason, courts in the United Kingdom are willing to 'defer', and, on the issue of justification, give weight to the decisions of Parliament (expressed in the policies inherent in Acts of Parliament) and of the executive and the administration.

15.4 'Private... life'

The ECtHR has developed a wide, inclusive understanding of 'private life'. In *Pretty v United Kingdom* (2002) 35 EHRR 1, the Court stressed that 'the concept of "private life" is a broad term not susceptible to exhaustive definition' (see paras 61–62):

> It covers the physical and psychological integrity of a person. It can sometimes embrace aspects of an individual's physical and social identity. Elements such as, for example, gender identification, name and sexual orientation and sexual life fall within the personal sphere protected by Article 8. Article

8 also protects a right to personal development, and the right to establish and develop relationships with other human beings and the outside world...the Court considers that the notion of personal autonomy is an important principle underlying the interpretation of its guarantees.

Private life includes the idea of being left alone. However, as *Pretty* shows, it also extends to concepts of self-development and autonomy. UK courts have adopted this definition under the HRA. Nevertheless doubt has been expressed about the concepts of 'identity' and 'personal development', referred to in *Pretty*. In *R (Razgar)* v *Secretary of State for the Home Department* [2004] UKHL 27, Lord Walker, at para 34, suggested that the meaning of these words was unclear and that the rights developed out of Article 8 could be 'abstract and volatile' in character.

15.4.1 **Physical integrity**

ECHR

States must have laws and procedures which give adequate protection to those who have suffered physical abuse or been subject to physical, bodily, interference: see, for example, *X and Y* v *The Netherlands*, at section 15.2.2. The suffering must reach an appropriate level of severity to engage Article 8(1), but this level is lower than that required for a breach of Article 3 (*Bensaid* v *United Kingdom* (2001) 33 EHRR 10, para 46). Treatment covered by Article 8(1), unlike under Article 3, may be acceptable if it is justified under Article 8(2) as being proportionate to the achievement of a social good. For example, forcible medical interventions (see Chapter 9, section 9.7.2) and requiring a person to undergo a strip search (*Wainwright* v *United Kingdom* (2007) 44 EHRR 40) engage Article 8(1) and therefore require justification under Article 8(2).

HRA

case close-up

Evans v Amicus Healthcare Ltd [2004] EWCA Civ 727

Under the Human Fertilisation and Embryology Act 1990, in vitro fertilisation treatment could only be given on the basis of the consent of both parties to the fertilisation. The claimant's former partner withdrew his consent. The claimant sought an injunction to compel her former partner to restore his consent and a declaration that the Act was incompatible with her rights under Article 8.

It was held by the Court of Appeal that the claimant's Article 8 rights were engaged but the requirement for continued consent, insisted on by Parliament, was proportionate and so was justified under Article 8(2).

The Court of Appeal found both that refusal of treatment by the clinic and the question of when a person can become pregnant, engaged Article 8(1). In *Burke* v *General Medical Council* [2005] EWCA Civ 1003, it was accepted that Article 8 was likely to be engaged on issues concerning consent to medical treatment.

15.4.2 **Psychological or moral integrity ECHR**

States also need to have laws and procedures to protect citizens from abuse causing psychological harm and threats to what is called 'moral integrity'. Moral integrity is something less than psychological illness. It can include, for instance, the humiliation and degradation of the person that can accompany physical abuse and ill-treatment. On these grounds Article 8 can be relevant in the context of abusive prison conditions and other forms of detention (see, for example, *Raninen* v *Finland* (1998) 26 EHRR 563, para 63).

Article 8 might involve duties on states to ensure adequate treatment for those suffering mental illness, though the extent of such a positive duty is unclear.

In *Bensaid* v *United Kingdom* (2001) 33 EHRR 10, the applicant sought to resist deportation on the grounds that, as a sufferer from schizophrenia, his treatment in Algeria, the country he was to be deported to, would be so inadequate as to violate his right to private life under Article 8. The ECtHR held that 'mental health must…be regarded as a crucial part of private life associated with the aspect of moral integrity' (para 47); though, on the facts, the alleged deprivations were probably not so serious as to come within the protection of Article 8 and, even if they did, the deportation could be justified under Article 8(2).

HRA

cross reference

For further discussion, with reference to Article 3, see Chapter 9, section 9.7.

Physical and psychological integrity can be in issue in the context of people's living conditions. The point is whether states have a positive duty to provide resources to remedy conditions which are so bad they violate Article 8.

In *R (Bernard)* v *Enfield LBC* [2003] LGR 423, it was held, and accepted by the Court of Appeal in *Anufrijeva* (section 15.2.2), that the failure of a local authority to support a disabled mother with six children, leaving them in 'hideous' living conditions, clearly engaged Article 8(1) both in terms of private life and family life.

15.4.3 **Personal and social identity**

Names

Legal restrictions on the names that people are entitled to adopt can engage Article 8(1) (as in *Johansson* v *Finland* (2008) 47 EHRR 14).

cross reference

The human rights of transgendered persons are considered in Chapter 19, section 19.4.

Gender

A person's sense of identity is closely related to their gender. Article 8(1) (as well as Article 12) has frequently been engaged in respect of national laws which discriminate against 'transsexuals'—persons who have gone through a psychological and, usually, a physical process of gender reassignment. In *Goodwin* v *United Kingdom* (2002) 35 EHRR 18, the ECtHR held that legal barriers imposed on a transgendered person violated their rights to private life.

Reputation

A person's reputation is an aspect of private life protected by Article 8. Thus rights and remedies to protect reputation (such as common law 'defamation') must be available (e.g. *Clift* v *Slough BC* [2010] EWCA Civ 1484) and, likewise, courts, when considering whether to allow parties or witnesses to be anonymous, must act compatibly with Article 8. The issue is discussed in *Re Guardian News and Media* [2010] UKSC 1, paras 37–42, which cites *Pfeifer* v *Austria* (2007) 48 EHRR 175, para 35.

15.4.4 **Personal information**

Access to personal information

A full sense of identity involves knowing the central facts about who one is and where one came from. For some people, crucial pieces of information may be held by public authorities or be unavailable under the law. Although Article 10 (the right to freedom of expression) includes a right to 'receive…information', the ECtHR has held that this does not create an obligation on the unwilling party (e.g. the authorities) to divulge secret information (*Leander* v *Sweden* (1987) 9 EHRR 433, para 74). However, the Court has accepted that there may be a right to receive information in the context of Article 8. This right has been asserted in respect of

- access to social work files where this is necessary for the applicant to have knowledge about his early childhood (*Gaskin* v *United Kingdom* (1980) 12 EHRR 36),
- information pertaining to the health risks of those involved in dangerous activities (*McGinley* v *United Kingdom* (1999) 27 EHRR 1),
- information for adopted children about their natural parents (*Odievre* v *France* (2004) 38 EHRR 43).

Protection of personal information

Making personal information available to the public without the person's consent raises an issue under Article 8(1). There have been a number of cases under the HRA. (Cases involving celebrities are discussed in Chapter 22, section 22.5.)

In *R (Robertson)* v *Wakefield Metropolitan District Council* [2001] EWHC 915 (Admin), the sale to a commercial buyer of personal information contained in the electoral register without the right of an individual to refuse, was held to engage Article 8(1) and not be justified under Article 8(2). It also violated EU law on data protection.

Police records and samples

- Under various powers in the Police and Criminal Evidence Act 1984 (PACE) and other statutes, the police have powers to take and retain fingerprints and body samples from suspects. This raises important issues, which are discussed in Chapter 20, sections 20.6.1 and 20.6.2.

15.4.5 Sexual orientation and sexual freedom

Private life 'includes...sexual life' (*Dudgeon* v *United Kingdom*, para 41). Laws regulating or restricting sexual orientation and sexual freedom deal with a person's most intimate feelings and relationships and engage Article 8. Cases such as *Dudgeon* v *United Kingdom* (1982) 4 EHRR 149 (criminalised male homosexual activity), *BB* v *United Kingdom* (2004) 39 EHRR 30 (age of consent), *ADT* v *United Kingdom* (2001) 31 EHRR 33 (group sex and privacy) make it clear that laws which treat homosexuals less favourably than heterosexuals cannot be justified under Article 8(2).

KEY POINT Under the Sexual Offences Act 2003, the age of consent in the United Kingdom is now the same for heterosexual and homosexual acts.

A remaining issue under the Convention is whether states are required to give full and equal recognition to same sex partnerships (this is discussed at section 15.5.3).

15.4.6 Personal development, autonomy and freedom

Personal development

The extent of the protection given by Article 8(1) is unclear. The summary in *Pretty* (paras 61–62 quoted at section 15.4) refers to 'personal development'. This gives protection beyond merely the right to be left alone:

It also secures to the individual a sphere within which he or she can freely pursue the development and fulfilment of his or her personality.

(Brüggerman and Scheuten v Germany (1977) DR 10, para 55)

cross reference

Prisoners' rights are discussed in Chapter 21. For ASBOs see Chapter 12, section 12.5.3. For TPIMs see Chapter 26, section 26.7.2.

Thus Article 8(1) is engaged when laws or official practices limit a person's ability to establish and develop relationships with other people and the outside world generally. In the United Kingdom, prisoners held in solitary confinement, persons under Anti-social Behaviour Orders or terrorist suspects subject to Terrorism Prevention and Investigation Measures (TPIMs), if they suffer significant restrictions on their right to meet and associate with whom they please, could, if the restrictions are sufficiently severe, find that their Article 8 rights are in issue.

Autonomy

In *Pretty* (see section 15.4), the Court also referred to personal autonomy, the idea that a person should, given their circumstances, be able to control his or her life and make important decisions for themselves, is an important guiding principle in Article 8.

In *Pretty* the ECtHR would 'not...exclude' the possibility that autonomy included, at least in the circumstances of the case, a right to choose to die (para 67). For UK law the application of Article 8(1) in 'right to die' cases was affirmed by the House of Lords in *R (Purdy)* v *DPP* [2009] UKHL 45. In *Haas* v *Switzerland* (2011) 53 EHRR 33, the right of a competent person to commit suicide (without assistance) was clearly brought within the scope of Article 8(1).

Freedom

The scope of these concepts of self-development and autonomy is not clear. First, Article 8(1) seems to extend to a person's right to go about his or her daily business and ordinary life without unjustifiable interference. Thus in *von Hannover* v *Germany* (2005) 40 EHRR 1, Princess Caroline of Monaco was able to assert a right to private life, which the German courts should have protected, against being hassled by paparazzi when doing ordinary things like shopping and playing tennis. Some senior UK judges would like this to go further and for private life to include activities that are of core importance to an individual's sense of him- or herself, or they would like Article 8 to embody a general right to freedom. On this basis, legal restrictions on a person's freedom of action that are not based on harm to others but on, for example, facilitating a policy that benefits others or stopping actions considered to be immoral or disgusting, will engage Article 8(1), and therefore need justification before the judges.

discussion topic

Has the 'human rights agenda' moved on and left the Convention looking rather old-fashioned and limited?

Should Article 8(1) express a right to freedom? The argument mentioned previously was developed, *obiter dicta,* by Lords Rodger and Brown in *R (Countryside Alliance)* v *Attorney General* [2007] UKHL 52, an unsuccessful challenge to the ban on hunting in England and Wales. All their Lordships accepted that the ban on fox hunting could not be sufficiently justified on the grounds of suppression of cruelty to animals (since alternatives to fox hunting are also cruel) and so part of the justification was a moral revulsion, on behalf of a majority of MPs, to fox hunting.

The views of Lords Rodger and Brown ('Why should it [Article 8(1)] not encompass a broad philosophy of live and let live') are at paras 95–101 and 137–141; and can be compared with the view of Baroness Hale ('In my view there is no human right to be left alone to do as one likes') at paras 110–116. Lords Rodger and Brown both accepted that the Article 8 case law had not gone as far as they would like.

15.4.7 **Public places**

As the *von Hannover* case makes clear, the simple fact that a person is in a public place, such as a street, does not mean that they have thereby lost all rights to private life. After all, private life, in its positive aspect, includes the idea of being able to interact with others and it would be arbitrary if that freedom could only be exercised in private places. It is the nature of the activity and the circumstances that are important. Being photographed by police whilst engaged in a political demonstration (whose point is public awareness) is unlikely to engage Article 8(1) (see *Friedl v Austria* (1996) 21 EHRR 83). On the other hand there was a breach of Article 8 when CCTV footage of a man attempting suicide in a town centre was used by the media without his full consent (see *Peck v United Kingdom* (2003) 36 EHRR 41). The Court distinguished between the simple monitoring of people in public places, which will not normally engage Article 8, and the keeping of personal records or other uses of the information which may well do so. See further, Chapter 5, section 5.1.4. In *R (Countryside Alliance) v Attorney General* [2007] UKHL 52, all the Law Lords agreed that the public and spectacular nature of hunting made it impossible for Article 8(1) to be engaged.

15.4.8 **Surveillance**

Surveillance activities, by police, security services and others, engage Article 8(1). Justification for surveillance is discussed later in this chapter, section 15.10.2.

15.4.9 **Private life and economic activity**

The idea of personal development can make Article 8 significant in respect of legal barriers that prevent people from leading normal lives, such as refusing passports or creating legal barriers to people working in their chosen careers (e.g. *Sidabras and Dziautas v Lithuania* (2006) 42 EHRR 6, where barriers to former members of the KGB working violated Article 14 linked to Article 8).

The concept of 'private life' is indeterminate in scope and could be applied in a commercial and professional context, as in *Niemietz*, at section 15.6.1. Individuals construct their lives in ways in which there is intermingling of the private and the public.

15.5 **'Family life'**

15.5.1 **Introduction**

States have duties not to interfere in arbitrary ways with those close, personal and psychologically important relationships which are contained in the concept of 'family'. Interferences with the relationships between close blood relations, husband and wife, parents and children, and parents and their adopted children will all come within the scope of Article 8(1). In *Huang v Secretary of State for the Home Department* [2007] UKHL 11, Baroness Hale, summarising Strasbourg case law, defined family in terms of deep social, emotional and financial dependency (para 18).

15.5.2 Family and informal relationships

From early days the ECtHR has sought to define the idea of a family relationship in a way that recognises social change and development and which does not allow legal forms (e.g. marriage) to prevail over 'biological and social reality' (*Kroon* v *The Netherlands* (1995) 19 EHRR 263, para 40). So-called 'ad hoc' relationships are recognised. These relationships are not defined in advance. Their acceptance by the Court as being family relationships depends on 'real' (as distinct from legal) factors, such as whether there is sufficient closeness and longevity for it to be familial in quality. If so it must be respected by the national laws. Laws and official practices which discriminate between legitimate and illegitimate children (*Marckx* v *Belgium* (1979–80) 2 EHRR 330) or which base family life solely on marriage, or which focus on legal formalities rather than personal realities (*Abdulaziz, Cabbales and Balkandali* v *United Kingdom* (1985) 7 EHRR 471) are likely to raise Article 8(1) issues and require justification under Article 8(2).

> **case close-up**
>
> ***Kroon* v *The Netherlands* (1995) 19 EHRR 263**
>
> Before being divorced from her husband, K formed a relationship with A. It was a stable relationship although K and A did not live together. They had a child but, under The Netherlands' law, the child could not be registered as A's child because only the husband could authorise legal steps which denied the legitimacy of his wife's children. The ECtHR held that there was a violation of Article 8.

Various points follow from this case:

* Familial relationships, which the laws must respect, do not depend on marriage.
* Given factors of strength and stability, a relationship can be familial even if the couple are living apart.
* Relationships between parents and children must be protected by national laws and legal presumptions (here about legitimacy) must not be allowed to interfere with the biological and social realities.

15.5.3 Same-sex relationships

Same-sex relationships are included in family relationships and are protected by Article 8(1), *Schalk and Kopf* v *Austria* (2011) 53 EHRR 20, paras 90–94). This involves a deliberate change by the ECtHR from its earlier rulings. There is not yet a positive duty on states to provide for homosexual marriage or 'civil partnership', though the latter, at least, is a discernable trend in European societies.

15.5.4 Social policy

There are a number of areas of social policy in which states, acting in pursuit of legitimate policy objectives, take actions which interfere with family life, given its broad definition. These include steps taken:

* To protect children, by taking them from their parents and placing them in the care of the local authority who then make important decisions about whom the children are to

live with and whether the biological parents have rights of access etc. These actions must respect the rights to family life of those involved including the children themselves and the biological parents (*C* v *United Kingdom* App 14858/03, admissibility decision of 14 December 2004).

- Immigration. Under the Convention it is recognised that states are entitled to take steps to control immigration. Immigration policies on who may enter the country or who is to be deported may involve decisions about whether family members can be together. Such actions must respect the rights to family life of those involved (*Abdulaziz, Cabalas and Balkandali* v *United Kingdom* (1985) 7 EHRR 471, para 57).

15.6 'Home'

15.6.1 The concept of 'home'

Under Article 8, states have obligations not to interfere in arbitrary ways with a person's 'home'. 'Home' is not defined but the implication is that it is the place where a person lives or intends to live on a settled basis.

case close-up

Buckley v United Kingdom (1997) 23 EHRR 101

B was a gypsy who, for two years, had lived in caravans placed on land that she owned. She sought retrospective planning permission for herself and her family. The application was refused by the local authority. B was offered a place on an official site, which she turned down. The local authority issued enforcement notices requiring the caravans to be removed. She alleged a breach of Article 8. The ECtHR held that the refusal to grant planning permission was an interference with B's home but it was one which was within the margin of appreciation of the United Kingdom's planning authorities and hence was justified under the terms of Article 8(2).

In finding that Article 8 was engaged, the ECtHR adopted a Convention specific, 'autonomous' meaning of home. In particular:

- A person's home exists independently of whether or not it is 'lawful' under the national laws.
- No abstract definition of home is provided.
- The main issue involves the intentions and attitude of the applicant towards the land in issue—an intention now or in the future to treat the place as home.
- It is not necessary for a person to have lived all the time on the land in question—a home is not lost just because a person is living abroad for a while. But it is necessary to show sufficient, continuous links with the place in issue and, perhaps, that no other permanent home has been established.

In *Giacomelli* v *Italy* (2007) 45 EHRR 38, the ECtHR described a home as 'the place, the physically defined area, where private and family life develops', para 76. This is clearly not a complete definition since home can include company offices (*Société Colas Est* v *France*, section 15.1.4) and the place where an individual works.

***Niemietz v Germany* (1993) 16 EHRR 97**

A lawyer's offices were searched by the police acting on the basis of a warrant. The ECtHR held that a person's place of work could be considered as part of their home. Because of the intermingling of the private and the professional in the way individuals construct and value their lives, such a broad definition of home was necessary given that the underlying purpose of Article 8 is to prevent arbitrary interference by states in individual lives. The search was not justified under Article 8(2), and so there was a breach of Article 8.

15.6.2 **Respect for a home**

cross reference

Peaceful enjoyment of possessions is also a right under Article 1 of the First Protocol, see Chapter 23

Article 8 places a duty on states to 'respect' a person's home. This can mean, for example, that states must ensure access and a right to live in their home (such as did not happen in *Gillow v United Kingdom* (1989) 11 EHRR 335); that states must protect a person's peaceful enjoyment of their property (taking reasonable steps to prevent harassment, for example, as in *Whiteside v United Kingdom* (1994) 18 EHRR CD126).

Right to a home?

Article 8 does not mean that states have general social duties to house the homeless and provide secure accommodation to people who do not have, or have lost through lawful eviction, a place they can call home.

Article 8 applies to evictions by public landlords.

***McCann v United Kingdom* (2008) 47 EHRR 40**

M's wife left him because of alleged domestic violence. M lost his legal right to remain in the family home and the local authority landlord successfully evicted him. The legal procedure it used gave M no opportunity to argue that, on the basis of his personal circumstances, eviction was unlawful. The ECtHR found that there was a breach of Article 8.

In *McCann* the ECtHR said that eviction was 'a most extreme form of interference with the right to respect for the home' (para 50). Even though the tenant had no legal right to remain it should still, 'in principle', be possible for the proportionality of the eviction to be measured by a court that had a jurisdiction to deal with all the relevant factual as well as legal issues.

The principle in *McCann* has now been adopted into the law of England and Wales under the HRA.

***Manchester CC v Pinnock* [2010] UKSC 45**

P lived in a property let by MCC as a 'demoted tenant'. This meant, in essence, that MCC could seek a possession order from the County Court, which would be granted on the sufficient grounds that he had breached the terms of the demoted tenancy and that the authority had followed a statutory procedure (i.e. the County Court was not required to consider whether it was reasonable to evict in the circumstances). Continued anti-social behaviour by P's children led to his eviction. The Supreme Court applied Article 8 to the eviction:

- Article 8(1) is engaged when public landlords exercise lawful powers to evict people from their homes.

- Section 3 HRA could be used to read into the statutory duties of the County Court the power to consider justification for the eviction under Article 8(2).

- The tenant must raise the issue of proportionality; otherwise public landlords can proceed on the assumption that Article 8 is complied with.

- There was a high threshold for the tenant to cross. Fair balance, required by 'proportionality' (Article 8(2)), would give great weight to public landlords' legal rights and also to their judgment on housing policy and balancing the various interests engaged by social housing (though the court refused to say that disproportionate eviction would be 'exceptional').

- The case has no implications for private landlords.

discussion topic

Do you agree with the decision in *Pinnock*? Perhaps the 'high threshold' means that a tenant's right is illusory in practice? On the other hand, perhaps the effect of the decision will make it harder for public landlords to deal with anti-social behaviour or to allocate homes according to needs.

There may even be extreme examples where the Convention does impose a duty to provide a home. In *R v North East Devon Health Authority ex parte Coughlan* [2001] QB 213, a Health Authority promised a severely disabled young woman a 'home for life' in a specially built facility. Under English administrative law the promise established a 'legitimate expectation', but the question for the courts was whether this was merely a legitimate expectation to be consulted about any proposed changes to her situation or whether it gave her a right to go on living in the facility. The Court of Appeal took the latter view and, in part, saw this as giving effect to Coughlan's Article 8 rights.

15.7 'Correspondence'

The term 'correspondence', like private life is given a wide definition under the Convention. Both terms can embrace interferences with personal communications in all their forms: letters and telephone calls and, presumably, other methods such as fax and e-mail (see *Klass v Germany* (1979–80) 2 EHRR 214, para 41).

As with private life and home, the ECtHR recognises that it not possible to make a clear distinction between the private sphere and other aspects of a person's life such as their working life.

In *Halford v United Kingdom* (1997) 24 EHRR 523, a senior police officer, who was bringing a sex discrimination case against her force, had both her home telephone and her office telephone, bugged by the police authority. The ECtHR held that Article 8 applied both to the interceptions on her home phone and the office phone (see also *Copland v United Kingdom* (2007) 45 EHRR 37).

'Respect' for correspondence means that states must justify, under Article 8(2), actions such as opening and reading letters or e-mails, metering and tapping phones, censoring correspondence and so on. States may have positive duties to ensure adequate access to communication by vulnerable groups, including prisoners.

15.8 Environmental law

cross reference
The applicability of the Convention to the modern political agenda is discussed in Chapter 2, section 2.3.5.

No provision in the Convention expressly requires environmental rights; there are, for instance, no express rights to clean air or a quiet environment.

Despite this, the ECtHR has implied environmental rights into Article 8(1). Where environmental damage has a serious direct effect upon a person's private and family life or their home, there can be an issue raised under Article 8.

In *López Ostra* v *Spain* (1995) 20 EHRR 277, the ECtHR held that there had been a breach of Article 8 in respect of the authority's failure adequately to deal with a waste treatment plant built only 12 metres from the applicant's home and which was responsible for fumes, bad smells and contamination causing health problems.

cross reference
Environmental failures causing death can engage Article 2, see Chapter 8, section 8.3.5.

In *Guerra* v *Italy* (1998) 26 EHRR 357, the applicant lived one kilometre from a chemical factory which had released highly toxic substances into the atmosphere, which were responsible for serious poisoning of the population. The ECtHR held that there had been a violation of Article 8 in respect of both the failure properly to regulate the factory and also the failure to make proper information available to the population.

In *Moreno Gomez* v *Spain* (2005) 41 EHRR 40, noise pollution from night clubs raised an Article 8 issue.

The general principles are summarised in *Fadeyeva* v *Russia*.

case close-up

Fadeyeva v *Russia* (2007) 45 EHRR 10

F was one of thousands of people who lived within a 1000-metre buffer zone that was supposed to isolate the biggest steel smelter in Russia from any residential area. The smelter, which was old and inefficient, was the cause of major air pollution which caused serious respiratory and blood illnesses amongst many of the population. Schemes to rehouse the residents were not put into full effect. The resident was one who was not rehoused. No remedy was available to her from the Russian courts. The ECtHR held that there had been a violation of Article 8.

- Though there is no explicit right to a clean environment in the Convention, Article 8 is engaged if pollution has a direct effect on a person's private and family life, or on his or her home.

- Pollution will only engage Article 8(1) if it surpasses a minimum level of severity. This level depends on the particular circumstances such as the intensity and duration of the pollution.

- The facts must be proved. The standard of proof is beyond a reasonable doubt; the burden of proof is on the applicant but, given the fact that obtaining information may be difficult and that much of the information will be controlled by the authorities, the Court adopts a flexible approach. It will make inferences and work on the basis of presumptions about the responsibilities of the authorities if direct causal evidence of the effects on the applicant is not available.

The need for significant severity in pollution before Article 8 is engaged has been emphasised for the purposes of domestic UK law in *Barr* v *Biffa Waste Services* [2011] EWHC 1003 (see paras 305–310 for a summary of cases).

cross reference
For margin of appreciation see Chapter 6, section 6.3.

It is rarely the state itself which does the polluting. In *Fadeyeva,* as in all the cases mentioned, the pollution was done by a commercial company. In the environmental context, therefore, states have 'positive duties' to regulate commercial industrial processes to the extent necessary to protect private and family lives and people's homes. Positive duties are not absolute. The ECtHR must be satisfied that the state has achieved a fair balance between the interests of the applicant, other parties involved (e.g. the commercial owners of the plant) and the wider public interest. Factors explicit in Article 8(2) can be relevant to such a judgment.

It is emphatically not the Court's job to determine a state's environmental laws and policies. The Court's role is to ensure that the states have given due weight to the applicant's Article 8 rights and not just ignored them. States have a wide margin of appreciation. Only in exceptional circumstances will the Court be prepared to find that the states, acting lawfully, in good faith and giving full weight to individual's rights, have made a wrong judgment on where the fair balance lies.

15.9 Article 8(2)

How individuals wish to lead their private and family lives and what they may wish to do regarding their homes and correspondence can have a significant impact on others and on the interests of the public. Under the Convention a state, acting through public authorities, can restrict the private and family lives, the right of access to, and enjoyment of, home and the correspondence, of individuals. But such restriction or interference is only possible if it is

- done for one of the purposes listed in Article 8(2) and not for any other purpose;
- done 'in accordance with the law', i.e. is based on law and is compatible with the rule of law;
- 'necessary in a democratic society'—it is a proportionate way of meeting a pressing social need.

15.9.1 **Public authorities and positive duties**

cross reference
For a fuller discussion of the 'state' see Chapter 2, section 2.4.3.

Article 8(2) refers only to 'interference by a public authority'. This term refers to the full range of executive and administrative bodies through which the authority of the state is exercised (ministers and civil service, police, local councils, 'quangos', etc.) and also to other bodies for which the state is responsible, such as the FE college in *Copland* v *United Kingdom* (2007) 45 EHRR 37.

States may also have positive duties to regulate interferences with the Article 8 freedoms which come from private sources such as the media or private landlords. States may have to alter national laws, including those, such as laws of contract and property, which govern private relations; or establish regulatory agencies which control the activities of private or commercial bodies. Likewise the UK courts need to fashion the private law in ways that recognise Article 8 rights. Under the HRA, of course, UK courts are public authorities under a duty to act compatibly with the Convention rights (see Chapter 4, section 4.5.4).

cross reference
For positive duties see section 15.2.2, and Chapter 6, section 6.6.

Where an interference is based on a freely entered into contract, Article 8(1) may not be engaged at all (there will have been no interference as recognised under the Convention) or it will be easily justified under Article 8(2) as being to protect the rights of others, namely the rights under the contract of the other party. Thus, while states may have positive duties to regulate the private media in order to protect privacy, it is less likely that the same will apply to private landlords whose power over tenants is entirely contractual (see *Pinnock* at section 15.6.2). Nevertheless, context means a lot under the Convention and there may be circumstances where this is not true (as in *Ghaidan* v *Godin-Mendoza* [2004] UKHL 30, discussed in Chapter 4, section 4.4.7).

cross reference

The pervasive concept of law and legality is discussed in Chapter 6, section 6.2.

15.9.2 'In accordance with the law'

Under Article 8(2) any interference with the freedom in Article 8(1) must be 'in accordance with the law'.

The concept of law and legality which pervades the Convention applies in respect of Article 8(2).

That is, the interference must be

- in accordance with the national law as determined by the national courts;
- the national law must also meet the Convention requirements of 'accessibility' and 'foreseeability' (see Chapter 6, section 6.2);
- legality also requires that the applicant's rights are protected by a fair, adversarial, legal procedure. The applicant must have an opportunity to assert his or her fundamental rights and this applies, albeit subject to context, even in situations such as where the state acts to protect national security (see, for example, *Al Nashif* v *Bulgaria* (2003) 36 EHRR 37, paras 123–124).

Officials may exercise **discretion.**

Where this is so, the law must indicate the scope and limits of discretion. Otherwise the application of the laws by officials may not be sufficiently 'foreseeble'. Whether the legality test is met will depend upon contextual factors such as the purpose being pursued and the availability of adequate safeguards. The protection of children, for example, may justify wider discretion than that enjoyed by officials in the context of surveillance and national security.

· ·

discretion

Often the law identifies a general purpose officials (like police officers or civil servants) are to pursue but says little about the ways and means for doing this. The matter is left to the officials who thereby exercise 'discretion'.

· ·

15.9.3 Legitimate purposes

An interference with private life etc. must not only be in accordance with the law but can be only for one or more of the purposes listed in Article 8(2). It is often (though not always) easy for the state to prove that it is acting for a legitimate purpose.

'In the interests of national security'

'National security' has been accepted by the Court as justifying interferences with private and family life, home and correspondence in a number of circumstances such as surveillance by security services and information gathering (e.g. *Klass* v *Germany* (1979–80 2 EHRR 214, para 46).

Historically it has been all too easy for states to invoke national security to justify their actions and national courts have been reluctant to allow this claim to be challenged before them. Under the Convention, however, national law and procedures must give an opportunity for the government's claims to be tested to ensure that they have some reasonable basis. The person whose private life has been interfered with must be able, under national law, to

> challenge the executive's assertion that national security is at stake. While the executive's assessment of what poses a threat to national security will naturally be of significant weight, the independent

authority [i.e. a court] must be able to react in cases where invoking that concept has no reasonable basis in the facts or reveals an interpretation of 'national security' that is unlawful or contrary to common sense and arbitrary.

(*Al-Nashif* v *Bulgaria* (2003) 36 EHRR 37, para 124)

KEY POINT UK courts do require the government to give a proper explanation of why national security is at stake, though they also recognise that the government is the primary decision taker and, on this matter above all, is in possession of the main evidence, all or much of which may legitimately be secret or only available to special tribunals. On such a matter, context, including the nature of the burden on the individual, is all-important. See, for example, *A* v *Secretary of State for the Home Department* [2004] UKHL 56, para 177, per Lord Rodger.

'In the interests of ... public safety'

This purpose seldom stands in its own right but is more likely to be linked with other purposes such as the prevention of crime. The purpose may justify, for example, public disclosure by the police or other authorities of personal information.

'In the interests of ... the economic well-being of the country'

This phrase is unique to Article 8 and, unlike most of the others, does not appear in Article 9(2), 10(2) or 11(2). It appears to have been inserted at the behest of the (old) Labour government in the United Kingdom, which was concerned that Article 8 rights might be used to inhibit the programme of nationalisation (government ownership of basic industries) they were pursuing.

further study

See Wicks, E. 'The United Kingdom Government's Perception of the European Convention on Human Rights at the Time of Entry' [2000] *Public Law* (Autumn) 438, 438, 444.

It is, in principle, hard to explain a situation in which an individual's rights can be restricted in order to promote the general wealth of the community since one of the central aims of human rights is to ensure that individuals and minorities are protected as society pursues its collective interests. Nevertheless this category has been used in the context of cases that involve the deportations of foreigners who have established family links and also environmental protection cases.

'for the prevention of disorder or crime'

This category can justify surveillance by the police and security services; it has also been accepted by the ECtHR as a legitimate purpose underlying the deportation of foreigners with criminal offences.

'for the protection of health'

Article 8(1) can be in issue in respect of a range of difficult issues relating to health and medical treatment. Respect for private life may be interfered with by, for example, the withdrawal of treatment or by forced treatment. The state may seek to justify such measures as being 'for the protection of health' but cannot do so if the measures were merely to exercise physical control. Issues about the care and custody of children may also fall to be considered as being for the protection of health.

'for the protection of . . . morals'

Governments and Parliaments may wish to restrict personal behaviour on the grounds that it is immoral in itself or harmful to the person involved or harmful to others. Such restrictions on personal behaviour may be found in respect, for example, of sexual behaviour or sexual orientation.

'for the protection of the rights and freedoms of others'

This is a broad and inclusive category, which is often linked with other purposes when states are seeking to justify interferences with Article 8(1) rights. The 'rights and freedoms' are not just those secured in the Convention but the term is used more generally to include legal rights and other freedoms that the ECtHR recognises. Similarly, the right to private life under Article 8(1) is itself a 'right' which can be asserted against, for example, the claims of the media to publish or broadcast personally intrusive stories.

15.9.4 'Necessary in a democratic society'

cross reference
See Chapter 14, section 14.4.3 for general discussion.

By signing the Convention, the states agree that they will not interfere with the private lives of their population unless each and every individual interference meets the test of being 'necessary in a democratic society'. This involves courts in a judgment of proportionality and whether a fair balance has, in the detail of the case, been achieved between the various private and public interests involved.

15.10 Particular interferences

Article 8 has an important impact on many important aspects of social, economic and political life. Where there has been a direct interference by a public authority it must be justified in terms of Article 8(2). Where it is state inaction that is in issue, justification is in terms of the fair balance between maintaining the essence of Article 8 rights and the competing individual and collective interests that are at stake.

In the last part of this chapter a number of topics will be discussed in relation to justification directly under the Convention or, for UK law, the HRA.

15.10.1 Environmental law

ECHR

Environmental hazards or state policies to protect the environment can raise issues under Article 8 (see section 15.8).

Where, for example, pollution affects private and family life then a state's failure to enforce its own anti-pollution laws may mean a violation of Article 8 (as in *López Ostra* v *Spain* (1995) 20 EHRR 277, section 15.8). However, where an interference comes as a consequence of a carefully conceived, lawful regulatory regime, the ECtHR may be persuaded that a fair balance has been achieved.

In *Hatton* v *United Kingdom* (2003) 37 EHRR 28, a Grand Chamber reversed the Chamber's decision and held that the night flying regulations at Heathrow were proportionate interferences with the private and family life of the applicants and in the interests of the economic well-being of the country.

In *Hatton*, the Court gave considerable weight to the fact that noise pollution from night flying at Heathrow Airport served the economic interests of the nation, a legitimate purpose allowed under Article 8(2). Such a purpose is, of course, capable of supporting the claims of most industrial and commercial polluters. The concern is that decisions such as *Hatton* seriously weaken the environmental protection allowed under the Convention. *Fadeyeva* v *Russia* (section 15.8), however, may indicate that the Court is still prepared to find important environmental protection in the Convention for the worst cases.

HRA

Environmental issues under Article 8 have arisen in a number of contexts. For example:

- Noise pollution was considered in *Dennis* v *Ministry of Defence* [2003] EWHC 793: very loud aircraft noise from a nearby RAF base interfered with D's enjoyment of his home. The High Court held that any fair balance of D's rights under Article 8(1) with the public interest in an effective air force, could only be achieved on the basis of (considerable) financial compensation.

- In *Marcic* v *Thames Water* [2003] UKHL 66, M's home and garden were repeatedly flooded and affected by sewage discharge. The cause was pipes which needed to be replaced. The water company, acting under a statutory scheme, had a system of priorities for replacing pipes and M was a low priority. The House of Lords held that the statutory scheme was a fair balance between the different interests. (*Hatton*, discussed earlier in this section, was followed).

15.10.2 **Surveillance**

Surveillance and other forms of secret investigation engage Article 8(1) (see section 15.4.8).

ECHR

From its earliest cases the ECtHR has accepted that states may conduct secret surveillance (*Klass* v *Federal Republic of Germany* (1979–80) 2 EHRR 214). The surveillance must be strictly necessary to protect democratic institutions from threats to national security (as in *Klass*) but can also be used for the prevention of crime (e.g. *Valenzuela Contreras* v *Spain* (1999) 28 ECHR 483). For example, in *Erdem* v *Germany* (2002) 35 EHRR 15, the ECtHR accepted that the monitoring of the correspondence of a terrorist suspect was for the legitimate purpose of protecting national security (para 60).

The Court stressed the need for proper legal regulation of surveillance and of effective review.

case close-up

***Malone v United Kingdom* (1985) 7 EHRR 14**

M was convicted of a criminal offence and challenged the use of evidence against him which had been obtained by phone tapping. Under English law at the time, authority for the police to tap telephones was based on a warrant issued by the Home Secretary. The effectiveness of the warrant was recognised in various Acts of Parliament. The warrant itself, however, was issued by the Home Secretary on the basis of unwritten, common law powers whose lawfulness under national law was only expressly established after M took his challenge to the English courts. The ECtHR held that there had been a violation of Article 8, because the tapping had not been in accordance with the law.

The Court reasserted the basic requirements of legality (national lawfulness, accessibility and foreseeability: see Chapter 6, section 6.2) but noted the importance of context. Laws on surveillance did not aim to restrict the behaviour of individuals but, rather, to regulate the behaviour of officials. Legal 'forseeability' did not mean that a person is entitled to know when his or her phone was likely to be tapped. But, surveillance, by its secrecy, means that there is a serious risk of arbitrary actions by officials. In this context 'in accordance with the law' means that the law must be

> sufficiently clear in its terms to give citizens an adequate indication as to the circumstances in which and the conditions on which public authorities are empowered to resort to this secret and potentially dangerous interference with the right to respect for private life and correspondence.
>
> (*Malone* v *United Kingdom*, para 67)

Fear of arbitrariness means there need to be safeguards against abuse. In particular, there needs to be effective review of surveillance decisions by a judicial-type body which is independent, impartial and based on proper procedures. In *Valenzuela Contreras* v *Spain* (1999) 28 EHRR 483 the Court suggested that the national laws permitting surveillance should at least identify

- the categories of people who might be subject to surveillance (e.g. those suspected of spying or terrorism);
- the criminal offences for the prosecution of which surveillance might be used,
- time limits on any particular authorisation,
- the procedures for reporting the results of surveillance,
- the uses that can be made of surveillance information, and
- provision for the destruction of such information.

further study

Other leading cases on surveillance include:

- *Kruslin* v *France* (1990) 12 EHRR 547
- *Halford* v *United Kingdom* (1997) 24 EHRR 523
- *Kopp* v *Switzerland* (1999) 27 EHRR 91

HRA

Following *Malone* and other cases, statutory regulation of surveillance was introduced. It is now found in statutes such as the Regulation of Investigatory Powers Act 2000 (interception of communications) and both the Police Act 1997 and the Intelligence Services Act 1994, which deal with other forms of surveillance which would, without a warrant, be unlawful. These provisions are supplemented by Codes of Practice. A tribunal, the Investigatory Powers Tribunal, provides a degree of judicial supervision. In *Kennedy* v *United Kingdom* (2011) 52 EHRR 4, the ECtHR considered significant aspects of the legal, administrative and judicial system governing surveillance in the UK and found, overall, that it was compatible with Article 8.

In *R* v *H* [2004] UKHL 3, the House of Lords has adopted the general principle, in *Klass* above, that properly regulated surveillance is not itself a breach of Article 8 (para 23). There have been a number of cases in which there has been a violation of Article 8 by the police when surveillance has taken place without proper authorisation. In such a circumstance, the interference with Article 8(1) is not in accordance with the law and cannot therefore be justified under Article 8(2). The question for the courts is whether the information obtained is admissible as evidence in a trial or whether it should be automatically excluded under section 78 PACE (see Chapter 12, section 12.1.1). The answer is that the law does not require the automatic exclusion of such evidence.

cross reference
See Chapter 5, section 5.5 for remedies under the HRA.

Does this answer leave Article 8 largely ineffective in the context of police surveillance? The remedies, such as they are, should be from the police or other authorities who violate Article 8. A simple declaration of a violation may be enough; police disciplinary actions are also possible.

Journalists and others may undertake secret surveillance. Whilst intercepting communications is likely to be unlawful in English law, other forms of surveillance, like secret filming, will not necessarily be so unless it involves trespass or some other form of illegality. Where invasions of privacy are committed by the media, complaints to the appropriate regulator (Ofcom, for instance) may be appropriate.

In *Jones* v *Warwick University* [2003] EWCA Civ 151, the Court of Appeal accepted that secret filming by an employer's insurer aimed at testing an employee's claim to be unable to work, engaged Article 8(1). The invasion of privacy was by the employer's insurers, a private body. For the Court the issue was whether to admit the evidence. Was it justified in doing so, under Article 8(2)? On the one hand the secret filming was 'improper and not justified'; on the other hand the employee's behaviour was outrageous. Overall it was in the interests of justice to admit the evidence.

15.10.3 **Sexual life**

Laws may restrict forms of consensual sexual activity on 'moral' grounds. On such questions the ECtHR allows a wide margin of appreciation. This is now narrowed greatly regarding homosexual acts, but bans on other forms of sexual activity, such as sadomasochism, have been allowed.

In *Laskey, Jaggard and Brown* v *United Kingdom* (1997) 24 EHRR 39, convictions of men for participating in consensual sadomasochistic acts were held not to violate Article 8.

The situation is different where it is sexual identity rather than sexual acts that are in issue.

In *Smith and Grady* v *United Kingdom* (2000) 29 EHRR 493, the ECtHR accepted that a ban on homosexual men and women being in the armed forces was an interference in their private life done to maintain the efficiency of the armed forces. This was encompassed by 'the interests of national security' and 'the prevention of disorder' in Article 8(2) (see para 74). The Court went on to find that the interference was disproportionate and that there was a breach of Article 8.

KEY POINT Morally based restraints on activity are also in issue when the authorities seek to censor films, plays and DVDs. These are discussed in Chapter 17, section 17.12. There is a general argument concerning whether states should be allowed to suppress behaviour on the sufficient ground that it is immoral; this 'enforcement of morals' debate is discussed in Chapter 17, section 17.12 (Discussion Topic).

15.10.4 Abortion

As we have seen in Chapter 8, section 8.4.9, a foetus is not directly protected by Article 2. Article 2 does not define when 'life' begins. There is no legal, moral or scientific consensus in Europe on these matters. A wide margin of appreciation is to be allowed to the states (*Vo v France* (2005) 40 EHRR 12, paras 75–82 and, in particular paras 80 and 82). An absolute ban on abortion even when the mother's life was in danger, particularly in the early stages of pregnancy, could be incompatible with the right to life of the mother (para 75, endorsing an earlier Commission case); but allowing mothers to go abroad for terminations may satisfy this (see *A, B, C v Ireland*, section 15.10.4).

Abortion engages the mothers right to private life (*Tysiac v Poland* (2007) 45 EHRR 42, para 107). However, this does not mean that a woman has an unlimited 'right to choose' (*Brüggemann and Scheuten v Germany* (1977) 3 EHRR 244). Her private life is closely connected with the foetus and must be weighed against other competing rights and freedoms, including those of the foetus (see *A, B, C*, section 15.10.4, para 213). Therefore restrictions on abortion can be justified under Article 8(2).

323

case close-up

A, B, C v Ireland **(2011) 53 EHRR 13**

Ireland's constitution banned abortion unless it was necessary to protect the mother's life. Two women (whose lives were not in danger but who both had serious health and social problems) travelled to the UK for abortions and alleged the Irish ban on abortion had detrimental consequences for their subsequent care. They challenged the Irish law. The Grand Chamber, held that:

- The Irish ban on abortions for reasons of health and well-being was an interference with the women's private lives and needed justification. The Convention neither imposes a positive duty on states to allow women the right to choose, nor, on the other hand, does it give states an entirely free hand to restrict abortion.

- The ban was in accordance with the law.

- It served a moral purpose.

- On the issue of proportionality, of balancing the competing rights and freedoms, the Court has the final word. However, a wide margin of appreciation is allowed to the states. Even though most European states have more liberal laws than Ireland, this does not narrow the margin of appreciation. This is because proportionality involves weighing the interests of mother and foetus and there is no consensus on whether the latter counts as a life. The Irish people still retained a profound moral opposition to abortion and this was an important factor in the fair balance. There was no breach of Article 8.

Of great importance is that decisions about abortion should be taken in accordance with the law—on the basis of proper procedures rather than the whim of doctors (*Tysiac*, section 15.10.4, where a refusal to allow an abortion caused the mother to go blind). States have a positive duty to enshrine in accessible and foreseeable legal rules the abortion rights that women do have. The third applicant in *A, B, C* succeeded in showing a violation of Article 8. The Irish constitution allowed abortion to protect a mother's life but this provision had not been given specific enactment. Doctors and women were unable to be certain about what was legally permissible.

15.10.5 **Child care**

Under the Convention

States accept legal responsibilities to protect and care for children in need. In England and Wales local authorities have various powers under the Children Act 1989 to identify children in need and, by court order, assume parental responsibilities for them. Local authorities exercise a range of powers including removing a child from his or her parents under a 'care order'. The exercise of such powers engages the Article 8 rights of the children, the parents and others.

case close-up

Haase v Germany [2005] 40 EHRR 19

The applicants' children, one of which was newborn, were removed into care without a hearing and on the basis of what turned out to be flawed expert evidence. The ECtHR held that the removal failed the 'necessary in a democratic society' test and so violated Article 8.

Some general principles emerge from paras 82–94:

- Protection of children involves interferences with their private and family life which must be justified in terms of Article 8(2).

- Laws aiming at the protection of children are likely to give officials quite a wide discretion over how they act. Given the fact that the situations in which children may be harmed are impossible to predict in advance, such discretion is likely to be in accordance with the law (see *Eriksson v Sweden* (1990) 12 EHRR 183, paras 59–60).

- Care orders etc. can be necessary to protect the health and morals, and the rights and freedoms of children.

- A decision may be proportionate if based on the 'best interests' of the child.

- An international court must respect the decisions of the national authorities but it must be satisfied that the national authorities have acted for sufficient reasons and on the basis of proper procedures. The removal of a newborn child from his or her parents requires 'extra-ordinarily compelling' reasons.

further study

See also *P, C and S v United Kingdom* [2002] 35 EHRR 31, paras 113–138.

Under the HRA

The Children Act 1989 does not contain provisions that are necessarily incompatible with Article 8: see *Re V (A Child) (Care Proceedings: Human Rights Claims)* [2004] EWCA Civ 54. In particular, the court said, section 1(3) of the Act has a list of factors to be taken into account when identifying the best interests of the child. Following this list enables an authority to give proper weight to the competing Article 8 rights of the child and other parties (see para 8). Where a local authority makes a judgment in good faith about a child's best interests it is unlikely that an Article 8 challenge will succeed on the issue of the need for the order proposed (see, for example, *Re G* [2006] UKHL 43 in which the House of Lords assessed a child's best interests in a residency dispute without mentioning Article 8).

further study

In *Re S* [2002] UKHL 10, the House of Lords held that the relatively limited rights of parents under the Act did not necessarily conflict with their Article 8 rights. In *S v L* [2012] UKSC 30, the Supreme Court held that statutory rules allowing a court to dispense with parental consent to adoption were not incompatible with the parent's Convention rights.

Social workers and others have powers under the Act that not only can but must be exercised compatibly with Convention rights.

In *Langley* v *Liverpool CC* [2005] EWCA Civ 1173, an emergency protection order was obtained to protect children from their father who, though registered blind, persisted in driving. The police, exercising powers to assist social workers, forcibly removed one of the children after he had gone to bed. The Court of Appeal held the police action was unlawful and a breach of Article 8.

15.10.6 Protection of personal information

Disclosure of personal or confidential information about a person engages Article 8(1) and so must be justified under Article 8(2). Any system which involves the storing and release of information and which fails to allow adequate means for the information to be challenged for accuracy, will raise issues under Article 8(1).

In *Leander* v *Sweden* (1987) 9 EHRR 433, a system of security vetting for people working in a naval dockyard was accepted as a justified restriction on Article 8(1) rights.

Under the HRA, the protection of personal information under Article 8 has been significant in a number of areas.

Police records

Taking fingerprints and other samples is an interference with respect for private life. If it is done according to the procedures in the PACE and Codes of Practice, it is likely easily to be justified under Article 8(2). Retention raises other issues. These are discussed in Chapter 20, sections 20.6.1 and 20.6.2.

Health records

Disclosure of health records must be justified under Article 8(2). The ECtHR weighs a person's right to confidentiality in this area very highly—it is of fundamental importance not only to protect a person's private life but also general confidence in a willingness to use a country's health service (see *Z* v *Finland* (1998) 25 EHRR 371, para 95). Any interference can only be justified by weighty reasons.

case close-up

Ashworth Hospital Authority v MGN Ltd [2002] UKHL 29

The *Daily Mirror* published articles clearly based on the medical records of Ian Brady, a notorious murderer serving a life sentence in a secure mental hospital. The House of Lords considered that the right to medical confidentiality was one of the reasons (para 63) which outweighed freedom of the press and the principle that journalists should not be compelled to disclose their sources. The order that the newspaper disclose its source was confirmed.

The newspaper disclosed that its source was a freelance journalist. In subsequent proceedings, however, the Court of Appeal refused to order the freelance to disclose his original source. Given the passage of time and other factors and given the importance of press freedom under Article 10, the need for disclosure was no longer pressing; nevertheless the general principle of protecting medical records was strongly endorsed (*Mersey Care NHS Trust* v *Ackroyd (No 2)* [2007] EWCA Civ 101).

Disclosure of confidential information

Making public information about people can engage Article 8 rights. The courts must decide whether any interference is justified.

In *R (H)* v *A City Council* [2011] EWCA Civ 403, a married, disabled, couple (H and L) were active in a disability organisation and ran a company seeking contracts from public bodies. The local authority, without notice to H and L, informed the various charitable and public organisations with which they were involved that H faced trial for an alleged sex offence (for which he was latter acquitted), and that in the past, when applying for a job, he had failed to disclose a sex conviction. It was held that these disclosures breached H and L's substantive and procedural rights under both Article 8 and common law. The critical point in the fair balance was that H and L did not work with children.

This can be compared to *R (X)* v *Chief Constable of the West Midlands Police* [2004] EWCA Civ 1068. Here the Court of Appeal upheld a decision by the Chief Constable to communicate to a social work employment agency the fact that an applicant for employment had been charged with indecent exposure but acquitted. Section 115 of the Police Act 1997 required police to communicate any information they considered relevant to an employer who was considering employing a person for working with young people. The court accepted that section 115 was compatible with Article 8(2) and that the particular exercise of his powers by the Chief Constable was a proportionate exercise of those powers.

cross reference
See Chapter 9, section 9.8.1 for definition and legal grounds of extradition, deportation and removal.

15.10.7 **Deportation and Article 8**

We have seen that Convention rights, being applied in the UK, can prevent removals, deportations and extraditions if there is a real risk of death, torture or inhuman treatment in the receiving country (discussed in Chapter 9, section 9.8).

Likewise a real risk of a 'flagrant' denial of other rights in the receiving country should prevent a deportation or extradition, and this includes a risk that the person will be tried on the basis of evidence obtained by torture (discussed in Chapter 12, section 12.17).

Deportations can engage Article 8 rights. A distinction is drawn between 'foreign' and 'domestic' cases.

Foreign cases concern the conditions in the receiving country.

> **case close-up**
>
> ### R (Razgar) v Secretary of State for the Home Department [2004] UKHL 27
>
> R's application for asylum failed. He feared that, if removed to Germany and perhaps back to Iraq, his mental health would seriously deteriorate. The House of Lords, following Strasbourg principles (see *Bensaid* v *United Kingdom* (2001) 33 EHRR 10), held that R might have a claim to resist deportation under Article 8 even if the consequences were not so severe as to engage Article 3. The evidence should show that the denial of Article 8(1) rights will be flagrant (para 72). The Secretary of State had acted unlawfully in deciding that his Article 8 claim was hopeless. An immigration adjudicator might have found it justified.

'Domestic cases' concern the family ties that have been established in the deporting country.

> **case close-up**
>
> ### Üner v The Netherlands (2007) 45 EHRR 14
>
> A Turkish national was deported from the Netherlands as a consequence of his conviction for serious crimes. On account of his relationship with his partner and sons he alleged there would be a violation of his article 8 rights if he was deported.
>   A Grand Chamber
>
> - confirmed that states may control immigration, including by expelling aliens;
>
> - however, actions must be compatible with Convention rights and there are circumstances in which an expulsion (removal, extradition, deportation) can engage Article 8(1) and require justification under Article 8;
>
> - relevant criteria, which courts must consider in seeking a fair balance between the public interests served by immigration control and the interests of the person being removed, are listed (following *Boultif* v *Switzerland* (2001) 33 EHRR 50) at para 57 and 58. They include the length of time the applicant has been in the country; the seriousness of offences committed by the applicant; the applicant's family situation, such as the length of marriage, age of children, the seriousness of difficulties that the family may experience in the receiving country; the interests of children and the relative solidity of ties with the host and receiving country (para 60).

These principles have been followed and adapted by UK courts under the HRA.

> **case close-up**
>
> ### R (H) v Deputy Prosecutor of the Italian Republic [2012] UKSC 25
>
> Three individuals appealed against the decision to extradite them from the UK on the basis of a European arrest warrant. They claimed that extradition would have a serious effect on their family life.

The Supreme Court weighed the various interests (based on the *Boultif/Üner* criteria, above) and allowed one of the three appeals on the grounds of the very severe consequences for family life. The court emphasized:

- The weight to be given to the public interest might be different as between extradition (involving criminal punishment for serious crime) and deportation (the removal of undesirable aliens), but in all cases that weighing of interests was central to Article 8.

- Of particular importance were the rights of children. The Supreme Court building on *Üner* and other Strasbourg case law, and other sources such as the UN Convention on the Rights of the Child, held that the best interests of the children were 'a primary consideration'—very important but not 'the' primary or 'the paramount' consideration. They were, therefore, capable of being outweighed by the public interests involved in a deportation or extradition.

It is clear that these issues of removal, deportation or extradition involve a complex weighing of interests. In England and Wales this is to be done by the tribunal or court hearing an appeal. The tribunal should decide for itself, giving little deference to the authorities (*Huang* v *Secretary of State for the Home Department* [2007] UKHL 11).

15.10.8 **Privacy and the media**

A person's desire for privacy may conflict with the desire of the media to publish stories about them. Such conflicts involve the balancing of the person's rights under Article 8 and the media's rights to freedom of expression under Article 10. This issue is explored in Chapter 22.

15.10.9 **Prisoners**

Prisoners retain their Convention rights (lawful imprisonment is consistent with Article 5). Prisoner's rights under Article 8 are in issue in a number of different contexts. They are discussed in Chapter 21.

Summary

- Article 8 requires states to respect people's private life, family life, home and correspondence.

- These terms (private life etc.) are given a wide and inclusive definition.

- States may have positive duties to ensure that Article 8 rights are effective.

- There are many circumstances in which it is reasonable and in the public interest for private life etc. to be interfered with.

- Article 8 allows such interferences but only if they are by a public authority and only if they are lawful (as that term is understood by the Convention), necessary in a democratic society (a proportionate means of achieving a pressing social need) and only for one or more of the purposes listed in Article 8(2).

Questions

For suggested approaches, please visit the Online Resource Centre.

1 What is meant by 'private life' in the context of Article 8? Do you agree that, as developed by the ECtHR, the term is imprecise and there is a lack of certainty over what is encompassed by it?

2 What approach should national courts take in deciding an Article 8 case? Is it necessary to distinguish between cases involving direct interferences by public authorities and alleged failures of positive duties by states?

 # Further reading

LEADING TEXTS ON ARTICLE 8

Amos, M. (see Preface) Chapters 11–13

Harris, D. et al (eds), *Harris, O'Boyle and Warbrick: Law of the ECHR* 2nd edn (2009) Oxford: OUP, Chapters 8 and 9 (by Warbrick and Kilkelly)

Lester, A., Pannick, D. and Herberg, J. (see Preface) Chapter 4, Article 8

Moreham, N. 'The Right to Respect for Private Life in the European Convention on Human Rights: A Re-examination' [2008] 1 *EHRLR* 44–79

Maciolek, N. 'Defining Privacy and the European Court of Human Rights: Assessing the Court's Application of Article 8(1)' (2009) 15 *UCL Juris Rev* 94–118

Article 9: freedom of thought, conscience and religion

Chapter overview

- The importance of religious belief and the 'neutral' role of the state.
- The absolute protection of a person's religious, moral and other beliefs.
- 'Manifestations' of religious belief and the exclusive conditions under which they can be lawfully interfered with.
- The importance of Article 9 regarding a range of important questions such as the law on blasphemy and restrictions on religious dress.

Article 9   Freedom of thought, conscience and religion

(1) Everyone has the right to freedom of thought, conscience and religion; this right includes freedom to change his religion or belief and freedom, either alone or in community with others and in public or private, to manifest his religion or belief, in worship, teaching, practice and observance.

(2) Freedom to manifest one's religion or beliefs shall be subject only to such limitations as are prescribed by law and are necessary in a democratic society in the interests of public safety, for the protection of public order, health or morals, or for the protection of the rights and freedoms of others.

Introduction

A hallmark of a totalitarian state is its attempt to control the thoughts, beliefs and ideas of its citizens and to insist that only officially sanctioned ideas and attitudes are allowed. Mind control may be attempted by, for example, endless propaganda or by imposing a particular curriculum on schools. More usually, the totalitarian state simply closes down the places of worship, the societies, the university departments, the trade unions, etc. where unwelcome ideas and beliefs are expressed. Article 9 is one of the articles which embodies the 'pluralism' inherent in the Convention: states are not allowed to enforce particular ideologies or religions on their population; these are matters for individuals and the state must accept, tolerate and protect a plurality of beliefs.

The assertion of beliefs in public ('manifestations of belief') can interfere with the rights and freedoms of others or with important public interests. In the early years of the twenty-first century there is, perhaps, a sense that, for many, religion is ceasing to be a matter of a private relationship with God, albeit mediated by a church, and is, in some circumstances, being 'politicised'. Matters of the school science curriculum, sex education, abortion, the performance of plays, the dress of women, the right to vote and a host of other issues are matters that have involved the exercise of political and social power by religious groups. Religion, for many, must be asserted publicly and powerfully, involving adjustments to their lives by others. In this context we can expect Article 9 to have an increasing emphasis in the modern world.

16.1   **General**

16.1.1 **The structure of Article 9**

Article 9(1) establishes:

- A general right to freedom of 'thought, conscience and religion' which cannot be restricted by the state.

- A right to 'manifest' (demonstrate) religion or belief in 'worship, teaching, practice and observance'. The Convention recognises that there can be circumstances in which it is reasonable to restrict the manifestation of a belief and these circumstances are identified, in abstract terms, in the second paragraph, Article 9(2).

The job of a court dealing with an Article 9 issue is:

- To decide whether there has been an interference, for which the state is responsible, which either restricts a person in holding religious beliefs or which restricts the manifestation of belief.

- If it is a restriction on the holding of belief then the restriction is a violation of Article 9(1). There is no question of justification.

- If it is a restriction on a manifestation of belief, the court must decide whether the state has demonstrated that the restriction is justified under the terms of Article 9(2): it has been imposed on the basis of 'law', it is for one of the purposes listed in Article 9(2) and that the particular restriction was 'necessary in a democratic society'.

Thus the approach to Article 9 is similar to that to Articles 8, 10 and 11.

cross reference

The common features of Articles 8, 9, 10 and 11 have been introduced in Chapter 14.

further study

For a summary of the general principles applicable to Article 9, see *Church of Bessarabia* v *Moldova* (2002) 35 EHRR 13, paras 101–119.

KEY POINT Under Article 34 of the European Convention on Human Rights (ECHR), and therefore section 7 of the Human Rights Act 1998 (HRA), a church or other religious organisation can bring actions in order to protect the Article 9 rights of its believers (*Church of Bessarabia* v *Moldova* (2002) 35 EHRR 13, para 101).

16.1.2 **Links with other rights**

Article 9 can often be invoked in tandem with other Convention rights which also help to secure freedom of religion and belief. Thus, Article 10 can be engaged where there are restrictions on religious expression, Article 11 may be relevant to restrictions on religious organisations and associations and Article 8 can be involved if restrictions on religion interfere with a person's private life. Where the issue centres on manifestations of religion, Article 9 is likely to be the Court's focus, with the other articles being relevant only if they raise serious and distinct issues.

cross reference

Article 2 of the First Protocol is the topic of Chapter 24.

The most important other right relevant to freedom of belief is Article 2 of the First Protocol. This gives a right to parents (not to anyone else) that the education of their children shall be 'in conformity with their own religious and philosophical convictions'. A restriction on a manifestation of religion that is justified under Article 9(1) is likely to be also compatible with Article 2 of the First Protocol. This is because Article 2 is not an absolute right: it, too, is subject to reasonable restrictions.

16.1.3 **Section 13 HRA**

During its passage through Parliament, the Human Rights Bill came under criticism from religious groups who feared that the Act would impose unreasonable restraints on their freedom to conduct their affairs in the ways that enabled them to preserve their religious and moral ethos. For example, there was a concern the Act would make it hard to employ only people with a sufficient degree of religious belief or acceptable moral rectitude. Though these fears were probably groundless, the government conceded a special provision in the Act for the protection of religion.

Section 13   Freedom of Thought, Conscience and Religion

(1)   If a court's determination of any question arising under this Act might affect the exercise by a religious organisation (itself or its members collectively) of the Convention right to freedom of thought, conscience and religion, it must have particular regard to the importance of that right.

(2)   In this section 'court' includes a tribunal.

Whether this provision has any significance at all, or was just a sop to religious groups when the bill was going through Parliament, is debatable. It requires no more of a court than it is already required to do—to consider the proper significance of Article 9 in the situation before it. It does not give Article 9 any priority or greater weight or importance in respect of other rights and freedoms.

16.2   Article 9(1): the unrestrictable right to thought, conscience and religion

The right to freedom of thought, conscience and religion, including the right to change religion, cannot be restricted under the terms of the Convention (though a derogation is possible under Article 15 (see Chapter 7, section 7.2). Manifestations of religion or belief, on the other hand, can be restricted if the state can show it was necessary so to do under the terms of Article 9(2). It can be important, therefore, to distinguish between actions which are a necessary consequence of having a belief and actions which involve the manifestation of that belief. Restrictions on the former cannot be allowed. Thus, for example, restrictions on movement which prevent a person getting to his place of worship may be a simple breach of Article 9 without there being any need to consider whether the restriction was justified.

16.2.1   The importance of religion and belief

The great importance of freedom of thought, conscience and religion is recognised by the European Court of Human Rights (ECtHR).

> [Freedom of thought, conscience and religion] is, in its religious dimension, one of the most vital elements that go to make up the identity of believers and their conception of life, but it is also a precious asset for atheists, agnostics, sceptics and the unconcerned. The pluralism indissociable from a democratic society, which has been dearly won over the centuries, depends on it.
>
> (*Kokkinakis* v *Greece* (1994) 17 EHRR 397)

In *R (Williamson)* v *Secretary of State for Education and Employment* [2005] UKHL 15, the House of Lords called beliefs, religious or not, 'part of the humanity of every individual. They are an integral part of his personality and individuality' (para 15, per Lord Nicholls—the case is discussed later in the chapter). Time and again the ECtHR emphasises that the Convention acknowledges only one general form of government: a plural and liberal democracy. All states must support, through their laws, the diversity of people's religious, moral and political views and recognise that, in any society, people will hold many different views of how best to live and what to believe. Article 9 is clearly central to this.

16.2.2 'Thought, conscience and religion'

Religion

Religion includes the major, organised, world religions such as Buddhism, Christianity, Hinduism, Islam, Judaism and Sikhism, and the various traditions, denominations and sects that make up their parts. Other beliefs which claim, in one way or another, to be 'religious' have also been recognised. Druid ceremony, for example, was recognised by the Commission as being religious in nature in *Arthur Pendragon* v *United Kingdom* App 31416/96, admissibility decision of 19 October 1998. Under the HRA, English courts have accepted that Rastafarianism is a religion (*R* v *Taylor* [2001] EWCA Civ 2263). There is no need for an abstract discussion of the nature of religion by the Court since if a matter is not religious it is likely, nevertheless, to be a 'belief' and so enjoy the same protection.

Thought and conscience, non-religious beliefs

Article 9 is not confined to religion. Freedom of belief is a 'precious asset' for atheists (who deny the existence of God), agnostics (who accept the possibility of the non-existence of God) and sceptics (who doubt the claims of religion). Belief is also defined widely to include specific social and moral ideas that have direct consequences for people's actions. Pacifism (*Arrowsmith* v *United Kingdom* (1981) 3 EHRR 218) and 'vegetarianism and temperance' (*Williamson* (section 16.4.5)) have been accepted as beliefs for the purposes of Article 9. This approach was followed in *Grainger* v *Nicolson* [2010] ICR 360 (paras 20–31), where Article 9 jurisprudence was followed in holding that a belief in climate change could be a 'philosophical belief' (for the purposes of domestic law on discrimination) if genuinely held as a serious belief, not a mere opinion, and worthy of respect in a democratic society (see Evaluation of beliefs, section 16.3).

16.2.3 The role of the state

Neutrality

Article 9 presupposes a pluralist, liberal democracy. In that context the role of the state is to be neutral, not to promote one religion over another, and not to act on the basis that a particular belief is false or lacks credibility or is in some way bad.

In *Hasan* v *Bulgaria* (2002) 34 EHRR 55, the ECtHR held that there was a violation of Article 9 when the Bulgarian government intervened in a dispute between Bulgarian Muslims over who should be their national leader in post-Communist Bulgaria. The state had ceased to be neutral over a religious matter (see, in particular, para 78).

KEY POINT When it comes to the manifestation of belief, however, the state may be entitled to form of judgment about the content of the belief. This point is addressed below.

Established religion

Article 9 does not forbid state or **established** religions.

establishment

An established religion is one that has been recognised by law as, in some sense, the religion of the state. The Church of England is the established religion in the UK. Some states, such as the USA, are constitutionally banned from establishing a religion. The old Reformation principle *cuius regio, cius religio* (whose rule, his religion) by which the religion of the ruler was imposed on the people, can no longer apply. Any attempt to impose religion on the population would violate the Convention.

But establishment does not justify propaganda through the education system (see Chapter 24 on the right to education). Nor can adherence to a particular religion or doctrine be a requirement of public office.

In *Buscarini* v *San Marino* (2000) 30 EHRR 208, the ECtHR found that Article 9 was violated when Parliamentarians were required to take a religious oath before taking their seats.

discussion topic

In the United Kingdom, the monarch, by law, must not be a Roman Catholic. Does this violate Article 9?

Legal recognition

If a state refuses or unreasonably delays the legal recognition of a religious group (so that it cannot enjoy legal protection of its assets and advantages such as tax breaks), the approach of the ECtHR is to consider the matter under Article 9 with due regard to Article 11 (freedom of association). An unjustified refusal or delay may violate either Article read in the light of the other; e.g. *Moscow Branch of the Salvation Army* v *Russia* (2007) 44 EHRR 46 (violation of Article 11); *Religionsgemeinschaft der Zeugen Jehovas* v *Austria* (2009) 48 EHRR 17 (violation of Article 9).

Positive duties

States may have positive duties under Article 9 to protect believers, particularly religious believers, from the intolerance, contempt and hatred of others (see *97 Members of the Gldani Congregation of Jehovah's Witnesses* v *Georgia* (2008) 46 EHRR 30. Here the indifference of the authorities in the face of attacks on Jehovah Witnesses was a breach of Article 9).

16.2.4 Freedom to change religion

Article 9 provides an 'absolute' right (a right that cannot be restricted in terms of Article 9(2)), to change religion and beliefs. States cannot have laws which compel people to have particular beliefs or which punish a person who renounces beliefs. Nor can atheism or agnosticism be crimes. Islamic states (of which there are none in Europe) can have difficulties with this provision as found in international law since 'apostasy' (the renunciation of a particular religion) may be contrary to some of the traditions on which Islamic law is based and may, indeed, invite the death penalty. However, there is no unanimity by Islamic jurists on the point.

further study

For discussion, see Baderin, M. *International Human Rights and Islamic Law* (2003) Oxford: OUP, Chapter 4, pp 123–125.

16.3 Article 9(1): the manifestation of religion

Under Article 9 a person has the right to manifest his or her religion or belief. This can be done 'alone or in community with others and in public or private'. Manifestation can be 'in worship, teaching, practice or observance'. A clear instance of this is where the state prevents people worshipping by, for example, refusing to give the necessary legal recognition to a religious organisation, as in *Church of Bessarabia* v *Moldova* (2002) 35 EHRR 13.

Definition and examples of manifestations of belief

Manifestation goes further than just acts of worship. It includes actions which are 'intimately linked' to the belief. The action must be a direct expression of the belief, though it need not be a definite, universally acknowledged, requirement. Examples of manifestations of belief are

- forms of dress (such as the Islamic headscarf in *Leyla Sahin* v *Turkey* (2007) 44 EHRR 5);
- dietary requirements (such as ritual slaughter of animals as required by Judaism in *Cha'are Shalom Ve Tsedek* v *France* App 27417/95, judgment of 27 June 2000);
- views on school punishment, including corporal punishment (such as in ECHR case *Campbell and Cosans* v *UK* (1982) 4 EHRR 293 and the HRA case *R (Williamson)* v *Secretary of State for Education and Employment* [2005] UKHL 15, see section 16.4.5).

English courts have considered the matter under the HRA. For example:

- Burial in a cemetery recognised by the religion was treated as a manifestation of belief (the disinterment of a Jew, buried in a Christian cemetery at the behest of his Christian wife (now deceased), to be reinterred in a Jewish cemetery in accordance with the wishes of his Jewish relatives), *Re Durrington Cemetery* [2001] Fam 33.

On the other hand:

- A conscientious objector who refused to return to duty was not manifesting his belief (see *Khan* v *RAF Summary Appeal Court* [2004] EWHC 2230 (Admin); see further, section 16.4.6).

Religious or other motivation is not sufficient

An action that is merely motivated by religious belief or individual conscience is not a manifestation of that belief (see *Arrowsmith* v *United Kingdom* (1981) 3 EHRR 218, para 71).

The following are examples of conduct motivated by a religious or other belief that the Strasbourg authorities (Court or Commission of Human Rights) have held not to be manifestations of religious belief, protected by Article 9, but actions merely motivated by religious belief for which the Article gives no protection.

- the distribution of pacifist leaflets to soldiers (*Arrowsmith*, section 16.2.2),
- refusing to sell contraceptives that had been prescribed to women (*Pichon and Sajous* v *France* App 49853/99, admissibility decision of 2 October 2001),
- assisting in another's suicide (as in *Pretty* v *United Kingdom* (2002) 35 EHRR 1, para 82),
- commercial advertising to promote a belief (as in *X and Church of Scientology* v *Sweden* [1979] ECC 511, para 14).

Article 9 does not therefore protect the right of a person to behave in public situations in a manner dictated by religious belief.

> Article 9 does not always guarantee a right to behave in a manner governed by religious belief…and does not confer on people who do so the right to disregard rules that have proved to be justified.
>
> (*Leyla Sahin* v *Turkey*, above, para 121)

The right to 'manifest belief' does not, for example, mean that a person can use his or her religious beliefs as a defence for what would otherwise be a criminal offence (such as drugs offences). Nor does a religious motivation entitle a person to avoid duties and obligations that they have voluntarily accepted or that have been embodied in rules and practices (e.g. school rules) that are justified and proportionate.

Under the HRA these principles have been confirmed by the House of Lords in *R (Williamson)* v *Secretary of State for Education and Employment* [2005] UKHL 15 (see section 16.4.5) and followed in *R (Boughton)* v *Her Majesty's Treasury* [2006] EWCA Civ 504. Here the Court of Appeal (following clear Strasbourg authority) rejected a claim by a group of tax payers that the Treasury had a duty, based on Article 9, to set up a fund into which those with conscientious objections to defence spending could pay their taxes.

KEY POINT Actions motivated by political, religious or other belief, though not protected by Article 9, may come within the terms of Article 10 (freedom of expression) or Article 11 (freedom of assembly and association).

Evaluation of beliefs

What about the manifestation of extreme or utterly eccentric beliefs, religious or otherwise? In some of its statements the ECtHR has suggested that, regarding manifestations of belief, states may depart from the position of neutrality. In *Campbell and Cosans* v *United Kingdom* (1982) 4 EHRR 293, the ECtHR suggested that Convention protection might be confined to 'views which attained a certain level of cogency, seriousness, cohesion and importance' and to 'convictions as are worthy of respect in a "democratic society"…and are not incompatible with human dignity'. *Campbell and Cosans* involved Article 2 of the First Protocol, which requires states to respect the 'religious and philosophical convictions' of parents in educational provision (see Chapter 24). Nevertheless, the Court's view refers to the basic values of the Convention and might be thought to extend to Article 9.

This view appears to give state officials and courts the power to make controversial judgments about which beliefs are worthy or not of respect in a democracy. In the HRA case *Williamson* (see section 16.4.5), Lord Walker found the prospect 'alarming', arguing that courts are not equipped to evaluate religious and other beliefs in this way and that the ECtHR begged too many questions. In fact, there are few, if any, cases in which the Court has evaluated the worth of a belief; and there are many cases in which it has asserted the need for state neutrality on matters of belief.

Article 9(2): restrictions on the manifestation of religion or belief

Genuine manifestations of religion or belief, such as those given above, can be restricted by the state under the terms of Article 9(2). The right to have such beliefs and the right to change religion cannot be restricted. Restrictions on manifestations of religion may be necessary to protect a plural, democratic society in which peoples of different religions, beliefs and interests live together.

> in democratic societies, in which several freedoms coexist within one and the same population, it may be necessary to place restrictions on this freedom in order to reconcile the interests of the various groups and ensure that everyone's beliefs are respected.
>
> (*Kokkinakis* v *Greece* (1994) 17 EHRR 397, para 33)

The second paragraph to Article 9 has the same structure as that of Articles 8, 10 and 11.

16.4.1 **The existence of an interference**

If a state takes actions which interfere with the manifestation of a belief, then possible justification under Article 9(2) is relevant. This must be distinguished from the situations in which Article 9(2) is not relevant such as

- where states interfere with or fail to secure the general right to freedom of thought, conscience and religion (there will be an unjustifiable violation of Article 9(1));
- where the state interferes with an action which is motivated by religion but which is not a manifestation of it (Article 9 is not engaged at all).

16.4.2 **'Prescribed by law'**

cross reference
The Convention concept of 'law' is discussed in Chapter 6, section 6.2.

The interference imposed on the manifestation of a belief must meet the Convention test of lawfulness: the interference must not only be based on a provision of national law but that provision must be 'accessible' and 'foreseeable' and compatible with the rule of law.

In *Kokkinakis* v *Greece* (1994) 17 EHRR 397, the ECtHR accepted that the Greek laws on proselytism (seeking converts), despite the general way they were expressed, were sufficiently precise and developed by a body of known and accessible case law to satisfy the Convention requirements.

16.4.3 **The restriction is for a legitimate purpose**

Restrictions by the state of a manifestation of religion or belief can only be for one of the purposes listed in the second paragraph of Article 9, and not, as Article 18 makes clear, for any other purpose. The purposes in Article 9(2) (public safety, public order, health, morals, or the rights and freedoms of others) are the same as in Article 18 of the International Covenant on Civil and Political Rights (ICCPR). It is not possible to argue that manifestations of religion can be restricted in order to advance the economic interests of society (as is possible for restricting the right to private life) or to protect national security (as is possible for justifying restrictions under Articles 8, 10 and 11) nor to protect the reputations of others (as can justify a restriction on freedom of expression under Article 10). In practice it is normally not difficult for the state to relate its reasons for restriction to one of the listed purposes. In *Kokkinakis* v *Greece* (1994) 17 EHRR 397, for example, the ECtHR accepted that one of the 'rights of others' was the right to be free of attempts by others at conversion, at least in so far as this involved 'immoral or deceitful means' (see para 46).

16.4.4 'Necessary in a democratic society'

A restriction on the manifestation of religion must also be 'necessary in a democratic society', and this is the issue on which much of the case law depends. The general approach is identified by the ECtHR in *Kokkinakis* v *Greece*.

> The Court has consistently held that a certain margin of appreciation is to be left to the Contracting States in assessing the existence and extent of the necessity of an interference, but this margin is subject to European supervision, embracing both the legislation and the decisions applying it, even those given by an independent court. The Court's task is to determine whether the measures taken at national level were justified in principle and proportionate. (para 47)

Essentially a court (including a national court such as in the United Kingdom under the HRA) must examine

- whether the state's actions were justified in general terms (e.g. that the state had sufficiently and properly worked through reasons for laws restricting manifestations of religious or other belief and that it was an option that the state could reasonably adopt in its circumstances); and
- whether the application of the law in the particular case represented a 'fair balance' (was 'proportionate') between the freedom of the individual and the benefit to others or to society generally that the restricting law aimed to achieve.

case close-up

Surayanda v *The Welsh Ministers* [2007] EWCA Civ 893

S represented a Hindu community for whom the killing of cows was akin to killing a human being. It was held that Welsh Ministers were entitled to order the slaughter of Shambo, the community's bullock, as part of a campaign to prevent the spread of bovine tuberculosis. The minister's decision not to make an exception under Article 9(1) was justified under Article 9(2).

16.4.5 Corporal punishment in schools

cross reference
See also Chapter 24, section 24.4.1, on Article 2 of the First Protocol.

Parental views about school discipline, including the use or non-use of corporal punishment ('beating' or 'smacking', depending on your views), engage Convention rights in at least two ways: as a manifestation of a belief that, parents argue, should be protected by Article 9, and as a 'religious or philosophical conviction' that, under Article 2 of the First Protocol, should be respected by the state in the education of children.

The issue has come before the House of Lords under the HRA.

case close-up

R (Williamson) v *Secretary of State for Education and Employment* [2005] UKHL 15

Parents and teachers in Christian schools challenged the ban on corporal punishment in all schools, state or independent, by section 548 of the Education Act 1996. They alleged that their rights under Article 9 (as well as Article 2 of the First Protocol) had been violated. The House of Lords held that there had been an interference with the manifestation by the parents of their beliefs. It was, therefore, necessary to consider whether the interference was justified under Article 9(2). They held that the interference was prescribed by law (it was found in a clear statutory rule). It was for a legitimate purpose: the rights of others, in particular the rights of children to protection. Finally, it was necessary in a democratic society: states had a wide margin of appreciation and a ban on corporal punishment was an appropriate way of achieving this and one which a legislature was entitled to choose.

Corporal punishment has also been in issue in respect of Article 3, see Chapter 9, section 9.6.1; school cases include *Costello-Roberts* v *United Kingdom* (1995) 19 EHRR 112; *Warwick* v *United Kingdom* App 9471/81, Commission Report of 18 July 1986 and *Y* v *United Kingdom* (1994) 17 EHRR 238.

16.4.6 Conscientious objection

Many countries in the world, including in Europe, have military conscription (this ended in the United Kingdom in the 1960s). Many, but not all, recognise a right of conscientious objection. This usually requires an objector to perform substitute social service and authorises punishment if the objector refuses. It is much rarer for a society to recognise a right to conscientious objection in the full sense of allowing a person, on grounds of conscience, to avoid military or substitute social service altogether without punishment. Similarly, it is quite common for conscientious objection to be recognised in respect of military service generally but not in respect of particular wars and causes.

The ECtHR's long-standing view was that Article 9 did not provide a right of conscientious objection to military service or to substitute social service (see *Grandrath* v *Germany* (1967) 10 YB 626, 627 and other cases). Article 9 was read in the light of Article 4(3)(b), which expressly exempts both normal military conscription and alternative, substitute, forms of social service, from the ban on forced or compulsory labour (and does not require states to permit conscientious objection).

However, there is a clear tendency in Europe to phase out conscription and permit conscientious objection. Likewise there has been a strong movement towards recognising a right to conscientious objection at the international and European level. In particular, the EU's Charter of Fundamental Rights explicitly recognises conscientious objection (Article 10).

In response to such developments, the ECtHR, still unwilling to separate Article 9 from Article 4, had sought to protect conscientious objection indirectly. In *Thlimmenos* v *Greece* (2001) 31 EHRR 15, for example, the treatment of a conscientious objector was dealt with as discrimination in violation of Article 14 taken with Article 9. The discriminatory action needed to be merely in the 'ambit' of Article 9 (which was easy to show); there was no need to show there had been a breach—which the court refused to consider.

As late as 2003, however, the House of Lords in the United Kingdom held that there was not yet established an internationally recognised human right to conscientious objection (*Sepet* v *Secretary of State for the Home Department* [2003] UKHL 15).

The ECtHR has now shifted its position.

Bayatyan v Armenia (2012) 54 EHRR 15

The applicant was a Jehovah's Witness who declined, for conscientious reasons, to do compulsory military service. He was sentenced to two-and-a-half years in prison. A Grand Chamber held that there had been a violation of Article 9.

• Because of international developments favouring conscientious objection and phasing out of conscription, Article 9 should no longer be limited in its application by reading it in conjunction with Article 4(3)(b).

- Although Article 9 does not expressly mention conscientious objection, opposition to military service motivated by a 'serious and insurmountable conflict between the obligation to serve in the army and a person's conscience or his deeply and genuinely held religious beliefs' could come within the protection of Article 9.

- Whether there has been a violation will depend on justification under Article 9(2), in particular proportionality.

- Because of European developments, the margin of appreciation for states is limited.

- In the circumstances of the case the ban was disproportionate.

It is important to stress that *Bayatyan* simply makes it possible for Article 9 to apply to conscientious objectors; the question of justification remains.

case close-up

R v *Lyons* [2011] EWCA Crim 2808, Courts-Martial Appeal Court

L voluntarily joined the Royal Navy. He formed the view that UK involvement in Afghanistan was morally wrong. He refused to obey orders to be trained in order to be sent there. He was court-martialled and convicted. Following *Bayatyan* the Courts-Martial Appeal Court held:

- Article 9 could apply to volunteers as well as conscripts.

- Nevertheless, being a volunteer would affect the balancing exercise under Article 9(2).

- Nothing in Article 9 requires a conscientious objector to be immediately removed from duty.

- The Navy's procedures meant that all the issues under Article 9(2) were properly considered. There was no violation.

16.4.7 **Dismissal and discrimination law**

cross reference

UK discrimination law is summarised in Chapter 7, section 7.1.1.

The UK has an extensive body of anti-discrimination law. This is now based on EU law and embodied in the Equality Act 2010 and regulations made under it. Amongst other things it makes discrimination, on a wide range of grounds, unlawful in respect of employment and the provision of services.

Under the HRA, of course, such legislation must be interpreted compatibly with Convention rights and, likewise, public authorities, with duties under the law, must act compatibly.

The application of discrimination law can lead to claims that rights protected by Article 9 have been violated. Employees or office holders may be dismissed for refusing to work on their Sabbath or to do duties that they think are otherwise inconsistent with their religious beliefs. The Convention, and therefore the HRA, gives them little support.

Persons who voluntarily accept employment or an office (such as being a magistrate) that cannot always be exercised in a manner consistent with their beliefs will find that Article 9 will generally not accord them a right of conscientious objection—so long as they remain free

case close-up

Islington LBC v *Ladele* [2009] EWCA Civ 1357

L was a registrar of births, marriages and deaths who was disciplined by her employer for refusing, on grounds of religious belief, to conduct civil partnerships between persons of the same sex. An Employment Tribunal upheld her claim of unlawful discrimination, but this was set aside by the Employment Appeal Tribunal whose position was confirmed by the Court of Appeal. The central point in the judgment is that Article 9 does not protect an action merely because it is motivated or inspired by religion. Furthermore, there is no express 'right to employment' in the Convention and employees are not under any pressure from the state to change their beliefs since they are free to resign (*Copsey* v *WBB Devon Clays* [2005] EWCA Civ 932 (following *Stedman* v *United Kingdom* (1997) 23 EHRR CD 168)).

to manifest their beliefs outside the role (see *R (Begum)* v *Governors of Denbigh High School* [2006] UKHL 15, para 23).

Likewise, in *McFarlane* v *Relate Avon Ltd* [2010] EWCA Civ 880, the Court of Appeal upheld the dismissal of a Relate counsellor who refused, on religious grounds, to give sex counselling to same-sex couples.

For these reasons, Article 9 offers, in UK law, little assistance to employees who are unable, because of employers' uniform policy, to display a religious symbol, such as a cross, at work. This applied in *Eweida* v *BA* [2010] EWCA Civ 80 (uniform code for airline check-in staff) and *Chaplin* v *Royal Devon and Exeter NHS Trust* (Exeter Employment Tribunal, April 2010) concerning hospital uniform policy for nurses.

further study

The cases of *Ladele*, *MacFarlane*, *Eweida* and *Chaplin* are currently (2012) before the ECtHR.

Though there are no rights to employment in the Convention, employment law must be interpreted, if possible, to be compatible with Article 9. Employers who are public authorities have a direct duty under the HRA to protect the Convention rights of their employees. Also, though, Article 9 can guide the courts when applying employment law in a private context. In *Grainger* (section 16.2.2) it was held that an employee could have a valid claim of discrimination on grounds of philosophical belief when he was dismissed for taking actions against his company which were motivated by his strongly held views on climate change.

KEY POINT Under the Equality Act 2010 (see Chapter 7, section 7.1.1) 'religion or belief' are 'protected characteristics' (section 10).

16.5 Blasphemy

Laws of blasphemy, in their modern forms, aim to protect religious believers from being seriously insulted and offended by written or spoken words or images. Blasphemy does not imply that there has been an incitement to violence or hatred. Broadcasters, film makers, novelists and so on can find themselves censored or even at risk of criminal punishment for publishing matter that causes this type of offence to others.

A principal argument in favour of a law against blasphemy is that religion can be central to a person's sense of well-being and self-respect and this is worthy of protection by the criminal law. In particular, there is the need to protect minority groups who may, in part, be defined in terms of religion and for whom contemptuous attacks increase a sense of social vulnerability. Laws against blasphemy also remove any cause radical groups have to take the law into their own hands.

The central argument against a law of blasphemy is that insult or offence to a religious group is not enough to justify censorship in a free society. Blasphemous words do not undermine the faith of believers nor prevent people from worshipping in the way they wish. The very essence of freedom of speech is that people should be able to say offensive or unpopular things: it is actions that can be suppressed, not words.

The ECtHR has been not unsympathetic to national laws which criminalise blasphemous expression. The issue is dealt with, normally, on the basis of a claim under Article 10 (freedom of expression) brought by the broadcaster, film maker, etc. who is subjected to a blasphemy law. Under Article 10(2) restrictions on expression may be justified if done to protect the rights of others. These can include the rights to freedom of religion in Article 9, which can legitimately be protected by blasphemy laws applied in a lawful and proportionate manner. This position has been adopted by the ECtHR in cases such as *Wingrove* v *United Kingdom* (1997) 24 EHRR 1 and *Otto-Preminger Institute* v *Austria* (1995) 19 EHRR 34. The Court makes it clear, however, that the laws must not be applied in ways that prevent religious beliefs from being denied or criticised. Indeed, there is a reciprocal duty of the religious to tolerate criticism. By reference to the 'duties and responsibilities' provision in Article 10(2), however, states can place legal limits requiring appropriate respect in the manner of such criticism (the prosecution in *Wingrove* could be justified because of the highly offensive nature of the video). It should be noted that, at least according to the Commission (*Choudhury* v *United Kingdom* App 17439/90), nothing in Article 9 places a positive duty on states to adopt general laws against blasphemy.

In the United Kingdom the law of blasphemy, which, as an offence, was somewhat revived in the 1970s, came in for severe criticism. It seemed partial (because it only protected Christianity, see *Choudhury*, in the previous paragraph) and impossible to reconcile with freedom of speech (as in, for example, the failed attempt to get the authorities to prosecute 'Jerry Springer: The Opera'—*R (Green)* v *City of Westminster Magistrates Court* [2007] EWHC 2785). As a result the common law offences of blasphemy and blasphemous libel have been abolished for England and Wales by section 79 of the Criminal Justice and Immigration Act 2008. The alternative approach that has been adopted in England and Wales is to criminalise expressions of religious hatred. This is done by Part IIIA of the Public Order Act 1986. Here, expressions of 'hatred' are distinguished from expressions of 'antipathy, dislike, ridicule, insult or abuse' (section 29J).

343

16.6 Religious dress and the manifestation of religion

discussion topic

Freedom to manifest religion and religious dress

Should Article 9 secure the right of Muslim women, who so wish, to wear headscarves and whatever other forms of dress, including veils, they believe to be appropriate for, or required by, their religious beliefs?

This is a topic of great controversy in a number of European countries.

Arguments in favour of the view that women have a right to wear headscarves etc., which the Convention should protect, include:

- A number of Muslim women feel that such dress is a requirement of their religion or at least it feels appropriate to wear it as an aspect of their religious identity; this feeling needs to be respected.

- The Convention embodies the values of tolerance and broadmindedness.

- Adult women should be allowed to choose for themselves what they wear.

- Other religious symbols, such as crucifixes worn as neck pendants, are allowed.

- The alleged problems caused are exaggerated. There is no necessary connection between religious dress and problems such as extremism. Dress harms no one. If a person wishes to wear something that others think is a badge of subordination, so be it: that someone is 'harming' themselves is their business and not grounds for the state to interfere.

Where state laws, or institutional practices within states, have restricted headscarves and other forms of Islamic dress for women, the arguments for restriction include:

- In a context of religious diversity, states and institutions are entitled to take steps to preserve secularism (the idea that public institutions should not embody the beliefs of any religion).

- The wearing of a headscarf may, in some contexts, be associated with 'proselytism' (putting pressure on others to conform to a particular set of religious beliefs), particularly if it is alleged to be a requirement of the religion. Some restriction may be reasonable to protect the freedom of others not to wear the dress.

- The argument that it is only women but not men who are subjected to a dress code may be hard to square with gender equality; highly valued under the Convention.

16.6.1 **Some case law**

The ECtHR has found that particular restrictions on, specifically, the wearing of headscarves, do not violate Article 9.

In *Leyla Sahin* v *Turkey* (2007) 44 EHRR 5, a Grand Chamber of the ECtHR found that a ban, imposed by a Turkish university, on its female students wearing headscarves, did not violate Article 9. There was an interference with the applicant's rights under Article 9(1) but it was justified in the terms of Article 9(2). Turkey has a large Muslim population.

As a state it is committed to secularism and gender equality, and this was recognised by the Court. The university's ban was prescribed by law in its regulations and the ban served legitimate purposes, including protecting the rights of others and public order. The ban was proportionate. It resulted from a careful weighing of the issues and interests of all those involved. The university, and the Turkish courts that found in its favour, had acted within the state's margin of appreciation, being best placed to decide the matter in context. (See also *Dahlab* v *Switzerland* App 42393/98, judgment 15 February 2001.)

In the United Kingdom a more accepting approach has, perhaps, been signalled.

R (Begum) v *Governors of Denbigh High School* [2006] UKHL 15, the House of Lords held that the exclusion of SB, a Muslim girl, from her school (a public authority under the HRA) was compatible with Article 9. She was excluded because she insisted, for religious reasons, on wearing a more concealing form of dress than was permitted under the school's rules. The purpose of the uniform rules was to protect the majority of Muslim female pupils (who were happy with the uniform policy) from pressure being exerted on them to adopt a more fundamentalist conception of their religion. The House of Lords followed Strasbourg case law. The restriction was prescribed by law (a carefully thought out uniform policy), its purpose was to protect the rights and freedoms of others (other pupils) and its application to SB was proportionate. The school had striven to achieve a fair balance of different interests to which a court had to defer.

Other cases include *R (X)* v *Y School* [2007] EWHC 298 (a school's refusal to allow a pupil to wear the niqab was, given alternative options, justified under Article 9(2)) and *R (Playfoot)* v *Millais School* [2007] EWHC 1698 (banning a pupil from wearing a purity ring did not violate

Article 9). UK and EU discrimination law (which must be interpreted compatibly with Article 9) was in issue in *Azmi* v *Kirklees MBC* [2007] ICR 1154 (a teaching assistant dismissed for insisting on being fully veiled in the presence of male teachers was not unlawfully discriminated against); in *R (Watkins-Singh)* v *Aberdare High School* [2008] EWHC 1865, on the other hand, there was unlawful discrimination of a pupil excluded for insisting on wearing a Kara (Sikh bracelet)— *Begum* was distinguished on the facts.

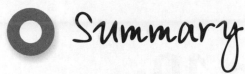 Summary

- The protection of belief itself is absolute in the sense that, unless there are grounds for derogation under Article 15, the state cannot interfere with religious and other beliefs and may have a duty to secure religious freedom.

- Manifestations of belief can be restricted by the state subject to the provisions of Article 9(2). The important point here is to distinguish between actions which manifest belief and those which simply are motivated by belief. The latter do not raise issues under Article 9.

- Nothing in Article 9 allows a person to manifest their beliefs whenever they wish and so Article 9 gives little support to conscientious objection in the employment context.

? Questions

 For suggested approaches, please visit the Online Resource Centre.

1 How does the ECtHR distinguish a manifestation of a belief from an action motivated by a belief?

2 For what kinds of purpose is it legitimate to restrict a person's manifestation of belief?

? Further reading

Addison, N. *Religious Discrimination and Hatred Law* (2007) London: Routledge-Cavendish

Ahdar, R. and Leigh, F. *Religious Freedom in the Liberal State* (2005) Oxford: OUP

Lester, A., Pannick, D. and Herberg, J. (see Preface) Chapter 4, Article 9

Pitt, G. 'Keeping the Faith: Trends in Religion or Belief Discrimination' (2011) 40(4) *ILJ* 384–404.

Taylor, P. *Freedom of Religion* (2005) Cambridge: CUP

Article 10: freedom of expression

Chapter overview

- The importance of freedom of expression.
- 'Expression' and the scope of Article 10(1).
- Media freedom.
- Restrictions on freedom of expression as permitted under Article 10(2).
- Political speech (which has the highest levels of protection).
- Permissible restrictions of political speech.
- Artistic speech.
- Commercial speech.

Article 10   Freedom of Expression

(1) Everyone has the right to freedom of expression. This right shall include freedom to hold opinions and to receive and impart information and ideas without interference by public authority and regardless of frontiers. This article shall not prevent states from requiring the licensing of broadcasting, television or cinema enterprises.

(2) The exercise of these freedoms, since it carries with it duties and responsibilities, may be subject to such formalities, conditions, restrictions or penalties as are prescribed by law and are necessary in a democratic society, in the interests of national security, territorial integrity or public safety, for the prevention of disorder or crime, for the protection of health or morals, for the protection of the reputation or rights of others, for preventing the disclosure of information received in confidence, or for maintaining the authority and impartiality of the judiciary.

Introduction

Freedom of expression is widely acknowledged as a fundamental right in a liberal, democratic society. There are, however, important and legitimate reasons why freedom of expression may need to be restricted in order to protect other important rights and freedoms such as the right to a fair trial or to private life. Article 10 (following the pattern found in Articles 8, 9 and 11) establishes, in its first paragraph, a general right to freedom of expression and then, in its second paragraph, identifies the only basis upon which the right can be restricted. The necessity for such restrictions must be established by the state and must be subject to scrutiny by the courts. As is made clear in the rest of this chapter:

- The essential role of a free media in a democracy is recognised.

- The protection of Article 10 extends to ideas that offend, shock or disturb.

- Expression relating to public affairs has the highest level of protection.

17.1   Freedom of expression as a value in common law

Freedom of expression is a well-recognised principle of the common law (the basic judge-made law of England and Wales) which had been established before, and independently of, the Human Rights Act 1998 (HRA). British judges have, on a number of occasions, insisted that there is no incompatibility between the degree of protection afforded expression under the common law with the protection under Article 10: there is simply a difference of approach. The following quote, from Lord Goff in one of the *Spycatcher* cases of the 1980s, expresses the point.

I can see no inconsistency between English law on this subject and art 10 [ECHR]. This is scarcely surprising, since we may pride ourselves on the fact that freedom of speech has existed in this country perhaps as long as, if not longer than, it has existed in any other country in the world. The only difference is that, whereas art 10 of the convention, in accordance with its avowed purpose, proceeds to state a fundamental right and then to qualify it, we in this country (where everybody is free to do anything, subject only to the provisions of the law) proceed rather on an assumption of freedom of speech, and turn to our law to discover the established exceptions to it.

(*Attorney General* v *Guardian Newspapers (No 2)* [1988] 3 All ER 545, 659)

The importance of freedom of expression in common law continues to be asserted by the judges. It has been recognised by Law Lords as attaining 'the status of a constitutional right with attendant high normative force' (*McCartan Turkington Breen* v *Times Newspapers* [2000] 4 All ER 913, 926).

Under the law of England and Wales issues of freedom of speech can arise, for example

- in 'defamation' proceedings where a person seeks damages for false statements made which damage their reputation;
- to protect confidential information through an action for 'breach of confidence';
- to protect intellectual property rights such as copyright and trade marks;
- in the criminal law, such as public order offences which may have been committed by political demonstrators.

Some of these issues will involve the HRA directly, for example where the interpretation of an Act of Parliament is involved or where it is alleged that the police or some other public authority have failed to respect freedom of expression. Where, like defamation or breach of confidence, it is essentially a matter of private law, freedom of expression is still relevant, either because the courts are public authorities required to act compatibly with Convention rights or, irrespective of the HRA, because freedom of expression is a long-standing value in the common law. As Lord Steyn said, in *Reynolds* v *Times Newspapers Ltd* [1999] 4 All ER 609, 628, 'freedom of expression is the rule and regulation of speech is the exception requiring justification'.

further study

For a summary of the law and importance of freedom of expression in English law, taking Article 10 into account and including references to significant cases, see *R (BBC)* v *Secretary of State for Justice* [2012] EWHC 13, paras 35–54.

17.2 Article 10: general issues

17.2.1 Importance

From one of its earliest cases, *Handyside* v *United Kingdom* (1979–80) 1 EHRR 737, onwards the European Court of Human Rights (ECtHR) has continuously recognised the importance of the right to freedom of expression within the Convention scheme (see para 49). Freedom of expression is

- necessary for individual self-fulfilment, and
- an essential foundation of a democratic society. A democratic society, characterised by pluralism, tolerance and broadmindedness, is a necessary condition in which human rights can be protected and justice and peace can flourish.

further study

Other major cases in which the importance of freedom of expression is discussed include *Lingens* v *Austria* (1986) 8 EHRR 407, para 41; *Cumpana* v *Romania* (2005) 41 EHRR 14, paras 88–91 and *Editions Plon* v *France* (2006) 42 EHRR 36, paras 42 and 43.

17.2.2 General structure

Despite the importance of freedom of expression, the text of Article 10 makes it clear that there is no absolute right to freedom of expression. Freedom of expression, like the freedoms in Articles 8, 9 and 11, can be restricted if certain conditions are present. The nature and scope of freedom of expression is established in the first paragraph (Article 10(1)), and the exclusive conditions under which that freedom can be restricted are identified in the second (Article 10(2)). Thus the approach of the ECtHR (or any national court) to freedom of expression cases is to ask itself:

- is an act of speech, writing or some other type of expression in issue in the case? If it is, then:
- is it a type of expression that is protected under the terms of the first paragraph of Article 10? If it is, then:
- has the speech etc. been restricted (usually this will have been by a court or by a state agency such as the police)? If so, then:
- has the state shown that the restriction is justified in terms of Article 10(2), i.e. that it was imposed 'by law', that it aimed to achieve one of the purposes listed in paragraph 2 and that it was 'necessary in a democratic society' in the sense of being a proportionate means of meeting a pressing social need?

On the basis of this approach, a court's job involves balancing freedom of expression with the arguments for restricting expression. The latter may be in terms of the collective good or the rights of other individuals that restricting speech promotes or protects. In this balancing exercise the ECtHR gives greatest weight to political speech, broadly defined as speech involving the discussion of public and social affairs; only the most compelling reasons will justify restrictions. Other forms of speech, such as commercial or artistic speech, are still within the scope of the protection of the first paragraph, but restrictions are more easily brought within the terms of the second paragraph.

17.2.3 Role of the European Court of Human Rights (ECtHR)

The ECtHR has the final say on whether any restriction on freedom of expression is compatible with Article 10. National laws permitting restriction must be narrowly construed and government actions be subject to close scrutiny. On the issue of the need for an interference with free expression, the Court has summarised its role in this way (similar wording is used in many cases):

> The Court's task, in exercising its supervisory jurisdiction, is not to take the place of the competent national courts but rather to review under Article 10 the decisions they delivered in the exercise of the power of appreciation. This does not mean that the supervision is limited to ascertaining whether the respondent State exercised its discretion reasonably, carefully and in good faith; what the Court has to do is to look at the interference complained of in the light of the case as a whole and determine whether it was 'proportionate to the legitimate aim pursued' and whether the reasons adduced by the national authorities to justify it are 'relevant and sufficient'.
>
> (*Association Ekin* v *France* (2002) 35 EHRR 35, para 56)

Depending on the issue, the ECtHR allows a margin of appreciation to states (wide on moral questions, very narrow for political speech).

UK courts

Under the HRA the question of the degree to which UK courts should defer to the way Parliament, the executive or various administrative bodies have balanced free speech with other interests, arises. The tendency is for UK courts not to defer to the authorities. The protection of freedom of expression is an established role for the courts.

case close-up

Ashdown v Telegraph Group Ltd [2001] EWCA Civ 1142

A, who had been leader of the Liberal Democrats, alleged breach of copyright by the *Daily Telegraph*. The newspaper had published, without his permission, excerpts from his diary detailing meetings with the Prime Minister. Under the Copyright, Designs and Patents Act 1988 there is a defence of 'fair dealing', but this was not available to the *Telegraph*. The question was whether the *Telegraph* could rely on wider rights to free expression under Article 10. The Court of Appeal expressly rejected the view that the 'fair dealing' defence was Parliament's way of dealing with the freedom of expression issue and that the courts should defer to this. Rather it was the court's duty to make its own assessment of whether there were overriding public interests which justified publication. On the facts there were not.

There are exceptions. See *Pro-Life Alliance v BBC* [2003] UKHL 23, discussed at section 17.8.3.

17.2.4 **Positive duties or obligations**

National authorities have limited obligations to take positive steps to protect freedom of expression. In *Palomo Sánchez v Spain* (2012) 54 EHRR 24, a Grand Chamber found no violation of Article 10 when domestic Spanish employment law allowed the sacking of trade unionists, by their private employer, for publishing defamatory cartoons of managers. Confirming earlier cases, the Court held that 'in certain cases the State has a positive obligation to protect the right to freedom of expression, even against interference by private persons' (para 59). The case, which, because of the trade union connection, also involved Article 11, was an example. Whether it means that Article 10 applies generally to dismissals on the basis of expressions by the employee, is unclear.

cross reference

For 'deference' see Chapter 4, section 4.6.2. For 'positive duties' see Chapter 6, section 6.6.

Positive duties are not absolute, a positive obligation should not be 'interpreted in such a way as to impose an impossible or disproportionate burden on the authorities', *Özgür Gündem v Turkey* (2001) 31 EHRR 49, para 43. In *Özgür Gündem* there was a breach of Article 10 because of the state's inadequate investigation of violence and harassment against the owners and editors of a newspaper.

17.2.5 **Prior restraint**

One of the debates about the law of freedom of expression generally is whether the law should be used to prevent publication in the first place (e.g. through an injunction) or whether freedom of expression is best protected by allowing publication even of material which, after publication, can be the subject of legal action against the speaker.

The main argument in favour of banning prior restraint orders is that it maintains the 'hearers' interests' in the content of the expression. In particular, it makes it difficult for government and powerful individuals or groups to prevent information and ideas getting into the public domain.

The main argument for allowing prior restraints is that some legitimate restrictions on speech would lose their force altogether if publication were allowed. If, for example, the point of a legitimate restriction on free speech is to protect information obtained in confidence, there is little point if the law cannot protect the confidence by restraining publication.

Two examples from English law are given here.

- Defamation. Following *Bonnard* v *Perryman* [1891] 2 Ch 269, English courts will not, other than exceptionally, issue an injunction to prevent a publication which impugns a person's reputation, particularly where, in legal proceedings for defamation, the defence would claim justification. The legal approach is 'publish and be damned'. (The rule has been held to be compatible with Convention rights in *Greene* v *Associated Newspapers* [2004] EWCA Civ 1462.)

- Breach of confidence. An injunction is more easily available where a newspaper, for example, intends to publish information obtained in confidence (whether true or false, whether defamatory or not). If the law accepts that some information is legitimately confidential (such as medical records or trade secrets) then it will protect it by issuing an injunction. The underlying issue is whether, on balance, the public interest justifies publication or secrecy; see, for example, the refusal of the Court of Appeal to issue a temporary injunction to preserve the confidentiality (in reality the privacy) of the Michael Douglas–Catherine Zeta-Jones wedding photographs: *Douglas* v *Hello!* [2001] 2 All ER 289.

Prior restraint is not incompatible with the ECHR (see *Markt Intern Verlag GmbH* v *Germany* (1990) 12 EHRR 161, for example). Nevertheless, the inherent dangers call 'for the most careful scrutiny on the part of the Court', particularly in restraining the media in news reporting: 'for news is a perishable commodity and to delay its publication, even for a short period, may well deprive it of all its value and interest' (*Association Ekin* v *France* (2002) 35 EHRR 35, para 56).

17.3 Freedom of expression and section 12 HRA

During the passage of the HRA, Parliament expressed concern that some Convention rights, in particular the right to privacy in Article 8, might be used to limit freedom of expression, especially media freedom, more than was acceptable. Section 12 was introduced and applies whenever a UK court is considering whether to grant a civil remedy (including an injunction prior to publication or damages after publication) which affects the exercise of freedom of expression.

Section 12(2) requires that, unless there are compelling reasons to the contrary, a remedy affecting freedom of speech should only be granted if the person against whom the injunction is made is present or represented.

Section 12(3) deals with interim injunctions. These are holding injunctions whose effect is to prevent publication of a matter in the period before the full trial to decide whether or not the law permits publication is held. An interim injunction can be issued on the basis of a 'balance of convenience', which does not deal with the legal rights and wrongs but relates to the issue of whether it is the applicant or respondent who has most to lose if publication is allowed in this interim period. Given the 'perishable nature' of much news and information, issuing an interim injunction can have the effect of stopping the story once and for all. For this reason, under section 12(3) an interim injunction affecting freedom of expression can only be issued if the court goes beyond the balance of convenience and considers, by reference to the merits of the case, that the claimant would 'probably' (more likely than not) succeed at the final trial. The degree of probability required depends on the circumstances (*Cream Holdings Ltd* v *Banerjee* [2004] UKHL 44, para 22).

Section 12(4) requires a court to have 'particular regard' to the importance of Article 10. In respect of matters affecting journalistic, literary or artistic material, the court must consider the extent to which the material is or is about to be available to the public, whether publication is or would be in the public interest and 'any relevant privacy code' (e.g. in the context of the media, the Codes of Practice of the Press Complaints Commission or, for broadcasting, Codes supervised by Ofcom and the BBC).

Section 12(4) may be of symbolic rather than real effect. As Sedley LJ noted in *Douglas v Hello!* [2001] 2 All ER 289 (paras 131–137), giving particular regard to Article 10 must include considering Article 10(2). This necessarily means seeking a fair balance with competing rights, such as private life in Article 8. It follows that section 12(4) does not give the right of free expression 'a presumptive priority' over other rights (para 137). This view has been accepted by the House of Lords in *Campbell v MGN Ltd* [2004] UKHL 22, para 111.

17.4 The scope of Article 10(1)

Article 10 protects 'freedom of expression', not just freedom of speech. Expressive activity is not confined to speech. It can, for example, extend to expressive acts that do not involve words at all, such as the playing of music, dancing or the wearing of particular clothes.

Political expression is given particular protection under Article 10. 'Political' has a wide definition and includes, for instance, participating in political demonstrations. Article 10 also extends to artistic and commercial expression, although restrictions may be easier to justify in these areas than in respect of political speech.

An expressive act can, of course, give rise to issues within the ambit of more than one article. Restrictions on dress, for example, could give rise to issues under Article 8, the right to private life, or under Article 9, the right to freedom of thought, conscience and religion. The tendency of the Court is to decide that one article is the one predominantly in issue and that all substantive issues can be dealt with under its terms.

Article 10 protects not just the substance of the ideas and information but also the chosen form of expression (*News Verlags GmbH v Austria* (2001) 31 EHRR 8, para 39). In *R (BBC) v Secretary of State for Justice* [2012] EWHC 13, for instance, the Justice Secretary allowed journalists to interview a prisoner and discuss the contents of the interview on air, but not to broadcast the interview itself. The High Court held the ban on broadcasting was disproportionate and incompatible with Article 10.

17.4.1 Freedom to receive information

Access to information held by government and other public bodies is essential for an effective political democracy. The judgments and choices of a political kind that citizens make depend on the information that is available and that depends, largely, on the ability of individuals and organisations and, most importantly, the media to obtain information. In a way receiving information is the most important aspect to freedom of expression since the overwhelming majority of people have no realistic access to the media in order to express their views and opinions.

The ECtHR has consistently held that the right to receive information prevents the government from restricting the flow of information that others are prepared to give. It cannot be used to compel the government or others to disclose information they wish to keep secret.

In *Leander v Sweden* (1987) 9 EHRR 433, the applicant claimed that he was entitled to see his security vetting, which had found that he was a security risk. He had been unable to challenge this and, as a result, he had lost his job. The ECtHR held that there had been no violation of Article 10. The right to receive information does not impose an obligation on the government to impart such information.

This view was confirmed by the Grand Chamber in *Roche* v *United Kingdom* (2006) 42 EHRR 30, para 172.

The ECtHR has, however, recognised that a right to receive information, even from an unwilling government, may arise not under Article 10 but, rather, where it is necessary in order to uphold other Convention rights and freedoms such as the right to private and family life under Article 8. Information that has a particular significance for an individual's private life, for his or her sense of identity, for example, may need to be disclosed (see *Gaskin* v *United Kingdom* (1990) 12 EHRR 36). Similarly, information necessary to enable an individual to assess environmental or other dangers to health (see, for example, *Guerra* v *Italy* (1998) 26 EHRR 357) may need to be disclosed.

The general position under the Convention has been followed by courts in England and Wales. In *R (Persey)* v *Secretary of State for the Environment, Food and Rural Affairs* [2002] EWHC 371, for instance, the Administrative Court followed *Leander* and refused to hold that Article 10 was engaged when the government refused to hold an inquiry into the foot and mouth outbreak of 2001 in public. This can be compared with *London Regional Transport* v *Mayor of London* [2001] EWCA Civ 1491, where the Court of Appeal ordered the publication of a commercially sensitive report, partly on the basis of a right to receive information in Article 10.

There is some indication that the ECtHR is, slightly, shifting its position. In *Tarsasag a Szabadsagjogkert* v *Hungary* (2011) 53 EHRR 3 (paras 35–38), the Court held that Article 10 was violated when the Hungarian Civil Liberties Union was denied access to details of a complaint made to the Hungarian Constitutional Court by an MP about the constitutionality of new drug laws. The ECtHR did not establish a general right to public information (so that all interferences would need to be justified by reference to Article 10(2)). Rather it moved in that direction in order to prevent the *Leander* principle being used to allow interferences by an 'information monopoly' with the ability of a 'watchdog' such as the media, to scrutinise public affairs. The extent of the shift in *Tarsasag* is unclear and, in *BBC* v *Sugar (No2)* [2012] UKSC 4, the Supreme Court refused to take it as indicating a shift towards a general right to receive information from an unwilling provider (paras 85–94). But the situation is complex. In England and Wales the Freedom of Information Act 2000 (FIA 2000) imposes a general duty on public authorities to disclose information. There are many exemptions and exceptions. In *Kennedy* v *Information Commissioner* [2012] EWCA Civ 317, the First Tier Tribunal had accepted Article 10 might mean that the force of exemptions under the FIA 2000 should be weakened. This could be done by reading down (under section 3 HRA) the exemptions on the basis of the *Tarsasag* approach. The Court of Appeal has considered the matter one the Supreme Court should return to.

17.5 Freedom of the media

The importance of a free media has been emphasised time and again by the ECtHR, and freedom of the press, broadcasting and other forms of media are clearly protected under Article 10(1).

The principles derived from leading Convention cases on media freedom such as *Lingens* v *Austria* (1986) 8 EHRR 407, paras 41–42 and *Fressoz and Roire* v *France* (2001) 31 EHRR 2, para 45 include:

- Safeguarding the freedom of the media is of particular importance for the maintenance of freedom of expression.
- The media has the 'task' of imparting information and ideas of public interest.
- The public has a 'right' to receive such information and ideas.
- The media has a vital 'watchdog' role to play in a democracy.
- It is incumbent on the media to 'impart information and ideas on political issues', including controversial ones.

- Nevertheless: (given, in particular, the 'duties and responsibilities' clause in Article 10) 'the press must not overstep the bounds set, *inter alia*, for the protection of vital State interests, such as national security or territorial integrity, against the threat of violence of the prevention of disorder or crime.' This is particularly true in the context of reporting political violence (e.g. *Sürek and Özdemir v Turkey* (1999) App 23927/94, Grand Chamber judgment of 8 July 1999, para 58).

The freedom of the media on the basis of Article 10 and the need to balance this with the rights of others, particularly under Article 8, involves the consideration of a number of important issues, both under the Convention and the HRA. These are the topic of Chapter 22.

17.6 Restrictions under Article 10(2)

Any restrictions on speech or expressive acts that are within the scope of Article 10(1) will be violations unless the state can prove that the restriction is justified in terms of Article 10(2).

Under the HRA, UK courts have adopted the basic Strasbourg principles under Article 10(2).

case close-up

> **R v Shayler [2002] UKHL 11**
>
> S had been a member of the security service. After leaving the service he disclosed various security matters to a national newspaper. Some of the disclosures suggested possible wrong-doing by the security services. On joining the service, and again on leaving, he had signed declarations accepting that he had both a contractual and a statutory duty not to disclose information relating to national security. He was prosecuted under the Official Secrets Act 1989. This makes it an offence for existing or former members of the security services to disclose security information. There is no 'public interest' defence in the Act. The issue was whether Article 10 ECHR provided S with the defence that the disclosure was necessary and in the public interest. The House of Lords held that there was no such defence in the Act and that this was compatible with Article 10.

The general principles, as discussed in the following sections, were summarised by Lord Hope (see paras 54–61).

17.6.1 Duties and responsibilities

The Convention text recognises that freedom of expression carries with it 'duties and responsibilities' and it is on this basis that speech can reasonably be restricted. Whilst the duties and responsibilities clause can influence the way a court views various issues, it does not relieve a court of the need for close scrutiny of the reasons adduced by states for restricting expression.

Duties and responsibilities have been emphasised by the ECtHR and UK courts in the following situations:

- The duties of publishers of books aimed at children which had allegedly obscene content (*Handyside v United Kingdom* (1979–80) 1 EHRR 737, para 49).
- The duties of the media, owners, editors and journalists, in the context of reporting terrorism and armed struggle, to ensure that their reports do not 'become a vehicle for the

dissemination of hate speech and the promotion of violence' (*Sürek v Turkey (No 4)* (1999) App 24762/94, Grand Chamber judgment of 8 July 1999, para 60).

- The duties and responsibilities of former members of the security services, as in *Shayler*, section 17.6.

- 'Responsible journalism' is discussed in Chapter 22, section 22.3.

17.6.2 **Prescribed by law**

Restrictions on freedom of expression must meet the standard of 'legality' which pervades the Convention. Specifically there must be

- a basis in law for the restriction,

- the law must be accessible to the individual likely to be affected by it,

- the terms of the law must be sufficiently precise for the individual to be able to regulate his or her conduct without breaking the law,

- the 'law' must not be arbitrary and incompatible with the 'rule of law'.

KEY POINT The principle of legality is discussed in Chapter 6, section 6.2. The leading case, *Sunday Times* v *United Kingdom* (1979–80) 2 EHRR 245, involved freedom of expression.

In the context of freedom of expression the standards of 'prescribed by law' can be quite undemanding. In *Chorherr v Austria* (1994) 17 EHRR 358, an offence of 'causing a breach of the peace by conduct likely to cause annoyance' was felt to be sufficiently precise for a person to regulate his or her conduct: the issue had to be approached in context (see para 25). Nevertheless, the concept has not lost all its significance.

case close-up

Gaweda v Poland (2004) 39 EHRR 4

A regional court in Poland refused an application to register periodical titles. The effect of refusal was that the periodicals could not be published. The relevant legislation said that registration could be refused if the application was 'in conflict with reality'. This provision normally meant that the statements in the application had to be true. However, the Polish regional court refused the application because the proposed titles, one of which was 'Germany—A Thousand-Year-Old Enemy of Poland', suggested a false picture of social reality.

The ECtHR held that the Polish court had introduced its own criteria of what was in conflict with reality, which was an unforeseeable development of the law. The refusal to register was not prescribed by law.

Restrictions based on Codes of Practice (non-statutory guidance from government or other bodies) have been considered under the HRA.

In *R* v *Advertising Standards Authority ex parte Matthias Rath BV* [2001] EMLR 22, the High Court accepted that the ASA's Code of Practice was sufficiently clear to meet the prescribed by law standards for the purposes of advertising.

Given the number of 'codes of practice' which are part of the regulatory machinery of modern life, this is an important decision.

17.6.3 Legitimate purposes

Restrictions are only legitimate if for one of the purposes listed in Article 10(2). Article 18 ECHR makes it clear that restrictions for other purposes are not permissible. These purposes are described in loose and open-textured phrases, such as 'national security' or 'protection of morals', and it is usually relatively easy for states to show that their reason for restricting expression can be brought within one or more of them.

'the interests of national security'

The 'interests of national security' has been accepted as a legitimate purpose in situations such as the following:

- bans on the direct reporting of the speech of members of alleged terrorist organisations (*Purcell* v *Ireland* App 15404/89, admissibility decision of 16 April 1991),
- preserving order in the armed forces by suppressing unofficial magazines distributed amongst soldiers (*Vereinigung Demokratischer Soldaten Österreichs and Gubi* v *Austria* (1995) 20 EHRR 56, where the Court held that, though for a legitimate purpose, there was a violation of Article 10).

National security is likely to be relevant in respect of areas of UK law such as

- crimes that can be committed if secret government information is passed on to others without permission. Compatibility of the Official Secrets Act 1989 with Article 10 was accepted by the House of Lords in *Shayler*, section 17.6;
- the civil remedy of an injunction to prevent a breach of confidence can be sought by the government to try and prevent publication in the media of secret government information (e.g. *Ministry of Defence* v *Griffin* [2008] EWHC1542, where the court enforced the terms of a confidentiality agreement signed by a member of UK Special Forces).

KEY POINT Injunctions restraining publication of confidential information were accepted (by the ECtHR) as compatible with Article 10, for so long as the information remains confidential. See the discussion in *Observer and Guardian Newspapers* v *United Kingdom* (1992) 14 EHRR 153, section 17.7.3.

'territorial integrity and public safety'

The 'interests of . . . territorial integrity' has been accepted as a legitimate purpose in situations such as the following:

- expelling a member of the European Parliament who had taken part in a banned anti-nuclear march in French Polynesia (*Piermont* v *France* (1995) 20 EHRR 301),
- anti-terrorism laws, such as those restricting freedom of expression in the context of armed struggle aimed at constitutional change including separatism. The armed struggle between Turkey and the PKK over 'Kurdistan' in 1990 has provided many examples, such as *Sürek* v *Turkey (No 4)* App 24762/94, Grand Chamber judgment of 8 July 1999, paras 46–49.

'the prevention of disorder or crime'

This is widely used as part of the claim of justification for restrictions on, for example

- political meetings, marches and demonstrations, such as in *Steel* v *United Kingdom* (1999) 28 EHRR 603;

- inciting members of the armed forces to desertion, which even in times of peace can have a weakening effect on the social 'order' (*Arrowsmith* v *United Kingdom* (1981) 3 EHRR 218);
- provisions in anti-terrorism legislation which restrict speech and other forms of expression. In a number of cases involving Turkey, the ECtHR accepted that anti-terrorism measures, including prohibiting 'separatist propaganda' or the publication of material from banned organisations, were, at least in the context of violent struggle between the PKK and the Turkish state, for 'the protection of national security and territorial integrity and the prevention of disorder and crime' (e.g. *Baskaya and Okçuoglu* v *Turkey* (2001) 31 EHRR 10, para 56).

cross reference

The application of Article 10 in the context of political demonstration is discussed further in Chapter 18, section 18.1; Article 10 and political speech generally is discussed in section 17.7.

Under the HRA, the courts of England and Wales have to deal with restrictions on freedom of expression imposed, for example, under public order legislation such as the Public Order Act 1986, the common law power to arrest for 'breach of the peace' or offences of incitement, including to racial or religious hatred. The main issue, usually, is whether some restraint on free expression is necessary and proportionate.

'Disorder' need not involve threats to public order. It can, for instance, apply to areas where regulation is necessary, such as telecommunications (*Groppera Radio AG* v *Switzerland* (1990) 12 EHRR 321, paras 69–70 and *Autronic AG* v *Switzerland* (1990) 12 EHRR 485, para 59).

'the protection of health'

This purpose has been accepted, under the HRA, as part of the justification for restrictions imposed on advertising and publicity promoting health products (as in *R* v *Advertising Standards Authority ex parte Matthias Rath BV* [2001] EMLR 22).

'the protection of…morals'

This purpose is used as part of the justification for legal measures taken against speech and other forms of expression on the grounds of obscenity and indecency (e.g. *Muller* v *Switzerland* (1991) 13 EHRR 212). It can also be relevant to laws which aim at upholding deeply held moral values in a society.

case close-up

> **Open Door Counselling and Dublin Well Woman v Ireland (1993) 15 EHRR 244**
>
> Irish law imposed a legal ban on giving advice and counselling to Irish women seeking abortions in the United Kingdom. It was challenged on Article 10 grounds. The ECtHR held that the ban embodied 'the profound moral values concerning the nature of life', which the Irish people had, in those days, endorsed in a referendum (paras 61–63). However, in all the circumstances, the Court went on to find that the ban was disproportionate.

Article 10 and laws against obscenity are discussed in section 17.12.

cross reference

The issue of the media and qualified privilege is discussed in Chapter 22, section 22.3.

'protection of the reputation…of others'

This provision is part of the justification for:

- Actions for defamation. 'Libel' and 'slander' (in English law terms) involve a claim for damages against a person who has expressed him or herself in ways that undermine the reputation of the person seeking damages. Convention cases have involved actions brought to defend the reputation of public officials (see section 17.8.4). Article 10 is also relevant to defamation proceedings brought between private persons, including the media. This is because the courts are 'public authorities' under section 6 HRA and so must develop common law actions like defamation in ways that are compatible with Convention rights and also because of section 12 HRA, discussed in section 17.3.

further study

Defamation cases include:

- *Jameel* v *Wall Street Journal Europe Sprl* [2006] UKHL 44,
- Actions for defamation *Loutchansky* v *Times Newspapers* [2001] 4 All ER 115.

- Hate speech. Laws that criminalise various forms of hate speech, such as incitements to violence on racial or religious grounds can be justified by reference to protecting the reputation of others. This issue is discussed later in the chapter.

'protection of the...rights of others'

This provision can be part of a state's justification of a restriction on freedom of expression designed to protect some legal right that others enjoy. This includes the protection of other Convention rights, such as the right to respect for private life under Article 8. Balancing Article 10 and Article 8 is central to breach of confidence cases brought, for example, by celebrities against what they see as intrusive newspaper reporting (see Chapter 22, section 22.5).

The protection of ordinary property rights can also be a legitimate purpose which might justify an interference with freedom of expression. Examples include

- the protection of intellectual property rights through, for example, laws of copyright, trade marks and patents (*Ashdown* v *Telegraph Group Ltd* [2001] EWCA Civ 1142). In *Twentieth Century Fox* v *British Telecommunications* [2011] EWHC 1981, an injunction was issued requiring BT to block access by its ISP subscribers to Newzbin2, a website which facilitated film downloads in breach of the claimants' copyrights. The injunction was compatible with Article 10;
- the protection of other forms of property such as the rights of shopping mall owners to restrict political demonstrations (*Appleby* v *United Kingdom* (2003) 37 EHRR 38).

Protecting the 'rights of others' has been used by the Court to protect certain background rights that have not been clearly established in law. In *Chassagnou* v *France* (2000) 29 EHRR 615 this was recognised but confined, by the ECtHR, to important rights embodying an 'indisputable imperative', para 113. Examples, relating to freedom of expression, from both the ECtHR and UK courts are rights of

- people not to be offended or insulted in their religious beliefs (*Otto-Preminger Institute* v *Austria* (1995) 19 EHRR 34),
- people not to suffer gratuitously offensive material broadcast into their own home (*Pro-Life Alliance*) v *BBC* [2003] UKHL 23),
- victims of racial abuse (*Jersild* v *Denmark* (1995) 19 EHRR 1),
- candidates and electors to a fair election which is not distorted by the power of money (*Bowman* v *United Kingdom* (1998) 26 EHRR 1, para 38).

further study

For discussion of the rights of others in a freedom of expression context see *Connolly* v *DPP* [2007] EWHC 237, paras 23–27.

'for preventing the disclosure of information received in confidence'

cross reference

Disclosure of journalists' sources is discussed in Chapter 22, section 22.4.

This provision can be part of the justification by states in situations such as the following:

- legal actions requiring the disclosure by journalists of their sources;
- legal actions to prevent the disclosure of medical records and other forms of confidential, personal information.

'for maintaining the authority and impartiality of the judiciary'

Laws and measures designed to protect fair trials, such as, in England, a range of measures preventing 'contempt of court', are likely to have this purpose as part of their justification.

On contempt of court, see Chapter 12, section 12.9.2, discussed in the context of the right to a fair trial.

17.6.4 'Necessary in a democratic society'

cross reference

These general principles have been discussed in Chapter 6, section 6.5 and Chapter 14, section 14.4.3.

Not only must the authorities prove that the restriction on freedom of expression is 'by law' and is aimed at one or more of the purposes listed in the second paragraph of Article 10, but also they must show that the restriction is 'necessary in a democratic society'. Most Article 10 cases turn on this issue.

The general Strasbourg principles have been summarised, in the context of Article 10, by Lord Hope in *Shayler* (section 17.6), paras 54–61:

- Restrictions must be based on relevant and sufficient reasons.
- Restrictions must aim to meet a pressing social need.
- The pressing social need must be met in a 'proportionate' way.
- Proportionality involves a balancing of interests, but the starting point is freedom of expression, with the burden of proof on the authorities to justify the need for the restrictions and that the restrictions are no more than are necessary.
- The authority's reasons must be subject to close scrutiny by a court.

17.7 Expression on political and public issues

In assessing the democratic 'necessity' of any restriction on speech, the ECtHR has emphasised, again and again, the importance of protecting political speech. Very little, if any, margin of appreciation is allowed in respect of such speech. Likewise, UK courts are unlikely to defer overmuch in this context. Restraints on speech which, for example, involve criticism of ministers, officials or government policy will be hard to justify.

17.7.1 Broad definition of 'political' speech

Political speech is given a very broad definition. It is not confined to party political matters but includes information about, and comment on, matters of general public interest. The political or public dimension to speech can trigger Article 10 protection even if there may be other aspects to it (such as commercial self-interest) which, without the political aspect, might make restriction easier to justify.

In *Barthold* v *Germany* (1985) 7 EHRR 383, a private veterinary surgeon gave an interview in which he was critical of the lack of emergency vet services at night in Hamburg. His practice provided such services. Proceedings were successfully brought against the vet for breaching professional rules relating to advertising and publicity. The ECtHR held that there had been a violation of Article 10. By focusing on the fact that the applicant vet gained publicity for his practice, the German court had not recognised that the primary purpose of the interview was to address an important issue of concern. The ban was disproportionate.

Political marches, meetings, demonstrations and other types of political activity can be forms of 'expression' and so within the scope of Article 10; if 'peaceful' they may also be within the scope of Article 11.

case close-up

Steel v *United Kingdom* (1999) 28 EHRR 603

Demonstrators were detained for breach of the peace. The first and second applicants had attempted to disrupt, in the first case a grouse shoot, and in the second case the construction of a motorway. The third, fourth and fifth applicants had handed out leaflets and held up banners at an arms fair.

The ECtHR held that Article 10 applied to the situation of all five applicants; although it found that there had been a breach of the Article only in respect of the third, fourth and fifth defendants.

Likewise Article 10 gives protection to activists.

case close-up

Steel and Morris v *United Kingdom* (2005) 41 EHRR 22

S and M published leaflets which made serious allegations against McDonalds who sued them for libel. The main point of the case deals with whether they had a fair trial given the absence of legal aid (see Chapter 12, section 12.7.2). The ECtHR held that states had a margin of appreciation over whether or not massive commercial companies could sue individual campaigners for libel. However, the importance of freedom of expression meant that if companies did have this right the law needed to ensure that the defendants were properly represented so that all the issues could be raised and freedom of speech not unreasonably 'chilled'. The failure to provide legal aid, therefore, was also a breach of Article 10.

cross reference
Convention law relating to political meetings, marches and demonstrations is discussed in fuller detail in Chapter 18.

The ECtHR said, at para 89:

> in a democratic society even small and informal campaign groups...must be able to carry on their activities effectively and that there exists a strong public interest in enabling such groups and individuals outside the mainstream to contribute to the public debate by disseminating information and ideas on matters of general public interests such as health and the environment.

17.7.2 General principles

General principles that the Court follows in assessing the need for restrictions of political speech include:

- Freedom of expression is recognised as an essential condition of a 'democratic' society, as that term is understood by the Court.

- The courts, not the authorities, have the last word on whether or not a restriction on political speech is 'necessary'; such restrictions must be subject to the closest scrutiny by the Court.

- Pluralism, the recognition that different people have different standards, means that Article 10 must protect ideas and expressions even if they 'offend, shock or disturb' the majority of respectable citizens.

- The protection offered by Article 10 extends to groups or individuals who are seeking constitutional change such as the abolition of the monarchy (or even the possible break-up of the state or at least considerable autonomy for certain regions); such expression may be protected even when it takes place against a background of violent disorder (there are a number of cases involving Turkey which relate to this).

cross reference

The Court's understanding of 'democracy' is discussed in Chapter 6, section 6.4.

However:

- Article 10 permits states to adopt appropriate measures to guarantee public order and, in particular, to use the criminal law to suppress incitement to violence.

17.7.3 Restrictions on political speech

Despite the importance of expression dealing with public and social affairs, the ECtHR does recognise the right of states to suppress speech in certain circumstances. Proportionate restrictions aimed at protecting national security, for example, are permitted. An important example arose out of the long-running *Spycatcher* saga of the late 1980s.

case close-up

Observer and The Guardian v *United Kingdom* (1992) 14 EHRR 153

Peter Wright, a retired member of the security services, published his memoirs. These contained serious allegations about illegal or at least improper activity by the security service (they 'bugged and burgled their way around London' and their targets included the homes of members of the then Labour government). Peter Wright was liable to prosecution under the Official Secrets Act (which he avoided by living in Australia). More importantly, Mrs Thatcher's government sought to prevent the press from discussing the book or publishing excerpts from it. This they did by seeking a civil injunction on the grounds, recognised by English courts, of protecting confidential information. The House of Lords upheld an 'interlocutory', or holding, injunction that had been issued by the courts to maintain confidentiality until the issue could be finally decided. This injunction was maintained even after *Spycatcher* was published in the United States and copies were widely available throughout the world.

When the injunction was tested before the ECtHR, it was upheld on the grounds of being a lawful, proportionate restriction on freedom of expression, done in the interests of national security. However, maintaining the injunction after publication in the United States was disproportionate and a breach of Article 10. Like it or not, confidentiality was lost and so the injunction could not be 'necessary'. The government's argument that continuing the injunction was necessary in order to protect the general integrity of the security services was rejected.

17.8 Political expression and the political process

17.8.1 Politicians and the political process

It is particularly important that the laws must protect the freedom of speech of political actors, particularly elected representatives and those putting themselves forward for election.

In *Jerusalem* v *Austria* (2003) 37 EHRR 25, a member of the Vienna Municipal Council was subject to an injunction prohibiting her from repeating remarks she had made about religious sects in the Council chamber. The ECtHR found a violation of Article 10 and upheld the importance of free speech for elected representatives (para 36).

17.8.2 Parliamentary privilege

The freedom of elected representatives in Parliament is achieved by effective rules of **parliamentary privilege**, and the necessity for these has been recognised by the ECtHR.

. . . .

Parliamentary privilege

This is the freedom of Parliament to organise itself and conduct its own affairs free from any legal control enforced by the courts or from other forms of improper influence (see *R* v *Chaytor* [2010] UKSC 52). In particular, MPs enjoy freedom of speech (see Article 9 of the Bill of Rights 1688) and so it is not possible to seek either criminal or civil remedies against an MP for things said in Parliament. Fair and accurate media reports of things said in Parliament, including additional explanatory material which does not take the matter beyond what was said under privilege, are protected by 'qualified privilege': see *Curistan v Times Newspapers Ltd* [2008] EWCA Civ 432.

. . . .

In *A* v *United Kingdom* (2003) 36 EHRR 51, an MP, speaking in a Parliamentary debate, had connected the applicant to anti-social behaviour. She claimed that the absolute nature of parliamentary privilege prevented her from suing for defamation (in violation of her right to a fair trial). The ECtHR held that parliamentary privilege performed a necessary function in a democratic society of allowing Parliament to work effectively, and protecting it by limiting the right to sue for defamation did not violate Article 6.

17.8.3 Election restrictions

Freedom of expression can be restricted in the context of elections. The aim is to achieve a 'level playing field' on which political parties can set the political agenda at election time, present their policies and compete for votes. The law can be used to try to ensure that, at election time, the political agenda is not hijacked by wealthy and powerful pressure groups. This is a complex matter. In the United Kingdom there is

- a complete ban on the broadcasting (TV and radio) of paid-for political advertisements but no restrictions on press and poster political advertising (indeed, such advertising receives less regulation than ordinary commercial advertising);
- registered political parties have the right to make party political and party election broadcasts;
- at election times there are strict limits on expenditure at the constituency level—the amounts are quite small and, generally, only the candidates and their agents can spend money. Third

parties who wish to spend money to influence an election in a particular constituency are limited to £500. National expenditures (e.g. on poster campaigns) are restricted but the limits are quite high (both political parties and third parties could spend up to about £20m if they campaigned throughout the United Kingdom).

Political advertising

The complete ban on broadcast political advertising was upheld by the English courts in *R* v *Radio Authority ex parte Bull* [1997] 2 All ER 561. This involved advertising by Amnesty International aimed at promoting human rights, specifically in the context of Rwanda. However, in *VgT Verein gegen Tierfabriken* v *Switzerland* (2002) 34 EHRR 4 a similar ban was held to violate Article 10: a complete ban prevented political speech by an animal charity, by no means powerful, that was seeking to counter claims made in commercial advertising by the meat industry.

Despite this case, UK law has retained (in sections 319 and 321(2) of the Communications Act 2003) the outright ban on broadcast political advertising. The minister introducing the bill acknowledged, under section 19 HRA, that it might, on this point, not be compatible with Convention rights (see Chapter 4, section 4.9.2).

case close-up

R (Animal Defenders International) v Secretary of State for Culture, Media and Sport [2008] UKHL 15
. . . .

ADI, an animal charity, campaigning to change animal welfare law, was prevented, under the Communications Act 2003, from using broadcast adverts to promote its 'My Mate's a Primate' campaign aimed at raising public awareness of the treatment of primates. Despite the similarities with the *VgT* case, the House of Lords refused a declaration of incompatibility and upheld the ban. The sole issue was whether the clear and complete statutory ban was proportionate. It was held that

- the ban went no further than was necessary to achieve the important purpose in a democracy of fair elections that are not determined by money;

- there was no practical way of achieving this purpose by a more flexible rule which would, for example, allow advocacy on social issues by pressure groups (the policy could be hijacked by powerful interests);

- a high-level of deference was owed to Parliament on such an issue which affects the processes of British democracy.

discussion topic

The *Animal Defenders* case confirms that pressure groups representing the poor, the marginal and the dispossessed are unable to pursue political campaigns aimed at changes in the law or government policy through TV advertising (probably the most effective form of advertising). Is this a necessary consequence of maintaining a fair democracy in which all voices are equal or is it an undesirable constraint on political life?

Party political broadcasts

Who has the last word on the content of party political broadcasts in the UK? Is it the political parties or the broadcaster? The issue arose, under the HRA, in *Pro-Life Alliance* v *BBC*.

case close-up

Pro-Life Alliance v BBC [2003] UKHL 23

. . . .

The Pro-Life Alliance was entitled to a Party Election Broadcast and proposed to use the opportunity to broadcast graphic and disturbing images of abortions. The BBC, which has a legal responsibility not to broadcast matter which offends 'taste and decency', prohibited the broadcast of the images even though, normally, political parties control the content of election broadcasts. The courts were divided. The Court of Appeal held that the BBC had indulged in unlawful censorship; the House of Lords, by a majority, found for the BBC and decided that the broadcaster had simply exercised the discretion it was allowed over these matters by the law.

- The general rule (here in the BBC's Licence and Agreement with the government) that matters offensive to taste and decency should not be broadcast, was not itself tested against Article 10 (it might well have proved justifiable under Article 10(2)).

- In issue, rather, was the way the BBC had put the rule into effect. A majority of the House of Lords deferred to the broadcaster's decision on this matter. The court's job was just to ensure that the broadcasters had thought about freedom of expression and not behaved eccentrically. This was in stark contrast to the Court of Appeal, which imposed its own view of what freedom of speech required.

- Critics of the case suggest the House of Lords did not do enough to uphold freedom of speech. This was political speech at election time and it was also speech that was restricted just because it was thought shocking and disturbing. Article 10 is supposed to give a high priority to protecting such speech. Supporters of the decision argue that Parliament had approved the principle that decisions on taste and decency should be taken by the broadcasters and not the courts. The House of Lords had merely upheld this principle.

- The BBC did not object to the message but to the particular way in which the Pro-Life Alliance chose to express itself. Critics of the decision argue that not enough weight was given to the principle, found in the Strasbourg case law, that Article 10 protects not just what a person wants to say but must also allow people to express themselves in the way they think appropriate.

further study

Critical articles include Barendt, E. 'Free Speech and Abortion' [2003] *Public Law* (Winter) 580–591. Supportive articles include Geddes, A. 'What Future for Political Advertising on the United Kingdom's Television Screens?' [2002] *Public Law* (Winter) 615–625—commenting on the Court of Appeal's decision.

KEY POINT The importance at election times of allowing free speech about candidates by other candidates has been recognised by the High Court in *Culnane* v *Morris* [2005] EWHC 2438 (QB). The High Court upheld the argument that a leaflet published by the Liberal Democrat candidate, allegedly defamatory of the British National Party candidate, could be shown to enjoy qualified privileged, thus making it harder for the BNP candidate to sue.

Campaign expenditures

UK law (as was said at the beginning of this section) places significant restrictions on the amounts non-candidates can spend on promoting candidates or causes at elections. These obviously have an impact on the freedom of expression of the individuals, companies and pressure groups concerned. Restrictions which are absolute or which allow only very low expenditures by non-candidates, can be disproportionate and violate Article 10.

case close-up

Bowman v *United Kingdom* (1998) 26 EHRR 1

PB belonged to an anti-abortion campaign group which published information about the voting records on abortion of the candidates standing in a particular constituency. The election laws then (1992) prohibited expenditures in constituencies, other than by the candidates, to £5 (the figure is now £500). PB was prosecuted for breaking the election laws. The ECtHR held that there had been a violation of Article 10(2). The law served a legitimate purpose (the rights of others). Nevertheless £5 was so low that it amounted to an absolute bar on expenditures and so was a disproportionate restriction of PB's right to freedom of expression.

17.8.4 Criticising politicians and defamation

The importance of political speech means that the law may restrict the right of a public body to protect its reputation by an action for defamation (libel or slander). To succeed in such an action, a public body may have to prove that the speaker who made the defamatory statement (e.g. a newspaper) was motivated by malice. This is because the public body may be met by a rule of law that denies it the right to bring an action to protect its reputation in the absence of malice (the principle was adopted in England and Wales in *Derbyshire County Council* v *Times Newspapers* [1993] AC 534, and extended to political parties in *Goldsmith* v *Bhoyrul* [1998] QB 459). Or it may be that individuals (elected officials, for example, who are not covered by the rule in *Derbyshire* and may seek to protect their reputations) who sue newspapers are met with the defence of qualified privilege, which, again, requires proof of malice (see *Reynolds* v *Times Newspapers*, discussed in Chapter 22, section 22.3).

The justification for restricting the legal rights of politicians or public bodies to sue for defamation lies in the protection of freedom of speech. It is too easy for those in power to inhibit or 'chill' freedom of speech by using the law against their critics.

KEY POINT It has been argued that similar restrictions should apply to commercial companies, who, unlike public bodies, are able to defend their reputations through actions for defamation. After all, by means of their economic power, they can exercise considerable power and influence over social and economic life. This extension of the law has been rejected by the House of Lords (*Jameel* v *Wall Street Journal* [2006] UKHL 44, para 27) and finds no favour with the ECtHR (*Steel and Morris* v *United Kingdom*, section 17.7.1, para 94).

Under the Convention the issue is not clear cut. The Convention upholds the need to ensure that politicians and political bodies can be effectively and robustly criticised (e.g. *Lingens* v *Austria* (1986) 8 EHRR 407). Nevertheless, it is also an accepted principle that politicians and public figures do not lose their other Convention rights, such as their right to respect for private life, under Article 8 and their right to protect their reputation. Cases often involve a court seeking a fair balance between the Article 8 rights of a public figure and the rights of the media to freedom of expression (see, for example, *von Hannover* v *Germany* (2005) 40 EHRR 1).

For the Court, the proportionality of defamation proceedings brought by politicians may depend on whether it is a statement of 'fact' or 'opinion' that is objected to. Statements of opinion about politicians are much more strongly protected by Article 10.

In *Lindon* v *France* (2008) 46 EHRR 35, for instance, Jean-Marie Le Pen (the leader of a nationalist, some say neo-fascist, political party in France) had successfully sued the writers of a novel in which he was a named character to whom violently racist sentiments were attributed. The ECtHR (by a majority with strong dissents) held there was no violation of Article 10. An important part of its reasoning was that the novel had gone far beyond opinion and fiction and was, in effect, making unproven factual statements about the real politician.

discussion topic

Politicians and the media

Is the cause of democracy advanced or retarded by legal rules that give politicians and public officials lesser protection from the unfair, untrue or unreasonable criticism of others?

The cause of democracy is advanced because:

- Politicians exercise power and they often have considerable resources at their disposal. It is wrong that they should be able to use the law to prevent criticisms of their actions.

- They accept and enjoy the rewards of power and public life and as such they should be prepared to accept public criticism.

- Unlike most people, politicians are likely to be part of a representative assembly and have access to the media. They are therefore able to answer their critics. Political argument should take place in such places rather than in the courts.

The cause of democracy is retarded because:

- Politicians are normally trying to serve the public as best they can and should not be subject to damaging accusations of fact or slurs on their reputations which they are unable to refute.

- In a democracy we should encourage people to enter public life and serve their country or community; the threat of unfounded criticism and attack is likely to be a deterrent.

17.9 The limits to political speech: hate speech, racism and incitement

The extent of tolerance of intolerant political speech is one of the ongoing dilemmas of a liberal society. Article 10 protects political speech which disturbs, shocks or offends. Therefore, if it is legitimate under the Convention to restrict political speech, something more than the speech being merely offensive etc. must be at stake. Individual cases must, of course, meet the tests of Article 10(2). The test for being 'prescribed by law' is normally satisfied if the suppressing laws are formulated by statute. Often, the suppression of such speech can have the aim of preventing 'disorder or crime' or protecting 'the rights of others'. Compatibility with Article 10 then depends on the proportionality of any ban in the circumstances of the case.

17.9.1 Political outcomes which would violate human rights

cross reference
This topic, although it raises freedom of expression issues, is discussed in more detail in Chapter 18, section 18.7.2.

One issue is the extent to which political parties and others are free to advocate the passing of laws which, if they were brought into effect, would create a society in which important human rights would be violated. The ECtHR has shown itself willing to uphold bans on, for example, Islamist political parties in Turkey, which, if they came to power, might bring about such a state of affairs.

17.9.2 Advocacy of political violence

Article 10 does not protect speech which aims at inciting violence or hatred. The reaction of the Turkish government to the insurrection against it by part of its Kurdish population has given rise to a large case law on the issue. Whether speech or other expression is an incitement depends not just on the dictionary content of the words but also on the context. Issues such as

- who is speaking (whether in an official capacity or not),
- the nature of the medium (suppression of the mass media may be easier to justify than of a small circulation magazine),
- the area in which the words will be read or listened to,

are the kinds of issues that are relevant to a context-dependent judgment.

KEY POINT The advocacy of violence by officials raises different issues. International law bans 'propaganda for war' (Article 20 of the International Covenant on Civil and Political Rights (ICCPR)) and such a ban should extend to public officials. However, the lawful use of force can be legitimate for a state, and so propaganda for war is unlikely to exclude reasoned arguments for lawful war. Arguing for unlawful war could, of course, raise an Article 20 point.

17.9.3 Hate speech

Article 20 ICCPR requires states to ensure that

> Any advocacy of national, racial or religious hatred that constitutes incitement to discrimination, hostility or violence shall be prohibited by law.

Article 10 ECHR does not expressly require the suppression of hate speech, such as racist speech. Nevertheless, in *Jersild* v *Denmark* (1995) 19 EHRR 1, the ECtHR held that the expression of vicious racist sentiments would not be protected by Article 10. They were likely to go beyond being merely disturbing, shocking or offensive.

> There can be no doubt that the remarks [made by racists during a television programme] were more than insulting to members of the targeted group and did not enjoy the protection of Article 10. (para 35)

Jersild was about the prosecution of journalists who had allowed a group of racists (the Greenjackets) to broadcast their racist views as part of a programme on Danish television dealing with the rise of racism in that country.

HRA

In England and Wales, Part III of the Public Order Act 1986 (POA 1986) creates a range of offences dealing with incitements to racial hatred in various contexts. Legislation dealing with football hooliganism criminalises racist chanting. Under the Crime and Disorder Act 1998, some offences can be more severely punished if there is evidence of a racial motive and, since 2001, an anti-religious motive. All these Acts criminalise expression and must be interpreted consistently with Article 10.

The Racial and Religious Hatred Act 2006 amends the POA 1986 by making the 'stirring up' of religious hatred, by threatening words, behaviour or displays, a crime (and hatred on grounds of sexual orientation is added by section 74 Criminal Justice and Immigration Act 2008). The links between religion and ethical and moral issues mean that the criticism of religion is not necessarily unreasonable. Section 29J POA 1986 therefore makes the protection of freedom of expression a statutory principle. The offence of stirring up religious hatred is not committed by those who express 'antipathy, dislike, ridicule, insult or abuse' of religions and their adherents (there is no similar defence in respect of race or sexual orientation).

However, there is also section 5 POA 1986, which allows, amongst other things, for the prosecution of a person who causes 'harassment, alarm or distress' by using 'insulting words or behaviour'; the crime can be committed, therefore, without there being any threat of violence and on the basis of words or other expressions alone. The provision has been widely used in the context of aggressive but non-violent demonstrations and racist or other offensive forms of speech and signs made for political purposes. There is a defence under section 5(3) for the defendant to show that his or her conduct was reasonable, and at this point the fact that they were otherwise lawfully exercising their rights to freedom of expression under Article 10 can be relevant.

discussion topic

The use of section 5 POA 1986 in reference to politically motivated demonstrations, speech and actions involves difficult questions of the limits of freedom of expression. Has section 5 got the balance right?

- In *Percy* v *DPP* [2001] EWHC 1125, P burnt the US flag, seen by some Americans as a desecration, as part of a protest against US defence policy: her conviction was quashed as being a disproportionate interference with freedom of expression.

- In *Norwood* v *DPP* [2003] EWHC 1564 (Admin), the defendant was convicted under section 5 POA 1986 for an ordinary public order offence aggravated by an anti-religious motive. He had displayed posters advocating 'Islam out of Britain' and associating Islam with the attacks on the World Trade Center. The Administrative Court held that the prosecutions were compatible with Article 10.

- In *Hammond* v *DPP* [2004] EWHC 69, the conviction, also under section 5 POA 1986, of a religious campaigner who had preached against gay rights, thereby stirring up a hostile reaction, was also held to be compatible with Article 10.

Norwood and *Hammond* raise the issue of the value of Article 10. The expressions in issue did not incite violence. They were, no doubt, offensive, but offensive words about public affairs are supposed to enjoy protection under Article 10(1). The High Court held both convictions were justified in terms of Article 10(2) as proportionate ways of protecting the rights of others. The danger is that English courts may be creating a right not to be offended, which renders the protection of offensive speech under Article 10(1) of little worth. On the other hand, supporters of the judgment could say the morality behind human rights law clearly stands against forms of discrimination that are based on assumptions that other people, their identity or their beliefs are in one sense or another inferior. The recognition of the dignity of others, on which human rights is based, involves respect for others as equals, and applying section 5 in this way puts that important moral principle into effect. A decent society requires laws such as this: there is no right to offend.

Inciting violence and expressions of hate (rather than criticism, dislike or insult) are dealt with in other legislation, in particular Parts 3 and 3A Public Order Act 1986 dealing with stirring up hatred on grounds of race, religion and sexual orientation.

17.9.4 **Morally worthless speech**

cross reference
Article 17 is discussed in Chapter 7, section 7.3.

Convention case law on Article 10 suggests that some expression is outside the protection of Article 10 (and therefore can be subject to criminal penalties) because it is morally worthless. It is worthless in the sense that it is expression which contradicts the basic values on which the Convention is based and may involve the denial of clearly established facts. Article 17 can be invoked against such speech. Under Article 17 a person cannot claim Convention rights in order to suppress the rights of others.

Examples of such expression include:

- Holocaust denial. Denying the Holocaust is an offence in some countries. In *Remer* v *Germany* App 25096/94, admissibility decision of 6 September 1995, the Commission found there could be no breach of Article 10 in respect of Holocaust denial; the speech was unprotected because of Article 17. In *Lehideux and Isomi* v *France* (2000) 30 EHRR 665, the ECtHR accepted that there is a 'category of clearly established historical facts—such as the Holocaust—whose negation or revision would be removed from the protection of Article 10 by Article 17' (para 47).

- Overt religious (and racist?) prejudice. In *Norwood* (see Discussion Topic in section 17.9.3), the defendant applied to Strasbourg. The ECtHR held it was inadmissible because of Article 17 (N's freedom of expression was aimed at the destruction of the rights of others). The posters involved a 'general, vehement attack against a religious group, linking the group as a whole with terrorism'. It was 'incompatible with basic Convention values of tolerance, social peace and non-discrimination' (*Norwood* v *United Kingdom* (2005) 40 EHRR SE 11).

Legitimate debate about controversial and sensitive matters is protected by Article 10 so long as the debate does not involve attitudes, assumptions and the assertion of falsehoods which are incompatible with the basic values underlying the Convention. (The reassessment of the reputation of Marshall Pétain, the leader of the Vichy government in France, which, during the Second World War collaborated with the Nazis, was legitimate, see *Lehideux and Isomi* v *France* (2000) 30 EHRR 665.)

17.10 Freedom of expression and Article 8

The right to freedom of expression, especially freedom of the media, can often lead to challenges brought by those who feel that their privacy, protected by Article 8, has been violated. These issues are explored in Chapter 22, section 22.5.

17.11 Freedom of expression and contempt of court

Legal limits on the way in which trials and matters before the courts are reported involve one of the most significant interferences with freedom of expression, especially media freedom. The issue is considered in Chapter 12, section 12.9.2, Contempt of court.

Artistic expression

There is no expressed protection for 'artistic' speech in Article 10 (unlike Article 19(2) ICCPR, which protects a person's freedom of expression 'orally, in writing or in print, in the form of art, or through any other media of his choice'). Nevertheless, the ECtHR has made it clear that the protection of Article 10(1) extends to artistic works: both the freedom to create artistic works and the freedom to disseminate them through exhibitions and other methods. In *Müller* v *Switzerland* (1998) 13 EHRR 212, the ECtHR understood artistic expression as affording 'the opportunity to take part in the public exchange of cultural, political and social information and ideas of all kinds'.

Works of art that have overt political and social themes can enjoy the high degree of protection given to political speech. However, Article 10 also protects works that have no social or political purpose and which aim, for example, simply to be beautiful. However, works without an overt social and political purpose may have a lower degree of protection. In other words, absent a clear political purpose, it is easier for the state to show that an act of censorship or restriction is justified in terms of Article 10(2).

Work which is merely pornographic and makes no claim to be otherwise enjoys little protection under the Convention. The problem here is that the right to freedom of artistic expression under Article 10 may give little assistance to artists whose work is vulnerable to state claims that it is indecent or pornographic but who are seeking, through artistic production, to challenge conventional conceptions of 'art' or conventional moralities (for a statement of the issue see *Belfast City Council* v *Miss Behavin' Ltd* [2007] UKHL 19, para 38, Baroness Hale).

Any such bans on artistic work must meet the tests in Article 10(2). First, a ban must be 'prescribed by law'. The vagueness of terms like 'obscenity' or 'indecency' might, in principle, create a problem, though this has not generally occurred.

case close-up

S and G v United Kingdom App 17634/91, Commission admissibility decision of 2 September 1991

. . . .

An artist and gallery owner had displayed sculptures in an art gallery that included modelled heads to which earrings made from freeze-dried human foetuses had been attached. They were prosecuted for the common law offence of outraging public decency. The Commission of Human Rights found that the application was manifestly unfounded and inadmissible.

The offence of outraging public decency, although a common law offence and vague when considered in abstract terms, had been defined by the UK courts with sufficient clarity for it to meet the Convention standards for 'law' of 'foreseeability' and 'accessibility'.

The prosecution was a proportionate way of achieving the purpose of protection of morals.

Second, any ban must be to further one of the purposes listed in Article 10(2). In the context of art works and alleged obscenity or indecency, the ECtHR has accepted that bans and prosecutions, etc. can be for 'the protection of . . . morals'.

Third, therefore, any such ban or prosecution must be 'necessary in a democratic society'. In the context of expression that is banned or prosecuted in order to protect morals, the ECtHR has allowed a wide margin of appreciation (at least since *Handyside* v *United Kingdom* (1979–80) 1 EHRR 737, one of its earliest cases). The ECtHR does not accept that there is a tension between its insistence that expression is protected by Article 10 even if (in the often repeated formula) it 'offends, shocks or disturbs' and giving states a wide margin of appreciation over the banning of works on the grounds that they are seriously offensive though not otherwise harmful. Nevertheless, context and changing social standards are very important.

In *Müller* v *Switzerland* (1988) 13 EHRR 212, a group of artists and others were prosecuted for obscenity offences. Some of the pictures depicted, in large and graphic scale, acts of sodomy, fellatio, bestiality and also erect penises. The ECtHR held that, in the circumstances (the pictures were displayed in a free and public exhibition) the prosecutions were within the state's margin of appreciation.

In *Vereinigung Bildender Kunstler* v *Austria* (2008) 47 EHRR 5, an injunction preventing the public display of a picture containing sexually explicit caricatures of well-known people, including a prominent politician, was a violation of Article 10.

Prosecutions in England and Wales under, for example, the Obscene Publications Act 1959, are measured against Article 10.

---

case close-up

R v *Perrin* [2002] EWCA Crim 747

P was convicted of publishing obscene images on the Internet. The Court of Appeal held that the conviction was compatible with Article 10. In particular:

- The margin of appreciation and the relatively low level of protection for non-political speech left states room to make choices balancing Internet freedom with other interests such as the protection of children.

- There was little if any public interest in the publication of merely pornographic images.

---

discussion topic

The enforcement of morals

Should the protection of morals in itself ever justify restriction of free expression?

- In a famous passage from his book *On Liberty* (Chapter 1), John Stuart Mill argued that 'the only purpose for which power can rightfully be exercised over any member of a civilised community against his will is to prevent harm to others'. Expression that does not lead to physical harm or harm to the property or interests of others (i.e. it does not have the effect of preventing others leading their lives as they wish) should not be suppressed. Suppression on grounds of immorality, in the absence of harm to others, is simply giving vent to prejudice and to an intrusive sense of disgust etc. at the thought of the lives that others lead. Article 10, as the Court has often said, protects speech which is shocking, disturbing or offensive.

- Even if we do allow 'immorality', in the absence of harm to others, to be suppressed, who is to determine what is or is not 'immoral'? Moral standards are endlessly controversial. There is no full social consensus on what is immoral; standards change and claims that behaviour is immoral may simply reflect the prejudices of the majority, those in positions of power or loud minorities.

On the other hand, it can be suggested that:

- Mill's concept of 'harm' is very hard to make sense of. A powerful feeling of disgust may be harmful. It is a very subjective test.

- In any case, a society, if it is to have some degree of coherence and unity, is bound to reflect cultural values that are important to men and women in terms of their sense of identity, well-being and belonging. The importance of these values means they can, reasonably, be enforced against dissident minorities and individuals. Such values are identified through the considered judgments of legislators, judges and juries dealing with particular cases and situations. Arguments such as these are important to discussion of, for example, laws on pornography: should pornography be banned only if there is evidence that it is harmful, in the sense, for example, that it leads to attacks on women; or should it be banned because it can be disgusting and degrading and leads to a diminishing sense of self-worth for both men and women?

The leading texts in the 'enforcement of morals' debate are

- Devlin, P. *The Enforcement of Morals* (1965) Oxford: OUP;
- Hart, H.L.A. *Law, Liberty and Morality* (1963) Oxford: OUP.

The debate is summarised and discussed in jurisprudence texts such as

- Bix, B. *Jurisprudence* 2nd edn (1999) London: Sweet and Maxwell, Chapter 15.

 17.13 # Commercial expression

Commercial speech, such as that found in catalogues or advertising, is capable of protection under Article 10(1). However, the ECtHR accepts that states have a very wide margin of appreciation over the need for restrictions. Speech which is entirely or predominantly commercial enjoys only a low level of protection: it is relatively easy for the authorities to show that the public good requires restriction on speech (see *Markt Intern Verlag* v *Germany* (1990) 12 EHRR 161, para 33). If commercial speech also has political overtones, then it will enjoy greater protection, as in *Barthold* v *Germany* (1985) 7 EHRR 383, see section 17.7.1.

Restrictions on advertising are also, usually, compatible with Article 10 so long as the public interest served by the ban outweighs the interest of the public in hearing about the products in issue.

In *R (British American Tobacco)* v *Secretary of State for Health* [2004] EWHC 2493 (Admin), the ban on tobacco advertising in the United Kingdom was upheld by the Administrative Court. It satisfied the need for proportionality where restrictions on human rights are concerned. Proportionality was measured against the wider margin of appreciation left to the national authorities by the ECtHR.

 # Summary

- Freedom of speech is protected in both common law and as a Convention right.

- Article 10 of the Convention involves asking, first, whether some form of expression is protected by the first paragraph of Article 10 and then whether any restriction on expression can be justified in terms of Article 10(2).

- Under the Convention, the highest degree of protection is accorded to speech and other expressions which concern political and public affairs. Media freedom is protected.

- Nevertheless, Article 10(2) permits restriction to freedom of expression on various grounds, such as national security and protecting the authority of the judiciary; also racists and others may be denied protection for their speech under Article 17.

- Artistic and other forms of expression, including commercial expression, are protected, although on moral issues, such as laws on obscenity, states enjoy a wide margin of appreciation.

? Questions

For suggested approaches, please visit the Online Resource Centre.

1 Suppose that a local government department bans all officials from wearing any badge or insignia with racist overtones, and does so, as required under the Race Relations Act 1976 (amended in 2000), to 'promote good race relations'. If the ban is challenged, how would the issue be approached by an English court?

2 What approach is taken by the ECtHR regarding restricting expenditure on advertisements, pamphlets, etc. during elections. Is the Court's approach consistent with 'democracy'?

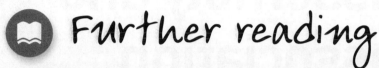

Further reading

Barendt, E. *Freedom of Speech* (2001) Oxford: OUP

Davis, H. 'The Rights Approach to the Right to a Public Hearing' [2012] (Jan) *Public Law* 11–18

Khan, A. 'A "Right Not to be Offended" under Article 10(2) ECHR' [2012] 2 *EHRLR* 191–204

Lester, A, Pannick, D. and Herberg, J. (see Preface) Chapter 4, Article 10

Ovey, C. and White, R. *The European Convention on Human Rights (Jacobs and White)* 4th edn (2006) Oxford: OUP, Chapter 13

Scott, A. 'A Monstrous and Unjustifiable Infringement? Political Expression and the Broadcasting Ban of Advocacy Advertising' (2003) 66 *MLR* 224–244

Schauer, F. *Freedom of Speech: A Philosophical Inquiry* (1982) Cambridge: CUP

Article 11: freedom of assembly and association

Chapter overview

- The right to peaceful assembly, including political meetings, marches and protests (Article 11(1)).
- The grounds on which the right to peaceful assembly can be legitimately interfered with, considered with reference to the law of public order in England and Wales.
- The right to freedom of association.
- The grounds on which the right to association can be legitimately interfered with.
- Trade unions.
- Restrictions on the political activity of public officials.

Article 11 Freedom of assembly and association

(1) Everyone has the right to freedom of peaceful assembly and to freedom of association with others, including the right to form and to join trade unions for the protection of his interests.

(2) No restrictions shall be placed on the exercise of these rights other than such as are prescribed by law and are necessary in a democratic society in the interests of national security or public safety, for the prevention of disorder or crime, for the protection of health or morals, for the protection of the reputation or rights of others. This article shall not prevent the imposition of lawful restrictions on the exercise of these rights by members of the armed forces, of the police or of the administration of the state.

Introduction

Article 11 protects the rights of people to 'peaceful assembly', which means, in effect, to hold and take part in peaceful meetings, marches and demonstrations. This is an important right to protect and facilitate political activity and an important section of this chapter concerns the application of Article 11 to various aspects of UK (mainly English) law which deal with political meetings, marches and demonstrations.

Article 11 also protects people's rights to 'associate', and this refers to the right to join and be active in 'associations'—clubs and societies such as political parties, pressure groups and religious organisations; trade unions are expressly mentioned.

18.1 Political rights and the Convention

cross reference

On democracy see Chapter 1, section 1.1.1 (part of the jus-tification of human rights) and Chapter 6, section 6.4 (a per-vasive Convention concept).

Article 11 is one of the rights by which political freedom (the right to political action or to participate in public affairs) is secured under the Convention (see *R (Countryside Alliance)* v *AG* [2007] UKHL 52, paras 117–118, Baroness Hale). As such, it needs to be read and under-stood in the light of the Convention concept of democracy. The promotion of democracy is one of the aims of the Council of Europe and is central to the general philosophical justifi-cation of human rights. A 'democratic' political system is the only one acceptable under the Convention.

The right to vote, and the right to stand for election and, if elected, to take one's seat is guar-anteed in terms of Article 3 of the First Protocol.

cross reference

Article 3 is discussed in Chapter 25.

But it would be a narrow conception of democracy (as merely a four- or five-yearly competition for votes by political elites) that was sufficiently encapsulated by these rights. People need to pursue their political aims through extra-Parliamentary means such as joining political parties and pressure groups, promoting their aims through various media and by holding meetings and marches and taking part in demonstrations. This broader political freedom is protected in the Convention, in particular, by Article 10 (freedom of expression: see Chapter 17) and by

Article 11. Like Article 10, Article 11 is understood to be fundamental to a democracy. The right to peaceful assembly and association can only be interfered with by laws or actions which aim to protect democracy. As with Article 10, assembly or association can involve promoting ideas and policies that 'disturb, shock and offend'. Both rights can be interfered with by state action which is lawful (in the Convention meaning of the term), for one of the legitimate purposes listed in Article 10(2) or 11(2) and proportionate.

It is not unusual that a case could be decided by both Article 10 or Article 11. Political marches, meetings and demonstrations are protected under the Convention, and Article 11 has an important role to play in this. However, such activity can also be a type of expression and so within the scope of Article 10. It is not unusual that cases dealing with political demonstration are dealt with using Article 10. Any Article 11 claim is dismissed by the European Court of Human Rights (ECtHR) on the grounds that no new issues are raised which have not already been raised under Article 10 (see, for example, *Steel* v *United Kingdom* (1999) 28 EHRR 603, discussed in Chapter 17, section 17.7.1).

In such a case the courts will normally apply one Article only. This is the '*lex specialis*' and whether it is Article 10 or 11 will depend on the facts. Only passing reference is made to the other Article unless separate issues arise.

18.2 The structure of Article 11

Like Articles 8–10, Article 11 has a two-paragraph structure. A court (including the ECtHR) dealing with a case in which it is claimed that Article 11 is involved, must first decide whether the facts disclose an issue covered by the terms 'peaceful assembly' or 'association'. Then a court must decide whether the assembly or association has been interfered with. If so, finally, a court must decide whether the state has shown the interference to be justified in terms of Article 11(2).

cross reference
This basic structure is common with Articles 8, 9, 10 and is discussed in Chapter 14.

- Any interference must be 'prescribed by law'.

- Any interference must be for one of the purposes listed in paragraph 2, and not for any others.

- Any interference must be 'necessary' in the sense of being a proportionate exercise of power.

18.3 Peaceful assembly: meetings, marches and demonstrations

18.3.1 Peaceful assembly

Article 11 protects only the right to peaceful assembly. This right is recognised by the ECtHR as a 'fundamental right in a democratic society . . . one of the foundations of such a society' (*Adali* v *Turkey* App 38187/97, judgment of 31 March 2005, citing earlier cases).

Article 11 applies to both meetings and marches whether they take place on private land or in public places including highways.

Article 11 is not a licence for people to coerce others or the population at large. Violent demonstrations or actions taken for political reasons to stop others acting lawfully (scientists doing regulated experiments on animals, for example) will fall outside the protection of Article 11 altogether.

KEY POINT Whether a demonstration is peaceful or not, demonstrators continue to enjoy other Convention rights such as Article 5 (liberty), Article 2 (the right to life—which is not violated if lawful, potentially lethal, force is used to quell a 'riot or insurrection') and Article 3 (the right not to suffer inhuman or degrading treatment, for example at the hands of the police or others). Article 17, however, prevents demonstrators from using their Convention rights to undermine the rights of others.

18.3.2 **Peaceful and non-peaceful assembly**

The boundary between peaceful and non-peaceful protest is hard to draw. A peaceful protest is where organisers and participants do not have 'violent intentions' (*Stankov* v *Bulgaria* App 29221/95, judgment of 2 October 2001, para 77). The Convention does not confine 'peaceful' to meetings etc. which are entirely based on rational persuasion conducted by words alone. Non-violent but obstructive behaviour can be peaceful.

case close-up

MC v *Germany* App 13079/87, admissibility decision of 6 March 1989

MC participated in a demonstration in front of US military barracks. The demonstrators blocked the road for 12 minutes every hour and required the military and the police to close the road.

It was held by the European Commission of Human Rights that the prosecution of the demonstrators was an interference with their right to peaceful assembly, which could only be justified on the grounds provided for by Article 11(2). The interference was so justified.

The general principles derived from this and other cases are as follows:

• The right to protest in a democratic society is fundamental and important, so Article 11 should not be interpreted restrictively.

• A demonstration 'where the organisers and participants have violent intentions which result in public disorder' is not protected by Article 11.

• However, a person does not lose the protection of Article 11 just because of the violent actions of others. The exercise of a right to, specifically, peaceful assembly must be judged by the conduct of the applicant.

In *Ezelin* v *France* (1991) 14 EHRR 362, for example, there was a breach of Article 11 when a French lawyer was disciplined by his professional body for not disassociating himself from a demonstration when it began to turn disorderly. The Commission held that

generally speaking, an individual does not cease to enjoy the right to freedom of peaceful assembly simply because sporadic violence or other punishable acts take place in the course of the assembly, if he himself remains peaceful in his intentions and behaviour.

These words have been endorsed by the ECtHR in *Ziliberberg* App 61821/00, admissibility decision of 4 May 2004.

Demonstrations may interfere with the ordinary life of others (by obstructing traffic, for example). However it is necessary for the authorities to balance this against preserving the effectiveness of the right to peaceful assembly. The ECtHR has said 'it is important for the public authorities to show a certain degree of tolerance towards peaceful gatherings if [freedom of peaceful assembly under Article 11] is not to be deprived of its substance' (*Berladir* v *Russia* App 34202/06, judgment of 19 July 2012, para 38).

It is worth repeating that the principles given here concern the issue of whether Article 11 is engaged at all. If it is engaged, the attention then shifts (as it did in the cases noted earlier) to whether there was a justified interference with the applicant's freedom of assembly.

18.4 Positive duties

Given the fundamental nature of the right of assembly in a democracy, the question has arisen whether states have positive duties to promote democratic politics (e.g. by making facilities available for meetings etc.) and to protect those taking part in demonstrations. There is little case law on the former. However, states do have positive duties to protect those taking part in meetings from the violence and intimidation of those opposed to them. In *Plattform Ärzte für das Leben* v *Austria* (1988) 13 EHRR 204, a group of 'pro-life' doctors alleged that there was insufficient police protection of their march from a 'pro-choice' counter-demonstration. On the facts there was no violation of the Convention, but the ECtHR did say that

> Genuine, effective freedom of peaceful assembly cannot . . . be reduced to a mere duty on the part of the state not to interfere: a purely negative conception would not be compatible with the object and purposes of Article 11. Like Article 8, Article 11 sometimes requires positive measures to be taken even in the sphere of relations between individuals, if need be. (para 31)

However, the duty is not absolute—there is no duty to ensure that the peaceful assembly can take place. Rather, it is to take 'reasonable and appropriate' measures, over which the states have a wide margin of appreciation.

The duty to take positive measures requires states to inhibit the 'opposition veto'. The traditional English law on breach of the peace, for example, focused on the need of the police to keep order. They could take whatever action was most convenient to achieve this end. Arresting a person lawfully making a speech might be easier than confronting a violent mob. The mob, by threatening violence, exercises a veto on lawful demonstrators. English cases taking into account Articles 10 and 11 have begun to redirect the law on this matter.

case close-up

Redmond-Bate v *DPP* [2000] HRLR 249

A group of female Christians were preaching on the steps of Wakefield Cathedral. They began to irritate tourists and passers by. The police, fearing a breach of the peace, took action against the women. The High Court held that the arrest of the women for breach of the peace was unlawful under common law, partly as measured against the women's Convention rights.

The importance of this case is:

- Its stress on the need for the police to consider the reasonableness of the actions of the claimant.

- The police must do more than take the easiest way of preserving the peace. It is necessary to consider, for example, the source of the threat of violence and whether the claimant's actions are really provocative.

- If people are exercising their Convention rights, of free expression or peaceful assembly, then there is likely to be a presumption that their actions are reasonable and it is unreasonable for a person to respond violently.

- If, on the other hand, demonstrators are preventing others from lawful activities the possibility of violence is likely to be more reasonable and Convention rights less likely to offer a defence to the demonstrators (see, for example, *Nicol* v *DPP* (1996) 160 JP 155, which, though decided before the Human Rights Act 1998 (HRA), nevertheless refers to Convention rights).

further study

Local authorities in England and Wales have a statutory duty to make school and other premises available for election meetings, but whether there are broader positive duties is unclear. Over-broad refusals to allow political activity of any kind, at a local festival, for example, can already be unlawful exercises of power under common law, a point reinforced by Article 11 (see *R* v *Barnet LBC ex parte Johnson* (1990) 89 LGR 581 (QB)).

Positive duties are not absolute. Rights to demonstrate peacefully may, for example, be restricted in order to give recognition to the rights of others, such as property owners. This can be so even if the property owner controls a large shopping area which has, as it were, taken over the centre of a city (see *Appleby* v *United Kingdom* (2003) 37 EHRR 38).

discussion topic

Should political activists have the right to protest and demonstrate if, in so doing, they interfere with the freedom of others and, perhaps, break laws or prevent activities which have been endorsed by the majority of the population through the process of electoral politics and representative government? Does the Convention provide the basis for a reasonable solution to the problem?

- Consider the concept of 'peaceful' in the idea of a peaceful assembly.

- Consider the 'rights of others' provision in Articles 10(2) and 11(2).

- Is there a difference between, on the one hand, interfering with people going about their ordinary daily tasks and, on the other hand, trying to prevent a lawful activity which the protestors oppose?

- Is there a difference (as some political theorists contend) between a range of issues which are appropriate for decision on the basis of majority votes (and so we should all accept the majority view as embodied in the law), and other more fundamental issues which are more like moral absolutes. If the law allows actions which are inconsistent with these 'moral absolutes' then, perhaps, law breaking by demonstrators or interfering with the freedom of others might be justified? If this distinction can be made, what examples might be given?

The legal (and also moral) limits to the rights of demonstrators are discussed by Lord Hoffmann in *R* v *Jones* [2006] UKHL 16, see paras 74–89.

18.5 Interference with rights

Any restrictions, by the police and other authorities, on the right to peaceful assembly and association, including the right to demonstrate, must be justified in terms of Articles 10(2) and 11(2).

cross reference
For the concept of 'law' see Chapter 6, section 6.2; a good summary by the Court is Rekvényi v Hungary (2000) 30 EHRR 519, para 34.

18.5.1 Is the restriction 'prescribed by law'?

Public order law often gives the police and magistrates wide discretionary powers. Such powers must be prescribed by law and not only be lawful under national law, but the national law must also fulfil the Convention requirements of being 'accessible' and 'foreseeable'.

In the context of meetings, marches and demonstrations, the ECtHR takes a tolerant view of open-textured powers granting wide discretion.

In *Chorherr v Austria* (1994) 17 EHRR 358, the ECtHR accepted that a legal power to arrest for an offence of 'conduct likely to cause annoyance' was, in the circumstances, sufficiently precise.

By contrast, in *Hashman and Harrup v United Kingdom* (2000) 30 EHRR 241, the ECtHR held that the power of magistrates in the United Kingdom to bind over for 'good behaviour' failed the 'foreseeablity' test. (A person could agree to restrictions on their behaviour, not to take part in future demonstrations, for example, often as an alternative to a criminal conviction.) What good behaviour might require could not, in the view of the Court, be predicted by the person bound over. The distinction with other cases is that they refer, no matter how vaguely, to the effects of actions; good behaviour limits only conduct, irrespective of results.

In *Gillan v UK* (2010) 50 EHRR 45, the ECtHR held that the exercise by the police of powers of random stop and search (stop and search without the need for reasonable suspicion in the individual case) under the Terrorism Act 2000 was a breach of Article 8. The ECtHR held that the power could be exercised on grounds and under conditions that did not meet the requirements of foreseeability (for further discussion see Chapter 26, section 26.8.1).

18.5.2 Is the interference for a legitimate purpose

Police action against demonstrators must also be justified, under Article 11(2), as being for one of the purposes listed in Article 11(2). The 'prevention of disorder or crime' will normally be sufficient and easy to establish.

18.5.3 Is the restriction 'necessary in a democratic society'

Such action must also be 'necessary in a democratic society'. This requires a judgment of proportionality. The issue will depend very much on the specific facts. The case law suggests that the Strasbourg authorities tend to give a wide margin of appreciation to states on whether there is a real threat of disorder.

In *Christians against Racism and Fascism v United Kingdom* App 8440/78 (1980) 21 DR 138, the applicants were unable to hold a non-controversial march because of a general ban on all marches imposed, under public order legislation, in order to stop a controversial racist march. UK law only permitted general bans in order to protect the political impartiality of the police and authorities. The Commission took the view that a general ban was only justified if necessary to prevent disorder, not just to protect official impartiality. On the facts, however, they held that the ban was proportionate.

18.6 English law and the Human Rights Act

18.6.1 Introduction

There is in the United Kingdom a long tradition of political dissent and protest, which has expressed itself through extra-Parliamentary activity, some of which has aimed at deliberate disruption of lawful but disapproved-of activities, and some of which has resulted in violent confrontations with the police. Recent years have seen such protests against war, nuclear weapons, the arms trade, free trade, racist politics, environmental degradation, the exploitation of animals, abortion and other matters. The policing of these activities is itself often controversial, with allegations being made of disproportionate reactions, which both fuel violent reactions and also involve improper restrictions on demonstrator's rights. On the other hand the police can be faced with demonstrators some of whom they, the police, have good grounds to believe are aiming at damaging property, are prepared to intimidate and may use violence against people.

The underlying issue is the extent of police discretion and how the exercise of this discretion can be compatible with Convention rights.

The police are a public authority under section 6 HRA and so can be proceeded against in court, under section 7 HRA, if they fail to act compatibly with Convention rights; alternatively a breach of Convention rights can be part of a defence or of some other cause of action.

cross reference
Breach of the peace is discussed in section 18.6.3.

- Police have, as we shall see, an important common law power to act against breaches of the peace. Such a power must be exercised consistently with Articles 10 and 11.

- Police have statutory powers which relate to public order, and these statutes, under section 3 HRA, must be read and given effect (if possible) compatibly with Convention rights. Of particular importance is the Public Order Act 1986 (POA 1986), which authorises a range of police powers and creates a number of offences in the public order context. This is in addition to their general powers (stop and search, arrest, etc.) in the Police and Criminal Evidence Act 1984 (PACE) (see Chapter 20).

18.6.2 Use of land

Any meeting, march or process must, obviously, take place on land, which will be in the possession of someone: an individual, a corporate body or a public authority. Likewise, if a person uses a highway for an obstructive or otherwise improper purpose, they lose their right to be there and the owner of the underlying land can seek a remedy.

For private, including corporate bodies, ordinary property law applies and permission can be refused on any ground (or for no reason). If the meeting etc. goes ahead despite the refusal of consent it will be trespassory. The occupier has various civil remedies available. The police could remove the trespassers but only if a breach of the peace was apprehended or a criminal offence committed.

The courts issue the remedies (e.g. an injunction) and, as public authorities, should only do so if an injunction would be compatible with Convention rights. If the possessor of the land is a public authority (e.g. a local council) then its action in seeking a remedy must, under section 6 HRA, be compatible with the Convention. Clearly any injunction will interfere with peaceful assembly, so the issue of justification under Article 11(2) will be central. Injunctions and other judicial remedies have a well-established legal basis in English law, so the issue of legality is unlikely to be decisive. Likewise one of the purposes for which interference with freedom of assembly is legitimate is to 'protect the rights . . . of others' and property rights come within this concept. It follows that the main focus of justification will be on the proportionality of any interference.

Of great importance is the role of a corporate land owner. Large areas in the centre of many cities, areas where the public go, are occupied by great shopping malls owned by commercial bodies. As public areas they are places where political activists may want to promote their cause. The conflict between the activists' claims to be exercising political rights and the property rights of the occupiers tend to be resolved in favour of the latter.

case close-up

Appleby v United Kingdom (2003) 37 EHRR 38

. . . .

An environmental pressure group sought to obtain signatures for a petition by setting up a stall in a shopping mall in the centre of Washington, in Tyne and Wear. The owners refused permission on the grounds of maintaining political neutrality. The ECtHR held that the property rights of the owners (Article 1 of the First Protocol) had to be taken into account. The political rights of the applicants had not been fully extinguished since there were other places where they could go to seek signatures. The Court did suggest that if there were no effective alternatives then, perhaps, the state would have positive duties to allow political activity.

It is clear that the courts will take into account the Article 11 rights of protestors, even against private, corporate landowners. At the same time they have been prepared to protect the corporate interest by issuing injunctions to control large demonstrations by binding many unidentified persons.

- In *Heathrow Airport Ltd v Garman* [2007] EWHC 1957, Heathrow Airport obtained an injunction restraining the organisation of a climate change demonstration at Heathrow Airport. It was obtained against alleged disrupters (three organisers and an unincorporated association 'Plane Stupid') but also 'anyone acting in concert' with these.

This was clearly a very broad injunction and potential interference with Convention rights (though Article 11 was not discussed). 'Acting in concert' has an uncertain scope raising Convention issues of legality. However, the judge made it clear that the injunction was much narrower than that originally sought by Heathrow and that it was targeted not at peaceful protesters but at disrupters (see para 120). Breach of an injunction would make those covered by it liable in contempt of court.

- In *City of London v Samede* [2012] EWCA Civ 160 the City of London successfully sought possession orders and injunctions in respect of land occupied (as part of the Occupy Movement) by S and others. The court agreed that S was exercising her rights under Articles 10 and 11, however, these Articles could not justify requiring a court to allow a permanent occupation. The importance of the issues behind the protest are relevant matters but not decisive. The court also agreed that case management powers could be used by a judge in future cases to limit the exposition of political views in the court.

18.6.3 Police powers: common law

In policing demonstrations, the police have available to them a range of statutory powers, in particular those under the POA 1986. Of equal if not greater importance are their common law powers to take reasonable steps to maintain the peace.

The power to take steps, including detention, in order to prevent a breach of the peace was reiterated by the House of Lords in *R (Laporte)* v *Chief Constable of Gloucester Constabulary* [2006] UKHL 55:

> Every constable, and also every citizen, enjoys the power and is subject to the duty to seek to prevent, by arrest or other action short of arrest, any breach of the peace occurring in his presence, or any breach of the peace which (having occurred) is likely to be renewed, or any breach of the peace which is about to occur. (para 29)

cross reference

Steel is discussed in Chapter 11, section 11.4.3; see also Chapter 20, section 20.1.2.

The general principle that a person may be detained for an apprehended or anticipated breach of the peace has been accepted as being compatible with Convention rights in *Steel* v *United Kingdom* (1999) 28 EHRR 603. In that case it had been suggested by the applicants that the exercise of the power, based on common law rather than specific statutory provisions, was too discretionary and therefore inconsistent with the principle of legality which pervades the Convention. The ECtHR rejected this on the grounds that there was a body of English case law which had clarified the power in ways that gave proper recognition to Convention rights and made the exercise of the power, in the context, foreseeable.

In *Redmond-Bate* v *DPP* [2000] HRLR 249 (see section 18.4), for example, the need for the police to consider the relative reasonableness of the conduct of the person detained in comparison with third parties who had been provoked to threaten violence, was stressed. *Nicol and Selvanayagam* v *DPP* [1996] Crim LR 318 made clear that where a person was lawfully exercising his or her fundamental rights it would not normally be possible for a third party (including officials) to claim they had been reasonably provoked and therefore their violence was reasonable.

case close-up

R (Laporte) v *Chief Constable of Gloucestershire* [2006] UKHL 55

Police prevented a coachload of anti-war protesters from reaching RAF Fairford, a base used in the invasion of Iraq in 2003 and where the demonstrators intended to hold a demonstration. They were stopped about 5km, by road, from the base. Police intelligence suggested that some of the protestors were 'WOMBLES' (White Overalls Movement Building Libertarian Effective Struggles) who were set on disruption and violence. The police identified only eight known WOMBLES on the coach. The protestors were sent back to London under police escort (a disproportionate exercise of the breach of the peace power which violated the law: see [2004] EWCA Civ 1639). The House of Lords found the initial stop to be unlawful.

- *Laporte* contains a full discussion of the history and development of the law on breach of the peace. In considering the common law their Lordships took into account the requirements of Article 11.

- The police case was that they had reasonable grounds to apprehend a breach of the peace in the future (at the base).

- Importantly, the House of Lords held that reasonable grounds were not sufficient. The decisions stresses that the apprehended threat to the peace has to be imminent. What counts as 'imminent' depends on context, including the role that technology such as mobile phones can play in organising demonstrations etc. In this case the police had accepted that a breach of the peace was not imminent and so the stop (as well as the return to London) was unlawful. A court must consider the reasonableness of the police view of whether a threat is imminent (i.e. was there evidence upon which the police could reasonable form the view that a threat was imminent) and not substitute its own view on the matter (*R (McClure and Moos) v CPM* [2012] EWCA Civ 12).

18.6.4 Control of meetings, marches and demonstrations: statutory powers

Police powers and the HRA

In addition to their common law powers, police officers, acting in the office of constable, have a range of statutory powers dealing with the control of meetings, marches and demonstrations. These powers, of course, should be interpreted by the courts, on the basis of section 3 HRA. This means that, if it is 'possible', they can only authorise (and make lawful) police actions which are compatible with Article 11 and other Convention rights. It can be said with confidence that the wording of, and Parliamentary intention behind, the legislation in issue is sufficiently open-textured to allow Convention-compliant interpretations. Furthermore, the requirements of Article 11, as interpreted by the ECtHR, are relatively flexible and context-dependent with significant margins of appreciation allowed the states. Declarations of incompatibility (under section 4 HRA) have not been necessary in the public order context.

cross reference

Sections 3, 4 and 6 HRA are discussed in Chapter 4.

In particular this means that the police will not be able to escape liability under section 6 HRA (a public authority must act compatibly with Convention rights) on the section 6(2) HRA grounds that they were putting into effect an incompatible statute.

Prior notification, section 11 POA 1986

Section 11 POA 1986 requires prior notice of political or commemorative processions to be given, by organisers, to the police (there are exceptions on practicality grounds).

A requirement for notice, even prior authorisation (not a requirement under POA 1986), is in itself compatible with Article 11. This is so the authorities are able to take appropriate steps to ensure the march is peaceful.

case close-up

Ziliberberg v Moldova **App 61821/00, admissibility decision of 4 May 2004**

Z was arrested for participating in an unauthorised demonstration against the withdrawal of student transport privileges. He had behaved peacefully. The ECtHR held that there had been an interference with Z's right to assembly but it was justified under Article 11(2). In particular it held that a prior authorisation procedure for meetings in public places, enabling the police to ensure a peaceful gathering, is compatible with Article 11; consequently criminal sanctions to enforce such a procedure must also be acceptable (see The Law, 2).

The position in *Ziliberberg* was adopted in respect of prior authorisation in the POA 1986 in *Laporte* (section 18.6.3), para 82.

Imposing conditions on marches, section 12 POA 1986

If voluntary negotiations with marchers fail, section 12 POA 1986 allows the police to enforce conditions on the marchers such as route or timing. The exercise of this power will clearly interfere with the right of peaceful assembly and will require a justification under Article 11(2). First, the interference must have a clear legal basis in the Act. Second, if exercised lawfully, the powers will be for the 'prevention of disorder or crime'. This is because, under the Act, they are triggered only when necessary to prevent serious disorder, serious damage, serious disruption to the community or intimidation. Any challenge based on the HRA, therefore, is likely to focus on the necessity and proportionality of the individual interference. The general power of the police to impose conditions on meetings has been held to be compatible with the Convention in *Laporte* (section 18.6.3), see para 130 (following *Ziliberberg*).

There are other statutes that empower the police to impose conditions on marches:

- The Metropolitan Police Act 1839, section 52 (which applies only in London);
- The Town Police Clauses Act 1847.

These powers are less precise and more easily triggered than under POA 1986. They are, therefore, more vulnerable to an Article 11 challenge on the grounds of not being prescribed by law—their application not being adequately foreseeable.

Imposing conditions on meetings, section 14 POA 1986

There are similar powers, triggered by the same concerns, to impose conditions on 'public assemblies'. The exercise of these powers by the police can be challenged by judicial review or using the HRA directly but, again, a lawful and proportionate exercise of the power is likely to be compatible with Article 11.

In *R (Brehony)* v *Chief Constable of Greater Manchester Police* [2005] EWHC 640, a police use of section 14 POA 1986, based on the disruption trigger, was held compatible with Article 11 as well as Article 10. The case involved a demonstration against Marks and Spencer because of that company's alleged support for Israel. For the Christmas period there was a counter-demonstration and protestors were required to move away from outside the store to a park. Of particular importance was

- the duty on the police to give reasons for the section 14 order, and
- the recognition that there is a right to counter-demonstrate but not for the counter-demonstrators to seek to create conditions in which all demonstrations would need to be banned.

The power in section 14 can be used during a meeting, though this requires the police to be lawfully present. Whilst the police have the general freedom enjoyed by civilians to be in public places, they need specific lawful authority to be at a meeting on private land (whether or not open to the public) if the organisers refuse or withdraw consent to a police presence. Section 17(1) PACE allows police to enter private premises to arrest where they believe an indictable offence has been committed (but not to prevent the commission in the first place). Political speech offences such as sedition or some anti-terrorism offences could be relevant here. More importantly, section 17(6) gives statutory footing to the powers the police have to enter private premises to deal with breaches of the peace. In *Thomas* v *Sawkins* [1935] 2 KB 249, these powers were said to include situations where the breach of the peace is anticipated. In

cross reference
Counter demonstrations and an 'opposition veto' is discussed in section 18.4.

cross reference
For breach of the peace see section 18.4.

McCleod v *United Kingdom* (1999) 27 EHRR 493 the general power of entry for breach of the peace was upheld and this suggests that the power in *Thomas* can be exercised compatibly with Convention rights. Clearly a police presence at a meeting can have a distinctly 'chilling' effect on freedom of assembly and also expression. Articles 8, 10 and 11 could be engaged and this means that the legal basis of the power needs to be clear and the need in the particular case very strong if there is to be justification under the second paragraphs to these articles.

Banning marches, section 13 POA 1986

Where the police believe that the section 12 power to impose conditions on a march is not sufficient to prevent serious disorder, they may apply, under section 13, to the local council for a banning order. The council can then make an order, but only with the consent of the Secretary of State. In London, the order is made by the police directly with the consent of the Secretary of State. This is a draconian power, which must be exercised compatibly with Article 11. There are various safeguards:

• Only the anticipation of serious public disorder can justify a ban.

• A ban is limited to no more than three months, but a new order can always be sought.

• The ban is limited to a district. However, this can be very large, such as the whole of Greater London.

• A ban must encompass all public processions or at least a class of public procession: there is no power to ban a single march. The point of this blanket ban is to enable the police to appear neutral as between competing political ideologies. It means, however, that entirely peaceful marches can be caught up in the ban.

The issuing of the banning order can be challenged in the courts of England and Wales by way of judicial review. Cases based on the law prior to POA 1986, suggest that the legal test both in the UK courts and by the ECtHR applying Article 11 directly may not have been very demanding on the authorities.

• In *Kent* v *Metropolitan Police Commissioner* The Times, 15 May 1981, a traditional *Wednesbury* test was used by the court; this involved a low level of judicial scrutiny of the police's reasons.

• In *Christians against Racism and Fascism* v *United Kingdom* (1978) 21 DR 138, a ban over the whole of the London area, imposed in respect of a racist march but also covering the claimant, was held, by the Human Rights Commission, to be compatible with Article 11.

A post-HRA challenge, based on Article 11 and using a proportionality approach rather than one based on traditional *Wednesbury* principles, ought to require a much more intense scrutiny by the courts. Following *Moos* (section 18.6.3), however, it seems that the judicial inquiry will still focus on the reasonableness of the police's assessment rather than permit the court to make its own assessment of the proportionality of the ban.

cross reference
Wednesbury
grounds of review
and proportionality
are compared in
Chapter 4,
section 4.6.1.

In *Laporte* (section 18.6.3), para 130, Lord Brown took the view that the banning power in section 13 POA 1986 could, if the conditions were properly followed, be exercised in a manner compatible with Article 11—as interpreted in *Ziliberberg* (above). This might be optimistic. It has been suggested (Helen Fenwick, *Civil Liberties*) that the blanket ban approach might be hard to make compatible with Article 11. It can lead to the ban of a peaceful march solely to enhance police neutrality—which is not expressly a legitimate purpose in Article 11(2).

Banning meetings, section 14A POA 1986

The power to ban meetings in English law is more limited. Section 14A POA 1986, allows the police to apply for an order from the appropriate local authority prohibiting for a specified period the holding of trespassory open air meetings. Bans require the consent of the Secretary of State and are for no more than four days and apply to all trespassory meetings in the area. Trespassory meetings are meetings on land in the open air on which the public has no right to hold meetings—such as on private property where the occupier has refused permission.

The authorising of such bans must, of course, be compatible with Article 11.

In *DPP* v *Jones* [1999] 2 AC 240, the House of Lords held (by a majority) that a non-obstructive, static, political meeting held on a highway could be by right (and so not trespassory). A highway can be used by right in order to pass and repass, and also for incidental uses, and the question was whether these had to be in the context of passage or whether there could be a right to use the highway for a range of reasonable purposes, including static ones. The court accepted that holding a political meeting could be an incidental or a reasonable use of the highway. Though this was a pre-HRA case, two Law Lords based their reasoning on the influence of Article 11 ECHR.

The power is triggered by the police's belief that, if the meeting were to go ahead, a 'serious disruption to the life of the community' may result. It is not clear that this rather open-ended condition provides sufficient structure to police discretion to meet the prescribed by law test in Article 11(2) (though, as mentioned previously, the ECtHR allows considerable police discretion in the public order context). As with the banning of marches under section 13 POA 1986 (see earlier in this section), the meetings ban in section 14A extends to all trespassory assemblies for the period, including any which are entirely peaceful. It may be hard to show that the banning of these peaceful demonstrations is for one of the legitimate purposes in Article 11(2). Again, though, the Strasbourg institutions are sympathetic to the authorities in these situations. The Commission of Human Rights, for example, accepted that an order, made because of previous damage to Stonehenge by New Age Travellers, which prevented the holding of peaceful Druidic ceremonies near to the monument during the summer solstice, was proportionate (*Arthur U Pendragon* v *United Kingdom* App 31416/95, admissibility decision of 19 October 1998) and, from cases such as *Christians against Racism* (section 18.5.3), it seems that a legitimate ban on potentially violent assemblies which also catches peaceful assemblies is not thereby seen as based on an overbroad power which was incompatible with Article 11.

18.7 Freedom of association

18.7.1 Association

The right of individuals to join, and take part in the activities of, associations is recognised by the ECtHR as being fundamental to the concept of a democratic society if it is to be pluralist and tolerant. Article 11 protects association in the sense of a relatively organised group with a common aim rather than association in the sense of being in the company of others (see *Anderson* v *United Kingdom* (1998) 25 EHRR CD172).

Political parties and associations, religious organisations, pressure groups, professional bodies, etc. are the typical forms of association protected by Article 11. They are non-governmental. Professional bodies which also have a statutory, regulatory function (such as the Law Society for England and Wales) may be outside the scope of Article 11—*Le Compte* v *Belgium* (1982) 4 EHRR 1, paras 64–65. Associations within the scope of Article 11 should be properly recognised by the laws of the signatory states. The laws of a state should enable people to form, join and participate in the activities of such organisations. Any restrictions are interferences which need to be justified under the terms of Article 11(2). The fact that a group is not recognised as an association under the laws of states is not sufficient. States should not be able to close down opposition groups, for example, by simply declaring them not to be an association. The concept of association under Article 11 is, therefore, another autonomous Convention concept.

The extent that the right of association includes the right of the association to exclude people from membership is controversial. Associations are private bodies with their own rules and should be able to accept and reject members as they see fit. On the other hand, some associations have a form of monopoly power (the major political parties, for example, control access to the legislature and, thereby, to representative public service) and should not be allowed to exclude people on arbitrary grounds.

In *RSPCA* v *Attorney-General* [2001] 3 All ER 530, the High Court held that attempts by the Royal Society for the Prevention of Cruelty to Animals to exclude fox hunting supporters from membership did not breach Article 11. Article 11 includes the right to exclude from membership those it honestly believes are damaging the interests of the society.

18.7.2 **Proscription of political organisations**

Some of the most difficult and controversial decisions of the ECtHR involve cases brought by political parties or associations that have been banned.

. . . .

proscription

This is the legal term used for banning organisations, particularly political organisations. The government's powers to proscribe terrorist organisations are described in Chapter 26, section 26.6. **Note:** care needs to be taken to distinguish 'proscription' (banning) from 'prescription' (permitted or required). Thus, under Article 11, an organisation can be 'proscribed' so long as the process is 'prescribed' by law.

. . . .

case close-up

United Communist Party of Turkey v *Turkey* (1998) 26 EHRR 121

. . . .

The Turkish Constitutional Court upheld the dissolution of the Communist Party of Turkey before it was able to start acting as an association. The reasons for the ban were connected with the alleged support of the party for constitutional change in Turkey, including support for separatism and other values held to be inconsistent with the Turkish constitution.

The ECtHR held that there was a violation of Article 11. The Communist Party had been banned because of its name and programme, not its actions. The ban, though prescribed by law and for a legitimate purpose, was not proportionate to the aim pursued and hence not necessary in a democratic society.

- States can take actions to protect their major institutions and, as in the case of Turkey, their national unity.

- Nevertheless, both Article 11 and Article 10 require that the laws permit the advocacy and promotion of constitutional change.

- This advocacy and promotion of constitutional change needs the protection of the laws even if it takes place against a background of political violence (as in Turkey at the time, with the ongoing insurrection of the Turkish Kurd population).

Freedom of political association has its limits under the Convention. This is illustrated by one of the most significant decisions the ECtHR has ever made.

case close-up

Refah Partisi (the Welfare Party) v *Turkey* (2003) 37 EHRR 1

Refah Partisi, the Welfare Party, was the largest single party in the Turkish Parliament and, in 1996, in coalition with another party, it was part of the government. Opinion polls suggested that at the next general election, in 2000, it could obtain an overall majority of seats with as much as 67% of the vote. In 1998 the party was banned by the Turkish Constitutional Court on the grounds that the party intended to introduce Islamic law (Sharia), which was incompatible with the secular nature of the Turkish state. A Grand Chamber of the ECtHR held that there had been no violation of Article 11. There had been an interference with the party's right of association under Article 11(1), but it was justified under Article 11(2). The ban was legally based, it was for a number of the purposes listed in Article 11(2) and, in all the circumstances, it was necessary in a democratic society for the protection of Turkish democracy.

This case involves no less than the banning of a party that had non-violent aims and methods, which participated in the democratic political process and had won a general election for the legislature. Nevertheless, the ECtHR upheld the ban and, in doing so, asserted the strong commitment of the Convention to the principles of maintaining democracy and the egalitarian approach to human rights.

- Following *United Communist Party*, the Court accepted that states can take reasonable steps to preserve their institutions. Here the main reason for the ban was the struggle by Turkish state institutions to protect the secular character of the state (as distinct from the predominantly Moslem character of society).

- States can ban political parties and groups which incite or promote violence. They can also act against groups which advocate unlawful action. This is a more complex issue: incitement depends upon context. The Refah Partisi did not advocate violence.

- States may ban (they may even have a duty to ban) groups and organisations that promote a state of affairs which is undemocratic or which would be likely to undermine the human rights of others. This was the position accepted by the ECtHR in *Refah Partisi*.

- Pre-emption. As part of the protection of democracy, states can use the law to pre-empt (prevent) an anti-democratic outcome. The Welfare Party sought the introduction of Islamic law (Sharia). In the Court's analysis such a legal system, if introduced in the Turkish context, would create a legal and constitutional system which would, in important ways, be incompatible with the Convention. The Moslem population of Turkey would be governed by a law whose ultimate authority was divine revelation rather than the consent of the people and, in particular, the evidence was that this would have significantly detrimental effects on the rights of women. The need to defend democracy extends, in the view of the Court, even to restricting the outcomes that the people can vote for.

KEY POINT This idea, that 'democracy' and human rights may need to be defended by means which seem to be undemocratic is accepted by the ECtHR, especially in the context of Article 17. It is discussed more fully in Chapter 7, section 7.3.

18.8 Trade unions

Article 11 expressly includes a person's 'right to form and to join trade unions for the protection of his interests'. This right is widely accepted by Council of Europe states. It is also enshrined in other instruments of international law, such as the statutes of the International Labour Organization (ILO).

KEY POINT The ILO is the United Nations, specialist agency to promote the rights of workers. Its Convention 87 requires states to guarantee the rights of workers to organise.

Article 11 does not require any specific system of trade union regulation, and states have a wide margin of appreciation on how trade unions are controlled and what powers they may have (see *Swedish Engine Drivers' Union* v *Sweden* (1979–80) 1 EHRR 617).

The issue in modern capitalist societies is the extent to which laws must ensure that workers have the effective freedom to join a trade union when their employers put economic or other pressures on them not to join. In the past, the issue has been whether workers have a right not to belong to a trade union. This has been particularly important where the trade union negotiates the workers' terms and conditions and gives them some power in the workplace.

Non-membership, in such circumstances, can seem like a form of free riding in which non-members avoid the costs of membership but benefit from the willingness of members to contribute to and support the union. In *Young, James and Webster* v *United Kingdom* (1982) 4 EHRR 38, the ECtHR declined to rule that a 'closed shop' in itself violated Article 11. Since this case, however, the ECtHR has moved further towards accepting that Article 11 includes both the positive right to join and the negative right not to join associations including trade unions. In *Sorensen* v *Denmark* (2008) 46 EHRR 29, a Grand Chamber ruled that though compulsory membership may not always be contrary to the Convention, it will be if compulsion strikes at the heart of freedom of association by, in effect, forcing trade union membership on reluctant workers (see para 54).

Where there is no closed shop, trade unions have greater freedom to reject members who also support racist or other political causes the union opposes: *ASLEF* v *United Kingdom* (2007) 45 EHRR 34.

18.9 Political restriction

The last sentence of Article 11 expressly allows national laws to restrict the rights of assembly and association of 'members of the armed forces, of the police or of the administration of the State'. In the United Kingdom, for example, there are severe restrictions on the freedom of the police, the military, senior civil servants and some local government officers to do things like stand for Parliament or take part in the activities of political parties. The House of Commons Disqualification Act 1975 lists a large number of posts and offices, the occupiers of which are unable to sit in the House of Commons. The reasons for these restrictions are to ensure that the public services maintain the appearance of political impartiality and that elected representatives do not have divided loyalties.

The scope of the restrictions and the need for them in respect of thousands of workers who neither deal directly with the public nor have a major impact on policy has been questioned. However, the ECtHR has not found such restrictions to be incompatible with Article 11.

In *Ahmed* v *United Kingdom* (2000) 29 EHRR 1, the ECtHR held that political restrictions on certain local government workers were compatible with Articles 10, 11 and Article 3 of the First Protocol (there were strong dissenting judgments).

In 1983 the government banned the workers at the General Communications Headquarters in Cheltenham (a centre for electronic intelligence-gathering) from being members of an independent trade union. The taking of industrial action by such workers endangered national security, according to the government. The Commission held that the ban was justified in terms of the second sentence of Article 11(2), as it was a restriction on the rights of association of members of the 'administration on the State': *Council of Civil Service Unions* v *United Kingdom* (1988) 10 EHRR CD 269.

Summary

- Article 11 represents one of the important political rights guaranteed by the Convention, under which people have rights of 'assembly' (which includes the right to take part in political demonstrations), and rights of 'association' (which includes the right to form, join and take part in the activities of a political party).

- These rights are subject to restriction under the terms of Article 11(2). The importance of Article 11 rights for democracy is fully recognised and any restrictions will need to be consistent with the principles of tolerance and pluralism.

- The promotion of constitutional change is a protected purpose under Article 11, but assemblies or associations which incite violence or promote anti-democratic outcomes may be restricted by states acting lawfully and proportionately.

- Article 11 protects trade union activity.

- Article 11 permits significant restrictions on the political freedom of police, civil servants and other public officials.

Question

For suggested approaches, please visit the Online Resource Centre.

If the government is concerned that a political party is promoting ideas to which it is opposed, what are the conditions which the ECtHR requires before any action against the party could be consistent with the Convention?

Further reading

Fenwick, H. *Civil Liberties and Human Rights* 4th edn (2007) Abingdon: Routledge-Cavendish, Chapter 9

Fenwick, H. 'Marginalising Human Rights: Breach of the Peace, "Kettling", the Human Rights Act and Public Protest' [2009] (Oct) *Public Law* 737–765

Lester, A., Pannick, D. and Herberg, J. (see Preface) Chapter 4, Article 11

Sottiaux, S. and Rummens, S. 'ECtHR Case Law on Freedom of Expression and Freedom of Association' (2012) 10(1) *IJCL* 106–126

Stone, R. *Textbook on Civil Liberties and Human Rights* 8th edn (2010) Oxford: OUP, Chapter 9

Article 12: right to marry

Chapter overview

- The right to marry and the kinds of relationships that are included in the concept of 'marriage'.
- The states' rights to regulate marriage and the kinds of purposes such regulations can promote.
- The right to found a family.
- The rights of non-married couples.

Article 12   Right to Marry

Men and women of marriageable age have the right to marry and to found a family, according to the national laws governing the exercise of this right.

Introduction

Article 12 creates a right to marry and found a family. The right is qualified by reference to 'national laws'. This permits states to regulate and restrict marriage so long as the 'essence' of the right is not compromised.

Marriage is recognised as the central relationship in organised civil society. Article 23 of the International Covenant on Civil and Political Rights (ICCPR, see Chapter 1, section 1.4.4) refers to marriage as the 'natural and fundamental group unit of society'. Marriage can be fundamental to social status. A human right to marriage also gives public recognition and legal protection to the primary unit through which children are conceived and brought up. It can be argued that marriage is also a source of human happiness, but Lord Millett's view, in *Ghaidan* v *Godin Mendoza* [2004] UKHL 30, is also correct and avoids sentimentality: marriage gives 'legal status to a relationship between men and women (which need not be loving, sexual, stable, faithful, long standing or contented)' (para 78).

Article 8 and other rights

Article 12, marriage and founding a family, complements Article 8, the right to respect for private and family life. A number of issues, such as the rights of transsexuals, discussed at the end of this chapter, involve both Articles. The focus on marriage means that different legal issues can arise under the two different Articles, and this is reflected in the case law. Likewise, issues of discrimination on the grounds of marriage can engage Article 14 when linked to Article 12.

Traditionally, marriage has been central to the legal status of adult women and too often that status has been low. The need to ensure legal protection for married women and freedom from oppression and subordination within marriage is embodied in other international instruments such as the UN Convention on the Elimination of All Forms of Discrimination against Women (CEDAW), which, in Article 16, requires states to secure equality between the sexes in all aspects of their marriage laws.

19.1 Marriage

Marriage, in the context of Article 12, is defined as the 'formation of a legally binding association between a man and a woman', which thereby involves the acquisition of legally recognised social status (see *Hamer* v *United Kingdom* (1982) 4 EHRR 139). Marriage has a particular status in Article 12 and is not to be equated with other forms of relationship or simple cohabitation (*Burden* v *United Kingdom* (2008) 47 EHRR 38, Grand Chamber, para 63).

Article 23 ICCPR expressly requires marriage to be based on the full and free consent of spouses, asserts the need for equality between spouses regarding the rights and responsibilities of marriage, and accepts the fact of divorce and the need for adequate protection for children if that happens. Such matters as consent and equality are not expressly mentioned in Article 12 of the European Convention on Human Rights (ECHR) but may be implied from its text.

19.1.1 Homosexual marriage and civil partnership

Article 12 refers to 'men and women'. The European Court of Human Rights (ECtHR) takes the view that marriage is, by definition, a relationship between men and women. In *Rees* v *United Kingdom* (1987) 9 EHRR 56, the Court said:

> In the Court's opinion, the right to marry guaranteed by Article 12 (art. 12) refers to the traditional marriage between persons of opposite biological sex. (para 49)

cross reference
See Chapter 15, section 15.5.3 on same-sex relationships.

It follows that there is no positive duty on states to recognise marriages between homosexuals or civil partnerships, see, for example, *Estevez* v *Spain* App 56501/00, admissibility decision of 10 May 2001. This has been accepted by English courts, see *Wilkinson* v *Kitzinger* (2006) EWHC 2022, paras 44–48. The recognition of such relationships as warranting full legal status is a discernible trend in Europe (civil partnerships for gay men and lesbian women were introduced to the UK in 2005). The 'evolutive' nature of the Convention (the values it embodies develop as the cultural values of Europe develop) suggests that this may be a development for the future.

KEY POINT The right to marry and found a family in Article 9 of the European Union's Charter of Fundamental Rights is expressed without reference to gender— though it is unclear whether this places a positive duty on states to recognise civil partnerships or homosexual marriage.

19.1.2 Divorce

Neither Article 12 nor Article 8 require states to allow divorce, see *Johnston* v *Ireland* (1987) 9 EHRR 203 (see paras 51–58). Since Article 15 of the UN Declaration of Human Rights refers to the dissolution of marriage but this reference is not repeated in Article 12 ECHR, the ECtHR was convinced that the absence of a right to divorce in the Convention was therefore deliberate.

19.1.3 Right not to marry and forced marriage

Marriage would not be a 'right' if there were not an equal and opposite right not to marry. The voluntary, consensual nature of the relationship would be lost. Nevertheless, the issue has not been authoritatively decided by the ECtHR, though Lord Bingham, in *R (Pretty)* v *DPP* [2001] UKHL 61, was 'inclined' to support it (para 6). A non-consensual marriage that is valid under foreign law may not be recognised in the United Kingdom: *City of Westminister* v *C* [2008] EWCA Civ 198. In *XCC* v *AA* [2012] EWHC 2183, the Court of Protection (which deals with the interests of those with limited mental capacity) refused, despite arguments about cultural issues, to recognise the 'marriage' of a woman, with significant learning difficulties, which lacked consent and was probably done to enable the husband to obtain a visa.

A marriage that is forced or coerced will be incompatible with Article 12. International law (e.g. Article 23 ICCPR) requires voluntary marriage and it must be assumed that, even though express words on this point are absent from Article 12, states have a duty to ensure that their marriage laws require freely given consent. The extent to which the duty goes further and requires, for example, state support for those threatened with, or embroiled in, a non-voluntary marriage is unclear and the lack of clear words is to be regretted. In the United Kingdom, for example, there is an acknowledged problem of 'forced marriage', which is treated as an abuse of human rights. Administrative action (e.g. by consular offices abroad) and legal remedies (orders and directions issued by a court) are available. This is done under the common law in particular, but may also be a duty required under Article 12 and Article 8.

further study

On legal action see *Re SK* [2004] EWHC 3202. On administrative action see the website of the Forced Marriage Unit (see: http://www.fco.gov.uk/en/travel-and-living-abroad/when-things-go-wrong/forced-marriage/). Civil remedies are available on the basis of the Forced Marriage (Civil Protection) Act 2007; in June 2012 the government announced that forcing someone to marry would be made a criminal offence.

However, any attempts at regulation which interfere with the right to marry and with private life must be proportionate. In *R (Aguilar Quila)* v *Secretary of State for the Home Department* [2011] UKSC 45, regulations meant that marriage visas would only be granted to spouses aged over 19. The regulations were designed to help prevent forced marriage. However, they had a severe impact on couples whose marriages were entirely voluntary. The Supreme Court subjected the regulations to careful analysis and held that the Secretary of State had failed to demonstrate that they were proportionate to the aim.

discussion topic

The legal response to forced marriage

What is the correct response to the problem of forced marriage? Consider:

- Is there a need for a criminal offence?
- Is it right to regulate if this affects the rights of others (do you support the majority or Lord Brown in *Aguilar* (in the previous paragraph)?
- How much weight should be given to cultural traditions by the courts (see *XCC*, above)?

19.2 Founding a family

19.2.1 Married couples

Article 12 also gives men and women a right to 'marry and to found a family'. There is no assumption that the right to marry does not apply in the absence of an intention or ability to have children at the time of marriage (so transsexuals may have rights under Article 12 even though the couple have no physical ability to have children—see *Goodwin* v *United Kingdom* (2002) 35 EHRR 18, para 98).

The main effect of the right to found a family is to bring within the scope of Article 12 national laws and regulations on the means by which married couples can have children. Adoption and artificial insemination are the main examples. On such issues states have a wide margin of appreciation on the kinds of regulations they impose.

There is a presumption in favour of married couples having a right to live together (see *Abdulaziz* v *United Kingdom* (1985) 7 EHRR 471, para 62). In that case the ECtHR said that Article 8(1) did not impose a positive duty on states to admit non-national spouses to residence. Different views have been taken in later cases (e.g. *Tuquabo-Tekle* v *Netherlands* [2006] 1 FLR 798) and, in *Aguilar* (section 19.1.3), the Supreme Court held that Article 8(1) was engaged in respect of entry decisions affecting private life, which, therefore, needed justification under Article 8(2).

19.2.2 **Unmarried persons**

However, the human right to found a family under Article 12 probably does not apply to unmarried persons. Therefore their position and status on this issue can be more freely regulated (or ignored) by the state. In a case dealing with the rights of illegitimate children, the ECtHR denied that Article 12 rights should apply equally in other marriage-like situations (*Marckx* v *Belgium* (1979–80) 2 EHRR 330, para 67).

- Cohabiting unmarried couples. The Court has not extended the full range of Article 12 rights in this context. For example, an unmarried father's claim to the custody of his children cannot be based on Article 12 rights (*B, R and J* v *Germany* (1984) 36 DR 130).
- Homosexual relationships. As stated previously, there is no positive duty on states to recognise homosexual relationships as being capable of acquiring legal status.
- Legitimacy. From some of its earliest case law, the Court has required states to recognise equality in their laws between legitimate and illegitimate children. However, this is based on developing Article 8 rights rather than the right to found a family in Article 12 (see *Marckx*).

These are all matters of social change and development in Europe. As the position of transsexual men and women discloses (discussed in section 19.4) the ECtHR is capable of changing its case law, within the terms of Article 12, to reflect a changing consensus. As large proportions of children are brought up in unmarried families, and as homosexual couples are increasingly given legal status and allowed to adopt children, etc., it may be that the case law of Article 12 will need to develop. Issues can arise under Article 14 in respect of discrimination within the 'ambit' of one of the articles, such as Article 12 (see Chapter 7, section 7.1.4).

Regulating marriage

19.3.1 **General principles**

The right to marriage is 'according to the national laws governing the exercise of this right'. The meaning of the terms 'marriage' and 'founding a family' are governed by the laws of the signatory states. States have their own rules, policies and practices on the matter and the ECtHR accepts that a wide margin of appreciation must exist in this context. The familiar language of proportionality and the 'fair balance' between individual freedoms and social benefits is found in respect of the Court's evaluation of these laws. Nevertheless, the Court retains the final word on what is required by Article 12 and, as illustrated from the transsexuals' cases discussed in section 19.4, is prepared to limit the margin of appreciation if the circumstances so warrant.

General principles were stated in *F* v *Switzerland* (1988) 10 EHRR 411 (involving Swiss laws which imposed a temporary ban of up to three years on a person remarrying after divorce). The ECtHR said (in para 32):

- The institution of marriage 'gives rise to personal, social and legal consequences'. Therefore it is necessary for it to be regulated and limited by law.

- The normal regulations are those that apply 'procedural' limits (such as requiring marriage to be a public matter or stipulating some minimal ceremonial requirements) and 'substantive' limits such as those relating to capacity (e.g. age, gender or not being already married), consent and other impediments to marriage such as those describing the 'degrees' of marriage by which marriage to relatives is barred.

- Any such limitations must not impair the 'very essence' of the right. It is the Court's job to ensure that this has not happened in the particular cases that are brought before it. Thus in the case the majority felt that the fact of a ban on marriage impaired the essence of the right, whilst the minority, by focusing on its temporary nature, disagreed (see also *B and L v United Kingdom* App 36536/02, judgment of 13 September 2005).

19.3.2 **The purposes of regulation**

But for what purposes can marriage be regulated? Can they go beyond factors about marriage itself and extend to other legitimate state purposes such as immigration control and the good order of prisons? The issue has arisen under the Human Rights Act 1998 (HRA).

Immigration

case close-up

R (Baiai) v *Secretary of State for the Home Department* [2008] UKHL 53

Section 19 of the Asylum and Immigration (Treatment of Claimants) Act 2004, in essence, allowed the Secretary of State to refuse permission to marry (other than under the rites of the Church of England) to a person subject to immigration control (a person who requires leave to enter the UK). In many situations the policy adopted under the Act was to refuse permission on the assumption that the proposed marriage was a 'sham'.

The House of Lords held that the Secretary of State was pursuing an inflexible policy that caught genuine as well as 'sham' marriages. But (save for the provision discriminating in favour of Anglican marriage) section 19 could and should be read down (under section 3 HRA) to mean that permission to marry could not be refused except where there was a marriage of convenience. Nor could section 19 authorise other conditions that were incompatible with Article 12 (regulations that imposed a high, deterrent, fee on applicants were to that extent unlawful). The instructions on which civil servants worked were incompatible with the proper reading of section 19.

The Law Lords adopt a narrow and focused approach to the subject matter of legal restrictions on marriage. These must relate to the terms of lawful marriage. Restricting marriage for social purposes, such as immigration control, is unlawful. Article 12 allows no balancing of individual rights and social interests as is possible under Article 8(2). However, only real marriages are protected by Article 12 and so a state is permitted to regulate against accepting marriages of convenience and this is what section 19, properly interpreted, does.

Prisoners

The regulation of the rights of prisoners to marry is discussed in Chapter 21, section 21.9.2.

Transsexuals

The position of transsexuals—persons who have gone through a physical as well as emotional process of gender reassignment—has always been difficult. In the past states have refused to give such persons full legal recognition in their acquired gender. In particular, states have refused to allow a change of birth certificate, thus making marriage (legally defined as being between a man and a woman) impossible, and with this comes a range of other legal obstacles, difficulties and unfairness.

The original position of the ECtHR was that the failure by states to give full legal recognition to transsexual men and women did not involve a violation of either Article 8 or Article 12, because states enjoyed a wide margin of appreciation over the issue. However, from as early as *Rees* v *United Kingdom* (1987) 9 EHRR 56, the Court was aware of medical, social and attitudinal developments in European society and culture, and suggested that states keep the issue under review. The Court fully revised its view in *Goodwin* v *United Kingdom*.

case close-up

Goodwin v *United Kingdom* (2002) 35 EHRR 18

Christine Goodwin was a post-operative male-to-female transsexual. She complained of a range of legal disadvantages stemming from the fact that UK law did not allow her to change her birth certificate. These included not being able to bring a sexual harassment case, having to pay higher car insurance premiums and not being able to marry. The ECtHR held that there had been a violation of Articles 8 and 12.

399

The Court's underlying view was that there was now a clear European consensus emerging which required legal recognition for transsexuals in their acquired gender. The margin of appreciation on the matter was withdrawn. States can no longer base their legal definitions of gender solely on 'biological criteria' determined at the time of birth. Given present-day attitudes and conditions, and given the seriousness of the problems faced by transsexuals, there was an overriding need for the Court to depart from its earlier case law.

further study

Goodwin and UK law

In *Bellinger* v *Bellinger* [2003] UKHL 21, the House of Lords had to rule on the validity of a marriage between a male-to-female transsexual and a man. The Matrimonial Causes Act 1973 made marriages void unless between a man and a woman. The House of Lords refused (under section 3 HRA) to read and give effect to the 1973 Act so that transsexual persons would be recognised in their acquired gender. They preferred to issue a Declaration of Incompatibility under section 4 HRA (see Chapter 4, section 4.4.3). The Government responded with the Gender Recognition Act 2004. This establishes a Gender Recognition Panel to which transsexual people can apply for legal recognition, in the form of a gender recognition certificate, in their acquired gender.

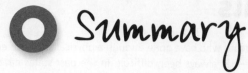

Summary

- Article 12 establishes both a right to marry and to found a family. The right is often asserted in tandem with Article 8.

- This right can be regulated by states according to their laws. Restrictions and regulations on issues such as age, capacity and ceremony are acceptable, but any limits which undermine the essence of the right will be a violation.

- Though marriage does not imply an intention to found a family, specific rights related to founding a family are not available to unmarried persons.

Question

For suggested approaches, please visit the Online Resource Centre.

On what principles and for what purposes is a state entitled to regulate and restrict a person's freedom to marry and to found a family?

Further reading

Leech, S. and Young, R. 'Marriage, Divorce and Ancillary Relief under the Human Rights Act 1998: An Introduction' [2001] 3 *EHRLR* 300–311

Lester, A., Pannick, D. and Herberg, J. (see Preface) Chapter 4, Article 12

Tew, Y. 'And They Call It Puppy Love: Young Love, Forced Marriage and Immigration Rules' (2012) 71(1) *CLJ* 18–19

Applications: police powers

Chapter overview

The impact of Convention rights on the law of England and Wales respecting the general powers of the police at common law and in statute, in particular the Police and Criminal Evidence Act 1984.

Introduction

cross reference
For the definition of a core public authority see Chapter 4, section 4.5.5.

In *Aston Cantlow* v *Wallbank* [2003] UKHL 37, the police were 'instinctively' listed as a 'core' public authority (para 7): policing is self-evidently a public function (they exercise directly the coercive authority of the state). This means police are required, by section 6 of the Human Rights Act 1998 (HRA), to act compatibly in all they do with Convention rights. Failure to do so means they can be acted against under section 7 HRA.

cross reference
For the interpretation of legislation under the HRA see Chapter 4, section 4.4.

Equally, as discussed in this chapter, the authority of the police (their legal right to do the things they do) is largely (though not exclusively) based on legislation which, under section 3 HRA, must be interpreted, so far as possible, for compatibility with Convention rights.

20.1 Police powers in general

20.1.1 Outline

Statute

The Police and Criminal Evidence Act 1984 (PACE) provides the principal statutory basis for police actions. The powers of the police lawfully to stop and search, arrest, detain suspects, take fingerprints and samples, search property and seize items, etc. are found in this Act. In the Act these powers are specified, the circumstances in which they can be exercised detailed and the safeguards enjoyed by those affected identified. Failure to act according to the statutory provisions can be unlawful and can be the basis of an action against the police or can give rise to other consequences such as the possibility of evidence being inadmissible at a trial. Many other Acts of Parliament also give police powers to search and arrest, etc. Examples are the Public Order Act 1986, the Firearms Act 1968 and the Misuse of Drugs Act 1971. Significant increases in police powers are found in anti-terrorism legislation, in particular the Terrorism Act 2000 (discussed in Chapter 26).

Police powers in PACE and other statutes have to be exercised in the light of guidance in Codes of Practice (with attached 'Notes for Guidance') produced under the Act by the Home Secretary (section 66 PACE). Failure to comply with a Code is not in itself unlawful but police compliance can be taken into account in determining the outcome of criminal and civil trials (section 67 PACE).

further study

The Codes are regularly updated. There are eight Codes (A–H) (updated between 2006 and 2012), available on the Home Office Police website:

http://www.homeoffice.gov.uk/publications/police/operational-policing/pace-codes/

Common law

cross reference
For breach of the peace see Chapter 18, section 18.6.3.

As well as statutory powers, the police have common law powers. These are the ordinary powers that all persons in England and Wales enjoy: to walk the streets, enter premises such as shops that are open to the public, etc. An important power (which private persons also have) is to take reasonable steps to deal with a breach of the peace, including one that has not occurred but is anticipated. A great deal of ordinary public order policing is done on this basis.

20.1.2 The Human Rights Act: legality

cross reference
For the Convention concept of legality see Chapter 6, section 6.2.

The compatibility of these provisions with the substantive Convention rights in Schedule 1 HRA will be considered in the rest of this chapter. The general point is that, in so far as the police take action that interferes with individual's rights (as arrest interferes with the right to liberty in Article 5 or a search may interfere with the right to private and family life, home and correspondence in Article 8), they must act in accordance with the law. This means that compliance with the Convention requires not only that the police act lawfully in terms of domestic (national) law but that the domestic law itself meets the standards of accessibility, foreseeability and non-arbitrariness that are at the heart of the autonomous Convention concept of law and the rule of law.

The European Court of Human Rights (ECtHR) accepts a wide definition of law. The rules that must be accessible and foreseeable need not only be in legislation but can also be in non-statutory written sources (such as Codes of Practice) and in 'unwritten' sources such as common law. The ECtHR has held that the legal basis on which the common law power to detain for breach of the peace is exercised with sufficient clarity to be consistent with the Convention concept of law (*Steel v United Kingdom* (1999) 28 EHRR 603, paras 54–55).

20.1.3 The use of force by the police

cross reference
On the lethal use of force including that based on an honest mistake, see Chapter 8, sections 8.2.1 and 8.2.5.

The police can use force in the exercise of their powers. There is a general provision, that applies to all, including the police: section 3 of the Criminal Law Act 1967 allows a person to use 'such force as is reasonable in the circumstances in the prevention of crime, or in effecting or assisting in the lawful arrest of offenders or suspected offenders or persons unlawfully at large'. Under section 117 PACE a constable may use 'reasonable force, if necessary' when exercising a power conferred on the police by PACE.

Under the HRA, of course, this use of force must be exercised in ways that are compatible, in particular, with Article 2 (the right to life: see Chapter 8, section 8.2.1), Article 3 (the prohibition on torture etc.: see Chapter 9, section 9.5) and Article 8 (the qualified right to private life etc.: see Chapter 15).

20.1.4 Assaulting and obstructing the police

It is an offence under section 89 of the Police Act 1996 to assault or obstruct a constable 'in the execution of his duty'. People are, however, allowed to use force that is reasonable in the circumstances to resist a police officer who is not executing his duty. The importance of section 89 is that it can be the judicial vehicle through which the precise scope of police powers under the law are determined.

20.1.5 **Remedies against the police**

In respect of unlawful or improper actions by the police, a range of remedies are available. These include

- a civil action for damages;
- an action under section 7 HRA;
- judicial review (e.g. where the challenge is to a policy the police are pursuing);
- a judge's exercise of his or her discretion, in section 78 PACE, not to admit evidence obtained unlawfully (breach of PACE, for example) or in breach of one of the PACE Codes (though neither common law nor Article 6 of the Convention requires unlawfully obtained evidence to be inadmissible);
- a complaint to the Independent Police Complaints Authority (IPCA).

cross reference
For Article 13 see Chapter 5, section 5.1.

The Convention point is that, under Article 13 ECHR, these remedies must provide adequate protection for those who allege that the police behaviour they complain of is a breach of their Convention rights. The courts and the IPCA have to be able to provide a forum in which all the issues relating to the alleged violation can be properly and fairly determined.

Many serious issues start out as a complaint to the IPCA. This body was created, in part, because its predecessor, the Police Complaints Authority, was held, in *Khan* v *United Kingdom* (2001) 31 EHRR 45, not to be sufficiently independent of government and the police to meet the standards of Article 13. Article 13 is not one of the scheduled Convention rights in the HRA so, if domestic remedies cannot be given effect to give proper consideration of alleged Convention violations, a complaint to Strasbourg will be necessary.

20.2 **Stop and search**

20.2.1 **General**

The police have powers to compel people to stop and be searched whilst they are in public places; people can be detained by the police for that purpose. The main power, which is in Part 1 PACE, is to stop, detain and search for stolen or prohibited articles including articles with blades and prohibited fireworks. If found, such articles may be seized. A number of other statutes also have stop and search powers, such as in relation to firearms (Firearms Act 1968, section 47(3)) or drugs (Misuse of Drugs Act 1971, section 23(2)). Stops and searches under all these Acts are subject to the guidance in PACE Code A.

20.2.2 **Restrictions and safeguards**

The stop and search power, particularly in PACE, is highly controversial. It is an interference with people's basic liberty to be in public places and it has often been alleged that the power is used in discriminatory ways, disproportionately against young, black males. (Code A makes it clear that it is unlawful to exercise the power in a way which involves direct or indirect racial discrimination.)

There are important safeguards:

- A stop and search under PACE can only be conducted on the basis of 'reasonable suspicion' that the person is carrying stolen or prohibited articles. Code A (paras 2.2–2.11) gives extensive guidance on this. In particular there has to be an objective basis for the suspicion. Controversially, however, there are a number of other powers the police have that allow stop and search without the need for specific suspicion against the individual searched (a random search). This includes some powers under the Terrorism Act 2000 (discussed in Chapter 26, section 26.8.1) and under section 60 Criminal Justice and Public Order Act 1994. This allows the police to designate an area in which random stops and searches may take place for a limited period and under certain conditions.

- A search is limited in its nature: the person cannot, in public, be required to remove any clothing other than coats, jackets or gloves. A more intensive search can only be done out of the public view and searches involving the exposure of intimate bodily parts must be done at a police station (Code A, para 3.7).

- A search is unlawful unless certain information about the officer conducting the search and the reason for it is given before the search commences (section 2 PACE) and a full record is made afterwards (section 3 PACE). Code A gives additional detail.

KEY POINT The majority of stops and searches are done with the consent of the person searched and so do not need the authority of PACE. Usually, of course, a person 'consents' because there is no real option. Code A (appearing to lay down a rule of law) says that even fully consensual searches must not be done unless the search would also be lawful under PACE (para 1.5).

20.2.3 Convention compliance: Articles 8–11

A person's physical integrity, correspondence, etc. is protected by Article 8(1) and may be interfered with by a personal search. Furthermore PACE gives police a power of seizure of prohibited articles and these include offensive weapons. Any object can be an offensive weapon depending on the context. This can include, for example, political banners whose seizure could raise an issue under Articles 10(1) and 11(1) (freedom of expression and freedom of assembly) and require justification under Articles 10(2) or 11(2).

The *Gillan* case, which is discussed in Chapter 26 (section 26.8.1; see also Chapter 11, section 11.4.2) involved the compatibility with Convention rights of a random stop and search conducted under section 44 Terrorism Act 2000. Remarkably the House of Lords, in *R (Gillan)* v *Metropolitan Police Commissioner* [2006] UKHL 12, found that the lawful and proper conduct of a stop and search will normally be superficial and not a sufficiently serious interference with these rights to require justification. If there are circumstances where a stop and search does involve an interference then, assuming it is lawfully and properly conducted, it is likely to be capable of justification under the second paragraphs of Article 8, 10 or 11. The ECtHR (*Gillan* v *UK*) (2010) 50 EHRR 45) took a dramatically different view and found that the random basis of selection for search and the lack of adequate controls meant that the powers could not be exercised lawfully, in the Convention sense of the term. As discussed in Chapter 26, section 26.8.1, the power was revised and replaced in 2012.

A search conducted in an inhuman and degrading way would be incompatible with Article 3 but it would also be inconsistent with Code A. This requires the powers to be used 'fairly, responsibly, with respect for people being searched and without unlawful discrimination' (para 1.1).

Depending on context, articles with religious significance can be seized, raising issues under Article 9. Part 1 PACE makes no particular reference to religion; however, in the Notes for Guidance attached to Code A, it is made clear that religious headdress cannot be removed unless the police officer believes it is being worn for the purpose of disguise (other than the simple fact that it has the effect of disguise) and removals may have to take place away from public view.

further study

Other police powers to seize items, such as knives, give a statutory defence that the item was for a religious purpose: see Criminal Justice Act 1988, section 139(5)(b).

20.2.4 **Convention compliance and Article 5**

cross reference
For Article 5(1) see Chapter 11, section 11.4.

Stop and search powers, including under Part 1 PACE, authorise the police to 'detain' the suspect for the purposes of the search. If such a detention were to involve a 'deprivation of liberty' then a stop and search would engage Article 5 of HRA Schedule 1. This would mean it could only be done for the purposes listed in Article 5(1). The point of stop and search is to allow officers to 'allay or confirm suspicions' without needing to arrest on reasonable suspicion of an offence and so Article 5(1)(c) would normally be breached.

In *Gillan* (the UK case), the House of Lords held that:

- An ordinary stop and search, lawfully and properly conducted, is unlikely to involve a deprivation of liberty (para 25).

- If there are additional factors (the person stopped and searched is detained for more than a brief period, is taken to a police station for a more intimate search or handcuffed, for example) there may have been a deprivation of liberty. In that case the stop and search is likely to fall within Article 5(1)(b) as being necessary to fulfil 'an obligation prescribed by law'; namely the obligation of submitting to a stop and search where the grounds (reasonable suspicion, for example, of carrying stolen or prohibited articles) exist (para 26).

In *Gillan v UK*, the ECtHR found it unnecessary to rule on this specific issue and so the House of Lords' position remains authoritative in the UK.

cross reference
On Article 5(1)(b) see Chapter 11, section 11.4.2.

KEY POINT The search in *Gillan*, under the Terrorism Act, did not require reasonable suspicion. This was because the area in which it was conducted (central London) had been designated, under the Act, as an area in which random searches could take place. The House of Lords rejected the view that, because the designation had not been made known to the public, the stop and search was not done on the basis of foreseeable and accessible rules and so the Convention concept of 'law' had not been complied with.

20.3 **Arrest**

20.3.1 **The concept of arrest**

An arrest is a crucial moment in the criminal justice process. It means that the arrested person loses his or her physical liberty and is brought under the compulsory control of the police. Both police and private persons can (on significantly different grounds) effect an arrest. Reasonable force can be used for a lawful arrest, though, equally, a person can use reasonable force to resist an unlawful arrest. Under the law of England and Wales an arrest requires an act of physical restraint by the arrester or clear words indicating to the person, and understood by him or her, that he or she is now under compulsion (*Alderson v Booth* [1969] 2 QB 216).

20.3.2 **Arrest under the law of England and Wales**

Warrant

Arrest on the basis of a warrant means there has been at least some degree of judicial supervision of the decision to arrest. The main general power is in section 1(1)(b) of the Magistrates' Courts Act 1980 under which a magistrate can issue an arrest warrant on the basis of information laid before them that a person is suspected of an indictable (usually the more serious) criminal offence. Magistrates can also issue a summons that requires the person to appear in court but does not involve arrest. Failure to answer a summons, however, can be the grounds of a warrant, issued under section 13. Section 17 PACE allows police to enter premises in order to execute a warrant.

Summary arrest

Summary arrest is done by the police (or a private person) without any form of prior judicial supervision. Police have the power of summary arrest under a large number of statutes. The general power for a police officer is contained in section 24 PACE, with guidance in Code G. A person can be arrested for any offence so long as certain conditions apply. For the police these are (in summary) that

- the person is about to commit, is committing or has committed a criminal offence; *and*
- to arrest the person is necessary (compared with the alternatives of obtaining a summons to appear in court or a warrant for an arrest from a magistrate, for example); *but*
- the officer must have reasonable grounds for believing the arrest is necessary in order to identify the suspect, to prevent injury to the suspect or others, prevent loss or damage to property, to prevent the suspect committing offences against public decency, to prevent the suspect causing an obstruction of the highway, to protect a child or vulnerable person, to allow the prompt and effective investigation of the offence or to prevent any prosecution being hindered by the disappearance of the suspect.

20.3.3 **Convention compliance: reasonable suspicion**

cross reference
For Article 5(1)(c) see Chapter 11, section 11.4.3.

Arrest, by definition, involves a deprivation of liberty and so the laws allowing the issuing of warrants and summary arrest such as under section 24 PACE must be applied in ways that are compatible with Article 5(1)(c). This requires that any arrest must be lawful, effected for the purpose of bringing the arrested person before the competent legal authority and based on 'reasonable suspicion' of the offence or 'when it is reasonably considered necessary to prevent his committing an offence or fleeing after having done so'. Lawfulness includes the requirement that the decision to arrest needs to be a proportionate exercise of power.

Section 24 PACE is generally compatible with Article 5. In particular the terms of section 24 mean either that the arrest is based, as a matter of law and fact, on an offence being committed or on the arresting officer having reasonable suspicion. An arrest on a lesser standard, such as mere suspicion based on a hunch, would not be lawful under either the Act or the Convention.

cross reference
*For reasonable sus-
picion, see Chapter
11, section 11.4.3.*

Under Article 5 the suspicion must be honestly held and based on 'facts or information which would satisfy an objective observer that the person concerned may have committed the offence in question' (see *Fox, Campbell and Hartley* v *United Kingdom* (1991) 13 EHRR 157, para 32).

The application of Article 5 ECHR to English law in this context was considered in *Cumming* v *Chief Constable of the Northumbria Police*.

> **case close-up**
>
> **Cumming v Chief Constable of Northumbria Police [2003] EWCA Civ 1844**
>
> ·
>
> CCTV footage that contained evidence of a crime appeared to have been tampered with. All the local authority employees controlling the CCTV were arrested on suspicion of perverting the course of justice. They were all innocent. They sought damages from the police for wrongful arrest and false imprisonment. The Court of Appeal agreed with the trial judge that their arrests had been lawful.

The pre-HRA law was found in *Castorina* v *Chief Constable of Surrey* (1988) 138 *NLJ* 180. The test was:

- did the police suspect the arrested persons had committed the offence,

- were there reasonable grounds for that belief, and

cross reference
*'Proportionality'
and 'reasonable-
ness' in admin-
istrative law are
discussed in
Chapter 4,
section 4.6.1.*

- in all the circumstances was it reasonable to arrest?

Under the HRA, these basic principles are retained but revised to ensure Article 5 is taken into account. The Court of Appeal in *Cumming* said:

> The court must consider with care whether or not the decision to arrest was one which no police officer, applying his mind to the matter could reasonably take bearing in mind the effect on the appellants' right to liberty. (para 43)

In *Shields* v *Chief Constable of Merseyside* [2010] EWCA Civ 1281 the Court of Appeal said that the law on arrest, which was given its present form in 2006 'takes into account the principles of Article 5, which therefore do not require separate consideration'. So a lawful arrest under section 24 PACE will be compatible with Article 5.

KEY POINT Private people also have the power of arrest. This is specified in section 24A PACE. The power is significantly limited—in particular there is no power to arrest someone who is about to commit an offence.

20.3.4 **Lawfulness and breach of the peace**

Arrest on the basis of a warrant or summary arrest is statute based and thereby likely to meet the requirement that a deprivation of liberty be consistent with the Convention concept of 'law' and 'legality', which is explicit in Article 5. The police retain a common law power to 'detain' for 'breach of the peace'. As said previously (section 20.1.1) the ECtHR has found that, given the way this power has been defined by the English courts, it can only be lawfully exercised in a way that is compatible with the Convention conception of law and legality.

20.3.5 **Information on arrest**

Article 5(2) requires that everyone 'arrested' 'shall be informed promptly, in a language which he understands, of the reasons for his arrest and of any charge against him'. Such a requirement has long been part of common law (see *Christie* v *Leachinsky* [1947] 1 All ER 567) and is confirmed by section 28(3) PACE. Section 28 requires that arrested persons be informed both of the fact that they are under arrest and also of the reasons for their arrest. This information must be given 'as soon as is practicable'. In *Taylor* v *Chief Constable of Thames Valley Police* [2004] EWCA Civ 858 the formula adopted by the ECtHR in *Fox, Campbell and Hartley* (1991) 13 EHRR 157, para 40 (see Chapter 11, section 11.5) was accepted as part of English law:

> having regard to all the circumstances of the particular case [the accused] was told in simple, non-technical language that he could understand, the essential legal and factual grounds for his arrest.

The point is to allow the arrested person to instigate a legal challenge and so the information given must be sufficient for that purpose (*Clarke* v *Chief Constable of North Wales Police* The Independent, 22 May 2000).

20.4 The treatment of an arrested person

20.4.1 General

Part V PACE deals with the treatment of arrested persons being held in custody in a police station. Code C on Detention, Treatment and Questioning applies.

Under the Convention and the HRA, there is the need to treat arrested persons in a manner that does not involve inhuman or degrading treatment in violation of Article 3; also to ensure that the interferences with private life that are likely can be justified under the terms of Article 8(2). Questioning must not be oppressive (Code C, para 11.5). A confession obtained by oppression is not admissible as evidence (section 76 PACE) and other kinds of improperly or unfairly obtained evidence can be excluded at the discretion of the judge (section 78 PACE).

An arrested person being held in custody has the right to have someone informed, though this can be delayed for up to 36 hours by the police (section 56 PACE and Code C, para 5).

20.4.2 Article 6 and access to a lawyer

As said many times, the rule of law pervades the Convention (including Article 5) and so police behaviour in respect of an arrested person must adhere strictly to the law and the Convention conception of the rule of law. Given that arrest may lead to charge and then to prosecution, the lawfulness of what happens to an arrested person under the control of the police can affect their right to a fair trial under Article 6. Article 6 'has some application at the pre-trial stage' (*Reinprecht* v *Austria* (2007) 44 EHRR 39, para 37). The significance of Article 6 over pre-trial events depends upon the circumstances, specifically whether what happens could prejudice the likely outcome of the trial.

Access to legal advice during police questioning is likely to be necessary in this context. Legal advice is particularly important since, under English law, a jury at the trial can draw a presumption of guilt from the accused person's silence or failure to mention certain matters whilst under police questioning (sections 34, 36 and 37 Criminal Justice and Public Order Act 1994). In *Murray* v *United Kingdom* (1996) 22 EHRR 29 the ECtHR held that in circumstances where what the accused does or says under police interrogation can have decisive consequences at the resulting trial, Article 6 normally requires that the accused have legal assistance; though this right, since it is only implied from Article 6, may be 'subject to restrictions for good cause'.

Section 58 PACE gives a suspect held in custody in a police station the right to consult a solicitor privately. A senior police officer can authorise a delay of up to 36 hours under certain circumstances, such as a belief that exercising the right will lead to interference with evidence. Most importantly, regarding Convention rights, the relevant provisions of the Criminal Justice and Public Order Act 1994 have been amended so that presumptions tending to guilt cannot be drawn if, whilst in custody, the suspect did not have access to legal advice.

20.5 Detention

20.5.1 The power to detain

An arrested person should be charged or released. Detention is possible under certain circumstances.

- **Detention after charge.** Section 37 PACE requires the 'custody officer' to decide whether there is sufficient evidence to charge the arrested person. If there is and the person is charged he or she will then be released, either with or without bail, unless the custody officer thinks it is necessary to detain the person, under section 38 PACE. There are various grounds for this, such as a fear that the person will not voluntarily attend court. A person so detained must then, under section 46, be brought before a magistrate on the same day or the day following.

- **Pre-charge detention.** If there is insufficient evidence for an immediate charge, section 37 requires that the arrested person should be released (with or without bail). However, PACE permits the police to detain an arrested person against whom, at the time of arrest, there is insufficient evidence to charge. This is where detention is considered 'necessary to secure or preserve evidence relating to an offence for which he is under arrest or to obtain such evidence by questioning him' (section 37).

- Pre-charge detention is for a maximum of 96 hours but after 36 hours judicial authority from a magistrate is required: see sections 41–44 PACE:

  - The initial police detention can be for up to 24 hours.

  - That can be extended by another 12 hours, to a maximum of 36, but only with the authority of a senior police officer and only in respect of **indictable** offences.

  - Detention beyond 36 hours requires a warrant from a magistrate.

  - A warrant from a magistrate can be for no more than 36 hours although it can be renewed for a second time so long as the overall period in detention without trial does not exceed 96 hours.

....

indictable and summary offences

The most serious offences are tried on 'indictment'. This involves jury trial before a Crown Court. The indictment is the document that specifies the alleged offence. 'Summary' offences are the less serious offences which are dealt with by magistrates. Accused people receive a 'summons' to the court. Many offences can be tried 'either way' giving the defendant an option to choose jury trial.

....

20.5.2 **Article 5(3) and detention**

Pre-charge detention is a deprivation of liberty and thus must be done compatibly with Article 5. Assuming detainees have been arrested on reasonable suspicion of an offence, their detention is in principle permitted under Article 5(1)(c). The important provision is Article 5(3). This embodies the idea of the rule of law and the need that the police's power to detain should be in accordance with law and properly supervised by an independent judiciary.

In *McKay* v *United Kingdom* (2007) 44 EHRR 41, a Grand Chamber distinguished the 'arrest period' part of Article 5(3) from the 'pre-trial or remand' part.

Arrest period

This requires a detained person to be brought 'promptly' before a judicial body who can exercise judicial power by, for example, ordering the release of a person unlawfully detained.

As discussed in Chapter 11, section 11.7.1, the ECtHR has been reluctant to lay down definite periods to correspond with the word 'promptly'. *Brogan* v *United Kingdom* ((1989) 11 EHRR 117) was an anti-terrorism case and even here a delay of more than four days was held to be a breach. The PACE provisions, given above, seem to meet Article 5(3) requirements. They require judicial involvement after 36 hours (in the case of pre-charge detention) and within a day or at the first possible moment regarding detainees who have been charged.

The job of the magistrates dealing with the arrest period aspect of Article 5(3) is to give a proper examination of the grounds for detention. In *Re McAuley's Application* [2004] NIQB 5, para 24 (a Northern Ireland terrorism case concerned with the effect of Article 5(3)) this was said to include examining the basis for reasonable suspicion, the basis for the charge and whether there have been any procedural defects. At this stage it is not necessary for the magistrate to consider the issue of bail: *McKay* v *United Kingdom* (above, paras 35–40).

Under the Convention, detainees also have a right that the investigation will be reviewed and conducted with due diligence. PACE meets this requirement by the requirement of a review, conducted by a review officer independent of the investigation, after six hours and then at nine-hourly intervals (section 40 PACE and Code C, Notes for Guidance, note 15A).

Pre-trial or remand period

Article 5(3) requires 'trial within a reasonable time or release pending trial'. Section 37 PACE gives the police the power to release where there is insufficient evidence to charge (section 37(2)) or, where there is sufficient evidence to charge, either with or without bail (section 37(7)). These provisions must be exercised compatibly with Article 5(3), which creates a presumption in favour of release. Issues of bail or remand then fall to the courts to determine under the Bail Act 1976.

KEY POINT Different provisions apply under anti-terrorism legislation and these are discussed in Chapter 26, section 26.8.2.

Fingerprints and samples

Normally fingerprints and bodily samples cannot be taken from a person without their consent (sections 61, 61A, 62 and 63 PACE). However, the requirement for consent can be dispensed with where a person who is detained in a police station has been arrested or charged for a recordable offence. In those circumstances the police can, without consent, take

- fingerprints (section 61(3) and (4) PACE);
- an impression of the person's footwear (section 61A(3) PACE);
- non-intimate samples, such as head hair, saliva and mouth swabs or a skin impression (section 63 PACE).

Intimate samples (defined as blood, semen, other tissue fluid, urine, pubic hair, a dental impression or a swab from an orifice other than the mouth) can only be taken with written consent (section 62 PACE). However, under section 62(10) inferences can be drawn (e.g. by a jury in a subsequent trial) if a police request for an intimate sample is unreasonably refused. It is, of course, from these samples that DNA information can be obtained. Code D applies to the exercise of these powers.

The fingerprints and samples taken can then be checked against others, such as those found at the scene of a crime (section 63A PACE).

20.6.1 **Taking and Convention rights**

PACE confines the non-consensual taking of fingerprints and samples to persons under reasonable suspicion of an offence (for which they have been arrested or charged) and it limits the use of such material to, broadly speaking, the investigation of crimes. The taking of samples and fingerprints clearly involves a person's physical integrity and so is an interference with private life under Article 8(1); therefore, in principle, it requires justification under Article 8(2). Normal applications of the power in PACE are likely to be easily justified under Article 8(2). This was the view of the House of Lords in *R (Marper)* v *Chief Constable of South Yorkshire Police* [2004] UKHL 39 (para 21), following the view of the Commission of Human Rights in *McVeigh* v *United Kingdom* (1983) 5 EHRR 71, para 224:

- the PACE provisions are clearly accessible and the circumstances in which they will be invoked reasonable foreseeable,
- the taking of samples etc. is done for the 'prevention of crime', and
- is necessary for that purpose.

20.6.2 **Retention and Convention rights**

Attention and concern is focused less on taking and more on the power and the policy of retaining samples or, more importantly, the DNA information that can be obtained from them.

Authority to retain samples (from which the DNA profiles are obtained and which can then be stored on a database) is found in section 64 PACE. It permits the retention of samples etc. after they have fulfilled the purpose for which they are taken, but only for purposes related to the prevention, detection, investigation and prosecution of crime or to assist with the identification of a dead person or a body part (section 64(1A) PACE). Between 2001 and 2011, samples, including DNA profiles, could be retained indefinitely from juveniles and also from people arrested and charged with an offence but who had been acquitted or whose case did not come to trial. Similarly, samples etc. given by people never suspected in the first place (which are supposed to be destroyed) could be retained if some other person had been convicted of the offence and that convicted person had a sample etc. taken from them.

This wide, inclusive power of retention and storage of DNA profiles was challenged on Article 8 grounds in *R (Marper)* v *Chief Constable of South Yorkshire Police* [2004] UKHL 39. The claimants were an 11-year-old child who had been acquitted of attempted robbery and a man arrested and charged with harassment whose case had been discontinued by the Crown Prosecution Service. In both cases fingerprints and DNA samples were taken and retained. The House of Lords held that the general policy of retaining samples did not normally amount to an interference with private life, and so Article 8(1) was not engaged and that if, in exceptional circumstances, there was an interference it was likely to be justifiable under Article 8(2).

This judgment, however, was successfully challenged in Strasbourg. In *Marper* v *United Kingdom* (2009) 48 EHRR 50, a Grand Chamber held that:

cross reference
For discussion of the direct consequences of Marper v UK see Chapter 4, section 4.4.7.

- The storage of cellular samples, DNA and fingerprints was an interference with private life. Individuals could be identified and fears of future, improper uses, were a relevant factor.

- The interference was not justified under Article 8(2). The Court accepted the utility of retention in fighting crime. However, this would have to be compatible with human rights. The Article 8(2) requirements that interferences be in accordance with law and proportionate were merged. In these and other matters (such as secret surveillance) there need to be detailed rules and proper safeguards, dealing with issues like storage, accessibility and destruction. These were needed in order to minimise the risk of arbitrariness. In the Court's view, the legal provisions failed to offer these safeguards. There was a breach of Article 8 because the 'blanket and indiscriminate' policy of retaining the samples and fingerprints of all suspected but unconvicted persons (persons presumed innocent) was disproportionate and not justifiable under Article 8(2).

Following *Marper* v *United Kingdom* the law has been amended. The Protection of Freedoms Act 2012 (PFA 2012) amended PACE with a detailed scheme for the retention and destruction of DNA profiles. Thus, for instance, DNA profiles of those arrested, charged but not convicted must be destroyed after three years; profiles of those convicted of serious offences, however, can be retained indefinitely; and the profiles of juvenile offenders should be destroyed after five years. Section 23 PFA 2012 requires retained profiles to be put on the DNA database. This database is run by the Home Office (since 2012) but its operation must be overseen by an independent body—the National DNA Database Strategy Board (section 24 PFA 2012). The effect of these provisions should be to remove the arbitrary and indiscriminate quality of the retention of data prior to the *Marper* litigation.

discussion topic

Irrespective of the post-*Marper* reforms, is the DNA database still an intrusion into private life which should be closed or reformed further?

For:

- The DNA database is believed to be the biggest of any country. One estimate in 2012 is that there are nearly 6 million profiles. This is a significant intrusion by the state into private life. No matter how stringent the laws, mistakes and misuse are always a possibility. Even under PFA 2012 profiles of the innocent can be retained for three years.

Against:

- The Home Office make a strong case for its usefulness in solving crimes. In the period April–June 2012, profile matches contributed to the investigation of 29 murders, 91 rapes and 6,094 other crimes (figures from the National Police Improvement Agency, wound up in 2012 but which until then had responsibility for the database).

- The reforms in PFA 2012 now provide sufficient protection against abuse.

Entry, search and seizure

The police have extensive powers to enter and search premises and seize matters found there. As we shall see these can raise issues involving Convention rights, such as under Article 8 (respect for private and family life, home and correspondence) and Article 1 of the First Protocol (peaceful enjoyment of possessions).

20.7.1 Consent to enter, search and seizure

No particular authority is needed for a police officer to enter homes, offices, shops, factories, etc. with the consent, express or implied, of the owners or occupiers. In that sense the police are in the same position as everybody else. If the occupier withdraws consent then the police (assuming they have no other legal basis for being there) should leave and, if they do not, reasonable force can be used.

Consent to enter is not the same thing as consent to a search. PACE Code B (para 5.4) makes it clear, for example, that the occupier should be reminded of their right to refuse if the police seek consent to search.

There is, of course, no freedom to seize goods and items from places just because there was an express or implied right to enter. Goods could be taken with consent, of course. However, if the police are in premises lawfully (e.g. with the occupier's consent) they have a broad statutory power to seize anything believed to be there as a consequence of a criminal act, so long as seizure is believed to be necessary to prevent the thing being 'concealed, lost, altered or destroyed' (section 19 PACE).

20.7.2 Statutory power to enter without consent

Section 17 PACE abolished most of the pre-existing common law powers police had to enter premises without consent. A few remain, such as the power to abate a nuisance. Section 17 PACE gives the police statutory authority to enter premises in order to arrest persons, under various circumstances or to save life and limb. This is a power the police exercise without the need for judicial authority from a warrant. Section 17(6) expressly reserves the common law power to enter premises to deal with a breach of the peace.

case close-up

McCleod v United Kingdom (1999) 27 EHRR 493

Police, advised by Mrs McCleod's ex-husband's solicitors that there might be a breach of the peace, assisted the ex-husband whilst he removed property from Mrs McCleod's house. The husband was trespassing since, under a legal settlement between them, ownership of the property, at that time, had not yet transferred to him. The police refused Mrs McCleod's request to restore the property. The courts held that the police had acted lawfully under section 17(6) PACE. The ECtHR held that there had been a violation of Article 8.

The Court held that

- the entry under section 17 was an interference with the rights protected by Article 8(1) and so the interference must be justified under Article 8(2);

- breach of the peace was defined with sufficient clarity to be 'in accordance with the law';

- the power was used for a legitimate purpose, the 'prevention of disorder or crime';

- however, the exercise of power, especially because not enough attention was paid to Mrs McCleod's legal rights under the court order, was disproportionate and so there was a breach.

Given the narrow, proportionality, ground on which this case was decided, it is likely that, in general terms, the powers in section 17 (not just subsection (6)) will be, if properly exercised, compatible with Article 8.

Of course section 17 does not give a power of search for goods or seizure. Section 19 (above), however, applies since the arresting officers will have entered the premises lawfully.

20.7.3 Statutory power to search premises

Section 32 PACE gives the police power to search the premises where an arrested person was immediately before being arrested. There must be a reasonable belief that there is evidence relating to the offence on the premises. Under section 18 PACE, a constable may search premises 'occupied or controlled' by an arrested person. The power is to search for evidence connected to the arrest. In a Convention-related case, the Court of Appeal has adopted an objective test on whether the property is occupied or controlled.

case close-up

Khan v Commissioner of Police for the Metropolis [2008] EWCA Civ 723

. . . .

M was arrested by the police. He gave a false address—the claimant's home. The police searched the claimant's home and found nothing. The claimant sued the police for trespass. The police defence was that they had acted under section 18 and so were on the property lawfully. The judge awarded damages against the police and the police appeal was rejected by the Court of Appeal.

The Court of Appeal held that:

- Section 18 should be given its ordinary meaning—it referred to an arrested person's actual address. There was nothing in the section that referred to the police needing only reasonable grounds for believing it was the arrested person's address.

- The police could have used section 32 or obtained a warrant under section 8.

- This approach flowed from a section 3 HRA reading of section 18 PACE and, with regard to Article 8, gave proper respect to a person's home.

The police have powers of entry and search under other statutes. In addition there are some circumstances where the police are able to rely on traditional common law powers which have not been superseded by PACE. Search of premises after the arrest of a person in pursuit of an extradition warrant is outside PACE, because the offence in question is under the law of a foreign country. Nevertheless, the House of Lords, in *R (Rottman)* v *Commissioner of Police for the Metropolis* [2002] UKHL 20, held that the police retained a common law power of entry and search.

20.7.4 Power of entry, search and seizure on the basis of a warrant

Section 8 PACE allows a constable to apply to a magistrate for a search warrant. An indictable offence must have been committed, the officer must have reasonable grounds for believing that a search will give rise to material of 'substantial value' to an investigation and the warrant must be necessary for various reasons such as that entry would otherwise be refused. There are many other statutes that also authorise the issuing of warrants to the police. Section 8(2) allows a police officer to seize any matter for which the search was warranted.

A warrant means that there is some element of judicial supervision of this power of significant interference with premises, including a person's 'home'. It helps to establish that searches are, for the purposes of Article 8, in accordance with the law. The courts have stressed the serious-ness of a warrant and the need that it is issued with proper care. ('The obtaining of a search warrant is never to be treated as a formality. It authorises the invasion of a person's home': *Redknapp* v *City of London Police* [2008] EWHC 1177, para 13.)

The malicious procurement of a warrant (when the police do not act in good faith) is a tort and can give rise to an action for damages. Mere negligence (not checking an address for instance) is not enough.

case close-up

Keegan v *United Kingdom* (2007) 44 EHRR 33

Acting on the basis of a warrant, police forced an entry to the home of Mr and Mrs Keegan. The address had been used by the mother of a suspected armed robber, but she had left six months previously when the Keegans moved in. The Court of Appeal found that the police had been negligent (they had not made elementary checks) but had acted in good faith. Therefore the tort of malicious procurement of a warrant was not made out (*Keegan* v *Chief Constable of the Merseyside Police* [2003] EWCA Civ 936). The Keegans, therefore, had no remedy under English law. The ECtHR held that the failure to check meant that the interference with the Keegans' right to a home was disproportionate and so a breach of Article 8. Furthermore, the insistence on their having to prove malice meant they had no effective remedy and so there was also a breach of Article 13.

cross reference
For Article 13 see Chapter 5, section 5.1.

Sections 15 and 16 of PACE introduce a range of procedural protections and these are empha-sised in Code B. Section 15 deals with issuing, e.g. the warrant must specify who it relates to, the date issued and the premises to be entered and searched. Section 16 deal with execution, e.g. the execution should normally be at a reasonable hour unless this would frustrate the purpose of the search. A warrant undertaken in breach of these provisions may be unlawful, but it needs to be remembered that there is no absolute bar in the law of England and Wales, nor under Article 6, to unlawfully obtained evidence being admitted as evidence.

The normal and lawful exercise of these powers (both statutory and common law) is likely to be compatible with Article 8 as being in accordance with law (even the common law power is sufficiently well defined), for a legitimate purpose (the prevention of crime) and, because of the safeguards, proportionate (see *R (Rottman)* v *Commissioner of Police for the Metropolis* [2002] UKHL 20, para 80, a decision on the common law power).

20.7.5 Protected material

Section 8 cannot be used to search for certain kinds of material. These are:

- Material subject to legal privilege, such as communications between the person searched and his or her legal advisor. The principle of upholding legal privilege is firmly entrenched in common law and is also fully recognised as necessary to a person's right to a fair trial under Article 6 and private life under Article 8 (see, for example, *Niemietz* v *Germany* (1993) 16 EHRR 97 and *Campbell* v *United Kingdom* (1993) 15 EHRR 137). Nothing in section 8 or other provisions of PACE authorise a search for privileged material and section 9 repeals any earlier Acts under which this might have been possible. In *R (Daly)* v *Secretary of State for the Home Department* [2001] UKHL 26, the House of Lords, referring to Article 6, upheld the importance of legal privilege in relation to the powers of a prison governor to search prisoners' correspondence in their absence. There are serious problems about searching a body of correspondence some of which may be privileged: Part 2 of the Criminal Justice and Police Act 2001 provides a scheme for this.

- 'Excluded' or 'Special Procedure' material cannot be searched for under section 8. Excluded material describes professionally held confidential records relating to physical or spiritual health or welfare; or human tissue taken for medical purposes and held in confidence. Special procedure material describes other types of confidential records (see PACE, sections 10–14). This is confidential and personal material that is given extra protection under the law; a protection that Article 8 may also require.

Under section 9(1) and Schedule 1 PACE the police may seek a court order from a circuit judge requiring the handing over of such material. The main procedural protection for this kind of confidential and private material lies in the fact that the police must apply to a circuit judge rather than just a magistrate and that there is the opportunity for a proper hearing to oppose the application (ordinary warrants under section 8 PACE are obtained *ex parte* without the person involved knowing).

Journalistic material can be either excluded or special procedure material depending on whether it is personal records held in confidence or other material held in confidence. Therefore it can only be obtained under Schedule 1.

A judge can order journalistic material, which is special procedure material, to be disclosed if the material would be of substantial value to an investigation and disclosure would be in the public interest having regard to that value. However, even if these 'access conditions' are made out, the judge still has a residual discretion to decide whether to make a disclosure order. It is at this point, in particular, that freedom of the press must be considered. In *R* v *Central Criminal Court ex parte Bright* [2001] 2 All ER 244, the police sought the disclosure of files held by a journalist which might disclose that an offence under the Official Secrets Act 1989 had been committed. The judgment in this pre-HRA case contains strong words in favour of media freedom (see especially the opinion of Judge J) and a concern that 'investigative journalism will be discouraged, perhaps stifled'. These general principles are reflected in post-HRA cases.

ss reference

protection of
rces see also
pter 22,
ion 22.4.

case close-up

R (BSkyB) v Chelmsford Crown Court [2012] EWHC 1295

Essex Police sought the disclosure of footage recorded by broadcasters of the controversial and violent eviction of travellers from Dale Farm. On appeal by the broadcasters, the Divisional Court stressed the need for the judge to make a careful, evidence based, analysis of whether the access conditions (such as the 'substantial value' test, section 20.7.4) are made out. Furthermore, assuming they are made out, Article 10 then requires a careful balancing exercise between the public interest in the suppression of crime and the public interest in media freedom (para 24). Eady J stressed the relevance of the issue that effective reporting of controversial issues might be discouraged if judges, by issuing disclosure orders too easily, compromise the impartiality and independence of broadcasters and put cameramen at risk (para 25).

The broadcaster's appeal succeeded because the police had not given sufficient evidence of the need for disclosure.

further study For discussion of a similar power under the Terrorism Act 2000, see *Shiv Malik* v *Manchester Crown Court* [2008] EWHC 1362.

KEY POINT Section 12 HRA requires the courts to have particular regard to the importance of freedom of expression in this context (see Chapter 17, section 17.3).

Summary

Police have extensive powers under common law and PACE. As public authorities these need to be exercised compatibly with Convention rights, especially Article 5 (regarding arrest and detention) and Article 8 (regarding searches and seizure). English and Welsh courts adjudicating on these powers have generally found them to be compatible with Convention rights at the general level. Attention is focused on particular applications in individual cases.

Question

 For suggested approaches, please visit the Online Resource Centre.

How do Articles 5 and 8 have an impact on the exercise of their powers by the police?

Further reading

Austin, R. 'The New Powers of Arrest: Plus ça Change: More of the Same or Major Change?' [2007] *Crim LR* 459–471

Bowling, B. and Philips, C. 'Disproportionate and Discriminatory: Reviewing the Evidence on Police Stop and Search' (2007) 70(6) *MLR* 936–961

Fenwick, H. *Civil Liberties and Human Rights* 4th edn (2007) Abingdon: Routledge-Cavendish, Part IV

Stone, R. *Textbook on Civil Liberties and Human Rights* 9th edn (2012) Oxford: OUP, Chapters 3–5

Applications: prisoners' rights

Chapter overview

The impact of Convention rights on the law of England and Wales respecting prisoners' rights.

Introduction

In this chapter the application of Convention rights in the field of prisoners' rights is considered.

The approximately 88,000 prisoners in the United Kingdom are under the complete control of the state as regards their everyday life. Whilst some are violent and repellent, the majority are also psychologically vulnerable, often suffering from alcoholism and drug dependency. Despite imprisonment they remain human beings and so are within the protection of the European Convention of Human Rights (ECHR). It is the scope of that protection, through the Human Rights Act 1998 (HRA), that is explored in this chapter.

21.1 Prisons and the Human Rights Act

Within its territory the state exercises a 'monopoly of legitimate force'. Given the abolition of capital punishment, the ultimate expression of that force is imprisonment—depriving individuals of their liberty. Not surprisingly, therefore, it is a public function for which the state is responsible under the Convention.

21.1.1 Legislation

The Prisons Act 1952 provides the basic authority for prisons in England and Wales. The Act authorises the making of subordinate legislation, in particular section 47 authorises the Secretary of State to make rules for the regulation, management, discipline, etc. of prisons and prisoners. The Prison Rules, thus made, deal with the general regulation and management of prisons and are regularly updated. The Prison Service Orders and Prison Service Instructions, authorised by the Rules, deal in detail with long-term and short-term matters.

The Act, the Rules, the Orders and the Instructions all come within the definitions (in section 21 HRA) of primary and subordinate legislation that (under section 3 HRA) must be interpreted, if possible, for compatibility with Convention rights. Some Prison Rules have been redrafted to build in Convention compliance.

21.1.2 Public authorities

Prisons legislation authorises the actions of a range of officials and authorities. In England and Wales it is the Secretary of State for Justice (prior to 2007 it was the Home Secretary) who has ultimate responsibility for prisons and prisoners. Direct, day-to-day, responsibility lies with the Prison Service, an executive agency that has a degree of independence from ministers. Individual prisons are under the direct control of a prison governor, who is a civil servant. Some prisons are privately owned and operate on the basis of a contract with the Prison Service.

These officials and agencies are 'public authorities' under section 6 HRA and so must act compatibly with Convention rights (private prisons are performing a public function and so, also, are public authorities under section 6(3)(b) HRA).

cross reference
See Chapter 4,
sections 4.4 and 4.5
for sections 3 and
6 HRA.

KEY POINT In Scotland, matters concerning prisons are non-reserved and therefore a devolved responsibility of the Scottish Parliament and Executive; likewise in Northern Ireland, since 2010, they are the responsibility of the Northern Ireland Executive and Assembly.

21.2 The rights of prisoners in general

Prisoners in England and Wales are not outlaws. In *Raymond* v *Honey* the House of Lords confirmed that

> a convicted prisoner, in spite of his imprisonment, retains all civil rights which are not taken away expressly or by necessary implication. (Lord Wilberforce [1983] 1 AC 1, at p 10)

A general power to make rules, such as section 47 of the Prisons Act, does not allow the making of rules that deny prisoners their fundamental rights. Only express and clear statutory words can do this. This common law recognition that prisoners retain those rights that are not necessarily incompatible with imprisonment is also found in the ECHR. In *Hirst* v *United Kingdom (2)* (2006) 42 EHRR 41, for example, a Grand Chamber made it clear that

> prisoners in general continue to enjoy all the fundamental rights and freedoms guaranteed under the Convention save for the right to liberty. (para 69)

Of particular importance is the recognition that both remand and convicted prisoners are under the more or less total control of the state and so are particularly vulnerable to abuse. The state has a clear duty to provide a proper and safe regime in which prisoners can enjoy the Convention rights and freedoms they retain.

21.2.1 Access to court

cross reference
*The Convention
right of access to
court is discussed in
Chapter 12,
section 12.7.*

Of the rights retained by prisoners, in a way the most fundamental is the right of access to a court to vindicate civil rights. It means that prisoners' retained rights are not illusory and they can obtain genuine remedies from the courts. Access to a court for prisoners has long been recognised both at common law (e.g. *R (Daly)* v *Secretary of State for the Home Department* [2001] UKHL 26, para 5) and under the Convention (*Golder* v *United Kingdom* (1979–80) 1 EHRR 524).

In England and Wales this means that prisoners can pursue:

- Private law rights such as actions for negligence, trespass, breach of statutory duty and misfeasance in public office. These include actions against the authorities based on either the behaviour of, for example, police or the Prison Service or the behaviour of fellow inmates, against whom the authorities should provide proper protection.

- Public law rights. These include the right that the prison authorities should only act within their powers, should exercise their discretion over policies and individual decisions in reasonable ways and, importantly, ensure that in disciplinary and other proceedings prisoners are given a fair hearing before an unbiased tribunal. These public law rights are obtained through the process of 'judicial review'.

cross reference

Section 7 HRA is discussed in Chapter 5, section 5.4.

- Convention rights. Where a prisoner alleges he or she has been directly affected by a violation of a Convention right they can use section 7 HRA. This can be by way of a direct challenge to the authorities or by using their Convention rights in other civil or criminal proceedings in which they are involved.

21.2.2 **The substance of prisoners' rights: general**

But what are the substantive rights that prisoner's enjoy? In England and Wales this is a matter of the judges interpreting and applying the relevant statutory and common law provisions. Of course, as public authorities themselves, the judges must do this in ways that are compatible with Convention rights—indeed sometimes they will be directly applying a Convention right. What must be stressed is that, mostly, prisoners' rights are not absolute but are flexible and context dependent, and this is true under both the common law and the Convention. The courts recognise the necessity for restrictions and qualifications on the application of rights to prisoners where such restrictions would not be acceptable in the situation of free persons. For instance, in *R (Cannan)* v *Governor of Full Sutton Prison* [2003] EWCA Civ 1480 the Court of Appeal held that a prisoner's right of access to the courts under Article 6 was violated in respect of conditions imposed on the transmission of documents between a prisoner and his legal advisor. However, restrictions on other types of communication with legal advisors served a legitimate purpose and did not violate Article 6.

21.3

The basis of imprisonment: Article 5

21.3.1 **Article 5(1)(a)**

Prisoners lose the right to liberty but their imprisonment must be compatible with Article 5, which establishes the only terms on which a person can be deprived of his or her liberty. In particular: any deprivation of liberty must be on the basis of a 'procedure prescribed by law' and Article 5(1)(a) allows 'the lawful detention of a person after conviction by a competent court'. This means that prisoners in England and Wales must have been convicted

- for offences that are properly defined in law (otherwise there could also be a violation of Article 7: see Chapter 13, section 13.3),

- through a fair criminal procedure. Defendants have the right to a fair trial under Article 6(1)–(3): see Chapter 12.

A prisoner's detention will not be 'lawful', even if it complies with domestic law, if it is 'arbitrary' as the European Court of Human Rights (ECtHR) understands that term. In *James, Wells and Lee* v *United Kingdom* App 25119/09, judgment of 18 September 2012, the ECtHR identified four requirements relevant to that understanding (paras 192–195):

- the authorities act with good faith;

- there is a clear link between the facts and circumstances of imprisonment with the purposes of permitted detention in Article 5(1)(a)–(f);

- likewise there must be a relationship between the permitted ground in Article 5(1)(a)–(e) relied on and the place and conditions of detention;

cross reference
For Article 5(1)(a)
see Chapter 11,
section 11.4.1.

- the decision to detain on one of the permitted grounds must be proportionate to that ground. The scope of proportionality depends on the context—the length of lawful imprisonment after conviction will normally be accepted, but decisions not to release for reasons that are not related to the original conviction might violate Article 5(1).

21.3.2 Article 5(4) and indeterminate sentences

Of particular importance for some convicted prisoners is Article 5(4). There must be legal procedures by which prisoners can make an effective challenge to the lawfulness of their detention.

In England and Wales there are 'determinate' sentences (where the number of years is given at the time of conviction—e.g. five years' imprisonment) and 'indeterminate' sentences (e.g. a life sentence, where the prisoner may only be released if it is safe to do so and he or she can be recalled to prison).

Determinate sentences

The prisoner should have been sentenced according to law by a properly constituted criminal court that is independent, impartial and follows fair procedures. The trial, including any subsequent appeals, are taken to satisfy the requirements of Article 5(4): a position confirmed by the House of Lords in *R (Giles)* v *Parole Board* [2003] UKHL 42, para 25.

Indeterminate sentences

The passing of an indeterminate sentence is compatible with Article 5(1). However, the decisions on release and recall must be taken in a manner consistent with Article 5(4) (see *R (Smith)* v *Parole Board* [2005] UKHL 1, para 36).

There are three main forms of indeterminate sentence:

- A 'mandatory' life sentence must be imposed by a court on a person convicted of murder.
- A 'discretionary' life sentence can be imposed as the maximum punishment for particularly grave offences.
- A life sentence must normally be imposed for a second, particularly grave offence (section 122 Legal Aid, Sentencing and Punishment of Offenders Act 2012). Indeterminate sentences for 'public protection' were abolished by this Act (section 123) and replaced by a power to impose a sentence extended by a maximum of 5 to 8 years (sections 123 and 125) allowing for release on licence during the extended period.

The basic structure of these sentences is that the prisoner serves a minimum term (the custodial period) for the purpose of punishment and can then be released on licence but only if the requirement of public safety is satisfied (the risk period). Under a life sentence the licence remains in place for life. The released person can be returned to prison for breaching the terms of the licence.

Under Article 5(1)(a) the minimum term should be determined judicially and, likewise, under Article 5(4) it should be possible to challenge the 'risk period' before a judicial body. In the past, under the law of England and Wales, the Home Secretary, a member of the executive, had a decisive role in both matters. A series of adverse decisions from the ECtHR led to changes in the law. Under the Criminal Justice Act 2003 the minimum custodial period, for all indeterminate sentences, is determined by the trial judge (see, regarding mandatory life

423

sentences, section 269). A 'whole life' tariff is allowed under English law. Compatibility with Article 5 was accepted by a majority in *Bamber* v *UK* App 33742/96, Commission admissibility decision of 11 September 1997. Compatibility with Article 3, upheld in *Vinter* v *UK* (2012) 55 EHRR 34, is to be re-examined before a Grand Chamber. Decisions on continuing risk and release of prisoners, including those serving a mandatory life sentence, are made by the Parole Board (section 239).

To satisfy Article 5(4), the Parole Board has to meet the requirements of independence, impartiality and fair procedures required by Article 5(4).

In *R (Brooke)* v *Parole Board* [2008] EWCA Civ 29, the Court of Appeal held that the Parole Board in England and Wales lacked the necessary independence from the government because Ministers issued directions to the board and influenced appointments. This led to a restructuring of the relationship between the Ministry of Justice and the Parole Board.

Prisoners must have a practical opportunity to demonstrate to the Parole Board that they are safe to release after serving the custodial period. The Parole Board has laid down a condition that some prisoners must have attended anger management or other courses before their case can be considered. The Prison Service has been unable to provide these courses. In *James* (section 21.3.1), the ECtHR held that the failure to provide the courses introduced an arbitrary element into the continued imprisonment and violated Article 5(1) (the judgment of the House of Lords, *R (Wells)* v *Parole Board* [2009] UKHL 22, had been mainly focused on Article 5(4), which, the ECtHR agreed, had not been violated).

21.4 General conditions

The ECHR has no provision equivalent to Article 10 of the International Covenant on Civil and Political Rights (ICCPR), which says:

cross reference
The ICCPR is discussed in Chapter 1, section 1.4.4.

(1) All persons deprived of their liberty shall be treated with humanity and with respect for the inherent dignity of the human person...

(2) The penitentiary system shall comprise treatment of prisoners the essential aim of which shall be their reformation and social rehabilitation.

Article 3, since it embodies a general requirement that everyone, including prisoners, should be treated with humanity and dignity, is being increasingly used in respect of prison conditions. In the early twenty-first century, this is particularly noticeable in relation to rather shocking prison conditions that can be experienced by prisoners in some east European and Russian prisons (see *Kolunov* v *Russia* App 26436/05, judgment of 9 October 2012, for a recent example). Given the vulnerability and powerlessness of prisoners, Article 3 imposes a positive duty on states to ensure that the punitive regime provides proper protection compatible with a prisoner's dignity.

The general principles concerning the application of Article 3 to prison are stated in, for example, *Kehayov* v *Bulgaria* App 41035/98, judgment of 18 January 2005, paras 62–65:

• There will only be a violation of Article 3 if the treatment is above a minimum level of severity required. This minimum level cannot be stated in general or abstract terms but depends upon a range of contextual factors.

• Article 3 can be violated even if there was no intention by the authorities to cause suffering or to humiliate and degrade.

- A violation of Article 3 only occurs in respect of prison conditions that go beyond conditions that are necessary for imprisonment: 'the suffering and humiliation involved must in any event go beyond that inevitable element of suffering or humiliation connected with a given form of legitimate treatment or punishment' (*Kalashnikov* v *Russia* (2003) 36 EHRR 34, para 95).

- It follows that the mere fact of, for example, imprisonment on remand, or imprisonment in a special prison regime does not, of itself, give rise to a violation of Article 3.

- In assessing the conditions for compatibility with Article 3, it is necessary to take into account not only the physical conditions (overcrowding, ventilation, food, etc.) but also the nature of the regime under which the prisoner is being held.

- In any event the general, positive duty of the state is to ensure that a person is detained in conditions that are compatible with respect for his human dignity, that the manner and method of the execution of any measures do not subject him to distress or hardship of an intensity exceeding the unavoidable level of suffering inherent in detention and that, given the practical demands of imprisonment, his health and well-being are adequately secured. When assessing conditions of detention, account has to be taken of the cumulative effects of those conditions and the duration of the detention (para 64).

The application of Article 3 to prison conditions is fully accepted under English and UK law (see, for example, *R (Spinks)* v *Secretary of State for the Home Department* [2005] EWCA Civ 275, para 35). Article 3 is only violated if the conditions are sufficiently serious to cross the threshold of severity. Where that threshold is situated depends on context and circumstances. In *Napier* v *Scottish Ministers* 2005 1 SC 229, the Scottish courts held that the sanitary provisions (where prisoners, confined to shared cells, had to urinate into bottles and defecate into chamber pots), combined with other factors, crossed that threshold. But in *Grant* v *The Ministry of Justice* [2011] EWHC 3379, the case was distinguished in respect of prisoners in single cells: the threshold for a violation of Article 3 had not been passed, nor had there been a violation of Article 8.

Article 3 has significance not just in respect of the physical conditions under which prisoners are kept but also to other aspects of their treatment. A strip search is not itself a breach but must be conducted in a way that minimises degradation.

- In *Valasinas* v *Lithuania* App 44558/98, judgment of 24 July 2001, the ECtHR held that a strip search of a male prisoner in front of a woman was such a violation.

cross reference

On handcuffs, see also Chapter 9, section 9.5.

- In *R (Carroll)* v *Secretary of State for the Home Department* [2005] UKHL 13, intimate searches properly conducted under Prison Rules did not directly raise an Article 3 issue.

The use of handcuffs and other restraints does not normally give rise to a breach of Article 3, but may do if it is unnecessary or particularly humiliating. Where they are used on, for example, very ill prisoners who are incapable of escape, there may be a violation of Article 3 (*R (Graham)* v *Secretary of State for Justice* [2007] EWHC 2940).

21.5 Seclusion

Prison Rules (Rule 45) allow a prisoner to be placed in seclusion if this 'appears desirable, for the maintenance of good order or discipline or his own interests'. In extreme situations this could violate Article 3; more likely it will engage Article 8(1) since the concept of 'private life' includes the idea of self-development, including through association with others. However, it is likely to be the case that properly taken decisions on seclusion will be justified under Article 8(2). In *R (Munjaz)* v *Mersey Care NHS Trust* [2005] UKHL 58, a hospital's policy regarding the seclusion of detained mental health patients was held to be justified under Article 8(2) in terms of the prevention of crime (see para 33).

Physically and mentally ill or disabled prisoners

States have positive duties in respect of prisoners who are particularly vulnerable on account of illness or disabilities.

> **Keenan v United Kingdom (2001) 33 EHRR 38**
>
> A seriously disturbed and sometimes violent young man committed suicide in prison. It was held by the ECtHR that there had been a violation of Article 3 based on inadequacies of the medical treatment that he received and the fact that, shortly before he died, a serious disciplinary punishment, segregation, had been imposed. (There was not, however, a violation of Article 2).

General principles relating to physically and mentally ill patients are discussed by the Court in paras 90–112:

- Nothing in Article 3 requires the state to refrain from imprisoning the ill, the old, the frail or those with mental or physical disabilities.

- However, Article 3 does require that the nature of the regime to which such persons are subjected is properly adapted to their needs. Given their greater needs, such people would otherwise suffer disproportionately; it will not do for the state to claim that such a person has been treated the same as an able-bodied person.

- A failure to give appropriate treatment, including proper medical treatment, to an ill, disabled or otherwise incapacitated prisoner is likely to be a violation of Article 3.

Examples of breaches of Article 3 include *Price* v *United Kingdom* (2002) 34 EHRR 53 (the failure to provide appropriately for a woman with severe physical disabilities) and *McGlinchey* v *United Kingdom* (2003) 37 EHRR 41 (the failure to give adequate medical treatment to a prisoner who was both asthmatic and a heroin addict).

These principles can apply to prisoners with serious illnesses requiring intensive treatment.

In *R (Spinks)* v *Secretary of State for the Home Department* [2005] EWCA Civ 275 the Court of Appeal found there was no violation of Article 3 in the case of a prisoner with terminal cancer. On the facts, a full risk assessment had been made and the difficulties he experienced were, in the circumstances, below the threshold of severity. The case was compared with *Mouisel* v *France* (2004) 38 EHRR 34, where a prisoner with leukaemia received treatment but no other special measures were taken. The ECtHR held that there had been a breach of Article 3.

KEY POINT In *Spinks* the Court of Appeal suggests that, if there is no way of treating seriously ill prisoners in a way that is compatible with Article 3, it may be necessary to release them—showing, again, the absolute nature of Article 3 (see para 52).

21.7

Deaths in custody

Deaths in custody engage Article 2. State responsibility for those it has taken into custody is clearly established.

21.7.1 The substantive duty

The 'substantive' duty under Article 2 means that the Prison Service must take adequate steps to ensure the safety of prisoners. In *Edwards v United Kingdom* (2002) 35 EHRR 19, the ECtHR found a violation of Article 2 ECHR in respect of a remand prisoner killed by his cell mate. The cell mate had a known history of violence linked to mental illness.

The *Osman* duty (that states must take positive measures to protect a person for whom they are responsible from a real and immediate threat to life) applies not only where there is a real risk of attack from other prisoners that was understood at the time by the prison authorities; it also applies to prisoners at risk of suicide.

cross reference
The Osman duty is discussed in Chapter 8, section 8.3.2.

Keenan v United Kingdom (2001) 33 EHRR 38, involved a seriously mentally disturbed prisoner who, although being monitored by the prison authorities for suicide, nevertheless hanged himself in his cell. The ECtHR stressed that the positive duties under Article 2 ECHR are not absolute and that, in all the circumstances, the authorities had done what could be reasonably expected of them (there was, however, a breach of Article 3 ECHR).

> **case close-up**
>
> **R (Bloggs 61) v Secretary of State for the Home Department [2003] EWCA Civ 686**
>
> ....
>
> The Prison Service removed Bloggs 61, a prisoner, from a protected witness unit back to the mainstream prison. The prisoner argued that he was at risk from his former associates (drug traffickers) against whom he was to give evidence.
>
> It was held by the Court of Appeal that returning Bloggs 61 to mainstream prison would not violate the Prison Service's positive duty under Article 2 to protect the prisoner's life (nor were other principles of administrative law breached).

Although in *Bloggs 61* the Court of Appeal stressed the need for anxious scrutiny in such cases, they also held that the duty is not absolute and that a court must give a measure of deference to the authorities over the assessment of the risk and its nature.

In non-prison cases UK courts have stressed that the *Osman* duty arises when a proposed action will increase the risk faced by the person at risk (*Re Officer L* [2007] UKHL 36) and that the assessment of the duty must be based on the facts as they were understood at the time (*Van Colle* [2008] UKHL 50).

In *R (MJ) v Secretary of State for the Home Department* [2004] EWHC 2069, the prisoner feared that, because he had given evidence against fellow prisoners, he would be attacked if moved to a different prison. The court held that there was no evidence that the transfer would result in a real and immediate threat to the prisoner. Much of the reasoning is based on the risk assessment carried out by the Prison Service.

21.7.2 The procedural duty

cross reference
For the procedural duty see Chapter 8, section 8.5.

The 'procedural' duty under Article 2 is for the state to provide a proper investigation into deaths of people for which it is responsible.

The duty arises in respect of violent deaths of prisoners. The leading case in England and Wales, *R (Amin) v Secretary of State for the Home Department* [2003] UKHL 51, involves the failure of the authorities to hold a full and independent investigation, with proper family involvement, in the case of a prisoner who was the victim of a racist killing by his cell mate. Where a prisoner commits or attempts to commit suicide the English courts also accept that an investigation under Article 2 is necessary. The nature and extent to which it must be the full 'enhanced' investigation (as described in *Jordan v UK* (2003) 37 EHRR 2) that is public and independent of the Prison Service depends on the circumstances.

case close-up

R (JL) v Secretary of State for Justice [2006] UKHL 68

JL, a remand prisoner, was known by the prison authorities to be a real and immediate suicide risk. He attempted suicide but was revived, though he sustained irreversible brain damage. The House of Lords held that Article 2 required an enhanced (more than in-house) investigation. Whether it required a fuller, public, investigation (which would be very expensive) would depend on the facts and the results of an independent preliminary investigation.

21.8 Discipline and security

21.8.1 Offences against discipline

Prisoners in England and Wales can be prosecuted in the ordinary courts for criminal offences they commit in prison. More usually, however, they will be punished for 'offences against discipline' as these are defined in Rule 51 of the Prison Rules (for example, disobeying a lawful order: Rule 51(22)). There are a range of punishments available to a governor (Rule 55). Under the HRA, these powers need to be exercised compatibly with Convention rights. There are other provisions in the Rules that, for reasons of good order and security, allow removal from association, close supervision and other forms of control and restraint.

21.8.2 The Convention

Nothing in Article 3 prevents the prison authorities from imposing disciplinary punishments on prisoners or from having special regimes for difficult or dangerous prisoners based on high levels of security. Such punishments or regimes must, albeit in context, not involve treatment that humiliates and degrades more than is necessary for the purposes of punishment or security.

In *Lorse v The Netherlands* (2003) 37 EHRR 3, the applicant had been convicted of drugs and firearms offences. He was kept in a special unit, which involved, amongst other matters, regular weekly strip searches, including anal inspections, and these were imposed automatically whether or not the prisoners had been out of their cells or the unit. The ECtHR could see no need for these humiliating practices and found that there was a violation of Article 3.

Strip searches, particularly involving intimate search, are likely to violate Article 3 unless they are clearly necessary and a proportionate way of achieving prison security. It is easy for such searches to be used by guards as a form of humiliation of prisoners.

21.8.3 England and Wales

Punishment

The imposition of a punishment and security measures must be compatible with the law, as expressed in the Prison Rules. For example, a governor has some discretion over the way food and clothing is provided. However, to withdraw food and clothing from a prisoner as a punishment would be unlawful and also likely to be a violation of Article 3 (reduced diet was one of the techniques used in *Ireland v United Kingdom*: see Chapter 9, section 9.2; see *R (Russell) v Governor of Frankland Prison* [2000] 1 WLR 2027).

Force-feeding

Prisoners may refuse food. The force-feeding of a prisoner on hunger strike can involve Article 3. The general position under the Convention is that where there is a genuine medical necessity (to save the life of the person, for example) then there is no objection in principle to force-feeding subject to procedural guarantees being complied with and that the method does not go above a minimum level of severity. Where these conditions do not apply, particularly if force-feeding is part of a disciplinary response or punishment, then Article 3 is likely to be breached and could, given the method, even amount to 'torture' (see, for instance, *Nevmerzhitsky v Ukraine* (2006) 43 EHRR 32, especially paras 93–99).

Under the HRA, in England and Wales, these are matters for the courts to decide on the basis of the full evidence and with little deference needing to be shown to the authorities (*R (Wilkinson) v Responsible Medical Officer, Broadmoor Hospital* [2001] EWCA Civ 1545). Where a prisoner of sound mind chooses to maintain a hunger strike, then his or her right to autonomy (recognised by the common law and reinforced under Article 8) is likely to outweigh any argument of medical necessity (*R (Robb) v Secretary of State for the Home Department* [1995] 2 WLR 722).

21.8.4 **Punishment and fair trials**

The right to a fair hearing before an unbiased tribunal has been extended to prisoners in England and Wales under the common law and this is reinforced, perhaps in a more hard-edged way, by the Convention, which recognises that prisoners have rights to a fair trial under Article 6.

In *Leech v Deputy Governor of Parkhurst Prison* [1988] 2 WLR 290, the House of Lords held (building on an earlier case involving the Board of Prison Visitors, who no longer have a disciplinary role) that Governors' disciplinary procedures were subject to judicial review and needed to meet proper fair trial standards. The basic principles are that the prisoner should know precisely what is alleged against him or her and have the opportunity to answer the charge.

The common law rights are context dependent and flexible. In *R v Home Secretary ex parte Tarrant* [1985] 1 QB 251, for example, it was held that the rules of natural justice did not mean that a prisoner was in all circumstances entitled to be represented when subject to governor's discipline. A similar situation was challenged before the ECtHR.

case close-up

ss reference
*Article 6 and
ninal charge'
Chapter 12,
ion 12.5.*

Ezeh v United Kingdom (2004) 39 EHRR 1

. . . .

Prisoners had been awarded 'additional days' (meaning they would stay in prison for longer than they would otherwise anticipate) in disciplinary hearings before their prison governor. Their claim, under the common law, to be represented had been denied. A Grand Chamber held that given the severity of the punishment, the governor had been determining a 'criminal charge', thus invoking Article 6(1)–(3). Article 6(3)(c) in particular gave an entitlement to representation that the English courts had denied.

KEY POINT Ezeh is an example of where Convention rights are more definite than under the common law. Following the case the Prison Rules were changed. A disciplinary charge that might result in an additional days punishment must now be heard not by the governor but by an independent adjudicator before whom there is a right of representation.

21.9 Prisoners and Convention freedoms: private life

Prisoners are subject to the continuous day-to-day control of the authorities over all aspects of their lives. At the same time they retain their Convention rights and their freedom under the common law to the extent that it is not necessarily restricted by imprisonment. A number of issues have arisen in which the policies of the authorities have been tested against Convention rights.

further study

For a listing of these rights by a Grand Chamber see *Hirst* v *United Kingdom (2)* (2006) 42 EHRR 41, para 69.

cross reference
For Article 8 see Chapter 15.

Of particular importance are prisoners' rights under Article 8, the right to private life and correspondence. Prisoners retain these rights, but the question is the extent to which, in the context of imprisonment, the authorities can show that some restriction they have imposed can be justified under the second paragraph of the Article: the restrictions must be imposed on the basis of law, be for a legitimate purpose and be proportionate. Proportionality often involves a requirement that the authorities are sensitive to individual circumstances and do not apply blanket rules.

21.9.1 Search

The prison authorities have powers, based in the Prison Rules, to search prisoners and their cells. This power clearly engages prisoners' rights to private life and correspondence under Article 8(1); it also engages Article 6, the right to a fair trial (especially the implied right of access to the courts) in so far as searches may involve a prisoner's correspondence with legal advisors.

In *R* v *Secretary of State for the Home Department ex parte Daly* [2001] UKHL 26, the House of Lords accepted that a policy of always removing prisoners during cell searches that could include searches of legal correspondence was disproportionate and hence not justified under Article 8(2).

21.9.2 Article 8, family life: artificial insemination

Separation means that long-term prisoners may not have the opportunity to conceive children. They retain the simple right to marry under Article 12 (*Hamer* v *United Kingdom* (1982) 4 EHRR 139) but the more extensive right to found a family in that Article requires balancing individual

cross reference

For Article 12 see Chapter 19.

interests with the need for prison order and security that Article 8 explicitly allows. There is no Convention right to 'conjugal visits' (e.g. *X* v *United Kingdom* (1975) 2 DR 105) and nothing in the Prison Rules permits these. The Home Office and Prison Service did not normally allow prisoners access to artificial insemination facilities and in *R (Mellor)* v *Secretary of State for the Home Department* [2001] EWCA Civ 472, the Court of Appeal had denied this policy was a breach of either Article 8 or Article 12.

---

case close-up

Dickson v *United Kingdom* (2008) 46 EHRR 41

. . . .

D, a long-term prisoner, was married to L. They had no children and applied for artificial insemination facilities to be provided. The Prison Service refused. A Grand Chamber, reversing the Chamber decision, held that there had been a violation of Article 8. The Court held:

- Artificial insemination engages Article 8(1).

- The automatic forfeiture of rights to assuage public opinion is not permissible; though states can act to maintain confidence in the penal system.

- The issue was of particular importance for the applicants.

- There is no European consensus on the issue; but nor had the policy been debated by Parliament.

- Though the Prison Service did not operate a blanket ban, the evidence did not suggest that proper consideration was given to individual cases to ensure that decisions were proportionate.

21.9.3 **Mothers and babies**

The issue of the treatment of prisoner mothers and their children engages Article 8(1).

---

case close-up

R (P and Q) v *Secretary of State for the Home Department* [2001] EWCA Civ 1151

. . . .

Prison policy meant that babies were separated from their prisoner mothers after 18 months. The Court of Appeal held that the policy was only justified under Article 8(2) if applied flexibly and in a way that centred on the consequences for the children. P was serving a long sentence and would probably be deported; Q was serving a short sentence and there were no suitable arrangements for her child outside the prison. In Q's case Article 8 had been violated.

21.10 **Prisoners and Convention freedoms: freedom of expression**

Prisoners retain their Convention rights including freedom of expression in Article 10 and under the common law they retain those rights that are not necessarily incompatible with imprisonment. Restrictions on prisoners' rights to freedom of expression may be seen by the authorities as necessary incidents to imprisonment. In which case they still have to be compatible with Article 10 but it may be relatively easy for the authorities to show that a restriction is justified. Alternatively they will be an interference with the Article 10 rights that is not strictly an incident of imprisonment, in which case it will need compelling justification under Article 10(2).

Article 10(1) includes the right to receive information. Some restrictions on the availability of reading and writing materials for prisoners may be a necessary incident of imprisonment; others may need justification under Article 10(2).

cross reference
For Article 10 see Chapter 17.

As regards prisoners' communications with the outside world, Rule 34 of the Prison Rules allows restrictions to be imposed by the authorities but only those that are compatible with Convention rights such as Article 10 (i.e. necessary incidents to imprisonment or justifiable under Article 10(2)). There are likely to be ample justifications for the Prison Service to retain powers to scrutinise writings by prisoners, though punishment of a prisoner for writing critically about prisons is likely to be a breach, as it was in *Yankov* v *Bulgaria* (2005) 40 EHRR 36. A ban on a prisoner seeking to publish his autobiography, which might contain discussion of his crimes, was upheld by the Court of Appeal in (*R (Nilsen)* v *Governor of Full Sutton Prison* [2004] EWCA Civ 1540).

One issue of increasing importance involves prisoners' contacts with the media.

- In *Bamber* v *United Kingdom* App 33742/96, admissibility decision of 11 September 1997, the Commission of Human Rights held that total bans on access to the media could, in individual cases, be disproportionate.

- In *R (Simms)* v *Secretary of State for the Home Department* [2000] 2 AC 115, the House of Lords accepted that there was a violation of Article 10 when the prison authorities had imposed a complete ban on interviews with journalists. The ban had disproportionate effects, specifically in respect of prisoners pursuing a claim that they were victims of a miscarriage of justice.

- In *R (BBC)* v *Secretary of State for Justice* [2012] EWHC 13, the SSJ's refusal to allow the broadcasting of an interview with a prisoner violated Article 10 (see Chapter 17, section 17.4).

case close-up

R (Hirst) v Secretary of State for the Home Department [2002] EWHC 602 (Admin)

A Prison Service Order banned, other than in exceptional circumstances, prisoners from telephoning to the media with material that might be broadcast. The Order was applied to Hirst, a serving prisoner who campaigned on prisoners' rights issues and wanted to be able to comment in broadcast media on prisoners' rights issues. The court held that the total ban involved a disproportionate impact on the defendant and was an unlawful policy.

21.11 The right to vote

The right of prisoners to vote, based on Article 3 of the First Protocol, became, in 2011, a major matter of political controversy in the United Kingdom. It is discussed in Chapter 25, section 25.3.2.

Summary

Prisoners retain Convention rights not necessarily lost as a consequence of imprisonment. These include not only rights to the non-arbitrary loss of liberty and rights to fair procedures, but also not to be disproportionately denied the rights and freedoms in Articles 8 to 11. These rights are applied in context and a wide margin of appreciation is allowed to the states.

Further reading

Easton, S. *Prisoner's Rights* (2011) London: Routledge

Livingstone, S., Owen, T. and Macdonald, A. *Prison Law* 4th edn (2008) Oxford: OUP

Applications: media law and privacy

cross reference
Article 10,
including polit-
ical speech, is
considered in
Chapter 17; Article
8 is considered in
Chapter 15.

This chapter deals with the tension between, on the one hand, the importance in a democratic society of freedom of expression, particularly the freedom of the media to inform and to comment on the full range of public affairs, and, on the other hand, the rights of others to protect their various interests particularly when these involve matters of privacy and confidentiality. In Human Rights Act 1998 (HRA) terms we are predominantly concerned with how the law of England and Wales deals with the tension between Articles 10 and 8.

22.1 | **The importance of the media**

The importance of the media is fully recognised by the European Court of Human Rights (ECtHR) (see Chapter 17, section 17.5). From early cases such as *Lingens v Austria* (1986) 8 EHRR 407, para 41, the ECtHR has spoken of the media as having something close to a duty to 'impart information and ideas of political issues' (defined very broadly and including unpopular and controversial ideas) and has referred to its vital 'watchdog' role of reporting on the activities of those in power. In performing this duty a certain leeway (journalistic exaggeration and provocation, for instance) is allowed. But the court has also recognised that, in performing this role, the press (given the 'duties and responsibilities' clause in Article 10) must not overstep the bounds set, for example, by the need to protect the reputations of others or the need not to incite violence or racial hatred. In the context of the modern media, this sense of restraining duty is being emphasised.

435

435

case close-up

Stoll v Switzerland (2008) 47 EHRR 59

A journalist published extracts from a confidential strategy document which was extremely critical of the Swiss ambassador to the United States over his approach to negotiating compensation for Holocaust victims. He was prosecuted, convicted and fined by the Swiss courts.

A Grand Chamber, reversing the Chamber judgment, found there had been no violation of Article 10. The Court emphasised that, Article 10 notwithstanding, journalists are bound by the criminal law. They must act in good faith and on an accurate factual basis and provide accurate and precise information in accordance with the 'ethics of journalism'. These considerations are particularly relevant to the modern world because, in it, the media do not just inform they also suggest how information is to be assessed. In this world 'monitoring compliance with journalistic ethics takes on added importance' (see paras 102–104).

Similar principles on the importance of a free media can be found in the law of England and Wales. For example:

> The proper functioning of a modern participatory democracy requires the media be free, active, professional and enquiring. For this reason the courts, here and elsewhere, have recognised the cardinal importance of Press freedom and the need for any restriction on that freedom to be proportionate and no more than is necessary to promote the legitimate object of the restriction.

> (*McCartan Turkington Breen v Times Newspapers* [2000] 4 All ER 913, 922, Lord Bingham)

22.2 | The Human Rights Act and the regulation of the media

These principles are given effect through the application not only of the general law as it applies to the media but also through the regulation of both the press and broadcasting.

22.2.1 The press

The press is commercially owned, typically by major corporations with a wide range of media interests. There are provisions under competition law (which includes European law) that, in the name of a free media, are designed to prevent market dominance. In the past individual owners have had a significant role over the broad editorial stance. This continues today, although, for a corporation, profitability is central.

Regarding content, there are no special laws that apply to the press. There is no formal censorship. However, newspapers are subject to the ordinary law on matters such as obscenity, defamation and breach of confidence. Some statutory provisions, though applying generally, have a particular relevance for the press and media. Section 5 of the Official Secrets Act 1989 is an example: a person (such as a newspaper editor) commits an offence if he or she makes a damaging disclosure of information known to have itself been obtained in breach of the Act. Other statutory provisions apply expressly to journalists, such as the protection given to 'journalistic material' in the context of police powers of entry, search and seizure.

cross reference
For indirect horizontal effect see Chapter 4, section 4.7.1.

Being privately owned, newspapers are unlikely to be 'public authorities' for the purpose of section 6 HRA (though, given the public importance of a free press, they might be thought to be performing a public function and thus covered by the Act under section 6(3)(b)). This does not matter much because newspapers tend to be subject to the 'indirect horizontal effect' of the Act.

The courts, as public authorities, will act compatibly with Convention rights and, depending on context, may develop the common law that relates to important issues involving the press in ways that reflect Convention rights. *Campbell* v *MGN* [2004] UKHL 22 involved a conflict between media freedom and the right to private life—it was expressly decided by the House of Lords by balancing the terms and values found in Articles 8 and 10 (paras 17–18; 132).

Serious, recurring, concerns about press intrusions into privacy led to demands for regulation, particularly as court action can be expensive and difficult. The industry has, so far, successfully resisted a statute-based external regulator (such as exists for broadcasting: see section 22.2.2). The industry itself established the Press Complaints Commission (PCC) as a 'self-regulatory' body. The industry funded it and its authority derived from the agreement of the press to abide by its decisions. However, for fear of an external regulator being imposed, a majority of members of the Commission were not involved in newspaper or magazine publishing. The PCC accepted that it was a public authority for HRA purposes and was amenable to judicial review (*R (Ford)* v *PCC* [2001] EWHC 683, para 11).

The main role of the Commission was to adjudicate on complaints that the voluntary Code of Practice, agreed to by the industry, had been breached. Paragraph 1 of the Code required the press not to publish 'inaccurate, misleading or distorted information' and to correct such inaccuracies. It allowed the press to be partisan but required clear distinctions to be made 'between comment, conjecture and fact'. In this, it mirrors the distinction found in Convention case law on Article 10 between factual claims, which depend upon a degree of responsibility in terms of checking stories etc., and value judgments, for which much greater freedom is allowed, though still need some factual basis (see, for instance, *Lingens v Austria* (1986) 8 EHRR 407, para 46; cf *Lindon v France* (2008) 46 EHRR 35, para 55).

The Code required the protection of privacy by journalists, including restrictions on photographing people in private places and on 'harassment'. However, the protection of privacy was subject to a 'public interest' justification. The public interest included, but was not confined to:

- detecting or exposing crime or a serious misdemeanour,
- protection of public health and safety,
- preventing the public from being misled by some statement or action of an individual or organisation.

The Code also recognised that 'There is a public interest in freedom of expression itself.'

The Commission was, therefore, empowered to seek a fair balance between public and individual interests as is required under Article 8. However, there had been concerns about whether the PCC was able to provide adequate remedies to meet the requirements of Article 8. It could require an offending newspaper to publish the PCC's judgment and an apology, but could not award damages or issue injunctions (see *Peck v United Kingdom* (2003) 36 EHRR 41). Article 8 may require stronger remedies against the press which only a court can provide. In *Venables v News Group Newspapers* [2001] EMLR 10, for example, the High Court accepted that the remedies available from the Commission were insufficient to protect the right to life of notorious child murderers after their release (para 97). This situation the court remedied by issuing a protective injunction. Under section 12 HRA, courts considering remedies involving freedom of the press must take into account any 'relevant privacy code'.

In 2011–2012 a major press scandal dominated British public life (the 'phone-hacking' scandal). At its heart were allegations of unlawful or unethical intrusions by journalists (and private investigators they employed) into the private lives not just of celebrities but of others, including the victims of crime. An important aspect of the scandal was the inability of the PCC adequately to investigate and deal with allegations made and its general lack of knowledge and of power to keep the press within the law and subject to decent ethical standards. As a result it has voluntarily wound itself up. In 2012 it declared it was operating in a 'transition' mode. The Leveson Inquiry reported on the scandal in 2012. Political decisions will be made in 2013 on how to replace the PCC.

KEY POINT The right to a fair trial, under Article 6, is an important issue in press regulation. Publishing articles that pre-judge the outcome of a trial, especially a jury trial, can be unlawful as a 'contempt of court': this is discussed in Chapter 12, section 12.9.2. Under the Code, no payments to witnesses should be made once a legal process has commenced; at earlier stages payments to potential witnesses are possible if justified in the public interest (para 15).

22.2.2 **Broadcasting**

Broadcasting companies are corporately owned, like the press, but, unlike the press, are subject to external, statute-based regulation. This is performed partly by Ofcom itself and partly by the broadcasters under the auspices of Ofcom. Ofcom's authority comes from the Communications Act 2003 and, as such, it will be a public authority under section 6 HRA or subject to Article 10 through judicial review (*Gaunt v Ofcom* [2011] EWCA Civ 692). Furthermore, it has statutory duties that must be applied in ways that are compatible with Convention rights. Much of the Communications Act is to do with technical matters but, under section 319, Ofcom produces a Broadcasting Code (covering standards, sponsorship, fairness and privacy), which licensed broadcasters must obey. Complaints can be made to Ofcom for breach of the Code, after a programme has been broadcast. The Code deals (in much more detail than the Press Code) with a range of issues, such as offensiveness, due impartiality in political matters, fairness and privacy. Ofcom, therefore, is a central part of the system for providing remedies for breaches of (in particular) Article 8 and to do so in ways that enable a fair balance to be achieved with freedom of expression in Article 10.

Any inadequacy in the Ofcom process for respecting private life and protecting media freedom can be brought before the High Court under section 7 HRA or 'ordinary' judicial review. *Pro-Life Alliance* v *BBC* [2003] UKHL 23 (where the House of Lords upheld the broadcaster's refusal to show an anti-abortion party election broadcast: see Chapter 17, section 17.8.3) suggests that the courts may show significant 'deference' to the regulators who have been specifically empowered with the task.

The BBC is different: it is established by Royal Charter. Nevertheless, the courts treat it as they would a statute-based organisation. Control over programme standards is, ultimately, the responsibility of the BBC Trust (who replaced the governors in 2007) and is derived from provisions in the Charter and the Agreement. Standards are based partly on the Trust's own codes (such an on due impartiality) whilst others are standardised with commercial broadcasting—this includes the provisions on fairness and privacy. Complaints can be made initially to BBC management with the Trust acting as a 'final court of appeal'. As with Ofcom, any inadequacies in human rights protection should (for compliance with Article 13) be dealt with in the courts.

KEY POINT Internet content is not regulated by Ofcom. It is, however, subject to ordinary law (defamation, for example), so long as there is someone responsible and within the jurisdiction of the law. English courts can, for example, force disclosure from a website owner (not an ISP) who hosts defamatory material (see, for example, *Sheffield Wednesday FC* v *Hargreaves* [2007] EWHC 2375). The website owner can then be proceeded against.

(22.3) Legal control: defamation and responsible journalism

As well as through regulation, content-related control of the media to protect people's rights to privacy can be based on the ordinary law. An important instance is an action for defamation. This provides a remedy to a claimant who can prove that a publication lowers his or her reputation in the view of reasonable people. If the claimant can satisfy the court that the publication does this, damages will be awarded unless the defendant can establish that what was published was true or that what was published was not a simple statement of fact but a value judgment that amounted to fair comment on a matter of public interest.

further study

For a full analysis of the law: Price, D. *Defamation: Law, Procedure and Practice* 3rd edn (2004) London: Sweet & Maxwell.

cross reference

The impact of defamation laws on political speech is also explored in Chapter 17, section 17.8.4.

Defamation is a restriction on freedom of expression that is likely to be justifiable under Article 10(2) as a legal and proportionate restriction aimed at protecting 'the reputation or rights of others'. Reputation is an aspect of private life respect for which must be secured under Article 8. But in practice this has a potentially 'chilling' effect on media freedom. This potential has been recognised by the courts in the way they attempt to balance Article 10 and Article 8 rights. Thus in *Cumpana v Romania* (2005) 41 EHRR 14, for example, a Grand Chamber accepted that journalists had defamed an official and had been properly convicted; however, there was a breach of Article 10 because the severity of the punishment did not take the protection of media freedom into account.

The need to counteract the chilling effect on freedom of expression that defamation proceedings may cause has led the UK courts to grant a qualified privilege to the press. Qualified privilege means that statements can be made without the threat of defamation unless the claimant can prove that the publication was made maliciously (intending harm to the claimant) or in bad faith. Qualified privilege applies to reports of various official matters including Parliamentary proceedings (see the Defamation Act 1996, section 15 and Schedule 1). Absolute privilege applies to fair and accurate contemporaneous reports of court proceedings (section 14).

There is also qualified privilege available in some situations under common law and it is this that the courts have extended to general media stories that would otherwise be defamatory and that are either in fact untrue or whose truth the defendant is unable to prove. The principles were established in *Reynolds* v *Times Newspapers* [2001] 2 AC 127 (see later in this section) and the law was confirmed and clarified by the House of Lords in *Jameel*.

case close-up

> ### Jameel v Wall Street Journal Europe Sprl [2006] UKHL 44
> ....
>
> A Saudi company alleged that an article in the *Wall Street Journal* had linked them to terrorist funding. The House of Lords allowed the newspaper's appeal from a finding that they had libelled the claimants. The newspapers had media privilege ('*Reynolds* privilege').

The central points of media privilege are:

- The publication, taken as a whole, must be in the public interest. This is a development of the law and means that media privilege is a distinct form of qualified privilege. In many earlier cases, qualified privilege required a duty to publish and a reciprocal duty or interest to receive the information. This duty/interest approach does not adequately encompass the situation of the media, who publish to the public in general, and so it has been adapted.

- The court determines whether the story is in the public interest. An important difference is recognised between stories that the public might like to know about (celebrity gossip, for instance) and stories of sufficient importance for their publication to be in the public interest. However, it is not necessary to go so far as proving that the public have a 'need to know'.

- Responsible journalism. Publication can only be in the public interest (and therefore privileged) if the journalists have behaved (considered in the context) properly and responsibly in the way they have obtained and checked the story.

Responsible journalism and factors that go to establishing the public interest in a story were considered in *Reynolds*.

case close-up

Reynolds v Times Newspapers [2001] 2 AC 127

R, the former Taoiseach (Prime Minister) of Ireland, alleged that Times Newspapers had defamed him by suggesting he had deliberately misled the Irish Parliament during a political crisis. In its defence the newspaper argued that, because of the importance of media freedom, it should enjoy 'qualified privilege' over political reporting. The House of Lords rejected the idea that there should be a blanket privilege for the media on political stories. Their Lordships developed the general principles confirmed in Jameel (above). On the facts of the case there was no public interest requiring publication.

In *Reynolds* Lord Nicholls (p 205) suggested that, in determining public interest, a range of factors need to be taken into account. These include (but are not confined to) the seriousness of the allegation, the nature of the information in issue, the source of the information, the steps taken to verify it, the status of the information, the urgency of the matter, whether comment was sought from the claimant, whether the 'gist' of the claimant's side of the story was published, the tone of the story (particularly if the newspaper adopts the allegation as fact) and the circumstances, including timing, of the publication.

case close-up

Flood v Times Newspapers [2012] UKSC 11

A national newspaper reported allegations of bribery and corruption against a serving, named police officer. The officer was exonerated; however, the allegations remained, unamended, on the newspaper's website. The officer brought defamation proceedings. The newspaper successfully argued that the original story and its continued presence on the website was protected by media (*Reynolds*) privilege. The Supreme Court, applying *Reynolds* and *Jameel*, agreed.

Part of the argument was to recognise that qualified privilege was necessary to ensure compatibility of common law defamation with Article 10 (paras 44–47). It was held that it could be in the public interest to publish mere allegations, despite the fear of 'trial by media'. The Supreme Court (unlike the Court of Appeal) accepted that the journalism had been 'responsible' because the journalists had done enough to justify their belief that there was a serious case against the officer.

Media (*Reynolds*) privilege aims at reducing the chilling effect of defamation proceedings on freedom of speech where there is a clear public interest in the publication. Its impact is not confined to the media (e.g. *Charman* v *Orion Publishing Group Ltd* [2007] EWCA Civ 972, where it is applied to book publishers, and *Seaga* v *Harper* [2008] UKPC 9, where it is applied to statements made at a public meeting).

22.4 Protection of sources

The need for journalists to protect the identity of their sources is an axiom of journalist ethics. It is reflected in the Press Complaints Commission Code ('Journalists have a moral obligation to protect confidential sources of information', para 14); under section 12 HRA this Code may need to be taken into account in freedom of expression cases.

The ECtHR has frequently recognised that 'the protection of journalists' sources is one of the cornerstones of freedom of the Press' (*Cumpana* v *Romania* (2005) 41 EHRR 14, para 106). In *Goodwin* v *United Kingdom* (1996) 22 EHRR 123, the ECtHR held that a court order requiring a journalist to disclose his sources, done in order to enable a company to identify a disloyal employee, was disproportionate. The Court said:

> Without such protection [the confidentiality of sources], sources may be deterred from assisting the Press in informing the public on matters of public interest. As a result the vital watchdog role of the Press may be undermined and the ability of the Press to provide accurate and reliable information may be adversely affected . . . such a measure [a court order requiring disclosure] cannot be compatible with Article 10 of the Convention unless it is justified by an overriding requirement in the public interest. (para 39)

Under English law, section 10 of the Contempt of Court Act 1981 (CCA 1981) establishes the general rule that journalists may not be compelled to disclose their sources but allows for disclosure to be ordered in certain circumstances.

10 Sources of information

> No court may require a person to disclose, nor is any person guilty of contempt of court for refusing to disclose, the source of information contained in a publication for which he is responsible, unless it be established to the satisfaction of the court that disclosure is necessary in the interests of justice or national security or for the prevention of disorder or crime.

First, a court must decide whether one of the three grounds of exception in section 10 CCA 1981 are engaged:

- Interests of justice. This has been said to mean: 'to exercise important legal rights and to protect themselves from serious legal wrongs'. This is a narrower meaning than 'justice as the opposite of injustice' but broader than justice as requiring a resort to the courts. The term encompasses the right of an employer to seek the name of a disloyal employee so that he or she might be dismissed (e.g. *X* v *Morgan Grampian Ltd* [1991] 1 AC 1; quotation is at p 43).

- National security. This has been used to identify a civil servant responsible for a leak to the media (*Secretary of State for Defence* v *Guardian Newspapers Ltd* [1984] 2 WLR 268).

- Prevention of disorder or crime. This has been used to require disclosure of evidence that might be used in a fraud prosecution: *Re an Inquiry under the Company Securities (Insider Dealing) Act 1985* [1988] AC 660.

Second, a court must decide whether disclosure is necessary in the public interest. Here the point is whether the public interest in, for example, preventing crime, could be secured other than by ordering disclosure. In *Interbrew SA* v *Financial Times Ltd* [2002] EWCA Civ 274, for example, disclosure was ordered as necessary to permit a company to take court action to seek to protect confidential commercial information.

Third, a court must decide whether the public interest in disclosure outweighs the public interest in media freedom and the protection of sources. On this point there was some evidence that greater weight was given to protection of sources in Strasbourg than in the United Kingdom, at least in some of the pre-HRA cases mentioned earlier.

When the *Interbrew* case (above) was considered by the ECtHR, it found a violation of Article 10. The company had other means available to it by which it might seek damages and minimise harm from future disclosures. Therefore there was no overriding requirement of the public interest that required an interference with freedom of expression by forcing the journalist to disclose his source (*Financial Times Ltd* v *United Kingdom* (2010) 50 EHRR 46).

Following the coming into force of the HRA, English courts unambiguously bring together section 10 and Article 10 on the issue of when the assumption in favour of protecting sources can be overridden.

case close-up

Ashworth Hospital Authority v MGN [2002] UKHL 29

MGN published in the *Daily Mirror* excerpts of the medical records of Ian Brady, a notorious child killer detained at a security hospital. The source was probably an employee of the hospital who disclosed them (via an intermediary) in breach of his contract of employment. The hospital obtained a court order requiring the newspaper to disclose the original source so that he could be dismissed (a matter 'in the interests of justice'). One of the issues was whether the journalist could be compelled to disclose his source. The House of Lords confirmed the order. (The matter was returned to the lower courts, which, in the end, did not order disclosure: *Mersey Care NHS Trust* v *Ackroyd* [2007] EWCA Civ 101.)

The House of Lords held that:

- Section 10 and Article 10 have the same purpose: to protect journalist freedom.

- Following *Goodwin*, any overriding of the right to protect sources requires an overriding public interest that must be 'convincingly established' and given, by the court, the most 'careful scrutiny' (paras 49 and 61).

- On the facts of the case great weight was given to the need to protect medical records, particularly in the context of psychiatry and the need, found in Article 8, that the law provide appropriate safeguards to protect medical records.

cross reference
Ashworth is also discussed in Chapter 15, section 15.10.6.

442

22.5 Celebrity cases

22.5.1 Introduction

The courts in England and Wales have had to deal with cases brought by public figures and celebrities who allege the media have interfered with their privacy. At the heart of the cases is the question of what weight to give to the competing interests of the media's freedom to publish (which may be commercially motivated and the story may have little public significance), contrasted with a celebrity's privacy (perhaps already compromised by those who use the media to create and advance their financially valuable images).

22.5.2 The Convention position

In *von Hannover (No 2)* a Grand Chamber has laid down the basic principles dealing with these cases.

case close-up

von Hannover v Germany (No 2) (2012) 55 EHRR 15

Following an earlier case ((2005) 40 EHRR 1), Princess Caroline of Monaco argued that the failure of the German courts to prevent the publication in magazines of photographs of her on a skiing holiday in St Moritz violated her right to respect for private life. The text, accompanying the photographs, referred to the illness of her father, Prince Rainier, with a possible implication that she was less than a dutiful daughter. The Grand Chamber laid down some basic guidance on balancing Article 8 and Article 10 rights in this context. Of particular importance was

- the sense that the photographs, in context, were a contribution to debate of general interest. Referring to its case law, the Court distinguished stories dealing with political issues, crime, the activities of sporting figures and performing artists. These were distinguished from stories about rumoured marital difficulties of the President of France or of the financial difficulties of famours singers;

- the public prominence of the person and the subject of the story. The Court distinguished between private individuals and 'persons acting in a public context' and between stories expressing facts 'capable of contributing to a debate in a democratic society' and merely reporting details of the private life of an individual who does not exercise public functions. Stories protected by Article 10 could relate to the private life of public ,figures but not where they were exclusively concerned with private life and aimed merely to satisfy public curiosity.

Other features related to the conduct of the person concerned (including previous dealings with the media), the content, form and extent of publication, and the circumstances in which the photos were taken (did they involve consent or subterfuge).

On the facts, the German courts had followed these principles and its decision was within the state's margin of appreciation.

At the heart of this decision is an attempt to find a way of accepting that public figures retain some rights of privacy but not ones that can interfere with the proper interest of the people in the conduct of public affairs.

In *Mosley* v *UK* (2011) 53 EHRR 30, the ECtHR rejected the argument that a proper aspect in any fair balance in cases involving the private life of public figures was to require pre-publication notification to enable an injunction to be sought by the public figure.

22.5.3 English law (breach of confidence) and the HRA

The common law of England and Wales has not developed an abstract, background right to privacy. Most of the concrete incidents of privacy are covered by existing law, such as laws of property and the torts of trespass to the person (see *Wainwright* v *Home Office* [2003] UKHL 53, paras 15–35).

cross reference
The 'indirect horizontal effect' of Convention rights is discussed in Chapter 4, 4.7.

But the HRA means that UK law needs to provide adequate remedies for breaches of Article 8, even in the private sphere (e.g. regarding newspapers and broadcasters). The UK courts, being public authorities, have duties to develop the common law in ways that secure these rights.

English courts have developed the common law remedy for breach of confidentiality into a more general protection of privacy. The traditional remedy was based upon a pre-existing relationship of confidentiality (as between doctor and patient, husband and wife, even secret service agent and the government). Under the influence of Article 8, the courts have developed this cause of action in the direction of protecting a person's privacy. It is no longer necessary to establish a pre-existing confidential relationship: a breach of confidence remedy can now be available if 'in respect of the disclosed facts the person in question had a reasonable expect-ation of privacy': *Campbell* v *MGN* [2004] UKHL 22, para 21.

cross reference
For confidentiality in a political context see Chapter 17, section 17.7.3.

case close-up

Campbell v *MGN* [2004] UKHL 22

Naomi Campbell, a celebrity supermodel, claimed that the publication in the *Daily Mirror* (owned by the defendant) of information about her receiving treatment for drug addiction and a photograph of her leaving a meeting of Narcotics Anonymous violated her privacy, and was arguably incompatible with her rights under Article 8. On the facts it was held (3–2) that the claimant's rights had been violated.

Important points in the judgment are:

- The House of Lords accepted that an action for breach of confidence was now to be understood as an action to uphold a person's reasonable expectation of privacy.

- It followed from this that the basic issue for a court is to balance rights to respect for private life under Article 8 with the media's freedom under Article 10.

- On the facts of the case the House of Lords departed from the Court of Appeal's assessment and, by a majority, found that Campbell's Article 8 rights outweighed the right of the press to freedom of expression. The fact that it was evidence of medical treatment that was disclosed had, in the context of a person's struggles with addiction, particular weight.

There have been many cases following *Campbell*. In *Mosley* v *Newsgroup Newspapers* [2008] EWHC 1777, the newspaper published pictures of M (who was a prominent figure in motor racing) engaging in consensual sexual activity on private property. It was held that this interfered with M's Article 8 rights and there was no public interest sufficient to justify the interference. An alleged Nazi angle to the sexual activity was shown to be false. This might have engaged the public interest especially, since M was the son of the leader of the British fascist movement in the 1930s.

Injunctions

Given that any confidentiality or reasonable expectation of privacy is necessarily destroyed by publication, the courts can issue an interim injunction to prevent publication in the first place. An interim injunction prevents publication pending the full hearing. An injunction has a major impact on media freedom and, in respect of Article 10, is not easily obtained (for example Catherine Zeta-Jones and Michael Douglas were unable to prevent unauthorised photographs of their wedding being published: *Douglas* v *Hello!* [2001] 2 All ER 289). Section 12 HRA means that interim injunctions should only be awarded if the applicant would be likely to win at a full hearing, and this applies as much to fully confidential information as it does to claims of simple privacy (*Cream Holdings Ltd* v *Banerjee Ltd* [2004] UKHL 44).

A major issue for UK courts has been the extent to which Article 8 (and common law protection of privacy) might require not only the injunction but also further restraints, such as anonymity or withholding even general facts about the case. In *JIH* v *News Group Newspapers* [2011] EWCA Civ 42, the Court of Appeal laid down general guidance (in para 21). The principle of open justice (Article 6 and common law) is important, but there may be overwhelming reasons for it to be restricted (see Chapter 12, sections 12.9.1 and 12.9.2). Judges should impose no more than the minimum restraints on publication necessary to protect Article 8. The question is whether the public interest in publishing names and normally reported subject matter outweighs the need to protect the person's privacy. These are fact-sensitive issues and an appeal court should not normally interfere with the way the judge at first instance has balanced the issues.

further study

The report of Lord Neuberger MR, *Super-Injunctions, Anonymised Injunctions and Open Justice*, contains a full discussion of these issues. True 'super-injunctions' (where the very existence of an injunction cannot be published) are shown to be very rare. Anonymity, discussed above is a much bigger issue.

⬤ Summary

Convention rights have had a significant impact, both directly and indirectly, on media law. However, often the issue involves balancing the clear commitment to media freedom derived from Article 10 with other rights such as in Article 8. Here the issue is less one of legal principle and more of application on the particular facts of cases.

❓ Question

For suggested approaches, please visit the Online Resource Centre.

How effectively does the law balance media freedom with the rights of individuals, including prominent ones, to protect their privacy?

📖 Further reading

Kenyon, A. and Richardson, M. (eds) *New Dimensions in Privacy Law: International and Comparative Perspectives* (2006) Cambridge: CUP

Pearce, R. 'Privacy, Superinjunctions and Anonymity: Selling My Story Will Sort My Life Out' (2011) *Denning LJ* 92–130

Robertson, G. and Nicol, A. *Media Law* 5th edn rev (2008) London: Penguin

Smart, U. *Media and Entertainment Law* (2011) London: Routledge

Article 1 of the First Protocol: protection of property

Chapter overview

- Article 1 of the First Protocol as a qualified right to property.
- The scope of Article 1: the concept of 'possessions'.
- Legitimate justifications for state interferences with possessions.
- Legitimate public interests that interferences with possessions can serve.
- The need for proportionality.

Article 1   Protection of Property

Every natural or legal person is entitled to the peaceful enjoyment of his possessions. No one shall be deprived of his possessions except in the public interest and subject to the conditions provided for by law and by the general principles of international law.

The preceding provisions shall not, however, in any way impair the right of a state to enforce such laws as it deems necessary to control the use of property in accordance with the general interest or to secure the payment of taxes or other contributions or penalties.

Introduction

A right to protect possessions (property) is controversial. On the one hand, it can be seen as essential to human flourishing. Without legal support for property there would be little security for individuals choosing the lives they wish to lead (albeit in conditions not of their own choosing) and taking rational steps to achieve it. On the other hand, property represents social and political power. It is distributed unequally and the minorities who own and control the land and the wealth of the country are able to exercise indirect control over the political, economic and social system. In the twenty-first century economic power and dominance is in corporate, non-personal, hands. The self-interested decisions of huge corporations have enormous social, economic and political impact and this is a power that depends upon the possession and exercise of property rights. Given the relationship between property and power, it is not surprising that governments have often sought the constitutional freedom to control the production and distribution of wealth in society and this may require limiting the right to property.

These kinds of arguments were very real at the end of the Second World War. They explain why the issue of the protection of property was not settled until after the European Convention on Human Rights (ECHR), in its original form, came into effect. In particular, Britain had an 'old' Labour government that, in the late 1940s, was pursuing a vigorous programme of nationalisation (public ownership). As Lord Hoffmann said in *R (Alconbury) v Secretary of State for the Environment, Transport and the Regions* [2001] UKHL 23, para 71:

> All democratic societies recognise that while there are certain basic rights which attach to the ownership of property, they are heavily qualified by considerations of the public interest. This is reflected in the terms of art 1 of Protocol 1 to the Convention.

447

Article 1 of the First Protocol— general features

Article 1 of the First Protocol (Article 1) is couched in terms which seem to accept wide powers of states to control property in the 'public' or 'general' interest. As we shall see, the European Court of Human Rights (ECtHR) has narrowed this power considerably in the way the Article has been interpreted.

23.1.1 Companies

cross reference
The position of companies and shareholders under the Convention is discussed in Chapter 5, section 5.4.6.

It should be noted that Article 1 expressly gives rights to any 'legal person'. This means that companies, in themselves, may seek the protection of the Article. Although companies have rights under other articles (e.g. Article 6, the right to a fair trial), Article 1 contains the only express reference to companies in the whole Convention. Thus companies, which are artificial legal persons, enjoy 'human' rights irrespective of the social power they can exercise on the basis of their economic strength. Shareholders, however, may not have a claim if the interference is really with the company's rights and the company chooses not to act.

23.1.2 Human Rights Act 1998

Property is, of course, firmly established in English law. It can be inherent in Acts of Parliament, such as those dealing with estates in land, credit controls or intellectual property. It is also inherent in common law principles relating, for example, to contract and to torts such as trespass to land or to property. Under the Human Rights Act 1998 (HRA) these statutory and common law provisions must be interpreted and developed for compatibility with Convention rights, especially Article 1.

case close-up

Wilson v *First County Trust Ltd* [2003] UKHL 40

....

FCT, a credit company, lent W money to buy a car. The credit agreement was regulated by the Consumer Credit Act 1974. The Act prevented the enforcement of an agreement by creditor against debtor unless, amongst other matters, the exact amount of the loan was expressed in the paperwork. In this case the expressed amount of the loan did not include a £250 administration fee. It was held that the agreement could not be enforced against W. The House of Lords held that FCT's right to possessions under Article 1 had not been violated. (Other important human rights issues are also raised in this case: see Chapter 4, sections 4.9.3 and 4.11.1.)

In *Wilson*:

- A majority of Law Lords held that Article 1 applied, either because the credit company had been deprived of their possessions or because it had been restricted in its enjoyment of its possessions.

- However, there was a 'fair balance' between the public interest in controlling credit and the fundamental rights of the creditors.

- Considerable deference was shown to Parliament's view on the proper balance the public interest required between debtors' and creditors' interests.

23.2 The definition of 'possessions'

The concept of a possession is an autonomous Convention concept (a concept developed by the ECtHR and not dependant on the way the matter is defined in national law). Possessions are defined in a broad and inclusive way which focuses on a person's entitlement to valuable assets of a tangible or intangible kind.

It includes the obvious such as land, personal property (things) and money. It also includes 'intangible' property, a right to something of value to the holder. Examples are licences to engage in economic activity (as in *Tre Traktörer Aktiebolag* v *Sweden* (1991) 13 EHRR 309 or to practice a profession with an existing business trade connection and goodwill (*Van Marle* v *The Netherlands* (1986) 8 EHRR 483). It includes intellectual property rights such as copyright, registered trademark and patents (*Anheuser-Busch* v *Portugal* (2007) 45 EHRR 36 and, for English law, *Ashdown* v *Telegraph Group Plc* [2001] EWCA Civ 1142).

But the issue is often not the nature of the property; rather it is the nature of the claim or the type of interest that the applicant enjoys. The clear cases are where the applicant has an already vested legal right to the property in question: a freehold or leasehold interest in land (to use English law terminology), ownership of an object in the sense of an immediate right of possession, an already recognised right to an intangible thing of value such as a registered trade mark or an economically valuable licence, or a legally recognised right to compensation. 'Possessions' also include contractual rights over personal property (as in *Wilson*, above).

23.2.1 The acquisition of possessions

No right to acquire possessions

From its earliest cases the Court has denied that Article 1 guarantees a right to acquire possessions not currently enjoyed. (In *Marckx* v *Belgium* (1979–80) 2 EHRR 330 the ECtHR held that Article 1 does not guarantee children's rights to acquire property by inheritance from their parents, see para 50.)

Legitimate expectations as 'possessions'

The ECtHR does accept that Article 1 can protect certain 'legitimate expectations'—property interests which are in the 'nature of a claim' which have a clear and uncontested basis in domestic law. Article 1 does not guarantee that the applicant will have the asset but, by treating it as a 'possession', requires that any refusal or withdrawal should be justified in terms of Article 1. An example is the right to bring a tort action, as in *Pressos Compania Naviera SA* v *Belgium* (1996) 21 EHRR 301, discussed below.

In *Centro Europa 7 SRL* v *Italy* App. 38433/09, Grand Chamber judgment of 7 June 2012, the applicant TV company had a licence for national terrestrial broadcasting in Italy. But it could only begin broadcasting once the Italian authorities had allocated frequencies; and over this there were considerable delays. A significant portion of the judgment concerns Article 10 (see Chapter 17)—the failure to allocate frequencies was, in the circumstances, an unjusitified interference with the applicant's right to 'impart information and ideas'. However, there was also a violation of Article 1 of the First Protocol. The allocation of the licence created a legitimate expectation of being able to broadcast, which was a 'possession'. Given that the interference with this 'possession' was unlawful (because in breach of Article 10) it was also a breach of Article 1.

Under the HRA, in *R (PCSU)* v *Minister for the Civil Service* [2011] EWHC 2041, the High Court accepted that the expectation to benefits under the civil service pension were possessions for the purpose of Article 1 (though government interference with these benefits was justified).

23.2.2 The right to practise a profession

A licence or other permission necessary to practise a profession may involve a possession but only if the applicant already enjoys a valuable asset in his or her practice, such as business goodwill.

- In *Van Marle* v *Belgium* (1986) 8 EHRR 483 Belgium law was changed to require existing accountants to register with a professional body. The ECtHR held that a refusal by the professional body to register the applicants (experienced accountants with an existing clientele) would be detrimental to their existing business with its valuable goodwill and was an interference with their possessions.

Van Marle can be compared with *R (Malik)* v *Waltham Forest NHS PCT* [2007] EWCA Civ 265, where the Court of Appeal denied that a doctor's inclusion on the medical performers list (entitling the doctor to provide NHS services) was a possession. Inclusion had no marketable value and amounted, in effect, to no more than an expectation of future earnings. The doctor's unlawful suspension from the list did not, therefore, engage Article 1.

23.2.3 Welfare payments

Nothing in the Convention imposes a duty on a state to provide welfare benefits. Disputes frequently arise over entitlements to the complex range of benefits that modern European states do provide their citizens in the context of the 'welfare state'. The question can arise whether rights to such benefits are possessions and so engage Article 1. Originally the case law, from both the Commission and the Court, suggested (though not consistently) that only contributory benefits (such as under a national insurance scheme to which individuals have made identifiable contributions and which are, in that sense, like private insurance schemes) were possessions. Non-contributory benefits (like the basic state old age pension, for example) which were funded from general taxation, were not possessions and so not protected by Article 1. The Court changed this in *Stec* v *United Kingdom*.

case close-up

Stec v United Kingdom (2005) 41 EHRR SE18, Grand Chamber admissibility

S alleged that a non-contributory benefit was distributed in a way that involved sex discrimination, contrary to Article 14. Article 14 would only apply if she could also show that she had a right to the benefit under Article 1 of the First Protocol (Article 14 is confined to discrimination in the way other Convention rights are secured). Although the ECtHR held that there had not been a violation of the Convention, it did accept that S's entitlement to the benefit was a possession and so Article 1 of the First Protocol was engaged.

In *Stec* the Court made it clear that Article 1 applied to all benefits whether contributory or non-contributory (see paras 38–53).

- The Court adopted an 'evolutive' approach to the Convention (one which recognises social and legal changes in Europe) which took into account the reality of the complex way in which states organised and funded their benefits systems. Many benefits are interlocking and it is artificial to distinguish contributory from non-contributory benefits.

- The Convention needs to be read as a whole and to be internally consistent. Article 6 (the right to a fair trial) no longer distinguishes between contributory and non-contributory benefits as regards the right to a fair trial and so the interpretation of Article 1 should be consistent with this.

- Nevertheless, the Court re iterated the point that nothing in Article 1 of the First Protocol gives an individual a right to a benefit which the state has not chosen to provide (para 53).

Under the HRA, the House of Lords has dealt (in cases decided before *Stec*) with tax allowances (*R (Wilkinson)* v *IRC* [2005] UKHL 30), state pension allowances (*R (Carson)* v *Secretary of State for Work and Pensions* [2005] UKHL 37) and young persons' allowances (*Carson*) as if they engaged Article 1. But this has mainly been based on concessions by the parties rather than a matter that has been fully argued.

The merging in *Stec* of contributory and non-contributory benefits has been followed by the House of Lords in *R (RJM)* v *Secretary of State for Work and Pensions* [2008] UKHL 63, holding that disability benefit was a possession, thus engaging Article 1. This case may cast doubt on the correctness of the Court of Appeal's refusal to treat jobseeker's allowance as a possession in *R (Couronne)* v *Crawley* [2007] EWCA Civ 1086.

23.3 General approach: three rules or one?

The approach of the ECtHR is to break Article 1 down into three separate but interrelated rules (see *Sporrong and Lönnroth* v *Sweden* (1982) 5 EHRR 35, para 61).

- Rule 1 (the first sentence of the first paragraph) invokes a general principle of peaceful enjoyment of possessions.

- Rule 2 (second sentence of the first paragraph) deals with the state depriving an owner of property.

- Rule 3 (second paragraph) deals with the state exercising control over the uses of property, short of deprivation.

In the text the rules appear to have different significance. Rule 2 seems to inhibit deprivation of property unless done 'in the public interest and subject to the conditions provided for by law and by the general principles of international law'. Rule 3, by contrast, does no more than require states to act in the 'general interest'. It could easily be read as imposing few if any justiciable restrictions on the freedom of the state to control the uses of property.

The ECtHR has not accepted this. Rules 2 and 3 are to be interpreted in the light of Rule 1, an unqualified right to the 'peaceful enjoyment of possessions'. Being unqualified Rule 1 is interpreted by the Court in terms of general Convention principles. In particular, interferences with property must be considered in respect of the general Convention concepts of 'lawfulness' and, above all, 'proportionality'. They must serve a 'legitimate purpose' and represent a fair balance between the achievement of the purpose and the burdens imposed upon the individual (see *James* v *United Kingdom* (1986) 8 EHRR 123, para 37).

> The court must decide whether a fair balance was struck between the demands of the general interest of the community and the requirements of the protection of the individual's fundamental rights.
>
> (*Sporrong and Lönnroth* v *Sweden* (1982) 5 EHRR 35 (a case decided under Rule 1))

The ECtHR has made it clear that this applies to Rules 2 and 3 as well. These rules are to be understood as

> particular instances of interference with the right to peaceful enjoyment of property [i.e. Rule 1] and should therefore be construed in the light of the general principle enunciated in the first rule.
>
> (*Broniowski* v *Poland* (2005) 40 EHRR 21, para 134)

Thus proportionality applies to Rule 2 and also, despite its wording, Rule 3. However, these rules refer to the 'public' and the 'general' interests, respectively. Proportionality in this context does not, therefore, mean that a court can substitute its own view for that of the authorities. Rather it is to ensure that, in determining the public or general interests, the authorities have not simply ignored the property owners but sought a fair balance with their interests.

23.4 Has there been an interference and, if so, of what type?

Assuming there is a possession, the next question is whether there has been an interference for which the state is responsible.

23.4.1 Positive duties

cross reference
Positive duties are discussed in general terms in Chapter 6, section 6.6.

As with many of the state's obligations under the Convention, the state may have 'positive duties' to act, or to ensure that a certain state of affairs exists, rather than a mere obligation not to do certain things.

To achieve a fair balance, the state may need to ensure, for example, that compensation is paid where necessary or that effective measures are taken to deal with environmental hazards which impact on property rights (as in *Öneryildiz* v *Turkey* (2004) 41 EHRR 20, see Chapter 8, section 8.3.5). Positive duties to maintain a system of law protecting property rights between private parties are illustrated by *James* v *United Kingdom* (discussed below, 23.6.1). Where, however, the interference with possessions is, in the Court's view, entirely a private contractual matter, and not a consequence of government action or inaction, then it may hold that Article 1 is not involved (see *Gustafsson* v *Sweden* (1996) 22 EHRR 409, involving a dispute between a restaurant owner and a trade union over which the government had no legal powers). As the ECtHR has often said, however, the distinction between negative and positive duties can seem arbitrary. The overriding question is not the type of duty but whether there has been an interference with property which involves state responsibility.

23.4.2 The basic approach

Where there is an interference for which the state is responsible the general method of the Court is to consider, first, whether there has been a deprivation of property or a control of use and, if possible, to deal with the matter under either Rule 2 or Rule 3. If the interference cannot be classified by either of those two terms, the Court will deal with the matter as an interference with peaceful enjoyment, under Rule 1. These classifications are not 'watertight' and little now seems to turn on them since the same basic issue, the existence of a fair balance between the individual and the collective interest, applies whichever of the three rules is in issue. In both Convention cases and cases under the HRA it is not necessarily made clear which rule is being followed.

23.4.3 Deprivation (Rule 2)

A 'deprivation' of property involves the idea that the reality of the interference suffered by the applicant is a compelled, full transfer of ownership rights. Examples from the case law include:

- **Nationalisation**, as in *Lithgow v United Kingdom* (1986) 8 EHRR 329, where aircraft and shipbuilding companies objected to the compensation terms of their nationalisation.

....

nationalisation

The taking of industries into state ownership. Many basic industries (such as coal, steel, railways) were nationalised by the 'old' Labour government of 1945–52 and a 'mixed economy' (public and private ownership) was accepted by both Labour and Conservative governments. The Conservative government of Mrs Thatcher began an extensive programme of 'privatisation', which has not been generally reversed, although the railway infrastructure was placed under a form of public ownership in 2002, as were a number of banks in 2007–8 following the credit crunch.

....

- Forced sale, as in *Hentrich v France* (1994) 18 EHRR 440, where the tax authorities had 'pre-emption' rights to force the sale of property bought below market price, in order to meet tax demands.
- Expropriation of land, as in *Scordino v Italy (No 1)* (2007) 45 EHRR 7, where the authorities expropriated the applicant's land under a general development plan; the case focused on compensation.

23.4.4 Control of use (Rule 3)

Where there has been no total loss of ownership rights, the Court will consider whether the interference complained of involves a control of use rather than the elimination of the rights of ownership.

- Development control (town and country planning) can give rise to issues under Rule 3. For example, in *Pine Valley Developments Ltd v Ireland* (1992) 14 EHRR 319, the ECtHR held that Rule 3 applied to a dispute over whether the Irish authorities could grant the applicant permission to build on 'green belt' land. Rule 3 is not always seen as applying to development control, which is sometimes treated by the ECtHR as involving an interference with the peaceful enjoyment of possessions under Rule 1.
- The loss of effective ownership may be the consequence of laws that control the use of property. These are dealt with under Rule 3. Confiscation and forfeiture of property, in the

context of the suppression of crimes, is an example (see *Air Canada* v *United Kingdom* (1995) 20 EHRR 150 (forfeiture of an aircraft on which smuggled drugs had been discovered) and *Allgemeine Gold- und Silberscheideanstalt AG* v *UK* (1987) 9 EHRR 1 (seizure and forfeiture of smuggled Krugerrands (gold coinage)). Adverse possession (the legal rule by which a landowner's title is extinguished if they have not objected, for at least 12 years, to another person's trespassory use of the land) was held by a Grand Chamber to be a restriction on use and not, as the Chamber had held, a deprivation of property: *Pye (Oxford) Ltd* v *United Kingdom* (2008) 46 EHRR 45, para 66.

- Rent control schemes that limit the economic freedom of landlords, such as in *Hutten-Czapska* v *Poland* (2007) 45 EHRR 4, engage Rule 3.

23.4.5 Peaceful enjoyment (Rule 1)

There can be interferences with property which, in the Court's view, do not cause a total loss of ownership rights nor are they conveniently understood as controls over use. In these circumstances, the ECtHR will deal with the issue under Rule 1, as interferences with the peaceful enjoyment of possessions. Examples include:

- Planning blight: planning issues are sometimes dealt with under Rule 3. Where government plans for redevelopment or other schemes diminish the value of property or involve other constraints, an issue under Rule 1 may arise (as in *Sporrong and Lönnroth* v *Sweden* (1983) 5 EHRR 35—various restrictions on property in Stockholm were imposed for up to 23 years to enable city council redevelopment plans that did not materialise).

- Restitution. Alleged failure of governments to provide effective compensation for losses of property can be considered in terms of Rule 1. This can include, for instance, failure to make proper restitution for the behaviour of previous regimes (see, for instance, *Papamichalopoulos* v *Greece* (1993) 16 EHRR 440 or *Broniowski* v *Poland* (2005) 40 EHRR 21).

- Pre-emption rights to prevent the sale abroad of an old master (in *Beyeler* v *Italy* (2001) 33 EHRR 52) were dealt with under Rule 3.

- In *Thomas* v *Bridgend CBC* [2011] EWCA Civ 862 section 3 HRA was used to read into section 19 Land Compensation Act 1973 a right to compensation in respect of noise nuisance from an unadopted road in order to make it compatible with Article 1.

Is the interference lawful?

An 'interference' with possessions is not itself a violation. The issue for the court is whether the interference can be justified. The interference must be lawful, for a legitimate purpose and proportionate.

23.5.1 Legality and the Convention

Article 1 will be breached if the state's interference with possessions is not lawful. It must be in accordance with national law (as determined by national courts) and also meet the Convention requirement of accessibility and foreseeability. In *Scordino* v *Italy (No 3)* (2009) 48 EHRR 9, the Italian courts had condoned an unlawful expropriation of land. The ECtHR awarded €3,300,000 for pecuniary damage and €40,000 for non-pecuniary damage.

A law that gives officials a wide discretion to interfere with property where it is very hard to determine in advance the circumstances in which that discretion is likely to be exercised may fall foul of the legality principle.

cross reference
Convention concept of 'law' is discussed in Chapter 6, section 6.2.

In *Hentrich* v *France* (1994) 18 EHRR 440, the ECtHR held that the power of 'pre-emption' exercised by the French tax authorities (by which they could force an individual to sell land if bought at a price so low it implied tax evasion) was highly discretionary and exercised in unpredictable ways. Therefore it failed the 'legality' test.

As well as acting on the basis of law, the legality principle requires that the state and its agencies themselves comply with judicial orders made against them (see, for example, *Amat-G Ltd* v *Georgia* (2007) 45 EHRR 35).

23.5.2 **International law**

Rule 2 requires any deprivation of property to be compatible with 'international law'. The main impact of this provision is on the principles dealing with compensation, and is considered below.

23.6 Justifications: legitimate purpose

There will be a violation of Article 1 unless the state can prove that the interference was for a legitimate purpose and, as regards the imposition on the individual claimant, was not an unreasonable burden on the applicant. Although the language of the three rules is different, the concept of seeking a fair balance between the common good aimed at by an interference and the individual burden imposed, applies to all. The Court has consistently made it clear that the second and third rules should 'be construed in the light of the general principle enunciated in the first rule' and that this compatibility with the first rule requires, in relation to the second and third rules, a '"fair balance" between the demands of the general interest of the community and the requirements of the protection of the individual's fundamental rights' (from *Pye (Oxford) Ltd* v *United Kingdom* (2006) 43 EHRR 3, paras 52–53).

However, the permissive language of Article 1 and its references to justifying interferences in the public or general interest, means that states have a wide margin of appreciation over the identification of what purposes and policies are in their public or general interest (see *Broniowski* v *Poland* (2005) 40 EHRR 21, para 149).

It also means, under UK law, that courts will defer to government and Parliament on the issue of where the public or general interest lies. In *Alconbury* (above), Lord Hoffmann said:

> the question of what the public interest requires for the purposes of art 1 of Protocol 1 can, and in my opinion should, be determined according to the democratic principle—by elected local or central bodies or by ministers accountable to them. There is no principle of human rights which requires such decisions to be made by independent and impartial tribunals. (para 72)

23.6.1 **Social policy and the redistribution of wealth**

Governments (often those of the 'old' left or associated with the 'social market') might want to distribute property in the name of social justice in order to improve the lives of the least well off in society or some other disadvantaged group. Article 1 does not seem a barrier to effective schemes of this kind. For example, in *James* v *United Kingdom* (1986) 8 EHRR 123 a statutory scheme by which tenants holding very long leases had the right to purchase the freehold of their dwellings from their landlords was held to be compatible with Article 1. This was so even though the landlords stood to make considerable losses and received no compensation beyond the sale price. The Act pursued a legitimate purpose (preventing the unjust enrichment of landlords) and the burden on the applicants was proportionate, including the level of compensation. The Court implicitly rejects, therefore, any view that the Convention somehow protects and insists upon freedom of contract and the values of the free market. Nationalisation (the taking of individual businesses or whole industries into public ownership) has also been accepted as a legitimate aim in cases such as *Lithgow* v *United Kingdom* (1986) 8 EHRR 329.

The views of the elected legislature on important social objectives will also weigh heavily against Article 1 claims by landowners. This is demonstrated by the Countryside Alliance's challenge to the Hunting Act 2004 under the HRA.

case close-up

R (Countryside Alliance) v Attorney General [2007] UKHL 52

The Hunting Act 2004 banned hunting with dogs. The Countryside Alliance and individuals sought a declaration of incompatibility under section 4 HRA that, amongst other things, the Act was incompatible with rights of their members in Article 1 of the First Protocol. The House of Lords accepted that Article 1 was engaged. Specifically, the ban interfered with land owners' use of their land for hunting; likewise the value of hounds and hunting equipment was reduced. However, Article 1 required justification in terms of the general interest. There is no 'necessity' test and so proper deference by the court to Parliament's view of the balance of rights and wrongs was appropriate.

23.6.2 Development control and town and country planning

Most states adopt policies to protect the environment by placing restrictions on building and development, such as producing plans to organise land use and requiring planning permission before developments can go ahead. Cases objecting to planning decisions are dealt with under Article 1 either as an example of Rule 3 (control of use) or Rule 1 (interference with peaceful enjoyment). The ECtHR is reluctant to interfere with good faith decisions taken in this regard (see, for example, *Katte Klitsche de la Grange* v *Italy* (1995) 19 EHRR 368). However, as in *Sporrong and Lönnroth* v *Sweden*, discussed below, section 23.7.1, procedural problems, like serious delay, may mean that the authorities have acted disproportionately.

Similar deference to the planning authorities is illustrated in HRA cases.

- In *Davies* v *Crawley* [2001] EWHC 854, the council adopted a street trading scheme which had a highly detrimental impact on D's mobile catering business. Nevertheless, there was a fair balance of competing interests and Article 1 did not require compensation to be paid.

- In *Belfast City Council* v *Miss Behavin' Ltd* [2007] UKHL 19, there was a challenge, partly on Article 1 grounds, to the refusal of Belfast Council to license a sex shop. It was held that, at best, the impact of Article 1 would be very weak with interferences easily justified; indeed Lord Neuberger referred to case law suggesting that a refusal of planning permission could, of itself, never give rise to a violation of Article 1.

23.6.3 **Prevention of crime**

Measures that have an impact on people's property may be taken in order to promote the prevention or punishment of crime.

In *Raimondo* v *Italy* (1994) 18 EHRR 237, the ECtHR held that there was no violation of Article 1 when a mafia suspect was arrested and his property confiscated whilst the criminal issues were decided. There was a breach, however, caused by the delay in returning the property after the applicant had been acquitted.

In this and other forfeiture cases (such as *Air Canada* v *United Kingdom* (1995) 20 EHRR 150, mentioned above), the matter is treated as a temporary transfer of property and is dealt with under Rule 3. Where full ownership transfers entirely to the state then there is likely to be a deprivation of property to be dealt with under Rule 2.

In the United Kingdom there are increasingly tough laws by which the state can impose what is, in effect, a levy aimed at denying a convicted person the proceeds of crime.

In *R* v *Rezvi* [2002] UKHL 1 and *R* v *Benjafield* [2002] UKHL 2, the House of Lords held that the procedures for dealing with confiscation orders under the Criminal Justice Act 1988 and the Drug Trafficking Act 1994 respectively, were compatible with Article 1. Confiscation had a legitimate aim of denying criminals the profits of crime, the measures in the Acts were rationally related to these aims and represented a fair balance of interests.

In *R* v *May* [2008] UKHL 28, the House of Lords held that the aim of such legislation (including the Proceeds of Crime Act 2002) was to deprive criminals of their gains. Conspirators, who acted together, are not (other than exceptionally) entitled, under Article 1, to an apportionment so that only their personal share of the proceeds is confiscated.

457

cross reference
See Lindsay, in section 23.7.2, for an example of a disproportionate exercise of this power.

23.6.4 **The seizure of goods to guarantee the payment of taxes**

Since this is expressly mentioned in the third sentence of Article 1, seizure of goods to enforce taxes is accepted as a legitimate activity by the state over which it is given a wide margin of appreciation (see, for example, *Gasus Dosier- und Fördertechnik GmbH* v *Netherlands* (1995) 20 EHRR 403).

(23.7) # Proportionality

The bite of Article 1 lies in the proportionality test. Demonstrating a legitimate purpose is not enough. The means chosen must be 'proportionate' and this applies whether the issue is dealt with under Rule 1, 2 or 3. There must be a fair balance or 'reasonable relationship of proportionality' between the demands on the individual and the public interest. If there is an 'individual and excessive burden' on the individual, the Court may find a violation of Article 1. However, in *James* v *United Kingdom* (discussed above) the ECtHR rejected an approach to proportionality which required proof that a burden was strictly necessary and no less onerous alternatives were available (para 51). Thus states have room to pursue legitimate objectives in their own way appropriate to the circumstances.

case close-up

***International Transport Roth GmbH v Secretary of State for the Home Department* [2002] EWCA Civ 158**

. . . .

A scheme made under the Immigration and Asylum Act 1999 made lorry companies liable for a fixed penalty fine of £2,000 for every illegal entrant found concealed in their vehicles. Vehicles could also be confiscated. There was no need to show an intention to smuggle people into the country. Defences available to the companies were hard to establish. The Court of Appeal held that the scheme was for a legitimate purpose but went beyond what was necessary and imposed an excessive burden on the companies. (Laws LJ dissented on the ground that the government's balancing of the interests needed to be respected.)

23.7.1 Delay, procedure and remedies

The fact that a person's rights over their property are suspended for long periods of time without a final resolution of the matter can be an important feature indicating a disproportionate burden on the applicant. This is often linked to the failure of the state to provide an adequate legal mechanism and set of remedies by which the tardiness of public bodies and officials can be challenged. Although Article 1 says nothing about procedural rights (i.e. rights to go to court and challenge the lawfulness of the actions of the authorities), their absence is taken seriously by the Court. In this context, Article 1 claims often include an Article 6 claim.

case close-up

***Sporrong and Lönnroth v Sweden* (1983) 5 EHRR 35**

. . . .

S and L owned property in central Stockholm which was scheduled for redevelopment. The city obtained legal permits enabling it to compulsorily purchase the land and to prohibit building. These permits were eventually cancelled but only after various periods between 12 and 25 years. Swedish law did not provide a legal process by which the city's need for the permits could be reconsidered, nor was there an effective system for compensation. The ECtHR held that there had been a violation of Article 1. The permits were for a legitimate purpose (development control) but the system was inflexible and so, in this case, imposed disproportionate burdens. The lack of a fair procedure also violated Article 6.

Bank Mellat v HM Treasury [2010] EWHC 1332 involved severe restrictions, imposed because of links with Iran, which excluded the Bank from UK financial markets. Access to the High Court to set aside the restrictions by applying judicial review grounds met the procedural requirements of Article 1 (paras 65-80).

23.7.2 An indiscriminate, blanket policy

State action which is based on applying a policy in a way that treats people the same who ought to be treated differently can be challenged on proportionality grounds. An HRA case illustrates the point.

Lindsay v Customs and Excise Commissioners [2002] EWCA Civ 267

. . . .

L purchased a new car for £12,000, which he later used to transport large amounts of cigarettes and tobacco from Calais to the UK. He was stopped by Customs and Excise who, alleging he was avoiding paying duty of about £3,500, confiscated not only the cigarettes and tobacco but also the car. A tribunal accepted, as fact, that the goods were for personal and family use (the Court of Appeal was sceptical). The Court of Appeal held that the policy of confiscating both goods and vehicle served a legitimate purpose. However, as a policy, it was potentially disproportionate and so violated Article 1. It did not distinguish between private smugglers and smugglers intending to make a profit. Regarding the former, the need for a fair balance required greater sensitivity to individual factors like the value of the confiscated goods, whether it was a first offence, potential hardship, etc. The decision had to be retaken in this light.

23.7.3 The conduct of the parties

The conduct of the parties is another feature that can determine whether an interference is proportionate.

Beyeler v Italy (2001) 33 EHRR 52

. . . .

B was a Swiss national who purchased a Van Gogh from a Rome art dealer. He did not disclose his identity but used an intermediary. B wished to sell his painting. The Italian state had legal powers of pre-emption by which, in order to preserve the Italian heritage, they could insist on buying a picture from its owner, thus preventing it from being sold abroad. The Italian government eventually exercised this power and obtained the painting for a sum below the market price. The ECtHR held that there had been a violation of Article 1. The burden on B was disproportionate.

The Court's reasons stress the conduct of both parties: some of B's actions were not as open and honest as they might be, whilst the authorities had delayed for five years in exercising its powers and had treated B in an ambivalent way, which left him uncertain of his situation. The extent of the discretion enjoyed by the authorities under the law also contributed to the finding that the burden on B was disproportionate.

23.7.4 Compatibility with the rule of law

State actions that are incompatible with the rule of law may also indicate that a disproportionate burden is involved.

Pressos Compania Naviera SA v Belgium (1996) 21 EHRR 301

. . . .

The Belgium legislature enacted retrospective legislation which removed from the applicant shipping companies a right, affirmed by a decision of the highest court in Belgium, to sue for negligence pilots working in Belgium waters. The ECtHR held there was a violation of Article 1. Although for a legitimate purpose, the burden on the applicant was disproportionate. One objection the Court had was to the retrospective nature of the legislation: had the legislation been prospective there would have been no Convention difficulty.

23.8 Compensation

23.8.1 Rule 2, deprivation of possessions

Convention principles

Where a person is lawfully deprived of their property under Rule 2, it will normally be a breach of Article 1 not to provide reasonable compensation. This is partly because compensation is normally a requirement of international law, which is expressly mentioned in Rule 2. More importantly, the payment of compensation is a crucial factor for determining whether or not a fair balance has been achieved between the public interest that justifies the deprivation and the burden placed upon the individual or company who loses a possession. However, compensation is not an absolute necessity: see, for example, *Jahn* v *Germany* (2006) 42 EHRR 49. Nor is the payment of full compensation always necessary since there may be significant social and economic reasons that justify a lesser amount (as in a nationalisation case, *Lithgow* v *United Kingdom* (1986) 8 EHRR 329). The Grand Chamber summed up the position in *Pye (Oxford) Ltd* v *United Kingdom* (2008) 46 EHRR 45, para 54:

> A taking of property under the second sentence of the first paragraph of Article 1 without payment of an amount reasonably related to its value will normally constitute a disproportionate interference that cannot be justified under Article 1. But full compensation is not guaranteed since legitimate objectives of 'public interest' may call for less than reimbursement of the full market value.

In *Scordino* v *Italy* (2007) 45 EHRR 7, building land was lawfully expropriated by the authorities, but the Court found the compensation paid under Italian law to be inadequate and awarded €580,000 and €12,400 to the applicants in two separate cases.

Human Rights Act 1998

These principles have been adopted under the HRA. In *Beaulane Properties* v *Palmer* [2005] EWHC 817, the High Court ruled that the application of 'adverse possession' laws was a deprivation of property engaging Rule 2, and so the total absence of compensation for the original owner was disproportionate and a violation of Article 1. (By conceptualising adverse possession as not a deprivation but an interference engaging Rule 3, the Grand Chamber, in *Pye (Oxford) Ltd* v *United Kingdom* has undermined the basis of this case: see above, section 23.4.4.)

R (SRM Global Master Fund) v *Treasury Commissioners* [2009] EWCA Civ 788 involved a dispute over the way shares in the bank Northern Rock were valued when it was nationalised. The effect of the method of valuation was that compensation paid to shareholders was minimal. The Court of Appeal found that Article 1 was not violated. The government had a wide margin of appreciation and had acted on the basis of coherent policy objectives.

23.8.2 Rule 1 and Rule 3

There is no general principle requiring compensation to be paid to a person whose use or peaceful enjoyment of their possessions has been restricted or interfered with.

In *R (Trailer Marina (Leven) Ltd)* v *Secretary of State for the Environment, Food and Rural Affairs* [2004] EWCA Civ 1580, the applicants had been prevented from the commercial exploitation of their canal for the purposes of nature conservation. Statutory changes meant that compensation could no longer be paid. The Court of Appeal held that there was no breach of Article 1.

In contrast in *Dennis v Ministry of Defence* [2003] EWHC 793, serious noise nuisance was caused by RAF planes. This, the High Court held, was an interference with W's Article 1 rights, which, as a matter of a fair balance of interests, required compensation (£950,000) to be paid.

discussion topic

Should property and possessions be the subject of human rights or should the state have a free hand in the distribution of wealth? Would it make any difference to your answer if 'human rights' were confined to human beings and companies were excluded?

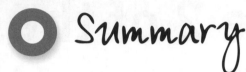

Summary

- Article 1 is analysed by the Court in terms of three rules (peaceful enjoyment, deprivation and control of use).

- Whatever rule is in issue, the same general concepts seem to apply: interferences by the state must be lawful, for a legitimate purpose and proportionate in the sense of there being a fair balance between the interests of the community and the restrictions imposed on individuals.

Question

For suggested approaches, please visit the Online Resource Centre.

In the context of a global economic recession affecting the housing market the Treasury takes into public ownership a major bank that would otherwise have gone bankrupt. The compensation is based on the bank's very low share price at the time of nationalisation. What are the main issues that a court in the United Kingdom would have to consider when dealing with a claim by the bank that its rights under Article 1 of the First Protocol have been violated?

Further reading

Allen, T. *Property and the Human Rights Act* (2005) Oxford: Hart Publishing
Lester, A., Pannick, D. and Herberg, J. (see Preface) Article 1 of the First Protocol
Waldron, J. *The Rule of Law and the Measure of Property* (2012) Cambridge: CUP

Article 2 of the First Protocol: right to education

Chapter overview

- The right to education: a right of access to the education system that is provided.
- The nature, scope and limits to the right of parents that their children's education should accord with their beliefs.

First Protocol

Article 2   Right to education

No person shall be denied the right to education. In the exercise of any functions which it assumes in relation to education and to teaching, the State shall respect the right of parents to ensure such education and teaching in conformity with their own religious and philosophical convictions.

Introduction

Article 2 of the First Protocol guarantees, first, a right of access to education and, second, an obligation on the state to ensure that the religious and philosophical convictions of parents over the education of their children are respected.

The second principle, regarding the religious and philosophical convictions of parents, is unremarkable in a human rights context: it reflects the fear of ideological indoctrination that has been associated with totalitarian regimes and is, predominantly, a negative obligation on states not to attempt to pervert the development of children's minds.

The first principle is one of the few places in which the Convention expressly refers to 'social rights' (there are no express rights to health or welfare, for example, and the reference to a person's right to 'respect for…his home' in Article 8 does not, other than very exceptionally, mean that states are required to house the homeless). Legally enforceable social rights are problematic because they can compel states to large expenditures and can distort democratically chosen priorities for expenditure (these matters have been discussed in Chapter 1, section 1.3.2). The important point is that Article 2 is expressed as a duty not to deny to persons the opportunities for education that are already provided; and it does not require states to create new opportunities for education.

Article 2 needs to be read in respect of other Convention rights, in particular Article 14 (no discrimination in the way Convention rights are given effect) and Article 9 (freedom of thought, conscience and religion).

24.1   **General principles and the basic right**

case close-up

***Belgian Linguistics Case (No 2)* (1979–80) 1 EHRR 252**

Belgium is a linguistically divided country. In the Walloon region French is the predominant language, Dutch is the predominant language in the Flemish region, and there are other areas in which no language predominates. French-speaking parents in the Flemish region complained to the European Court of Human Rights (ECtHR) that Article 2 of the First Protocol had been violated because the Belgian education system was organised on language grounds and they were effectively required to send their children to Dutch-speaking schools. The ECtHR held that, apart from the impact of laws on children living in the areas in which no language predominates, the Belgian education system did not violate Article 2.

From the case some important general principles regarding the 'right to education' can be identified:

- Although Article 2 is expressed in negative terms ('no person shall be denied') it does, nevertheless, create rights for individuals. However, these rights are limited.

- The basic right is the right of a child to access to the education system that exists; there is no right to a particular form or type of education.

- States are entitled to regulate and control the education system and the nature of the education that is available but in doing so must ensure that the education system

  – is compatible with the basic right of access;

  – does not discriminate in a way that is prohibited by Article 14;

  – is compatible with the other provisions of the Convention (an educational system that did not protect freedom of thought, conscience or religion, as recognised in the terms of Article 9, for example, would not be compatible with Article 2); and

  – respects the religious and philosophical convictions of parents, as required by the second sentence of Article 2.

- There is a right to the recognition of qualifications obtained: without this the right of access to education would lose much of its point and would not be effective.

- There is a right to be educated in one of the official languages of the state. This is implied from the principle that the education must be effective. As *Belgian Linguistics* generally showed, it cannot be inferred from Article 2 that there is a right to be educated in a language of choice.

24.2 The education system

24.2.1 The provision of education

States have a wide discretion over the education system. The negative formulation of the right has been taken to mean that the 'Parties do not recognise such a right to education as would require them to establish at their own expense, or to subsidise, education of any particular type or at any particular level' (see *Belgian Linguistics*, para 3). The Article 2 case law refers to states with well-established educational systems based on a mixture of state and private provision. It is not clear to what extent, if any, Article 2 could be relied upon in the situation of the complete absence of educational provision, though it is possible that the complete absence of state-funded provision of specifically elementary education might violate Article 2 since such education was recognised by all states at the time of signature.

24.2.2 The scope of the right of access to the education provided

The right of access to the education provision that is provided applies to all levels of education, including university education (*Leyla Sahin* v *Turkey* (2007) 44 EHRR 5 (the case is discussed in Chapter 16, section 16.6.1)). In *R (Hurley)* v *Secretary of State for Business, Innovation and Skills* [2012] EWHC 2012, the High Court held that Article 2 required effective, and (in respect of Article 14) non-discriminatory, access to whatever university education was provided. Tuition fees (here the £9,000 maximum charged in England) were restrictions. However, charging fees was justifiable and, given the scheme as a whole, was a proportionate restriction on access and did not violate Article 2.

24.2.3 The system

Regulation

There is no right to any particular form of educational provision. States have wide discretion over the type of education they provide and the right of access to this system is subject to the legitimate power of the state to regulate the education service. For example:

- There is no obligation on the state to provide education in a particular language (*Belgian Linguistics*, see section 24.1).

- There is no obligation on the state to fund schools for religious or ethnic groups, although discriminating in favour of some groups and not others could raise an issue under Article 14.

- Article 2 cannot be used to require a particular form of organisation or funding for schools (see a Scottish case, *Dove* v *the Scottish Ministers* 2002 SLT 1296).

- Article 2 cannot be used to compel the provision of a particular type of education for children with special needs (see *SP* v *United Kingdom* (1997) 23 EHRR CD 139). It is not clear what the position would be if there was a complete absence of provision for children with special needs.

- Separate education for children belonging to linguistic and cultural minorities is not necessarily a breach of Article 2 so long as there is a proper justification and sufficient safeguards (*DH* v *Czech Republic* (2008) 47 EHRR 3). If, however, the context and inadequacy of provision suggests discrimination, there may be a breach (*Orsus* v *Croatia* (2011) 52 EHRR 7).

Private education

Article 2 guarantees the existence of private or independent education. In *Kjeldsen* v *Denmark* (1979–80) 1 EHRR 711, at para 50, the ECtHR treats the legal possibility of private education as a necessary though not sufficient condition of freedom from indoctrination and to give proper respect to parental convictions, as required by the second sentence of Article 2. Based on this the Commission has expressly stated that Article 2 'guarantees the right to start and run a private school' (*Verein Gemeinsam Lernen* v *Austria* (1995) 20 EHRR CD 78). Nothing in Article 2 prevents states from regulating private schools on matters such as curriculum and standards and ensuring general compatibility with the wider system of public education. Nor do states have a duty to fund or to give indirect financial support to such schools (though it has been argued that the abolition of charitable status to British independent schools, which would impose significant financial burdens on them, may be incompatible with Article 2).

24.2.4 **Pupil exclusions**

The basic right is for persons to 'avail themselves of the means of instruction existing at a given time' (*Belgian Linguistics*, section 24.1, para 3). Excluding a child from one part of the education system, if done lawfully, is not necessarily a breach of Article 2. The issue has come up under the Human Rights Act 1998 (HRA).

> **case close-up**
>
> ### *Ali* v *Head Teacher and Governors of Lord Grey School* [2006] UKHL 14
>
> A was excluded from his school having been suspected of arson. Work was sent to his home and he was allowed to sit examinations. Later, A was referred to a Pupil Referral Unit for appropriate teaching. Charges for arson were not proceeded with. Neither A nor his parents attended meetings at the school whose aim was to facilitate his return. Only some months later did A and his parents indicate a desire to return to the school, by which time it was oversubscribed. The House of Lords held that there was no breach of Article 2.

The House of Lords stressed:

- Article 2 created a right to be educated to a minimum standard; there was no right to a particular type of education within the system.
- At all times the system had provided some form of education, or at least the opportunity of it.

If an exclusion results entirely from the difficulties of a child's circumstances and the authorities have behaved reasonably, there will be no violation of Article 2: see, for example, *A* v *Essex CC* [2008] EWCA Civ 364.

If exclusions result from children properly exercising their right to freedom of thought, conscience and religion (e.g. in a dispute over religious dress), then there is the potential for a breach of Article 2 (see *R (Begum)* v *Denbigh High School* [2006] UKHL 15, a case decided predominantly in respect of Article 9 and discussed in Chapter 16, section 16.6.1).

(24.3) **The curriculum: pluralism and diversity**

The education provided must meet reasonable standards of **pluralism** and diversity.

. . . .

pluralism

A general political perspective which assumes there is no ultimate truth on religious, moral and political issues (or at least no agreement on this) and so the social and political system must be open to a range of different ideas and principles.

. . . .

This is to meet the 'parental convictions' provision of the second sentence of Article 2 and also because pluralism and diversity is inherent in the idea of education appropriate to a democratic society and which avoids mere 'indoctrination'. Pluralism and diversity must be provided by the state through the policies and curriculum adopted in maintained schools and also in the way private schools are regulated. In *Kjeldsen* (see section 24.4.2) the ECtHR said that

> the state, in fulfilling the functions assumed by it in regard to education and teaching, must take care that information or knowledge included in the curriculum is conveyed in an objective, critical and pluralistic manner. (para 53)

As well as placing a duty on the state not to restrict educational diversity, pluralism and diversity also restrict the freedom that parents and others may have to object to the kind of education their children are getting in terms of standards and curriculum.

24.4 Parental convictions

The second sentence of Article 2 requires the state to 'respect' the religious and philosophical convictions of parents in the way it fulfils its educational functions. The second sentence reflects the fear of state indoctrination through education and embodies what is seen as the 'natural' parental functions of enlightening and guiding their children in terms of the convictions that they, the parents, consider valuable and important.

Respect means more than merely being acknowledged or taken into account: it imposes obligations on the state which limit the way in which its educational policy is performed. For instance, English courts, under the HRA, have said that parents' religious convictions need to be sought and taken into account when allocating children to schools (see *R (K) v Newham LBC* [2002] EWHC 405, paras 29, 38).

'Convictions' implies something more than just 'opinions' and 'ideas' referred to in Article 10. The state's duty is to respect only those religious and philosophical convictions which are reasonable in the sense of being 'worthy of respect in a "democratic society" and [which] are not incompatible with human dignity'. Furthermore, 'they must not conflict with the fundamental right of the child to education, the whole of Article 2 being dominated by its first sentence'. (Both quotations come from *Campbell and Cosans*, para 36: see section 24.4.1.)

In other words, the state has no duty to respect religious or philosophical beliefs which are unreasonable, particularly those which would have a significantly restrictive impact on a child's education. Parents who seek to withdraw their children from science classes that presuppose evolution, might not, on these grounds, be able to claim the support of Article 2. In *Williamson* (below), Lord Walker found this judgmental approach to other people's convictions 'alarming' (para 60). On the other hand, he agreed that allowing parents too much influence on the basis of the second sentence of Article 2 could have the effect of damaging a child's education.

24.4.1 Punishment

The duty to respect parental convictions applies not just to the classroom curriculum but to the full range of education regulation that the state legitimately performs, including school discipline and punishment.

Convention law

> **case close-up**
>
> **Campbell and Cosans v United Kingdom (1982) 4 EHRR 293**
> . . . .
> Parents objected to the potential use of corporal punishment (being hit on the hand with a 'tawse') in the Scottish state schools which their children attended. The local authority refused to assure Mrs Campbell that the tawse would not be used on her son, and Mrs Cosans' son was suspended from school for refusing the punishment. The ECtHR held that parental convictions about punishment involved a 'weighty and substantial aspect of human life, namely the integrity of the person' and that there had been a breach of Article 2.

HRA

The converse to *Campbell* failed under the HRA.

> **case close-up**
>
> **R (Williamson) v Secretary of State for Education and Employment [2005] UKHL 15**
> . . . .
> A group of parents, through the teachers and governors of a group of private Christian schools, objected to the statutory ban, applicable to all schools in England and Wales, on corporal punishment. They argued, following *Campbell and Cosans*, that views about school discipline could be expressions of philosophical and religious convictions. The House of Lords accepted that both Article 2 of the First Protocol and Article 9 were engaged but that Parliament had adopted a reasonable and proportionate policy in banning corporal punishment even though it limited parental choice. Neither article, therefore, had been violated.

24.4.2 The curriculum

In *Valsamis* v *Greece* (1997) 24 EHRR 294, the ECtHR said, in respect of the curriculum:

> democracy does not simply mean that the views of a majority must always prevail: a balance must be achieved which ensures the fair and proper treatment of minorities and avoids any abuse of a dominant position. (para 27)

If the curriculum meets these objectives, if it adopts a pluralistic but balanced approach to ethical and political matters, for example, and is informative rather than aiming at indoctrination, it is likely that parental objections to the curriculum and other school activities will fail.

In *Kjeldsen, Busk, Madsen and Pedersen* v *Denmark* (1979–80) 1 EHRR 711, parents objected to compulsory sex education lessons for their children in state schools. Given the ethically neutral and information-based way in which the sex education was delivered, the ECtHR held that the policy 'in no way offends the applicant's religious and philosophical convictions to the extent forbidden by the second sentence of Article 2'.

In *Folgero* v *Norway* (2008) 46 EHRR 47, on the other hand, a Grand Chamber found (by a narrow majority) that Article 2 was violated in respect of a compulsory course on Christianity, religion and philosophy. Christianity was given a particular emphasis and seeking exemption involved parents in having to disclose matters of personal belief.

In contrast: in *Lautsi v Italy* (2012) 54 EHRR 3, a Grand Chamber held that the Italian tradition of displaying a crucifix in classrooms did not amount to indoctrination nor did it influence the content of educational provision. Given this, it was a matter over which the state enjoyed a wide margin of appreciation.

24.5 The UK's reservation

When the United Kingdom signed the First Protocol, in 1952, it reserved its position regarding parental convictions:

> the principle affirmed in the second sentence of Article 2 is accepted by the United Kingdom only so far as it is compatible with the provision of efficient instruction and training, and the avoidance of unreasonable public expenditure.

cross reference
For 'reservations' in general, see Chapter 2, section 2.4.4.

This reservation is maintained under section 15 HRA, but, under section 17, is due for review. The impact of the reservation is unclear and, if it were asserted by the government in any proceedings, it is likely it would be challenged on the grounds that it lacks the precision and clarity as to its scope that is required under Article 57 (this was suggested in *SP* v *UK* (1997) 23 EHRR CD 139).

discussion topic

Values and parental choice
....

The second sentence of Article 2 embodies, though in a qualified way, the principle that parents be allowed to control the values and beliefs their children come into contact with through education. Is this a good principle?

The case in favour of parents having this influence might include considerations such as the following:

- Evidence from the first half of the twentieth century (Stalinism and Fascism, in particular) shows the danger of state indoctrination of children. The parents' role is vital in preventing this.

- Individual flourishing depends upon the transmission of religious and moral traditions. Without these we are all empty shells with no basic values and no language or symbols by which such values might be expressed. Parents have the right and duty to ensure that their children have a proper sense of identity and belonging.

The case against might include considerations such as the following:

- Even if it is true that individuals benefit from access to traditions of belief and understanding, it is also true that human flourishing requires a degree of openness and curiosity, and a willingness to consider the ideas of others and to adopt a reflective, even critical, approach towards one's own traditions. Without this, the traditions themselves will become mere orthodoxies.

- Traditions and systems of belief very often hide the exercise of social and political power which, in a democracy, should be open to criticism and challenge.

- Parents should not have strong rights to insist that their children be educated according to their philosophical and religious convictions. It is enough that the state is under an obligation to educate the children in a manner that is non-doctrinaire and is liberal, pluralist and diverse. To allow parents further rights may enable them to impose their own doctrinaire, even bigoted, approach to life on their children and so deny to the latter the very opportunity that education should provide.

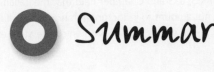

Summary

- Article 2 of the First Protocol contains the basic right of a child not to education in itself but of equal access to the educational provision that is available and to establishing the effectiveness of such education through the recognition of educational qualifications.

- What else Article 2 provides in terms of a child's rights to education is unclear; states have a wide margin of appreciation over issues such as the education system, the types of schools and the content of the curriculum. Nevertheless, there is a duty to maintain diversity and pluralism in education.

- The second sentence of Article 2 gives parents rights to have their religious and philosophical convictions respected in the way their children are educated. States must take this duty into account in the way they discharge their educational function, but it is not a right which will always restrict states in their reasonable attempts to regulate education in the public interest.

Questions

For suggested approaches, please visit the Online Resource Centre.

1   What kind of right to education, if any, does Article 2 of the First Protocol seek to guarantee for children?

2   What right is given, to whom, by the second sentence of Article 2? How extensive is this right?

Further reading

Kearns, P. 'Religion and the Human Rights Act 1998' (2001) 151 *NLJ* 498

Lester, A., Pannick, D. and Herberg, J. (see Preface) Article 2 of the First Protocol

Mountfield, H. 'The Implications of the Human Rights Act 1998 for the Law of Education' (2000) 1(3) *Education Law* 146–158

Article 3 of the First Protocol: right to free elections

Chapter overview

- The obligation on states to hold elections.
- Implied individual rights to vote, stand and take a seat if elected.
- Wide but not unlimited scope over the electoral system.
- Wide but not unlimited scope for reasonable limits and restrictions on individuals' rights to vote etc.

First Protocol

Article 3   Right to free elections.

The High Contracting Parties undertake to hold free elections at reasonable intervals by secret ballot, under conditions which will ensure the free expression of the opinion of the people in the choice of the legislature.

Introduction

The Preamble of the Convention suggests that the best way of maintaining 'justice and peace' is not only through the recognition of fundamental freedoms and the human rights by which those freedoms are protected, but also by upholding 'an effective political democracy'. At the heart of democracy is the idea of self-government by the people and there are many different theories of how that is to be achieved. For example, some theories focus on the people's choice of representatives; other theories find that too limiting and argue the need for a full range of rights and opportunities for people to participate in the collective decisions of the society. There is no human right to democracy. That would not mean much. Human rights require states to respect various rights and freedoms which are necessary for any system if it is to be democratic. Thus self-government is meaningless unless individuals and groups enjoy rights including the following:

- freedom of expression (Article 10);
- freedom of association, that people can form and join political parties and other groups (Article 11);
- freedom to hold meetings and marches; freedom of protest and the right to demonstrate (Articles 10 and 11);
- freedom from state oppression such as torture or inhuman treatment or arbitrary detention, etc. imposed by the state on its political opponents (Articles 2, 3 and 5).

There also need to be rights to vote for the government and to participate in the political process and public life of the nation. It was these last rights that proved difficult to agree upon and which were left out of the original Convention, to be added a year later in the First Protocol. At the heart of the disagreement was the fear of states that the Convention would require a particular form of political system. In fact, the final agreed text, on its face, merely obliges states to hold free elections for the legislature. As is clear from what follows, this obligation has been worked up by the European Court of Human Rights (ECtHR) into a set of (highly qualifiable) rights.

25.1 General principles

The general principles dealing with Article 3 were first laid down, authoritatively, by the ECtHR in *Mathieu-Mohin and Clerfayt v Belgium* (1988) 10 EHRR 1; they have been recently restated by a Grand Chamber in *Yumak and Sadak v Turkey* (2009) 48 EHRR 4, paras 105–108 and 109(i)–(vi).

case close-up

> ### Mathieu-Mohin and Clerfayt v Belgium (1988) 10 EHRR 1
>
> The case involved the complex constitutional arrangements in Belgium for establishing a system of government acceptable to the two principal language groups in the country. The applicants were French-speaking 'Walloons', who lived in a Dutch-speaking ('Flemish') area of Brussels. Like all people in the area, they were subject not only to the laws passed by the Belgian national parliament but also, on matters like education and the environment, to those passed by the Flemish Council. Membership of the Flemish Council was confined to Dutch-speaking members of the national parliament and it was not open to French speakers. As French-speaking members of the national parliament the applicants could not be members of the Flemish Council; furthermore French speakers living in a Dutch-speaking area could only be represented by Dutch-speaking representatives.
>
> The ECtHR departed from the view of the Commission and held that this system did not involve a violation of Article 3 of the First Protocol. The Court considered the place of the Flemish Council in the constitutional system as a whole, particularly the Belgian approach to dealing with the rights of and relations between the two principal language communities in the country. It decided that the restriction complained of was reasonable and proportionate to these legitimate aims.
>
> The Court took the opportunity to lay down some general principles (in paras 46–54).

cross reference
'Democracy', as a Convention concept, is discussed in Chapter 6, section 6.4.

25.1.1 The importance of democracy

The right to fair elections in Article 3 of the First Protocol is of great importance to the Convention. It 'enshrines a characteristic of democracy'. An effective political democracy is one of the principal means of protecting human rights, peace and democracy.

25.1.2 Individual rights

Taken at face value Article 3 does no more than impose a general duty on states to hold effective elections. In *Mathieu-Mohin* the Court implied individual rights into Article 3. These are:

- a right to vote in elections,
- a right to stand for election,

and, from later cases:

- a right to sit as a member of the legislature if elected (see *Sadak v Turkey* (2003) 36 EHRR 23, para 33).

The significance of implying individual rights from Article 3 is that individuals can assert these rights in the courts without having to prove that the will of the people has been thwarted because there would have been a difference to the outcome of the election.

25.1.3 **The Convention does not require any particular electoral system**

The Court recognised that there are many different political and electoral systems in Europe which can all claim to be reasonably effective democracies. The countries of Europe are different from each other in terms of history, culture and social make-up, and internal tensions. These will determine the political and election system. It is not for the Court to insist that all states adopt a particular electoral or legislative system. In particular, a system of proportional representation (where each party ends up with broadly the same proportion of the seats in the legislature as they had of the votes cast in the election) is not required.

25.1.4 **Article 3 rights may be subject to reasonable conditions; these conditions must not deprive these rights of their essence and effectiveness**

The individual rights to vote, to stand and, if elected, to sit, are not expressed in Article 3 but are implied from it. The ECtHR recognises that these rights may be subject to a range of restrictions and conditions. States have a wide margin of appreciation over the electoral system and individual rights. However, it is the Court's job to ensure that the essence of the rights in Article 3 is maintained.

> It has to satisfy itself that the conditions [imposed on the rights to vote or stand] do not curtail the rights in question to such an extent as to impair their very essence and deprive them of their effectiveness.

Any conditions and restrictions imposed on the rights to vote, stand and sit if elected must

- have a legitimate aim;
- not involve means which are disproportionate, and, above all;
- not 'thwart the "free expression of the opinion of the people"' in the choice of the legislature.

case close-up

> **Zdanoka v Latvia (2007) 45 EHRR 17, Grand Chamber**
>
> Z complained that she was the victim of a range of restrictions imposed on the political activity of former Communists and supporters of the Soviet Union by Latvia, formerly part of the Soviet Union. The Grand Chamber held that there was no violation of Article 3 of the First Protocol.
>
> - The Court reviewed the basic principles relating to Article 3 of the First Protocol, in particular, that the Article created individual rights which were subject to reasonable restriction.
> - It held that restrictions on political rights under Article 3 were not to be measured with the same rigour as restrictions on freedom of expression etc. Articles 8–10. There was no need for the state to demonstrate a pressing social need. The focus of judicial scrutiny was on whether the restriction was arbitrary and disproportionate.
> - The wide margin of appreciation was stressed. And so, on the facts, the Grand Chamber, by a majority, reversed the original decision of the Chamber that there had been a violation.

cross reference

The case is considered in Chapter 7 in respect of Article 17, see Chapter 7, section 7.3.

Zdanoka illustrates the point, accepted later by a Grand Chamber in *Yumuk and Sadak* v *Turkey* (above), that states have greater freedom to impose legitimate restrictions on the right to stand than they have to restrict individual voting rights (*Yumuk and Sadak*, para 109(vi)).

25.1.5 **Equality of treatment is the essential requirement**

The essence of the rights in Article 3 is that each person enjoys equal treatment under the electoral system, whatever it is. There is no requirement, for example, that every vote should have the same impact on determining the outcome of an election or that all candidates should have equal chances of winning, since these would require particular electoral systems and are not required by Article 3.

25.1.6 **The electoral system must be judged in terms of its specific social and cultural evolution**

It follows from the emphasis on the margin of appreciation and the refusal of the Court to interpret Article 3 as requiring any particular electoral system that

> For the purposes of Article 3 of the First Protocol, any electoral system must be assessed in the light of the political evolution of the country concerned; features which would be unacceptable in the context of one system may accordingly be justified in another.

In deciding whether some restriction on a person's Article 3 rights is allowable, the ECtHR has to be fully aware of the particular constitutional context within which the restriction has been imposed.

25.2 **The electoral system**

States have a wide margin of appreciation over their political and electoral system.

25.2.1 **Pluralism**

cross reference

Pluralism is discussed in Chapter 6, section 6.4.2, and Chapter 18, section 18.7.1.

The right to fair elections is part of the Convention's commitment to democracy. Part of this is the upholding of 'pluralism'. This involves states acknowledging the existence of different social groups in society and accepting that these may wish or need to protect their interests politically, through standing in elections, for instance. Article 3 (as well as Article 11 (freedom of assembly and association)) has an important function here (see, for instance, *Sadak v Turkey* (2003) 36 EHRR 23).

25.2.2 **The voting system**

A range of different voting systems is compatible with ensuring the 'free expression of the opinion of the people in the choice of the legislature'. Different systems can derive from the different aims of an election and reflect the historical and cultural evolution of societies. In particular, the court recognises that an electoral system can have the primary purpose of creating a legislature which can express a clear electoral will rather than one which represents the full range of political views.

Proportional representation is not a requirement, nor is there a need for each vote cast to have the same weight, or the same ability to determine the outcome of the election, as every other vote.

In *Liberal Party* v *United Kingdom* (1982) 4 EHRR 106, the Commission held that the first-past-the-post system in the United Kingdom satisfies Article 3 despite evidence that it systematically disadvantages third parties.

Similarly, election systems that require evidence of support before a party can put up candidates in an election, or take seats under a system of proportional representation, is normally acceptable. A demonstration of a minimum level of support is reasonable in order to maintain the public nature of the right to stand. Many cases, mainly decided by the Commission of Human Rights, demonstrate the point. For example:

In *Tete* v *France* (1989) 11 EHRR CD91, the requirements that parties had to pay FF100,000, with limited rights of refund, was held to be compatible with the Article 3 right to stand.

KEY POINT Monetary deposits are a requirement under the election system in the United Kingdom.

25.2.3 **Maintaining the essence of the right to free elections within the political system**

cross reference
Article 14, prohibition of discrimination, is discussed in Chapter 7, section 7.1.

Article 3 of the First Protocol is not without teeth. There can be violations of the right to free elections if restrictions allowed by the electoral system violate the 'essence' of the Article; specifically, if they mean that the opinion of a significant section of the people cannot be freely expressed, or that individuals or groups are not treated equally under the rules of the system. Above all, any disputed features of an electoral system must not be such as to 'thwart the free expression of the opinion of the people over the choice of the legislature'.

There is no requirement under Article 3 that ethnic, national or other minorities should have special standing or protection in the election system. However, an electoral system that systematically discriminates against a national or ethnic minority or which treats members less favourably under the system, is likely to fall foul of both Article 3 and Article 14 in respect of Article 3.

In *Aziz* v *Cyprus* (2005) 41 EHRR 11, for example, Article 3 was violated when Turkish Cypriots living in the Republic of Cyprus (effectively the southern, Greek Cypriot part of Cyprus) were unable to vote for the Cypriot House of Representatives. This can be contrasted with *Yamuk and Sadak* v *Turkey* (2009) 48 EHRR 4. The Grand Chamber found no violation in respect of an electoral system that resulted in a Parliament in which approximately 45% of the population was not represented by the party of their choice. In the context of Turkish history and politics, a system that inhibited the progress of parties representing narrow regional interests was legitimate.

A system that puts disproportionate burdens on political parties might be a violation of Article 3. An example is where disproportionately large monetary deposits by candidates are required (as in *Sukhovetskyy* v *Ukraine* App 13716/02, judgment of 28 March 2006). Similarly, violations of Article 3 are possible if there are long gaps between elections (see *Timke* v *Germany* (1995) 20 EHRR CD 133), or where there is widespread evidence of fraud but no action being taken by the authorities.

If the system imposes burdens on individuals which deter voting, then there may be a violation of Article 3. This issue has arisen under the Human Rights Act 1998 (HRA).

case close-up

R (Robertson) v Wakefield MDC [2001] EWHC 915 (Admin)

R objected to the sale of the electoral register to commercial organisations but the Electoral Registration Officer refused to remove his name from the saleable list. The High Court held that R's rights under Article 3 had been violated. Entry on the register is a necessary condition for being able to vote yet there were no means by which people could have their names removed for the non-voting, commercial purposes to which the register was put. (The case also involved a violation of Article 8 (see Chapter 15, section 15.4.4) and of EU law.

KEY POINT The law of the United Kingdom has been changed. There is now a right of exemption from the commercially available electoral register.

25.3 Individual restrictions

25.3.1 Acceptable and unacceptable restrictions

As stated in section 25.1.2, Article 3 of the First Protocol creates individual rights to vote, to stand as a candidate, and to sit as a member of the legislature if elected. Since these rights are not expressed in the text, but are implied from it, they are subject to reasonable restrictions over which the states have a wide margin of appreciation. These restrictions are subject to review by the Court. The Court must ensure that the 'essence' of the rights is not impaired and that restrictions are a proportionate means to a legitimate end and, above all, that the free expression of the will of the people is not thwarted (see, also, section 25.1.4).

A wide range of restrictions have been accepted by the Strasbourg authorities.

Acceptable restrictions on the right to vote include that

- voters be resident in the country (see, for example, *Hilbe* v *Liechenstein* App 31981/96, admissibility decision of 7 September 1999);
- married women register to vote in their husband's name (*X* v *Netherlands* App 9250/81, (1983) 32 DR 175).

Acceptable restrictions on the right to stand in elections include

- a ban on members of foreign legislatures (*M* v *United Kingdom* App 10316/83 (1984) 37 DR 129);
- age requirements, well over the voting age, for members of the legislature (*W, X, Y and Z* v *Belgium* App 6745/74 (1975) 2 DR 110).

Political restrictions on police, civil servants and other officials are also, in principle, compatible with Article 3. This issue has been discussed in the context of Article 11: see Chapter 18, section 18.9.

Acceptable restrictions on the right to sit once elected include

- the denial of Parliamentary services to an MP who refused to take the oath of allegiance to the Crown and hence could not take his seat (*McGuiness* v *United Kingdom* App 39511/98, admissibility decision of 8 June 1999).

477

But not all restrictions on individual rights are non-arbitrary and acceptable. It is the Court which has the final word. For example, in *Podkolzina* v *Lativia* App 46726/99, judgment of 9 April 2002, the applicant, who was from the minority Russian community in Latvia, was removed from the list of candidates because of insufficient knowledge of Latvian, the official language. The ECtHR held that there had been a violation of Article 3 not because the principle of a language requirement was wrong but because of the arbitrary and politically partial way in which the language test had been applied.

25.3.2 **Prisoners' right to vote**

A number of countries, including the United Kingdom, ban all or some convicted prisoners from voting in elections. Whether it is right for the ECtHR to hold such bans incompatible with Article 3 has been and remains highly controversial in the United Kingdom. As noted in Chapter 21, prisoners retain their human rights except for those necessarily lost as a consequence of imprisonment; however, as noted in section 25.3.1, the right to vote in Article 3 is subject to reasonable restrictions over which states have a wide margin of appreciation.

case close-up

Hirst v *United Kingdom* (2006) 42 EHRR 41

Section 3 of the Representation of the People Act 1983 (ROPA 1983) (as amended in 2000) excludes serving prisoners from the right to vote. In *R (Pearson)* v *Secretary of State for the Home Department* [2001] EWHC 239 (Admin), a challenge to this ban was brought in the English courts under the HRA. It failed on the grounds that the interference with rights was within the state's margin of appreciation. However, when the case was taken to Strasbourg, a Grand Chamber of the ECtHR held that there was a violation of Article 3. The Grand Chamber in *Hirst* ruled (see paras 76–85):

(1) Imprisonment should mean that prisoners lose only the right to liberty, not all other Convention rights.

(2) Disenfranchisement plays no overt role in sentencing in the UK; there is no evidence that it deters crime. Furthermore, the penalty is arbitrary: the vote is lost only if a prisoner is in prison at the time of an election.

(3) People convicted of crimes with a strong anti-social element but not put in prison do not lose the vote; some convicted prisoners, on the other hand, may have committed offences which may have some moral excuse or public support (e.g. the murder of a violent husband) but will nevertheless lose the vote.

(4) Parliament had not, seriously and deliberately, considered the competing arguments for and against the ban; this affected the operation of the margin of appreciation.

At the heart of the Grand Chamber's position, therefore, is an objection to the 'blanket' nature of the ban: that it is 'automatic' (i.e. applied with no thought as to its appropriateness to the individual concerned), 'general' (i.e. applied to all convicted prisoners) and 'indiscriminate' (i.e. applied without reference to relevant criteria such as seriousness of offence or length of sentence).

cross reference
On implementation of judgments, see Chapter 2, section 2.5.3.

The UK, therefore, was under an obligation, in Articles 1 and 46 ECHR, to give effect to this judgment.

The issue was highly controversial, government consultations were inconclusive and there was no political will to change the law.

Likewise, judicial enforcement in domestic courts had only limited success. A declaration of incompatibility was made in Scotland regarding section 3 ROPA 1983 (*Scott* v *Smith* 2007 SC 345). English courts declined, in *R (Chester)* v *Secretary of State for Justice* [2010] EWCA Civ 1439, either to read down the provision under section 3 HRA to create some flexibility or to issue a second declaration. The Court of Appeal saw the solution as a political one and noticed that there is no power in the HRA to compel a positive response to a section 4 declaration. Likewise, in *Tovey* v *Ministry of Justice* [2011] EWHC 271, the High Court (following *Greens*, see later in this section) held that a court would not award damages to individual prisoners, nor would a declaration that an individual prisoner's rights had been violated be likely.

cross reference

Greens and the pilot judgment procedure is discussed further in Chapter 2, section 2.5.3.

Meanwhile, at the Convention level, the Committee of Ministers (which has responsibility for supervising the enforcement of ECtHR judgments, expressed, in various documents, its concern at the UK's lack of action. At the judicial level, the ECtHR took further steps. In *Greens* v *UK* (2011) 53 EHRR 21, it confirmed its opposition to a blanket ban in *Hirst* and then used the 'pilot judgment' procedure to impose a six-month time limit on the UK (after years of inaction) to remove the blanket ban and come up with a Convention-compliant solution.

The ECtHR did, though, confirm that damages were not appropriate at this stage and that its general policy of not awarding exemplary damages applied.

The UK then obtained a further stay to await a further Grand Chamber decision.

case close-up

Scoppola v *Italy (No 3)* App 126/05, Grand Chamber judgment of 22 May 2012

The case involved a challenge to the Italian law under which certain categories of prisoners are denied the vote. The Grand Chamber

- confirmed, with its final authority, the position in *Hirst*: that bans which are 'automatic, general and indiscriminate' are arbitrary and disproportionate denials of the right to vote and violate Article 3;

- refused to confirm an earlier Chamber judgment (*Frodl* v *Austria* (2011) 52 EHRR 5) that removal of the right to vote had to be a judicial act linked to sentencing: Parliament, by statute, could establish non-arbitrary criteria on this matter;

- found that the Italian law was not arbitrary—loss of the vote depended on proportionate criteria, such as the type of offence and the length of sentence: it was within the margin of appreciation.

The Grand Chamber makes clear, therefore, that so long as there is no automatically imposed ban on all convicted prisoners, states have a wide margin of appreciation over the criteria (e.g. of type of offence or length of sentence) that can be used to determine whether prisoners may vote or not. In *Tovey* (above), for example, the judge thought it unlikely that, even if the Strasbourg rulings were implemented in the UK, prisoners facing a minimum term of four years would gain the vote.

Following *Scoppola*, the United Kingdom is required to come up with a system which allows some prisoners to vote. The alternative is a stand-off between the United Kingdom and the Council of Europe. This may have been signalled by David Cameron, the Prime Minister, who, following *Scoppola*, repeated the view that the matter was for Parliament and not a 'foreign court' (HC deb 23 May 2012, col 1127).

In November 2012 the government produced a draft bill (Cm 8499). This seeks pre-legislative scrutiny on three options: (1) a ban on prisoners serving four years or more, (2) a ban on prisoners serving more than six months and (3) retain the total ban.

discussion topic

Should disenfranchisement be used as a punishment?

. . . .

The moral arguments for and against prisoner voting are well covered in the *Hirst* decision. Where do you stand on the issue? Remember the argument has two basic strands:

(a) whether, as a matter of principle, all or some prisoners should be denied the vote;

(b) whether this is an issue that ought, properly, to be decided by an international court applying an agreed text or whether it is a matter for national courts, Parliaments or executives.

further study

Bates, E. 'British Sovereignty and the ECtHR' (2012) 128 *LQR* (July) 382–411.

Foster, S. 'The Long and Winding Road: The Battle for the Prisoner's Right to Vote' (2011) 16(1) *Cov LJ* 19–28

25.4 'The legislature' and wider rights of political action

25.4.1 The legislature

The major point is that Article 3 of the First Protocol only applies to elections for the 'legislature'. The meaning of 'legislature' was discussed in *Matthews v United Kingdom*.

case close-up

Matthews v United Kingdom **(1999) 28 EHRR 361**

. . . .

Residents of Gibraltar were subject to European Community law. They were unable to vote for the European Parliament. The UK's Convention obligations extended to Gibraltar and the question for the ECtHR was whether the inability of Gibraltarians to vote in European elections was a violation of the UK's obligations under Article 3. The issue turned on whether the European Parliament was a legislature for the purposes of Article 3.

The ECtHR held that there had been a violation of Article 3.

The Court held that:

- The legislature involves those institutions with decisive roles in the enacting of primary legislation in the country.

- The legislature can only be identified in terms of the constitutional structure of the state. In a federal or devolved constitution there is likely to be more than one body with primary legislative responsibilities.

- The legislature can, therefore, be made up of more than one body. It can include, but is not necessarily confined to, the national parliament. Other bodies such as regional parliaments in a federal structure and, as in the case of the European Parliament, an international body with a role which affects national laws, can also be part of the legislature.

- Where a body is part of the legislature there must be evidence in the constitution of power to initiate and adopt primary legislation or at least (as in the case of the European Parliament) to have a decisive role in the legislative process. This role must be more than merely 'advisory and supervisory' or 'purely consultative'.

- A body which has only subordinate legislative powers, which makes rules only in so far as it is authorised to do so by primary legislation, is not part of the legislature.

On this definition, the legislature includes federal and regional assemblies (like the German Lander, the Belgium regional councils and the assemblies of Spain's Autonomous Communities).

The United Kingdom legislature includes the Scottish Parliament and the Northern Ireland legislative assembly (both of which have primary legislative responsibility for matters such as health and education). The application of Article 3 to elections for the Northern Ireland Parliament is confirmed by the High Court in Northern Ireland in *Re McKinney's Application* [2004] NIQB 73, para 33. The Welsh Assembly (which originally had a more subordinate legislative role) has had its powers increased and may now, also, be part of the UK's legislature. As *Matthews v United Kingdom* demonstrates, the European Parliament is part of the legislature of the member states. The European Parliament is treated as a unique institution whose democratic role within the European Union should be recognised.

25.4.2 **Public participation**

As a consequence of this narrow definition of legislature, wider rights of participation in the political and public affairs of the country are not protected by Article 3 (though it should not be forgotten that politically active people have other Convention rights such as rights of association (Article 11) and rights of free expression (Article 10)). There is no equivalent in the Convention to, for example, Article 25 of the International Covenant on Civil and Political Rights, which refers to the rights of citizens to 'take part in the conduct of public affairs, directly or through freely chosen representatives'. In particular, Article 3 does not apply to:

- Local government elections. The powers of local councils, including making 'byelaws', are entirely dependent on primary legislation from the national parliament. Local councils are not part of the legislature.

- Referendums. Article 3 does not give a right to vote in referendums no matter how important they may be for the future of the country. If there is a direct link between the outcome of a referendum and legislation it is arguable that the referendum is part of the legislative process.

- Consultative assemblies. There are no Article 3 rights in respect of a body, such as the Northern Ireland Political Forum, which was established as a consultative link between the people and government (*Lindsay v United Kingdom* (1997) 23 EHRR CD 199).

- Public regulatory bodies. There are no Article 3 rights in respect of various 'quangos', which may have regulatory as well as adjudicative powers over individuals, usually in a commercial or business context (*X v Netherlands* App 9926/82 (1983) 32 DR 274).

Most importantly, Article 3 does not apply to election for a government or executive President who is entirely 'separated', under separation of powers, from the legislature. This is probably misleading. Article 3 does not apply to elections for a largely ceremonial head of state (such as the Federal President of Austria, see *Habsburg-Lothringen* v *Austria* App 15344/89, admissibility decision of 14 December 1989). However, where there are significant legislative powers associated with the office (a power to propose legislation or veto it, for example) it must be presumed that Article 3 will apply. In *Boskoski* v *Former Republic of Macedonia* App 11676/04, admissibility decision of 2 September 2004, the Court said:

> Should it be established that the office of the Head of State had been given the power to initiate and adopt legislation or enjoyed wide powers to control the passage of legislation or the power to censure the principal legislation-setting authorities, then it could arguably be considered to be a 'legislature' within the meaning of Article 3 of Protocol 1.

Nevertheless, by not applying to wholly executive office or to significant areas of political activity such as local government elections and referendums, the reach of Article 3, measured against the range of democratic activity, is surprisingly narrow.

 # Summary

- Though Article 3 of the First Protocol appears to provide only a collective right to fair elections, the Article has been interpreted to provide for individual rights to vote, to stand and to sit, if elected.

- States are given a very wide margin of appreciation over, first, the kind of electoral and voting system they have and, second, the kinds of restrictions and limits they can impose on the individual rights.

- Nevertheless, the ECtHR has the last word on whether the 'essence' of the collective and individual rights in Article 3 has been adhered to. Restrictions in the system or on individual rights will violate the Article if held to be for an improper purpose, imposed unlawfully, disproportionately or likely to 'thwart' the free expression of the people.

- Article 3 does not provide wide rights to participate in the political processes (the main political rights are in Articles 10 and 11). Its scope is confined to elections for 'the legislature', a complex, multi-institutional term, which does not include local elections or referendums.

 # Question

 For suggested approaches, please visit the Online Resource Centre.

Should the Convention support a wider range of rights to public participation in the public and political life of the nation than it does?

Further reading

Briant, S. 'Dialogue, Diplomacy and Defiance: Prisoners' Voting Rights at Home and in Strasbourg' (2011) 3 *EHRLR* 243–252.

De Meyer, J. 'Electoral Rights' in R. St. J. MacDonald *et al* (eds) *The European Sysem for the Protection of Human Rights* (1993) Dordrecht: M. Nijhoff

Lester, A., Pannick, D. and Herberg, J. (see Preface) Article 3 of the First Protocol

Anti-terrorism law and human rights

Introduction

Terrorism is notoriously difficult to define. Broadly speaking, it is the unlawful use of violence for political, religious or social ends, particularly where the violence aims at change through terrorising the civilian population. It is to be contrasted with the lawful use of violence for such ends by states acting in accordance with the UN Charter and international law (the Iraq war, of course, raises the issue of how, if at all, the legality of war is to be tested). The lawfulness of the use by states of military violence against their own populations is even more problematic. It mainly depends upon national laws and their enforcement, and it is here that the contrast with terrorism can seem unconvincing.

Responses by states to the threat of 'terrorism' is a major theme of global politics. Specifically, the dominant risk in the early twenty-first century is said to be from jihadists (Islamic proponents of holy war, particularly the Al'Qaeda network) promoting a political programme aimed, at least, at the removal of Western capitalist influence from the Islamic world. Methods used by states (such as special powers, alleged torture and internment beyond the reach of the normal law) raise significant human rights dilemmas.

26.1 Special powers

Terrorist actions, such as bombing a civilian building, are likely to involve the commission of crimes such as murder, firearms and explosive offences. But states may feel these are insufficient to deal with the threat. Therefore state responses have included the use of special powers: laws which give extra powers to the executive, the police, the security services or courts and tribunals which only apply in a 'terrorist' context. Such special powers can raise significant problems for human rights law. Many countries do not see the need for such powers. In the United Kingdom, by contrast, they have been extensively adopted. They were introduced in respect of the 'troubles' in Northern Ireland and have been reinvigorated to deal with international terrorism. Special powers can include

- banning ('proscribing') political or religious organisations or political parties (which can raise issues under Article 11, freedom of assembly and association—see Chapter 18, section 18.7.2),

- extended periods of arrest and detention for questioning (which can raise issues under Article 5, the right to liberty and security—see Chapter 11),

- detention or other forms of deprivation of liberty without conviction (also likely to involve Article 5),

- increased powers for the police and security services to conduct searches and undertake secret surveillance (which can raise issues under Article 8, the right to respect for private and family life—see Chapter 15),

- new offences specific to the promotion and organisation of terrorism, and

- restrictions on various forms of speech and expression which might involve the advocacy or encouragement of terrorism (such restrictions might be incompatible with Article 10, freedom of expression—see Chapter 17).

26.2 The underlying principles

The issue of terrorism and how to deal with it is, and has been, a major concern of the Council of Europe. The Council of Europe Convention on the Prevention of Terrorism 2005 came into force in June 2007 (it has been signed but not ratified by the UK). The basics are that

- states have an obligation to protect the human rights of their populations (in particular, the right to life in Article 2), and agree to take a range of measures; but
- any measures taken must be in conformity with human rights (see Article 12 of the 2005 Convention).

The general position of the European Court of Human Rights (ECtHR), interpreting the European Convention on Human rights (ECHR), reflects these basics (see, for example, *Klass* v *Germany* (1979–80) 2 EHRR 214, paras 49–50).

26.2.1 Special measures may be necessary in a democracy

From early cases (which pre-date the problem of international terrorism), the Court has accepted that special measures may be necessary if a democracy is to defend itself from terrorism.

- The need for secret surveillance to meet a terrorist threat was accepted in *Klass* v *Germany* (1979–80) 2 EHRR 214 (para 48).
- The need for longer periods of detention for terrorist suspects (in the Northern Ireland context) was accepted in *Brogan* v *United Kingdom* (1989) 11 EHRR 117 (para 61).

In *Fox, Campbell and Hartley* v *United Kingdom* (1991) 13 EHRR 157, the Court said (in relation to Article 5 (1)(c))

the Convention should not be applied in such a manner as to put disproportionate difficulties in the way of the police authorities of the Contracting States in taking effective measures to counter organized terrorism. (para 34)

And in *Othman* v *United Kingdom* (2012) 55 EHRR 1 the Court emphasised that

throughout its history it has been acutely conscious of the difficulties faced by States in protecting their populations from terrorist violence, which constitutes, in itself, a grave threat to human rights. (para 183)

26.2.2 Safeguards and the avoidance of abuse

Though accepting that special powers may be legitimate, the ECtHR is insistent that they must be exercised in a manner that is compatible with the Convention (this is made clear in all the cases mentioned in the previous paragraphs and reflected in their outcomes). Special measures are open to abuse and a democracy is in danger of destroying its democratic quality unless the essential protections of the different Convention rights are maintained. In particular, the application of special powers must be

- proportionate to the threat they deal with, and
- embody adequate safeguards for those affected.

States are given a wide margin of appreciation over issues such as the need for special measures. The proportionality of the application and the adequacy of the safeguards, however, remains a matter for proper judicial supervision.

Of course a great deal depends on which Convention right is in issue.

Article 3 (the prohibition on torture and inhuman treatment, the topic of Chapter 9) applies 'absolutely'. The ban is absolute. Torturing a terrorist suspect (or subjecting him or her to inhuman treatment) in order to get information is prohibited even if that information might directly save lives (see Chapter 9, section 9.1).

Other Convention rights are more flexible and context-dependent in their application. Questions such as whether a deprivation of liberty is 'arbitrary' (see Article 5) or whether restrictions on freedom of expression or association (see Articles 10 and 11) are 'necessary in a democratic society' are context-dependent. What is required (say, of police exercising their powers) may be different, the controls less exacting, regarding special powers when compared to 'ordinary' crime. Likewise some of the specific components of a 'fair trial' in Article 6 can be applied, in a terrorist context, in a way that would not be tolerated in respect of 'ordinary' trials.

The focus is, therefore, on the safeguards and the need to ensure the 'essence', the basic requirements of a right, are secured. Terrorist suspects cannot be simply denied their rights. The language of 'balance' is, as so often, appropriate. Necessary limitations on application of rights for terrorist suspects need to be counterbalanced by special safeguards if the requirement of proportionality is to be satisfied. In particular, proper procedural safeguards, usually involving some form of effective judicial scrutiny, may be necessary in order to achieve Convention compatibility.

487

26.3 Anti-terrorism legislation in the United Kingdom

The legal basis of United Kingdom anti-terrorism law is found in

- the ordinary law (such as criminal offences which apply to terrorist offences as much as to 'ordinary' crime) and general police powers under the Police and Criminal Evidence Act 1984 (PACE); and
- a body of specific anti-terrorism laws, which has been developed in response to the threat as understood by the government. This legislation was subject to review (Review 2010) by the Coalition government that came to power in May 2010 and there have been important consequential reforms.

further study

The pre-2010 strategy is described in *Countering International Terrorism: The UK's Strategy* Cm 6888, 2006. The independent review (Review 2010) of the law which underlies the post-2010 reforms is *Review of Counter-Terrorism and Security Powers Review Findings and Recommendations* Cm 8004.

The major pieces of special powers legislation are now outlined.

26.3.1 Terrorism Act 2000

The basic legislation is the Terrorism Act 2000. It was enacted before the '9/11' attacks in Washington and New York but after there had been a significant reduction in political violence associated with Northern Ireland. The central point about the Terrorism Act 2000 is that it enacts, as general law, a range of special powers which, previously, had been confined to the particular problem of Northern Ireland (though this was beginning to change). The Terrorism Act 2000 is general, in the sense that it applies to terrorism in all contexts and in respect of any political goal, and permanent, in that it does not require regular renewal by Parliament (although there is a requirement for reports by the Home Secretary to Parliament).

The Terrorism Act 2000 is a long and complex piece of legislation, which has been subject to amendment. It is outside the scope of this book to give it full examination. Its principal parts deal with

- proscription: to allow the Home Secretary to ban ('proscribe') political parties and other organisations on the grounds that they are terrorist; and the Act creates a number of offences for activities connected with banned organisations;
- requiring disclosure of information about terrorism to the police;
- terrorist property: the Act creates a range of offences and powers linked to the use of money and other property for terrorist purposes;
- police powers: the Act increases police powers over terrorist investigations, including powers to arrest and detain for questioning, stop and search, and search of property;
- offences: the Act creates a number of terrorism offences such as inciting terrorism overseas.

Although the Terrorism Act purported to be general and permanent, and followed a thorough investigation by Lord Lloyd into the nature of the threat to the United Kingdom, it seems, for the government, not to have been adequate. It has been added to by other Acts, which have been the legislative responses to particular terrorist outrages. These other Acts depend upon the Terrorism Act 2000 at least insofar as they are all based on the definition of terrorism found in the 2000 Act (see section 26.4). The 2010 Coalition government has been clarifying, perhaps reducing, and focusing the powers in legislative and other changes.

26.3.2 Anti-Terrorism, Crime and Security Act 2001—detention without trial

This was enacted after the 9/11 attacks. It creates a wide range of powers over terrorist property, it strengthens duties to disclose information to the police and contains a range of other powers over various matters, most of which are not earth-shattering but which steadily increase the powers of government. It has been widely criticised because some of the powers within it are of general application and not confined to terrorism, and yet it was pushed through as an emergency response to a terrorist outrage.

Its most notorious power authorised the Home Secretary to imprison indefinitely, without charge, trial or conviction, foreigners who were suspected of 'international terrorism'. In *A v Secretary of State for the Home Department* [2004] UKHL 56, a nine-judge House of Lords held that the derogation from Article 5, which was necessary for the power to be compatible with the Convention, was unlawful because it did not meet the requirements of Article 15 of the

Convention; consequently a declaration of incompatibility in respect of the relevant sections of the 2001 Act was made.

This power was then repealed in 2005.

26.3.3 Prevention of Terrorism Act 2005—control orders

The House of Lords held that detention without trial of foreign terrorist suspects was unlawful (see section 26.3.2). The government's response was to introduce 'control orders' in the Prevention of Terrorism Act 2005. These allowed a variety of restrictive measures (short of imprisonment) to be imposed on terrorist suspects, including British nationals. These powers were highly controversial and have been replaced by terrorism prevention and investigation measures (TPIMs). These are discussed in more detail in sections 26.3.6 and 26.7.2.

26.3.4 Terrorism Act 2006—control on speech and other measures

This Act introduces a number of measures creating criminal offences regarding acts which are preliminary to terrorism. Thus the encouragement of terrorism (through its 'glorification') or doing acts preparatory to terrorism are made offences. The Act also has a range of miscellaneous provisions which amend proscription and increase the powers of the police and others in respect of terrorist investigations. Some of these provisions are of great importance and are considered further in section 26.10.

26.3.5 The Counter-terrorism Act 2008

The Act increases police powers in various matters such as seizure of documents, the sharing of information with the security services and powers to act against terrorist financing. Since July 2012, as part of the reform programme, it has allowed post-charge questioning of terrorist suspects to be authorised.

26.3.6 Terrorism Prevention and Investigation Measures Act 2011

This Act, as part of the reform programme, abolishes control orders by repealing the Prevention of Terrorism Act 2005. Control orders are replaced by TPIMs, which moderate the most onerous effects of control orders. TPIMs in respect of human rights issues, are discussed in more detail in section 26.7.2.

A draft bill, which, if enacted, would give the government more draconian powers in a significant emergency, has been published (see section 26.7.2).

26.3.7 The need for special powers

Commentators have challenged the need for such special powers. Arguments include:

- The 'ordinary law' is sufficient to meet the challenges of terrorism. Terrorism involves ordinary crimes such as murder, and there is no reason why these should be treated differently just because the crimes are done with a political or religious motive. The police and other agencies already have considerable powers and do not need any more (this is especially challenging to the legislation passed after the 2000 Act). Part of the argument is that special measures may not work, may be counter-productive (they may alienate parts of society) and seem to be motivated by a desire of government to placate public opinion by being seen to be responding.

- Special measures involve the restriction of the traditional civil liberties enjoyed by British people. The real threat to our institutions and way of life comes from government overreaction rather than from terrorism itself. Insofar as this argument seeks support from British traditions, it is worth reminding ourselves that at times of national crisis (e.g. the French Revolutionary and Napoleonic Wars of the late eighteenth and early nineteenth centuries, and the First and Second World Wars in the first half of the twentieth century) special powers and invasion of civil liberties have been regularly used by the British government.

- The acceptability of special powers depends on their being proportional to the threat. The problem here is one of trust. Special powers are justified, if at all, by the need to protect the population from a credible threat. The existence of the threat is based on intelligence. There is some scepticism about the effectiveness of intelligence. The intelligence failure over the invasion of Iraq and over particular issues such as the intelligence-led police raids in Forest Gate, London, in June 2006, caused great concern.

26.3.8 **Constitutional processes**

The way in which special powers are introduced can be constitutionally controversial. Special powers legislation, though controversial and invasive of fundamental rights and liberties, tends to get less scrutiny by Parliament than ordinary legislation. There may be pre-legislative discussion (such as, for the Terrorism Act 2000, the Lloyd Report, mentioned previously, and numerous papers produced by the Home Office). Nevertheless, Parliamentary procedures are often curtailed. Characteristically, the House of Commons accepts government pressure and passes the measure quickly; and although fuller scrutiny is undertaken by the House of Lords, given their constitutional position, in the end the House of Lords gives way if the government, through the Commons, refuses to accept their amendments.

The Anti-Terrorism, Crime and Security Act 2001 is a good example. It was enacted in the months following 9/11. This was in the year following the enactment of the Terrorism Act 2000 and the government pushed through the new Act without waiting to see whether the 2000 Act would be sufficient. Though introducing the draconian measure of detention without trial, the 2001 Act went through all its Commons stages in three days, though it received eight days' scrutiny in the House of Lords. The Terrorism Act 2006 was enacted only after six rounds of 'Parliamentary ping pong' (the process by which amendments made in the House of Lords are considered by the House of Commons and, if rejected, returned to the House of Lords); in the end the House of Lords gave way to the Commons.

The situation should not be exaggerated, however. Important concessions, bearing on human rights and civil liberties, can be extracted from government. Originally, for instance, the 2006 Act would have extended the period for which a terrorist suspect can be detained for questioning from 14 to 90 days. This was defeated in Parliament and a compromise of 28 days agreed.

The definition of terrorism

The Terrorism Act 2000 defines terrorism. This definition applies to that Act and also to the other anti-terrorism Acts mentioned in section 26.3. The new offences created by all these anti-terrorism statutes and the numerous special powers for the Home Secretary, the police and other agencies that they authorise, all depend upon this definition.

Section 1 of the Terrorism Act 2000 defines terrorism in terms of a person or persons using or threatening action which has certain characteristics.

26.4.1 The action is designed to force a political change directly or by intimidating the public

The action must be 'designed to influence the government or an international governmental organisation, or to intimidate the public or a section of the public'.

26.4.2 The action must have a political, religious, racial or ideological purpose

The action must be 'made for the purpose of advancing a political, religious, racial or ideological cause' ('racial' was introduced by the Counter-Terrorism Act 2008).

26.4.3 The action must involve serious violence or damage to others

It must be action which

- involves serious violence against a person;
- involves serious damage to property;
- endangers a person's life, other than that of the person committing the action;
- creates a serious risk to the health or safety of the public or a section of the public; or
- is designed seriously to interfere with or seriously to disrupt an electronic system.

KEY POINT There is no standard definition of terrorism accepted internationally. Countries and international organisations develop their own definitions. The European Union's definition, for example, includes the words: 'seriously destabilising or destroying the fundamental, constitutional, economic or social structures of a country or an international organisation' (Council Framework Decision of 13 June 2002 on Combating Terrorism). There is a discussion of definitions in Lord Carlile, *The Definition of Terrorism* Cm 7052 (Lord Carlile is the independent reviewer of terrorist legislation).

26.4.4 Analysis

The definition given in section 1 of the Terrorism Act is controversial.

- Most importantly, it makes no distinction between 'armed struggle' aimed at an undemocratic tyranny and violence used against civilians in a democracy, albeit an imperfect one. The presumption in the definition (and the presumption of the UK government) is that violence and serious damage to property can never be legitimate, even for a proper cause. Critics are unconvinced by the government's view that, in the early twenty-first century, no population group anywhere in the world has a just cause of war against its own state or against some other state that is in occupation of what it takes to be its land.

- In *R* v *Gul* [2012] EWCA Crim 280, the defendant was accused of the offence of encouraging terrorism (section 2 Terrorism Act 2006) by uploading videos onto the internet showing attacks on coalition forces in Afghanistan and Iraq. His defence was that these attacks were legitimate acts of resistance against a foreign invader, not terrorism. For the Court of Appeal, however, the definition of terrorism clearly included attacks by insurgents on the armed forces or a state and there was nothing in international law that could justify using section 3 Human Rights Act 1998 (HRA) to restrict this definition so as to exclude the kinds of attacks in issue.

- The definition appears to exclude terror used by states against their populations or a section of their populations. From the point of view of the victims, actions by state agents can be indistinguishable from other forms of terror (actions by the Turkish state against the Kurds or by the Israelis against the Palestinians are examples).

- The definition could involve the suppression of radical politics such as those practised by environmental and animal rights groups. Actions such as destroying crops or animal laboratories might become subject to special powers rather than the normal criminal law. For some people there are important moral differences between violence against people and damage to property, which the definition does not acknowledge.

26.5 Convention compatibility

The definition of terrorism triggers a range of offences and powers. In the next sections of this chapter some of the special powers introduced by the UK's anti-terrorism legislation are considered from the point of view of their compatibility with Convention rights. The law is very complex and there is no attempt here to explore its details. The aim is to point out the main areas in which the policies of the law raise questions of compatibility with human rights.

The HRA needs to be recalled:

- Anti-terrorist legislation must be read and given effect 'so far as it is possible to do so' in a manner that is compatible with Convention rights. If this is not possible the legislation remains valid and effective, although the courts may issue a declaration of incompatibility.

- Ministers, the police, the security services, etc. are 'public authorities'. They act illegally if they act incompatibly with the Convention unless such actions are required by valid legislation (i.e. legislation that cannot be read for compatibility).

26.6 Proscription

26.6.1 Proscription and deproscription

The Terrorism Act 2000, Part 2, gives a power to the Secretary of State to ban or proscribe organisations. The test is that the Secretary believes the organisation is 'concerned in terrorism'. A proscribed organisation can apply to the Secretary of State to be 'deproscribed' and any refusal to deproscribe can be appealed to a special tribunal, the Proscribed Organisations Appeals Commission, which has the power to require the Secretary of State to lift the ban. It is the Commission (rather than the High Court) which has the principal jurisdiction to determine HRA challenges to proscription and provide remedies as required by Article 13 (see *R (Kurdistan Workers Party)* v *Secretary of State for the Home Department* [2002] EWHC 644).

26.6.2 **Article 11**

cross reference
Proscription in general is discussed in Chapter 18, section 18.7.2.

Proscription is a major interference with the political freedom of both the proscribed party or organisation and the individual members and supporters. Proscriptions must be compatible with the Convention, in particular Article 11, freedom of assembly and association.

Major issues under Article 11 include:

- Whether the ban is 'prescribed by law'. Being 'concerned in terrorism' is a vague expression. It says little about the degree of involvement in or knowledge of political violence by an organisation and its supporters that is required to justify proscription. There must clearly be doubt as to whether the Convention requirement that the law on which state power is exercised should be 'accessible' and 'foreseeable' will easily be met.

cross reference
See United Communist Party v Turkey—a case discussed in Chapter 18, section 18.7.2.

- Whether the ban is for one of the legitimate purposes listed in Article 11(2) (see Chapter 18, section 18.5.2). This is likely to be easy for the government to satisfy since the protection of national security and public safety are two of the purposes.

- Whether the ban is 'necessary in a democratic society'. The state must be able to show that the ban has been imposed to prevent a political organisation pursuing its aims by violent means. It is the actions of the organisation and not just the rhetoric associated with it that is decisive. A political organisation should not be proscribed just because it is pursuing radical, constitutional change against a background of political violence.

cross reference
Article 17 is discussed in Chapter 7, section 7.3.

- Article 17. The Convention cannot be used by organisations wishing to avoid a ban in order to pursue a political programme that is likely to lead to violations of the rights of others. The Court's support for pluralism, and its recognition that 'democracy' is the only political system compatible with the Convention, means that a political organisation whose aim is a non-democratic society or a society in which important human rights would not be respected, will find it difficult to show that its Convention rights have been violated (and this may apply even if it uses non-violent means).

26.6.3 **Fair trials**

Appearing before the Proscribed Organisations Appeal Commission can place a proscribed organisation under considerable procedural disadvantages. It may not know the full extent of the evidence against it or be able to challenge that evidence. Article 6 (the right to a fair trial) may be engaged, though this depends upon it being accepted that a 'criminal charge' against the association is being determined (unlikely) or that a civil right (perhaps a right under Article 11) is being decided.

Even if Article 6 is involved, restrictions on fair trial rights such as 'equality of arms' can be acceptable so long as there are adequate safeguards. The use by the Commission of 'special advocates' (barristers who represent, as best they can, the interests of the applicants without letting the applicants see the evidence) may be a sufficient safeguard, particularly because the liberty of an individual person is not at stake.

26.7 **Treatment of terrorist suspects**

The most controversial aspects of the special powers introduced in UK law involve the treatment of terrorist suspects. These are individual men and women who have not been convicted of any offence (whether under the general laws or anti-terrorism legislation) but whose personal liberty is severely restricted because they are suspected of being terrorists or supporting terrorism.

From the government's point of view, the issue is its duty, under general principles of good government but also under Article 2 of the Convention, to take appropriate measures to try and ensure the safety of the population. The typical situation is said to be one in which the suspect is probably involved in terrorism but the evidence does not demonstrate this beyond a reasonable doubt (i.e. to the criminal standard which would justify a prosecution); or the evidence does suggest terrorist involvement without doubt, but the evidence is inadmissible (e.g. because it would disclose the workings of the intelligence services); or, most likely, a combination of these two situations. At the heart of the matter is the intelligence on which the suspicions are based and whether it is reliable and the way it has been interpreted. Of particular concern, therefore, about the treatment of such suspects is their inability to know of, and challenge, the evidence against them.

26.7.1 **2001 to 2011**

As described earlier, the official response to this problem, at the height of the terrorist fears was, first, to use powers in Part IV of the Anti-terrorism, Crime and Security Act 2001 and detain in prison a small number of foreign terrorist suspects who could not be deported (usually because they might be tortured in the receiving country). Following *A v Secretary of State for the Home Department* (section 26.3.2) this power was repealed and replaced, in the Prevention of Terrorism Act 2005, by control orders. Control orders were controversial and have themselves been replaced by TPIMs. Some of the case law concerning the compatibility of control orders with Convention rights is still relevant in respect of TPIMs.

26.7.2 **Terrorism prevention and investigation measures**

The Terrorism Prevention and Investigation Measures Act 2011 (TPIMA 2011) allows the Secretary of State (Home Secretary) to impose a TPIM if he or she

- 'reasonably believes' that the individual is or has been 'involved in terrorism-related activity' (some of which must be 'new');
- 'reasonably considers it necessary' for protecting the public to impose the measures;
- has obtained prior permission by application to the High Court; or
- uses the urgent cases procedure, by which the Secretary of State can impose the TPIM, subject to consideration by the High Court within seven days.

Involvement in terrorism is defined widely in section 4 to include not just commissioning, preparing or instigating terrorist acts, but also encouraging, supporting or assisting such acts by others.

Schedule 1 specifies the restraints that can be imposed by a TPIM. These include 'requirements, restrictions and other provisions' relating to residence, travel, places where the person may be and where they may go, finance and property, computer use, association with others, and work and study. Individuals may be required to report to the police and be subjected to monitoring devices. It is a criminal offence to break the terms of a TPIM.

In a number of ways, TPIMs are less severe than control orders, and this makes it more likely that, even though they remain a departure from the norms of ordinary criminal justice, they will be compatible with human rights.

- The standard of proof that the Home Secretary needs is raised from 'reasonable suspicion' to 'reasonable belief'.
- TPIMs do not, generally, last beyond two years (one year which can be extended for another year by the Home Secretary so long as conditions still apply).
- There is a greater emphasis on using the criminal justice system against terrorist suspects—the police must be consulted on whether there is a realistic possibility of prosecution as an alternative (section 10).
- Individual TPIMs must be kept under review.

The Act is not permanent. The powers to make TPIMs will lapse after five years unless the Home Secretary revives them with the approval of Parliament (section 21).

Judicial supervision of TPIMs is important. First, the role of the court (in non-urgent cases) is to consider whether the Home Secretary's application is 'obviously flawed' and, if not, whether to give permission for the measures. Second, there must be a 'review hearing' at which the court must consider whether the relevant conditions authorising a TPIM have been met. The standard of review is that of judicial review—which is a highly variable standard of review, but one which can be compatible with intense scrutiny by the court, though this is not stipulated in the Act.

cross reference
JJ and deprivation of liberty is discussed in Chapter 11, section 11.2.1

TPIMs are likely to be compatible with Convention rights. In particular they do not authorise the Home Secretary to deprive a person of his or her liberty—which would engage and probably violate Article 5. The United Kingdom is not bound by Protocol 4 ECHR and so there are no Convention rights engaged by provisions which merely restrict movement. Schedule 1, Part 1 does give a power to require a person to stay overnight at a particular residence between hours specified by the Secretary of State. Control order cases, such as *Secretary of State for the Home Department v JJ* [2007] UKHL 45, make it clear that a long period of 'house arrest' (in that case 16 hours), coupled with other factors, can be a deprivation of liberty. The Act does not expressly authorise anything like this and its provisions can be read down, under section 3 HRA, to exclude them.

TPIMs and other rights

The restrictions that can be imposed under Schedule 1 can engage other Convention rights such as the right to respect for private life (Article 8), the right to manifest religious beliefs (Article 9) and freedom of expression (Article 10). Of course such interferences can be justified under the terms of the second paragraph to each article, and in the counter-terrorism context this may be relatively easy for the government to do. In *R (AP) v Secretary of State for the Home Department* [2010] UKSC 24, for instance, the judge had found that a control order requiring the controllee to live 150 miles from family and friends was a proportionate and justified interference with his Article 8 rights (though the interference could be a factor in deciding whether there had been, also, a deprivation of liberty).

Fair trials

Although TPIMs are subject to judicial approval, there are significant procedural barriers that a person may face when seeking to challenge the measure before the High Court. The Act itself and procedural rules made under it allow for the exclusion of the person and his or her representatives from proceedings, possible determination without a hearing and the non-disclosure of information relating to the reasons for the order (Schedule 4). Since similar restraints are found in respect of other counter-terrorist measures, their compatibility with Convention rights is discussed in section 26.9.

Draft Enhanced Terrorism and Investigation Measures Bill

The review of counter-terrorism powers (Review 2010) recognised that tougher control might be necessary if terrorist threats became more pressing. The government has produced a draft bill which, if enacted, would authorise somewhat more stringent restrictions than can be imposed under the TPIMA 2011. For example, it would allow the Home Secretary to require the person to remain at a specified residence within defined hours (i.e. more than just overnight), or to exclude the person from a defined area of the United Kingdom. As a draft bill it is not law, but is available for pre-legislative scrutiny. The idea is that it should be available for swift enactment by Parliament if circumstances so require. The draft bill is closely linked to TPIMA 2011 and adopts its provisions on most issues, including the process of application, the nature of judicial supervision and the procedures before the court. There will be a similar need to ensure that the application of the measures do not (in the absence of any derogation) violate Article 5 and are consistent with other Convention rights, including Article 8 and, in particular, the fair hearing provisions in Article 6.

26.7.3 Deportation of terrorist suspects

The nature of the alleged threat from international terrorism means that a number of terrorist suspects are likely to be foreigners and so are liable to exclusion from the country. This might be because

- they can be removed if they came to, or remain in, the United Kingdom illegally;
- they may be deported following conviction and punishment for a crime.

In particular, in this context:

- they may be deported because the Home Secretary believes their staying in the United Kingdom is not in the public interest,
- they may be 'extradited' (returned to another country to stand trial).

Under the Convention (and international law generally) a person cannot be excluded if they face a 'real risk' of torture, ill-treatment or the gross violation of other Convention rights in the receiving country.

cross reference
This issue is discussed in general terms in Chapter 9, section 9.8.2.

Reassessing *Chahal*?

The leading authority, *Chahal* v *United Kingdom* (1997) 23 EHRR 413, prevents any weighing of the danger a terrorist suspect may pose to national security against the degree of real risk of torture etc. in the receiving country. In the case, dissenting judges argued that, in such circumstances, a weighing exercise was reasonable, so that a suspect might be deported if, for instance, the threat he or she posed was considerable and the likelihood of being tortured not very great or very difficult to assess in advance. The UK government intervened in a terrorist deportation case to argue that weighing the risk of torture etc. to the individual against the threat he or she poses in the expelling country, was reasonable in a national security context and where the risk of torture did not come from the expelling state. A Grand Chamber, specifically addressing these points, rejected them and confirmed the established position in *Chahal*: *Saadi* v *Italy* (2009) 49 EHRR 30, paras 137–142.

Diplomatic agreements

The UK government has also entered into diplomatic agreements with countries against which torture allegations are made, that suspects can be deported without a danger of torture. Whether such agreements will pass muster with judges authorising deportation will depend upon the circumstances.

case close-up

Othman v _United Kingdom_ (2012) 55 EHRR 1

O, born in Jordan, had leave to live in the UK. He was suspected of involvement in terrorism. He was detained (under the Anti-terrorism Crime and Security Act 2001: see section 26.3.2) and, on the Act's repeal, made subject to a control order (under the Prevention of Terrorism Act 2005: see section 26.3.3). The Home Secretary sought to deport him to Jordan on public interest grounds. Convincing allegations are made that, in Jordan, torture of prisoners is widespread (para 191). The UK government had obtained specific assurances from the Jordanian authorities that O would not be tortured.

The ECtHR held that deporting O to Jordan would not violate Article 3.

- The Court noticed that, in general terms, the use of diplomatic assurances in this context was controversial; but it was not concerned with their general acceptability (para 186).
- The Court's task was to rule on whether the assurances meant that there was no longer a real risk of torture etc. in the particular case.
- Assurances are, therefore, a relevant factor in determining that question; however, the mere fact there were assurances is not sufficient in itself. The Court has to concern itself with the practical effect of the assurances in the particular circumstances of the case (the Court referred to the Grand Chamber in _Saadi_ v _Italy_ (2009) 49 EHRR 30 on this point).
- In assessing the practical worth of assurances the Court will consider the general human rights position in the receiving country (though it would be unusual for this to be such that assurances could never be valid). More importantly, it identified a range of factors (para 189) that need to be considered. These include the degree to which the assurances are specific, whether assurances given at a national level are likely to filter through to local authorities who will have specific responsibility for the person, and the receiving state's record in abiding by its assurances (there are 11 criteria altogether).

The Court then applied these factors, carefully and in detail, to the instant case and found that the assurances had, indeed, removed the real risk of torture if the applicant was returned to Jordan (paras 190–205).

UK courts will, therefore, have to follow the main lines of this judgment. In the domestic hearing of Othman's case, _RB (Algeria)_ v _Secretary of State for the Home Department_ [2009] UKHL 10, the House of Lords had decided, following earlier Strasbourg cases, that the issue of the credibility of diplomatic assurances was not a matter of law but of fact. The Special Immigration Appeals Commission (see section 26.9.2) deals with appeals involving public interest deportations and, unless wholly unreasonable, its factual judgments would be accepted. Such a focus on the factual circumstances would seem in line with _Othman_ v _UK_.

26.7.4 **Torture**

cross reference
This issue has been considered in Chapter 9, section 9.4.4.

The fear that terrorist suspects may be subjected to torture, if not in the United Kingdom, then in other countries, is a real one. The issue for the United Kingdom is whether government powers, such as making someone subject to a TPIM, might be based on intelligence gained from people under torture. The general principle is that, although it is unlawful for a court knowingly to admit evidence based on torture, it is not illegal for the executive, the minister, the police, etc. to act on the basis of such evidence: they do not need to enquire into its origins.

discussion topic

What should be done with terrorist suspects?

....

Is there any appropriate policy that (a) is compatible with Convention rights; and (b) can be applied to persons who, on the basis of intelligence, are 'probably' terrorists but who cannot be prosecuted for a number of reasons to do with the degree of proof the evidence discloses or the secret nature of the intelligence? Can the circle of security and human rights be squared?

26.8 Police powers

The Terrorism Act 2000 authorises a number of increased powers for the police. These include powers to create a 'cordon' around an area and require people to leave; stop and search a person reasonably suspected of being a terrorist; and increased powers to obtain search warrants, remove documents, take fingerprints and samples, share information with other agencies, etc. All these powers are predicated on the wide definition of terrorism found in the Act.

26.8.1 Stop and search

A major objection to the special powers in the Terrorism Act and other legislation is that there is little to prevent their use in the context of 'ordinary' politics, including meetings, marches and demonstrations. In Britain there is a long history of disorder breaking out in a political context. It is suggested that this is perfectly well dealt with under general public order legislation. Counter-terrorism powers should be more carefully defined to maintain the distinction between demonstrations (which might be disorderly and even violent) and the deliberate, deadly attacks on civilians which are at the core of the moral case against terrorism.

cross reference
'Ordinary' stop and search is discussed in Chapter 11, section 11.4.2.

Section 44 of the Terrorism Act 2000 was particularly controversial. It allowed an 'authorisation' to be made by a senior officer which then permitted police to make random stops and searches (for articles that could be used for terrorism) in the area and for the duration of the authorisation. Under regular police powers (such as in Part 1 PACE), stop and search powers require 'reasonable suspicion', relating to the individual being searched, that some prohibited article will be found.

No such person-specific suspicion was required under section 44. The grounds for making the authorisation was merely that the police believed it 'expedient' to prevent terrorism.

case close-up

Gillan v Commissioner of Police of the Metropolis [2006] UKHL 12

....

G, a student, and Q, a journalist, attended a demonstration in London against the arms trade. They were stopped and searched by police exercising section 44 powers. Nothing was found. An authorisation under section 44, covering the whole of London, had been made and continually renewed since February 2001. It had not been publicised. The House of Lords found that the police had acted lawfully.

On compatibility with Convention rights the House of Lords held that

- stop and search (in a terrorist or non-terrorist context) would not normally be a 'deprivation of liberty' engaging Article 5;
- nor, in the context of political demonstrations, would a stop and search be a sufficiently serious 'interference' with private life, freedom of expression or the right of assembly to bring it within the ambit of Articles 8(1), 10(1) and 11(1). In any event, non-trivial interferences would normally be justified under the terms of these articles;
- despite the lack of publicity, the authorisation was, in the context, sufficiently 'accessible and foreseeable' to be compatible with the Convention.

case close-up

Gillan v United Kingdom (2010) 50 EHRR 45

At the ECtHR, however, an entirely different view of Convention compatibility was taken. It was held that section 44, which the police had lawfully put into effect, involved an interference with private life which was unjustified under Article 8(2). At the heart of this judgment was the view that the police's discretion was not properly controlled by 'law'.

cross reference

The Convention concept of 'law' is discussed in Chapter 6, section 6.2.

The effect of the statute was not foreseeable in respect of the purposes; likewise there was insufficient control and safeguards over the operation of the section through, for example, the process of authorisation by senior officers. As well as Article 8 there could also be a violation of Articles 10 or 11 based on the same lack of legal control under which the exercise of the powers could be foreseeable. Because of the Article 8 finding, the ECtHR did not consider whether there was a deprivation of liberty which engaged and perhaps breached Article 5.

Following *Gillan v UK*, the power was suspended using a remedial order under section 10 HRA; further criticism was expressed in the Review 2010. Section 44 was repealed and the power replaced by sections 59 and 60 of the Protection of Freedoms Act 2012. The new power still allows individuals to be stopped and searched without reasonable suspicion, but the trigger for the necessary authorisation is raised from a belief that stop and search is expedient to a reasonable belief that an act of terrorism is likely, that the power is necessary, and the area and time for the authorisation is no greater than necessary. Other controls, including the introduction of a Code of Practice, are designed to ensure that the new power, when lawfully exercised, is foreseeable in its effects and subject to sufficient controls. The House of Lords' position, that a stop and search will not normally be a deprivation of liberty, or if there is one it will be allowed under Article 5(1)(b), still stands. This is strengthened, domestically, by the position articulated in *Austin v Commissioner of Police of the Metropolis* [2009] UKHL 5 (see Chapter 11) that proportionate actions by the police in a public order context are unlikely to involve deprivations of liberty.

cross reference

See the references to Brogan v United Kingdom (1989) 11 EHRR 117 (para 51) and Steel (1999) 28 EHRR 603 (paras 54–55) in Chapter 11, section 11.4.3, 'of an offence'.

26.8.2 **Arrest and detention for questioning**

Terrorism as an offence

Under the Terrorism Act 2000, someone who is suspected of an offence under that Act can be detained for questioning (and to preserve evidence) for up to 48 hours by the police. The same applies to someone suspected of being involved in terrorism. The problem is that, in this context, Article 5 only permits detention on reasonable suspicion that an 'offence' has been committed (Article 5(1)(c)). Terrorism is not an offence. However, terrorism implies actions which are likely to be offences, and it is likely to satisfy the Convention so long as the questioning relates to specific events.

Judicial authorisation of detention

Article 5(3) requires that a person, deprived of his or her liberty by being arrested for a criminal offence, be brought before a judge 'promptly' in order that the legality of the detention can be tested before an independent and impartial judicial body. In *Brogan v United Kingdom* (1989) 11 EHRR 117 (relating to Northern Ireland under the old Prevention of Terrorism Act) the ECtHR held that holding a suspect for four days without access to a judge was not 'prompt' and so violated Article 5(3): see Chapter 11, section 11.7.1.

The principle of judicial supervision has been adopted into the Terrorism Act. After an initial 48 hours of detention by the police, a person can be detained for a further 12 days (14 days in total). The detention beyond 48 hours requires judicial authority and a court hearing. A long period of detention will, roughly speaking, require weekly judicial authority. Given that the extended detention must be authorised by a court with opportunities for a hearing, the provisions of Article 5(3) are likely to be met by these provisions. So long as there is judicial supervision, review and the active pursuit of the case by the authorities, the absolute length of detention is unlikely to violate Article 5(1).

KEY POINT The Protection of Freedoms Act 2012 reduced the detention period from 28 days to 14. However, a draft bill which would allow 28 days to be restored in time of emergency was published in 2012.

26.9 Fair trials

26.9.1 Equality of arms

Although the reforms to counter-terrorism laws since 2010 have reduced their severity, they still sit uncomfortably with the rule of law and British traditions of political and civil freedom under the law. A crucial aspect of the proportionality of these powers and their ability to offer those affected sufficient safeguards to protect their rights, is the requirement that such powers are exercised under judicial supervision. The quality and effectiveness of this supervision depends greatly on the ability of the person affected knowing the evidence against him. They can then understand, challenge, answer and explain the facts on which the suspicions of the Secretary of State are based. The problem is that, from the police and government viewpoint, disclosing the evidence may compromise national security—it may, for instance, show that a political group has been infiltrated by informants, or it may involve evidence obtained from a foreign country on condition that it is kept confidential. Therefore the law on, for instance, proscription, TPIMs and detention without charge for questioning, can require judicial supervision to be conducted on the basis of 'closed evidence', which is not known to the person or his or her legal representative and so cannot be directly challenged.

cross reference

Fair trial rights in Article 5(4) are discussed in Chapter 11, section 11.8; equality of arms in Chapter 12, section 12.12.3.

Where there is a deprivation of liberty (e.g. detention for questioning: see section 26.8.2), a fair trial procedure is required by Article 5(4). Likewise Article 6 (right to a fair trial) is likely to be engaged because TPIMs are likely, like control orders before them, to involve the determination of a 'civil right'. The use of closed evidence looks, on its face, to violate the Article 6 principle of equality of arms (that the defence has equal access to the information on which the court decides the case).

However, it is not the case that fair trial rights apply in a standard way whatever the situation. The ECtHR (e.g. in *Chahal v United Kingdom* (1997) 23 EHRR 413, para 131) recognises that there can be legitimate reasons, relating to counter-terrorism or national security situations, for a court to determine an issue on the basis of confidential evidence kept from the parties. What is required are counterbalancing safeguards. The Court appeared to approve, at para 144, the use of 'security-cleared counsel' who would act on behalf of the detained or controlled person.

cross reference

Special advocates are discussed in Chapter 12, section 12.12.3.

In the United Kingdom, special advocates are available for use in the counter-terrorism context (before special courts, section 26.9.2, and in the procedures discussed here). The interests of the person are represented by an advocate who has access to the closed material. The system is controversial because the special advocate, after seeing the closed material, cannot contact the person involved to take instructions in respect of the particular allegations. Special advocates are also used in a number of other, non-terrorist contexts.

Secretary of State for the Home Department v MB/AF [2007] UKHL 46 concerned the control order regime (replaced by TPIMs). A major issue in the case was the compatibility with Article 6 of the closed materials procedures, including the use of special advocates, used during judicial supervision of the order. The House of Lords decision was complex. It required the closed materials provisions to be read down to achieve compatibility with Article 6 and returned the case to the Administrative Court to be retaken on that basis. The Court of Appeal (disagreeing with the Administrative Court's retaken decision) understood the House of Lords not to be laying down a rule that the person had to be given at least the absolute core of the evidence against them, use of special advocates notwithstanding ([2008] EWCA Civ 1148).

Then came a crucial Grand Chamber decision from Strasbourg. *A v UK* (2009) 49 EHRR 29 was the case brought by foreign terrorist suspects who had been detained without trial under the Anti-Terrorism Crime and Security Act (see section 26.3.2). The detention could be challenged before the Special Immigration Appeals Commission (see section 26.9.2), but on the basis of closed material procedures, including the use of special advocates. The Grand Chamber laid down an absolute rule:

> Where, however, the open material consisted purely of general assertions and SIAC's decision to uphold certification and maintain the detention was *based solely or to a decisive degree* on closed material, the procedural requirements of article 5(4) would not be satisfied. (emphasis added)

This position, which has the authority of a Grand Chamber, was adopted for UK law by the House of Lords when the Court of Appeal's judgment was appealed: *Secretary of State for the Home Department v AF (3)* [2009] UKHL 28. Lord Phillips said that the Strasbourg ruling established that the person

> must be given sufficient information about the allegations against him to enable him to give effective instructions [to special advocates] in relation to those allegations. (para 59)

Therefore judicial supervision can continue, even if the person is not informed of sources of the evidence or other detail, so long as the essential core of the case is disclosed.

It was accepted that the legislation could be read down under section 3 HRA to achieve this effect.

Detention without trial and control orders have been repealed. Nevertheless, the 'sole or decisive' principle, articulated in *AF*, is a general principle concerning the impact of both Article 5(4) and Article 6.

It has been applied in other contexts such as in special courts (see section 26.9.2). It will apply in the context of judicial supervision of TPIMs because the TPIMA allows closed procedures and special advocates but only in so far as these are compatible with Article 6 (Schedule 4, para 5), and this includes the 'sole or decisive' rule in *AF*. The principle seems to have less impact in the context of detention for questioning. In *R (Sher)* v *Chief Constable of Greater Manchester Police* [2010] EWHC 1859, following *Ward* v *Police Service of Northern Ireland* [2007] UKHL 50, the overall fairness of the procedures in Schedule 8 Terrorism Act 2000 (and therefore compatibility with Article 5(4)—though this is presumed rather than decided) was upheld.

further study

Consider, in contrast, the reaction of the UK Supreme Court to a similar rule applied to non-terrorist criminal trials; and to following Strasbourg judgments generally. This is discussed in Chapter 4, section 4.3.1.

26.9.2 **Special courts**

The use of special courts and tribunals in an anti-terrorist context is not necessarily inconsistent with the Convention. In the United Kingdom, the Special Immigration Appeals Commission (SIAC) has been created to hear appeals against deportations which have been ordered because the Home Secretary believes the deportee's presence is not in the public interest, because they threaten national security, perhaps on suspicion of terrorism. The court can see secret intelligence that the Home Secretary has relied upon but which would not be admissible in an ordinary court. The Proscribed Organisations Appeal Commission, mentioned in section 26.6.1, is another example.

Such courts, because they enable at least some judicial supervision of intelligence, can be important in balancing individual rights against national security and so achieving proportionality in the way special powers are applied. However, such tribunals cannot fulfil this role if, given their purpose and given the context, they are unable to provide a fair trial. If they lack independence and impartiality, for example, or if their procedures involve a disproportionate restriction on equality of arms between state and suspect, then there will still be a violation of Article 6 or 5(4). SIAC, for example, uses special advocates whose compatibility with the Convention is uncertain. In *R (U)* v *Special Immigration Appeals Commission* [2009] EWHC 3052, the principle in *AF*, section 26.9.1, that the applicant was entitled to know of the case against him to give effective instruction to special counsel, was applied to SIAC.

KEY POINT The controversial Justice and Security Bill 2012 aims to introduce closed material procedures into ordinary civil actions where rules preventing the disclosure of sensitive material might otherwise prevent the trial from proceeding.

discussion topic

Does judicial supervision of the exercise of special powers provide an effective, counter-balancing protection for the persons involved or is it just a misuse of the courts aimed at providing a cloak of respectability?

26.10 Glorification of terrorism

The European Convention on the Prevention of Terrorism places a duty on states to make 'public provocation to commit a terrorist offence' an offence. The response of the United Kingdom is in the Terrorism Act 2006. This makes the direct or indirect encouragement of terrorism an offence, and a statement which 'glorifies' past or future terrorism is deemed to be such a direct or indirect encouragement (see section 1). Disseminating information with the purpose of directly or indirectly encouraging terrorism is also an offence.

The argument in favour of such restrictions is partly a practical one: speech may encourage terrorists and, indirectly, cause more attacks. It is also an argument about civility: expressions of support for political violence are improper ways of conducting the public life of a democratic society, whether or not such expressions actually cause others to commit violent acts.

The following statement, taken from trial evidence against Sheik Abdullah el Faisal, illustrates why the offence may be necessary.

> The way forward can never be the ballot. The way forward is the bullet... We spread Islam by the Sword and so what, and today we are going to spread by the Kalashnikov and there is nothing you can do about it... if you see a Hindu walking down the road you are allowed to kill him and take his money.

> (*R v Faisal* [2004] EWCA Crim 456, para 15)

The European Convention on the Prevention of Terrorism clearly states that the offences must be compatible with the ECHR, most obviously with Article 10, freedom of expression. The offences in the 2006 Act have been strongly criticised on the grounds that they fail this test of compatibility.

Glorification is an uncertain term. It seems to go further than incitement to violence (which can be prohibited under Article 10), but it is not clear how much further. When this uncertainty is linked to the wide meaning given to terrorism (see section 26.4), there are doubts whether the Article 10 requirement that an offence be defined in ways that make its application foreseeable and hence prescribed by law will be met. These concerns are partly answered by the fact that prosecutions require the consent of the Director of Public Prosecutions, and that the most serious prosecutions will be before a jury. Supporters of the jury system are likely to argue that jurors will only convict if their common sense tells them that the prosecution was properly made and non-oppressive.

There is doubt whether the interference is 'necessary' given that there already exist offences that cover much of the ground of the glorification offence. An example is 'solicitation to murder' (section 4 of the Offences against the Person Act 1867), which makes it an offence to 'solicit, encourage, persuade or endeavour to persuade' a person to commit murder. Sheik Abdullah el Faisal, referred to earlier, was convicted under section 4 (February 2003).

The offence has been used against persons responsible for uploading videos onto the internet (see *R v Gul*, section 26.4.4).

26.11 Conclusion

There are many other counter-terrorism powers that have not been mentioned, such as powers over surveillance, disclosure of information, property, finance and so on. Because these powers are special they are controversial. They are hard to make compatible with the rule of law because they involve serious restraints on individual freedoms whilst, at the same time, often denying the normal rights to a fair trial which are associated with a society committed to the rule of law. At the heart of the reason for these powers is that the UK government, along with other countries, believes it is facing a threat equivalent to war, which cannot be met by the ordinary criminal law. The problem is that the degree of threat cannot be publicly tested. The government's understanding of the threat is based on intelligence which is not available either to the public or to the individuals directly affected. There is, therefore, a problem of trust. Reforms, following Review 2010, have moderated the most severe effects but, significantly, the government has published draft bills which would allow tough measures to be restored (see section 26.7.2). Restoration will require parliamentary scrutiny and, perhaps, a derogation from the Convention under Article 15. The scale of any new threat justifying such restored powers would, therefore, need some degree of public assessment.

The on-going question is whether the special powers can be applied in ways that are compatible with human rights. In the context of counter-terrorism, Convention rights seem to be at their most open-textured and amenable to adjustment to the circumstances. Nevertheless, there is evidence that the courts are taking a more demanding line in which the essence of rights, to a fair trial in particular, will not be compromised in the name of the alleged emergency.

 # Summary

- The fight against terrorism is conducted in the United Kingdom partially on the basis of special powers. These include, for example, TPIMs, powers of extended detention for questioning and random stop and search. Special powers may be linked to restricted procedures which make it difficult for a person to obtain a fair trial.

- Special powers are not necessarily inconsistent with the Convention. Many (but not all) Convention rights are open-textured and their application can be context-dependent and involve 'weighing' individual rights with important public interests such as the safety of the population and the protection of democratic institutions.

- Nevertheless, special powers which are applied disproportionately and which totally undermine an individual's Convention rights will violate the Convention.

 # Questions

 For suggested approaches, please visit the Online Resource Centre.

1   What are the general principles applied by the ECtHR to the adoption by states of special counter-terrorist measures?

2   Have the post-2010 reforms of counter-terrorism law created a regime which is reasonable in the circumstances and not oppressive?

Further reading

The Reports of the House of Lords, House of Commons Joint Committee on Human Rights are an important source. All counter-terrorism bills are closely and critically scrutinised.

GENERAL TEXTS ON COUNTER-TERRORISM LAWS

Council of Europe, *The Fight against Terrorism Council of Europe Standards* 3rd edn (2005)

Fiss, O. 'The War against Terrorism and the Rule of Law' (2006) 26(?) *OJLS* 235–256

Walker, C. *Terrorism and the Law* (2011) Oxford: OUP

Walker, C. 'The Terrorism and Investigation Measures Act 2011: One Thing but Not Much the Other? [2012] *Crim LR* 6, 421–438

Wilson, R. *Human Rights in the 'War on Terror'* (2005) Cambridge: CUP

Conclusion

For many the Human Rights Act 1998 (HRA), building on the United Kingdom's membership of the Council of Europe, has been a major success. It has had a significant impact in many areas of life, not always major, which have made Britain a kinder and more civilised place to live; one in which the basic rights of everyone have been better secured and the position of unpopular individuals and groups has been protected against official indifference and populist hostility. The aim has been to achieve this not only through providing rights actionable in the courts, but also by cementing human rights into the culture of public administration. The report of the Equality and Human Rights Commission, *Human Rights Inquiry*, in 2009, discusses the issue in critical detail.

There remains a lively academic debate about the structure and effects of the HRA. As indicated in Chapter 4, the Act constructs a particular constitutional balance between courts and Parliament. The courts, interpreting Acts of Parliament and delimiting the discretion of public authorities, can construct and impose their own interpretation of Convention rights; and in doing this, they assess the proportionate balance of individual rights and collective interests. However, the Act is clear that Parliament can insist on a contrary view (can disregard Convention rights or assert its own interpretation thereof) so long as it does so with clarity.

For some critics this structure hands too much power to the judges, but does so in a manner that is detrimental to human rights. An academic critique, from the left, takes this view. They see the HRA as shifting power from Parliament (elected) and the executive (accountable to Parliament) to an unaccountable (because independent) and unelected judiciary. They are sceptical of judicial claims to the impartial administration of the law. They point out that human rights norms are often highly controversial. The proper way to deal with such issues is through a strengthened Parliament, which is better able to ensure that the interests of all, including the least well off, are taken into account. The HRA is 'futile' (to quote the title of an essay written by a member of this tendency). The Act is good at fiddling at the margins, at protecting the interests of wealthy celebrities seeking to protect their privacy, but, they say, has had little significant effect in areas where it ought really to matter, in particular, the war on terror. Here the judges have been unable to use the Act to protect fundamental rights against serious challenge by the executive pursuing its national security agenda.

An alternative criticism feels that the Act does not give the judges enough power—they cannot strike down incompatible legislation. The Act encourages judges to use the interpretative power in section 3 and this leads to compromising on fundamental rights. Where the 'left' critique (in the previous paragraph) sees the way forward in a strengthened Parliament, this position would strengthen the judicial role. It embodies a liberal belief in the independent judiciary, deciding issues on principle rather than partisanship, as the best way of standing up to an over-mighty executive. This view assumes that there is a clear conceptual distinction between matters of policy and matters of rights, that policy must respect rights and that this is best achieved through the activity of impartial, principle-based, adjudication.

However, human rights law and practice has become politically controversial. Human rights law appears to be unpopular amongst some of the people of Britain, and this unpopularity has been taken up, in particular, by elements of the Conservative Party in government.

Criticism is not new. In 2006 the Labour government responded to concerns, including a fear that concern for human rights was undermining public safety, by setting up an investigation. Its conclusions were that many concerns were exaggerated and stimulated by media sensationalism, but that there was some evidence that officials had allowed individuals' rights to outweigh public safety concerns rather than undertake a proper balancing of individual rights and social interests. Much of the post-2010 political criticism is, likewise, a reaction to particular decisions. Unpopular individuals and groups enjoy rights and decisions vindicating these rights in matters such as counter-terrorism powers and deportation of foreign criminals, and this can cause a degree of outrage amongst elements of the media.

Such controversy is focused, in particular, on tension between Parliament and the European Court of Human Rights (ECtHR). The major issue was the total ban on convicted prisoners' voting, which the ECtHR has consistently said is arbitrary and therefore violates Article 3 of the first protocol (it is discussed in Chapter 25, section 25.3.2). Indeed, in the main case, *Hirst* v *United Kingdom (2)* (2006) 42 EHRR 41, the ECtHR argued that the ban had not been subject to specific parliamentary consideration, a matter that was remedied in February 2011 with parliamentary support for the total ban confirmed at 234 to 22 against (though few MPs who wanted change attended). At the heart of this dispute is not necessarily the view that a legislature should never have its powers limited by judicial human rights norms. Rather it is an argument about where the boundary lies between those issues which embody human autonomy and so need protection as human rights from even an elected Parliament and those which are the legitimate concern of Parliament. The majority refused to accept that this was a matter that should engage the will of the Strasbourg court.

Another area of criticism focuses on the relationship between the ECtHR and the UK courts. Under the HRA, individuals who fail in their claim before the UK courts can then apply to the Strasbourg court (section 11 HRA). Prisoners denied the vote lost their HRA case brought before the UK courts, before winning in Strasbourg. This has happened in other high-profile cases, such as over the DNA database (see Chapter 20, section 20.6.2) and the stop/search powers in respect of terrorist suspects (Chapter 26, section 26.8.1). This is seen by many as a process of 'dialogue' on rights between the domestic and the national courts. It is, though, a dialogue in which the ECtHR has the last word. Some UK judges have shown concern that their careful assessments of human rights law are then contradicted by the Strasbourg court. The concern involves questioning the point of the HRA if rulings and interpretations which are in favour of the authorities can be reassessed and set aside by the ECtHR (state agencies cannot bring a case before the Strasbourg court). Partly this relates to the ECtHR simply taking a different view of the proportionality, the balancing of interests, of an issue. Then the criticism is that the ECtHR is acting like a fourth tier of appeal. But there can also be significant differences of principle, and UK courts may be unwilling always to follow the Strasbourg line (see the discussion of section 2 HRA in Chapter 4, section 4.3.1). A further issue is the extent to which the authority of the common law is damaged by any axiomatic duty on the courts to follow Strasbourg rulings in principle. The Lord Chief Justice said, in his speech referred to in Chapter 4, that there has, perhaps, been too much focus on Strasbourg and not enough on the common law. This has a rich heritage, a strong commitment to liberty, and its organic growth should not be restricted by the Strasbourg court. We saw in the *Horncastle* case (discussed in Chapter 4, section 4.3.1) a strong assertion of the commitment to fairness in criminal trials, found in statute as interpreted in line with the common law, which could, perhaps, be damaged by the more rigid and inflexible Strasbourg position.

There are, therefore, a range of criticisms, some merely based on dislike of particular decisions, others more principled, which had public prominence in the first decade of the twenty-first century. The important point is that these had the ear of the Coalition government, which has taken them forward. Elements within the Conservative Party would like more radical changes, but any reforms have to be acceptable to the Coalition partners, the Liberal Democrats, for whom both the authority of the ECtHR and the HRA are very important.

Two things have happened here.

First, at the level of domestic law, the government has established a Commission to consider options for repealing the HRA and replacing it with a 'British Bill of Rights'. The terms of reference of the Commission require that it contains and builds upon the rights in the Convention.

There are at least three general problems with this:

- First, it is already the case that there is nothing to stop the United Kingdom at the moment from enacting legislation, or following policies, that provide for a more generous account of human rights than that provided under the Convention. There are indeed a number of cases in which the courts have noticed that, by interpreting the HRA in terms of the 'mirror principle' (that the point of the HRA is to provide the same standard of human rights as is available from Strasbourg, no less but also no more), they have been prevented from finding for claimants in cases where they would like so to have done. Proponents refer to jury trial but not much else. Most of the debate is about giving some kind of rights-based weight to social and economic policies such as rights to welfare etc. This, of course, just raises all the well-known questions about whether such political goals should be expressed as 'rights', given they involve major questions about social policy and the distribution of resources—matters, critics argue, essentially for the political rather than the judicial realm.

- Second, human rights represent universal standards (subject to a variable margin of appreciation) so it is not clear that distinctly British human rights makes a lot of sense.
- Conversely there is the issue of 'Britishness' anyway. The whole concept of 'Britishness' is in dispute. The United Kingdom is becoming increasingly disunited as claims are made on behalf of a distinctly Scottish, Welsh and Northern Irish culture, and, consequently, a distinctly English culture. How all this can be brought together in a 'British' bill of rights is unclear.

The second set of reforms aim at reforms of the Strasbourg system. This is a complex and long reform process which must engage with the interests and ideas of all the member states of the Council of Europe. This reform process has been discussed in Chapter 2, section 2.8. The tenor of these reforms is to place more responsibility for human rights protection with the member states. The United Kingdon would have liked to emphasise the background role of the court; even to say that, if an issue had been given a full human rights assessment by national courts, the Strasbourg court would have little to say. As we have seen, under the Brighton Declaration this is not the case. The reform process will be completed in 2015, with possible amendments to the Convention, such as more demanding admissions criteria.

Whether these reforms will satisfy critics, especially those in the Conservative Party, is hard to judge. In particular, there is little appetite for radical reforms of the Court amongst many states whose consent is necessary. Furthermore, it is not clear that it is helpful for mature democracies, such as the United Kingdom, to seek to undermine the powers of the ECtHR. The protection offered by this Court may well be very valuable to those living in some of the east European states whose traditions of democracy and the rule of law are less secure.

Further reading

Publications by the Commission on a Bill of Rights are found at: http://www.justice.gov.uk/about/cbr

Council of Europe, *High Level Conference on the Future of the European Court of Human Rights Brighton Declaration* http://hub.coe.int/20120419-brighton-declaration

Ewing, K. 'The Futility of the Human Rights Act' [2004] *Public Law* (Winter) 829–852

Justice, 'A British Bill of Rights: Informing the Debate' (2007) http://www.justice.org.uk/resources.php/11/a-british-bill-of-rights

Index

511

Index